KU-019-622

lonely planet

Walking in Spain

Miles Roddis
Nancy Frey & Jose Placer
Matthew Fletcher
John Noble

LONELY PLANET PUBLICATIONS
Melbourne • Oakland • London • Paris

SPAIN

CORDILLERA CANTÁBRICA
Limestone heart of the Picos; wild fluvial arteries cutting through gorges, dense forests, and pastures

GALICIA
A little known region of wild coasts, isolated beaches, gentle ranges, enchanting forests and riverways

SISTEMA CENTRAL
Accessible and rewarding walking, scrambling and climbing close to Madrid in the Sierra de Guadarrama; extended Alpine-style traverse in the Sierra de Gredos

BAY OF BISCAY

To Plymouth
To Portsmouth

Cabo Ortegal
O Ferrol
Viveiro
Ribadeo
Luarca
Avilés
Gijón
Ribadesella
Santander
La Coruña
Oviedo
Torre Ceredo (2648m)
Parque Nacional de los Picos de Europa
Cantabria
Bilbao
Asturias
Cordillera
Cantábrica
Reinosa
Santiago de Compostela
Lugo
León
Miranda de Ebro
Cabo Finisterre
Galicia
Ponferrada
Astorga
Burgos
Pontevedra
Orense
Montes de León
Palencia
Vigo
Tuy
Puebla de Sanabria
Benavente
Castilla y León
Aranda de Duero
Bragança
Chaves
Zamora
Valladolid
Braga
Guimarães
Tordesillas
Medina del Campo
Duero
Porto
Salamanca
Segovia
Sierra de Guadarrama
Guarda
Ciudad Rodrigo
Ávila
Béjar
Sistema Central
MADRID
Comunidad de Madrid
Coimbra
Sierra de Gredos
Almanzor (2592m)
Plasencia
Navalmoral de la Mata
Talavera de la Reina
Aranjuez
Toledo
Castilla
Santarém
Portalegre
Valencia de Alcántara
Cáceres
Sierra de Trujillo
Sierra de Guadalupe
Montes de Toledo
Alcázar de San Juan
Tejo
LISBON
PORTUGAL
Mérida
Extremadura
Parque Nacional de las Tablas de Daimiel
Ciudad Real
Manzanares
Setúbal
Évora
Badajoz
Guadiana
Zafra
Valdepeñas
Puertollano
Morena
Beja
Sierra
Bailén
Linares
Úbeda
Córdoba
Jaén
Sierra de Cazorla
Lagos
Faro
Huelva
Guadalquivir
Sevilla
Écija
Andalucía
Cordillera
Granada
Mulhacén (3478m)
Sierra Nevada
Osuna
Antequera
Las Alpujarras
Parque Nacional Doñana
Jerez de la Frontera
Cádiz
Sierra de Grazalema
Ronda
Málaga
Motril
Golfo de Cádiz
Marbella
Costa del Sol
Isla de Alborán
ATLANTIC OCEAN
Cabo de Trafalgar
Algeciras
Gibraltar (Brit)
Tarifa
Strait of Gibraltar
Ceuta (Sp)
To Islas Canarias
Tangier
Tetouan
To Islas Canarias (see inset map)
MOROCCO
Melilla (Sp)

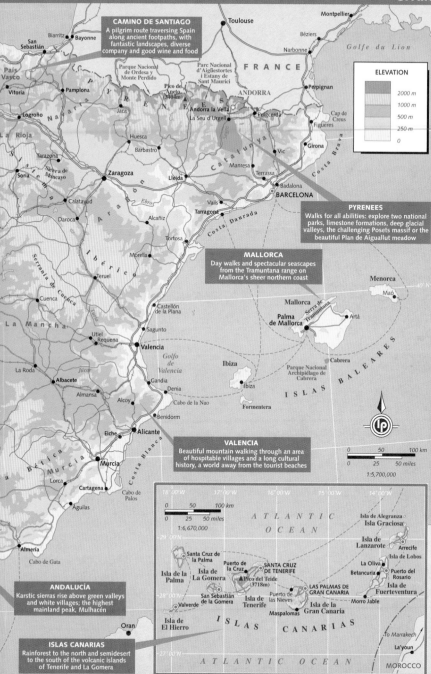

SPAIN

CAMINO DE SANTIAGO
A pilgrim route traversing Spain along ancient footpaths, with fantastic landscapes, diverse company and good wine and food

PYRENEES
Walks for all abilities: explore two national parks, limestone formations, deep glacial valleys, the challenging Posets massif or the beautiful Plan de Aiguallut meadow

MALLORCA
Day walks and spectacular seascapes from the Tramuntana range on Mallorca's sheer northern coast

VALENCIA
Beautiful mountain walking through an area of hospitable villages and a long cultural history, a world away from the tourist beaches

ANDALUCÍA
Karstic sierras rise above green valleys and white villages; the highest mainland peak, Mulhacén

ISLAS CANARIAS
Rainforest to the north and semidesert to the south of the volcanic islands of Tenerife and La Gomera

ELEVATION
2000 m
1000 m
500 m
250 m
0

Montpellier
Toulouse
Béziers
Narbonne
Golfe du Lion
Biarritz
Bayonne
San Sebastián
País Vasco
Perpignan
Cap de Creus
FRANCE
ANDORRA
Parque Nacional de Ordesa y Monte Perdido
Parc Nacional d'Aigüestortes i Estany de Sant Maurici
Pico de Aneto (3404m)
Andorra la Vella
La Seu d'Urgell
Puigcerdà
Figueres
Vitoria
Pamplona
Logroño
Jaca
Navarra
La Rioja
Sistema
Sierra de Moncayo
Tarazona
Soria
Zaragoza
Huesca
Barbastro
Costa Brava
Girona
Vic
Manresa
Terrassa
Badalona
BARCELONA
Lleida
Ibérico
Calatayud
Daroca
Aragón
Ebro
Alcañiz
Catalunya
Tarragona
Vails
Costa Daurada
Tortosa
Morella
Teruel
Serranía de Cuenca
Cuenca
Castellón de la Plana
Turia
Sagunto
La Mancha
Utiel
Requena
Júcar
VALENCIA
Golfo de Valencia
Menorca
Maó
Mallorca
Serra de Tramuntana
Palma de Mallorca
Artá
Ibiza
Cabrera
Parque Nacional Archipiélago de Cabrera
ISLAS BALEARES
Ibiza
Formentera
La Roda
Albacete
Almansa
Alcoy
Gandia
Denia
Cabo de la Nao
Benidorm
Elche
Alicante
Costa Blanca
Murcia
Bética
Lorca
Cartagena
Cabo de Palos
Águilas
Almería
Cabo de Gata
Oran

0 50 100 km
0 25 50 miles
1:5,700,000

ISLAS CANARIAS inset
18°00'W 17°00'W 16°00'W 15°00'W 14°00'W
0 50 100 km
0 25 50 miles
1:6,670,000
ATLANTIC OCEAN
29°00'N
Isla de Alegranza
Isla Graciosa
Isla de Lanzarote
Arrecife
Isla de Lobos
La Oliva
Betancuria
Puerto del Rosario
Isla de Fuerteventura
Morro Jable
Santa Cruz de la Palma
Puerto de la Cruz
SANTA CRUZ DE TENERIFE
LAS PALMAS DE GRAN CANARIA
Isla de la Palma
Isla de La Gomera
Pico del Teide (3718m)
Puerto de las Nieves
San Sebastián de la Gomera
Isla de Tenerife
Valverde
Maspalomas
Isla de la Gran Canaria
28°00'N
Isla de El Hierro
ISLAS CANARIAS
Oran
27°00'N
ATLANTIC OCEAN
To Marrakech
La'youn
MOROCCO

Walking in Spain
2nd edition – July 1999
First published – May 1990

Published by
Lonely Planet Publications Pty Ltd A.C.N. 005 607 983
192 Burwood Rd, Hawthorn, Victoria 3122, Australia

Lonely Planet Offices
Australia PO Box 617, Hawthorn, Victoria 3122
USA 150 Linden St, Oakland, CA 94607
UK 10a Spring Place, London NW5 3BH
France 1 rue du Dahomey, 75011 Paris

Photographs by
Matthew Fletcher, Nancy Frey, Richard Mills, John Noble, Jose Placer,
Ingrid Roddis, Damien Simonis, David Tipling – Windrush photos

Many of the images in this guide are available for licensing from
Lonely Planet Images.
email: lpi@lonelyplanet.com.au

Front cover photograph
Chewing the cud on the windswept Atlantic coast of Galicia
(Damien Simonis)

ISBN 0 86442 543 0

text & maps © Lonely Planet 1999
photos © photographers as indicated 1999

Printed by Craft Print International Limited, Singapore

Contents

The Walks	Duration	Standard	Transport
Sistema Central			
Alta Ruta de Gredos	3 days	Medium-Hard	Yes
Covacha Ascent	2 days	Medium-Hard	No
Sierra de Candelario	2 days	Medium	Yes
Valle de la Fuenfría	6½-7½ hours	Easy-Medium	Yes
Short Cuerda Larga Loop	2 days	Medium	Yes
La Pedriza Circuit	9-10 hours	Hard	Yes
The Pyrenees			
Cap de Rep & Riba Escorjada	4-4½ hours	Easy-Medium	No
Estanys de Siscaró	4-4½ hours	Medium	Yes
Pic de l'Estanyó	4¾-5¼ hours	Hard	No
Andorra to Catalunya*	2 days	Medium-Hard	Start only
Vall Ferrera & Vall de Cardós*	4 days	Medium-Hard	3rd day only
Espot to Refugi de Colomers*	6½-7 hours	Easy-Medium	No
Vall d'Aran*	3 days	Medium	Finish only
Estany Llong	5½-6 hours	Easy-Medium	No
Refugi de Colomina	2 days	Medium-Hard	Finish only
Port de Ratera d'Espot	4½-5 hours	Medium	No
La Ribagorça & into Aragón*	1½ or 2 days	Medium-Hard	Yes
The Frontier Ridge	3½ hours	Easy-Medium	Yes
Lago de Cregüeña	5-5½ hours	Medium	Yes
Posets Massif*	3-5 days	Medium-Hard	Start only
Parque Nacional de Ordesa y Monte Perdido*	2 days	Easy-Medium/ Medium-Hard	Finish only
Panticosa & Beyond*	4 days	Medium-Hard	Yes

* Stages of the Pyrenean Traverse

The Walks	Duration	Standard	Transport
Cordillera Cantábrica			
Senda del Oso	5 hours	Easy	Yes
Ruta de los Lagos	7-8 hours	Medium	Yes
Ruta de las Brañas	5-7½ hours	Medium-Hard	Yes
Saja-Besaya Traverse	2-3 days	Medium	Yes
Picos de Europa Circuit	9 days	Hard	Yes
Galicia			
Fraga do Eume	3½-4 hours	Easy-Medium	Yes
Monte Pindo	4½-5 hours	Medium-Hard	Yes
Spindrift Walk	2 days	Easy-Medium	Yes
Campa de Brego Loop	4½ hours	Easy-Medium	Yes
Ancares Ridge	5½-6 hours	Medium-Hard	Yes
Devesa da Rogueira	5-5½ hours	Medium-Hard	Yes
Río Lor Meander	5-5½ hours	Medium	Yes

The Walks *continued*	Duration	Standard	Transport
Valencia			
La Marina Alta	3-4 days	Medium	Yes
Sierra de Bernia	6½-7½ hours	Hard	Yes
Els Ports Loop	4-5 days	Medium	Yes
Mallorca			
Monestir de Sa Trapa	4½-5 hours	Easy-Medium	Yes
Sóller to Deià	3-4 hours	Easy	Yes
Barranc de Biniaraix & Embassament de Cúber	3½-4 hours	Easy-Medium	Yes
Valldemosa Loop	5½-6 hours	Medium	Yes
Sóller to Sa Calobra	5½-6½ hours	Medium	Yes
Torrent de Pareis	4-4½ hours	Medium-Hard	Yes
Andalucía			
Sierra de Cazorla Loop	6-6½ hours	Medium	Yes
Eastern Valleys Loop	5½-6½ hours	Easy-Medium	No
Río Borosa Walk	6-7 hours	Easy-Medium	Yes
Alpujarras Tour	4 days	Medium	Yes
Sierra Nevada Traverse	4 days	Hard	Yes
Cabo de Gata Coast Walk	2½ days	Medium	Yes
Grazalema Loop	6½-7½ hours	Medium	Yes
Benamahoma to Zahara de la Sierra	5 hours	Easy-Medium	Yes
Torrecilla & Peñón de los Enamorados	6-7 hours	Medium-Hard	No
Sierra Blanca Loop	5-6 hours	Medium	No
Islas Canarias			
Barranco del Infierno	2½-3 hours	Easy	Yes
Barranco de Masca	2¾-3 hours	Medium	Yes
Anaga Peninsula	6-6½ hours	Medium	Yes
La Caldera to El Portillo	5-5½ hours	Medium	Yes
Las Cañadas	4-4½ hours	Easy-Medium	Yes
La Rambleta & Pico del Teide	3¼-4 hours	Medium-Hard	Yes
Pajarito to Hermigua	5-5½ hours	Easy-Medium	Yes
Chipude to Alajeró	5½-6½ hours	Medium	Yes
Camino de Santiago			
Camino Francés	28 days	Medium	Yes

MAP INDEX

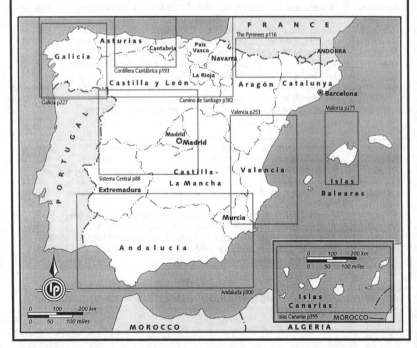

The Authors

Miles Roddis

Always an avid devourer and user of guidebooks, Miles came late to contributing. For more than 25 years he lived, worked, walked and ran in eight countries, including Laos, Iran, Spain and Egypt. He celebrated a new life by cycling 20,000km around the rim of the USA. Convinced that the bike is humankind's greatest invention (other than Velcro), he enjoys agitating for cyclists' rights and annoying motorists. Wild about wilderness, he's trekked the Zagros mountains in Iran, Britain's Pennine Way and the Pyrenees from the Atlantic to the Mediterranean. Now settled in Spain, he writes for outdoor and athletics magazines and has contributed to Lonely Planet's *Walking in Britain, Africa on a Shoestring* and *West Africa*.

Nancy Frey & Jose Placer

Nancy and Jose joined up in Roncesvalles on the Camino de Santiago. Nancy – on her way to a PhD in cultural anthropology from the University of California, Berkeley – was living in the village when Jose – on his way out of a law career – walked through on the way home to Santiago de Compostela. When not walking, Nancy continues her anthropological investigations in Galicia while Jose teaches outdoor education and carpentry. They also lead month-long educational walking tours for university students along the Camino de Santiago. Nancy has just published *Pilgrim Stories* based on her six-year investigation of this famous pilgrim's route. They live near the Galician coast, have a small farm and an adorable newborn baby.

Matt Fletcher

Matt's first major travels were along the northern coast of Spain in a Kombi van – an introduction to high mountain regions, red wine and the vagaries of an air-cooled engine. A 'sleeping rough and eating pasta' tour of Europe followed, plus summers in Germany and a trip to North Africa, where Matt spent just long enough in Morocco to get ripped off and climb Mount Tubkal.

After leaving art college with a degree in ceramics Matt traded a damp flat in England for camp sites under African skies. The northern coast of Mozambique and the Maralal International Camel Derby provided inspiration for a writing career which started at *Outdoors Illustrated*, an adventure sports magazine which soon folded (the two events are unrelated).

Freelancing ever since, Matt's travel and trekking articles have appeared in a wide range of newspapers and magazines. When not in distant mountains or down at the pub, Matt plays football, tries to improve his languages and sleeps.

John Noble

John Noble grew up at the bottom of a hill called Sawley Old Brow on the edge of England's Pennines and has been walking up, down, over and along hills ever since. Pendle Hill, home of the Lancashire Witches, was the first summit he conquered (*en famille*, at an age too early to remember). Numerous school trips up the hills of England's Lake District ingrained the habit. Studies and jobs in flat places like Surrey, Cambridge and London never had a chance of lasting long, and John soon took to perusing the bumpier, lumpier parts of the world – on foot whenever time permitted. He thinks he is the only person who has walked from Lamayuru to Padum, Wamena to Wolo *and* Palopo to Salurante. The steep streets of the Andalucian hill village he now calls home are the ideal springboard for exploring the many wonderfully rugged bits of southern Spain.

FROM THE AUTHORS

Miles Roddis A backpackful of thanks to Ingrid, the perfect Sancha Panza to a knight on the trail. Also, to Damon and Tristan for responding uncomplainingly to their Dad's can-you-find-out-by-yesterday requests.

To the well informed and genial refugio wardens Alejandro Gamarra, Albert and Esther Betrán, Juan Antonio Turmo and Masi Abajo: are they selected because they're so pleasant by nature (or does the job make them that way?).

Others who were generous with time and information include Jacinto Verdaguer, mountain guide; Joan Torres and Victoria Vilaret of the Grupo Excursionista de Mallorca; Jaume Comas of the national park office in Espot; Elisabet Alcántera and Lidia Aguerri of El Portillo's Centro de Visitantes in Tenerife; and Vicente Torrents and Nicola Stafford of Puerto de la Cruz's Oficina de Turismo.

Back at base camp, thanks to Dr Gerry Schofer of Rutgers University for reining in my artistic licence, in defiance of physical fact, on the geology of the Pyrenees. Dr Pep Banyuls helped with the Language chapter and colleagues Carlos, Sergio and Fernando of the Centre Excursionista de Valencia fielded requests for information patiently and efficiently. Pam and Jim Richards cheerfully rooted out US facts and figures and reader Jos vanden Akker sent in a particularly useful and detailed updating letter.

Nancy Frey & Jose Placer María and Wayne helped us open the door and for this we are grateful. Jane provided invaluable overseas assistance and moral support, always being available in a pinch. In Spain, we thank Teresa, Nino and Moncho for supplying information, and Toño who generously offered logistical support. Above all we thank our unknown walking companions who know and love their mountains and shared them with us. Finally, thanks to our little Jacob who accompanied us throughout the journey with barely a protest.

Matt Fletcher Firstly, I'd like to thank Clare for all her love and support over the last few years. Your calm, serene nature – even when in the company of a panicking, gibbering fool – is appreciated. I can't thank you enough.

Thanks to my Dad and uncle for instilling some literary nous, to Sue for all her Sunday lunches, encouragement and enthusiasm, and to the rest of the scattered tribe for showing confidence in me.

Thanks to Ag for all his patient editing; to David Else, who encouraged me to contact Lonely Planet in the first place; and to Bob Stansfield and Mary Gowland for helping me through Las Marinas. Also, to Rick for his ability to make the odd cup of tea and provide low-budget, in-house entertainment. Thanks also to all the poor souls in tourist information centres throughout Valencia and Castilla who have been pestered for months – I hope you feel your efforts have been rewarded.

John Noble Special thanks Mariano Cruz for good conversation and generous help; the Delegación Provincial de Granada of the Junta de Andalucía's Consejería de Medio Ambiente for information on the boundaries of the Parque Nacional Sierra Nevada; Isabella Noble for note-taking around Lanjarón; Susan Forsyth for blazing the Grazalema trail and holding the fort while I was away walking the sierras; and Miles, Nick, Chris, Emily, Glenn and all the crew for their patience and skilful work.

This Book

Material from the 2nd edition of Lonely Planet's *Spain* guide, updated by Damien Simonis, John Noble, Susan Forsyth, Tim Nollen and Fionn Davenport, was used for parts of this book. Miles Roddis was the coordinating author and wrote the introductory chapters and the Pyrenees, Mallorca and Islas Canarias chapters. Nancy Frey and Jose Placer wrote the Cordillera Cantábrica, Galicia and Camino de Santiago chapters, Matt Fletcher wrote the Sistema Central and Valencia chapters, and John Noble wrote the Andalucía chapter.

From the Publisher

This book was edited by Emily Coles, designed and mapped by Glenn van der Knijff and laid out by Andrew Smith in Lonely Planet's Melbourne office. David Burnett, Janet Austin, Kirsten John, Mary Harber and Sally Dillon assisted Emily with editing and proofing. Andrew Smith, Simon Tillema, Paul Piaia, Maree Styles, Sarah Sloane and Sonya Brooke helped with mapping and Mark Germanchis lent a hand with layout. Isabelle Young and Sean Pywell cast a specialist's eye over the Health & Safety and Flora & Fauna sections, respectively. Thanks to Quentin Frayne for the language section, Kate Nolan for helping us with new illustrations, Tim Uden for his layout assistance, the good people of Lonely Planet Images for help with the photographs and Maria Vallianos for the design of the cover.

THANKS

Many thanks to the travellers and walkers who used the last edition and wrote to us with their corrections, advice, hints and suggestions:

Stewart Black, Michael Borsdorf, Elaine R Bullard, Joseph F Cayne, Sarah Dunlop, Marjorie Hayes, Robin Kellett, Andrew Mylne, Ginny Quan, Caragh Salisbury, Michel Slinger, Jonathan Thomas, Jos vanden Akker, Pascal Vander Goten and MV Veelen.

Foreword

ABOUT LONELY PLANET GUIDEBOOKS

The story begins with a classic travel adventure: Tony and Maureen Wheeler's 1972 journey across Europe and Asia to Australia. Useful information about the overland trail did not exist at that time, so Tony and Maureen published the first Lonely Planet guidebook to meet a growing need.

From a kitchen table, then from a tiny office in Melbourne (Australia), Lonely Planet has become the largest independent travel publisher in the world, an international company with offices in Melbourne, Oakland (USA), London (UK) and Paris (France).

Today Lonely Planet guidebooks cover the globe. There is an ever-growing list of books and there's information in a variety of forms and media. Some things haven't changed. The main aim is still to help make it possible for adventurous travellers to get out there – to explore and better understand the world.

At Lonely Planet we believe travellers can make a positive contribution to the countries they visit – if they respect their host communities and spend their money wisely. Since 1986 a percentage of the income from each book has been donated to aid projects and human rights campaigns.

Updates Lonely Planet thoroughly updates each guidebook as often as possible. This usually means there are around two years between editions, although for more unusual or more stable destinations the gap can be longer. Check the imprint page (following the colour map at the beginning of the book) for publication dates.

Between editions up-to-date information is available in two free newsletters – the paper *Planet Talk* and email *Comet* (to subscribe, contact any Lonely Planet office) – and on our Web site at www.lonelyplanet.com. The *Upgrades* section of the Web site covers a number of important and volatile destinations and is regularly updated by Lonely Planet authors. *Scoop* covers news and current affairs relevant to travellers. And, lastly, the *Thorn Tree* bulletin board and *Postcards* section of the site carry unverified, but fascinating, reports from travellers.

Correspondence The process of creating new editions begins with the letters, postcards and emails received from travellers. This correspondence often includes suggestions, criticisms and comments about the current editions. Interesting excerpts are immediately passed on via newsletters and the Web site, and everything goes to our authors to be verified when they're researching on the road. We're keen to get more feedback from organisations or individuals who represent communities visited by travellers.

> Lonely Planet gathers information for everyone who's curious about the planet – and especially for those who explore it first-hand. Through guidebooks, phrasebooks, activity guides, maps, literature, newsletters, image library, TV series and Web site we act as an information exchange for a worldwide community of travellers.

Research Authors aim to gather sufficient practical information to enable travellers to make informed choices and to make the mechanics of a journey run smoothly. They also research historical and cultural background to help enrich the travel experience and allow travellers to understand and respond appropriately to cultural and environmental issues.

Authors don't stay in every hotel because that would mean spending a couple of months in each medium-sized city and, no, they don't eat at every restaurant because that would mean stretching belts beyond capacity. They do visit hotels and restaurants to check standards and prices, but feedback based on readers' direct experiences can be very helpful.

Many of our authors work undercover, others aren't so secretive. None of them accept freebies in exchange for positive write-ups. And none of our guidebooks contain any advertising.

Production Authors submit their raw manuscripts and maps to offices in Australia, USA, UK or France. Editors and cartographers – all experienced travellers themselves – then begin the process of assembling the pieces. When the book finally hits the shops, some things are already out of date, we start getting feedback from readers and the process begins again …

WARNING & REQUEST

Things change – prices go up, schedules change, good places go bad and bad places go bankrupt – nothing stays the same. So, if you find things better or worse, recently opened or long since closed, please tell us and help make the next edition even more accurate and useful. We genuinely value all the feedback we receive. Julie Young coordinates a well travelled team that reads and acknowledges every letter, postcard and email and ensures that every morsel of information finds its way to the appropriate authors, editors and cartographers for verification.

Everyone who writes to us will find their name in the next edition of the appropriate guidebook. They will also receive the latest issue of *Planet Talk*, our quarterly printed newsletter, or *Comet*, our monthly email newsletter. Subscriptions to both newsletters are free. The very best contributions will be rewarded with a free guidebook.

Excerpts from your correspondence may appear in new editions of Lonely Planet guidebooks, the Lonely Planet Web site, *Planet Talk* or *Comet*, so please let us know if you *don't* want your letter published or your name acknowledged.

Send all correspondence to the Lonely Planet office closest to you:

Australia: Locked Bag 1, Footscray, Victoria 3011
USA: 150 Linden St, Oakland, CA 94607
UK: 10A Spring Place, London NW5 3BH
France: 1 rue du Dahomey, 75011 Paris

Or email us at: talk2us@lonelyplanet.com.au

For news, views and updates see our Web site: www.lonelyplanet.com

Introduction

In 1998 Spain received more than 47 million visitors. So why, when perhaps walking's greatest joy is tramping alone or in congenial company, choose to walk in Spain?

For a start, a very high proportion of tourism, domestic and international, is confined to the Mediterranean coastal belt and star urban attractions such as Sevilla, Granada, Toledo, Barcelona and Madrid. Head for the hills and it's possible to spend the whole day without seeing another walker.

If you're staying in a coastal holiday resort, those hills aren't too far away. In the Valencia chapter we describe walks that are only a bus ride from Benidorm. Quite a few of the trails in the Andalucía chapter are within striking distance of the Costa del Sol and you can undertake day walks on Mallorca and in

the Islas Canarias which are easily accessible from a beachside base. Not that it's all communing with wilderness. If you visit some of Spain's spectacular and popular national parks, such as the Picos de Europa in Asturias, Ordesa y Monte Perdido in Aragón or Aigüestortes i Estany de Sant Maurici in the Catalan Pyrenees, the trails can be quite crowded. Yet walk no more than a kilometre from the car park or bus stop and you'll have the magnificent scenery almost to yourself.

The decision to change the name for this edition of the earlier Lonely Planet walking guide, *Trekking in Spain*, has been deliberate. Inside this completely revised edition, there's something for everyone: from hands-in-pockets family half-day walks to challenging sorties lasting several weeks.

Spain's most significant geographical feature is the Pyrenees, demarcating the frontier with France and for a long time a physical and psychological barrier to the rest of Europe. But Spain is now a fully fledged and enthusiastic member of the European Union, among the first wave of nations to adopt the euro, and the border posts at the head of the passes are no longer staffed.

A wonderfully varied and challenging resource for walkers, the Pyrenees range from the green, misty mountains of the País Vasco, which draw their humidity from the Atlantic Ocean, to the challenge of the Catalan mountains, into which the tiny, independent state of Andorra protrudes. We describe a three to four week traverse from Andorra through the heart of the Aragonese Pyrenees.

The Picos de Europa, in the Cordillera Cantábrica west of the Pyrenean isthmus, have long been a favourite destination for walking holidays, as gentle or as challenging as you care to make them. Within the Sierra Nevada, Europe's most southerly ski area in winter and a release from the summer heat of the Andalucian plains, rises Mulhacén, at 3478m the highest point in peninsular Spain. In the same region, the attractive Sierra de Alpujarras and Sierra de Cazorla are both excellent bases for walking holidays.

But walks needn't always involve mountain climbing. Galicia, with its own Atlantic mix of mist and greenness, recalls all the charm of the west coast of Ireland and other Celtic fringes, even down to the bagpipes. There, you can enjoy some fine coastal walking. And in eastern Andalucía on the Mediterranean shore, there's a fine three day coastal trail leading to the Cabo de Gata.

Spain is also crisscrossed by threads of ancient pilgrim ways, of which the best known is the Camino de Santiago. Its most famous variant, the Camino Francés, crosses the border from France at the pass of Roncesvalles and finishes in front of the cathedral in Santiago de Compostela. Nowadays it's travelled as much by lay people walking their history as by bona fide pilgrims and can be walked year-round.

And the enjoyment doesn't stop once you've pulled your boots off. As you'd expect from Europe's third-largest country, Spain impresses not only by the sheer variety of its scenery, vegetation and terrain but also by the diversity of its people, food, customs, domestic architecture and wines.

At a practical level, though it's wise to reserve your bed in advance during the peak summer months of July and August, even tiny villages in Spain can offer a clean, simple, reasonably priced room. In popular mountain areas such as the Pyrenees, Picos de Europa or Sierra Nevada, there are a network of *refugios* (refuges or mountain huts) and the climate is such that camping with a lightweight tent is a pleasure – but make it a strong one; storms, when they rage, can be powerful.

Facts about Spain

HISTORY

Spain's history is inseparable from its position on the globe. As a Mediterranean nation, its early history was marked by invasions – by Phoenicians, Carthaginians, Greeks and others, as well as by more longterm settlers such as the Romans and Muslims. To her short Atlantic coast, ships later brought unheard of treasure from Spain's colonies in the Americas.

The Pyrenees were long a barrier, isolating the peninsula from the mainstream of European thought and social development. In this century, the Spanish Civil War, though contained within its frontiers, was a bloody rehearsal for WWII and the global fight against fascism. Contemporary Spain, by contrast, is normally among the vanguard of countries within the European Union (EU) pressing for closer integration.

20,000-8000 BC – Magdelanian hunting culture in northern Spain.

2000 BC – Beginning of the Bronze Age.

1500 BC – The Iberians begin to arrive, probably from North Africa.

1200-600 BC – The Phoenicians, emanating from present-day Lebanon, establish coastal settlements, notably Cádiz.

1000-500 BC – Celts, originally from central Europe, begin to settle, bringing iron technology to the north of the country and merging with the Iberians in the central *meseta* (plateau) to become Celtiberians.

600 BC – The Greeks begin trading and establishing coastal colonies.

230 BC – The Carthaginians, from Carthage near contemporary Tunis, founding Barcelona and Carthago Nova, today's Cartagena.

218-201 AD – Rome defeats Carthage and begins a 600 year occupation of the Iberian peninsula (today's Spain and Portugal), later renaming the Spanish part 'Hispania' and establishing the Pax Romana, a long era of prosperity for the Roman Empire.

3rd century AD – Christianity spreads throughout Hispania.

418 – The first incursions by the Visigoths, who overrun most of the Iberian peninsula and establish their capital in Toledo.

711 – The Muslims invade from North Africa and remain the dominant force in the peninsula for nearly 600 years.

722 – The first battle in the long Reconquista (Reconquest) of the peninsula takes place when Christian forces are victorious at Covadonga, in contemporary Asturias.

929 – Abd ar-Rahman III declares the independent Caliphate of Córdoba, after which 'Al-Andalus' (Andalucía) reaches its cultural and political zenith.

1031 – The unified caliphate fragments into as many as 20 *taifas*, or small emirates, including among their most powerful those of Sevilla, Granada, Toledo and Zaragoza (Saragossa).

1086 – The Almoravids, a fanatical sect from North Africa, restores brief unity before being ousted in turn, after barely 50 years, by the equally extremist Almohads from the Atlas Mountains.

1118 – Alfonso I of Aragón recaptures Zaragoza.

1137 – In the north, Aragón and Catalunya (Cataluña in Spanish) unite to form the powerful new Kingdom of Aragón.

1212 – The combined northern Christian armies of Castilla, Aragón and Navarra crush the numerically superior Almohad army at Las Navas de Tolosa, Andalucía.

1230s – Jaume I of Aragón recaptures Las Islas Baleares (Balearic Islands), then Valencia.

1236 – Córdoba falls to Fernando III of Castilla.

1248 – Fernando III recovers Sevilla.

1469 – The marriage of Isabel of Castilla and Fernando of Aragón, known as the Reyes Católicos (the Catholic monarchs), unites the two states.

1478 – The beginning of the Spanish Inquisition, an ecclesiastical court which persecutes Jews, Muslims and Protestants and is only abrogated in the 19th century.

January 1492 – The fall of Granada, the last Muslim stronghold on the peninsula.

April 1492 – Fernando and Isabel order the expulsion of all Jews who refuse baptism. Thus begins the diaspora around the Mediterranean of the Sephardic Jews (of Spanish, Portuguese and Moroccan descent).

October 1492 – The Genoese Cristóbal Colón (Christopher Columbus), funded by the Reyes Católicos, 'discovers' the New World.

1494 – The treaty of Tordesillas, in which Spain and Portugal agree upon a division of the Americas.

1502 – All Muslims are ordered to convert to Christianity or leave. Those who convert and stay are known as Moriscos.

1519 – Carlos I of Spain, when only 19, inherits the Hapsburg territories in Austria and is elected Holy Roman Emperor (thus becoming Carlos V in that line).

1521 – In the New World, Hernán Cortés completes the conquest of the Aztec empire in contemporary Mexico. Ten years later, Francisco Pizarro and his conquistadors overthrow the Inca empire in present-day Peru. Looted treasure by the tonne is sent back to Spain.

1556 – Carlos abdicates, leaving most of his territories (including the Low Countries and all of Spain's American possessions) to his son, who becomes Felipe II.

1561 – Felipe II declares Madrid the capital of Spain.

1571 – Turkey, Spain's great Mediterranean sea rival, is routed at the battle of Lepanto.

1580 – Felipe II successfully claims Spain's neighbour, Portugal, upon the death of its reigning monarch.

1588 – Overstretching himself, Felipe II sees his Armada Invencible (Invincible Armada) destroyed by storm and the English fleet.

1609 – The Moriscos are expelled.

1618-48 – The Thirty Years' War in Europe. Spain's loss of Portugal (1641) and the Netherlands (1643) signals the end of her role as a European power.

1702-14 – The War of the Spanish Succession. Spain relinquishes Flanders, its last possession in the Low Countries.

1746-88 – Kings Fernando VI and Carlos III attempt to modernise Spain. Industry in Catalunya and the País Vasco (Basque country, known as Euskadi or Euskal Herri to the Basque people) prospers.

1805 – The British defeat of the combined Spanish-French fleet at Trafalgar ends Spanish sea power and heralds the loss of its American possessions.

1808-14 – The French emperor Napoleon's unilateral nomination of his brother Joseph as King José I of Spain sparks the Spanish War of Independence (Peninsular War). Spanish guerrillas, with British and Portuguese support, expel the invading French army.

1813 – In the Americas, Chile, Colombia, Paraguay and Uruguay, taking advantage of the war, are the first Spanish colonies to declare their independence.

1833-39 – The First Carlist War over who should succeed the conservative Fernando VII upon his death – his daughter Isabel, supported by liberals and the army, or his brother Carlos (hence the name, Carlist War).

1835 – The Desamortización decree, suppressing religious orders and confiscating their property.

1847-49 – The Second Carlist War.

1868 – The Septembrina Revolution. Liberals and discontented soldiers, led by General Juan Prim, overthrow Isabel, victor of the Carlist power struggle.

1872-76 – The Third Carlist War.

1873 – The First Republic, proclaimed by the liberal-dominated Cortes Generales (parliament, known as the Cortes), lasts a mere 11 months.

1874 – The army, church and rich landowning interests install Alfonso XII (1874-85), Isabel's son, on the throne.

1888 – The formation of the powerful socialist trade union, the Unión General de Trabajodores (UGT).

late 19th century – The emergence of strong Basque and Catalan separatist movements.

1898 – Defeated in the Spanish-American War, Spain loses Cuba, Puerto Rico and the Philippines, its last overseas possessions.

1902 – Accession of King Alfonso XIII, aged 16.

1909 – The Semana Trágica (Tragic Week) in Barcelona. A general strike leads to violence and repression.

1910 – The inauguration of the strong anarchist trade union, the Confederación Nacional del Trabajo (CNT).

1923-29 – The relatively benign dictatorship of General Miguel Primo de Rivera, with King Alfonso's concurrence.

1931 – The inauguration of the Second Republic (1931-36). Alfonso XIII abdicates. Universal suffrage is introduced.

1933 – Foundation of the right-wing Falange, headed by José Antonio Primo de Rivera, son of the ex-dictator.

1936 – The Popular Front, a left-wing coalition, wins the general elections. Elements of the army, fearful of outright revolution, mutiny, sparking the Spanish Civil War (1936-39). The nation is torn apart as the rebels, allied with the Catholic church and big business and styling themselves the Nationalists, are pitted against the Republicans. An estimated 350,000 Spaniards die.

1939-40 – An estimated 100,000 people are executed by the victorious Nationalist forces or die in prison.

1939-75 – The dictatorship of General Francisco Franco, the Nationalist commander. In 1945, diplomatic and UN recognition of Spain is withdrawn as a reprisal for her ambiguous role in WWII, despite her proclaimed neutrality.

1953 – The end of Spain's diplomatic isolation. In return for the right to establish military bases, the USA grants massive aid. The beginning of economic recovery, aided by remittances from emigre Spanish workers and the advent of mass tourism.

1975 – King Juan Carlos I, Franco's nominated successor, takes the throne upon the Generalísimo's death.

1977 – The newly elected Cortes, led by Prime Minister Adolfo Suarez of the Unión del Centro Democrático (UCD), agrees to a new constitution, declaring Spain a parliamentary monarchy with no official religion.

1982-96 – Spain is governed by the Partido Socialista Obrera Español (PSOE), a centre-left party headed by Felipe González.

1983 – In response to a widespread desire for regional autonomy, the country is divided into 17 Comunidades Autónomas, or Autonomous Regions, each with a high degree of local control. Despite this, the Basque terrorist organisation, ETA (Euskadi Ta Askatasuna, or Basques and Freedom), with a platform of full independence for the País Vasco, continues its campaign of violence.

1986 – Spain joins the EU.

1996 – The electorate, disaffected by an economic slump, rising unemployment and a handful of corruption scandals on the grand scale, votes in the centre-right Partido Popular (PP). Prime Minister José María Aznar begins a policy of wholesale privatisation of public assets.

1998 – After 30 years of violence and the loss of over 800 lives, the Basque terrorist group ETA declares a ceasefire.

Shoehorning 3000 years of Spanish history into a couple of pages of highlights is, of necessity, a highly selective operation, giving undue prominence to kings, battles and wars. For a more discursive treatment of trends and movements, refer to the History section in Lonely Planet's *Spain* or some of the titles recommended under Books in the Facts for the Walker chapter.

History of Walking

Until relatively recently, walking in Spain was primarily a utilitarian activity – to get you from A to B. The Pyrenees, for example, now regarded as a magnificent resource for walkers, were for centuries the preserve of

shepherds and hunters, and seen as an obstacle, a natural frontier separating Spain from the rest of Europe. The few passes leading into France were trodden mainly by merchants and smugglers, people walking to reach a goal, not trekking for its own sake.

There was one significant exception to this rule: the Camino de Santiago (Way of St James) pilgrim route, where walking the way was considered to confer just as much merit as arriving at the goal. Every year, between 500,000 and two million pilgrims would make the journey on foot from all corners of Europe to Santiago de Compostela in Galicia. Its cathedral, believers say, houses the tomb of Santiago (St James) the apostle, and a pilgrimage to Santiago ranked in its time with one to Rome or Jerusalem. Nowadays, it's not only the faithful who make the journey. Many undertake the route for its own sake, staying at the ancient *hospitales* (wayside guesthouses) which mark the way – or more accurately ways (see the Camino de Santiago chapter for details).

As in much of the rest of Europe, while shepherds went about their daily business in the mountains, walking for its own sake was the preserve of the leisured and wealthy. Many first-recorded ascents of the highest peaks were, however, achieved by surveyors or natural scientists, for whom the walk was merely the means to a greater end. It was, for example, the French botanist and geologist Louis-François Ramond de Carbonnières who, at the end of the 18th century, made the first known attempt to conquer the Glaciar de Maladeta in the Aragonese Pyrenees, while a Russian officer, Platon de Tchihatcheff, was the first to scale the nearby Pico d'Aneto in 1842. Similarly, it was as late as 1904 that the Spanish aristocrat El Marqués de Villaviciosa, Don Pedro Pidal, became the first to conquer the Pico de Naranjo de Bulnes in the Picos de Europa – guided by local shepherd Gregorio Pérez, who must have wondered what the point to it all was.

Charles Packe was both a gentleman and a scholar. A member of the English landed

The Colourful Count

The most eccentric of early walking pioneers must be the half-French, half-Irish Count Henry Patrick Marie Russell-Killough, who bagged 16 first ascents of Pyrenean peaks. Among his many idiosyncrasies, he rented a sizeable hunk of the Vignemale massif in the Aragonese Pyrenees for the princely sum of 1FF a year and proceeded to haul himself to its summit a total of 33 times, the last ascent in his 70th year.

When rather younger, the count marked a successful climb by having an impromptu grave dug on the summit into which he clambered, asking his guides to bury him up to the neck. Lower down the mountain, he excavated a number of caves and lived in one of them for long periods between spates of mountain walking. He was famous, too, for hosting dinner parties on the fringes of a glacier. Elegant Persian carpets were spread out and laden with fine food and wines carried up from the valley by a retinue of servants.

gentry, his meticulously researched *Guide to the Pyrenees*, first published in 1862, was the standard text for many years.

Nowadays, most major towns have their association of walking and climbing aficionados. The pioneer and first walking group to be established in Spain was the Centre Excursionista de Catalunya (CEC), founded in Barcelona in 1876 and still going strong.

GEOGRAPHY

Spain and Portugal share the Iberian Peninsula, a roughly square-shaped wedge perched on Europe's south-western corner. Separated from France by the formidable Pyrenees mountains and from Africa by less than 25km of sea across the Strait of Gibraltar (Estrecho de Gibraltar in Spanish), it's the continent's second highest country after Switzerland,

with more than a third of its area above 800m. Spread over 505,000 sq km, it's also Western Europe's second-largest country after France.

Spain is probably Europe's most geographically diverse country, with coastline on two seas and land ranging from the near-deserts of eastern Andalucía in the south of Spain to the deep coastal inlets of Galicia in the north-west; from the sunbaked uplands of Castilla-La Mancha in the centre to rugged, snowcapped Pyrenees.

The bombardment of names in this section may be a bit overwhelming unless you've already visited Spain. As an aid to navigation, flick to the colour country map at the front of this book, where you'll find the main features illustrated.

Meseta

At the centre of the peninsula spreads the meseta, a bleak tableland 400 to 1000m above sea level. Occupying some 40% of the country, it embraces most of Castilla y León, Castilla-La Mancha and Extremadura.

Apart from a handful of towns (including the capital city, Madrid), it's sparsely populated, with numbers still declining as the agricultural population of this harsh terrain continues to migrate to more hospitable areas. Grain is the most popular crop, though vineyards producing the strong reds of La Mancha plateau and huge olive groves stretch across the south, while Extremadura, in the west, boasts extensive pastures.

A land of boundless but unvarying horizons, boiling summers and harsh winters, it's not the stuff of great walking. There are, however, some enticing mountain chains running through and around the meseta.

Mountains

The Sierra de Gredos, to the west of Madrid, and the Sierra de Guadarrama, to its north, both rise above 2400m. Cleaving through the meseta, they form part of the Sistema Central mountain chain, which runs from north-east of the capital to the Portuguese border.

Mountain chains enclose the meseta on all sides except the west, where the terrain slopes more gently towards and then across Portugal.

On the meseta's northern limit, the Cordillera Cantábrica runs from near the Atlantic Ocean almost to the País Vasco, isolating central Spain from the Bay of Biscay (Mar Cantábrico in Spanish). Straddling the borders of Castilla y León, Cantabria and Asturias, it rises above 2500m in the spectacular Picos de Europa, one of Spain's most popular venues for walkers. In the north-west, the more modest Montes de León and their offshoots cut off Galicia from the meseta.

The Sistema Ibérico runs from La Rioja in the País Vasco to southern Aragón, varying from plateaus and high moorland to deep gorges and weird eroded rock formations as in the Serranía de Cuenca. The meseta's southern boundary is marked by the low, wooded Sierra Morena running across northern Andalucía.

Spain's highest mountains lie at or near its edges. The Pyrenees mark 400km of border with France, from the Mediterranean to the Bay of Biscay, with stubby fingers reaching southwards into Navarra, Catalunya and Aragón and with foothills extending west into the País Vasco. Aragón and Catalunya boast numerous 3000m peaks, the highest being Aragón's Pico de Aneto (3408m).

Across southern and eastern Andalucía stretches the Cordillera Bética, a rumpled mass of ranges that includes mainland Spain's highest peak, Mulhacén (3478m), in the Sierra Nevada and an unusual spur radiating north, the Sierra de Cazorla, source of the Río Guadalquivir. This same system continues east into Murcia and southern Valencia, dips under the Mediterranean, then re-emerges as the Balearic islands of Ibiza and Mallorca. On Mallorca it rises to over 1400m in the Serra de Tramuntana. The other main Balearic island, Menorca, is a tip of the same underwater massif as Sardinia and Corsica.

The anomaly is the Islas Canarias (Canary Islands), politically and culturally a part of Spain yet geographically an offshoot of Africa.

Lowlands

Five lower-lying areas spread around and between the mountains of Spain.

Fertile Catalunya, in the north-east, is mainly ranges of lower hills. The Ebro basin, between the Sistema Ibérico to its south and the Cordillera Cantábrica and Pyrenees to its north, supports wine production in La Rioja, the growing of grain in Navarra and vegetables in eastern Aragón. Other less watered parts of Aragón, by contrast, are near-desert.

The soil of Galicia in the north-west is poor and farming difficult. The green, hilly terrain, from which people sailed in their thousands to seek a new life in the Americas, resembles other Celtic lands of emigration such as Ireland or Brittany. There's some great walking to be had along its deeply incised coastal inlets.

The coastal areas of Valencia and Murcia in the east are dry plains transformed by irrigation into green *huertas* (market gardens and orchards). Similar areas farther south, around Almería in eastern Andalucía, where there's much less inland water to be tapped, are virtually desert and have provided the location for many a 'spaghetti Western'.

The Río Guadalquivir basin, stretching across Andalucía between the Sierra Morena and Cordillera Bética, is another highly fertile zone, producing, in particular, grain, olives and citrus fruit. Its delta, like that of the Río Ebro, is one of Europe's great bird sanctuaries.

Rivers

Spain has five major rivers: the Ebro, Duero (Douro), Tajo (Tejo), Guadiana and Guadalquivir, each draining a different basin between the mountains. Between them and their tributaries, they provide much of Spain's water and electricity.

The Ebro, largest in volume, is the only one to flow from west to east, entering the Mediterranean in southern Catalunya. Between the sinuous waters of its delta, rice paddies flourish and provide a vital resting place for migratory birds flying the north-south corridor between Europe and Africa.

All the other major rivers empty into the Atlantic Ocean. The Duero drains the northern half of the meseta, then continues across Portugal as the Douro. The Tajo and the Guadiana drain the southern meseta. The Tajo continues west across Portugal to Lisbon as the Tejo, while the Guadiana turns south into the Golfo de Cádiz.

The Guadalquivir flows from east to west across the middle of Andalucía.

GEOLOGY

The Iberian Peninsula was an early transatlantic traveller before finally settling down in its present position, separated from the main European landmass by the Pyrenees in the north and from Africa by the Strait of Gibraltar to its south.

Seen on a mega geographical and time scale, it's a small plate which has spun between the continental tables of Europe, Africa and America. In Paleozoic times, the bedrock crashed into America, at around about the level of Newfoundland.

In Triassic times, when the Atlantic Ocean rose, the three prototype mountain chains became islands surrounded by accumulating sediment. The whole mass tore free from the American continent and made its slow way eastward again to graft itself onto Europe and what is, today, France.

Erosion over the millennia was intense; by the Jurassic period, the giant mountains had been all but rubbed out and the landmass was once again a vast plain with little relief. By Cretaceous times, it had eased itself away from the European continent, rotating slowly on its axis and leaving behind a vast cavity – the Bay of Biscay.

In the Paleocene era, as the Iberian plate smashed into the Europe and Africa landmasses once again, large-scale folding took place. Today's major mountain chains were formed and the peninsula took on its approximate present shape – the major force for change, discounting erosion, until this day. But don't imagine that the peninsula has given up all movement; though it's unlikely to throw you off balance, the coastline of Galicia is dropping a few centimetres each

year, while the Mediterranean shore is rising correspondingly.

The oldest rock can be found on the meseta. Occupying much of central Spain, this high plateau is composed mostly of igneous and metamorphic materials. The Pyrenees, in addition to their east-west axial range, have more recent chains flanking them to north and south, known as the Prepirineos, or the pre-Pyrenees.

In the west of Spain and much of Portugal, the most common rock is igneous, commonly granite, but supplemented by metamorphic forms such as slate, schist and gneiss. In central and southern areas, limestone predominates, while along and deep inland from the Mediterranean coast and in the Ebro basin are mostly clays and marls.

Of Spain's two island chains, the Islas Canarias are but the tips of a vast volcanic range lying beneath the Atlantic Ocean. This was formed when the African tectonic plate was severed from the South American landmass, the resulting fissures and ruptures releasing lava and magma from deep beneath the earth's crust. The Islas Baleares, the product of similar primeval forces, were thrust up when the African plate burrowed under the more static European one.

For a description of the geology in different regions, see Natural History in individual walks chapters.

CLIMATE

The meseta and Ebro basin have a continental climate: scorching in summer, cold in winter, and dry. Madrid, for example, regularly freezes in December, January and February, while temperatures climb well above 30°C in July and August. Locals describe the weather as *nueve meses de invierno y tres de infierno* (nine months of winter and three of hell). The northern meseta and much of the Ebro basin are even drier, with only around 300mm of rain a year. Most of inland Andalucía positively broils in high summer, with temperatures of 35°C and above. The compensation comes in the form of much milder winters than the meseta's.

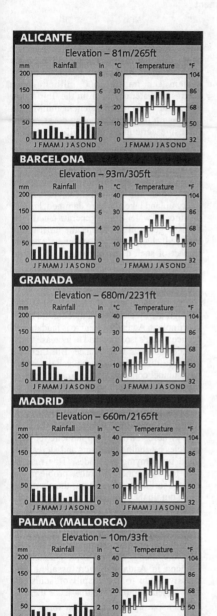

The western Pyrenees and the Cordillera Cantábrica abruptly halt the moisture-laden airstreams from the Atlantic Ocean, bringing moderate temperatures and heavy rainfall (three or four times as much as Madrid's) to the north and north-west coasts. Even in high summer you never know when you might get a shower.

The whole Mediterranean coast and the Islas Baleares get little more rain than Madrid, while the semi-desert regions of Murcia and Amería on the southern Mediterranean shores can be even hotter than the capital in summer. The whole of the coast experiences agreeably mild winters.

In general, you can rely on pleasant or hot temperatures just about everywhere from April to early November (plus March in the south, but minus a month at either end on the north and north-west coasts). In Andalucía there are plenty of warm, sunny days right through winter. In July and August, temperatures can get unpleasant, even unbearable, anywhere inland unless you're up high. At this time, Spaniards abandon their cities in droves for the coast and mountains.

You can't have greenness without getting wet. In Galicia, be prepared for drizzle and mist at any time. Other north-west regions – Asturias, Cantabria and the provinces of País Vasco – are similarly damp and lush, their climate determined by supersaturated clouds borne in from the Atlantic Ocean by the dominant winds.

In the Pyrenees too, where summer storms can be spectacular, rain, often intense but usually shortlived, can fall at any time. Snowfalls in Spain's high mountains can start as early as September and some cover lasts year-round on the highest peaks. Even key passes for walkers may have a residue of snowdrift well into July.

The Islas Canarias are, as in so many respects, the exception. Scattered off the coast of Africa, they seem to enjoy endless spring with average daily temperatures ranging from 18°C in what passes for winter to 24°C in summer. With the exception of Lanzarote and Fuerteventura, the two islands nearest Africa, there is a marked difference in climate between the damper, cloudier north side of an island and its more arid, hotter southern slopes.

For more detailed regional information, see the Climate sections in individual walks chapters. For on-the-spot sources of weather information, see Weather Information in the Facts for the Walker chapter.

ECOLOGY & ENVIRONMENT

Humankind has been shaping Spain's environment ever since hunter-gatherers scattered their first seeds and assumed a more sedentary life as cultivators of the land. Nor are large-scale environmental changes only a late 20th century phenomenon. It was the Romans who first began to hack away at the country's extensive woodlands, which until then had covered as much as half the meseta.

Over the ensuing 2000 years, further deforestation along with overcultivation of the land and overgrazing (notably by flocks of sheep several thousand strong) has brought about substantial topsoil erosion. Most of the 300 sq km delta of the Río Ebro, for example – today a vital staging post for migratory birds and a fertile area for rice paddy – has been formed by deposits of topsoil sluiced down from the meseta over the past 600 years. Change, whether inevitable or induced by humans, isn't always negative and one area's loss can be another's gain.

Spain generally supports a varied, often low-tech and mostly healthy agriculture. By European standards, the country is sparsely populated and most of its people live in towns and cities, reducing their impact on the countryside. There's still lots of wilderness and plenty of unpolluted wild land to roam. However, Spain has particular environmental problems, some imposed by nature and others the result of human negligence or indifference.

Spain shares the problem of unpredictable and often deficient rainfall with its southern Mediterranean neighbours. Drought is perhaps its most serious environmental problem. Last striking in the early 1990s, it brought seasonal water rationing to some 10

million people. To combat this, reservoirs cover a higher proportion of Spain than any other country in the world, and projects such as the Tajo-Segura water diversion system can transfer 600 million cubic metres of water a year from the Tajo basin in central Spain to the Valencia and Murcia regions on the Mediterranean coast, where intensive agriculture is heavily dependent upon irrigation.

Another particular consequence for walkers is that in areas of relatively high rainfall, which are confined mostly to the north coast and the Pyrenees, just about every upland lake has been dammed, both as a source of water and to generate electricity. Purists get uptight about the artificially induced changes in water levels and the impact of such dams upon the high mountain environment, but they reduce Spain's dependency upon nuclear or fossil fuels, and are small scale and relatively unintrusive.

The tunnels which have been bored through the Pyrenees are a much more negative implant. Again, the motive is laudable: to reduce Spain's isolation and to increase transfrontier contacts with France. But there's a palpable difference between valleys which have tunnel connection with France, such as the heavily commercialised Valle de Bielsa, and those which retain their original identity.

More fundamentally, the soil of much of Spain is unyielding and impoverished. As everywhere, farmers supplement its deficiencies by adding fertilisers and increase its yield by spraying pesticides. This may be fine for the farmer, but other problems are created farther downstream as the chemicals leech out. In the Albufera, a sweet-water lake south of Valencia, fish and eels flop belly up every so often because of contamination way, way upstream. Nor is it just the slow accumulation of toxic chemicals; in 1998, the fragile wetlands of the Parque Nacional de Doñana in Andalucía were assailed by a massive industrial overspill of acids and heavy metals into a river that feeds them.

Intensive agriculture in the form of *invernaderos* (huge plastic greenhouses) tends to drive out indigenous plants. A more pressing problem, however, is excessive irrigation, which can lead to a lowering of the water table.

All the above can be justified – and is, energetically – as a way of ensuring the continuation of rural life, based upon agricultural production and the raising of livestock. Less defensible, but just as ingrained in local culture, is hunting, an almost exclusively male preserve. The words '*coto privado de caza*' (private hunting area) daubed on rocks is a familiar sign and over 1.25 million shooting licences are issued annually. Birds are shot out of the sky, limed, netted and trapped, and older men especially resent limits on catches set for hunting and fishing seasons. Even though many species are now protected, poaching or winking at the law is commonplace and strict enforcement in Spain's vast countryside is impossible.

And yet, despite all the human odds stacked against them, species such as wild boar and red deer have recovered in some areas to the point where they are now legally culled. The Spanish ibex, a kind of mountain goat, was almost extinct by 1900 but protection since then has raised its numbers to around 10,000.

The private car remains one of Spain's principal polluters. There are ecological movements in major cities, led in the main by young activists, but the car rules. Politicians bend to the voting power of the car lobby, and the arteries of most large towns are clogged with traffic.

Conservation

In popular walking areas, however, there are signs of change. For example, you can now only enter the Parque Nacional de Ordesa y Monte Perdido on foot or by bus, while private vehicle access to the Parque Posets-Maladeta in Aragón, one of Spain's newest protected areas, is restricted to between 8 pm and 8 am.

More generally, controls and legislation are beginning to bite as environmental awareness increases. The PSOE government, in power from 1982 to 1996, made environmental pollution a crime and spurred on a range of actions by regional governments, which now have responsibility for most environmental matters. In 1981, Spain had just 35 environmentally protected areas, covering 2200 sq km. Today, there are over 400, embracing more than 25,000 sq km.

National Parks & Reserves

Spain's most ecologically important and spectacular walking areas – about 40,000 sq km if you include national hunting reserves – are almost all under some kind of official protection, with varying degrees of conservation and access. A *parque natural* (nature park), for instance, the most frequent category of protected area, may include villages with hotels and camp sites. In others, access may be limited to a few walking trails, while a few reserves allow no public access. Controlled hunting is often still permitted – indeed in some parks, such as the Parque Nacional de Cazorla, a combination of restocking and vigilance has actually led to an increase in the variety and quantity of larger species of wildlife. The most popular and interesting often have a visitor centre. Even though information is usually only in Spanish, illustrative panels and video transcend language, and you can frequently pick up useful suggestions for walking routes. For more about such centres, see Information Sources within the individual walks chapters.

National Parks A *parque nacional* (national park) is an area of exceptional importance for its fauna, flora, geomorphology or landscape. They're generally the most strictly controlled and protected, and embrace some of Spain's most spectacular areas for trekking.

For information on walks in the Parque Nacional de la Montaña de Covadonga, consult the Cordillera Cantábrica chapter.

The higher slopes of the Sierra Nevada, Spain's 12th and most recently designated national park, feature in the Andalucía chapter.

In the Pyrenees chapter we describe a selection of routes through the Parque

European Mink

One of northern Spain's most endangered natives is the diminutive European mink (*Mustela lutreola*) – you are most unlikely to see one and should count yourself very lucky if you do. Once common throughout Europe, the native mink has been reduced to just a few hundred individuals. Northern Spain has one of the last wild populations, though biologists are concerned that the number remaining in the world may already have fallen below the threshold needed for species survival.

The mink is a small, brown-black member of the weasel family and occupies an ecological niche similar to the beaver and the platypus, though it lacks their webbed feet and specialised tail. The animal's fatal attraction to the fashion industry results from its fine pelt, which has a thick layer of underfur for buoyancy and insulation.

Each animal requires a large territory (a male can range along 4km of stream), which is increasingly difficult to support as land has been swallowed up by farming and urban expansion. However, the main threat to the European mink's survival is the larger, more powerful American species which has steadily encroached on its traditional range, outcompeting its native cousin for prime habitat rather than interbreeding with it.

The last hope for the European mink may be a rescue plan coordinated by the Darwin Initiative, a British organisation dedicated to preserving species on the brink of extinction. The small island of Hiiumaa in the Baltic Sea is to be cleared of foreign invaders and attempts made to establish a breeding population in a last-ditch effort to save it.

Nacional de Ordesa y Monte Perdido and the Parque Nacional d'Aigüestortes i Estany de Sant Maurici (in the Aragonese Pyrenees and Catalan Pyrenees sections, respectively).

In the Islas Canarias chapter are walks through the volcanic Parque Nacional del Teide, on the slopes of Spain's highest mountain (the Pico del Teide) looming over the island of Tenerife, and in the Parque Nacional de Garajonay on La Gomera island, which was created to protect its unique subtropical rainforest.

Other Protected Areas These are administered by Spain's 17 regional governments. There are literally hundreds of such areas, falling into at least 16 classifications with a bewildering variety of terminology: *reservas naturales*, *parques ecológicos*, *áreas naturales*, *zonas protegidas*, just plain *parques* – and just about every other permutation of these names. They range in size from 100 sq m rocks off the Islas Baleares to the mountainous 2140 sq km Parque Natural de Cazorla, described in the Andalucía chapter. The Áreas Naturales de la Serra de Tramuntana offer protection to the spectacular mountain range in the north of Mallorca; walks within it are described in the Mallorca chapter.

Reservas Nacionales de Caza Some 15,000 sq km of wilderness areas around the country are *reservas nacionales de caza* (national hunting reserves), sometimes called a *coto nacional de caza*. These are usually well conserved for the sake of the wildlife that is to be hunted. Public access is usually unrestricted (some hunting reserves even include villages or towns) and you may well hike across one without even knowing it. In the hunting season (notices or gunfire will alert you to when that movable feast may be), brightly coloured clothing can reduce the risk of your being mistaken for a hapless chamois.

continued on page 35

FLORA & FAUNA
OF SPAIN

FLORA & FAUNA OF SPAIN

Many of the walking areas we describe are a treasure trove for botanists and birdwatchers. Springtime, even in those regions which are brown and arid for most of the year, is spectacular with wild flowers. Spain is on one of the main corridors for birds migrating between Europe and Africa, so if you manage to time your visit to coincide with the twice-yearly fly past, you'll encounter many birds of passage as well as a number of indigenous species you'll never see elsewhere.

Spain is also a country rich in mammalian fauna. Walking in the Cordillera Cantábrica and the Pyrenees, you stand a very good chance of seeing chamois, while the Sierra de Gredos in Castilla and the Sierra de Cazorla in Andalucía are havens for ibex. Many of the larger mammals, however, as in much of Europe's wilder regions, have been shot, poisoned and starved to near-extinction. There are, nevertheless, wild boars and a very few brown bears clinging on precariously in the north (we saw traces of bear in the Aragonese Pyrenees). You'll be lucky, however, to even hear the distant howl of one of the estimated 1000 surviving wolves.

Title page: The black-shouldered kite is commonly seen perching on posts or treetops and hovering over fields. Large numbers may congregate in areas where there are large rodent populations.

RICHARD MILLS

Fawns of the red deer are born in late spring and lose their spots, probably a form of camouflage protection, after three months.

FLORA

The variety of Spain's flora is astonishing, as anyone who witnesses the spectacular wild flower displays on roadsides and in pastures in spring and early summer will testify. Spain has around 8000 plant species, many of them unique to the Iberian Peninsula – a diversity due largely to the fact that the last Ice Age did not cover the entire peninsula, enabling plants which were killed off further north to survive in Spain. For this same reason, out in the Atlantic a good 50% of about 2000 plant species growing on the seven small islands of the Islas Canarias aren't to be found elsewhere.

High-Altitude Plants

Much of the variety of Spain's flora lies in its mountain areas. The Pyrenees have about 150 unique species, and even the Sierra Nevada in the south, covering a much smaller area, has about 60. When the snows melt, the alpine and subalpine zones – above the tree line in these regions – bloom spectacularly with small, rock-clinging plants and gentians, orchids, crocuses, narcissi and sundews. Particularly rich with orchids are the alpine meadows of the Picos de Europa (with 40 species) and the Serranía de Cuenca in the Sistema Ibérico.

Mountain Forests

Higher mountain forests tend to be coniferous and are often commercially harvested. The **silver fir** (*Abies alba*) is common in the Pyrenees and Sistema Ibérico, while the **Spanish fir** (*A. pinsapo*) is confined to the area around Ronda in Andalucía. The **Scots pine** (*Pinus sylvestris*), with its flaking red bark, is frequently found on the cooler northern mountains; the **umbrella pine** (*P. pinea*), with its large spreading top and edible kernel, grows more commonly near the coast. In the Islas Canarias, the **Canary Island pine** (*P. canariensis*), an indigenous variety, has resisted the competition of exotic species because of its ability to regenerate after forest fire.

Many pine forests are threatened by the hairy caterpillar of the pine processionary moth, which devours pine needles. The caterpillar's large, silvery nests are easy to spot in the trees and best steered clear of. Touching the caterpillar can provoke a nasty allergic reaction (for information on treatment, see Cuts, Bites & Stings in the Health & Safety chapter).

In ideal conditions the Scots pine can grows as tall as 40m, while its straight trunk can measure 1m across.

Deciduous forests – predominantly **beech** (*Fagus* spp) but also made up of **Pyrenean oak** (*Quercus pyrenaica*) and other trees – are found mainly on the lower slopes of the damp northern mountains. Many orchids grow on forest floors.

Lowland Forests

Mixed forests are dotted over the lowlands and *meseta* (the high tableland of central Spain), but can be found elsewhere, such as in Ronda. Many contain two useful evergreen oaks: the **cork oak** (*Q. suber*, alcornoque), the thick bark of which is stripped every nine years for *corcho* (cork); and the **holm** or **ilex oak** (*Q. ilex*; encina), its acorns gobbled up by pigs.

Where the tree cover is scattered, the resulting combined woodland pastures are known as *dehesas*. These mostly occur in the south-western meseta and bloom with flowers in early summer. Mixed forests may also contain conifers (grown for timber) or eucalyptus (grown for wood pulp). In the western Islas Canarias, and especially on the north-facing slopes of the small island of La Gomera – so significant that they've been declared a UNESCO World Heritage Site – survive areas of *laurisilva* (laurel forest). One of the world's last remaining Tertiary Era forests (wiped out just about everywhere else by the last of the Ice Ages), it is a mixture of laurels and lichen, holly, ash and heather (which resembles trees more closely than the ankle-high moorland tufts of northern Europe).

Scrub & Steppe

Where there's no woodland and no agriculture, the land is often maquis scrub or steppe. Maquis occurs where forests have been felled and the land then abandoned. Herbs such as **lavender** (*Lavandula* spp), **rosemary** (*Rosmarinus officinalis*) and **thyme** (*Thymus* spp) are typical maquis plants, as are shrubs of the rockrose family in the south, and **gorse** (*Ulex* spp), **juniper** (*Juniperus* spp), **heather** (*Erica* spp) and the **strawberry tree** (*Arbutus unedo*) in the north. If the soil is acid there may also be broom. Orchids, gladioli and irises may flower beneath these shrubs, which themselves can be quite colourful in spring.

Steppe is produced by overgrazing or occurs naturally in areas of hot, very dry climate. Much of the Ebro valley and Castilla-La Mancha are steppe, as is the almost desert-like Cabo de Gata in Andalucía. These areas burst into flower after rain.

Soft and deep red when ripe, the fruit of the strawberry tree is edible. Some like the taste, others agree with its Latin name *unedo*, meaning 'I eat one (only)'.

Some populations of brown bear in North America rank among the largest of terrestrial carnivores. Those in Spain, however, are often considerably smaller.

FAUNA

Spain's wildlife is among the most varied in Europe thanks to its wild terrain which has allowed the survival of several species that have died out in many other countries – though the numbers of some are now perilously small. Many of Spain's wild animals are nocturnal and you need to be both dedicated and lucky to track them down.

Mammals

In 1900 Spain had about 1000 **brown bears** (*Ursus arctos*; oso pardo). Today there are only about 50 still surviving in the Picos de Europa and further west in the Cordillera Cantábrica, as well as a few in the Pyrenees (mostly on the French side). Though hunting or killing these bears has been banned since 1973, numbers have continued to decline. The Pyrenean population is effectively extinct (though attempts are being made to import bears from Slovenia), while the Cantabrian bears are seriously threatened. Hunting and poisoning (accidental and deliberate) have been the main reasons for their decline.

As many as 1000 **wolves** (*Canis lupus*; lobo) survive, mostly in the mountains of the north-west, though there are a few in the south-western meseta and the Sierra Morena. While heavily protected, they're still regarded as an enemy by many local people.

Things look better for the **Spanish ibex** (*Capra pyrenaica*; cabra montés) – a stocky, high-mountain goat whose males have distinctive, long horns. It spends summer hopping agilely around high crags and descends to pastures in winter. Almost hunted to extinction by 1900, the ibex was protected by royal decree a few years later, and recent estimates suggest there are as many as 70,000. The main populations are in the Sierra de Gredos (see the boxed text 'The Gredos Ibex' in the Sistema Central chapter) and Andalucía's Sierra de Cazorla.

The **Spanish lynx** (*Lynx pardinus*; lince ibérico) is a uniquely Spanish wild cat, smaller than the lynx of northern Europe. Its numbers have been reduced to between 600 and 800 by hunting and by a decline in the numbers of rabbits, its staple diet. Now stringently protected, it lives in wild southern and western woodlands, including Parque Nacional de Doñana and Parque Natural Monfragüe.

Less uncommon beasts – though you'll still need to go looking for them – include the mainly nocturnal **wild boar** (*Sus scrofa*; jabalí), which likes thick

The Spanish lynx is mainly nocturnal and solitary, hunting small animals by stalking or waiting for hours in ambush.

woods, marshes and farmers' root crops; and the **chamois** (*Rupicapra pyrenaica*; rebeco, sarrio, isard or gamuza*)*, not unlike a smaller, shorter-horned ibex but actually a member of the antelope family, living near the tree line of the Pyrenees and Cordillera Cantábrica, and descending to pastures in winter.

Other more frequently sighted animals include the **red** (*Cervus elaphus*), **roe** (*Capreolus capreolus*) and **fallow** (*Dama dama*) **deer** (ciervo, corzo or gamo), found in forests and woodlands of all types; the nocturnal **genet** (*Genetta genetta*; gineta), rather like a short-legged cat with a black-spotted white coat and a long, striped tail, found in woodland and scrub in the south and north; the **red squirrel** (*Sciurus vulgaris*), living in mountain forests; the mainly nocturnal **Egyptian mongoose** (*Herpestes ichneumon*; meloncillo), inhabiting woods, scrub and marshes in the southern half of the country; the otter (*Lutra lutra*; nutria); the **beech marten** (*Martes foina*; garduña), found in scattered deciduous forests and on rocky outcrops and cliffs; and the **pine marten** (*M. martes*; marta), which inhabits pine forests in the Pyrenees.

Birds of Prey

Spain has many birds of prey – around 25 breeding species, some of them summer visitors from Africa. You'll often see them circling or hovering above the mountains or meseta. Parque Natural Monfragüe and the Serranía de Cuenca are two places particularly noted for birds of prey. (Identifying them is a different matter! See Books in the Facts for the Walker chapter for some useful field guides.)

The threatened **lammergeier** (*Gypaetus barbatus*), with its majestic 2m-plus wingspan, is slowly recovering in the high Pyrenees (55 pairs were counted in 1996) and is being reintroduced into the Sierra de Cazorla. Poisoned food and furtive hunting have been the bird's main threats. Its Spanish name, *quebrantahuesos* (bone-smasher), reflects its habit of dropping prey onto rocks from the air so that it can get at the bone marrow. Spain has a few hundred pairs of Europe's biggest bird of prey, the **black vulture** (*Aegypius monachus*; buitre negro), probably the world's largest population. Its strongholds are in the Sierra Morena, Parque Natural Monfragüe in Extremadura, Montes de Toledo in Castilla-La Mancha and Sierra de la Peña de Francia in Castilla y León.

Another emblematic bird is the **Spanish imperial eagle** (*Aquila adalberti*; águila imperial), which was almost killed off by hunting and a decline in the

Also known as the bearded vulture, the lammergeier sports long bristles on the chin. It ha brown plumage on top and a tawny underside

Pairs of golden eagles mate for life and can occasionally be seen performing aerial displays in which the male and female lock feet together and cartwheel towards the ground.

rabbit population and is now considered among the rarest birds of prey in Europe. Its white shoulders distinguish it from other imperial eagles. Around 100 pairs remain, about 20 of them in Parque Nacional de Doñana, and others in Parque Natural Monfragüe, the Pyrenees and Cantabria.

Other notable large birds of prey include the **golden eagle** (*A. chrysaetos*; águila real), **griffon vulture** (*Gyps fulvus*; buitre leonado) and **Egyptian vulture** (*Neophron percnopterus*; alimoche), all found in high mountain regions. Among smaller birds of prey, many of them found around deciduous or lowland woods and forests, are the **kestrel** (*Falco tinnunculus*; cernícalo) and **buzzard** (*Buteo buteo*; ratonero), which are both common, the **sparrowhawk** (*Accipiter nisus*; gavilán), various harriers (*Circus* sp; aguiluchos), and the acrobatic **red kite** (*Milvus milvus*; milano real) and **black kite** (*M. migrans*; milano negro). Black kites may be seen over open ground near marshes and rubbish dumps.

Water Birds

Spain is a haven for numerous water birds, thanks to some large wetland areas. Most famous and important of the wetlands is the Guadalquivir delta in Andalucía, large sections of which are included in the Parque Nacional de Doñana and its buffer zones. Hundreds of thousands of birds winter here and many more call in during spring and autumn migrations. Other important coastal wetlands are the Albufera de Valencia in Valencia and the Ebro delta and Aiguamolls de l'Empordà in Catalunya.

Inland, thousands of ducks (pato) winter on the Tablas de Daimiel wetlands in Castilla-La Mancha and at Laguna de Gallocanta, 50km south of Calatayud in Aragón. The Laguna de Gallocanta is Spain's biggest natural lake and supports a sizeable **crane** (*Grus grus*; grulla) population. Laguna de Fuente de Piedra near Antequera in Andalucía is Europe's main breeding site for the **greater flamingo** (*Phoenicopterus ruber*; flamenco), with as many as 13,000 pairs rearing chicks in spring and summer. This beautiful pink bird can be seen in many other saline wetlands along the Mediterranean and southern Atlantic coasts, including the Ebro delta, Cabo de Gata and Parque Nacional de Doñana.

Other Birds

Two rare, large birds famous for their elaborate male courtship displays are the **great bustard** (*Otis tarda*;

avutarda), which inhabits the plains of the meseta, and the **capercaillie** (*Tetrao urogallus*; urogallo), a kind of giant black grouse found in northern mountain woodlands. Spain has perhaps 8000 great bustards, more than the rest of Europe combined. Weighing as much as 14kg, the male in flight has been compared to a goose with eagle's wings.

More often seen is the large **white stork** (*Ciconia ciconia*; cigüeña blanca), actually black and white, which nests from spring to autumn on chimneys and towers right in the middle of towns like Cáceres and Trujillo in Extremadura, as well as on trees, pylons and other protuberances. The much rarer **black stork** (*C. nigra*; cigüeña negra), all black, has been reduced to perhaps 200 pairs in Spain by destruction of its woodland habitat and by pollution of its watering and feeding places. Its stronghold is the western part of the southern meseta, especially Parque Natural Monfragüe. Both types of stork winter in Africa.

Among the most colourful of Spain's many other birds are the **golden oriole** (*Oriolus oriolus*; oropéndola), found in orchards and deciduous woodlands in summer (the male has an unmistakable bright yellow body); the orange, black and white **hoopoe** (*Upupa epops*; abubilla), with its distinctive crest, common in open woodlands, on farmland and golf courses; and the gold, brown and turquoise **bee-eater** (*Merops apiaster*; abejaruco), which nests in sandy banks in summer. All are more common in the south. Various woodpeckers (pitos or picos) and owls (búhos) inhabit mountain woodlands.

And let's not forget the **canary** (*Serinus canaria*), that native of the Islas Canarias. Unlike its distant, inbred domestic relative, the island canary is a muddy brown colour, but its song is just as sweet – in fact all the sweeter because it is wild.

The wild canary is less colourful than its domestic counterpart, which has been selectively bred for more than 400 years to enhance its singing and plumage.

Other Fauna

Most of Europe's species of butterfly are found in Spain, including some unique to the Iberian Peninsula. There are 20-odd bat species, four types of salamander, midwife toads, chameleons (found in Andalucía's Axarquía region), numerous lizards and snakes.

Off Spain's shores are found 27 species of marine mammals, including several each of whale and dolphin. Cabo de Peñas, near Gijon on the Bay of Biscay, is a noted gathering ground. In the Mediterranean, some species are threatened by driftnet fishing (though this is not practised by Spanish fishing boats).

continued from page 26

POPULATION & PEOPLE

There's only space for a swift canter through one of Spain's greatest riches: the regional, linguistic and cultural diversity of its almost 40 million people. Though most take pride in being Spanish when the national football team is on a winning streak or when the Olympic Games come round, in other contexts regional loyalties often take precedence. It's quite possible, for example, for a Valenciano to refer to someone from the meseta as an *extranjero* – a 'foreigner' in literal terms, but in this context more accurately translated as 'stranger' or 'outsider'.

Distribution

Spain is one of Europe's least densely populated countries, with about 75 people per sq km. The spaces beckoning to the walker are, in fact, even wider and more open than this round figure suggests. More than half of all Spaniards live in cities nowadays and most of the rest live in towns of 10,000 or more inhabitants. In this century, the least fruitful soils of Andalucía, the meseta and Galicia have been abandoned in favour of the industrialised regions of Catalunya, the País Vasco and other areas with greater opportunity for employment.

In order to maximise the cultivable land, people in rural areas have for centuries concentrated in *pueblos* (villages), from where farmers travel out to their fields in the morning and back at night. (The País Vasco is the exception; only here are you likely to see the land dotted with single farmsteads, each relatively distant from its neighbour, as in much of the rest of rural Europe.) This, in a land of over 505,000 sq km, leaves an awful lot of space. Aragón, for example, has only around 20 people per sq km (if you exclude its capital, Zaragoza), and if you walk the Aragonese Pyrenees you'll wonder where even this small number got to.

Regional Differences

The peoples with the strongest sense of local identity, reinforced by the fact that each has its own language, are the Catalans, Basques and, to a lesser extent, Galicians. Each lives on the fringes of the country whose heartland, geographically speaking, is Castilla.

The Catalans are renowned for being hardworking, resourceful, artistic and adventurous. They can also be the most insular and their insistence upon the official use of the Catalan language in the public domain arouses the resentment of residents from other regions of Spain. They're great walkers; their network of refuges and trails is the most developed in the nation and there's a considerable body of trekking and mountaineering literature in Catalan. But even mountaineering isn't free from regional politics; when the first team from Catalunya to conquer Everest hauled themselves to the summit, they planted the Catalan flag, and only the Catalan flag.

The Andalucians, or Andaluz, live in the largest autonomous region in an increasingly decentralised Spain. Andalucía is home to several of the stereotypes often incorrectly attributed to the Spanish as a whole, such as sherry, flamenco, bullfighting, gazpacho, flamboyant fiestas and intense summer heat.

The Basques claim to be the original inhabitants of the Iberian Peninsula and there is a certain amount of evidence – from Basque place names in the Catalan Pyrenees and Andorra to the results of recent blood-group studies – which supports this argument. Traditionally conservative and ultra-Catholic, their sense of separateness is reinforced by their unique language, known to be non-Indo-European, which is perhaps the oldest in Europe and all but impenetrable to outsiders. Their rich cuisine alone is a powerful reason for a visit to the País Vasco.

Galicia, together with Andalucía in the south and Extremadura in the west, is one of Spain's poorest areas, from where many have emigrated over the years to other regions of Spain, Europe or the New World. Living amid mists and greenness, and surrounded by an often forbidding sea, Galicians frequently identify with Celtic peoples also living on the western fringes of

Europe; you'll even hear the bagpipes, a popular local instrument.

Spain has about 500,000 *gitanos* (Gypsies), half of whom live in Andalucía. The remainder are confined very much to the poorer quarters of large cities such as Madrid, Barcelona and Valencia. Originating in India, the first gitanos are reputed to have reached Spain in the 15th century.

A more recent movement of peoples is the southward push of northern Europeans, a high proportion of them retired and seeking sunshine. Concentrated in the main on the Costa del Sol and Costa Blanca, there are about 200,000 permanent residents from other EU countries, particularly Britain, Germany, Holland and Scandinavia, and an equivalent number of winter migrants.

SOCIETY & CONDUCT

There's little in local customs and behaviour that's likely to throw you. On the trail, you are likely to be greeted with a hearty *hola* at any time of day, *buenos días* up to midday and *buenas tardes* from then on. To these, you can reply in just the same way. Similarly, when entering a shop, bar or restaurant many people will give such a greeting, whether murmured discreetly or robustly sung out to all present. Similarly, when leavetaking, it's polite to throw out a generalised *adiós*. When in a restaurant many Spaniards will say *¡Que aprovecheis!*, the equivalent of *bon appétit* (enjoy your meal).

Anglo-Saxons are often struck by the more economical use by the Spanish of *por favor* (please) and *gracias* (thank you), and it's true that they occur less in Spanish than in many English social interactions. This doesn't mean that Spaniards are less polite, however. They often convey a sense of courtesy through other means: by intonation, gesture or facial expression. In some contexts, it's just not deemed necessary. Why, they will argue, should you say 'thank you' to a shopkeeper for handing over goods at the end of a straight commercial transaction from which both parties have benefited?

For walking – and, indeed, in any walk of contemporary Spanish life – the dress code is as informal as you care to make it. Whenever the weather allows, shorts are the trekking norm for both women and men. Some people may look askance at you if you visit a church with knees or shoulders bared, but they are a dwindling minority.

Don't expect to come down from the hills and top up on provisions at the village shop between 2 and 5 pm, when they normally close. On the other hand, shops, supermarkets and tourist information centres usually stay open until at least 7 and often 8 pm. Spaniards normally eat late and this is reflected in restaurant hours. Lunch will typically be served from around 2 pm and people won't look askance if you arrive as late as 4.30 pm, expecting to be served. Dinner is rarely on offer before 9 pm, so if you're ravenous after a long day hike, make sure you've some snacks in your backpack to tide you over. Outside normal opening hours, however, many burger joints and places offer *platos combinados*, literally meaning 'combined plate', a largeish serve of meat, seafood or omelette with trimmings – often advertised by photos on the cafe wall.

Those *refugios* (refuges or mountain huts) which are staffed usually have different hours, serving dinner earlier, often in two sittings if it's a large place and full to capacity. Unspoken refugio etiquette also usually observes lights out and silence from 10 pm or even earlier, and you're unlikely to be left sleeping after 6.30 am.

LANGUAGE

Spanish (Español) is the national language, understood by everyone and spoken fluently by nearly all. It's often referred to as Castellano, or Castilian, a term generally preferred by users of the three widely spoken regional languages, Catalan, Basque and Galician.

For more information on all four languages, plus a guide to the pronunciation of Spanish and a list of words and phrases particularly suitable for walkers, refer to the Language chapter later in the book.

Facts for the Walker

SUGGESTED ITINERARIES

With a week at your disposal, you might want to base yourself in one place and do a number of day walks. For suggestions, see What Kind of Walk? later in this chapter.

The Sistema Central and Valencia chapters contain several extended walks which can be combined to make up a walking holiday of a week or a little more (including travelling time). In the Sistema Central, combine a two day 'training run' in the Sierra de Candelario with the Alta Ruta de Gredos in the Sierra de Gredos. In Valencia, the dramatic four to five day Els Ports circuit followed by two or three days of gentler walking in La Marina are an ideal way to experience the region. Alternatively, after the Els Ports circuit it's possible, with good bus and train connections to Madrid, to sample some of the shorter walks in the Sistema Central.

The options widen if you have two or more weeks at your disposal. The Picos de Europa Circuit in the Cordillera Cantábrica takes nine days, but you don't have to complete the walk. After a brief taste of the mountains, continue onto Santiago de Compostela in Galicia to enjoy a couple of days by the ocean on the Spindrift Walk.

Highlights

- Scrambling around La Pedriza in the Sierra de Guadarrama, an adventure playground of eroded rock formations, fallen boulders, spires and tight gullies.

- Watching the sun redden the glacial corrie below El Calvitero in the Sierra de Candelario.

- Heaving yourself over the Coll de Mulleres to marvel at the Maladeta glacier and peaks of Aragón before you.

- The high-level Faja de Pelay route, clutching the contours way above the valley in the Parque Nacional de Ordesa y Monte Perdido.

- Reluctantly leaving the splendour of the Parc Nacional d'Aigüestortes i Estany de Sant Maurici and dropping down into the lake-stippled bowl of the Circ de Colomers.

- The challenge and stark beauty of the upper limits of the Picos de Europa.

- The lost trails of Galicia's Costa da Morte with the ocean at your feet.

- Sauntering through the Serra do Courel, Galicia's little-known crown jewel.

- After the dry, rugged slopes of the Las Marinas mountains, walking the spectacular Sierra de Bernia ridge, then descending to the warm waters of the Costa Blanca.

- The approach to Portell de l'Infern in Els Ports as the path winds its way under the huge overhanging limestone cliffs of an increasingly dramatic gorge.

- The superb seascapes from the clifftop Camino del Archiduque in Mallorca's Serra de Tramuntana range.

- The Sierra Nevada's awesome high-level rock wilderness.

- The Sierra de Grazalema and Parque Natural de Cazorla: beautiful mountainscapes and – rare in dry Andalucía – gorgeous green countryside.

- The stench of sulphur in your nostrils as, eschewing the easy route up by cable car, you gain the summit of the Pico del Teide in the Islas Canarias.

- Reaching Santiago de Compostela after 730km and one month on the Camino de Santiago pilgrim trail.

In Andalucía, which alone merits at least a fortnight, try two or three day walks in the Parque Natural de Cazorla and divide the rest of your time between the valleys of Alpujarras and the Sierra Nevada.

A walking holiday in the Pyrenees can be as long or as short as you care to make it: from a few days based in Andorra, Espot, Benasque or Torla to the 23 day traverse from Andorra to Sallent de Gállego. Few walkers will have enough time to accomplish it all. But shorter stretches such as from Andorra to Espot, followed by a few walks within the Parc Nacional d'Aigüestortes i Estany de Sant Maurici, or from Espot as far as the Vall d'Aran, or from Benasque to Torla just beyond the Parque Nacional de Ordesa y Monte Perdido, can give you something of the true flavour of this magnificent chain.

The main variant of the Camino de Santiago pilgrim trail from the French frontier to the holy city of Santiago de Compostela in Galicia requires a month or so to complete. Again, if you're pressed for time it's quite feasible to complete only a section of the route.

Spain's islands are destinations in their own right. Based in Sóller on Mallorca, you can enjoy a week of action-packed walking. With more time, it's well worth a trip by ferry to Denia on the mainland, walking for four or five days through the Sierra Bernia and Las Marinas mountains in Valencia.

Similarly, Puerto de la Cruz on Tenerife in the Islas Canarias (Canary Islands) makes an excellent base for a full week of day walks, interspersed with two or three walking days on the island of La Gomera, only a short ferry trip away.

A final piece of advice: distances from one walking area to another can be considerable and public transport, though usually reliable, may not be frequent. If in doubt, limit yourself to one walking area – and come back again the following year.

PLANNING
When to Walk

Whatever time of year you plan to walk, there'll be a region of Spain which will be at its best. If the climate of the moment on the mainland is too extreme, consider the offshore islands. In the Islas Baleares (Balearic Islands), Mallorca's snow-free Serra de Tramuntana offers bracing walking during and on either side of winter, while the climate of the Islas Canarias, rendered mild by the Gulf Stream and prevailing trade winds, makes hiking pleasant year-round. Similarly, the Camino de Santiago, at its best from June to July and September to October, can be walked at any time, though you may want to avoid the hottest and most popular months of July and August. Galician coastal routes are also accessible throughout the year, though heavy winter rains from the end of November until well into March can dampen enthusiasm.

The mild-season window for some of the high-level walks is open only briefly. In Andalucía's Sierra Nevada, the Picos de Europa in the Cordillera Cantábrica and on the higher walks in the Pyrenees, snow can block passes until the second half of June and again begins to fall in early September. Galician sierra routes are also primarily summer walks, though they are passable at any time between June and October. Snow dusting outside these months can make trail finding difficult.

Above 2500m in the Pyrenees, manageable snow can linger in the dips until well into July. *Refugios* (refuges or mountain huts) are usually staffed only during these months, though many keep a small wing open year-round.

Andalucía in general has a justified reputation for uncomfortably hot summers. Most of the walks described there are at their best between April and October, though some of the lower ones are best avoided in July and August. This said, they can be walked at any time, with one important exception: the Sierra Nevada – as mentioned above, best left to skiers in winter.

In the Islas Baleares and inland from Valencia's Mediterranean coast, July and August can be uncomfortably hot. This needn't necessarily inhibit you; take plenty of water, set off early and you can still enjoy some great walking. March to May when the wild flowers are at their best is the optimum time. For this same reason, the Els Ports region in the north of Valencia is best walked from late April to June.

Given their closeness to Madrid, parts of the Gredos and Guadarrama *sierras* (mountain ranges) can become quite crowded. These areas are best walked in early or late summer when the climate's relatively benign and the trails are freer.

In general, most of Spain and a fair percentage of Western Europe holiday in the peninsula from mid-July until the end of August, stretching facilities to the limit (Spain and its offshore islands receive more than 47 million visitors a year). At these times, as well as during Easter Week, it's essential to reserve accommodation in refugios in the Pyrenees and most other areas. Hotels in popular tourist areas then tend to jack up their prices and are almost invariably full.

Walkers and mountaineers do attempt the high mountain routes in winter – even scaling Pico de Aneto, the highest point in the Pyrenees – but we assume that most readers aren't so experienced and confine our recommendations to walking at less forbidding times of the year.

Overall in Spain, June and September are the optimum months of the year for walking. At these times, the nights are still relatively long, the heat is milder, camping grounds, refugios and hotels less overwhelmed and the trails less crowded. This said, there's quite a lot of variation between regions. For an overview, consult the section on Climate in the Facts about Spain chapter; for more specific regional information, see the Climate sections in the individual walks chapters.

What Kind of Walk?

Within this edition you'll find the whole spectrum of walks, from three-hour strolls to quite demanding walks of several days. Before deciding where to go, determine which area best fits the way you like to walk. Nearly all walks, however short or long, will require a certain degree of physical fitness,

for such is Spain – or rather such are its most attractive hiking areas – that you'll only rarely find yourself walking on the flat. For a description of the book's system of grading and a description of walk standards, see the section on Walking Routes later in this chapter. For information on a selection of walks most suitable for children, see Walking with Children, also later in this chapter.

In popular tourist areas, such as the islands of Mallorca in the Islas Baleares and Tenerife and La Gomera in the Islas Canarias, we concentrate upon day walks, accessible by public transport. On the mainland, you can radiate out each day from, for example, Oviedo and Santiago de Compostela in the north of Spain or Cazorla and Ronda in Andalucía. The walks included in each of these areas are sufficient for a hiking holiday of a week or more. All the chapters, except Mallorca and the Islas Canarias, describe linear or circular walks of much longer duration. With very few exceptions, each daily leg finishes where there's some form of accommodation, either a refugio or a village offering a range of options. Camping grounds with facilities are indicated, as are the most attractive sites for camping wild.

In Spain, it's not usual for walkers to hire a personal guide. However, in certain areas where walking is especially popular, it's possible to sign on for a guided group outing. Several private companies on Tenerife island, for example, or in Benasque in the Aragonese Pyrenees, organise trips. You can also sign on for a ranger-led walk in several of the protected parks, such as the Parque Nacional d'Aigüestortes i Estany de Sant Maurici. Explanations are normally given only in Spanish, or Spanish plus the regional language. And be warned: the signing-up procedure can sometimes be absurdly bureaucratic and complex.

Maps

For shops within Spain which have an extensive stock of maps, see the Books section later in this chapter. Generally, it's safer to buy all your maps in advance. Even in the most popular parts of the Pyrenees, for example, a shop in a tourist town or village might sell the Editorial Alpina map for its area, but you'd be lucky to find anything else.

In the UK, Stanfords (☎ 0171-836 1321, fax 0171 836 0189; from 1 June 1999 ☎ 020-7836 1321, fax 020-7836 0189), nearly 150 years in business, is the world's largest map and guidebook store. It has several Spain-specific catalogues listing all the maps and books on peninsula Spain, the Islas Baleares and Islas Canarias kept in stock. It also operates an efficient mail-order service; you can place orders by phone from anywhere in the world. Ring or write to 12-14 Long Acre, London WC2E 9LP.

Map World, otherwise known as Travellers World Bookshop (free call within Britain ☎ 0800-83 80 80, fax 01332-34 04 64, shop@map-world.co.uk), also operates a worldwide mail-order service. Visit their Web site at www.mapworld.com.

Small-Scale Maps If you want something more sophisticated than a tourist office map of Spain, the Michelin *España y Portugal* No 990 map at 1:1 million and the 1:500,000 map of the same title produced by García y Solis are both reliable. Michelin publishes six regional 1:400,000 maps which between them cover the whole country. Germany's RV Verlag publishes 10 regional maps at 1:300,000, plus one of the peninsula at 1:1 million.

Large-Scale Maps Two public sector bodies, the Instituto Geográfico Nacional (IGN) and the Servicio Geográfico del Ejército (SGE) of the Spanish army, produce maps.

Between them and often duplicating each other, they cover the whole country with over 1000 maps at 1:50,000 and contours indicated at 20m intervals. Nearly all areas of interest to walkers are covered, especially by IGN, which has a range of maps at 1:25,000 with contours at 10m intervals.

Traditionally working in isolation and almost in defiance of each other, there's greater cooperation nowadays. The tendency is for IGN to concentrate upon new and updated maps at 1:25,000 and for SGE to take responsibility for the 1:50,000 series.

SGE 1:50,000 maps (375 ptas) are generally better for walkers, particularly if you're undertaking a long walk. They're relatively recent, the most ancient dating back to the 1980s. The IGN's 1:25,000 series is being constantly updated but most are based upon an aerial survey and, though giving more topographical detail, have less footpath information.

Each has its own system of numbering. This, however, is scarcely a problem, since most sources quote both. Where SGE maps are cited in this book, the SGE number is given first, followed by the IGN number in brackets – for example, *Sóller* No 38-26 (670).

Each also has a different system of map reference. IGN maps use the familiar latitude/longitude coordinate system. Army maps, however, use UTM (Universal Transverse Mercator) coordinates. Neither system affects navigation on the ground. If you're a techno-walker with a GPS (Global Positioning System) receiver in your backpack, simply select the appropriate coordinate system for the map that you're using.

Both series suffer from the lack of any overlap between maps and the fact that map distribution accords to purely geographical criteria (some coastal maps can be as much as 75% sea, while a popular day walk might require two or even three maps). When buying maps, check carefully when a map was *actualizada* (updated or last revised) rather than the date of printing; the difference can be considerable.

Two private map companies, both relatively young, stand out for reliability and walker-friendliness. If they produce maps for the area where you intend to walk, choose them every time in preference to the IGN or SGE alternatives. PRAMES, a consortium in which the Federación Aragonesa de Montañismo (FAM) is the principal shareholder, produces excellent maps specifically for walkers. For more information, see Maps under Information in the Pyrenees chapter. Though maps are limited for the moment to Aragón, PRAMES has plans to branch out into other areas. Also very reliable, though regrettably more limited in coverage and distribution, are the few maps produced by Adrados Ediciones (☎ 98 578 06 11). You'll find them in major northern cities such as Oviedo and Santander in Cantabria, as well as in even the smallest villages around the Picos de Europa in the Cordillera Cantábrica.

For the Islas Canarias and Baleares, as well as the Alpujarras region in Andalucía, the UK-based Discovery Walking Guides (who also call themselves Warm Island Walking Guides) publishes reliable maps based upon IGN 1:25,000 originals. Each comes in a handy pack with a detailed route description in English. For current titles, check the Web site at www.walking.demon.co.uk.

Editorial Alpina (email for their latest list of titles, alpin@jet.es) produces over 50 *Guías Excursionistas y Turísticas*, each costing 675 ptas. These topographical maps with small accompanying guidebooks in Spanish or Catalan are targeted particularly at walkers and climbers. They are based on SGE maps, to which information has been added, and cover the Pyrenees and Catalunya fairly comprehensively, as well as areas such as the Picos de Europa, the Sierra de Cazorla and the Sierra de Gredos. They are mostly at a scale of 1:25,000, have contours at 20m intervals and five to seven shades of colour to indicate altitude.

While contours and villages are accurate, be very wary of other information as maps contain more than the occasional blinding, disorienting error. In particular, paths and tracks indicated on the map are sometimes little more than a cartographer's innovative thin red line or a long disappeared trail that nobody's bothered to research on the ground. Refugio locations, in particular, are often lackadaisically positioned.

Lastly, another anomaly: older maps usually adopt, with breathtaking ethnocentricity, Madrid as the zero point of longitude, while most recent maps follow international practice and opt for Greenwich.

You'll find details of relevant maps in the regional Information sections of each walks chapter and in Planning at the beginning of each walk section.

Maps in This Book Every walk described in this book has an accompanying map which gives the walk's general route. It is best used together with one of the commercial maps recommended in the Planning section for each walk.

A continuous brown line indicates the route of a walk, while a broken line indicates an optional side trip detailed in the text at the end of the walk description. You'll also find highlighted all significant natural features, starting and finishing points, camping grounds, the best camp sites for wild camping and exceptional viewpoints.

Contours appear in brown, and because of a map's scale they generally have large intervals. While they provide a broad indication of the topography, we recommend that you don't rely upon them alone for navigation as between each can be some fairly considerable ups and downs.

What to Bring

In a country as big as Spain, in addition to the usual seasonal variation, temperatures differ from region to region and from highland to lowland. Similarly, the probability of rain can oscillate between near-certain and highly improbable. In choosing what to bring on your trip, study the weather information under Climate in each walks chapter, then select according to your itinerary from the items recommended in this section. For suggestions on what to include in a basic medical kit, see the boxed text 'Medical Kit Check List' in the Health & Safety chapter.

Warm Weather Wear Summertime in Andalucía and the mountains of central Spain can be very hot. Wear light and loose clothing such as a T-shirt and shorts or a

Equipment Check List

This list is a general guide to things you might pack if you're planning to camp wild. If you're on a walk lasting several days but planning to stay in refugios or other accommodation, you can select from this list and travel much lighter.

Equipment
- [ ] tent
- [ ] backpack and day-pack
- [ ] waterproof backpack liner
- [ ] survival blanket
- [ ] insulating mat
- [ ] sleeping bag
- [ ] fuel stove and fuel
- [ ] small pan/saucepan and pot grip
- [ ] pocket knife, cup, plate and eating utensils
- [ ] water containers
- [ ] basic medical kit, toiletries and toilet paper
- [ ] water purification tablets or iodine
- [ ] camera and spare film
- [ ] map, guides and compass
- [ ] torch with spare batteries and globe
- [ ] matches or lighter and candles
- [ ] notebook and pencil
- [ ] whistle

- [ ] pot scourer
- [ ] spare length of nylon cord
- [ ] lightweight, high-energy food

Clothes
- [ ] windproof jacket
- [ ] waterproof jacket
- [ ] waterproof overtrousers
- [ ] T-shirt and long-sleeved shirt with collar
- [ ] thermal underwear
- [ ] spare underwear and socks
- [ ] warm hat and gloves
- [ ] sunhat
- [ ] sunglasses
- [ ] gaiters
- [ ] small pack towel

Optional Items
- [ ] backpack cover
- [ ] runners (training shoes)
- [ ] swimming costume
- [ ] walking poles or stick
- [ ] trowel
- [ ] altimeter
- [ ] binoculars
- [ ] Walkman/radio
- [ ] solar battery recharger

skirt. Sometimes a pair of light trousers are preferable, whatever the heat, if the undergrowth's thick and prickly. Should this be the case, it will be indicated in the What to Bring section of the introduction to a walk. Stuff a second shirt into your day-pack – useful as an extra layer – wear a hat with a brim that's wide enough to keep the sun off your face. Sunglasses, if there's intense glare, are more than a fashion statement.

When in the mountains – indeed anywhere where there's the least possibility of the weather taking a turn for the worse – learn to be sceptical of the clear blue skies of the moment and pack for the potential worst.

Cold Weather Wear The secret of happy walking is to wear several layers of light clothing. Though tedious to pull on and off, layers allow you to fine-tune your body temperature; the wind may be knifing into your face but, if you're walking hard uphill with a full backpack, the rest of you may feel as though it's in a sauna. A lightweight, windproof external layer will help to prevent your body from losing too much warmth. A tightly woven cotton or polycotton jacket, or a windproof synthetic fleece top, are all good choices. Underneath, you have an ideal opportunity to use up those old blouses or shirts that it would pain you to throw out. A synthetic base layer such as polypropylene, with its ability to wick the moisture away from the body and reduce chilling, is a good idea.

Below the waist, loose-fitting trousers, supplemented if it's really cold by a pair of polypropylene thermal leggings, will keep you cosy. Leave the Levi's at home; denim is inflexible and once it's wet it clings around your legs like a cold compress. Up top (bear in mind that up to 60% of body heat is lost via your head), pull on a cold-weather cap or balaclava and bring along a pair of gloves or mittens.

Rainwear It's well worth investing in a jacket containing Sympatex, Gore-Tex or a similar 'breathable fabric' which – though this sounds like a paradox – lets the sweat out but prevents the rain from penetrating. Whatever the material, make sure it is in good condition and proven against wet weather. It should have a hood which allows you some peripheral vision; this can be important in difficult terrain. If the jacket also has a storm flap over the main zip and drawcords at either waist or hem, so much the better.

If you're planning to walk where it's likely to be wet, a pair of waterproof over-pants made out of a breathable fabric – with slits for pocket access and zips so you don't have to pull your boots off as the downpour begins – are also worth the investment. Otherwise, pull on a pair of shorts; legs dry much more easily than soggy trousers.

A large, heavy-duty plastic bag inside your backpack (and optionally a backpack cover, elasticated and easily slipped over your backpack when the first raindrops fall) is almost as important as your own rain gear. It ensures that, whatever the elements throw at you, you've something dry to put on at the end of the day.

Footwear You can get by with all sorts of compromises above the ankles, but never sell yourself short on footwear. On easier walks, runners (training shoes) are adequate. For anything more challenging, a pair of good boots should be a serious consideration. They don't come cheap but, if

well cared for, they'll be your companions for years and it will be like losing a close relative when you finally have to throw them out.

The heavyweight, clumping mud collectors of yesteryear are now extinct, replaced by a wide choice of brands in quality fabric or lightweight leather. In fabric, choose a pair with a waterproof, breathable fabric lining. Firm ankle support is essential, while a sole with widely spaced treads and a stepped heel will help you to negotiate rough terrain. Lastly, do make sure you and your boots get to know each other on at least a couple of outings before you head off on a walking holiday; there's nothing worse for morale than throbbing, avoidable blisters at the end of the first day.

Choose appropriate socks, the vital inter-face between your feet and boots. Synthetic or a wool and synthetic mixture will give the best cushioning and the least friction. Around the toe area, check that there are no seams; these can cause blisters the size of baby mushrooms.

If you're camping or staying in refugios, don't forget to slip a spare pair of light-weight footwear, such as runners, into your backpack to give both boots and feet a rest at the end of the day.

Equipment If you're limiting yourself to day walks, you can happily skip most of what follows, with the exception of our advice on carrying water. Where it's scarce, you'll find springs and sources indicated on individual walk maps in this book, but you should always have a couple of containers in your backpack. Plastic bottles will do – they needn't be anything fancy – but keep them topped up.

On the road your backpack should shift as much weight as possible away from your fragile back and onto the much stouter hips. Check that the one you buy has a firm, well padded belt; the two shoulder straps serve only to keep your load evenly balanced. Consider also taking a smaller day-pack so that, whenever possible, you can dump the big one and walk light.

If you're hopping from refugio to refugio, the only special item you might need is an inner sheet, for reasons of hygiene.

If you're planning to camp wild, however, certain equipment is indispensable. If buying a tent, it's worth paying a bit extra for one that has a flysheet that completely covers an inner layer, and weight is another important consideration. Go for a three-season sleeping bag. It will keep you warm in other than extremely cold conditions. In hot weather, just lie on top and enjoy an extra layer between you and the ground. To reduce the space it occupies in your backpack, buy a compression sack. Under your body and bag, you need an insulating mat.

For heating food and water, we strongly recommend taking a Camping Gaz stove or analogue that uses butane/propane cartridges (Cointra is a locally popular brand of cartridge). It's not that they're necessarily any better than alternative systems, but their cartridges (*cartuchos*) are the only widely available fuel source. Many are the walkers from abroad who've brought in some state-of-the-art device only to find themselves eating cold food on the trail. Even Coleman and Primus cartridges can only be found in a few specialist shops in large towns. You might be lucky enough to come across kerosene (*keroseno*, also spelt *quereseno*) in a hardware shop (*ferretería*) or garage, but they'll often expect you to buy it in industrial quantities. Methylated spirits (*alcohol de quemar*) is sold in some *droguerías* (shops which sell household products).

If you decide to use an alternative, bring enough fuel to carry you through your stay – but, if you're flying in, bear in mind that it's a prohibited item on all airlines.

Think carefully about packing a pair of lightweight telescopic poles. Collapsed short and thrust into the slope ahead, they help you up inclines and, elongated and prodded into the ground below, they ease the jarring on your knees during steep descents. Whatever the terrain, they take most of the weight of your backpack away from your back and haunches. The real mountaineer's gear of ice axe and crampons is very much an optional extra, even for some of the highest-level walks.

Among the smaller but no less vital items, a compass – plus the ability to use it – is an essential tool. An altimeter, though by no means vital, can also be a valuable navigational aid. Other useful items include extra plastic bags, a map holder to keep your maps clean and dry, a whistle to signal help in an emergency, a pocket knife and a torch (flashlight). The most flexible torches are those which fit on your head like a miner's lamp, leaving your hands free. For the potential if unlikely emergency, pack either a polythene 'bivvy bag' or an aluminium 'space blanket'.

The equipment list in this section is a distillation of things taken – and, on occasion, forgotten – on long walks over the years. It's only a guide. Conditions can vary enormously from region to region, season to season and day to day, making one walker's essential item another's frivolous option. Regard it as a basic check list for you to personalise according to your own walking style or the dictates of the particular journey that you're about to undertake.

With everything assembled, lay it all out on the floor, decide what's indispensable and discard the remainder. Once you've tucked the residue into your backpack, reflect upon the advice of Georges Véron, the classic French mountaineer and writer who knows the Pyrenees like nobody else. For comfortable walking, he says, your backpack shouldn't exceed 14kg. So, like so many before you, spill it all out on the floor again and decide what's *really* essential. Pack everything back in and take off for a strenuous day walk. Back home again, ask yourself how you're feeling, and if the answer's less than positive sling out yet more.

Buying & Hiring Locally The best advice is to bring your gear with you, having tried out everything in advance so that your boots and backpack are comfortable and you can put up that new tent alone in a strong wind with your eyes shut. This said, Spain's a good place to pick up new items at reasonable prices – and if you're hiking through tax-free Andorra, bargains are even keener (for shops there, see Accommodation & Supplies in the Andorra section of the Pyrenees chapter).

Look for a *tienda de deportes*, a sports goods shop. Below is a list of a few suggested shops in Madrid and Barcelona, the two cities you're most likely to arrive in. Within individual walks chapters, you'll find other shops indicated under Accommodation & Supplies.

Madrid
    Vivac:
    (☎/fax 91 517 63 30)
    Calle Ercille 7 (metro: Embajadores)
    Gonza Sport:
    (☎/fax 91 527 57 48)
    Calle Ribera de Curtidores 10, El Rastro
    (metro: Latina or Tirso de Molina)
    Koala:
    (☎/fax 91 429 91 89)
    Calle León 29 (metro: Antón Martín)

Barcelona
    Edelweiss:
    (☎ 93 454 83 09, fax 93 451 92 60)
    Carrer Urgell 72-76 (metro: Urgell)
    Campanna Esport:
    (☎ 93 45 35 001)
    Carrer Comte de Urgell 95 (metro: Urgell)
    Decathlon-l'Illa:
    (☎ 93 444 01 54)
    Avingut Diagonal 577-565 (metro: Palau Reial)

There isn't any real tradition of renting out equipment in Spain, though in some towns such as Benasque in the Pyrenees it's possible to hire crampons and an ice axe.

Physical Preparation

There's no need to go overboard about preparations for a walking holiday in Spain. This said, some longish jogs or hikes in the two months before departure to build up stamina and a couple of weeks of preparatory stretching exercises will really pay off.

TOURIST OFFICES
Local Tourist Offices

All cities and many smaller towns have an *oficina de turismo* or *oficina de información turística*, as do many quite tiny villages in walking areas during the summer months. Look for a sign with a large 'i' on it.

In general, the more important tourism is to a region the better informed the staff are. So, for example, offices in Andorra la Vella or Puerto de la Cruz, Tenerife, stand out. Others, such as many of the small summeronly offices, are only as good as the brochures they carry. Generally reliable for information on accommodation and local transport, they usually have little that's specifically targeted at walkers.

By contrast, national and many nature parks have visitor centres where the staff and information, sometimes supported by a video or display panels, tend to be much more useful for walkers.

For information on tourist offices in the areas where you are walking, see Information Sources in the individual walks chapters.

Tourist Offices Abroad

Information is available from Spanish national tourist offices in 19 countries, including:

Canada
    (☎ 416-961 3131)
    2 Bloor St West, 34th Floor, Toronto, Ontario M4W 3E2
France
    (☎ 01 45 03 82 50)
    43 rue Decamps, 75784 Paris, Cedex 16
Italy
    (☎ 06-678 3106)
    Via del Mortaro 19 interno 5, Rome 00187
    (☎ 02-7200 4617)
    Piazza del Carmine 4, 20121 Milan
Germany
    (☎ 030-8 82 65 43)
    Kurfürstendamm 180, D-10707 Berlin
    (☎ 0211-6 80 39 80)
    Grafenberger Allee 100 'Kutscherhaus', D-40237 Düsseldorf
    (☎ 069-72 50 33)
    Myliusstrasse 14, D-60325 Frankfurt am Main
    (☎ 089-5 38 90 75)
    Schubertstrasse 10, D-80336 Munich

Netherlands
(☎ 070-346 59 00)
Laan Van Meerdervoort 8-8a, 2517 The Hague
UK
(☎ 0171-486 8077; from 1 June 1999 020-
7486 8077; brochure request ☎ 0891-669920
at 50p a minute)
22-23 Manchester Square, London W1M 5AP
USA
(☎ 212-265 8822)
666 Fifth Ave, 35th Floor, New York, NY
10103
(☎ 213-658 7188)
8383 Wilshire Blvd, Suite 960, Beverly Hills,
Los Angeles, CA 90211
(☎ 312-642 1992)
845 North Michigan Ave, Chicago, IL 60611
(☎ 305-358 1992)
1221 Brickell Ave, Suite 1850, Miami, FL
33131

DOCUMENTS

Where the best walks are located, it's extremely unlikely that you'll be robbed. In the rougher quarters of the big cities through which you may pass, however, fleecing the foreigner is almost a local sport. Before you leave home, it's prudent to photocopy all documents that are important to you (such as your passport, your credit cards, travel insurance papers, air ticket, driving licence and even your Youth Hostel card). Leave one copy with someone at home and keep another with you, separate from the originals.

You needn't worry about straying over the border between Spain and France in the Pyrenees or walking near the Portuguese frontier. Since the 1997 Schengen agreement between nations committed to a united Europe, border posts just don't exist any more.

Passports

Citizens of European Union (EU) member states and Switzerland can travel to and around Spain on nothing more than their national identity card. If such countries do not issue identity cards – as in the UK – travellers must carry a fully valid passport. (UK visitor passports are not acceptable.) All other nationalities must carry a passport.

Check that your passport's expiry date is at least some months off; otherwise, if you're from a country that needs a visa, you may not be granted one.

Spaniards wouldn't venture as far as the corner shop without their Documento Nacional de Identidad (DNI). By law you too are supposed to carry your passport or ID card at all times; in order to avoid an embarrassing confrontation with the police, it's best to comply. In practice, the only occasion when you'll regularly have to flash your ID is when registering at a hotel or camping ground – and that's more to ensure that you don't do a runner than because Big Brother wants to know where or with whom you're sleeping.

Visas

For tourist visits to Spain of up to 90 days, nationals of many countries – including Australia, Canada, Japan, New Zealand and the USA – require no visa. South Africans, however, do. Options include a 30 day or 90 day single-entry visa (in London these cost UK£17.75 and UK£21.30 respectively) or a 90 day multiple-entry visa (UK£24.85).

Apply for a visa before leaving home. If you put in for one in a country where you aren't resident, your request may be forwarded to Madrid and a reply could take weeks. In addition, you may be asked to present tickets for onward or return flights, evidence of hotel accommodation and solvency, or even an invitation from someone in Spain. Finally, you may not be allowed the option of the 90 day three-entry visa.

Walking Permits

You need a piece of paper to get to the summit of the Pico del Teide on Tenerife (for the arcane procedure, see the Information section in the Islas Canarias chapter). So far, the only other place in this book where access is restricted is the *área de reserva* at the heart of the Sierra de Grazalema in Andalucía, where you're obliged to join an organised group – and pay for the privilege. If you're proposing to walk the Camino de Santiago, it's worth picking up the optional

Credencial del Peregrino, the pilgrim's passbook, which gives you access to refugios en route (for details, see Permits under Information in the Camino de Santiago chapter).

Travel Insurance

If you're from an EU country, pick up an E111 form from your local health authority before you leave home. This will entitle you to free emergency medical but not dental treatment. For more details, see Medical Cover in the Predeparture Preparation section of the Heath & Safety chapter.

A personal travel insurance policy to cover theft, loss and medical problems, particularly if you're walking the high mountains, is important. Look closely at the small print, however, before signing up; some insurance policies specifically exclude 'dangerous activities' which might, if the compiler's never pulled on a pair of boots, include walking. Ensure too that your policy covers the cost of an ambulance and emergency flight home. If you have to stretch out, you'll need two or even three seats, and airlines don't give them away!

You may prefer a policy which pays doctors or hospitals directly rather than requiring you to pay up front and claim later. If you opt for the latter, make sure you keep all documentation. Some policies ask you to call back (reverse charges) to a centre in your home country, where an immediate assessment of your problem is made.

Other Documents

If you're from an EU country, your driving licence should suffice for hiring a car. This said, the surest course of action wherever you're from is to pick up an International Driving Permit before you set out, valid for 12 months and available from automobile clubs in your home country.

There aren't many youth hostels in Spain – and even fewer near popular walking trails. For a bed at one, you just need to present your Hostelling International (HI) or youth hostel card from your home country. If you haven't got an HI card, you can buy one at most HI hostels in Spain.

EMBASSIES & CONSULATES
Spanish Embassies & Consulates

Spanish diplomatic representation abroad includes:

Andorra
Embassy:
(☎ 82 00 13)
Carrer Prat de la Creu 34, Andorra la Vella

Australia
Embassy:
(☎ 02-6273 3555)
15 Arkana St, Yarralumla, ACT 2600
Consulate:
(☎ 03-9347 1966)
766 Elizabeth St, 3rd Floor, Melbourne 3000
Consulate:
(☎ 02-9261 2433)
Level 24, St Martins Tower, 31 Market St, Sydney 2000

Canada
Embassy:
(☎ 613-747 2252)
74 Stanley Ave, Ottawa, Ontario K1M 1P4
Consulate:
(☎ 416-977 1661)
Suite 400, 1200 Bay St, Toronto M3H 2D1

France
Embassy:
(☎ 01 44 43 18 00)
22 Ave Marceau, 75008 Paris, Cedex 08

Germany
Embassy:
(☎ 0228-21 70 94)
Schlossstrasse 4, D-53115 Bonn
Consulate:
(☎ 030-261 60 81)
Lichtensteinallee 1, D-10787 Berlin

Ireland
Embassy:
(☎ 01-269 1640)
17A Merlyn Park, Ballsbridge, Dublin 4

Japan
Embassy:
(☎ 03-3583 8531)
1-3-29 Roppongi, Minato-Ku, Tokyo 106

Netherlands
Embassy:
(☎ 070-364 3814)
Lange Voorhout 50, 2514 EG The Hague

New Zealand
Spain has no diplomatic representation

Portugal
Embassy:
(☎ 01-347 2381)
Rua do Salitre 1, 1250 Lisbon

UK
  Embassy:
  (☎ 0171-235 5555; from 1 June 1999 ☎ 020-7235 5555)
  39 Chesham Place, London SW1X 8SB
  Consulate:
  (☎ 0171-5899 8989; from 1 June 1999 ☎ 020-7899 8989)
  20 Draycott Place, London SW3 2RZ
  Consulate:
  (☎ 0131-220 1843)
  63 North Castle St, Edinburgh EH2 3LJ, Scotland
USA
  Embassy:
  (☎ 202-728 2330)
  2375 Pennsylvania Ave NW, Washington, DC 20037
  Consulate:
  (☎ 212-355 4080)
  150 East 58th St, 30th Floor, New York, NY 10155

Embassies & Consulates in Spain

All embassies are in Madrid and include:

Australia
  Embassy:
  (☎ 91 441 93 00)
  Plaza del Descubridor Diego de Ordás 3-2, Edificio Santa Engracia 120
Canada
  Embassy:
  (☎ 91 431 43 00)
  Calle de Núñez de Balboa 35
France
  Embassy:
  (☎ 91 435 55 60)
  Calle de Salustiano Olózaga 9
  Consulate:
  (☎ 91 597 32 67)
  Paseo de la Castellana 79
Germany
  Embassy:
  (☎ 91 557 90 00)
  Calle de Fortuny 8
Ireland
  Embassy:
  (☎ 91 576 35 00)
  Calle de Claudio Coello 73
Japan
  Embassy:
  (☎ 91 590 76 00)
  Calle de Serrano 109
Netherlands
  Embassy:
  (☎ 91 359 09 14)
  Avenida del Comandante Franco 32

New Zealand
  Embassy:
  (☎ 91 523 02 26)
  Plaza de la Lealtad 2
Portugal
  Embassy:
  (☎ 91 561 78 00)
  Calle del Castillo 128
  Consulate:
  (☎ 91 445 46 00)
  Paseo de General Martínez Campos 11
UK
  Embassy:
  (☎ 91 319 02 00)
  Calle de Fernando el Santo 16
  Consulate:
  (☎ 91 308 52 01)
  Calle del Marqués Ensenada 16
USA
  Embassy:
  (☎ 91 587 22 00)
  Calle de Serrano 75

CUSTOMS

If you fly into Spain from outside the EU, you can bring in or take out duty-free a 1L bottle of spirits, a 1L bottle of wine, 200 cigarettes and, for those intimate moments on the trail, 50mL of perfume. Allowances for the Islas Canarias, which are considered a duty-free zone, are slightly more generous. Duty-free allowances for travel between EU countries are due to be abolished on 30 June 1999. As for items bought locally – with tax already paid – if you're heading for another EU country, don't even bother to calculate; the allowances are generous enough to fill three or four backpacks.

There are duty-free shops at Spain's main airports.

MONEY
Currency

Spain's unit of currency is the peseta (pta), which will be superseded by the euro (€) on 1 January 2002. From this date, euro coins and notes will be used alongside the peseta for a few months until 1 July 2002, when the peseta will cease to be legal tender. The euro will have a fixed peseta value of about 166 ptas and be divided into 100 cents.

Exchange Rates

Exchange rates fluctuate, of course, but the table below will give you a more than approximate sense of the value of the peseta against other world currencies.

country	unit		peseta
Australia	A$1	=	96 ptas
Canada	C$1	=	100 ptas
euro	€1	=	166 ptas
France	1FF	=	25 ptas
Germany	DM1	=	85 ptas
Ireland	IR£1	=	212 ptas
Japan	¥100	=	126 ptas
Morocco	Dr 1	=	16 ptas
Netherlands	fl1	=	75 ptas
New Zealand	NZ$1	=	81 ptas
Portugal	100$00	=	83 ptas
UK	UK£1	=	246 ptas
USA	US$1	=	153 ptas

Exchanging Money

Major currencies, including all of the above except the New Zealand dollar – which for some reason comes as a surprise to most banks – can be changed without problem at most banks and exchange offices. Nowadays, the majority of banks in Spain have a *cajero automático*, or automatic teller machine (ATM), which will safely swallow and spit back just about any credit card you care to stick in. It's the quickest way to get at pesetas and the commission, normally 1.5%, is much the same as elsewhere.

Don't necessarily go for a bank or exchange office with the sign 'No Commission' in the window; they have to take their cut to stay in business and usually offer a poorer exchange rate. This apart, rates between one bank and another vary little – so little that it's not worth shopping around. By contrast, rates at exchange offices, though offering much quicker service, can differ quite markedly.

The exchange rate for travellers cheques is usually better – sometimes much better – than for cash. What's certain is that you'll be wasting your time and gaining nothing on exchange rates by arranging an international transfer. You may have to hang around for days until it arrives and the rate will be no better than if you'd presented a travellers cheque in the first place.

Banks are generally open from 8.30 or 9 am to 2 pm weekdays and until 1 pm on Saturday. In the peak summer months, however, you'll be lucky to find any bank open on a Saturday morning.

On the Walk

The safest way to travel, in general, is with a credit card supplemented by a fall-back of travellers cheques. Ensure that you have enough pesetas to live modestly for at least a week in the mountains as ATMs here are rare and confined to towns and larger villages, while banks are even rarer. Except in banks, travellers cheques are rarely accepted.

Costs

Transport costs which can really skew your budget needn't be too considerable if you stick to buses and trains (for more information on transport costs, see the Getting Around chapter). Transport aside, you can live like a monarch of the mountains on 6000 ptas a day, and still more modestly (3000 ptas) if you're camping wild and free and your only expense is food. In general, the cost of staying in cities (with some care) and resort areas such as Mallorca need be no more expensive than in the mountains.

A typical budget might include:

item	cost (ptas)
hostal or refugio	2000-3000
dinner in a modest restaurant	1500-2000
lunch-time loaf of bread and filling	260
a couple of beers, glasses of wine or soft drinks	250
sundries	500-2000

For more information on accommodation costs and standards, see Accommodation later in this chapter.

Taxes & Refunds

Value-added tax (VAT) on services and goods is known as IVA. The rate varies from 7% on accommodation and restaurant prices to 16% on retail goods and car hire (there's an equivalent tax of only 4% in the Islas Canarias). It's usually – but not always – included in quoted prices.

POST & COMMUNICATIONS

Post

Out on the trails you're on your own. Every post office has, in principle, a poste restante (*lista de correos*) facility, but it would be risky, not to say folly, to rely upon mail arriving in time for the day when you're planning to pass by. If you need to pass on a contact for incoming mail, it's a much better idea to give an address in the next large city you're heading for once the walking's over.

For poste restante, ask for letters to be addressed to 'Lista de Correos'. If correspondents write your family name in capitals, it can ease any sorting problems. It also helps if they add the postcode, if you know it in advance (if not, your mail will be sent to the major post office in the city you specify). A typical address might read:

> Jane SMITH
> Lista de Correos
> 08080 Barcelona
> SPAIN

Take your passport or ID with photo as proof of identity when you collect. Holders of Amex cards or travellers cheques can use the free client mail-holding service at American Express offices in Spain. You can obtain a list of these from any Amex office, within or outside Spain.

The creaking *correos*, the Spanish postal service, is worse than that of many a third-world country. Letters routinely take up to a week to reach the rest of Europe, 10 days or so to North America and two weeks or more to Australia and New Zealand. A lightweight letter costs 70 ptas to the EU, 115 ptas to the Americas and 155 ptas to Australia and New Zealand. The *urgente* (hah!) service might

clip a couple of days off delivery time and costs an extra 200 ptas. A day or two quicker than urgente service – but a lot more expensive – is Postal Exprés, sometimes called Express Mail Service (EMS). This is available at most post offices and uses courier companies for international deliveries.

If you put your postcard in an envelope, the price of the stamp is the same and it usually gets taken more seriously. Post your mail at post offices or in yellow street boxes (*buzones*) for normal mail, red ones for urgente; mail is normally quite safe but speed is a word yet to enter the postal service's vocabulary.

Post offices in villages are increasingly part-time concerns and may only be open for a few hours each weekday morning. Stamps can also be bought at *estancos* (tobacco shops).

Telephone

Streetside pay phones accept coins and phonecards (*tarjetas telefónicas*) issued by the national phone company, Telefónica, and increasingly by a number of private operators who have muscled their way into the market since deregulation. The cards come in 1000 ptas and 2000 ptas denominations and are sold at post offices and estancos. If there's no public phone around, ask at just about any bar or cafe. You might pay a little more, but for a local call it can save you a lot of wandering around. It's worth bearing in mind that international calls are a good 15% cheaper between 10 pm and 8 am and all day on Sunday.

The access code for international calls from Spain is ☎ 00. To make an international call dial the access code, wait for a new dialling tone, then dial the country code, area code and number you want. Dialling from abroad, Spain's country code is ☎ 34. Follow this with the full nine digit number you are calling. Andorra's country code is ☎ 376.

Fax

Fax can be useful for guaranteeing accommodation – and indeed some hotels may insist upon receiving one from you before confirming a reservation. Most main post offices offer a fax service but the cost borders on the scandalous: around 350 ptas per page within Spain, 920 ptas within the EU and 1700 ptas to 2000 ptas to other destinations. Rates are often cheaper at shops or offices with a 'Fax Público' sign.

Email
Email and the Internet are burgeoning in Spain, and larger towns may have several Internet cafes and other public Internet and email services, which you can use for a few hundred pesetas an hour. Elsewhere, unless you can communicate through your regular server, it's back to pen and paper.

INTERNET RESOURCES
The World Wide Web is a rich resource for travellers. You can research your trip, hunt down bargain air fares, book hotels, check on weather conditions or chat with locals and other travellers about the best places to visit (or avoid!). Search the Web under 'Spain, Travel' and it will throw up dozens of sites. The national tourist office, Turespaña, has a useful Web page called 'Discover Spain' (www.spaintour.com), which provides all sorts of links to other sites, though it suffers from being only irregularly updated. Another Turespaña site is at www.tourspain.es/inicioi.htm.

Lonely Planet's Web site (www.lonely planet.com) 'Destination Spain' page includes recent travellers' tips and links to a number of other sources of information on Spain.

BOOKS
Books are often published in different editions by different publishers in different countries. As a result, a book might be a hardback rarity in one country while it's readily available in paperback in another. Fortunately, bookshops and libraries search by title or author, so your local bookshop or library is best placed to advise you on the availability of recommended titles.

For walking guidebooks and natural history titles specific to a region, see Books in the regional Information sections of the individual walks chapters.

Lonely Planet
The 900-plus fact-packed pages of Lonely Planet's *Spain* guide are an ideal supplement to the general information in this book (as is the *Barcelona* guide if you plan to spend a few days in the city). Similarly, *Canary Islands* treats general themes more fully than we have room for here. If you're planning to walk down south, stow *Andalucía* in your backpack.

Lonely Planet's slim-fit *Spanish Phrasebook* has a range of terms for most situations you're likely to encounter and is compact enough to slip into a pocket for instant access.

Walking Guidebooks
There isn't a great deal available in English, with the exception of two British publishers, Cicerone Press and Sunflower Books.

Cicerone specialises in outdoor books, particularly on walking and climbing. Its books tend to be aimed very much at the serious walker – walk times, for example, are generally so spartan that they might have been set by Kenyan marathon runners. Current titles relating to Spain include *Mountain Walks on the Costa Blanca* by Bob Stansfield, *Walking in Mallorca* by June Parker, *The Mountains of Central Spain* by Jacqueline Oglesby, *Through the Spanish Pyrenees: GR11* by Paul Lucia, *Walking in the Sierra Nevada of Spain* by Andy Walmsley, *Walks and Climbs in the Picos de Europa* by Robin Walker, *Walks and Climbs in the Pyrenees* by the prolific Kev Reynolds, *The Way of St James: Spain* by Alison Raju and *Birdwatching in Mallorca* by Ken Stoba.

Much slimmer than the Cicerone series, the 'Landscapes' series from Sunflower Books is less ascetic and more leisurely in its approach to walks. Typically, these vary from a half-hour stroll to an all-day outing, and share space with routes for car driving and recommended picnic spots. The quality of writing varies quite significantly from book to book. The series concentrates on the major tourist destinations; titles include *Landscapes of Tenerife, Southern Tenerife and La Gomera, Gran Canaria, Catalunya, Mallorca* and *Menorca*.

Among the wide selection of guidebooks for walkers in both Spanish and Catalan, those published by PRAMES, dealing mainly with Aragón, stand out for reliability.

Travel & Exploration

To set your own walking endeavours in perspective, pack *As I Walked Out One Midsummer Morning* by Laurie Lee. When only 19, Lee walked away from his Gloucestershire home, hopped on a boat bound for Vigo in Galicia and then walked the length of Spain as far as Málaga, busking with his fiddle to pay his long way. This account of his journeys, written over 30 years later, records the sights, smells and contrasting moods of a turbulent period of Spanish history just prior to the Spanish Civil War.

For an even more impressive – and contemporary – walking endeavour, read *Clear Waters Rising*, an unputdownable account by Nick Crane of his epic trek from Finisterre, Galicia's most westerly tip, to Istanbul. The first third of the book describes his progress through Galicia, segments of the Camino Francés, Picos de Europa and Pyrenees. Alternatively, Adam Hopkins' *Spanish Journeys* ranks with the best of general travel writing about contemporary Spain.

The Camino de Santiago, in particular, has captured the imagination of writers in English and spawned a shelf or two of writing. For details of recommended titles, see Books in the Information section of the Camino de Santiago chapter.

Natural History

Wildlife Travelling Companion: Spain by John Measures is a good traveller's guide, focusing on 150 of the best sites for viewing flora and fauna, with details of how to reach them and what you can hope to see. *Spain's Wildlife* by Eric Robins covers the country's most interesting animals and birds – and their prospects for survival – in an informative

way, spiced with good photos and plenty of personal experience.

If you like to combine your walking with birdwatching, consider packing either *The Birds of Britain and Europe with North Africa and the Middle East* by Herman Heinzel et al or *A Field Guide to the Birds of Britain and Europe* by Roger Peterson et al, both published in Europe by Collins. For coastal birds, *Seabirds of Spain and Portugal* by Andrew Paterson is a good travel companion.

The single best guide to Spain's flowers and shrubs is *Flowers of South-West Europe: A Field Guide* by Oleg Polunin & B E Smythies. For serious botanists, the classic work remains the three volumes of *Wild Flowers of Spain* by Clive Innes.

General

For a colourful but thorough and not overly long canter through Spanish history, *The Story of Spain* by Mark Williams is hard to beat. Also concise and worthwhile is Juan Lalaguna's *A Traveller's History of Spain*. The keen journalist's eye of John Hooper in *The Spaniards*, written in 1987, captures the essence of post-Franco Spain and is a thoroughly entertaining read in its own right. More controversial, just as fascinating and making no claim to objectivity is *Fire in the Blood*, a book written by a respected academic, Ian Gibson, to accompany the British TV series of the same name. James Michener's *Iberia* is an often precious and excessively long anecdotal account of Spain in the late 1960s. For all its shortcomings, it's difficult to lay aside and you end up enjoying hating the man for his self-centred egotism.

There are two classic studies of the Spanish Civil War, both by British historians. *The Spanish Civil War* by Hugh Thomas is long and dense with detail, yet immensely readable, even-handed and humane. Raymond Carr's more succinct *The Spanish Tragedy* is another well written and respected account.

For an artist's viewpoint from a particular political standpoint, George Orwell's *Homage to Catalonia* is outstanding for its passion and commitment. It is an account of his experience of the Spanish Civil War from the euphoria of the early days of the conflict in Barcelona to Orwell's eventual disillusionment with the disastrous infighting of the Republicans.

Buying Books

In Madrid, La Tienda Verde (fax 91 533 64 54) has two shops opposite each other on Calle Maudes (metro: Plaza de Castilla). No 23 (☎ 91 535 38 10) specialises in guidebooks and natural history, while No 38 (☎ 91 534 32 57) has maps and mountaineering titles. Both branches accept orders by post. Also large and recommended is Librería Desnivel (☎/fax 91 369 47 27, libreria@desnivel.es) at Calle Amor de Dios 11 (metro: Antón Martín).

Barcelona's Librería Quera (☎ 93 318 07 43), Carrer Petrixol 2 (metro: Liceo), is Spain's oldest bookshop specialising in maps and books for walkers. Librería Montcau, Carrer Urgell 120 (metro: Urgell), and Librería La Pleta (☎/fax 93 494 09 62, lapleta@bcn.servicom.es) in Calle Mallorca 56 (metro: Entença) are also well stocked.

In Valencia, the friendly and recently established Librería Patagonia (☎/fax 96 391 52 47) on Calle Guillem de Castro 106, 46003, carries a good range of maps and books and will accept orders by mail. They carry a number of titles in English and French.

In the UK, you can contentedly spend a day or more of your life browsing around Stanfords (☎ 0171-836 1321, fax 0171-836 0189; from 1 June 1999 ☎ 020-7836 1321, fax 020-7836 0189), the world's largest map and guidebook store. It operates an efficient mail-order service and orders can be placed by phone from anywhere in the world. Ring or write to 12-14 Long Acre, London WC2E 9LP. Less central, the Travel Bookshop (☎ 0171-229 5260; from 1 June 1999 ☎ 020-7229 5260), 13-15 Blenheim Crescent, W11 2EE, also has a comprehensive range. (Check out its Web site at www.thetravelbookshop.co.uk.)

In the USA, mail orders can be placed with Mountaineers Books (☎ 1800 553 4453, fax 206 223 6306, mbooks@moun taineers.org), a nonprofit organisation based in Seattle.

You can also order books online through the Adventurous Traveler Bookstore (☎ 1800 282 3963 in the USA and Canada, 802 860 6776 elsewhere, fax 800 677 1821 in the USA and Canada, 802 860 6667 else where, books@atbook.com) and Pacific Travelers Supply (☎ 888 722 8728, fax 805 564 3138) in Santa Barbara.

CD-ROMS

Though the text and voice-over for each are in Spanish, there are four CD-ROMs of special interest to walkers. *Parques Nacionales de España*, produced by Indesmedia, is packed with information, supported by plenty of photos and video clips and has a useful plant and animal index. *El Camino de Santiago,* by Micronet SA, gives full information on all the variations within Spain of this traditional pilgrims' way, together with details of accommodation and camping grounds on and off route.

Visual Map Pirineo, produced by Visual GIS Engineering, is mainly devoted to the Aragonese Pyrenees, with some coverage of the Catalan mountains. It has a wealth of background information and practical details on accommodation, but isn't designed specifically for walkers. One that deals exclusively with walking is *Senderos de Canarias*, developed and, at 4500 ptas, heavily subsidised by the Islas Canarias government.

None of the above are available outside Spain.

NEWSPAPERS & MAGAZINES

The major national daily newspapers are the left-leaning *El País*, the highly conservative *ABC*, and *El Mundo*, the liveliest of the three. For solid reporting of national and international events, *El País* is hard to beat.

The thriving provincial newspapers, whether daily or weekly, are a useful source for finding out what's on locally and where and when. They're also fascinating for the way they reveal the concerns and preoccupations of smaller communities.

Spain's best specialist magazine for walkers and climbers is *Desnivel*, which appears monthly.

RADIO & TV

Spain has several hundred provincial radio stations, mostly broadcasting on FM. The majority offer the familiar diet of music interspersed with chat that can range from the stimulating to the inane. Radio Nacional de España (RNE) has five stations broadcasting nationally. Of these, Radio Cinco (Radio Five) is a round-the-clock news station.

For news and programs in English, tune to the BBC World Service, which beams to Spain and Portugal on 7325, 9410, 12,095, 15,070 and 17,705kHz. In the Islas Canarias, the best reception is normally on 12,095 and 15,485kHz. You can pick up Voice of America on various short-wave frequencies, including 9.700, 15.205 and 15.255MHz, depending on the time of day.

There's little point in going into detail about TV channels since, on the trail, you're unlikely to see much more than a flickering eye high in the corner of a bars. Suffice to say that serious programs are mostly on La 2, the second channel of Televisión Española (TVE), or on Canal Plus, a subscription channel. News programs are generally good and documentaries, many bought in from abroad, can be excellent. The regular diet of *culebrones* (soap operas), game shows, football, variety programs and mind-numbing talk shows are best left to flicker away above the bottles.

WEATHER INFORMATION

There are some times when it's useful to have a drink in a bar and keep an eye on the TV. Daily at around 9.30 pm, both TVE1 and Antenna 3, a private channel, show the weather forecast for the next 24 hours and beyond. Reading their symbols for sunshine, cloud, fog, rain and so on, plus their prediction of maximum and minimum temperatures, you can get a broad indication of the weather for your area. At more leisure

and in more detail, pick up a local paper where you'll find the weather prognosis in both visual and textual form.

If you speak Spanish well, you can call up Teletiempo (47 ptas per minute), the phone information service of the Instituto Nacional de Meteorología. We say 'well' since the system is touch-tone interactive and speakers tend to gabble. Unless you're confident, it's better to get a Spanish friend to call and interpret the information for you. To access it, dial ☎ 906 36 53, followed by the first two numbers of the postal code of the province you're interested in.

PHOTOGRAPHY

Most major brands of film for prints are widely sold. Film for slides, however, is less readily available and it's advisable to stock up in advance. If you're in a village which is used to walkers and tourists, the village will probably stock a brand or two. Check the expiry date.

For processing, it's better to wait until you return home, even though the service within Spain for prints is generally speedy and efficient. Unless a shop which advertises same-day service has its own processing plant, it's not worth taking the minor risk of losing a day's walking while you wait in frustration for your photos to come back.

A roll of print film (36 exposures, 100 ASA) costs around 650 ptas and can be processed for about 1700 ptas. The equivalent in slide film (*diapositiva*) is around 850 ptas, plus 850 ptas for processing; you're unlikely to find a place that can guarantee turnaround in less than three days. A roll is called a *carete*, though you'll generally be understood if you say 'film' – or just point.

In Spain, you're most unlikely to encounter the kind of paranoia which forbids the photographing of dams and bridges. However, as anywhere, it's common courtesy to ask permission before taking photos of people, their homes, animals or other possessions.

Your camera and film will be routinely passed through airport X-ray machines, which shouldn't damage film. The extra precaution taken by many professionals is to put films in a lead-lined bag. However, since every gram in your backpack counts, simply carry films on your person if you're worried and produce them for inspection by hand.

For the same reason, try to limit the weight of photographic equipment you carry. For example, rather than three or more separate lenses, if you use an SLR camera take a 28-110mm zoom lens. Compact cameras which have a mini-zoom lens with variable angle (usually 35-70mm) are in many respects ideal for walking.

Many of the trails can be dusty and the higher you climb the more intense can be the sunlight. Ensure, therefore, that whatever camera you use you equip it with a lens cap and plain glass or UV filter. Pack some lens-cleaning tissues and take special care to avoid dust blowing into the camera interior while you're changing film. Because of the dust and variations in temperature as the day progresses, it also makes sense to keep rolls of film in a simple insulated bag such as those sold to keep food and drinks cool.

A polarising filter is useful where there's intense solar reflection, such as middle-of-the-day shots of scenes with shimmering lakes or snow. Excessive light is generally a problem as the bright, harsh midday sun tends to bleach out your shots. One basic rule for straightforward shooting is to keep the sun at your back – checking, of course, that your shadow isn't caught in the frame!

VIDEO SYSTEMS

If you're thinking of buying a commercial videotape as a souvenir of your walk, check first that you can play it on your home video player; you won't get a picture if the image registration systems are different. Nearly all prerecorded videos on sale in Spain, and also Spanish TVs, use the PAL system common to most of Western Europe and Australia. France uses the incompatible SECAM system, and North America and Japan use the incompatible NTSC system. PAL videos can't be played on a machine that lacks PAL capability.

TIME

Peninsular Spain and the Islas Baleares are on GMT/UTC plus one hour during winter and GMT/UTC plus two hours during daylight-saving (from the last Sunday in March to the last Sunday in October). Most other Western European countries have the same time as Spain year-round. The Islas Canarias are an hour behind the Spanish mainland throughout the year and are in the same time zone as other western fringe countries of Europe: the UK, Ireland and Portugal.

Spanish time is normally USA Eastern Time plus six hours, and USA Pacific Time plus nine hours. In the Australian winter, subtract eight hours from Sydney time to get Spanish time; in the Australian summer, subtract 10 hours.

Intercontinental conversions may differ by a further hour for a couple of weeks each year where countries revert to and from daylight-saving time on different dates.

Timetables, as in most of Europe, usually follow the 24 hour clock.

ELECTRICITY

Electric current in Spain, like elsewhere in continental Europe, is 220V, 50Hz. If you're from the USA and your appliances work on 110V, you'll need to bring a small step-down transformer with you as they aren't readily available locally. Since North American appliances function at 60Hz, you may notice a certain reduction in performance. While this might be mildly annoying, it won't damage your machine.

Plugs have two round pins, so walkers from the UK, Australia and North America will require a plug adapter. Again, to save a hunt around the shops, bring one with you.

WEIGHTS & MEASURES

Spain uses the metric system (see the conversion tables on the inside rear cover of this book). Decimals are indicated by a comma, and thousands by a dot.

LAUNDRY

Self-service laundrettes are rare. Small laundries (*lavanderías*) are more common in larger villages and towns but don't come cheap. They often require a full load, which will be returned to you the same day, washed, dried and folded, for between 1000 ptas and 1200 ptas. Many camping grounds plus a very few budget *hostales* (budget hotels) and lowland refugios have washing machines for guests' use.

All of which means that you will probably be doing most of your own washing, either at a sink in your accommodation or in the open. If the former, be sure to pack a plug – though a sock well stuffed into the hole is almost as effective. If the latter, choose a running stream and avoid soap or detergent – and never, ever wash in mountain tarns and pools, where the ecosystem is particularly delicate and easily unbalanced.

WOMEN WALKERS

You'll be very unlucky if you have any problems on the trails which are related specifically to gender. Like walkers everywhere, Spanish hikers tend to be fairly socially enlightened. Younger ones are relaxed in their dealings with the opposite sex, and older walkers are usually free of the prurient interest in foreign women that some dinosaurs still carry over from the repressive social climate of the Franco era.

In towns, you may get the occasional unwelcome stare, catcall or unnecessary comment, to which the best – and most galling – response is indifference. And don't get too paranoid about what's being called; the *piropo* – a harmless, mildly flirty compliment – is deeply ingrained in Spanish society and, if well delivered, even considered gallant. Serious harassment is much less frequent than you might expect and Spain has one of the developed world's lowest incidences of reported rape.

Sleeping arrangements in many refugios are often a single or double-decker bench running from one side of the dormitory to the other where male and female, young and old snore side by side. If this worries you, better to pack a tent and retain your independence.

In general, as anywhere, it might be risky for a woman to hitch alone. Take a look also

On Spanish Trails

In general, Spain is a very safe country for a woman alone, especially in rural walking areas. Before going to Spain for the first time, I was warned about the attention I might receive from the stereotyped 'macho Ibérico'. Once there, however, I found that a firm 'No!' was enough to keep any unwanted advances at bay.

What did bother me at first were the long looks from both sexes. Rather than an invasion of individual privacy, however, I found they are part of a Spanish cultural code in which people-watching is the norm. 'Stares' don't necessarily have a secondary intent.

You don't see women walking alone in the mountains very often, and this does attract attention. Women on their own (mostly foreigners) provoke reactions among locals of surprise, admiration and concern. It's common to be warned not to go into the hills alone by both men and women repeating advice learned in childhood.

As a side note, it's a delight to live near Santiago de Compostela, a city of nearly 100,000 whose police have fired their sidearms only twice in the last six years – both times at cows running amok.

Nancy Frey

at the brief section on Hitching in the Getting Around chapter.

For advice that's not specific to either walking or Spain, consult the more general *Handbook for Women Travellers* by M & G Moss.

GAY & LESBIAN WALKERS

Gay and lesbian sex are legal in Spain and the age of consent is 16 years. Levels of tolerance towards lesbians and gay men vary from place to place, however. As in most countries, gay and lesbian scenes flourish more openly in urban centres.

WALKING WITH CHILDREN

There's no need to hang up your boots once you become parents, and walking with children in Spain is no more difficult than elsewhere in Europe.

In some respects, it's easier. The Spanish in general are fond of children, who play happily in and around restaurants and cafes until often quite late at night. There are no puritanical laws banishing them from places where alcohol is served and, since most cafes are open from breakfast until way after their bedtime, you can always pick up a soft drink or a snack. (Bear in mind, however, the late hour at which restaurants serve lunch and dinner, and ensure that you always have a cache of emergency provisions in your backpack.)

Baby food, nappies (diapers), creams and potions and all the other paraphernalia of travelling with the very young are readily available in Spanish towns, though you may not find your favourite brand. If you're planning to walk in less populated areas, stock up in advance.

Children can be slow to adapt to changes of diet, temperature and altitude, so before undertaking a route of several days, it might be wise to first establish a base camp and do a number of day or half-day walks to break yourselves in.

Think also of combining walking with other activities such as beach fun. You could, for example, stay at Port de Sóller on Mallorca, Puerto de la Cruz on Tenerife in the Islas Canarias or on the Costa Blanca in Valencia. Car-hire rates are much cheaper than in many parts of Europe and worth considering in preference to waiting for infrequent or nonexistent bus services.

There's a simple rule-of-thumb for calculating what kids can carry on a walk: most can comfortably walk their age and carry half of it. A 12-year-old, for example, should be able to walk about 12km per day in moderate terrain, carrying a backpack which weighs 6kg.

Lonely Planet's *Travel with Children* by Maureen Wheeler has lots of practical advice on the subject, along with first-hand travel stories from a host of Lonely Planet authors and others.

Walks suitable for families with children include Sóller to Deià and the Barranc de Biniaraix walks on Mallorca, the Barranco del Infierno walk in the Islas Canarias, the descent to Caaveiro monastery in Galicia's Parque Natural Fraga do Eume and the Campa de Brego Circuit in the same chapter.

Other possibilities are the walk from Benamahoma to Zahara de la Sierra in Andalucía's Sierra de Grazalema and a section of the Senda del Oso or Ruta de los Lagos in the Cordillera Cantábrica.

The Pyrenees aren't, in general, suitable for younger children. This said, Canillo or Ordino in Andorra both make good bases for undemanding half-day walks such as the Cap de Rep & Riba Escorjada. Side trips listed at the end of a walk description and Other Walks, which feature at the end of most chapters, can also be a source of ideas.

USEFUL ORGANISATIONS
Walking Clubs & Associations

The umbrella organisation representing walking and walkers' interests in Spain is the Federación Española de Montañismo (☎ 91 445 13 82). It encompasses all regional Federaciones – the organisations with which you're more likely to have contact. The Federación Español de Deportes de Montaña (FEDME), Calle Alberto Aguilera 3-4, 28015, Madrid, has a similar role.

Nowadays, almost every region has its own federation. For more information on useful regional organisations, see Information in the introduction to individual regions or chapters.

Most major cities have walking clubs which arrange outings both locally and further afield. In the capital, contact the Federación Madrileña de Montañismo (☎ 91 593 80 74, fax 91 448 07 24).

In areas where there are large expatriate communities, there are active walking groups usually composed of wiry pensioners who are happy to include visiting hikers. For details, check the small ads in the local

English-language press. One active group is the Costa Blanca Mountain Walkers, based near Benidorm. For contact details, see Information in the introduction to La Marina in the Valencia chapter.

Other Organisations

TIVE, the Spanish youth and student travel organisation, is good for reduced-price student and youth travel tickets, if you're under 26. It also issues various useful documents such as the International Student Identity Card (ISIC), International Teacher Identity Card (ITIC) as well as HI youth hostel and Federation of International Youth Travel Organisations (FIYTO) cards, all of which offer a range of discounts. TIVE has branches in many cities, but its head office (☎ 91 347 77 00) is at Calle de José Ortega y Gasset 71, 28006 Madrid.

For information on HI youth hostels, see the Accommodation section later in this chapter.

Keen birdwatchers might like to contact La Sociedad Española de Ornitología, the Spanish Ornithological Society, at Carretera de Húmera 63-1, 28224 Pozuelo de Alarcón, Madrid.

BUSINESS HOURS

Generally, people work from about 9 am to 2 pm and then again from 4.30 or 5 pm for another three hours or so, Monday to Friday. Shops and travel agencies are usually open during these same hours and also on Saturday, though some may skip the Saturday afternoon session. Big supermarkets and department stores often stay open every day except Sunday from about 9 am to 9 pm. A lot of government offices don't bother opening in the afternoon.

For bank hours, see Exchanging Money in the Money section earlier in this chapter. For post office times, see Post in the Post & Communications section, also in this chapter.

PUBLIC HOLIDAYS & SPECIAL EVENTS

Check in advance for public holidays, among the world's most generous, that might fall

within your walking dates. At such times, Spain takes to the roads and trails, it's often difficult to find a bed in a refugio or hotel and public transport operates a reduced service (on a Sunday schedule).

Every region of Spain has at least 14 official holidays a year, some of which are observed nationwide, while others (to compound your planning problems) are very local. When a public holiday nudges near to a weekend, Spaniards observe the excellent tradition of *el puente* – literally meaning 'bridge' – which permits them to take the intervening day off too. The seven national holidays, which are supplemented by those 'bridges' and locally observed holidays, are:

Año Nuevo (New Year's Day)	1 January
Viernes Santo (Good Friday)	March/April
Fiesta del Trabajo (Labour Day)	1 May
La Asunción (Feast of the Assumption)	15 August
Día de la Hispanidad (National Day)	12 October
La Inmaculada Concepción (Feast of the Immaculate Conception)	8 December
Navidad (Christmas)	25 December

To supplement these, each regional government decrees an additional seven days a year, which often include a local festival such as Las Fallas in Valencia in March; Madrid's fiesta in honour of its patron saint, San Isidro, in May; and Pamplona's famous San Fermín, when the bulls run through the streets, in July. Other commonly observed dates include:

6 January
Epifanía (Epiphany) or Día de los Reyes Magos (Three Kings' Day), when children receive presents
19 March
Día de San José (St Joseph's Day)
March/April
Jueves Santo (Maundy Thursday, the day before Good Friday); observed widely
June
Corpus Christi (the Thursday after the eighth Sunday after Easter Sunday); observed widely
24 June
Día de San Juan Bautista (Feast of St John the Baptist), King Juan Carlos' saint's day; observed widely

25 July
  Día de Santiago Apóstol (Feast of St James the Apostle), Spain's patron saint; observed widely
6 December
  Día de la Constitución (Constitution Day); observed widely

The two main periods when Spaniards go on holiday are Semana Santa (the week leading up to Easter Sunday) and the month of August. At these times, and also during much of July, pressure on accommodation, including mountain refugios, is intense and it's wise to reserve in advance.

WALKING ROUTES

At the beginning of the book, just before the Introduction, you'll find a table which summarises each walk's duration, standard, accessibility by public transport and the best time to undertake it, while also giving a brief indication of its main features.

Route Descriptions

To get the feel of a walk at a glance, consult the Facts Box at the beginning of each walk. You'll find the duration and standard listed as well as the starting and finishing points, the nearest town and whether or not the walk is accessible by public transport.

At the end of each day there's usually somewhere to stay. In the few instances where there are no refugios in the vicinity, an attractive spot to pitch a tent is indicated. When dividing up longer walks of several days, we've also taken into account access to public transport and the need to top up supplies of food. Bear in mind that the stages we recommend aren't, of course, immutable. On many long walks, particularly in the Pyrenees, several permutations are possible, especially if you're carrying a tent.

Within most walks, a bold highlight indicates just that, one of the day's highlights. At the end of a number of walk descriptions are suggestions for side trips, which range from a brief 20 minute detour to a full day's outing. Concise descriptions of other recommended walks are listed under Other

Walks at the end of the individual walks chapters.

Precise compass bearings are only given on those rare occasions when there's a possibility of ambiguity. For the most part, we give the general direction you need to take, such as 'head south', 'at the three-way junction, take the path leading north-east' or 'keep heading south-west along the flank of the mountain'.

Standards

Each walk is graded into one of five categories: easy, medium and hard, plus the intermediate categories of easy-medium and medium-hard. When allotting a grade, we take into account such features as a walk's length, the amount and steepness of uphill work, the degree of navigational skill required and whether the trail is well formed or rough. To an extent, such a judgment is subjective. A route's difficulty can also vary according to weather conditions and, in the high mountains, the presence or absence of snow. We strongly recommend, therefore, that you read through the whole of a route description before deciding to undertake it.

Easy routes present no navigational difficulties, don't require the use of all four limbs at any point and can comfortably be undertaken by a family with children over 10 years old.

Medium routes can be walked with just a little exertion by someone of average fitness. The relative difficulty may reside in route-finding, the length, changes of elevation or a combination of these factors. They assume that you're familiar with the use of a compass.

Walks graded hard are just that: tough in terms of navigation, ascent and length. They're gruelling and you may well be finding your way cross-country with no path to guide you.

Times & Distances

The times given in the introductory table to each walk are actual walking times. We give a range, since walking paces vary markedly. What we don't do is budget for lunch breaks, pee stops, photo calls, consulting the map, getting temporarily lost, pausing to take in the scenery, brewing a pot of tea and all the other little activities which break up the day and which, cumulatively, can add as much as a third or a half again onto the net walking time.

Within a walk description, we generally give measurements of time rather than distance from the starting point or from the last significant landmark since, on all but the easiest of terrain, the number of kilometres is a fairly meaningless figure.

Altitude Measurements

Altitude measurements in the text and on accompanying maps are based upon reference maps which we used while researching the walks. Spot heights sometimes vary from one commercial map to another – not least because some maps take sea level as the Mediterranean off Alicante, while others use the Atlantic Ocean off Bilbao as their zero point. Differences, however, aren't considerable.

Place Names & Terminology

With only rare exceptions, we use names the locals use. In monolingual areas we use the Spanish name, which differ from the form English speakers are more familiar with; for example, Islas Canarias for the Canary Islands, Islas Baleares for the Balearic Islands and Sevilla for Seville.

Where a regional language is spoken, we reflect predominant local usage; for example, in the Catalan Pyrenees we call a village, mountain or pass by its Catalan name, while in Galicia we use the Galician form. It's no big deal since the majority of names aren't significantly different from their equivalent in Spanish; for example, Mulleres for Molières, Urdiceta for Ordiceta and Astós for Estós.

The fairly standard terms 'true left' and 'true right' for describing the bank of a stream or river sometimes throw readers. The 'true left bank' simply means the left bank as you look downstream.

You'll find key words which occur in the names of natural features (such as Pic this or Río that) in the Glossary at the end of the book, in both their Spanish and Catalan forms.

A couple of abbreviations you'll meet in the book and on the road are GR and PR. A Sendero de Gran Recorrido (GR), or long-distance trail, is signalled by red-and-white striped trail markers. Spain has over 50 of them, each with a minimum length of 50km. The GR11, also known as the Senda Pirenáica, runs the length of the Pyrenees from Irún in the Bay of Biscay to the Cap de Creus on Catalunya's Mediterranean coast, east of Figueres. In addition to the principal route, it has many variants so that at times every path you come to seems to bear the familiar two-tone blazes. It's mirrored on the other side of the Pyrenees by the French GR10, which snakes its way along the northern slopes. Several GRs link in with trans-European trails. The GR65, for example, which follows the Camino de Santiago fairly closely through Navarra, has its beginning in the woods of Bohemia in the Czech Republic, while the GR10, also known as the E7, runs from Puçol, north of Valencia, to Lisbon on the Atlantic coast of Portugal. If you walk the Els Ports routes in the north of the Valencia region, you'll be following part of the GR7 at times. Also known as the E3, it has its beginnings in Crete, enters Spain via Andorra and runs down through Murcia and onto Gibraltar.

The shorter Senderos de Pequeno Recorrido (PRs) pop up everywhere. Normally indicated by yellow-and-white trail markers, they're administered locally. Usually selected because they're scenically attractive, they sometimes have an accompanying booklet or explanatory panel at the beginning or end.

RESPONSIBLE WALKING

The popularity of walking can place great pressure on the natural environment. Consider the following tips when on the trails and play a small part in helping to preserve the ecology of Spain's very considerable areas of natural beauty.

Fires

Every summer, large areas of mainland Spain are ravaged by forest fire. The Islas Canarias, especially Tenerife, are also at risk. In many areas, camp fires are expressly forbidden, both because of the danger of forest fire and because too many campers cooking over wood can rapidly destroy the natural cycle of growth, decay and regeneration.

If you're in an area where wood is plentiful and walkers few, dig a small hole for your fire (to reduce the risk of it spreading) and use only as many twigs as it takes to heat your dinner or pot of tea; it's amazing how few you'll need to bring water to a brisk boil. Never burn plastics or aluminium foil; always pack them out with you or don't bring them along. And never light a fire in peaty soil, which consists largely of organic matter that can continue to smoulder long after you've moved on. Use only dead, fallen wood and ensure that you fully extinguish a fire when dinner's over. Spread the embers and douse them with water. Remember that an extinguished fire is only truly safe to leave when you can comfortably place your hand in it. In refugios, where possible it's courtesy to leave wood for those who come after you.

In all other areas, use a fuel stove and be sure to carry empty canisters out with you; full or empty, they add only a few grams to your backpack.

Washing & Washing Up

Where possible, try to avoid the use of detergents. That little luxury you allow yourself can play havoc with the fragile ecosystems of high mountain tarns and streams. As a basic rule, never use detergents or toothpaste, even if they claim to be biodegradable, in or near watercourses.

When washing yourself, if you use soap be sure it's biodegradable and take your water container at least 50m away from the watercourse. Disperse the waste water widely to allow the soil or rock to filter it fully. In the same way, wash cooking utensils a good 50m from watercourses using a scourer – or sand, snow, even grit – instead of detergent.

Toilets

Contamination of water sources by human urine and faeces can lead to the transmission of all sorts of dire diseases to both other humans and wildlife, which often lack our defence mechanisms. Where you come across a toilet, take advantage; the next one could be miles or days away.

Where there's nothing so sophisticated, bury your waste. Dig a small hole a good 15cm deep and at least 100m from any watercourse. Some people carry a lightweight trowel for this purpose, though a sharp stone serves just as well. Cover the evidence with soil and top it with a rock. In stony, high mountain areas devoid of soil, simply turn over a large stone and replace it afterwards. In snow, dig right down to the soil and beneath.

Rubbish

Carry out all your rubbish. If you've managed to carry it in, you can backpack it out. Don't overlook tiny items such as silver paper, cigarette butts and plastic wrappers. Pack a small supermarket plastic bag to hold all such bits and unpleasant pieces. It's also worth making the small if sometimes mildly disagreeable effort to carry out rubbish left by others less responsible than yourself. The aphorism, 'Take only photos, leave only footprints', may be unduly twee, but it's based on sound common sense.

Never, ever bury your rubbish, which small animals will snuffle out and scatter almost as soon as you've left. It's also not good for their digestion. If the local fauna spurn it, your trash may take years to decompose, especially at high altitudes. Sanitary towels, tampons and condoms should also be carried out since they burn and decompose poorly.

Erosion

Hillsides and mountain slopes, especially at high altitudes, are prone to erosion. Stick to existing tracks and avoid short cuts that bypass a switchback. If you blaze a new trail straight down a slope, it's certain to become a watercourse with the next heavy rainfall and eventually cause soil loss and deep scarring.

Where to Camp

The higher you go, the more sensitive the vegetation. Wherever possible, camp lower down in valleys and glens where the land recovers more easily. Avoid popular places for wild camping. Your abstinence will reduce the pressure upon them – and the alternatives are usually more pleasant anyway.

At the end of the day – or rather, next morning as you prepare to move on – your site should bear no trace of your presence except some flattened grass which will soon spring back into shape.

Access

If walking through private property, stick to the path and be sure to close all gates behind you, particularly if there are livestock around.

ACCOMMODATION

Spain has a bewildering variety of names and categories for places to stay, which range from the exceedingly basic to the five star palace. Many have separate price structures for the low season (*temporada baja*), mid-season (*temporada media*) and high season (*temporada alta*), when prices in popular tourist areas are often jacked up significantly. The temporada alta can vary from region to region, but you should anticipate premium prices during August and probably July, from Christmas to 6 January and during Semana Santa. At such times it's wise – and in some regions essential – to reserve in advance. Rates are usually displayed on a notice at or near reception.

IVA tax is levied on accommodation at the rate of 7%. In more modest places, it's invariably included within the room price and you won't even be aware of it. Hotels vary in their way of quoting prices.

The annual *Guía Oficial de Hoteles* (1200 ptas), available from most bookshops, lists all but the lowest categories of accommodation with their facilities and prices.

Note that where no alternatives are given we quote the high-season tariff, so outside peak periods you might be in for a pleasant surprise.

In Cities, Towns & Villages

Camping In this book we've defined an area with facilities, where a fee is normally demanded, as a 'camping ground'. We reserve the term 'camp site' for more informal places where it's possible to pitch your tent.

Spain has around 1000 official camping grounds, known as *campings*, which are graded into three classes according to the facilities they offer. Their quality ranges from reasonable to very good. In July and August in popular tourist areas, tents and vehicles are packed cheek by jowl. This said, space will almost invariably be found for walkers.

Even 3rd class camping grounds often have hot showers and probably a small store and bar. A typical nightly fee for a 2nd or 3rd class operation is 300 ptas to 350 ptas for a small tent and the same again per head.

Now and again, you may come across a *zona de acampada* or *área de acampada*, an area where camping's permitted but there's no charge. There are no facilities, however, so they can be decidedly unhygienic.

When planning your walking holiday, it's worth investing 1000 ptas in the annually updated *Guía Oficial de Campings*. Available in most bookshops, it lists many of the country's sites, together with facilities and prices.

Hostels Spain's 180 or so youth hostels (*albergues juveniles*), not to be confused with *hostales* (budget hotels), are often the cheapest places for lone travellers, but two people can usually get a double room elsewhere for a similar price. Prices often depend on the season or whether or not you're under 26: typically you pay 900 ptas to 1500 ptas a night. Many hostels require you to rent sheets (around 300 ptas for your stay) if you don't have your own or a sleeping bag.

Most youth hostels are members of the Red Española de Albergues Juveniles

(REAJ, or Spanish Youth Hostel Network), the Spanish affiliate of Hostelling International (HI), which used to be called the International Youth Hostel Federation. REAJ's head office (☎ 91 347 77 00, fax 91 401 81 60) is at Calle de José Ortega y Gasset 71, 28006 Madrid.

Most hostels, however, are actually managed by regional governments. Each region usually sets its own price structure. Some have central booking services where you can make reservations for most hostels in the region. These include Andalucía (☎ 95 455 82 93, fax 95 455 82 92), Catalunya (☎ 93 483 83 63, fax 93 483 83 50) and Valencia (☎ 96 386 92 52, fax 96 386 99 51).

Some hostels require an HI card or membership card from your home country's youth hostel association; others don't (even though they may be HI hostels) but may charge more if you don't have one.

Fondas, Casas de Huéspedes & Pensiones At the cheapest end of the accommodation pyramid is the *fonda*, indicated by a white 'F' on a rectangular blue sign. Much the same is the *casa de huéspedes* (signed 'CH'), which translates literally as 'guesthouse', though nothing could be further from the image of genteel languor that such a term in English conjures up. Usually clean enough, though the plumbing may be eccentric, very few rooms have a bathroom attached. The *pensión* (signed 'P') is a small notch up, but here too you'll be lucky to find a room with bathroom.

There are many more pensiones than fondas or casas de huéspedes. In all three establishments, prices of singles/doubles are likely to be between 1000/2000 ptas and 1500/3000 ptas.

Hostales Next up the scale is the hostal, graded according to a three star system. Some are little different from pensiones, while a three star hostal may be considerably more comfortable and have a majority of rooms with bathroom. Prices range from pensión levels up to 6000 ptas. A *hostal-residencia* is a hostal which doesn't provide meals.

Casas Rurales In recent years, there has a been heavy investment in the development and promotion of rural tourism as a means of bringing income to what are often economically deprived regions. *Casas rurales* are usually comfortably renovated country houses or farmhouses, some offering meals and some self-catering. A double room typically costs from 3000 ptas to 8000 ptas. Tourist offices usually provide leaflets listing casas rurales and other country accommodation in their areas.

Hotels Hotels (*hoteles*) are graded from one to five. The stars, as for the grading of pensiones and hostales, reflect a place's facilities and not necessarily price or quality. There'll probably be a restaurant and even the cheapest room normally has a bathroom. Prices cover the whole gamut from 4000 ptas to over 50,000 ptas. Packing at least the relevant pages of the *Guía Oficial de Hoteles* can save you a detour to a place that may turn out to be beyond your price ceiling.

Paradores, officially *paradores de turismo*, are a state-run chain of 80-odd luxury hotels, many in converted castles, palaces, mansions or monasteries. Prices start at around 15,000 ptas for a double. You can book a room at any parador through their central reservation system (☎ 91 516 66 66, fax 91 516 66 57). They're also a great place just for a drink after a day's walking, and their restaurants, which usually offer regional specialities, though not cheap are normally excellent value for money.

On the Walk

Day walks and some stages of longer walks begin and end within a bus ride of a population centre, where you'll normally find accommodation and sometimes a camping ground. Two other options on many longer walks are camping wild and refugios.

Camping A lightweight tent confers liberty and independence. If you have one you can still opt for something more cosy, should the mood take you. If you haven't got one, you're obliged to head for the nearest refugio or village – where you may arrive to find all options full. Those three to four extra kilos will more than justify themselves every time you pitch your tent.

You can't expect untrammelled freedom, however. *Parques nacionales* (national parks) and many *parques naturales* (nature parks) and other protected areas prohibit camping within their boundaries, and walkers should respect this restriction in the wider interest of the park's health. There's also a regulation which says that you're not allowed to camp within 1km of a camping ground.

Apart from such legitimate restrictions, and others of more localised ambit, the opportunity for wild camping in Spain's open spaces is almost limitless. Within each walk we indicate particularly attractive or convenient sites, but there are many more waiting to be discovered.

Refugios The larger mountain huts are staffed and usually open from mid-June until the middle of September, though a minority of more accessible ones stay open year-round. In July and August, in popular regions such as the Pyrenees it's highly advisable to reserve in advance (you'll find contact details within the relevant walk descriptions). Refugios in the Sierra de Gredos and the Sierra de Guadarrama, both an easy bus ride away from Madrid, are usually packed solid every weekend.

Prices are between 1100 ptas and 1300 ptas for a bunk and 1400 ptas to 1800 ptas for dinner; if you think the latter's expensive, reflect upon the effort expended to get supplies in. There's rarely equipment for doing your own cooking, though many of the bigger ones set aside an area for this. Sleeping is normally in *literas*, long benches with mattresses running the length of the dormitory, and blankets are provided but not sheets.

Refugios are OK for a night or two – but check carefully how many sleepers there are to a room. Many are fine, like a high-altitude youth hostel; others, where you're one in a dormitory among 35 or more sweating,

snoring, farting others, are less fun. Their strong point is that the guardians are almost invariably friendly and well informed. Most come back season after season and are an invaluable source of information about walks in the vicinity.

In some regions, there are unstaffed refugios, the best of which can be surprisingly cosy. At the end of the day, however, they're only as clean as the last group passing through – and that can be anything from the most fastidious of fellow walkers to a herd of swine.

Most unstaffed refugios remain open year-round and many others will allow access to one wing outside the summer months.

All along the Camino Francés variant of the Camino de Santiago pilgrim route are a range of conveniently spaced refugios.

FOOD
Local Food
Most Spanish bar and restaurant food is hearty and plentiful rather than gourmet – just what you need after a day in the mountains. It's also generally healthy since it's based upon typically Mediterranean ingredients such as vegetable oil, garlic, onions, tomatoes and peppers.

For variety, you can munch your way through a selection of *tapas* (bar snacks) or *raciones* (larger portions of the same), though this can work out to be expensive. The price, range and quality of à la carte items vary enormously from place to place. However, there's almost always a *menú del día* (menu of the day) or a *menú de la casa* (house menu) available. Often simply called a *menú*, it has a set price and allows you a choice of items. It typically consists of a starter course, main course, a *postre* (dessert) and a beverage, with bread included.

Some places, especially in areas popular with tourists, offer *platos combinados* (literally, 'combination dishes'). These include a dish such as steak, sausage, a piece of fish or bacon and eggs, garnished with a salad and with a supporting cast of some kind of potato dish, all heaped together on one plate. There's often a labelled photograph of each

Seafood paella, despite its simplicity, is one of
Spain's most famous dishes

variation displayed on the wall, so you know
exactly what you're getting. Sophisticated
they're not, but they're wholesome and
usually good value for money.

Just about every region in Spain has its
specialities; the País Vasco and Catalunya are
particularly rich in their range of local dishes.
Originating in Valencia, *paella* is a delicious
saffron-coloured rice dish simmered in richly
flavoured stock which crops up on restaurant
menus throughout Spain. There are actually
two versions of paella: one with chicken,
rabbit, green beans, butter beans and sometimes a snail or two; and *paella de mariscos*,
a fancier version scattered with seafood.

Fabada asturiana is an Asturian speciality, a rich, meaty bean stew guaranteed to
dispel the chill of winter. It combines white
beans, black pudding, hunks of chorizo (a
spicy red sausage), cubes of pork fat and
stewing beef, diced smoked ham and, optionally, a pig's ear. It may not be subtle but
this heartwarming dish has been known to
bring tears to the eyes of a hungry walker.

For the vocabulary to help you navigate a
restaurant menu or a trip to the greengrocers,
consult Lonely Planet's *Spain* guide. Lonely
Planet's *Spanish phrasebook* gives an even
more comprehensive listing.

Where to Eat Even the tiniest village will
usually have a cafe or bar. Bars come in
various guises, including *bodegas* (old-style
wine bars), *cervecerías* (beer bars), *tascas*
(bars that specialise in tapas), *tabernas*

(taverns) and even pubs. Many serve tapas
and often have more substantial fare too.

Throughout Spain you'll find plenty of
restaurants serving good, simple food at affordable prices and featuring regional
specialities. There are also a minority of
fairly dire dumps, particularly in tourist
haunts. A *mesón* is a simple eatery with
home-style cooking, commonly attached to
a bar. A *venta* was probably once an inn,
and is usually off the beaten track, while a
marisquería is a seafood restaurant.

On the Walk
Refugios Most staffed refugios serve breakfast and dinner, while some of the larger ones
which stay open all day offer drinks, snacks
and occasionally lunch. It's advisable to
reserve dinner at the same time as your bunk,
though they'll never turn a hungry traveller
away. You don't have to be staying at a
refugio to order food, so it's quite possible to
enjoy an evening meal and then head away
to camp somewhere more tranquil.

Buying Food There's usually at least one
shop at the beginning and end of each walk
we've described. For walks of more than
one day's duration, places en route are indicated where you can pick up supplies.

For wild camping, most of the major
equipment shops in Madrid and Barcelona
(listed in Buying & Hiring Locally at the
end of the Planning section earlier in this
chapter) sell special dehydrated foods.
However, if you have particular favourites,
it's safer to purchase them before leaving
home. You shouldn't have trouble picking
up some form of high-energy food in even
the smallest one-shop village. For a glossary of camping food terms, see the boxed
text 'Camping Food'.

Cooking If you eat one meal a day or every
other day in a refuge, you can dispense with
a stove and fuel. A stove does confer extra
flexibility, however, and nothing in the
world rivals a post-dawn mug of steaming
tea or coffee. There's a wide range of titles
available on camp food and cooking.

Camping Food

The following is a list of Spanish food terms which may come in handy when shopping for camping supplies. Take only enough food to see you through the walk. Don't forget, though, to include an emergency supply in case the walk takes longer than planned.

Dehydrated & Powdered Foods

Dehydrated and powdered food products are ideal for walks of several days duration, where weight becomes an important consideration.

té or *té de infusiones* – tea or herbal tea
café – coffee (instant)
cacao – drinking cocoa
azúcar – sugar, sold almost always by the kilo and very difficult to find in smaller units
leche en polvo – powdered milk
puré de patatas – instant mashed potatoes
sopa en sobres – dehydrated soup in sachets

Staple Foods

Staple foods make an excellent, high-carbohydrate base for a meal.

copos de avena – oat flakes, cooked
muesli – muesli; available at health stores and some groceries
arroz – rice
pasta – pasta
lentejas – lentils
alubias – white beans
garbanzos – chickpeas; until recently, the staple carbohydrate of the poor. Buy them pre-cooked and decant them into a lightweight receptacle.

Semi-Perishable Foods

Try to choose foods such as cheese and sausages which will last in the heat over several days.

pan integral – wholemeal bread; not available at all bakeries

embutido – cured sausage
salchichón – salami; tends to be greasy
longaniza – pork sausage; less fatty than salchichón and better value
chorizo – the farmer's and hunter's favourite; a red, meaty sausage
jamón serrano – cured ham, lower in fat content than other cured meats
lomo – smoked pork loin
queso – cheese

Canned Foods

Cans are heavy, but carried in small quantities their contents make an excellent garnish to an otherwise bland meal.

atún – tuna; choose a more expensive brand, which will contain more tuna and less oil or salty water
sardinas – sardines
guisantes – peas
pimientos – peppers
pulpo en salsa – octopus in sauce
mejillones – mussels
calamares – squid

Dried Fruit

Frutos secos is the generic term for all kinds of nuts and dried fruit. Calorie per gram, they are among the most efficient foods to carry.

avellanas – hazelnuts
cacahuetes – peanuts
almendras – almonds
albaricoques – apricots
higos – figs
pan de higo – compressed figs and almonds
pasas – raisins
dátiles – dates
turrón – a delicious honey and almond nougat

Outdoor gear shops will usually have a few in stock or will at least be able to recommend a good one.

DRINKS
Nonalcoholic Drinks

Bottled spring water (*agua mineral*) is widely available. You can buy it *sin gas* (still) and *con gas* (sparkling, like soda water). The usual multinational brands of soft drink, called *refrescos*, are also sold everywhere. Freshly squeezed fruit juices (*zumos*) are delicious. You can also buy them cheaply by the litre or less in waxed cartons.

It's difficult to get a really bad coffee in Spain, where all but the humblest of bars will have an espresso machine hissing away. You can order coffee in three ways: *un cafe solo*, small, black and pungently strong; *un cortado*, a solo which is 'cut' with a splash or an equivalent amount of milk; and *cafe con leche*, coffee with milk. There's also *cafe americano*, black and weaker, but if you ask for one in the villages, you're likely to get a quizzical stare in return. If you ask for a cup of tea, you'll probably be served a cup of hot water with a tea bag on the side.

Alcoholic Drinks

Just to take a look at the array of bottles behind even the most modest bar is enough to make your liver protest. Most drinkers in a bar will be sipping *vino* (wine), either *tinto* (red), *rosado* (rosé) or *blanco* (white). In Andalucía and in fancier joints elsewhere, sherry – usually asked for as *un fino* – or its local equivalent are popular. In restaurants, the *vino de la casa* (house wine) can vary from the very palatable to toxic paint stripper. For draught beer, ask for *cerveza de barril* or *cerveza de presión*. If you just ask for *una cerveza*, you'll normally be served one in a bottle.

On the Walk

Water is by far the best thirst quencher when you're walking. It's also the most readily available way to rehydrate. In some mountain regions, well above the cultivation line and away from areas where livestock graze, it's safe to drink straight from flowing streams. Take advice from locals and refugio wardens and always keep water purifying tablets accessible. For information on how to treat water that seems suspect, see Water Purification in the Staying Healthy section of the Health & Safety chapter.

Health & Safety

Spain is, in general, a healthy place to visit; the climate, the food and the lack of pollution in areas where you're likely to walk all help to keep the bugs at bay. If you have any problems, they're likely to be of the kind that would arise wherever you're hiking: blisters, a minor strain, irritating insect bites (the horse flies can sometimes be voracious), sunburn (bear in mind that the higher you climb, the more intense are the sun's rays) or a touch of stomach trouble.

Travel health depends on your predeparture preparations, your daily health care while travelling and how you handle any medical problem that might develop. The sections that follow aren't intended to alarm. They are worth a skim, however – and could come into their own if you're unlucky enough to encounter other than routine irritants while walking.

Should you need treatment, ask for an *ambulatorio*, or government clinic. For the casualty department of a hospital, ask for *urgencias*.

Predeparture Preparation

MEDICAL COVER

Citizens of European Union (EU) countries are covered for emergency medical care upon presentation of an E111 form, which you need to get before you travel. In Britain, you can pick one up free at a post office. All you need to do is quote your name, address, date of birth and National Insurance number. In other EU countries, obtain information from your doctor or local health service.

Though the form will entitle you to free emergency treatment in government clinics and hospitals, you will have to pay for dental treatment, any medicines bought from pharmacies (even if a doctor has prescribed them) and also possibly for tests.

Once home, you may be able to recover some or all of these costs from your national health service.

HEALTH INSURANCE

Make sure that you have adequate health insurance. See Travel Insurance under Documents in the Facts for the Walker chapter for details.

IMMUNISATIONS

No special immunisations are required, but a few standard jabs are recommended, even if you're walking no further than the pub. These include inoculation against diphtheria, tetanus (a very mild risk if you cut yourself) and polio, as well as possibly measles, German measles (rubella) and mumps. They are normally administered in childhood but they do require a booster – every 10 years in the case of tetanus and polio.

OTHER PREPARATIONS

It's sensible to have had a recent dental checkup since toothache on the trail with solace a couple of days or more away can be a miserable experience. If you wear glasses, take a spare pair and your prescription.

If you need a particular medicine, take enough with you to last the trip. As an extra precaution, include part of the packaging listing the ingredients or generic name since this will make getting replacements easier. It's also a good idea to have a legible prescription or letter from your doctor to prove that you legally use the medication.

TRAVEL HEALTH GUIDES

Though neither of the following are written specifically for walkers, you might like to consult them. *Travellers' Health* by Dr Richard Dawood, which is comprehensive, authoritative and easy to read. It is too bulky to fit comfortably in your backpack, however, and best consulted before you set

Medical Kit Check List

Spain must have more *farmacias* (pharmacies) per head of population than anywhere else in Europe. They are, however, mostly confined to cities and towns, so ensure you have everything you need before you head for the hills. Consult your pharmacist for brand names available in Spain.

A basic medical kit might include:

☐ adhesive tape
☐ antifungal cream or powder – for fungal skin infections and thrush
☐ antihistamine – a decongestant for colds and allergies, to ease the itch from insect bites or stings and to help prevent motion sickness
☐ antiseptic – for cuts and grazes
☐ aspirin or paracetamol (acetaminophen in the USA) – for pain or fever
☐ bandages and safety pins
☐ blister plasters
☐ calamine lotion, sting relief spray or aloe vera – to ease irritation from sunburn and insect bites or stings
☐ cold and flu tablets, throat lozenges and nasal decongestant
☐ diphenoxylate or loperamide – 'blockers' for diarrhoea
☐ insect repellent
☐ elasticated bandage – for sprains, sore knees etc
☐ gauze pads
☐ pain relieving cream – for sore muscles
☐ prochlorperazine or metaclopramide – for nausea and vomiting
☐ rehydration mixture – to prevent dehydration, eg due to severe diarrhoea; particularly important when travelling with children
☐ small scissors and tweezers
☐ sterile alcohol wipes
☐ sticking plaster (such as Band-Aids)
☐ thermometer (note that mercury thermometers are prohibited by airlines)

out. *Travel with Children* by Maureen Wheeler is a Lonely Planet book which gives advice on travel health for younger children.

Staying Healthy

WATER

If it comes out of a tap, it's generally safe to drink. Village *fuentes*, the flowing spouts or fountains where people fill their containers, are also usually trustworthy. The sign '*agua potable*' (drinking water) will confirm. On the other hand, if you haven't been in the area long and your stomach is still adapting to the change of both water and food, it makes sense to take the extra precaution of purifying your drinking water. At even small shops you can buy bottled spring or mineral water (*agua mineral*), which costs between 40 ptas and 75 ptas for a 1.5L bottle.

Be sure you carry enough water with you. In some areas, topping up is no problem; in more arid areas, however, you could be a couple of hours away from the next source on a hot day, and dehydration's no fun. For more information on the compounded effects of dehydration, see Heat Exhaustion later in this chapter.

Water Purification

Vigorous boiling should be enough to zap most harmful elements. Remember, however, that at high altitudes water boils at a lower temperature, so keep the flame under the pan for longer. The big disadvantage of this method is that it uses up a lot of fuel.

The simplest purification method is to pop in a tablet. Chlorine tablets kill many pathogens, but not some parasites like giardia and amoebic cysts – a relatively minor risk in Spain. Iodine is more effective in purifying water; follow the directions carefully, since too much iodine can be harmful. It's also available in tablet form, which reduces the risk of overdosing. All of the above leave a taste in the water and wreck the flavour of a good cup of tea.

Most filters are no more effective than chemical treatment. They're also expensive and add weight to your backpack. You might want to bring a simple nylon mesh bag which filters out dirt and larger foreign bodies so that chemical solutions work much more effectively.

TIREDNESS

A simple statistic: more injuries of whatever nature happen towards the end of the day than earlier, when you're fresher. To reduce the risk, don't push yourself too hard and as the day declines slow down and walk with greater concentration.

During the day, stop for a rest, however brief, at least every couple of hours and build in a good half-hour's lunch break. As tiredness creeps up on you, chew something that will release energy rapidly into your system – things like nuts, dried fruit and chocolate.

Medical Problems & Treatment

ENVIRONMENTAL HAZARDS

Walkers are at more risk than most groups from environmental hazards. The risk, however, can be significantly reduced by applying nothing more than a dose of common sense.

Altitude Sickness

Lack of oxygen at high altitudes (over 2500m) affects most people to some extent. Since less oxygen reaches the muscles and the brain at higher altitudes, the heart and lungs have to compensate by working harder. Mild symptoms of Acute Mountain Sickness (AMS) include headache, breathlessness, lethargy, dizziness, difficulty in sleeping and loss of appetite. AMS may become severe without warning and can become fatal. Severe symptoms include breathlessness, a dry irritative cough (which may progress to the production of pink, frothy sputum), severe headache, lack of coordination and balance, confusion, irrational behaviour, vomiting, drowsiness and unconsciousness.

The real risk of AMS to walkers in Spain is fairly remote. However, there is no hard-and-fast rule as to the altitude at which more serious symptoms may develop.

If you feel mild distress, rest at the same altitude until recovery, usually a day or two, and take paracetamol or aspirin for headaches. If symptoms persist or become worse, however, an immediate descent is necessary; even 500m can help.

To reduce the risk of problems as you ascend higher:

- Ascend more slowly and build in more rest breaks.
- Drink extra fluids. The mountain air is cooler and normally drier and more moisture is lost as you breathe. Also, you're probably sweating much more than you realise. Both factors increase the risk of dehydration.
- Eat light, high-carbohydrate meals for more energy.
- Lay off the alcohol until you're down in the valleys since it increases the risk of dehydration.
- Avoid sedatives.

Heat Exhaustion & Sunburn

Dehydration compounded by salt deficiency can cause heat exhaustion. If you're working hard and it's hot, be sure to take in sufficient liquids to compensate for fluids lost through sweat. Salt deficiency is characterised by fatigue, lethargy, headaches, giddiness and muscle cramps. Salt tablets are overkill; just adding extra salt to your food is sufficient.

Protection against the sun should always be taken seriously. Particularly in the deceptive coolness of the mountains, sunburn occurs rapidly. Lather on the sunscreen and a barrier cream for your nose and lips, wear a broad-brimmed hat whenever the sun appears and protect your eyes with good quality sunglasses with UV lenses, particularly when walking near water, sand or snow. If, despite these precautions, you get yourself burnt, calamine lotion or Stingose will soothe.

Hypothermia

Too much cold can be just as dangerous as too much heat. Hypothermia, also known by its everyday name of exposure, occurs when the body loses heat faster than it can produce it, so the core temperature of the body falls. Even in summer, it's easy to progress from chilly to very cold to dangerously cold due to a combination of wind, wet clothing, fatigue and hunger.

Symptoms of hypothermia are exhaustion, numb skin (particularly toes and fingers), shivering, slurred speech, irrational, even violent behaviour, lethargy, stumbling, dizzy spells, muscle cramps and violent bursts of energy.

When walking in a region subject to rapid weather change – such as the Picos de Europa or the Pyrenees – pack clothing to equip you for wet and windy conditions, no matter how blue the sky is when you set out. Carry fluid to drink and food such as dates, raisins and chocolate, which contain simple sugars to generate heat quickly. For more detail on the clothing and equipment you should bring on a walk, see What to Bring in the Facts for the Walker chapter.

To treat mild hypothermia, first get the person out of the wind and/or rain, remove their clothing if it's wet and replace it with dry, warm clothing. Give them hot liquids – never alcohol – and some high-calorie, easily digestible food. Don't rub victims; instead, allow them to slowly warm themselves. This should be enough to treat the early stages of hypothermia. The speedy recognition and treatment of mild hypothermia is the only way to prevent severe hypothermia, which can be fatal.

INFECTIOUS DISEASES
Diarrhoea

Simple things like a change of water, food or climate can cause a mild case of the runs; a few rushed toilet trips with no other symptoms are no cause for concern.

Dehydration is the danger with any diarrhoea, particularly in children or the elderly. It can occur quite quickly, so fluid replacement in quantities at least equal to the volume being lost is essential. Weak black tea with a little sugar, soda water, or soft drinks allowed to go flat and then diluted 50% with water, are all good.

With really severe diarrhoea, downing a rehydrating solution will replace minerals and salts lost. You can buy oral rehydration salts (ORS) at most pharmacies; just mix them with water, swallow and clench your buttocks. If there's no pharmacy around, make up a solution of six teaspoons of sugar plus half a teaspoon of salt to a litre of water. Keep drinking small amounts often and stick to a bland diet as you recover.

Gut-paralysing drugs such as diphenoxylate and loperamide can bring relief from the symptoms, but they don't actually cure the problem. Only use these drugs if you can't rush to a toilet or rock big enough to provide privacy and never take them if you have a high fever or are severely dehydrated. They are not recommended for children under 12 years of age. Seek medical advice if you have diarrhoea with blood or mucus, any diarrhoea with fever or persistent and severe diarrhoea.

Fungal Infections

Long-distance walkers risk picking up a fungal infection by sweating liberally, probably washing less than usual and going longer without a change of clothes. While an unpleasant irritant, a fungal infection presents no danger and can easily be cured – once you stop walking.

Fungal infections are encouraged by moisture, so wear loose, comfortable clothes, wash when you can and dry yourself thoroughly. Try to expose the infected area to air or sunlight as much as possible and apply an antifungal cream or powder like tolnaftate (Tinaderm).

CUTS, BITES & STINGS
Snakes

It is very unlikely that you will encounter a poisonous snake. However, to minimise your chances of being bitten, always wear boots, socks and long trousers when walking through undergrowth where snakes may be present. Don't put your hands into holes and crevices and be careful when collecting firewood.

Snake bites do not cause instantaneous death and antivenenes are usually available.

Immediately wrap the bitten limb tightly, as you would for a sprained ankle, and then attach a splint to immobilise it. Keep the victim still and seek medical help, if possible with the dead snake for identification. Don't attempt to catch the snake if there is a possibility of being bitten again. Tourniquets and sucking out the poison are now comprehensively discredited methods of treating snakebite.

Insect Bites & Stings

Bee and wasp stings are usually painful rather than dangerous and ice packs will reduce the pain and swelling. In Spain, mosquitoes can be irritating but are not malaria-bearing, while some kinds of ant can be nasty little biters. In all cases, calamine lotion or Stingose spray will give relief, as will an antihistamine cream.

Beware too the hairy, reddish-brown caterpillars of the pine processionary moth, called *procesionarias*. They live in pine trees in a kind of giant, easily spotted web, but can be seen walking in long lines (hence their name). The hairs of the caterpillar can set off an extremely irritating allergic reaction of the skin.

Ticks

You should always check all over your body if you have been walking through a potentially tick-infested area – for instance, if walking near sheep or an abandoned sheep fold – as ticks can cause skin infections and other more serious diseases.

If a tick is found attached, press down around the tick's head with tweezers, grab the head and gently pull upwards. Avoid pulling the rear of the body as this may squeeze the tick's gut contents into the skin, increasing the risk of infection and disease. Smearing chemicals on the tick will not make it let go and is not recommended.

Cuts & Scratches

Wash well and treat any cut with antiseptic. It's better to avoid bandages and plasters, which can keep wounds wet.

TRAUMATIC INJURIES
Sprains

Ankle and knee sprains are common injuries in hikers, particularly when walking over rugged terrain. To help prevent ankle sprains in these circumstances, you should wear an all-leather boot that has adequate ankle support. If you do suffer a sprain, immobilise the joint with a firm bandage, and relieve pain and swelling by keeping the joint elevated for the first 24 hours and, where possible, by using ice (a packet of frozen peas is a good alternative) on the swollen joint. Take simple painkillers to ease the discomfort. If the sprain is mild, you may be able to continue your walk after a couple of days. For more severe sprains, seek medical attention as it may be necessary to have an X-ray to rule out the possibility of a broken bone.

Major Accident

Falling or having something fall on you, resulting in head injuries or fractures, is always possible when hiking, especially if you are crossing unstable terrain. Following is some basic advice on what to do if a major accident does occur; detailed first aid instruction is outside the scope of this guidebook. If a person suffers a major fall:

• Make sure you and other people with you are not in danger.
• Assess the injured person's condition.
• Stabilise any injuries, such as bleeding wounds or broken bones.
• Seek medical attention.

If the person is unconscious, immediately check whether they are breathing, and clear their airway if it is blocked; check whether they have a pulse – feel the side of the neck rather than the wrist. If they are not breathing but have a pulse, you should start mouth-to-mouth resuscitation immediately. In these circumstances it is best to move the person as little as possible in case their neck or back is broken. Keep the person warm by covering them with a blanket or other dry clothing; insulate them from the ground if possible.

Check for wounds and broken bones – ask the person where they have pain if they are conscious; otherwise, gently inspect them all over (including their back and the back of the head), moving them as little as possible. Control any bleeding by applying firm pressure to the wound. Bleeding from the nose or ear may indicate a fractured skull. Don't give the person anything by mouth, especially if they are unconscious.

Indications of a fracture (broken bone) are pain, swelling and discolouration, loss of function or deformity of a limb. You shouldn't try to move a broken bone unless it is obviously displaced, in which case you should attempt to straighten it if possible. To protect from further injury, immobilise a nondisplaced or straightened fracture by splinting it; for fractures of the thigh bone, try to straighten the leg gently, then tie it to the good leg to hold it in place. Fractures associated with open wounds (compound fractures) require more urgent treatment than simple fractures as there is a risk of infection. Dislocations, where the bone has come out of the joint, are very painful, and should be set as soon as possible.

Broken ribs are painful but usually heal by themselves and do not need splinting. If breathing difficulties occur, or the person coughs up blood, medical attention should be sought urgently, as it may indicate a punctured lung.

Internal injuries are more difficult to detect, and cannot usually be treated in the field. Watch for shock, which is a specific medical condition associated with a failure to maintain circulating blood volume. Signs include a rapid pulse and cold, clammy extremities. A person in shock requires urgent medical attention.

Some general points to bear in mind are as follows:

- Note that even large wounds can be sutured (sewn up) several days later, so there is no great hurry to close them unless you know what you are doing.
- Simple fractures take several weeks to heal, so they don't need to be fixed straight away, but they should be immobilised to protect them

from further injury. Compound fractures need much more urgent treatment.
- If you do have to splint a broken bone, remember to check regularly that the splint is not cutting off the circulation to the hand or foot.
- Most cases of brief unconsciousness are not associated with any serious internal injury to the brain, but as a general rule of thumb in these circumstances, any person who has been knocked unconscious should be watched for deterioration. If they do deteriorate, seek medical attention straight away.

OTHER MEDICAL PROBLEMS
Blisters
We've all had them and we'll all get them again, even though they're easily avoided. Be sure you and your walking boots or shoes know each other well before you set out on a walking holiday and that their fit is snug but not too tight. Seamless socks, where there's no join above the toes, are more expensive but worth the extra outlay. Even on a day walk, pack a spare pair of socks so you can change if they get wet or excessively sweaty. If you do feel a blister coming on, treat it sooner rather then later. Use a simple sticking plaster or one of the various 'second skin' spray or paint-on remedies.

Knee Pain
Many walkers feel the judder on long steep descents. When dropping steeply, to reduce the strain on the knee joint (you can't eliminate it) try taking shorter steps which leave your legs slightly bent and ensure that your heel hits the ground before the rest of your foot. Some walkers find that tubular bandages help, while others use high-tech, strap-on supports. Walking poles are very effective in taking some of the weight off the knees.

Women's Health

GYNAECOLOGICAL PROBLEMS
Antibiotic use, synthetic underwear, sweating and contraceptive pills can lead to fungal vaginal infections (thrush), especially when it's hot. Good personal hygiene,

loose-fitting clothes and cotton underwear will help to prevent them. Characterised by a rash, itch and discharge, fungal vaginal infections can be treated with a vinegar or lemon-juice douche, or with yoghurt. Alternatively, use Nystatin, miconazole or clotrimazole pessaries or vaginal cream. If you know you are prone to infection, bring your normal treatment with you.

Sexually transmitted diseases are another major cause of vaginal problems. Symptoms include a smelly discharge, painful intercourse and sometimes a burning sensation when urinating. Go to a doctor and bear in mind that male sexual partners must also be treated. Remember also that, in addition to such diseases, HIV or hepatitis B may also be acquired during exposure. It's essential to practise safe sex using condoms.

URINARY TRACT INFECTION

Cystitis, or inflammation of the bladder, is a common condition in women. Symptoms include burning when urinating and having to urinate frequently and urgently. Blood can sometimes be passed in the urine. Sexual activity with a new partner or with an old partner who has been away for a while can trigger an infection. The initial treatment is to drink plenty of fluids, which may resolve the problem. If symptoms persist, treat them with an antibiotic because a simple infection can spread to the kidneys, causing a more severe illness. Single dose (nonantibiotic) treatments, called Monuril, are available over the counter at pharmacies, but are generally effective only in the very early stages of mild cystitis. If you are prone to urinary tract infections, it is probably a good idea to bring along your usual medication.

Safety on the Walk

By taking a few simple precautions, you'll significantly reduce the odds of getting into trouble.

Allow plenty of time to accomplish a walk, particularly when daylight hours are shorter. Take the greater of the times we indicate for a walk, add a couple of hours and check that, given your planned departure time, it will still be light if you're delayed. Don't overestimate your capabilities. It's enormously tempting, when pitting yourself against a mountain, to drive yourself too hard. Don't. The mountain couldn't care less about you. If the going gets too tough, give up and head back, and if you're walking in a group and the pace gets too hot, tell them. It's no source of shame or embarrassment.

It's better not to walk on your own; this way, if something should go wrong, one person can stay put and the other can go for help. Every walker should let someone know their expected route. If setting off alone, however, it is especially important that others are alerted. If you're well organised, you can leave your itinerary at home with family or friends. Otherwise, simply tell someone responsible, such as the warden of the *refugio* (refugio or mountain hut) or the ranger at the park entrance, of your expected route and the return time.

For information on the clothes and equipment you should take with you when walking, consult What to Bring in the Facts for the Walker chapter.

Before you set out, make it a routine to check that you have a relevant map, a compass and whistle, and that you know the weather forecast for the area for the next 24 hours. In the high mountains, take advice on the probability of lingering snow on and beneath passes.

CROSSING RIVERS

You may have to ford a river or stream swollen with snowmelt which is fast flowing enough to be a potential risk. Before stepping out from the bank, ease one arm out of the shoulder strap of your backpack and unclip the belt buckle. In this way, should you lose your balance and be swept downstream, it will be easier to slip out of your backpack instead of being dragged under or flailing helplessly like an upturned tortoise. If linking hands with others, grasp at the wrist; this gives a tighter grip than a handhold. If you're fording alone, plant a stick or your walking poles upstream to give you greater stability and help you to lean against the current. Use them to feel the way forward and walk side-on to the direction of flow so that your body presents less of an obstacle to the rushing water.

LIGHTNING

If a storm brews, avoid exposed areas. Lightning has a penchant for crests, lone trees, small depressions, gullies, caves and cabin entrances, as well as wet ground. If you are caught out in the open, try to curl up as tightly as possible with your feet together and keep a layer of insulation between you and the ground. Place metal objects such as metal-frame backpacks and walking poles away from you.

RESCUE & EVACUATION

If someone in your group is injured or falls ill and can't move, leave somebody with them while another one or more goes for help. If there are only two of you, leave the injured person with as much warm clothing, food and water as it's sensible to spare, plus the whistle and torch. Mark the position with something conspicuous – an orange bivvy bag, or perhaps a large stone cross on the ground.

If you need to call for help, use these internationally recognised emergency signals. Give six short signals, such as a whistle, a yell or the flash of a light, at 10-second intervals, followed by a minute of rest. Repeat the sequence until you get a response. If the responder knows the signals, this will be three signals at 20-second intervals, followed by a minute's pause and a repetition of the sequence.

Telephone numbers worth learning by heart are ☎ 085 for a medical emergency, ☎ 112 for an emergency of any kind, ☎ 091 or ☎ 092 for the police and ☎ 062 for the *guardia civil*, who enforce law and order in rural areas. These numbers are nationwide. In the unlikely event that you find yourself in an emergency situation, ring them in the first instance rather than relying on your own resources.

Be ready to give information on where an accident occurred, how many people are injured and the injuries sustained. If a helicopter needs to come in, describe the terrain and weather conditions at the place of the accident.

Helicopter Rescue & Evacuation

If a helicopter arrives on the scene, there are a couple of conventions you should be familiar with. Standing face on to the chopper:

- Arms up in the shape of a letter 'V' means 'I/We need help'.
- Arms in a straight diagonal line (like one line of a letter X) means 'All OK'.

In order for the helicopter to land, there must be a cleared space of 25 sq metres, with a flat landing area of 6 sq metres. The helicopter will fly into the wind when landing. In cases of extreme emergency, where no landing area is available, a person or harness might be lowered. Take extreme care to avoid the rotors when approaching a landed helicopter.

Getting There & Away

As one of Europe's top holiday destinations, Spain has excellent air, rail and road links with other European countries. There are regular ferry services between the mainland and the Islas Baleares (Balearic Islands), and a weekly boat between Cádiz and both Tenerife and Gran Canaria in the Islas Canarias (Canary Islands).

If travelling to Spain from within Europe, unless you're keen to drive your own car, it's not only quicker but almost certainly less expensive to fly. It's also quite easy to hire a car on arrival. If travelling from outside Europe, check the cost of flying via London against the cost of a direct flight; the former is frequently less expensive.

For more detail on travel to and from the Spanish mainland and the Islas Canarias, see Lonely Planet's *Spain* guide.

AIR

On many European scheduled airline flights it's no longer strictly necessary to reconfirm your return booking or onward flight. For a charter flight, however, it's essential, both in order to ensure that you have a seat and because they're often subject to changes of schedule and even re-routing. For most intercontinental flights, you should reconfirm at least 72 hours before departure.

Airports & Airlines

The main gateways to Spain for scheduled flights are Barajas airport in Madrid, and El Prat de Llobregat in Barcelona. Many holiday-makers, however, arrive via the principal charter flight destinations of Málaga (for Andalucía), Alicante (for the Costa Blanca and Valencia region), Palma de Mallorca (for the Islas Baleares) and Fuertaventura, Gran Canaria and Tenerife (for the Islas Canarias). If planning to walk in Andorra or the Catalan Pyrenees, Barcelona is the handiest point of arrival, but look out for cheap charter deals to Reus or Girona (Gerona in Spanish), also in Catalunya.

The high season for air travel to Spain – and for ticket prices – is July and August, Easter and Christmas. Additionally, flights from the UK are normally fully booked and prices at a premium during British school half-term holidays.

Buying Tickets

The plane ticket will probably be the single most expensive item in your walking holiday, and the wide range of options from many European destinations can be baffling. Check the ads in a selection of newspapers and magazines. Then sit by the phone with paper, pen and a spare half-hour and ring around travel agents (airlines generally don't supply the cheapest tickets) to find out the fare and any restrictions. With your credit card before you, decide which is the best deal for you and phone to clinch it. Outside major vacation periods, if you decide on impulse to take a break there are some really cheap last minute charter flight deals from European destinations.

Use any fares we quote as a guide only. They're approximate, based on the rates advertised by travel agents at the time of writing, and are subject to fluctuation.

If you're travelling from the UK or the USA, you may find that the cheapest flights

---

WARNING

The information in this chapter is vulnerable to change: prices for international travel are volatile, routes are introduced and cancelled, schedules change, special deals come and go, and rules and requirements are amended. Similarly, walking companies may vary the destinations they cover. We give contact telephone numbers. From this point, it's over to you; our information is no substitute for your own careful, up-to-date research.

are being advertised by obscure bucket shops whose names haven't yet reached the telephone directory. Many such firms are honest and solvent, but there's the odd rogue who will take your money and disappear, to reopen elsewhere a month or two later under a new name. If you feel suspicious, don't hand over all the money at once; leave a deposit of 20% or so and pay the balance when you get the ticket. If they insist on cash in advance, go elsewhere. Once you have the ticket, ring the airline to confirm that you are actually booked on the flight. In Britain, ask whether an agent is 'ABTA-bonded', meaning that they've placed a bond with the Association of British Travel Agents so that clients will be refunded if they go bankrupt or do a runner. Most reputable agents belong to ABTA.

You may decide to pay more than the rock-bottom fare by opting for the safety of a better-known travel agent. Firms such as STA Travel, Council Travel in the USA, Travel CUTS in Canada, Flight Centres International in Australia and New Zealand, and Campus Travel or Trailfinders in Britain aren't going to disappear overnight and they offer competitive prices.

Once you have your ticket, write down its number and the flight details and keep this information somewhere separate. If the ticket is lost or stolen, it will help you get a replacement.

Departure Tax

On both scheduled flights and charters, departure tax is normally included within the ticket price. Not always, however, so when you're ringing around for the best quote, it's wise to ask.

The UK & Ireland

The weekend editions of the quality national newspapers have info on cheap fares. In London, try also the *Evening Standard*, the listings magazine *Time Out* and *TNT*, a free weekly magazine targeted at antipodeans. Those with access to TV Teletext will find a host of travel agents advertising; the Internet is another source.

Two among the many reliable travel agencies are STA Travel (☎ 0171-361 6161; from 1 june 1999 ☎ 020-7361 6161) and Trailfinders (☎ 0171-937 5400; from 1 June 1999 ☎ 020-7937 5400).

The fares advertised by bucket shops are invariably on charter flights (for the most popular destinations, many within striking distance of walking areas which feature in this book, see the section on Airports & Airlines earlier in this chapter). If you shop around, you can fly one way to Spain for around UK£80 outside the major holiday periods and should be able to pick up a return flight for under UK£150. There are a host of small and medium-sized operators fighting for the charter flight market. One such is Spanish Travel Services (☎ 0171-387 5337; from 1 June 1999 ☎ 020-7387 5337), 138 Eversholt St, London NW1 1BL, which has charter flights from as low as UK£104 return (plus UK£14 tax) to Madrid or Barcelona and does charters to Málaga from UK£109 return (including tax) – as always, depending on the season.

The downside of such a flight is that once it's reserved you can't change it. Make sure that your travel insurance policy (see the section on Documents in the Facts for the Walker chapter) has a clause to confirm that you'll be reimbursed if circumstances beyond your control prevent you from flying. Check also the time of departure; a 6 am flight for the saving of a pound or two isn't a great investment.

The two flag airlines linking the UK and Spain are British Airways (BA; ☎ 0345-222 111), 156 Regent St, London W1R, and Spain's Iberia (☎ 0171-830 0011 in London; from 1 June 1999 ☎ 020-7830 0011, or ☎ 0990-341341 elsewhere in the UK), 11 Haymarket, London SW1Y 4BP. BA's standard open-return ticket to Madrid costs UK£484 (UK£242 one way; bizarrely the monthly return is rather less at UK£210).

Nowadays, with deregulation and the abolition of the old cosy cartels, there's a third option, between the cheapo but sometimes inconvenient charter and the overpriced scheduled flight. Companies such as Debonair (☎ 0541-50 03 00 in the UK or ☎ 902-14 62 00 in Spain), EasyJet (☎ 0870-60 00 000, ☎ 902-29 99 92 in Spain) and Go (☎ 0845-60 54 321) have entered the market, offering no-frills scheduled flights at charter prices to destinations such as Barcelona and Madrid. If you book sufficiently in advance, EasyJet has tickets from London's Luton airport to Barcelona and Palma de Mallorca for as little as UK£49 each way (plus UK£10 departure tax). Many good deals are also available flying from regional airports in the UK.

If you're coming from Ireland, compare direct flights to flying via London; the latter may save you a punt or two. At the time of writing, Iberia is the only carrier operating between Dublin and Madrid or Barcelona. A single ticket costs 47,000 ptas and a return, valid for up to one month, costs 57,000 ptas.

Continental Europe

France In Paris, Voyages et Découvertes (☎ 01 42 61 00 01), 21 rue Cambon, offers reduced fares. In general, it's possible to find return flights for around 1000FF to Madrid and as little as 900FF to Barcelona (plus airport taxes of around 200FF). A more likely fare to Barcelona is 1450FF, and there are no charters to either.

From Spain, the choices are generally less attractive; at the time of writing, a standard return fare from Madrid to Paris was 44,000 ptas (31,000 ptas for students).

Germany Among the better of Munich's many budget travel agents are Council Travel (☎ 089-395 02 2), Adalbertstrasse 32, and STA Travel (☎ 089-399 09 6), Königstrasse 49. In Berlin, Kilroy Travel-ARTU Reisen (☎ 030-310 00 40) at Hardenbergstrasse 9 is good and has five other shops around the city. In Frankfurt am Main, you could try STA Travel (☎ 069-703 03 5), Bockenheimer Landstrasse 133.

Italy The best place to look for cheap fares is CTS (Centro Turístico Studentesco), with branches countrywide. The office in Rome (☎ 06-4 67 91) is at Via Genova 16.

Netherlands Amsterdam is a popular departure point. The student travel agency NBBS Reiswinkels (☎ 020-624 09 89), with branches throughout the city and over the border in Brussels, offers reliable service and reasonably low fares. Compare with prices in the bucket shops along Rokin before deciding.

Portugal Iberia and TAP Air Portugal have flights for around 34,000 ptas return, but unless you're in a real rush, you're better off travelling by train or bus.

The USA

On what is one of the world's busiest air corridors, prices vary enormously according to the season and whether you're travelling by charter or scheduled flight. As you shop around, bear in mind the alternative of flying to London and picking up a cheap onward ticket to Spain from there (see The UK & Ireland earlier in this section).

A peak return fare from the east coast of the USA to Spain will set you back over US$1000. By contrast, you should be able to pick up an off-season charter flight for between US$450 and US$550. Several airlines, including Iberia, BA and KLM-Royal Dutch Airlines (KLM), fly direct to Spain, landing in Madrid or Barcelona.

The *New York Times*, *LA Times*, *Chicago Tribune* and *San Francisco Examiner* produce weekly travel sections full of travel ads. The magazine *Travel Unlimited* (PO Box 1058, Allston, Massachusetts 02134) publishes details of cheap air fares.

Discount options from the USA include charter flights and stand-by fares. For a one-way flight, stand-by fares are often sold at 60% of the standard price. Airhitch (☎ 212-864 2000, ☎ 1800-326 2009 toll-free) has offices in several US cities and specialises in stand-by discounts. The Web site address is www.airhitch.org, and you can contact the representative in Madrid on ☎ 91 366 79 27 or check out the Spain Web site (www.collegeclub.com/~AHValencia).

Reliable travel agents include STA Travel (☎ 800-777 0112) and Council Travel

(☎ 800-226 8624), both of whom have offices in major cities. Their Web sites can be viewed at www.sta-travel.com and www.ciee.org/travel.htm. In New York, Discount Tickets (☎ 212-391 2313) specialises in budget air fares.

Canada

Between Canada and Spain, there's a similarly rich number of options. Travel CUTS (☎ 800-777 0112) has offices in all major cities. Its Web site address is www.trav elcuts.com. There are also plenty of bargains in the travel ads of newspapers such as the *Globe & Mail*, *Toronto Star* and *Vancouver Sun*. It can sometimes work out cheaper to head south and pick up a rock-bottom transatlantic fare out of Boston, New York, San Francisco or Los Angeles.

Australia

STA Travel (☎ 1300-660 960) and Flight Centres International (☎ 131 600) are major dealers in cheap air fares. Heavily discounted fares can often also be found at your local travel agent. In Australia, the Saturday travel sections of the *Age* (in Melbourne) and the *Sydney Morning Herald* carry a host of ads offering cheap fares to Europe.

As a rule, there are no direct flights from Australia to Spain. It's worth bearing in mind that on some flights between Australia and destinations like London, Paris and Frankfurt you can get a return ticket which includes a free return side trip from your destination to another European city. Madrid and Barcelona generally qualify for such deals.

New Zealand

The cheapest fares to Europe are generally routed through the USA, though in the case of Spain you may get a great deal via Latin America. A round-the-world ticket often works out cheaper than a normal return. Otherwise, you can fly from Auckland and pick up a connecting flight in Melbourne or Sydney.

STA Travel (☎ 09-309 0458) and Flight Centres International (☎ 09-309 0458) also operate in New Zealand. It's worth contacting your local travel agent to compare prices.

LAND

Interail (for residents of the European Union) or Eurail (for those from elsewhere) are two other concessionary schemes, but unless you're planning to travel by train across Europe as well as within Spain, neither is likely to justify the outlay. Interail costs 45,090 ptas (31,565 ptas for travellers under 26) for Spain, Portugal and Morocco, and 66,800 ptas (47,595 ptas for those under 26) including England and France.

Eurolines offers a Eurolines bus pass. Between mid-June and mid-September, a pass valid for 30/60 days costs UK£229/279 (UK£199/249 for those under 26 and senior citizens). With unlimited travel between 21 European cities, the inconvenience is that in Spain only Barcelona and Madrid are included in the scheme.

The UK

Bus Bear in mind that the rather gruelling bus journey to Spain may well work out no cheaper than hopping on a charter flight.

Eurolines (☎ 0990-143219) runs buses from London's Victoria bus terminal to Barcelona three times a week. The trip takes about 24 hours; one-way and return fares are UK£77/119 and UK£71/109 for those under 26 or senior citizens. A weekly bus heads for Madrid via San Sebastián year-round, leaving London on Friday at 10 pm and taking about 27 hours. From May to October, there's a second service, on Monday, and up to four extra services in summer, three via Paris (with an eight-hour stopover). One-way and return fares are UK£77/138 and UK£69/125 for those under 26 and senior citizens. Fares rise in the peak summer season and a major disadvantage of the bus is that you can't get off along the way.

Train You have to change trains in Paris. From London, there's a choice of train tickets, either crossing the Channel by ferry or taking the Eurostar train, which will whisk you through the Channel tunnel and to the heart of the French capital in under three hours.

One-way/return fares to Barcelona by train and ferry are UK£105/175 (rather less than the regular equivalent 2nd class fares by Eurostar only as far as Paris). For Eurostar information, ring European Rail (☎ 0171 387 0444; from 1 June 1999, 020-7387 0444) or Rail Europe (☎ 0990-848 848). For the train and ferry option, call Connex (☎ 0870 603).

Car & Motorcycle If you're planning on driving overland to Spain, inquire at any travel agent for information on the range of ferry companies which carry cars across the Channel. Another option is Eurotunnel, (also called Le Shuttle; ☎ 0990-353 535 for reservations), the Channel tunnel car train, a roll-up, around-the-clock service between Folkestone and Calais. You pay for the vehicle only and fares vary according to time of day and season: from UK£130 to UK£220 for a car and UK£65 to UK£100 for motorcycles.

Many people opt to fly to Spain, then rent a car once they arrive. Local operators can work out more cheaply than the multinational agencies with counters at the airport terminus; it may be worth your while looking into fly-drive combinations which allow you to pick up the vehicle on arrival and return it to a nominated point at the end of the rental period.

The minimum age in Spain for hiring a vehicle is 21 years and a credit card is usually required. For more details of petrol prices and rental options within Spain, see Car & Motorcycle in the Getting Around chapter.

Continental Europe

Bus Eurolines is the main long-distance bus service in Europe. It has buses between Paris and various Spanish cities, including Madrid, Barcelona, Santiago de Compostela, Alicante, Oviedo and Málaga, and stops at major towns en route. A one-way fare to Madrid is 11,300 ptas.

Eurolines and other companies operate services from major cities in Spain across France and into Germany, the Benelux countries, Italy, Switzerland and Eastern European destinations such as Prague.

Three Eurolines buses a week connect Lisbon and Madrid and there's a weekly run to and from Barcelona. There are also services to the Portuguese capital from Málaga (via Sevilla), Benidorm (via Alicante) and La Coruña (via Santiago de Compostela).

Local bus services cross the Franco-Spanish frontier at several locations.

From Portugal, Transportes Agobe (☎ 958 63 52 74 in Spain) runs three buses a week from Porto, Lisbon (☎ 01-796 61 48) and Albufeira to Sevilla, Málaga and Granada. Sevilla-Lisbon is 4500 ptas.

Train There's a nightly sleeper between Paris and both Madrid (809FF) and Barcelona (780FF). These apart, all other train journeys will mean a change somewhere en route.

The cheapest and most convenient option to Barcelona is the 10.02 pm from Paris Austerlitz, changing at Latour-de-Carol and arriving in Barcelona Sants at 11.27 am. It costs 485FF one way in a reclining seat or 555FF in a 2nd class couchette.

For speed, take a TGV high-speed train to, for example, Hendaye/Irún at the western end of the Pyrenees or either Montpellier or Narbonne on the French side of the border, and change there. A direct service connects Montpellier with Barcelona (252FF in 2nd class) and Valencia (366FF). With all these routes, prices and timetables vary according to season, so check the latest details.

Direct trains link Barcelona with Geneva and Zürich in Switzerland and Turin and Milan in Italy at least three times a week. Reaching other destinations in Europe will require a change in one of these cities or in Paris. There's also a daily service between Lisbon and Madrid (11 hours, 6900 ptas).

Car & Motorcycle The main crossings from France into Spain are the highways to Barcelona and San Sebastián at either end of the Pyrenees. There are several other attractive secondary passes, which are particularly convenient if you're planning to walk in the Pyrenees. These include Roncesvalles (Roncevaux in French), linking St Jean Pied-de-Port in France with Pamplona; the Puerto de Somport, north of Jaca in the Aragonese Pyrenees; the Puerto de Portalet, near Sallent de Gállego, convenient to the Parque Nacional de Ordesa y Monte Perdido; the Túnel de Bielsa; the Túnel de Vielha, which links the Vall d'Aran with the rest of Spain; and l'Hospitalet, on the border between Andorra and France.

SEA
The UK

P&O European Ferries (☎ 0990-980 980) operates a ferry from Portsmouth to Bilbao throughout the year, as a rule with two sailings a week (UK£200 return; UK£400 with car). Brittany Ferries (☎ 0990-360360) runs a twice-weekly ferry between Plymouth and Santander (24 hours) from mid-March to mid-November (UK£210 return; UK£445 with car). In other months, a weekly service departs from Poole or Portsmouth (30 to 33 hours). All ferries take both cars and foot passengers. Though the boats are well stabilised, seas in the Bay of Biscay can be quite rough.

Continental Europe

Línea Grimaldi has three sailings a week between Barcelona and Genova (17 hours). Boats leave Genoa on Monday, Wednesday and Friday, and Barcelona on Tuesday, Thursday plus the early hours of Sunday morning. For 8300 ptas, you can have a *butaca*, an airline-style reclining seat. For greater comfort, prices range from 9900 ptas for a bed in a four berth cabin to a luxury suite for two at 25,100 ptas. Book tickets with any major travel agent.

ORGANISED WALKS
Adventure Travel Companies

Most of the big British-based walking tour operators include Spain within their international programs. Favourite destinations for most include the Picos de Europa, Andalucía, Mallorca, the Islas Canarias and Aragón.

The British-based Alto Aragón (☎/fax 01869-337 339, 106604.3242@compuserve .com) organises walking, riding and cross-country skiing holidays in Aragón, one of the most attractive areas of the Pyrenees.

Explore Worldwide (☎ 01252-319 448, fax 01252-343 170, info@explore.co.uk) is ecosensitive and recommended. Sherpa Expeditions (☎ 0181-577 2717, fax 0181-572 9788; from 1 June 1999 ☎ 020-8577 2717, fax 020-8572 9788, sherpa.sales@dial.pipex .com) is experienced in offering hiking and trekking holidays in Spain. Exodus (☎ 0181-675 5550, fax 0181-673 0779; from 1 June 1999 ☎ 020-8675 5550, fax 020-8673 0779, sales@exodustravels.co.uk), similarly experienced, is unusual in including the Sierra de Gredos among its destinations.

Two other reliable companies which offer a range of walking opportunities are Headwater (☎ 01606-813 333, fax 01606-813 334, info@headwater.com) and Alternative Travel Group (☎ 01865-315 678, fax 01865-315 697, info@alternative-travel.co.uk). In addition to the more usual destinations, the latter also has a two week trip along the more interesting sections of the Camino de Santiago (Way of St James).

Lastly, there's the daddy of them all, Ramblers Holidays (☎ 01707 331 133, fax 01707 333 276, Ramhols@dial.pipex.com), an offshoot of the Ramblers Association and in business for over 50 years.

For information on walking tour companies based in Spain, see Organised Walks in the Getting Around chapter.

Getting Around

AIR

Generally speaking, internal flights within peninsular Spain are costly (a standard one way fare from Madrid to Barcelona ranges from 11,700 ptas to 15,550 ptas). Unless you're really pushed for time, it's more sensible to use the efficient and considerably less expensive train or bus services.

By contrast, a flight from the mainland to the Islas Baleares (Balearic Islands) is a serious alternative to the ferry from a Mediterranean port. Just about everybody flies to the Islas Canarias (Canary Islands). For details of services to each, see Getting There & Away in the relevant walks chapters.

Principal mainland airports include Madrid, Barcelona, Málaga, Santiago de Compostela and Valencia. Palma de Mallorca in the Islas Baleares and Tenerife and Gran Canaria in the Islas Canarias also have a massive daily number of flights, the majority of them charters.

Iberia (☎ 902-40 05 00), which has absorbed the once-separate airlines Aviaco, Air Nostrum and Binter Mediterráneo (even though they still sport their own livery), has an extensive network covering all Spain. Typical Iberia one-way fares are:

departure	destination	fare (ptas)
Madrid	Alicante	16,940
	Barcelona	16,290
	Granada	16,640
	Málaga	18,090
	Oviedo	18,240
	Santiago de Compostela	18,140
	Sevilla	15,240
	Zaragoza	17,440
Barcelona	Alicante	17,390
	Granada	23,590
	Madrid	16,290
	Málaga	24,390
	Oviedo	24,590
	Santiago de Compostela	27,540
	Sevilla	24,540
	Zaragoza	18,290

People under 22 or over 63 get 25% off return flights. A minifare return offers a reduction to all passengers of around 40%. To qualify, you have to reserve at least four days before travelling, spend a Saturday night away and return within a maximum of three months. Once the booking's made, it can't be altered.

Competing with Iberia and its subsidiaries are Spanair (☎ 902-13 14 15) and Air Europa (☎ 902-24 00 42). They used to be considerably cheaper, but the gap has closed in recent years.

BUS

It's usually cheaper – but not significantly so – to travel by bus rather than by train, particularly on long-haul runs. Intercity bus services in Spain are economical, reliable and reasonably frequent. The motorway service is faster and more direct than the normal one, which calls in at all towns of consequence along the route.

In most larger towns and cities, buses leave from one bus station, the *estación de autobuses*, usually but not always bang in the heart of town.

A return ticket often works out cheaper than buying two one-way tickets. People under the age of 26 should ask about discounts on long-distance trips. Some sample one-way fares include:

departure	destination	fare (ptas)
Madrid	Alicante	3270
	Barcelona	2940
	Granada	1945
	Oviedo	3655
	Santiago de Compostela	5500
	Sevilla	2730
Barcelona	Sevilla	8820
	Zaragoza	1640
Sevilla	Granada	2700

On most short regular runs between towns, the ticket you buy is for the next bus due to leave and cannot be used on a later one. For all longer trips (such as Madrid-Granada or Barcelona-Valencia), it's always prudent to buy your ticket in advance. At weekends and in peak season, this is essential.

Rural Services

Rural buses, alas, are a different story. As in many other European countries, routes and services have been sliced away to the bone and some villages are reliant on only two or three buses a week.

Schedules are subject to change, especially in more remote walking areas. Summer services are often more frequent than during the rest of the year (though on occasion this means nothing more than two buses a day rather than one). Where a morning or evening run serves primarily to transport children to school from outlying villages, the service may only operate during the school year.

Most buses connecting villages and provincial towns are run for the benefit of local inhabitants, not for the passing walker. Consequently, even frequent weekday services can drop off to a trickle at weekends. Indeed, many rural services don't operate at all on Sunday.

It's usually unnecessary – indeed, impossible – to make reservations; just arrive early enough to claim a seat. If you're planning to pick up a bus somewhere between population centres, arrive especially early since the moment of departure, whatever the timetable may say, is far from fixed.

In this book, if no alternatives feature, we've quoted the high-season schedule. Since a change of time could lead to a lost day, we strongly advise you to check the current schedule before setting out on a walk.

In smaller villages, buses tend to operate from a set street or plaza, often unmarked. Locals will know where to go. Usually a specific bar sells tickets and has timetable information.

In the Pyrenees and parts of rural Galicia, enterprising car owners in villages without public transport run an informal, on-demand taxi service. If you're stuck, ask at the local shop or bar.

TRAIN

Mainline trains of the national rail network, Red Nacional de los Ferrocarriles Españoles (RENFE), or Spanish Railway Network, are comfortable, reliable but rarely swift. Before you invest in a ticket, check the relative merits of the bus. Trains where you can stretch your legs and grab a meal or drink are more agreeable for long journeys, but they're usually slower, less frequent and more expensive (though not by much) than express buses. For information (in Spanish), call the local RENFE office, or have a look at their Web site (www.renfe.es).

Types of Train

A host of different train types cruise the narrow-gauge lines of the Spanish network. Bear in mind that a saving in time on a faster train can often mean a big hike in the fare.

Heading into and from the hills, you'll probably be travelling on a *regional*, a local train which tends to stop at every single station en route.

Between urban centres, there are the fastish, more comfortable and expensive Talgo or InterCity services. Both travel at much the same speed, the Talgo offering greater comfort for a slightly higher price. A *diurno* is a slightly slower (and correspondingly cheaper) option. Unless you're deliberately aiming to save a night's accommodation cost by sleeping on the train, avoid the *estrella* (star) which lumbers through the dark, picking up mail at every station.

The high-speed Alta Velocidad Español (AVE) train is the most expensive – and exciting – way to travel between Madrid and Sevilla. The Madrid-Barcelona line which would link up with the French TGV (Train à Grande Vitesse) has long been promised.

Passes

Nonresidents of Spain can buy a Tarjeta Turística rail pass at major train stations. Only really worthwhile if you're contemplating long-distance travel, they're valid for between three (22,545 ptas) and 10 days (55,277 ptas) of rail travel in Spain within a two month period.

Timetables & Reservations

There seems to be no comprehensive rail guide. Train timetables for specific lines are posted at most stations. *Llegadas* (arrivals) tend to be listed on white posters and *salidas* (departures) on yellow ones.

On local trains it's neither necessary or possible to book ahead. For long-distance trains, it generally costs nothing and is advisable to do so in the high season and at weekends. Bookings can be made at all RENFE stations and through many travel agents.

Costs

Some typical one-way 2nd class fares, which can vary according to the time of the day and the day or the week, include:

departure	destination	fare (ptas)
Madrid	Alicante	4500
	Barcelona	6200
	Granada	3300
	Málaga	6800
	Oviedo	4400
	Santiago de Compostela	5600
	Sevilla	9800
	Zaragoza	3800
Barcelona	Alicante	5700
	Granada	6300
	Madrid	6200
	Málaga	6700
	Oviedo	6100
	Santiago de Compostela	7200
	Sevilla	6600
	Zaragoza	3800

CAR & MOTORCYCLE

A car can be an advantage for getting to and from a walk. However, particularly in remote areas where buses may be few and far between, check the current timetable to ensure that you're going to meet up with it again. If you're in a group of four or five, a car can be really useful and save hours of waiting around if one person stands down each day or walks back to the car at the starting point and collects the rest of the party at the finish of the walk.

Be sure to pack your driving licence if you intend to get behind the wheel. If bringing your own car, remember to carry your insurance and other papers confirming that the vehicle is yours.

Road Rules

The speed limit ranges from 50 to 100km/h on major roads and 120km/h on *autopistas* (tolled dual-lane highways) and *autovías* (toll-free dual-carriage highways). Motorcyclists must use headlights at all times. Crash helmets are obligatory on bikes of any size.

Spanish truck drivers often have the courtesy to turn on their right indicator to show that the way ahead of them is clear for overtaking (and the left one if it is not and you are attempting this manoeuvre). This does not absolve you from exercising the usual caution, but can be a great help.

Vehicles already in roundabouts have right of way. Seat belts must be worn – both front and rear, if fitted. Fines for many traffic offences are tough, ranging from 50,000 ptas to 100,000 ptas. Nonresident foreigners can be fined up to 50,000 ptas on the spot – the minor compensation being that they get 20% off normal fines on immediate settlement. You can contest the fine in writing (and in English) within 10 days, but don't hold your breath for a favourable result.

Road Atlases

Several road atlases are available, including the *Mapa Oficial de Carreteras* for 1900 ptas. This even comes in a CD-ROM version! One of the best atlases on the market, available in and outside Spain, is the *Michelin Motoring Atlas: Spain & Portugal*. In Spain it's called *Michelin Atlas de Carreteras y Turístico: España Portugal* and costs 2575 ptas.

Both atlases include maps of all the main towns and cities, and can be bought in Spain at major bookshops and some petrol stations.

Road Assistance

The emergency 24 hour breakdown assistance service of the Real Automóvil Club de España (RACE) is available to members of foreign motoring organisations such as the RAC and AA. For assistance, call ☎ 900-11 81 18.

Tollways

Toll-free motorways are usually signed 'autovía'. Most paying autopistas are in the north of Spain. Keep in mind if you are driving into Spain from France that the A7 from the French border to Barcelona via Girona (Gerona) and down as far as Alicante, as well as the A8 from Irún to Bilbao, are quite expensive tollways. The frontier to Alicante, for example, will set you back 8155 ptas.

Tollways can sometimes be avoided in favour of virtually parallel and more scenic highways. The downside is that most other drivers of vehicles both big and small will have the same idea and they're too often clogged with traffic.

Petrol

Prices of *gasolina* tend to fluctuate. As an approximate guide, super costs 120 ptas per litre, diesel (*gasóleo*) is 91 ptas per litre and lead-free petrol (*sin plomo*) costs 114 ptas or 126 ptas per litre, depending on whether it's a 95 or 98 octane variant.

Car Rental

All the major international car rental companies are represented throughout Spain. Many visitors prebook car rental before arriving in Spain, for example in a fly-drive deal (see The UK in the Land section of the Getting There & Away chapter). Local operators, however, especially in popular tourist areas, are often significantly cheaper.

If you hire after arriving, you need to be at least 21 years old and have held a driving licence for a minimum of two years. It's easier, and with some companies obligatory, to pay by credit card.

Don't be misled by the price quoted up front. Once you've factored in the collision damage waiver plus theft and third party insurance and IVA (the Spanish equivalent of VAT) at 16%, it may even double. Hertz, for instance, will quote you a Fiat Punto for around 6900 ptas per day with unlimited kilometres. On top of this you pay 1900 ptas a day for the collision damage waiver as well as 950 ptas a day in theft and third party insurance. Add 16% IVA and you have the total daily cost.

In places frequented by foreign tourists, such as Málaga and Alicante airports, the Costa Brava, Costa Blanca and Costa del Sol, you can pick up a small car from a local agency for a net cost of around 20,000 ptas a week. Car rental in the Islas Baleares and Islas Canarias is also markedly cheaper than on the mainland.

HITCHING

Hitching can never be entirely safe and you should be aware that you're taking a very small but potentially serious risk. Women should be wary of hitching alone. This said, you're probably less at risk in popular walking regions or rural areas where everybody knows each other than on an intercity highway.

Indeed, there may be occasions where the options are hitching or a long walk along an asphalt road. In walking areas, hitching is often more common than elsewhere. It can also be easier since your backpack identifies you as a walker and may reduce the anxiety of drivers who might otherwise be reluctant to pick you up. Also, it's easier to establish eye contact with a driver who's travelling slowly on a country road. If your destination isn't obvious, it's worthwhile displaying a sign to indicate it.

Elsewhere in Spain, away from walking areas, hitching is neither a popular way of getting around nor easy. It's prohibited on autopistas and autovías (you can try to pick up lifts before a tollbooth or highway slipway).

BOAT

Ferries and boats link the mainland with the Islas Baleares and there's a weekly car ferry from Cádiz to the Islas Canarias. For more details on prices and times, see the Getting There & Away sections in the relevant walks chapters.

ORGANISED WALKS

Most Spaniards tend to walk independently in small groups of friends or in larger packs from outdoor clubs or scout groups. Organised tours do exist, such as the guided day walks led by *parques nationales* (national parks) and *parques naturales* (nature parks) staff. In big tourist areas such as Tenerife and Mallorca, outings are organised by private companies. In general, unless your Spanish is good – or sometimes German, as Spain is a popular destination for German walkers – you'll miss out on a lot.

In the Islas Canarias, several companies, most of whom also offer other outdoor activities, arrange guided day walks. Among the major ones are Canarias Trekking (☎/fax 922 20 10 51), Gaiatours (☎ 922 35 52 72) and Aden (☎ 922 24 62 61).

Spain Step by Step (☎/fax 93 245 82 53, nicholas.law@teclata.es) is a small, upmarket Barcelona-based English-run operation which prepares tailor-made organised tours for groups of between two and eight people.

A number of British companies arrange all-inclusive walking holidays of one or two weeks, though only some include the flight from the UK. For details of organised walking tour companies based outside Spain, see the Organised Walks section at the end of the Getting There & Away chapter.

Sistema Central

Mountain wilderness such as the Sistema Central offers is not the first thing that comes to mind when pondering Spain's vast and at times bleak interior. The reality of Castilla is very different to the picture commonly held of a landscape of endless arid wheat fields and Don Quixote-style windmills.

To the east is the Serranía de Cuenca, with its strange rock formations and traces of prehistoric occupation. To the north are the Montes de Toledo, a tranquil and crowd-free area for walking. North-east of Madrid, on the border of the País Vasco (Basque Country), are the Sierra de Urbión and Laguna Negra lake – popular with both hunters and weekenders.

For a rewarding alpine walking experience, however, you are not restricted to the fringes of the Castilla regions. The Sistema Central cuts straight through the middle of the *meseta* (the high tableland of central Spain) and lies within easy access of Madrid. This chapter describes some of the most spectacular walks through the two sierras of the Sistema Central: the Sierra de Gredos and Sierra de Guadarrama.

The Sierra de Gredos forms the western and most dramatic section of the mountain range. The Sierra de Guadarrama, while less grand than its western neighbour, is a popular getaway and ski destination for day-trippers from Madrid. Some of the earliest evidence of human activity in Castilla – wall carvings dating back to the Neolithic period – can be found in this area.

HISTORY

The history of the Sistema Central closely reflects events unfolding in the rest of central Spain. Politically and culturally the mountains were for a long time a part of the old kingdom of Castilla, known as Castile. As it was swept by successive invasions over the centuries by Romans, Visigoths and Muslims, the Sistema Central resisted and succumbed, repeatedly changing hands. The Sierra de

HIGHLIGHTS

The rocky pinnacles of Circo de la Pedriza are a popular destination for climbers.

- The El Morezón ridge in the central Gredos, which overlooks Almanzor, Laguna Grande and the savage cliffs of Los Tres Hermanitos

- The beautiful glacial corrie below Calvitero in the Sierra de Candelario

- La Pedriza in the Sierra de Guadarrama, an adventure playground of eroded rock formations, fallen boulders, tall spires and narrow gullies

- The wonderful ridge walk from Puerto del Arenal across the central Gredos to Refugio Elola, a great base from which to explore the Gredos mountains

Guadarrama was once called the Mons Carpetani, meaning the protector of Madrid.

During the Spanish Civil War Castilla was divided as the Republicans sought to hold onto Madrid, and for a while the front line

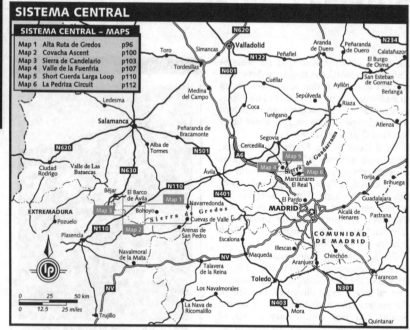

ran close to the mountains. In 1978 Spain was made a constitutional monarchy and in a bid to decentralise power the country was separated into 17 regions. Castilla was divided and the Sistema Central is now governed by three regions: Castilla-La Mancha, Castilla y León and Extremadura.

Over the course of the 20th century the population of the Sistema Central has gone into a decline. With changing agricultual methods and the lure of jobs, many have chosen to move to the cities. More recently, however, a new emphasis on rural tourism has begun to bring money and jobs back into the mountain communities which have suffered most from the urban pull.

NATURAL HISTORY

The Sistema Central reveals a huge diversity of fauna and flora to those prepared to look for it. While deforestation has taken its toll

on the slopes of both sierras, they still support a number of species of oak. Both areas contain a rich assortment of heathland scrub species and wild flowers.

Various subspecies of Spanish ibex (*Capra hispanica victoriae*) are common in many areas, and the mountains provide habitats for the rare pardel lynx (*lince ibérico* in Spanish), wild boars, fallow deers, red deers, civets, red partridges and wild turkeys. Both regions are also renowned havens for birds of prey, harbouring a range of eagle, vulture and buzzard species.

For more detail on the flora and fauna in each region, see Natural History in the introduction to the Sierra de Gredos and Sierra de Guadarrama sections.

CLIMATE

In general, Castilla has a climate of extremes. It's fiercely hot in summer and bitterly cold in winter, with icy winds blowing from the north. Rainfall (an average of 400-600mm per year) is concentrated in the autumn and spring. Within the Sistema Central, snow is common (the Sierra de Guadarrama has a number of ski resorts) and winter walkers should be prepared for blizzard conditions.

INFORMATION
Maps

The Instituto Geográfico Nacional (IGN) produces a series of Mapas Provinciales 1:200,000 maps that cover the 15 provinces in Castilla. But for planning, buy Michelin maps *Central Spain* No 444, *Northern Spain* No 442, and *Central and Southern Spain* No 445, at a scale of 1:400,000.

Books

All the mountain regions in Castilla are covered by at least one Spanish walking guide. At the time of writing, however, the only widely available English-language guide to the region is *Madrid and Castile* by Catherine Clancy, though many guides to Madrid touch on the Sierra de Gredos and Sierra de Guadarrama. Lonely Planet's *Spain* guide gives a good background to trekking regions in Castilla and is recommended.

Information Sources

In Madrid, Oficina de Promoción Turística de Castilla y León en Madrid (☎ 91 554 37 69, www.jcyl.es/turismo) is on Calle Espronceda 43 (metro: Ríos Rosas). The staff are not great with specific queries, but for background information it's first class. The main Castilla-La Mancha tourist office is in Toledo (☎ 925 26 98 00, fax 925 26 78 74).

A better plan is to contact the Federación Española de Montañismo (☎ 91 445 13 82) on Calle Alberto Aguilera 3 (metro: Anguelles) or the Federación Madrileña de Montañismo (☎ 91 593 80 74, fax 91 448 07 24) on Calle Apodaca (metro: Bilbao), which can give you specific advice and information.

As a general rule it is better to purchase maps in the big cities before leaving for the

Sistema Central. La Tienda Verde (☎ 91 535 38 10, fax 91 533 64 54) at Calle Maudes 38, Madrid (metro: Plaza de Castilla), is by far the best hiking and mountaineering map and bookshop in Castilla. Friendly, helpful and well stocked, La Tienda has an expanding range of walking maps and books and runs a mail-order operation.

ACCOMMODATION & SUPPLIES
Madrid

With both major walking areas within two hours of Madrid, Spain's transport hub, the capital is an obvious base and resupply point.

Close to Plaza de Santa Ana (metro: Antón Martín), a 20 minute walk from Atocha station, are dozens of pensiones and hostales. *Hostal La Isla (☎ 91 429 51 72, Calle del Prado 12)* is basic but clean and close to the action (singles/doubles for 1800/3200 ptas). Within walking distance of the airport bus terminal (metro: Alonso Martínez) at Colón is the very cheap *Hostal San Saturio (☎ 91 319 4048, Calle Fernando VI 23)*. At *Hostal Castilla (☎ 91 310 2176)*, just off Plaza Santa Barbara, rooms cost 1900/3500 ptas and the owner speaks English (metro: Alonso Martínez).

Madrid has a clutch of good camping shops. A short walk from La Tienda Verde (the best map shop in Madrid) is Ama Dablamat (☎ 91 553 05 31), Calle Comandante Zorita 13. However, Lepazpi (☎ 91 527 04 37), Ribera de Curtidores 8, and Gonza Sport (☎ 91 527 57 48), Ribera de Curtidores 10, have a wider selection (metro: Tirso de Molina). Koala (☎/fax 91 429 91 89) on Calle León 29 (metro: Antón Martin) is also very good, though more expensive. All these shops sell screw-fit gas canisters.

Ávila

In Ávila – a historic, tourist-oriented town west of Madrid on the N110 – try *Pensión Continental (☎ 920 21 15 02, Plaza de la Catedral 6)*, which has singles/doubles for 2200/3700 ptas, or *Hostal Mesón del Rastro (☎ 920 21 12 18, Plaza del Rastro 1)* where the restaurant is good and rooms start at 3550/4950 ptas.

El Barco de Ávila

El Barco de Ávila doesn't have very many accommodation options, but *Pensión Casa Gamo* (☎ 920 34 00 85, *Campillo 12*) is cheap and *Hotel Bellavista* (☎ 920 34 07 53, *Carretera de Ávila 15*) provides great post-walk luxury (4500/7500 ptas). The *bars* and *restaurants* around Plaza de España are the best in town for food and drinks (*Restaurante El Casino* is a cut above the rest).

Arenas de San Pedro

Arenas is an excellent springboard into the southern Gredos and a reasonable place to resupply.

There are a number of places to stay, the most pleasant of which are gathered around the 15th century Castillo de la Triste. *Hostel El Castillo* (☎ 920 37 00 91, *Caretera de Candeleda 2*) has spartan singles/doubles for about 1500/3000 ptas. Next door, *Pensión Yeka* (☎ 920 37 21 87) has some decent rooms with private bathrooms for 2500/4000 ptas, while *Hostería Los Galayos* (☎ 920 37 13 79, *Plaza de Condestable Dávalos 2*) has some expensive (7000 ptas) doubles and a restaurant – the *menú del día* (a fixed-price meal, sometimes only available at lunch time) costs about 1600 ptas. The food and accommodation at *Hostel Avenida* (☎ 920 37 09 88) on Los Regajales is more reasonably priced (doubles for 5000 ptas).

Béjar

If catching an early bus from Béjar, *Bar Restaurant El Puchero*, 200m down from the bus station in Béjar, is the most convenient place to stay (singles/doubles cost 1500/3000 ptas). However, *Hostal Casa Pavón* (☎ 923 40 28 61), 20 minutes away on the Plaza Mayor, is more convivial, has rooms for 2500/4400 ptas and the restaurant is excellent.

GETTING THERE & AWAY

Regular and charter flights from all over the world arrive at Madrid's Aeropuerto de Baraja, 13km north-east of the city. For information on flights between Madrid and destinations outside Spain, see Air in the Getting There & Away chapter.

Madrid has two main railway stations: Chamartín in the north, which generally handles destinations to the north of Madrid; and Atocha, south of the city centre, which services areas to the south of Madrid. *Cercanía* (trains operating within a short range of Madrid) and *regional* (travelling to longer-range destinations) services will get you into the major walking areas of Castilla. For train information call ☎ 91 328 90 20.

Madrid's main bus station, Estación Sur de Autobuses (☎ 91 468 45 11) on Calle de Méndez (metro: Méndez Álvaro) services a bewildering number of destinations. Most buses have a ticket office here, even if their buses depart from elsewhere. There are as many as eight smaller bus stations dotted around the capital.

Sierra de Gredos

Rising rather unexpectedly from the dry plains of Castilla y León and Castilla-La Mancha, the Sierra de Gredos is an oasis of alpine walking in a formidably hot and arid part of Spain.

The range consists of three overlapping ridges which begin just inside the region of Extremadura and stretch north-east, before blending into the Sierra de Guadarrama due west from Madrid. It forms the western and most dramatic section of the Sistema Central. Many of the peaks are above 2000m and the dark, granite cliffs on the southern side are a formidable barrier. Indeed, the northern and southern slopes differ greatly. On the northern side the terrain drops away in rolling *paramera* (moorland) to the Río Tormes valley (around 1300m). To the south, the terrain drops rapidly from 2000m passes to villages in the Río Tiétar valley, only 500m above sea level.

Villages on both sides of the main range are serviced by reasonable bus services (both from local towns and direct from Madrid) and most have some accommodation. In the mountains a network of *refugios* (refuges or mountain huts) provides shelter, though huge numbers of people choose to camp close to the highlights of Circo de Gredos and Cinco Lagunas in the centre of the range. A short trip up to a high ridge or pass will leave the crowds behind.

While the Gredos might be dismissed as minor league by aficionados of the Pyrenees and Picos de Europa, the area has undeniable attractions – principally the accessibility of the alpine area, the good condition of the most important trails and the varied challenges presented by a relatively small and underpopulated area. Long ridge walks, peak bagging, leisurely strolls and serious mountaineering can all be undertaken on a short trip from Madrid.

HISTORY

The Sierra de Gredos has been settled since the Iron Age. While Roman settlement in the area was limited, the road over Puerto del Pico remains as testament to their presence. The sierra marked the limits of the Muslim occupation.

It wasn't until after the Reconquista that permanent colonisation began as the native oak forests were cleared for the cultivation of vegetables, cereals, olives and vines on the southern side of the mountains and the rearing of sheep on the northern slopes. Patterns of land use remained relatively unchanged until the 20th century. The high mountains areas were the domain of shepherds and hunters. It wasn't until 1834 that the first recorded exploration of the mountains took place and not until 1899 that someone climbed Almanzor, at 2592m the region's highest peak.

General interest in the Gredos began with Alfonso XIII, who liked to hunt in the region. He set up a *coto real* (royal hunting reserve) in order to protect dwindling stocks of Gredos ibex (see the boxed text on the following page), and in 1926 actively encouraged the building of Spain's first *parador* (one of a chain of luxury state hotels) in Navarredonda, though mountaineering refugios had been established in the area 10 years before (sadly, many are now in ruins).

However, it wasn't until the 1970s that the region was 'discovered' by tourists. Today active discussion is taking place about the future of the area and the impact of tourism on the environment.

NATURAL HISTORY

Formed more than 300 million years ago during a period of mountain building in the late Paleozoic period, then resculptured 275 million years later, the Gredos is a natural haven for wildlife. Due to the nature of the rock (predominantly granite), numerous springs well up relatively close to the summits. The valleys, carved out by massive glaciation during the last Ice Age (obvious upon reaching the Circo de Gredos or Circo de Cinco Lagunas), remained unchanged until the Middle Ages when humans began to make a significant impact on the environment. Up till then the Gredos had a thick cover of deciduous trees such as holm, Pyrenean and cork oaks, with indigenous Scots pine appearing on the higher slopes. Most of the oak forests are gone, except for remnants in the river valleys and more inaccessible areas. Where there has been reforestation, the preferred species has been black or Corsican pine.

Sheltered from icy northerly winds in winter, the southern slopes enjoy a slightly milder climate than north of the range. From late March to May the slopes are awash with colour. Flowers include crocuses – the *Crocus carpetanus* is only found in Central Spain and northern Portugal – early purple orchids thriving in the shelter of the scented cistus thickets, and conspicuous St Bernard's and martagon lilies. In June and July the smell of French lavender, rosemary and thyme floats across the slopes, while the pale pink and purple of *Merendera montana* brings colour to the Gredos in September. *Crocus asturicus*, smaller and more delicate than the spring varieties, appears in forest clearings after the autumn rains. Thick carpets of broom, the bane of the walker, are very common on higher slopes.

Birdlife is fairly abundant and includes a few exotics: the azure-winged magpie

The Gredos Ibex

You are almost guaranteed to see the Gredos ibex (*Capra pyrenaica gloriae*) while walking in the Sierra de Gredos. Large herds graze the remote high pastures at dawn and dusk (Fuente de la Mira is a popular spot), and you can often stumble across smaller groups on the high ridges or see solitary males perched on seemingly inaccessible peaks, silhouetted against the sky.

The Gredos ibex – a subspecies of the Spanish ibex (*Capra hispanica victoriae*) – is a small, agile mountain goat with a medium-brown coat, black markings, and lighter areas on the neck and thighs. Its eyes are large and alert and you will often hear the animals' warning signal (a short, piercing whistle) before you see them. Males and females live in separate herds, except during the rut between November and the end of January. Herds of females and young can number up to 30; male mixed-age groups are smaller, while old males are solitary.

At the beginning of the 20th century, when the Gredos was the preserve of wealthy hunters, ibex were hunted almost to extinction. The species was saved by the intervention of King Alfonso XIII, who liked hunting the beautiful animals so much that in 1905 he decreed that the area be made a *coto real* (royal hunting reserve) in order to protect the last stock.

For the ibex it was a perverse kind of salvation, but since then the population has steadily increased from a low point of less than 10 (so legend would have it). Today there are thousands of animals in the Reserva Nacional del Macizo Central de Gredos. No longer instantly threatened by people, the ibex are tame to the point of being cheeky. In fact, there are now so many of these animals that disease and overgrazing have become a problem. Hunting – still practised in the area – does little to manage these problems as it is mainly the healthy adult males, with their metre-long curving horns, that are shot by hunters, rather than the mangy and diseased animals.

(which survives only in this corner of Europe), rollers, bee-eaters and visiting hoopoes. Look out for griffon vultures soaring around the high peaks. With wing spans of up to 3m they are an awe-inspiring and wonderfully frequent sight. Down in the valleys other common birds of prey include red and black kites, buzzards, harriers, kestrels and Egyptian and Bonelli's eagles.

Of the smaller high-mountain birds, rock buntings – identified by their striped heads – are the most common, with wheatears, crested larks and black redstarts also present. Crossbills and fire-crests inhabit the coniferous forests and the sound of cuckoos and woodpeckers (both the green and greater spotted varieties) can be heard in the valleys during summer. Occasionally, in the broom and long grass you may be startled by the flight of a red-legged par-tridge. There is also a huge variety of insects; the most striking is a fierce-looking (but harmless) cricket with a red thorax, striped wing cases and long, protruding barb.

Many common Spanish mammals are present in the mountains, while wild boar and red deer are still said to roam the valleys. You are virtually guaranteed to see Gredos ibex (see the boxed text) clinging to the rocks above 2000m, especially between the cirques of Laguna Grande and the Cinco Lagunas.

Also above 2000m you may see a striking turquoise and black mottled lizard called verdinegro, and in quieter areas you may see snakes. The grumbling or scowling viper (*Vibora hocicuad*) is a local species and you will need to get medical attention if bitten. Scorpions, though they exist, are very rare.

INFORMATION
Books

The only English walking guide to the region other than this one worth considering is *Mountains of Central Spain* by Jacqueline Oglesby, a good in-depth route guide. Spanish speakers have a wealth of publications to choose from, including the excellent *Gredos: Turismo-Desporteo-Aventura* published by Desnivel.

Information Sources

The main tourist offices for the Gredos are in El Barco de Ávila (☎ 920 340 844) and Navarredonda (☎ 920 348 001) on the northern side of the range and Arenas de San Pedro (☎ 920 372 368) on the southern side. Expect erratic opening times. The Spanish mountaineering federations (see Information Sources in the introduction to this chapter) often provide better insights into the region.

Béjar also has a tourist office opposite the bus station and there's a small information centre in Candelario off Calle Mayor (at the start of the Sierra de Candelario walk). The village has its own Web site (www.arrakis.es/~arnanz).

Alta Ruta de Gredos

Duration 3 days
Distance 51km
Standard Medium-Hard
Start Puerto del Pico
Finish Bohoyo
Public Transport Yes
Summary A challenging traverse of the central Sierra de Gredos including an ascent of Almanzor (the highest peak in the range) and a side trip to the Cinco Lagunas. Huge scope for further exploration of the peaks around Refugio Elola.

This fine ridge walk traverses the best of the central Gredos without relying on popular paths, conventional routes or complicated transport connections. It's possible to do this walk in three long, hard days (as described here), but at least two nights at Refugio José

Antonio Elola (referred to simply as Refugio Elola) is recommended.

From the trailhead at Puerto del Pico a tricky, cross-country traverse leads to Puerto del Arenal. From there it's simply a matter of heading west to Refugio Elola beneath the Circo de Gredos. Staying at the refugio puts you in the heart of the range, with ample opportunity for side trips. Climbers have no problem finding challenging routes here or at Los Galayos south of La Mira.

Exits to the south and north are simple from Refugio Elola, while by walking from Bohoyo to Nava del Barco (11km) the traverse west can be extended across Covacha and beyond (see the Covacha Ascent walk later in this chapter). A loop back to Puerto del Pico could be completed by simply following the Río Tormes east from Bohoyo to Camping Navagredos, then the Roman road to the pass.

Though refugios are scattered across the Gredos, campers have a major advantage as camp sites are plentiful. When climbing Almanzor we found a group of people camped on ledges 2m below the summit!

PLANNING
When to Walk

Facilities and bus schedules are geared toward July and August visitors when the shore of Laguna Grande becomes a sea of campers and intense heat plagues ascents from the south. The best time to walk is early June (when the snow on the high peaks has melted) or late summer when the crowds disappear (Elola and Reguero Llano refugios are open daily from the beginning of June to the end of September). Avoid the busy summer weekends.

Maps

A combination of Editorial Alpina's *Sierra de Gredos* at 1:40,000 and the IGN's *Mapa Guía del Macizo Central de Gredos* at 1:50,000 covers the route well. The former provides detail of footpaths and tracks (as well as a small guidebook to the range), while the latter gives a clear topographical overview of the area plus the route down to Bohoyo.

What to Bring

Bring all your supplies from Ávila or Madrid and wear a strong pair of walking boots. Few people bother to pitch a tent in summer – a sleeping bag will suffice.

PLACES TO STAY & EAT

Transport connections make spending a night in Ávila, El Barco de Ávila or Arenas de San Pedro a probability – see Accommodation & Supplies in the introduction to this chapter.

The *Hostal Moli* (☎ 920 38 30 48) is the only accommodation available in Cuevas del Valle. It's rather expensive (en suite singles/doubles/triples cost 3600/5000/6000 ptas including breakfast), but the food's good and it's beside the bus stop and Roman road leading to Puerto del Pico. There are a couple of *bar-restaurants* around the corner in the Plaza de Constitución.

The early morning bus north on the N502 means you can stay in Mombeltrán or Arenas de San Pedro, which have more accommodation, and still get to the trailhead in the early morning. Below Mombeltrán's 14th century Castillo de los Duques de Alburquerque in Plaza de la Soledad are a number of bars, restaurants and *Hostel Alburquerque* (☎ 920 38 60 32), which is small but has doubles for 5000 ptas and a restaurant. Alternatively, *Hostel Marji* (☎ 920 38 60 31, Calvo Sotelo 64) is at the south end of town.

The nearest camping ground to Mombeltrán, *Prados Abiertos* (☎ 920 38 60 61), is 4km south of the town on the N502. It also offers simple roofed accommodation. Alternatively, camp discretely at Puerto del Pico at the beginning of the walk.

Bohoyo, at the end of the walk, has several bars and restaurants but no accommodation. An official *camping ground* lies 2km north of the village beside the Río Tormes. Unofficial *camp sites* are not difficult to find beside the Garganta de Bohoyo, upstream from the *Restaurante El Vergel la Fuente de Gredos*.

GETTING TO/FROM THE WALK

The easiest way to get to the trailhead is from Ávila, a 1½ hour train ride (835 ptas) from Madrid. From the Ávila bus station (☎ 920 22 01 54), catch the 3 pm Robles bus to Cuevas del Valle (600 ptas), passing through Puerto del Pico. Between October and June there's also a 5.30 pm departure.

Alternatively, Donaldi (☎ 91 530 48 00) run regular services from Estación Sur de Autobuses in Madrid to Arenas de San Pedro (1175 ptas). You can stay overnight in Arenas and catch the early morning Robles bus (6.25 am) to the trailhead.

Leaving Bohoyo is more complicated, but during the summer you can catch an early morning or mid-afternoon bus direct to Madrid or El Barco de Ávila (only 10km away). El Barco de Ávila has regular bus connections with Madrid and Ávila.

THE WALK
Day 1: Puerto del Pico to La Mira

8 to 8½ hours, 19.5km

The first day of walking involves 911m of ascent. From Puerto del Pico (1½ hours walk north along the Roman road from Cuevas del Valle), all maps show a path traversing the southern slopes of La Casa (1845m) and Fría (1986m). In reality only ibex tracks snake across the slopes. However, the path leaving from a point east of the war memorial at the very top of the pass is the best option. Prepare yourself for a cross-country 'best fit' traverse, climbing gradually to a meadow and jumble of rounded boulders on Risco del Cuervo, the name of the spur to the southeast of La Casa. North of the meadow the slope climbs sharply to La Casa.

Head west through the meadow past a *fuente* (spring, fountain or water source) and good *camp site* shaded by tall pines, and into the broom. The path is now marked with cairns and traverses west across a rocky spur (where it disappears for a while) and across Río del Horcajo. With La Mira in the distance before you, make for a large pine tree on the spur to the south-west. If you're lucky, in 30 minutes you'll reach a goat shed at the end of a dirt road. An ancient track (with granite marker posts) leads north to Puerto del Arenal, passing a fuente after 20 minutes.

At the top of the pass head for a large cairn to the north-west, then follow a trail west around a boulder-strewn peak. You have two options: either continue west across the ridge to Puerto de la Cabrilla or traverse north-west to Fuente del Cervunal (a possible *camp site*) then west across a meadow to the source of Cuervo Garganta de Cabrilla. However, before you reach the source a path crosses the stream. Turn left here and head south-west through the broom to Puerto de la Cabrilla.

From here the ridge trail is straightforward, passing into Reserva Nacional del Macizo Central de Gredos and across several peaks to Peñón del Mediodía (2224m).

Continue west to a granite pole then south-west to Puerto del Peón where the well marked main trail across the central Gredos begins (the Fuente de Herveros is a little way down from the pass). After an hour or so the track zigzags up a scree slope to the remains of Refugio de los Pelaos – an excellent, sheltered *camp site*. La Mira (2543m) is due south and the Fuente de la Mira is a few yards away across the meadow, a favourite ibex grazing area. *Refugio Victory* (☎ *989 05 58 86*), only open at weekends, is reached by way of a long, 400m descent to the south-east which you'll have to climb back up in the morning if you don't camp on the ridge.

From the raised triangulation point of La Mira (once an optical telegraph station) it's easy to see why the granite cliffs and vicious, teeth-like ridges of Los Galayos are popular with climbers. These jagged southern pinnacles and the gentle spurs to the north illustrate the geological differences between the two sides of the range.

Day 2: La Mira to Refugio José Antonio Elola

5 to 6 hours, 12.5km

Head west from the ruined Refugio de los Pelaos and pick up a well worn path that turns south-west along the ridge. The path is well constructed in places and well marked. After crossing a rocky section below a 2166m peak there is a view to the north-west of a wide valley and meadows leading to Refugio Reguero Llano (which has similar capacity and services to Refugio Elola – see the end of this day's walk description) close to the Plataforma roadhead. The main path (unmarked on Editorial Alpina's *Sierra de Gredos* 1:40,000 map) duly swings northwest. Don't follow it; instead, turn left onto a path heading south-west to a saddle then onto Puerto de Candeleda (a popular route onto the mountains). Continue west along the ridge, with views of the Los Tres Hermanitos cliffs straight ahead, then loop north-west to the ruins of Refugio del Rey perched above a grassy bowl.

From the ruins you have two choices. The standard route leads north-west past Navasomera (2305m) to the Trocha Real (King's Way), a path linking the Refugios Elola and El Plataforma. A more adventurous route passes via a rocky ridge and the summit of Morezón (2379m) with its stunning views down to Laguna Grande and across to Almanzor (2592m).

The former route leads past the fuente close to the ruins and follows a well worn path around Navasomera (which lies directly west of the ruins of Refugio del Rey), down into a small valley and then traverses the hillside up to the Trocha Real west of Paredes Negras (2272m). Turn left for Refugio Elola and the end of this day's walking.

The alternative route also passes by the fuente before climbing west over the northern flank of Navasomera to an isolated meadow bordered on its western side by a rocky ridge. This wall of rock is part of the Circo de Gredos cirque which leads southwest from Morezón to the peaks of Los Tres Hermanitos and encircles the Laguna Grande below. There is considerable confusion as to the precise names and locations of many of the peaks on this section of ridge, but for the sake of continuity we have followed the height and position of Morezón as marked on the IGN *Macizo Central de*

Gredos 1:50,000 map. (Others maintain that the highest point on the southern end of this ridge section, marked by a cross, is Morezón at a spot height of 2393m.)

To reach Refugio Elola and the end of this stage from the ruins of Refugio del Rey, pick any of the marked paths you can see in front of you and climb to the ridge. Turn right and walk north-east down along the ridge and across the broad plateau of Morezón until reaching and descending into a small, rocky corridor. Exits to the eastern and western sides of the ridge are possible from here. Turn left (west) and zigzag down a narrow, steep gully onto the Trocha Real leading south to *Refugio José Antonio Elola* (☎ 920 20 75 76 or ☎ 920 22 83 93 in Ávila). Open from June to the end of October, and at weekends the rest of the year, it has capacity for 59 (650 ptas per person) plus a permanently open annexe.

There's a restaurant and a shop selling emergency rations including wine and camping gas. Everything is brought up on horseback so prices are high. Some English is spoken.

Side Trip: Almanzor & the Cinco Lagunas

6½ to 7½ hours, 10km

This excellent side trip, with 841m of ascent and descent, joins two separate excursions with one simple traverse, saving time and unnecessary climbing. Climb La Galana (2564m), the second-highest peak in the range, at the same time.

From the refugio follow the cairned path that climbs south-west beside a stream to the end of a bold spur leading down from Ameal de Pablo (2498m), which is reached after 40 minutes. Continue south-west and scramble up a rocky gully until, 15 minutes later, the path bears right away from the main slope

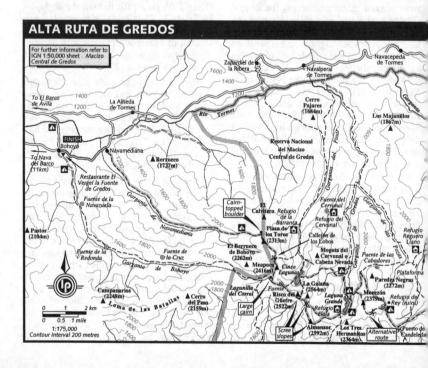

ALTA RUTA DE GREDOS

up a narrow boulder-filled gully east of Almanzor. After reaching a small col (2550m) turn right (north) and work your way around to Almanzor's western face. The **summit** (2592m) is reached after a scramble, during which some simple climbing is required. With the whole of the Gredos below you, enjoy the magnificent views.

Return to the col beneath the peak and turn right (north) onto the eastern side of the ridge (avoiding the path on the western side) and traversing to Portilla del Venteadero, which is reached in about 45 minutes. **La Galana** is due north from here. The summit can be reached after some straightforward climbing that involves crossing a dramatic split in the rock and a narrow clifftop traverse.

From south of La Galana an obvious path leads north-west to a small pass overlooking Risco del Güetre, which is reached via a scree

slope. Turn left and pick your way down a boulder field to the Cinco Lagunas. To complete the loop, follow the cairn-lined path on the eastern side of the largest lake up a 300m scree slope to Portilla del Rey (2374m), where an obvious path leads into the Gargantón valley, across Risco Negro and back to the *Refugio Elola* (about 2½ hours). Other exits from the Cinco Lagunas are possible – north past Refugio de la Barranca (also known as Chozo del Barranca) to Navalperal de Tormes or west up to Callejón de los Lobos and on to Bohoyo.

Day 3: Refugio José Antonio Elola to Bohoyo
7½ to 8½ hours, 19km

A signpost beside the refugio points west to Portilla del Venteadero. A couple of routes lead up through the slabs of rock to the long spur emanating south-east from Ameal de

ALTA RUTA DE GREDOS

Ice Climbing in the Gredos

While the Gredos is primarily a summer walking destination, Refugio Elola is open on weekends throughout the winter to cater for mountaineers, adventurous skiers, walkers and ice climbers. The north-facing cliffs of Circo de Gredos, high above Laguna Grande, are particularly suited to ice climbing and provide some excellent, challenging routes, most up frozen waterfalls.

Several climbing and mountaineering companies operate from the refugio, and some run ice climbing classes for beginners. Run by professional mountain guides, Espacioaccion (☎ 91 578 00 33) is recommended (see also their Web site at www .infornet.es/espacioaccion.com).

February and March are the best times for winter sports. For further information contact the Federación Española de Montañismo (☎ 91 445 13 82) or the Federación Madrileña de Montañismo (☎ 91 593 80 74, fax 91 448 07 24).

Pablo. The simplest route repeats the approach to Almanzor (described as part of the side trip immediately above) until, after 30 minutes, it crosses a small stream and heads north straight up a steep, narrow scree slope to a ridge of the spur. A line of cairns now leads north-west up to and around the cliffs on the southern side of Ameal de Pablo. Pass through a small bowl and west up a scree slope to Portilla del Venteadero. From the pass a path heading north-west traverses beneath cliffs encircling the Cinco Lagunas past Portilla de Cinco Lagunas and over flatter ground to a fuente. About 100m further north a wall running east-west marks the boundary of the Reserva Nacional del Macizo Central de Gredos.

From here there are two options. From the marker just beyond the wall a path leads north-west down to the Garganta de Bohoyo and follows it downstream to Bohoyo. A second path (recommended and described

here) leads north-east from the same point, skirting the summit of Meapoco (2416m) before following a stone wall past Callejón de los Lobos (a pass leading to the Cinco Lagunas) and north-west around Plaza de los Toros (2313m) to a huge cairn-topped boulder. In a large meadow to the north, Fuente del Regajo Largo signals the start of the Garganta de Navamediana.

Walk along the true right bank of the stream, climbing to a rocky path where the stream (now joined by the Arroyo del Gargantón) cascades over a set of falls. Ignore the walled lane that leads from a cattle corral and stick to the cairned path beside the stream which, after 3½ hours and as the valley becomes increasingly wooded, arrives at Navamediana. It's then a 30 minute road walk (west) to Bohoyo. For a more direct route to Bohoyo, cross the river close to Navamediana (marked on the IGN *Macizo Central de Gredos* map) and scramble west, then north-west through oak woodland to the sealed road east of Bohoyo, close to the *Restaurante El Vergel la Fuente de Gredos* – a welcome rest stop.

Nava del Barco, the start of the one-day ascent of Covacha described below and a continuation of the Gredos traverse, is 11km west of Bohoyo along sealed roads.

Covacha Ascent

Duration 2 days
Distance 23.5km
Standard Medium-Hard
Start Nava del Barco
Finish Puerto de Tornavacas
Public Transport No
Summary An extension of the Alta Ruta de Gredos traverse. A quiet part of the range, you're likely to have Covacha mountain and the beautiful Laguna de los Caballeros lake to yourself.

This ascent of Covacha, the highest mountain in the western Gredos, shadows the Garganta de Galin Gómez up a long glacial valley before passing over a saddle to a second valley and up to the summit. From the peak there's a wonderful, looping ridge walk high above Laguna del Barco before a long descent to Puerto de Tornavacas.

This would be an apt continuation of the Alta Ruta de Gredos traverse (described earlier in this chapter). An ideal route would never leave the ridges but continue from Portilla del Venteadero across to Cancho (2275m) south of Navalguijo village, then north-west to Covacha. However, I only received wry smiles when inquiring about this possibility.

The peak is a launching point for other traverses. Possibilities include routes west down to the cherry orchards of the Valle del Jerte, south into the valley of the Río Tiétar, or north-west from Puerto de Tornavacas onto the Sierra de Candelario.

It is possible to complete this walk in one day but this is hard work (1249m ascent, 1124m descent). Camping at Laguna de la Nava or Laguna de los Caballeros, before the final ascent, is recommended – especially if you have walked from Bohoyo on the previous afternoon – and this is how the walk is described here. (By camping at the latter you could plausibly make an ascent of Covacha and be out in time to catch a morning bus back to Nava del Barco.)

Note that there are no refugios along this route – those taking two days will have to camp. The consolation is the spectacular setting of the recommended camp sites.

PLANNING
Maps
Editorial Alpina produces a useful map, *Valle del Jerte*, at 1:50,000 (750 ptas). Unfortunately, there are a couple of errors: the path shown snaking up the true right bank of the Garganta de Galin Gómez is a non-starter and, disappointingly, the Refugio Palomo marked on the map near Puerto de Tornavacas has long since closed. The SGE *Cabezuela del Valle* 13-23 (576) 1:50,000 map therefore serves as a good additional reference map. The IGN *Macizo Central de Gredos* map at 1:50,000 is an excellent guide to the eastern approaches.

For more information on planning walks in the Sierra de Gredos, see the Information and Planning sections for the Alta Ruta de Gredos walk earlier in this chapter.

PLACES TO STAY & EAT
Neither Umbrías nor Nava del Barco have accommodation. Nava del Barco sports a couple of grocery shops and a few *bars*. and there are popular *camping sites* just south-west of the village.

In Puerto de Tornavacas, at the end of the walk, there are no facilities, though a large lookout was at the time of writing being constructed and there is a good chance that some simple facilities may soon be in place (inquire locally before setting off).

About 5km south of the pass at the 357km point along the N110 is *Hostel Puerto de Tornavacas* (☎ 927 47 01 01), which has some straightforward accommodation and a *restaurant*.

GETTING TO/FROM THE WALK
Unless you have your own car, getting to the trailhead is an 11km road walk from Bohoyo or a 4km walk from Umbrías. To get to Umbrías by public transport, take the Cevesa bus (☎ 91 539 31 32) linking Madrid and El Barco de Ávila to villages in the Valle del Jerte. It will drop you off at the turn-off to Umbrías on the N110. The village is about 2km away. The bus leaves Estación Sur de Autobuses in Madrid at 4 pm (8.30 am on Sunday), returning through Puerto de Tornavacas, at the end of the walk, around 10.15 am the next day. Additional buses in each direction (8.30 am from Madrid, returning through the pass at 3.30 pm) run between July and September.

THE WALK
Day 1: Nava del Barco to Laguna de los Caballeros
4½ to 5 hours, 11km
Over the course of the day the trail ascends 980m. From the fuente in Nava del Barco's central square walk south down Calle la Fuente, past *Bar La Fuente* to a dirt road parallel to Arroyo de la Garganta de Galin

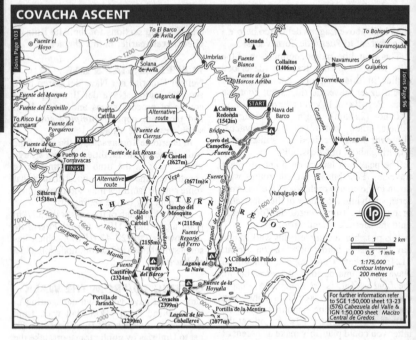

COVACHA ASCENT

Gómez. Ignore two right turns, taking the third across a stream. Bear left, descending to a restored mill. Turn right (west) past a number of suitable overnight *camp sites* and down a walled path, finally emerging onto a dirt road.

Do not walk down to the river, but turn right and walk up to a T-junction. Turn left and continue south-west parallel to the river before taking a left turn (south) down to a bridge. Cross this and follow the dirt road as it swings around the eastern flank of Cerro de Camocho before heading south-west again. About 20 minutes after passing a fuente the track turns south, passing through a set of green metal gates. From here a couple of trails head south up the valley, keeping to the true left of the stream (take either).

An hour later, shortly before a boulder field, cross to the true right bank. Pass a

shrine up a series of well constructed zigzags, taking the path around a set of falls and past an open-fronted shelter. Continue across a high meadow and follow the cairns to Laguna de la Nava – the dam wall is a popular (flat) *camp site*. The lake is a classic glacial creation surrounded by towering peaks and scree slopes on three sides.

Head west around the lake and then south-east up the boggy slope to a stream (a source of the Garganta de Galin Gómez). Walk roughly south-west to a fork in the stream, then cut left (south) up barren ground to a ridge. Turn right and walk along the ridge as it bends slowly west until the ground falls away, revealing a meadow and **Laguna de los Caballeros** lake to the west.

Traverse rough terrain towards the lake, passing Fuente de la Hoyuela en route. The lake area is one of the most secluded and tranquil *camp sites* in the Gredos.

Day 2: Laguna de los Caballeros to Puerto de Tornavacas

5 to 5½ hours, 12.5km

The day is mainly downhill (1124m). The path to Covacha, visible from afar, zigzags up to a col from the southern side of the lake. From the col turn right (west) and follow red arrows into a narrow pass, then right to the summit. There is a log book tucked beneath the summit.

The exit to Puerto de Tornavacas takes four hours and sticks to the main ridge that leads roughly north-west from Covacha to the N110. It's a simple and enjoyable descent which starts with a scramble across a jagged, high ridge. The ridge slowly bends north from Covacha, over Castifrío (2324m) to a third major peak (2155m) and, beyond, Collado del Carbiel, high above Laguna del Barco. Turn north-west away from the 2155m peak and follow the stone wall (the southern side is best) that marks the border between the provinces of Ávila and Cáceres. A cairned path leads along the ridge down to Sillares (1518m), from where a dirt road on the right continues descending to the N110 and a viewpoint overlooking the pass. Purists can stick to the ridge for this last section.

Alternative exits from Covacha are many: to the north a marked path descends from Covacha to Laguna del Barco and then follows the Garganta de la Vega to the village of Gilgarcía; to the south a trail leads across Cerro del Estecillo (2290m) and down to Jarandilla de la Vega via Refugio de las Nieves, which is roughly halfway (the village also has some accommodation). There is a large number of possible exits to the west and south-west, all via Carro del Estecillo. If you are determined, it's possible to walk along the ridges of the Sierra de Tormantos to the far end of the Valle de Jerte. For those wanting bigger challenges, the path up to **Risco la Campana** (2091m) and the Sierra de Candelario (see the next walk) starts opposite the car park and information board at Puerto de Tornavacas. Editorial Alpina's *Valle del Jerte* 1:50,000 map covers all these possibilities and more.

Sierra de Candelario

Duration 2 days
Distance 23.5km
Standard Medium
Start/Finish Candelario
Public Transport Yes
Summary A leisurely two day walk. The real pleasures of this route are camping in one of the most beautiful corries in the Sierra de Gredos and negotiating the Devil's Step before the summit of Calvitero.

At the western end of the Sierra de Gredos, the Sierra de Candelario forms a separate range divided from the main ridge by the N110 that continues on through the Valle del Jerte to Plasencia in the region of Extremadura. To the north of the short range, above the town of Béjar, is Candelario, one of the most beautiful villages in the Gredos. This sierra does not provide the scale and variety of landscapes found elsewhere in the Gredos, but good bus connections from Ávila and Madrid and an enjoyable summit ridge make it ideal for day walks and leisurely traverses.

The walk is a lengthy, but enjoyable, ascent up the Cuerpo de Hombre valley to Calvitero (2401m), the highest peak of Sierra de Candelario, reached after a short descent called the Devil's Step. The upper Cuerpo de Hombre valley rises in three distinct steps and shows obvious evidence of glaciation. The tranquil, boulder-strewn corrie (cirque) at the head of the valley is ringed by the towering cliffs of Los Tres Hermanitos and Calvitero, plus the Sierra de Candelario ridge.

Though possible in one long day, this walk (which entails 1304m of ascent) is best extended into a leisurely, two day trek with scope for exploration, as described here. Variations include an ascent of Canchal Negro (2369m) or exploration of the ridges south-west to La Nijarra (2214m) and east to Canchal del Turmal (2315m), both of which exit into the Valle del Jerte (see the Covacha Ascent walk earlier in this section).

If completing the walk in one day, a shorter variant can be taken. From behind Refugio de Hoya Cuevas climb up the scree slope to the Sierra de Béjar ridge, then head south-east across Los Hermanitos to Calvitero.

The corrie below Calvitero has permanent running water and many great camp sites. Two refugios in the valley (mainly used by climbers drawn to the sheer granite cliffs of Los Hermanitos) provide basic alternative shelter.

In planning this walk, Béjar is the best place to shop for supplies, though Candelario has a number of grocery shops and an ATM (Automatic Teller Machine; cash dispenser). You'll need to buy your camping gas in Madrid.

PLANNING
When to Walk
If you are walking in winter, don't underestimate the terrain or weather. A group of experienced French mountaineers once got completely lost on the sierra, splitting up in a blizzard and emerging in two separate valleys. The altitude makes walking in high summer quite possible.

Maps
Editorial Alpina's *Valle del Jerte* 1:50,000 map covers the western Gredos and picturesque Valle del Jerte – the gateway to Extremadura – though, confusingly, El Calvitero (2401m) is misidentified as El Torreón (and the name El Calvitero is given to the 2405m peak north of Chanchal La Ceja). A useful booklet is included. This map is occasionally available in Béjar and in the Candelario tourist office, which sometimes holds the SGE *Béjar* No 13-22 (553) 1:50,000 map needed for further exploration of the area.

The SGE *Cabezuela del Valle* 13-23 (576) 1:50,000 map is a good reference for those exploring further south (see the Covacha Ascent walk earlier in this chapter). At the time of writing the IGN 1:25,000 series did not cover the sierras Candelario and Béjar. Play it safe – buy your maps in Madrid.

PLACES TO STAY & EAT
The walk begins from Candelario. For accommodation, try *Hostal Christi (☎ 923 41 32 12, fax 923 41 31 19, Plaza de Béjar 1)*. This grand old establishment also trades as *Hotel Restaurant Candelario* and is a fine place to stay, though often full. Rooms cost 1900/3400 ptas without a bath and 3400/5600 ptas with. Not far away is *Mesón La Romana (☎ 923 41 32 72, Nuñez Losada 4)*, probably the best (and most expensive) restaurant in Candelario. A blow-out here costs between 2500 ptas and 3500 ptas. Another good option for food and accommodation is *Hostal Restaurante La Sierra (☎ 923 41 33 15, Calle Mayor 69)*.

Bars and cheap eateries are located along the tree-lined Avenida Del Humilladero and around Plaza de Solano. At the top of Calle de Pedro Muñoz Rico is *Bodega la Regadera*, an excellent bar specialising in meat snacks and cheap red wine.

About 1km out of town on the road to La Garganta is the well equipped *Camping Cinco Castaños (☎/fax 923 41 32 04)*, which has a bar-restaurant. Camping costs 450 ptas per person and 450 ptas per tent.

It is feasible to sleep the night before beginning the walk in Béjar, but you will need to add another 4.5km onto the total distance of the first day (there is no public transport between Béjar and Candelario). For information on places to stay and eat in Béjar and also Ávila (another feasible option), see Accommodation & Supplies in the introduction to this chapter.

GETTING TO/FROM THE WALK
Ávila-Piedrahita-Barco Automotives (☎ 920 22 09 98) run services to Ávila, El Barco de Ávila (1490 ptas) and Béjar (1695 ptas), leaving Madrid at 8.30 am and 4.10 pm Monday to Saturday and at 8.30 am on Sunday, with additional departures during holidays and fiestas.

On the return journey, buses from Béjar leave for Ávila and Madrid at 7.50 am and 4 pm on weekdays.

Cevesa (☎ 91 539 31 32) also runs services to Béjar from Madrid via El Barco de

Ávila (1595 ptas). Buses leave Estación Sur de Autobuses at 4 pm all year (8.30 am on Sunday). The return service leaves Béjar at 10 am. Between 1 July and 15 September there are additional departures (8.30 am from Madrid, returning at 3.15 pm from Béjar).

From Béjar it's a hitch or a 4.5km walk up to Candelario and the start of the trail.

THE WALK
Day 1: Candelario to Refugio Cueva de Hoya Moros
5 to 5½ hours, 11.5km

This is the day of steepest climbing. Leave Candelario walking south-west past a timber yard and onto the road to La Plataforma El Travieso (or El Quemal as it is called on some maps). Turn left off the road before *Camping Cinco Castaños* and walk along a dirt track (marked with yellow-and-white trail markers) that heads steadily south-east to the sealed La Garganta road east of Embalse de las Angosturas. Turn left and head south until turning off down a forestry road on the left, close to the fuente at El Peñón de los Avellanares. Go through the green metal gates and follow the track through a patchwork of oak woodland and meadow until it rises to a T-junction. Turn right (west), then bear right (south) where a track cuts back north-east. Ford the stream and follow the track west, then east, along zigzags (look out for a fuente on the right). At a left hairpin bend, climb to an open ridge and well marked path parallel to the road.

Follow the path along the ridge to a small meadow where, after 30 minutes and with Los Hermanitos and the Cuerpo de Hombre valley in full view, the track bears left through chest-high broom across rock slabs close to the river and up to a meadow. The rather decrepit *Refugio de Hoya Cuevas* (a brick shell with an unlocked steel door; the windows are gone, but the roof is relatively sound) and access to the Sierra de Béjar ridge is on a ledge to the south-west. Keeping left of the meadow, climb up the jumble of rocks to a second narrow meadow with a meandering river. Find a suitable path south through the moraine and make

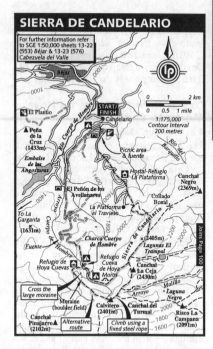

for the large cairn-topped boulder at the beginning of the corrie – *Refugio Cueva de Hoya Moros* (a shallow-walled cave, dry in summer, but flooded in winter) is due east; its entrance is south-facing.

Side Trip: Ascent of Calvitero
3½ to 4 hours, 6km

This 315m ascent is possible on Day 1, but by leaving it until the second day you'll avoid repeating the steep 200m climb that begins close to the refugio.

From the refugio head north-east across the meadow and up a steep, rocky slope (the lichen-covered rocks are treacherous when wet) that levels off after 30 minutes into a flatter barren landscape. Turn right (south-east) and follow the remains of a fence up to a path below a jumble of large, rounded rocks. South of here is the level summit of Canchal La Ceja (2430m), marked with a small metal rocket. Turn right along the well marked trail, following the cairns south-east over a saddle to **Calvitero** (2401m), reached after negotiating the Devil's Step – a steep channel in the rock (a fixed steel rope aids the simple climb).

Day 2: Refugio Cueva de Hoya Moros to Candelario

4 to 4½ hours, 12km

Repeat the first stage of the Calvitero ascent, but turn left along the trail north of Canchal La Ceja and follow it north-east across the saddle above Lagunas del Trampal and right (east) of the 2405m summit marked (wrongly) as El Calvitero on the Editorial Alpina map. (The summit is worth a visit for the views across to the Sierra de Béjar.)

North-east of the summit the trail forks. Bear left, following the trail in a more northerly direction as it descends through broom, past a giant cairn to a fuente. With La Plataforma el Travieso in full view the path splits. Turn left and pick your route down to the trailhead. Turn right along the road, then after a left bend bear right through a gap in the crash barrier and down a steep shortcut to *Hostal-Refugio La Plataforma* (☎ 923 40 18 00) – look out for the radio mast – 8km south of Candelario. It's a place with good views and a gentle breeze. The menu del día is 1300 ptas; singles/doubles are 2000/4000 ptas.

By walking underneath the electricity pylons that lead down from the hostal, Candelario is reached in an hour. The path is steep in places and crosses the road a couple of times before reaching a sealed road and flatter land beside the Navidul juice factory south of Candelario. After passing a sign for Casa Isidzo, turn left onto a dirt road and walk north through pine woodland to a picnic area with a fuente. Turn right (east) and walk past a fire lookout, then fork left down to a viewpoint and three stone crosses, directly above the village. Continue down to and across the road and into more woods, until finally emerging on the road 200m east of Camping Cinco Castaños. Retrace your steps back into town.

Sierra de Guadarrama

Slightly overshadowed by its grander neighbour on the Sistema Central, the Sierra de Guadarrama should not be dismissed as a walking destination. The ski resorts and large number of day-trippers from Madrid have certainly taken their toll on some regions, but the high ridges and remote peaks are remarkably undisturbed. Certain areas demand attention despite being overcrowded – ascents of Peñalara and Siete Picos and walking through the La Pedriza area are highly recommended, while the GR10 and Cuerda Larga long-distance paths cross the bulk of the mountain chain.

Only 50km from Madrid at the closest point, these mountains are well within daytrip range of the capital and efficient train and bus services bring the urban hordes into the mountains each weekend. The town of Cercedilla is the best bet for a base in the mountains, though there are some good low-altitude routes from El Escorial. During the week, and out of the main summer season, you're likely to have the place to yourself.

HISTORY

Other than a few caves containing Neolithic wall carvings, and a squabble between Segovia and Madrid after the Reconquista, the history of the Guadarrama is similar to that of the Gredos. The greatest differences are due to the Guadarrama's proximity to Madrid. In the 16th century Felipe II had a huge, austere palace and monastery built at San Lorenzo de Escorial as a summer retreat and alternative, cooler seat of government – good hunting in the area was also a factor. The Guadarrama was touched by the Napoleonic Wars of the 19th century. During the Spanish Civil War Republicans defending Madrid (including the International Brigades) fought along the ridges around the watershed of the range – evidence of trenches and other fortifications can still be seen.

Top: The view from the summit of La Mira (2543m) in the central Gredos, an area popular with climbers.
Bottom: Walking through the rocky labyrinth of the Circo de la Pedriza in the Sistema Central, a landscape of balancing boulders, rocky pinnacles and natural arches, easily accessible from nearby mountain villages.

MATTHEW FLETCHER

MATTHEW FLETCHER

MATTHEW FLETCHER

Top: Alpine meadow at the head of the Arroyo Cuerpo de Hombre in the Sierra de Candelario.
Bottom Left: Refugio José Antonia Elola, below the peaks of the Circo de Gredos, has a restaurant and shop and is a popular base for climbing the area's many desirable summits.
Bottom Right: A well earned rest on top of Almanzor, at 2592m the highest peak in the Sierra de Gredos.

Thirteen years before civil war broke out, tourism had begun in the range with the opening of a narrow-gauge railway from Cercedilla to the 1830m high pass of Puerto de Cotos. The subsequent influx of *madrileños* (people living in Madrid) who disturbed the mountain tranquillity upset the Los Doce Amigos mountaineering society, which had established refugios in the range 10 years earlier. Increased car ownership and the greater affluence that arrived in the 1970s led to the development of the limited, north-facing ski fields of the central Guadarrama and the large number of second homes and chalet housing developments which sprouted below the southern slopes.

NATURAL HISTORY

North of Madrid, the Sierra de Guadarrama has been subject to similar geographical processes as the Gredos (see Natural History in the Sierra de Gredos section earlier in this chapter) and shares the same dramatic difference between southern and northern slopes, though often not as pronounced. Geologically, the smaller range is made up of granite and gneiss.

The area of La Pedriza is an exception to these general rules. Here, numerous faults and extensive erosion of the softer, warmercoloured rock have produced a strange landscape of towering, rounded pinnacles, narrow passes, smooth domes and balancing rock sculptures.

After extensive deforestation the Guadarrama was replanted with random patterns of Scots pine (*Pinus silvestris*). The northern side of the range is almost completely covered by plantation forest. Spanish bluebells and toad flax (*Linaria triornithophora*) – which has large, snapdragon-like flowers – can be found in the pine forests. Also common are thickets of broom and cistus (rock rose or sun rose) – a tall, scratchy bush with large, white, papery-looking flowers in May and June.

The snake or Spanish short-toed eagle (*aguila culebrera* in Spanish) has an almost pure white underside with a broad, dark head. White storks, considered a good omen, are found in most villages in the mountains and foothills. Large colonies of seven or eight nests can be seen at Manzanares El Real and Soto del Real. If you're lucky you'll see Spanish ibex, wildcats or wild boar. The hairy brown-and-black caterpillars of the pine processionary moth produce an irritating rash, so watch out for their large nests (like a dense spider's web) in pine trees.

INFORMATION
Books
100 Excursiones Por La Sierra de Madrid by Domingo Pliego (who has written dozens of guides to the Sistema Central) is a comprehensive Spanish-language guide, while Jacqueline Oglesby's *Mountains of Central Spain* covers the area in depth.

Information Sources
Spanish mountaineering federations (see Information Sources in the introduction to this chapter) are your best bet for general information about the Sierra de Guadarrama. However, the Centro de Información Valle de la Fuenfría (☎ 91 852 22 13), a 2km walk up from Cercedilla train station, provides useful information about activities in the immediate vicinity. Its leaflet detailing the colour-coded walking trails in the valley is useful. The helpful staff are on duty from 10 am to 6 pm.

Valle de la Fuenfría

Duration 6½ to 7½ hours
Distance 23km
Standard Easy-Medium
Start/Finish Cercedilla
Public Transport Yes
Summary One of the most accessible and rewarding walks in the Sierra de Guadarrama. Includes an ascent of Siete Picos as a side trip and a ridge walk across Cerro Peña Águila.

This is probably the most accessible walk in the whole of the Sistema Central. From the train station in Cercedilla marked trails form a great, easy loop around Valle de la Fuenfría – easily achievable as a day trip from Madrid – which can be enjoyed at a leisurely pace without having to worry about missing the last train home, even including an ascent of Siete Picos. For these reasons, the valley is popular with madrileños (residents of Madrid) throughout the year, ski-mountaineering taking over from walking once winter arrives. The long route described here avoids the crowds until Puerto de Fuenfría. On Siete Picos in mid-September we didn't meet a soul other than a man on horseback on his way to fix a fuente!

Cercedilla can feel like a ski resort out of season. Many of the properties which line the Roman road north of Puerto de Fuenfría are second homes, and many businesses close in mid-September or only open at weekends. However, it's still a good walking base thanks to great transport links, restaurants and bars.

If you want to extend this walk, continue east from Siete Picos to Puerto de Navacerrada and pick up the Cuerda Larga long-distance path at Bola del Mundo (see the Short Cuerda Larga Loop walk later in this chapter). Alternatively, head south-west on the GR10 and pick a route to El Escorial.

PLANNING
When to Walk

Due to its popularity with madrileños the area is busy all year, but can be swamped in midsummer. Many refugios, restaurants and tourist-oriented shops wind down after the local fiesta in the first week of September, some opening only at the weekend (including Refugio Giner in La Pedriza). Avoid weekends if you don't like crowds, and visit in late spring if you can.

Maps

Two 1:25,000 Editorial Alpina *Sistema Central* maps cover the region: *La Pedriza* and *Guadarrama* (the general shop opposite Cercedilla station stocks them for 650 ptas each). However, they are woefully vague and inaccurate despite the large scale. La Tienda Verde's *Sierra de Guadarrama*

1:50,000 map (875 ptas) covers a greater area to better effect, and its *La Pedriza del Manzanares* 1:15,000 map is essential if you plan to spend any serious time in La Pedriza. The SGE *Cercedilla* No 18-20 (508) map is also a useful reference.

PLACES TO STAY & EAT

With great train and bus connections you don't have to stay in the Guadarrama. However, the large and friendly *Hostal Longinas/El Aribel* (☎ 91 852 15 11), 50m from the train station in Cercedilla, makes a good base. The restaurant is not open all the time, but the bar is; singles/doubles with and without bathrooms cost 2500/4000 ptas and 4800/6000 ptas, respectively. Alternatively, *La Maya* (☎ 91 852 22 52, Carrera del Señor 2) has four doubles with bathroom at 6000 ptas. The *raciones* are not bad, but the food at *La Muñza* on Plaza Mayor or at *El Frontón* on Calle Emilio Serrano is better. Cercedilla's two youth hostels – *Las Dehesas* (☎ 91 852 01 35) and *Villacastora* (☎ 91 852 03 34) – are open briefly during midsummer, but are usually full of school children on organised trips from Madrid.

GETTING TO/FROM THE WALK

There are regular trains and buses to Cercedilla. Cercanía and regionale train services leave from Madrid's Atocha and Chamartín stations (550 ptas weekends, 475 ptas weekdays), heading for Segovia. Connections to Ávila are also possible. Regular Larrea (☎ 91 530 48 00) buses leave from Madrid's Montcloa bus station. Apart from the five trains a day that struggle up and down to Puerto de Cotes and Puerto de Navacerrada, however, local communities are not linked by public transport.

THE WALK

Turn left out of the station, walk down the road, pass left under the railway and cross a bridge over the Río de la Venta. Cross to the western side of the road and walk past Fuente de Marino before bearing right up Paso de

VALLE DE LA FUENFRÍA

For further information
refer to SGE 1:50,000
sheet 18-20 (508) Cercedilla

Joins Page 110

0   0.5   1 km
0   0.25   0.5 mile

1:70,000
Contour Interval 50 metres

Canalejas. Turn right at the next junction and right again at a T-junction. Head along Camino de los Campamentos for the next 30 minutes, past Campamento La Peñota and the fire service helicopter station, to a green barrier before a large clearing. Turn left and walk up to the fuente. From here a local trail, La Calle Alta (marked with red dots), leads north-west through the woods to a forestry track, reached after 45 minutes.

Go left 20m down the track and onto a path leading diagonally north-west to the ridge, a stone wall and the GR10 trail. On the ridge, head north past a lesser peak with a ruin at its base to the summit of **Cerro Peña Águila** (2009m), which is named Peña del Águila on the Editorial Alpina *Guadarrama* map. Enjoy the views across the northern side of the Gredos, out over the meseta of Castilla y León and east to Siete Picos (2138m), Peñalara (2430m) and beyond.

Descend north-east on the western side of the wall to a road (turn left), then past a fuente to Puerto de la Fuenfría (1796m), which is reached 40 minutes after joining the road. There's another fuente just beyond the pass. Alternatively, a trail on the left leads up from Collado de Cerromalejo to Alto de la Peña o Peña Bercial (2001m) and over Cerro Minguete (2024m) before descending to the pass.

Two hundred metres south of here a wide track rises south-east from the dirt road to a viewpoint overlooking the whole of Valle de la Fuenfría. A path then climbs east to Collado Ventoso, a grassy saddle with a fuente to the south-west, from where a number of paths diverge. If not climbing the peak, head south-west along the local trail to Pico de Majalasna (marked with yellow trail markers) which leads from below (west of) the southern saddle to a peak of the same name.

If climbing to the peak follow cairns south from the col up to Umbría de Siete Picos ridge (30 minutes). Once on the ridge, traverse east through a jumble of rounded peaks to **Siete Picos**, marked with a triangulation point. The boulder-strewn summit is best approached from the north-east. To return to the main walk, retrace your steps to the saddle before the western peak and pick up a cairn-lined path descending south-west through a stretch of open pine woodland to Pico de Majalasna.

Head south through the meadow beside the peak past a fuente, then follow yellow trail markers down a series of tracks to meet a dirt road that heads south along a flat spur, until looping round before **Los Miradores** viewpoint.

Continue south and follow yellow trail markers down the slope on a path that swings east before heading back west and finally north to a recreational area on the valley floor. Head west past a fuente to a sealed road. Turn left to return to Cercedilla (a 40 minute road walk) or right for the bar-restaurant ***Las Dehesas Casa Cirilo*** (☎ 91 852 02 41), a very welcome stop after a long day in the mountains. Undergoing renovation at the time of writing, it's open year-round and may in the future offer accommodation.

Short Cuerda Larga Loop

Duration 2 days
Distance 39km
Standard Medium
Start Puerto de Cotos
Finish Puerto de Navacerrada
Public Transport Yes
Summary This introduction to the high ridges and deserted valleys of the Sierra de Guadarrama links well with the La Pedriza Circuit and offers the possibility of an ascent of Peñalara.

This loop is a simple, two day walk along a short section of the Cuerda Larga long-distance patch. The complete Cuerda Larga, a classic 18km walk, stretches across a section of high ridge that runs north-east from Puerto de Navacerrada to Puerto de la Morcuera. The short Cuerda Larga loop described here starts from the end of the Guadarrama narrow-gauge railway at Puerto del Paular o de los Cotos (Puerto de Cotos). It leaves the ski infrastructure of Valcotos and Valdesquí behind and climbs to the summit of Cabeza de Hierro, before turning off the main ridge at Asomate de Hoyos and descending into the Parque Regional del Alto Manzanares. It continues through La Pedriza and returns to Navacerrada along the tranquil valleys of the Río Manzanares.

The description of this walk has deliberately been kept short as there are a number of possible extensions and deviations that can be made: an ascent of Peñalara (2429m) from Puerto de Cotos, including a loop through the Lagunas de Peñalara overnighting in Refugio Zabala; two days in La Pedriza scrambling around the eroded peaks; a continuation from Puerto de Navacerrada across Siete Picos (2138m) and into the Valle de la Fuenfría; or simply a continuation along the Cuerda Larga to Puerto de la Morcuera, Canencia and beyond!

PLANNING

For information on the best times to walk and on the appropriate maps to take, see

Planning in the introduction to the Valle de la Fuenfría walk earlier in this section.

PLACES TO STAY & EAT
Puerto de Cotos
Options near the station include *Refugio del Club Alpino Español* and *Venta Marcelivo* (both are open year-round). About 10 minutes along the road to the Valdesquí ski area a side road leads to *Refugio El Pingarrón* (☎ 91 580 42 16). Perched high above Arroyo de las Guarramillas, it's open at weekends, with a permanently open annexe. Ski lifts blight the view south, but north-east the beautiful Valle de Lozoya is fair compensation.

Puerto de Navacerrada
If you get stuck at Puerto de Navacerrada, *Hotel Pasadoiro* (☎ 91 852 14 27), 50m south of the pass, and *Hostal Nueva Venta Arias* (☎ 91 852 11 00) both have doubles for around 6000 ptas. Also try *Albergue Álvaro Iglesias* (☎ 91 852 31 20).

GETTING TO/FROM THE WALK
For information on getting to the regional centre of Cercedilla from Madrid and Ávila, see the Getting to/from the Walk section for the Valle de la Fuenfría walk. Alternatively, regular Larrea (☎ 91 530 48 00) buses direct to Puerto de Navacerrada and Puerto de Cotos leave from Madrid's Montcloa bus station.

From the station at Cercedilla (☎ 91 852 00 57), five trains a day go to Puerto de Cotos via Puerto de Navacerrada. The first leaves at 9.35 am, the last at 7.35 pm. The last return train is at 8.43 pm.

THE WALK
Day 1: Puerto de Cotos to Manzanares El Real
5½ to 6 hours, 21km
From the station, walk past the refugios and turn right at the crest of the pass to head down a wide sealed road leading to the Valdesquí ski area. After 10 minutes turn left (east) onto the track which leads to Refugio El Pingarrón.

From the refugio, a path (marked with yellow trail markers) descends south to the Arroyo de las Guarramillas before looping west around a spur and down through pine woodland to a junction. Fork right and traverse above the Arroyo Cerradillas to a small clearing. Head east (still following yellow trail markers) across three streams, then turn right onto the true left (west) bank of a fourth stream. Head upstream along a cairn-lined path. The Cuerda Larga ridge should be visible to the south-east. After climbing south-east for 45 minutes a saddle (and fuente) is reached.

Proceed west to a grassy slope, then climb south-west to meet the Cuerda Larga and GR10 at a col. Red-and-white trail markers lead to the summit of **Cabeza de Hierro Mayor** (2380m). The views are magic. Much of the Cuerda Larga can be seen and the cliffs of Circo de la Pedriza Posterior are as dramatic as anything in the Sistema Central.

Trail markers lead along the ridge to Asomate de Hoyos (2230m), where the Cuerda Larga bears left (north-east) to La Najarra (2106m). A cairn-lined path leads south past Alto de Matasanos (2106m) to a col (Cancho de los Gavilanes) – the back entrance to La Pedriza. Follow a worn path south-west to a saddle, where the PRC1 and PRC2 walking trails meet. The PRC1 leads around La Pedriza, while the PRC2 continues south on a marked path to the car park at Canto Cochino beside the Río Manzanares (the descent takes 1½ hours).

Refugio Giner de los Rios (☎ 91 522 87 43) is reached after an hour. Well equipped, it's open at weekends year-round and daily between June and mid-September. Book in advance.

In the village of Canto Cochino there are two *bar-restaurants* (same opening hours as Refugio Giner). *Largo Ganta Zona de Campara* (a camping ground with some facilities, but no drinking water) is 1.5km west past the medical centre. In Manzanares El Real, 30 minutes downstream, is the *El Ortigal* camping ground (☎ 91 853 01 20), the expensive *Parque Real* (☎ 91 853 99 12),

SHORT CUERDA LARGA LOOP

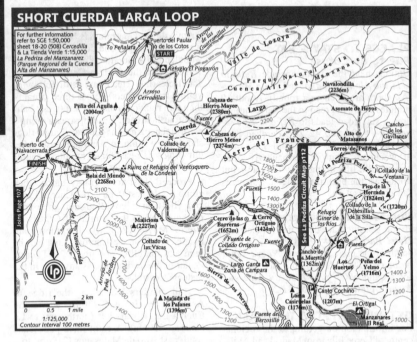

For further information refer to SGE 1:50,000 sheet 18-20 (508) Cercedilla & La Tienda Verde 1:15,000 La Pedriza del Manzanarez (Parque Regional de la Cuenca Alta del Manzanares)

0   1   2 km
0   0.5   1 mile
1:125,000
Contour Interval 100 metres

Joins Page 107

See La Pedriza Circuit Map p112

---

and *El Tranco* (☎ 91 853 00 63), which has doubles for 4500 ptas. The 15th century Castillo de los Mendoza is worth a visit.

Day 2: Manzanares El Real to Puerto de Navacerrada

5 to 5½ hours, 18km

For almost all of its length this route follows the Río Manzanares through gorges and valleys back to the Cuerda Larga, from where it's a simple descent to Puerto de Navacerrada.

Walk upstream from Canto Cochino on the true left bank of Río Manzanares After 15 minutes a bridge allows you to cross over the river. Turn right onto the road leading north past two fuentes to a bridge across the river. Use the steps on the left to climb up to a path that quickly leads to a reliable fuente before crossing to the true left bank of the river. The marked path then heads west, meeting the

Arroyo del Berzoso before turning south, then west (keep close to the river) to meet a dirt road due north of Maliciosa (2227m). Walk left along the road to a bridge where a path on the true left bank follows the river north-west through tranquil, grass-covered valleys to the ruins of Refugio del Ventisquero de la Condesa, 200m above the TV transmitters on Bola del Mundo (2268m) – it's a steep climb (due west) to the peak.

There are expansive views from the triangulation point. The evening light beautifully illuminates the flat, arid plains of Castilla-La Mancha to the south and the outline of the Sierra de Gredos to the southwest – Madrid looks like a mirage in the desert. A side trip to Maliciosa also looks inviting. From the TV transmission station, a concrete road descends through ski infrastructure to Puerto de Navacerrada, which has a clutch of *bar-restaurants*.

La Pedriza Circuit

Duration 9 to 10 hours
Distance 17km
Standard Hard
Start/Finish Manzanares El Real
Public Transport Yes
Summary The La Pedriza area is an adventure playground for climbers, scramblers and adventurous walkers. If you can, take two days to explore the weird rock formations, sheer cliffs and narrow gullies.

The Parque Regional del Alto Manzanares is something of a one-off for the Sistema Central; particularly spectacular is the Circo de la Pedriza, a near-perfect horseshoe of tall, rounded cliffs with a nearby rocky labyrinth and an 'adventure playground'. Take the opportunity to crawl through tunnels formed by huge balancing boulders, scramble up tall boulder stacks and squeeze across high, narrow passes. Needless to say it attracts climbers, scramblers and walkers year-round.

The complete circuit of La Pedriza on the PRC1 walking track will take around 10 hours of hard walking and scrambling (it gets a little easier after Las Torres de la Pedriza). It's better to spend two days in the park or cut the route short, especially if walking the Cuerda Larga. The nature of the terrain means that runners (training shoes), while not offering as much protection, may serve you better than heavy walking boots. You will also need at least 2L of water as there are no fuentes close to the ridges. The walk involves roughly 1000m of ascent.

There are several side trips to the circuit which haven't been described in any detail. In particular, the ascent of Peña del Yelmo is a popular walk which involves a couple of basic climbing moves and is best to approach from the north-east.

As an alternative to completing the circuit in one long day of walking, you could turn right (west) along the GR10 at the Collada de la Dehesilla o de la Silla and continue down to Refugio Giner de los Rios, about 2 to 3km away. For details of accommodation

at the refugio, see Day 1 of the Short Cuerda Larga Loop walk earlier in this section.

PLANNING

For information on the best times to walk and on the appropriate maps to take, see Planning in the introduction to the Valle de la Fuenfría walk earlier in this section.

PLACES TO STAY & EAT

The walk begins and ends in Manzanares El Real, though you could start walking from Canto Cochino, about 30 minutes upstream along the Río Manzanares. For information on food and accommodation in Canto Cochino and Manzanares El Real, see Day 1 of the Short Cuerda Larga Loop walk earlier in this section.

GETTING TO/FROM THE WALK

This walk is best approached from Madrid. Frequent buses to Manzanares El Real leave from Plaza de Castilla close to Chamartín station, taking around 40 minutes (300 ptas).

THE WALK

From Manzanares El Real follow the GR10 route upstream along the Río Manzanares, reaching Canto Cochino 30 minutes later. From the bridge at Canto Cochino leading from the car park (a 30 minute walk north-east of Manzanares El Real), head north-west up the slope following a set of yellow-and-white flashes to a junction. Turn right and follow the PRC1 (often marked as the PR1) across Cancho de los Muertos and down to an intersection at a saddle. Turn left then right (north-west) along a well used path. After a steep scramble over La Campana there is a sharp descent to a T-junction. Turn left and head north through pine woodland to another very steep, long scramble that puts you right among the tall rock pinnacles. The path now cuts to the eastern, then the western side of the ridge, providing great views of the waterfalls on the Río Manzanares and Cabeza de Hierro to the west.

After another hour the track meets the PRC2 (a short cut back to Canto Cochino)

LA PEDRIZA CIRCUIT

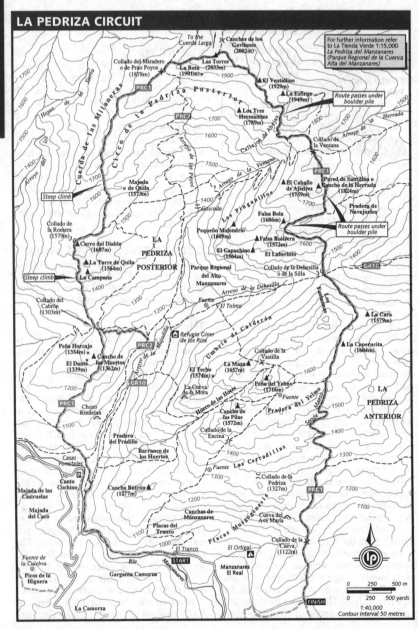

To the Cuerda Larga

Canchos de los Gavilanes (2002m)

Collado del Miradero o de Prao Poyos (1878m)

Las Torres (2033m)

La Bota (1901m) ▲

El Ventalino (1929m) ▲

La Esfinge (1949m) ▲

Route passes under boulder pile

For further information refer to La Tienda Verde 1:15,000 La Pedriza del Manzanares (Parque Regional de la Cuenca Alta del Manzanares)

PRC1

Circo de la Pedriza Posterior

PRC2

Los Tres Hermanitos (1789m) ▲

Collado de la Ventana

Cuerda de las Milaneras

Callejón de Agujas

Arroyo de los Poyos

Arroyo de la Ventana

Los Pingajillos

El Caballo de Ajedrez (1759m) ▲

PRC1

Pared de Santillán o Cancho de la Herrada (1824m)

Pradera de Navajuelos

Route passes under boulder pile

Steep climb

Majada de Quila (1513m) ×

Cascada

Pequeño Mojondrio (1609m) ▲

Falsa Bola (1686m) ▲

Falsa Ruitzera (1572m) ▲

Collado de la Romera (1579m)

Carro del Diablo (1607m) ▲

LA PEDRIZA POSTERIOR ×

El Capuchino (1564m) ▲

El Laberinto

La Cara (1579m) ▲

La Torre de Quila (1564m) ▲

La Campana ▲

Parque Regional del Alto Manzanares

Collado de la Dehesilla o de la Silla

GR10

Steep climb

Collado del Cabrón (1303m) ×

Arroyo de la Dehesilla

Fuente El Tolmo

La Caperucita (1604m) ▲

Peña Horcajo (1354m) × ▲

El Dante (1339m) ▲

Cancho de los Muertos (1362m) ×

PRC2

Refugio Giner de los Ríos

Umbría de Calderón

Collado de la Vastilla

La Maza (1657m) ▲

El Techo (1574m) ×

Peña del Yelmo (1716m) ▲

LA PEDRIZA ANTERIOR

GR10

La Cueva de la Mora

Fuente

PRC1

Chozo Kindelan

Hueco de las Hoces

Cancho de las Pilas (1572m) ▲

Pradera del Yelmo

Pradera del Pradillo

Collado de la Encina

Majada de las Casiruelas

Barranco de los Huertos

Casas Forestales

Canto Cochino

Fuente Las Cerradillas

Cancho Butrón (1277m) ▲

Collado de la Pedriza (1327m) ×

PRC1

Majada del Caco

Canchas de Manzanares

Cueva del Ave María

Placas del Tranco

Placas Mugrogénesis

Fuente de la Culebra

Picos de la Higuera

El Tranco

Río Manzanares

START

El Ortigal

Manzanares El Real

Garganta Camorza

Collado de la Cueva (1122m)

La Camorza

FINISH

0   250   500 m
0   250   500 yards

1:40,000
Contour Interval 50 metres

at Collado del Miradero o de Prao Poyos (1878m), a wide col. Continue north-east around Las Torres. Wind through the maze of boulders, spires and cliffs to Callejón de Abejas where the trail passes through a small tunnel before reaching a wide, grassy col – Collado de la Ventana. Continue along the PRC1 to the nearby crest and follow the trail as it descends sharply around the eastern side of the cirque. After about 1km it cuts south-west back to the centre of the

ridge and passes under a fallen boulder. The path now swings east and descends sharply down the eastern side of the ridge to the GR10 walking track at Collado de la Dehesilla o de la Silla. (The GR10 continues westwards to Refugio Giner.)

Follow the PRC1 as it winds its way south-east around the eastern flank of Peña del Yelmo (1716m). It keeps to the east of the peak, descending past Cueva del Ave María to Manzanares El Real.

The Pyrenees

This chapter features a 23 day traverse from the principality of Andorra in the east to Sallent de Gállego, well into Aragón in the west. It is divided into three sections: Andorra, the Catalan Pyrenees and the Aragonese Pyrenees. In addition to the full journey, there are also numerous side trips and separate walks – the full panoply needing more time than most walkers have at their disposal.

However, the chapter is organised so that walkers can either complete the Pyrenean Traverse in its entirety or just sample certain stages of it. Each section has been written as an independent walk with information on accommodation and transport.

Our aim has been to provide as flexible an itinerary as possible to cater for walkers with varying amounts of time and levels of fitness. Numerous camp sites and *refugios* (refuges or mountain shelters) have been included to allow walkers to finish early or push on beyond the official end of the day. Similarly, a number of walks offer alternative routes of varying lengths and standards of difficulty.

If you want to make one place your base for a week or so of walking, there are several points along the traverse with a concentration of day trips. As a warm-up to the full traverse, there are three one-day walks radiating out from Canillo in Andorra, of deliberately varying standards of difficulty. Highlighted in a section to itself, the Parque Nacional d'Aigüestortes i Estany de Sant Maurici features several walks through some of the most spectacular country in the Pyrenees. Other recommended walking bases include the Parque Nacional de Ordesa y Monte Perdido, the Vall d'Aran and Benasque.

Apart from in the two *parques nacionales* (national parks) during the height of the summer walking season, trails are rarely thronged with walkers. If you like to walk alone, you'll scarcely see another walker between Canillo in Andorra and Espot in the Catalan Pyrenees (Days 1 to 6 of the Pyrenean Traverse). You're also guaranteed

solitude on the long and quite tough route between the Hospital de Vielha (Day 10) and Benasque (Day 12), as well as on the walk from Bujaruelo to Panticosa (Day 20) in the Aragonese Pyrenees.

HISTORY

The distressing news for walkers is that the Pyrenees 'no longer exist'. Physically they are as impressive as ever, but many Spanish use this metaphor to describe the end of centuries of relative isolation from the rest of Europe – a process that began soon after the death of General Franco in 1975 and culminated in Spain's entry into the EU in 1986. In the process, much of the traditional lifestyle of the mountain communities has begun to disappear.

The Pyrenees contributed to the economic recovery which followed the ravages of the Spanish Civil War. In the 1950s and 1960s, Spain invested massively in the development of small-scale hydroelectric plants, mainly to service the towns and villages of the Pyrenean valleys. Most of the reservoirs are natural, though their depths have often been augmented by dams at their heads.

Traditionally the mountains have maintained an agricultural economy based on sheep and cows. Summer pastures were used not only by local villagers but also by shepherds and cowherds who transmigrated from much further afield (see the boxed text 'La Trashumancia' in the Andorra to Catalunya walk in the Andorra section of this chapter).

Many of the trails followed in this chapter were created to provide access to these lush, upland grasses. And many of the fanciful tracks still indicated on maps were once shepherds' routes, now overgrown and rarely used except by occasional walkers hacking their own way with compass and map.

NATURAL HISTORY
Geology

The history of the Pyrenees is long and turbulent. Some 350 million years ago they were already a formidable mountain chain of igneous rock formed by solidified magma from the earth's molten heart, and with summits capable of dwarfing today's 3000m giants.

Over tens of millions of years of slow erosion, the mountains were ground down to a vast plain, invaded by the sea. Grain by grain, shell by shell, sediments accumulated in layers on the ocean bed. (In places such as the Parque Nacional de Ordesa y Monte Perdido you can still see sandstone bands, sometimes straight, often in convoluted whorls.)

About 25 million years ago the Iberian tectonic plate slammed into the European one with a force sufficient to compress, fragment and fold upwards slabs as big as today's peaks, from which the seas streamed and departed.

From this moment on, erosion has been the principal force shaping the range we see today. During the successive Ice Ages of the last million years, ice covered all but the highest peaks and has left a distinctive imprint on the landscape (see the boxed text 'Signs of a Glacial Past' later in this section).

Flora

The trees and bushes of the Pyrenees can be divided – albeit crudely – into three roughly overlapping categories: alpine, subalpine and mountain.

Above 2500m there's little but bare rock to which a few alpine plants cling tenaciously, working themselves into crannies as protection against wind and snow. Below this height begin to appear the first tough, stringy grasses, collectively known as alpine, or upland, meadow.

Charlemagne & the Thistle

As the emperor Charlemagne's army was passing through the Pyrenees on its way to do battle with the Arab occupiers of Spain, the plague struck. Legend has it that when the emperor prayed to God for help an angel appeared and instructed him to fire an arrow into the air – whichever plant it pierced would prove to be an effective remedy. The arrow fell upon a kind of ground-hugging thistle, still common in the Pyrenees and still used as a natural remedy. It's called 'carlina' in both Catalan and Spanish after Carlomagno – Charlemagne.

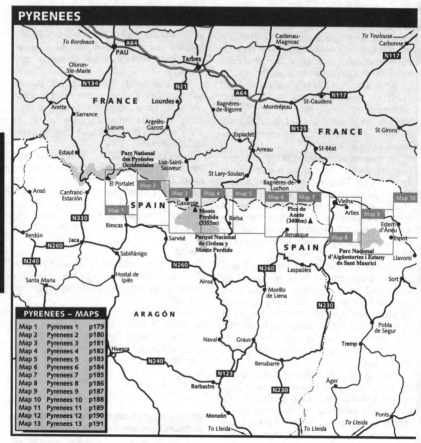

PYRENEES

Then come the hardiest of the trees: mountain, or black, pine (*Pinus uncinata*), small and squat with grey-black bark, sparse on the windward side and more abundant to the lee. At lower altitudes, as the land becomes less forbidding, the Scots pine (*P. sylvestris*) grows. It's known in Catalan as the *pi roig* (red pine) because of its characteristic reddish, deeply fissured bark.

As soil and temperature become more hospitable at subalpine altitudes (roughly 1600m to 2300m), fir trees (*Abies* sp) and the first of the deciduous trees appear.

These include rowan (*Sorbus aucuparia*), hazel (*Corylus avellana*) – a rich source of nutritious nuts in autumn – silver birch (*Betula pendula*), elms (*Ulmus* sp), mountain oak (*Quercus petraea*), elder (*Sambucus recemoso*) and, particularly in Aragón, beech trees (*Fagus* sp).

Down in the damp, lower valleys, goat willows (*Salix caprea*), common ashes (*Fraxinus excelsior*) and aspens abound.

In all but alpine environments, low banks of rhododendrons brush against your knees, their flowers startling splashes of vivid this section); the poet's, or pheasant's eye, narcissus (*Narcissus poeticus*); common and yellow monkshoods (*Aonitum napellus* and *A. anthora*), arnica (*Arnica* sp); and various varieties of gentian including great yellow (*Gentiana lutea*), spring (*G. verna*) and – found everywhere when in season – bright blue trumpet (*G. acaulis*) gentians.

Most of these flowers flourish in meadows along with the pink stars of moss campions (*Silene acaulis*), alpine pasques (*Pulsatilla alpina*), wild daffodils (*Narcissus pseudonarcissus*) and plenty of mountain irises (*Iris xiphioides*).

Fauna

At several points along the Pyrenean Traverse you stand a good chance of seeing chamois (*rebeco* in Spanish, *sarrio* in Aragonese and *isard* in Catalan), albeit at a distance. Roe and red deer are less timid but are also less widely distributed. Only a few brown bears survive in the Pyrenees and there's a positive but contentious program under way to reintroduce them. Though widely supported, it has come up against orchestrated opposition from livestock owners and property developers. Marmots, shaggy clowns of the high boulder fields, live in small colonies. Listen for their characteristic warning whistle. Strangest of all is the shy, rare desman, an aquatic, mole-like creature peculiar to the Pyrenees, whose closest relatives live in the Caucasus mountains of Georgia.

Wheeling above the upland valleys and peaks are a variety of birds of prey. Several eagle species inhabit the Pyrenees, including golden (*Aquila chrysaetos*), booted (*Hieraeetus pennatus*) and Bonnelli's (*H. fasciatus*) eagles. Other birds you may catch a glimpse of are griffon vultures (*Gyps fulvus*) and their Egyptian cousins (*Neophron percnopterus*) plus the rarer bearded vultures (*Gypaetus barbatus*). The Spanish name for the bearded vulture, *quebrantahuesos*, means bone-smasher, a term which graphically describes its habit of flying high and dropping bones onto the rocks so that it can peck at the marrow.

colour. Around them grow juniper bushes with their characteristic greyish berries, broom with bright yellow flowers, bilberries and wild raspberries (ready to pick in late summer), heather, dog roses and, at lower altitudes, clumps and stands of boxwood.

In general, June is the best time for viewing wild flowers. Common flowers at a subalpine level include white and leafless crocuses (*Crocus albiflorus* and *C. nudiflorus*); the carline thistle (see the boxed text 'Charlemagne & the Thistle' earlier in

Signs of a Glacial Past

Many of the world's finest walks are through landscapes which have been substantially shaped by glaciers. As a glacier flows downhill under its weight of ice and snow it creates a distinctive collection of landforms, many of which are preserved once the ice has retreated or vanished.

The most obvious is the *U-shaped valley* (1), gouged out by the glacier as it moves downhill, often with one or more bowl-shaped *cirques* or *corries* (2) at its head. Cirques are found along high mountain ridges or at mountain passes or *cols* (3). Where an alpine glacier – which flows off the upper slopes and ridges of a mountain range – has joined a deeper, more substantial valley glacier, a dramatic *hanging valley* (4) is often the result. In a post-glacial landscape, hanging valleys and cirques commonly shelter hidden alpine lakes or *tarns* (5). The thin ridge which separates adjacent glacial valleys is known as an *arête* (6).

As a glacier grinds its way forward it usually leaves long, *lateral moraine* (7) ridges along its course – mounds of debris either deposited along the flanks of the glacier or left by sub-ice streams within its heart. At the end – or snout – of a glacier is the *terminal moraine* (8), the point where the giant conveyor belt of ice drops its load of rocks and grit. Both high up in the hanging valleys and in the surrounding valleys and plains, *moraine lakes* (9) may form behind a dam of glacial rubble.

The plains which surround a once-glaciated range may feature a confusing variety of moraine ridges, mounds and outwash fans – material left by rivers flowing from the glaciers. Perched here and there may be an *erratic* (10), a rock carried far from its origin by the moving ice and left stranded in a geologically alien environment; for example, a granite boulder sitting in a limestone landscape.

THE PYRENEES

View of area before glacier's retreat

CLIMATE

The walking season, unless you're an experienced mountain trekker comfortable with snow and ice, is in the window between mid-June and early September. Come earlier and you face intimidating snowbanks; come later and the weather is increasingly unreliable.

The weather in the Pyrenees is never stable and change, when it comes, can be rapid. In particular, be prepared for summer mountain storms which build up during the afternoon and break in the early evening. While they usually pass quickly, they can be intense – hailstones the size of marbles are common even at the height of summer. When planning a walk, it's always wise to be aware of the weather forecast for at least the next 48 hours. For more information on how to prepare for a walk in the Pyrenees, see What to Bring under Planning in the Facts for the Walker chapter.

INFORMATION
Maps

The Pyrenees are well endowed with maps for walkers.

Small-Scale Maps Firestone produces a good, small-scale overview map of the Pyrenees at 1:200,000, covering both the French and Spanish sides of the frontier. Editorial Everest does a worthy alternative, available in either book or folding format at 1:230,000.

Large-Scale Maps Editorial Alpina maps are the most readily available, and come with scales of 1:25,000, 1:40,000 and an eccentric 1:30,000. For topography, they're reliable and are based for the most part upon either Instituto Geográfico Nacional (IGN) or Servicio Geográfico del Ejército (SGE) originals. The location of superimposed features such as refugios, as well as tracks and trails (many of them are just not there on the ground), should be treated with deep scepticism.

Until recently Editorial Alpina has had little or no competition. Now, however, it has two excellent rivals: the Institut Cartogràfic de Catalunya (ICC) and Proyectos y Realizaciones Aragonesas de Montaña, Escalada y Senderismo (PRAMES). In consequence, Editorial Alpina is improving the presentation, though not always the content, of its maps.

For the Catalan Pyrenees, the Mapas Comarcals de Catalunya series, produced at 1:50,000 by the ICC, is excellent. Its deficiency is the opposite of Editorial Alpina's; many existing tracks and trails aren't indicated. But in all other respects these maps are very dependable.

For the Aragonese Pyrenees, the maps produced by PRAMES at 1:25,000 are composed with walkers in mind and are by far the best. PRAMES also produces a handy ring binder of text (in Spanish) and maps at 1:50,000 covering the whole Sendero de Gran Recorrido (GR) 11 long-distance route from the Atlantic Ocean to the Mediterranean (for more information, see Books later in this section). It also sells a pack of 15 maps at 1:50,000 (2100 ptas) which covers the section of the GR11 trail through Aragón.

The French map publisher Randonnées Pyrénéennes (Rando Éditions) covers the whole of the Pyrenees in a series of 12 maps at 1:50,000. Coverage normally extends well over the frontier into Spain, though some areas are blotted out by the map legend and other information. Contours are at intervals of 20m and areas of steep terrain have elevation shading.

In a fruitful example of trans-frontier collaboration, Rando Éditions and the ICC have jointly published two 1:50,000 maps covering the area around Andorra and the Parc Nacional d'Aigüestortes i Estany de Sant Maurici. There's the promise of other trans-frontier maps in the pipeline, to eventually cover most of the Catalan Pyrenees.

In short, the best option in the Catalan Pyrenees is to go for the ICC 1:50,000 maps. In Aragón, PRAMES publications are unrivalled. For both areas, Rando Éditions maps are also excellent – but be sure that the area on the Spanish side which you intend to walk actually appears.

For information on maps required for individual walks, see Maps under Planning in the introduction to each walk.

Books

Both *Walks & Climbs in the Pyrenees* by Kev Reynolds and the more recent *Trekking in the Pyrenees* by Douglas Streatfield-James are well written and offer a wide range of walks, from half-day trips to demanding treks of a week or more. However, both concentrate more upon France than Spain, so check the areas they cover against your proposed route before you buy.

Compared with the above, *Landscapes of the Pyrenees* by Paul Jenner & Christine Smith is slight stuff with little of weight for walkers and even less of consequence about the Spanish slopes.

Much more stimulating is *Pyrenees High Level Route*, an abridged and fairly pedestrian – forgive the pun – translation of *La Haute Route des Pyrénées*, the classic French work by the grandad of all Pyrenees walkers, Georges Véron. His route, however, isn't for beginners or even intermediates. A master of navigation with an unparalleled knowledge of the mountains, his descriptions are minimal and often strike out where no path exists.

If you can read Spanish, think of investing 3500 ptas in *GR11: Senda Pirenaica* by PRAMES. It comes in a ring binder so you can pull out only the pages that are relevant to your traverse, and has a reliable map for each daily stage at 1:50,000. Information, however, isn't always reliable and some of the timings are wildly optimistic. *Through the Spanish Pyrenees: GR11* by Paul Lucia, published in book format by Cicerone Press, is based very closely upon this original, though it lacks the Spanish version's flexibility of format and supporting maps.

For flowers, *Wild Flowers of the Pyrenees* by AW Taylor is worth picking up. Amateurs who just enjoy identifying flowers from a clear photo will find the *Guia de Flors d'Andorra*, with photos and minimalist text by Doreen Lindley, excellent. It's only available in Catalan, but each photo is accompanied by the flower's Spanish, French, English and Latin names – most entries are valid for the Pyrenees in general.

Information Sources

It's safer to buy all your maps and books in advance (see Maps and Books under Planning in the Facts for the Walker chapter). Shops in popular tourist towns and villages such as Andorra la Vella, Espot, Vielha, Benasque, Bielsa and Torla often sell the local Editorial Alpina map but few alternatives.

Place Names

This chapter adopts local place names, opting for Catalan in Andorra and the Catalan Pyrenees, and Aragonese where it differs from the Spanish elsewhere. This isn't as easy in practice as it might sound. You'll often find a variety of spellings from one published map to another and even within the same text. One of the cols where the Vall d'Aran meets the limit of the Parc Nacional d'Aigüestortes i Estany de Sant Maurici, for instance, is labelled Port d'Onhla Crestada (Aranese), Port de Collcrestada and Güellicrestada (Catalan).

The confusion isn't only between Catalan, Aranese and Spanish. It can also reflect a shift in dialect from one valley to another and the fact that, until quite recently, some place names had never been written down by anyone.

Warnings

If you're walking in late summer you may find that what we or your map present as a small lake, tarn or pool is nothing more than cracked mud. Such pools come and soon go after heavy rain or the early summer snow thaw.

Bear in mind that what may be a clearly identifiable track in late summer may be nothing more than a red line on the map after the snows have melted and the fresh spring grass begins to grow. Those same winter snows will also probably have demolished any small stone cairn last year's walkers have laid.

ACCOMMODATION & SUPPLIES

For information on accommodation and supply centres within reach of the Pyrenees, see the Accommodation & Supplies sections under Andorra and the Aragonese Pyrenees later in this chapter.

GETTING THERE & AWAY

For information on transport services between the Spanish Pyrenees and other points in Spain and France, see the Getting There & Away sections under Andorra, the Catalan Pyrenees and the Aragonese Pyrenees later in this chapter.

GETTING AROUND

Public transport, rarely frequent at any time, runs rather more regularly during the summer months. Since most services are few and far between, it's always prudent to check times with the local tourist office or train station.

Where buses no longer operate, most villages have a taxi service, whether formally established or just someone who's prepared to do a run when asked. Inquire at the tourist office – in summer there's a small office in most villages with tourism aspirations – or, for the real lowdown, in the local bar. A small investment can save you an hour or more of unexciting walking along the road.

ANDORRA

Slip Andorra into the conversation and people will tell you, with horror or joy, that it's all skiing and shopping. They'll also probably add that it's a one-road, one-town mini-state, its only highway, which links Spain and France, cutting a swathe through its only town, Andorra la Vella – which in turn is little more than a vast traffic jam bordered by cut-price temples to human greed.

They're right to a degree, but also very wrong. Slip out of Andorra la Vella along good-quality secondary roads and you'll find villages as unspoilt as any in the Pyrenees. Despite the fact that Andorra, with a population of no more than 65,000 and an area of only 464 sq km, manages to absorb some 8 million visitors a year, there are still areas where you can be completely alone. And Andorra's small, friendly tourist offices offer support that's second to none.

HISTORY

According to legend, Andorra was founded in around 784 AD by the great emperor Charlemagne to thank the locals for guiding his troops through the mountains on their way to face the Arabs occupying the Spanish peninsula. Charlemagne's grandson granted the Valls d'Andorra (the valleys of Andorra) to the count of Urgell from La Seu, further south in present-day Catalunya. He in his turn bequeathed the valleys to the local bishop of La Seu d'Urgell.

Following an obscure 13th century dispute, a modus vivendi (working arrangement) was established sharing Andorra between the Catalan bishop and a feudal count over the French border. The contemporary consequence is that the very nominal suzerainty over Andorra – an independent state and member of the United Nations – is shared between France and Spain, which only get upset if the smuggling, particularly of tobacco, gets out of hand.

Andorra is also at the intersection of two GR trails: the GR11, which links the Atlantic Ocean with the Mediterranean on the Spanish side of the Pyrenees, and the GR7, which runs from Lisbon all the way to the Black Sea.

NATURAL HISTORY

Andorra's lines of communication are largely determined by its river valleys, created long before the cataclysms of successive Ice Ages. The principal river, Riu Gran Valira, flows southward into Spain. It is formed by the confluence of the Riu Valira del Nord, fed by waters funnelled down the Arinsal and Ordino valleys, and the Riu Valira d'Orient, which collects the headwaters of the catchment area around Soldeu.

THE PYRENEES

INFORMATION
Maps

The most up-to-date and accurate maps of Andorra are a series of four produced by the Spanish IGN at 1:25,000, which are intended to cover the whole of this small country. *Llorts* No 183-I and *Andorra La Vella* No 183-III were published in 1997, while Nos 183-II and 183-IV were in the pipeline at the time of writing.

The Rando Éditions *Haute-Ariège-Andorre* map at 1:50,000 is reliable and walker-friendly, though some of its trails, indicated in firm red lines, are much less obvious on the ground. The government of Andorra's own map, *Andorra* at 1:50,000, is also trustworthy. Editorial Alpina covers the whole of the principality in one map, *Andorra*, at 1:40,000.

For general orientation within the country, pick up a free map of Andorra at 1:145,000 from any tourist office.

Books

The Comú (local authority, or parish) of Ordino and La Massana publishes a free booklet in English, *Thirty Interesting Itineraries on the Paths of the Parishes of Ordino and La Massana*. Similarly, the excellent, if no longer easy to find, *Guide to Canillo* compiled by the Comú de Canillo (650 ptas) has a wide range of suggestions for day walks.

Information Sources

In Andorra la Vella, staff of the tourist office (☎ 82 02 14) on Carrer Dr Vilanova and the municipal tourist office (☎ 82 71 17) on Plaça de la Rotonda are impressively polyglot and well informed. The former publishes a free brochure entitled *Sports Activities* in its English version, which gives details of walks throughout the principality. You can also pick up a free map showing all the refugios together with information on sleeping capacities.

For more local walking information, contact the small tourist offices in Canillo (☎ 85 10 02) or Ordino (☎ 83 69 63). They

also post information on weather conditions for the coming 72 hours.

If you read Spanish, French or Catalan and enjoy maps and books, whether contemporary or collectors' items, Jaume Caballé's shop (☎ 82 94 54) on Avenida Fiter Russell 31 carries a comprehensive stock of maps.

ACCOMMODATION & SUPPLIES
Andorra la Vella

Andorra la Vella is the place to stock up on mountain gear since prices can't be beaten anywhere in western Europe. There's no shortage of sports shops. One of the best for walkers is Viladomat which has three branches, the largest (☎ 80 08 05) at Avenida Meritxell 110. But it's not alone; browse around – if you can stand the intrusive traffic.

There are also plenty of accommodation and eating options in town. At the budget end of the market, the helpful, 15 room *Residència Benazet (☎ 82 06 98, Carrer de la Llacuna 21, 1st floor)* has large, serviceable rooms with with shared bathroom for up to four people at 1300 ptas a person.

Canillo

Hotel Comerç (☎ 85 10 20) has singles/doubles for a bargain 1450/2900 ptas. Be sure to ring in advance since those in the know come back year after year. *Hotel Casa-Nostra (☎ 85 10 23)*, with rather less character, has rooms for 3750 ptas, while a bed at the mid-range *Hotel Pic Blanc* costs 3800 ptas. Of the five camping grounds in the village, *Camping Santa Creu* is the greenest and, since it's furthest from the highway, the quietest.

It's the usual hotel fare in town – reasonable value but nothing outstanding – with one sterling exception: the restaurant at *Hotel Comerç*, known to all as Chez Maria in honour of the cook, 60 years old and still going strong. Her standard menu, which you'll need to order in advance, is magnificent value at 2000 ptas. There's also a supermarket and a couple of grocery stores on the main road.

You can relax after a day in the mountains at the sauna or swimming pool of the Palau de Gel, Canillo's sports complex and ice rink.

GETTING THERE & AWAY
Andorra la Vella

Unless you walk over the mountains, the only way in or out of Andorra is by road. Alsina Graells (☎ 82 73 79 in Andorra, ☎ 93 265 68 66 in Barcelona) has at least five runs a day between Andorra and Barcelona. Samar/Andor-Inter (☎ 82 62 89 in Andorra, ☎ 91 468 41 90 in Madrid) runs three buses a week between Andorra and the Spanish capital.

Alternatively, you can vary the journey by taking the 9.18 am train from Barcelona's Sants station to Latour de Carol in France, from where a connecting Auto Pujol Huguet bus at the train station leaves for Andorra at 1.15 pm (there's another daily bus at 10.30 am).

From Andorra la Vella, a bus departs at 7.30 am for Latour de Carol, arriving at 9.40 am and allowing you to connect with several trains to Toulouse in France or Barcelona, while the second and last bus of the day departs Andorra la Vella at 10.30 am.

From L'Hospitalet, an alternative entry point to Andorra from France, buses of La Hispano Andorrana company leave daily for Andorra la Vella at 7.35 am and 7.45 pm. In high summer there's an extra service departing at 5 pm. In the reverse direction, buses leave Andorra la Vella at 5.45 am, 1.30 (summer only) and 5 pm. On Saturday there are as many as five buses from L'Hospitalet to Pas de la Casa in Andorra, from where you can travel onward by local bus to Canillo and Andorra la Vella.

For the latest information on Autos Pujol Juguet and La Hispano Andorrana services, ring ☎ 82 13 72.

Canillo

From 8.05 am until 8.05 pm, an hourly bus service links Andorra la Vella and Canillo and continues up the valley to Soldeu.

Cap de Rep & Riba Escorjada

Duration 4 to 4½ hours
Distance 10.5km
Standard Easy-Medium
Start CS241 road, 3.5km above Canillo
Finish CS241 road, 5km above Canillo
Public Transport No
Summary A circular route which, after taking in three minor peaks in quick succession, drops to the winter ski area of Riba Escorjada before meandering through mixed wood above the Vall de Canillo.

The route is clearly marked as far as Cap de Rep and from the Riba Escorjada plateau onwards. In between is an invigorating cross-country ridge walk over springy grass, followed by a brief scramble down to the ski station.

PLANNING
Maps

For a map covering this walk, see Maps under Information in the introduction to the Andorra section.

What to Bring

Be sure to carry water. Once the snows have melted (between April and May), there's not a trickle on this walk until you reach Riba Escorjada.

GETTING TO/FROM THE WALK

To get to the starting point you can either walk 3.5km up the lightly trafficked CS250 road, which becomes the CS241, or order a taxi in Canillo (☎ 85 10 32). For a more flexible but expensive alternative, Europcar (☎ 82 00 91), Hertz (☎ 82 64 04) and Avis (☎ 82 93 92) are all represented in Andorra.

THE WALK (see map on page 191)

Several bends before the end of the sealed road leading to the hamlet of El Forn, a sign indicates 'Cap de Rep', 'Pic dels Maians' and 'Pic d'Encampadana'. Disregard the times it quotes to these peaks since all are significantly out. Take the path from the signs leading upwards towards a lone house, beyond which it briefly becomes a distinct cart track. From here, you can soon distinguish the long, lateral line of the ridge extending from Cap de Rep to Pic dels Maians and beyond. Keep heading resolutely south-east, bearing away from a seductive dry-stone wall which seems to offer a more direct route to the saddle. You're now briefly in open grassland. There are occasional yellow trail markers to guide you across the clearing, but it's easier to pick your own course, aiming for the base of a steep valley strewn with dead pines.

Head up the valley in a southerly direction, picking your way between fallen trees, following the yellow trail markers. You should reach the ridge after 1½ to 1¾ hours of unremitting but not too arduous ascent.

From here, turn right to arrive after no more than 10 minutes at the four-way pole on the summit of **Cap de Rep** (2316m). In the valley to the south march the pylons of the giant, state-of-the-art cable car which in season lifts skiers from Encamp to the ski fields. Enjoy also views of Encamp, Andorra la Vella and the Coll d'Ordino; beyond it to the west are the distant hills of Spain.

From here until the ski centre at Riba Escorjada, you're walking cross-country with only the occasional hairline track to guide you. Unless the day is misty, this presents no problem. Looking along the ridge from Cap de Rep, the large cairn on top of the Pic dels Maians (2451m), your next landmark, is clearly visible, its knife-edge spur trailing away north-west. After a brief descent to a col, head away from the cliff edge on a north-east bearing; the cairn is a 15 minute ascent over tussocks of tough, upland grass.

Don't be confused by the bald mountain and ski lifts to the east, which probably won't feature on your map (unless it is a recent one). Instead, drop to another minor col where you cross a 4WD track and mount the opposite flank, heading for the marker pole at the summit of the **Pic d'Encampadana** (2476m). Below, to the north-east, are the ski lifts and cabins of Riba Escorjada, your next landmark, with the Vall de Ransol beyond.

From the peak, head north-west along the crest for some five to seven minutes, dropping slightly. Then – the exact point is up to you – turn east and work your way to the stream at the valley bottom, aiming to hit it about 250m upstream from a prominent, white chairlift. Though the descent begins steeply, the latter part, where the lusher turf affords more grip underfoot, is easy.

It's a strange experience to wander alone in this high valley among barren ski installations, all the winter animation of the ski resort difficult to imagine. You don't need to descend as far as the resort, which in summer is locked and deserted. Instead, cross the stream to pass beside the tiny **Refugio de Riba Escorjada** with its green doors and shutters. You could spend the night here, though there's not much incentive to do so.

From the refugio, the last hour is pleasantly undemanding as a clearly marked footpath drops gently through a pine forest and past banks of rhododendrons. In season, the opposite mountainside, where the Vall de Riu meets Vall de Canillo, blazes with yellow broom – a sure indicator of recent forest fire since this hardy shrub is among the first to repossess the land. Finally, the path intersects with the CS241 at a sharp bend, some 15 minutes above your starting point.

Estanys de Siscaró

Duration 4 to 4½ hours
Distance 12km
Standard Medium
Start/Finish Soldeu
Public Transport Yes
Summary A 750m ascent to the col of Port Dret, a steep drop to the Estanys de Siscaró, down to the marshy Basses de Siscaró and on through woods covering the flanks of the Tosa d'Incles.

The route is marked in red for the first 45 minutes or so, then by red-and-yellow trail markers from the Estanys de Siscaró to the Refugi de les Basses, and in yellow from there to the finish, some 300m west of Soldeu. We grade this walk medium because of the degree of route-finding required in the intervening stage.

You'll probably be walking alone for most of the day apart from the stretch between the Estanys de Siscaró and the refugio. The twin lakes are a popular destination for walkers who leave their vehicles at the end of the road beside Camping d'Incles.

PLANNING
Maps

For a map covering this walk, see Maps under Information in the introduction to the Andorra section.

GETTING TO/FROM THE WALK

Buses leave Canillo for Soldeu every hour, on the half hour, from 8.30 am. To return, they leave hourly, on the hour, until 8 pm.

For information on transport between Canillo and Andorra la Vella, see Getting There & Away in the introduction to the Andorra section earlier in this section.

THE WALK (see map on page 191)

At the head of the small lane opposite Supermercat Pirineu, near Soldeu's eastern limit, a sign reads 'Coma Bella', 'Clots de l'Os' and 'Port Dret'. Head eastward along the lane away from the village, following the often faded red dots. Beyond a small farm, reached after about 10 minutes, you'll arrive at a junction; keep to the left, following the main cart track. Soon after, take a small path which climbs just to the left of a water tank beside the stream's true left bank, zigzagging its way up the mountainside in an easterly direction.

After 45 minutes to an hour, the path enters a small, pine-stippled bowl. On a rock in the stream trickling through it are a pair of red arrows. Take the right option, and that's it; the signs dry up and you're on your own. Walk directly east up the lush turf to where a rock field begins, then bear north before swinging east once again. You'll soon meet the first of a series of small cairns leading up and over the lip of the valley.

Once over the brow a little less than 1¼ hours from Soldeu, the bare ridge appears ahead. Stick to the valley's eastern flank in order to avoid the rough ground of the lateral moraine. About 30 minutes later, at the cairned col of **Port Dret** (2564m), there's a magnificent view down upon the twin lakes of the **Estanys de Siscaró**, like a pair of blue eyes gazing back at you.

It takes about 30 minutes of steep descent, guided by red-and-yellow markers, to reach the bank of the right-hand, eastern lake – an ideal spot for a breather or lunch break. They take their name from the Catalan *siscall*, or glasswort, a rush-like plant that grows at their edges and in the flood plain below. Leave the pool at its northern corner to drop steeply and in tandem with the stream flowing from it to reach a flood plain, Les Basses de Siscaró, with the tiny *refugio* of the same name in its north-east corner.

Leave the main beaten path about two-thirds of the way along the side of this soggy plain. You may well need to cast around to your left for a couple of hundred metres to find the first of the yellow dots which lead you uphill and, after around 10 minutes, through a gate, over a clearing and into woodland. Every now and again you'll catch glimpses of the Vall d'Incles below, but for the most part it's just you, the trees and their welcome shade. Stick to the yellow trail markers – keep your gaze high since many of them are up on the trees – and you'll soon find yourself on an evident track. Threading its way through woodland, punctuated by clearings and streams, it leads to a crossroads after about another hour of walking, where a sign points right to Incles and left to Soldeu. Ignore the injunction to turn left and instead continue along the track for about 30 minutes to reach the main road, some 300m before the first buildings of Soldeu. Follow the road back to the starting point.

Side Trip: Vall d'Incles

1½ hours, 6km

Not so much a side trip, this well trodden way back to Soldeu from Basses de Siscaró is an attractive alternative to the higher route home through the woods, even though it's along sealed road from shortly beyond the Camping d'Incles onwards. It's a gentle stroll along the flat, wide Vall d'Incles with its pastures and understated local stone architecture.

Pic de l'Estanyó

Duration 4¾ to 5¼ hours
Distance 12.5km
Standard Hard
Start CS240 road, 4.6km from Canillo
Finish CS240 road, 3.6km from Canillo
Public Transport No
Summary An ascent to the Coll d'Arenes (2539m), a scramble and clamber along the Cresta de l'Estanyó to the Pic de l'Estanyó (2912m), followed by a descent of the Vall de Riu.

The difficulty of this route lies in the narrow (at times no more than 2m wide), jagged spine of the Cresta de l'Estanyó. If this sounds daunting, the first and last sections of the walk can be undertaken separately. Each is a pleasant up-and-down walk of medium difficulty passing through meadows with *bordas* (mountain huts used in summer by shepherds and cowherds). The return trip to the Coll d'Arenes takes three to 3¼ hours and the return trip to the lakes at the base of the Pic de l'Estanyó, 4¾ to 5¼ hours. Allow an extra two hours if you include an ascent to the peak. The total ascent for the walk as described is 1112m.

PLANNING
When to Walk

Don't attempt the Cresta de l'Estanyó ridge on a wet day, when the slippery rock can be treacherous.

Maps

For a map covering this walk, see Maps under Information in the introduction to the Andorra section.

What to Bring

If you're planning to climb the Cresta de l'Estanyó, keep your day-pack light in case the wind throws you off balance.

GETTING TO/FROM THE WALK

The starting point of this walk is only a short distance north of Canillo along the CS240 road. For information on taxis or hire cars, see Getting to/from the Walk in the Cap de Rep & Riba Escorjada walk earlier in this section.

THE WALK (see maps on pages 190-1)

From a sign 'Coll d'Arenes' beside the CS240, follow the east (true left) bank of the stream. Within five minutes a yellow arrow directs you right and up the steep flank of the Vall de Montaup, even though there's no evident path. Aim for a pair of stone buildings, at which point you turn left along a broad cart track. Just beyond the second borda, bear right along a path which rises gently to reach a series of waterfalls at a point where the valley closes in and becomes decidedly steeper.

About 45 minutes from the starting point you round a bend to enter a vast green amphitheatre. Just beyond a locked well, a faint path climbs parallel to the tumbling stream. From here to the pass the route is marked sporadically in red. Just beyond a steep 15 minute clamber to a false col, there's a deep, shady overhang where the path crosses the stream. Refill your bottles here or at the pipe just above – there's no more water until you reach a tarn beyond the Pic de l'Estanyó.

Keep to the left (west) side of the valley above this false col and don't worry if you deviate from the red blobs; it's easy, cross-country work up to a clear stony track which leads to the **Coll d'Arenes**.

From here until beyond the Pic de l'Estanyó, follow the red-and-white trail markers of one of the GR11's less responsible variants; a full backpack on the ridge is positively dangerous.

From the pass, a smudge of a path leads due north, soon turning right towards the ridge. On the ridge, progress is slow because of the jagged, friable rock. Here, the trail markers are invaluable indicators of the best passage to take along its narrower, more rugged stretches.

Views from the large, stone windbreak at the summit of the **Pic de l'Estanyó**, a good hour beyond the Coll d'Arenes, are spectacular. Be sure to sign the visitors book which you'll find in a sturdy metal box. To the south-east is the pine-clad valley through which you'll pass on the return to Canillo. Your immediate landmark, however, is a small tarn below and almost due east of the peak (at the end of a particularly dry summer this may be no more than a stain of darker grass). Continue along the ridge until the first small dip (in about 10 minutes) where you turn right to head down into the bowl in which the tarn nestles.

Cross eastward over a minor ridge, just beside a second and smaller tarn (which can also be seasonal) and continue to a pair of more substantial pools. Near the far corner of the western one, pick up the yellow trail markers of the signed route from L'Armiana which continues to the largest of the pools, known collectively as the Estanys de la Vall de Riu. Follow the yellow trail markers eastward to pass (in less than five minutes) above and south of yet another medium-sized tarn. High on the eastern flank of the Vall de Riu, the small Cabana de la Vall de Riu (2050m) is visible, still an hour or more away.

The last of the day's boulder fields are followed by a brief squelch through the marshy headwaters of the eponymous *riu* (Catalan for river) which tumbles down into the main valley. Head south along the east side of the valley to the Cabana de la Vall de Riu, which has a trough of flowing water.

After a stretch of easy walking across a meadow beyond the refugio, turn right at a pair of cairns to drop gradually down towards the valley bottom. Some 15 to 20 minutes beyond the refugio, pass an intact borda. Fifteen minutes later the path executes a series of zigzags before crossing the torrent by a wooden bridge.

It curls gently westward around the hill, leaving the stream to plunge away below. About 20 minutes beyond the bridge, beside the abandoned houses of **L'Armiana**, the path joins a road which you follow for a rather anticlimactic 15 minutes to a junction with the CS240 road.

Andorra to Catalunya
(Days 1 & 2 of the Pyrenean Traverse)

Duration 2 days
Distance 32.5km
Standard Medium-Hard
Start Canillo
Finish Refugi de Vall Ferrera
Public Transport Start only
Summary A couple of cols and a descent to the ski station of Arinsal, followed by a popular route to the Refugi de Coma Pedrosa, then wilderness walking over the Port de Baiau to the Vall Ferrera.

Here begins the 23 day east-to-west traverse of the Pyrenees which, if you cover the whole route, will take you as far as Sallent de Gállego in the Aragonese Pyrenees.

We add a qualifying 'hard' to the medium grading of this walk for two features, both met on Day 2: the possibility of snow above the Estany Negre and the very steep descent from Port de Baiau.

Though this walk represents the first stage of the Pyrenean Traverse, Day 1 can also be done as a day walk, returning to Canillo from Arinsal by bus via Andorra la Vella. Similarly, the first part of Day 1 to Ordino makes a pleasant half-day excursion, leaving you time to explore the village before returning by bus to Canillo via Andorra la Vella.

PLANNING
Maps

Two Editorial Alpina maps cover this stage of the walk: *Andorra* and *Pica d'Estats*, both at 1:40,000. The French Rando Éditions map *Haute-Ariège-Andorre* No 7 gives complete coverage at 1:50,000.

What to Bring

Telescopic poles are valuable walking aids on Day 2, both in the snow you may find above the Estany Negre and down the very steep descent on shale from the Port de Baiau.

PLACES TO STAY & EAT
Canillo

For information on places to stay and eat in Canillo, see Accommodation & Supplies in the introduction to the Andorra section.

Refugio de Vall Ferrera

For information on food and accommodation in Vall Ferrera and Áreu at the end of this walk, see Places to Stay & Eat in the introduction to the Vall Ferrera & Vall de Cardós walk in the Catalan Pyrenees section.

GETTING TO/FROM THE WALK

The walk begins in Canillo. If leaving the walk at the end of Day 1, buses leave Arinsal for Andorra la Vella at 8 and 10 am and 3 pm. For Canillo, they depart from Andorra la Vella on the hour until 8 pm. From Andorra la Vella, buses head for Arinsal at 9.30 am, 1 and 6 pm. If you leave the Day 1 route in Ordino, buses leave there for Andorra la Vella every half hour until 8.30 pm.

For transport to and from Refugi de Vall Ferrera at the end of this walk, see Getting to/from the Walk in the introduction to the Vall Ferrera & Vall de Cardós walk in the Catalan Pyrenees section.

THE WALK (see maps on pages 189-90)
Day 1: Canillo to Arinsal

7 hours, 17.5km

Walk 1.4km from Canillo on the Andorra la Vella road to the Mobil petrol station, where you take a path to the right signed 'Coll d'Ordino'. This soon begins to climb steeply westwards up the flank of a valley. After about 30 minutes, follow two sides of a rectangular boundary wall around a meadow, then pass well to the left of the ruined Borda

de N'Andrieta, cross the head of the valley and re-enter the pine forest. At the Planell de les Basses – a fine, open meadow on the other side of the forest – aim for a broad, double-trunked pine in front of you as you leave the forest. Some 50m beyond, a wide track with yellow and red markers crosses the path at right angles. Turn right along it to reach the **Coll d'Ordino** (1979m) after a total walking time of 1¼ to 1½ hours.

At this point, pick up the red-and-white trail markers of the GR11. A well defined track drops westwards towards the tight valley of the Riu de Segudet. After a little over 15 minutes, turn sharp right beside a metal fence to pass a *merendero* (picnic spot) and the Font de la Navina spring. Thirty minutes or so later, turn right at a T-junction to describe a hairpin around another merendero with a small pool. The path follows a stream which leads from the pool and frequently hops from bank to bank, passing beside the Casa Redort farm.

Thirty minutes from the T-junction, turn right at a second T-junction and follow the twists and turns of the track as it climbs the west flank of the Vall de Casamanya. At a signpost, take the left-hand option indicating Sornás. Soon after, it's easy to miss a sharp turn left beside a wooden fence. From here on, the path crosses several small *barrancos* (gullies or ravines) – steep, narrow but mercifully brief.

Back again at valley level, **La Cortinada**, with its 1630 church and restored waterpowered flour mill and sawmill, merits a stop. To reach Arans (1385m), take the cart track on the true left (east) bank of the river to avoid the sealed road. Both are attractive villages, now almost entirely given over to rural tourism.

Should you wish to postpone the ascent to the Coll de les Cases until the next day, both villages have limited accommodation. In La Cortinada, *Hostal la Cortinada* (☎ 85 01 51) has singles/doubles for 2500/4200 ptas, while in Arans there are two choices: *Hotel Arans* (☎ 85 01 11), with rooms for 4900 ptas, and *Hotel Cal Daina* (☎ 85 09 88), where rooms cost 3500/6000 ptas.

In Arans, the route crosses the sealed road beside the Restaurante la Font d'Arans, meandering its way through the village to a sign pointing to 'Camí del Coll de les Cases'. At the first bend in the track, go directly ahead up a narrow footpath which heads straight and steadily up to the **Coll de les Cases** (1964m), a good *camp site*. The descent to Arinsal (1465m) is more winding, varied and altogether more pleasant, though the stark buildings of this nouveau riche ski resort represent a somewhat brutal return to civilisation.

In Arinsal, the no-frills *Hostal Pobladó* (☎ 83 51 22) costs 2600 ptas per person, while rooms at *Hotel Comapedrosa* (☎ 83 51 23) are 3000/5500 ptas. One of the more popular top-end places is *Hotel Solana* (☎ 83 51 27, fax 83 73 95), where large rooms with bathroom are 5500/8000 ptas.

The nearest camping ground is *Camping Xixerella* (☎ 83 66 13), about 4km south of Arinsal near Erts. If you're camping wild, consider stopping early and pitching your tent on the grass at the Coll de les Cases, saving the descent to Arinsal until the next morning.

Day 2: Arinsal to Refugi de Vall Ferrera

6 to 6½ hours, 15km

At Arinsal's northern extremity, take a path which climbs between Aparthotel Crest and an ageing chairlift. After barely five minutes, bear right onto a track. This descends to cross and mount the true left bank of a stream which has its origin on the upper slopes of Pic de la Coma Pedrosa (2964m), Andorra's highest mountain.

At Aigües Juntes, about 30 minutes out, recross the stream and its tributary to ascend the flank of a valley coming in from the west. After a further 30 to 45 minutes of steady ascent, a broader valley opens up beyond a false col.

Just up to the left of the col is the *Refugi de Coma Pedrosa* (☎ 32 79 55), the only staffed refugio in Andorra and a favourite day-trip destination from Arinsal. Food and drinks are served from June to late September (1000 ptas for a bunk and 1700 ptas for

dinner). It's advisable to reserve a bunk. If you decide on a side trip to the Pic de la Coma Pedrosa, the refugio makes a good staging post – take the time to enjoy the Estany de les Truites, a little beyond it.

Continue up the main valley until you reach the cirque of the Coma Pedrosa (Rocky Bowl), from where the path zigzags steeply north-east. Some 45 minutes from the refugio you reach a small tarn. The much larger **Estany Negre** (aptly if unimaginatively named Black Pool) is no more than 10 minutes further on.

From here to the pass at **Port de Baiau** (2756m), thick but manageable snow can linger well into July. About 30 minutes beyond the pool it's worth pausing at a stone windbreak to savour the view back to the Estany Negre and north-east to the cairned summit of the Pic de la Coma Pedrosa.

At the col the trail leaves Andorra to drop down into the Spanish province of Lleida. The descent to the Estany de Baiau is decidedly steep, requiring all your attention, particularly if you're carrying a full backpack. Scree and loose stones are followed by what seems an interminable clamber over boulders. Be guided by the mini-cairns which are more plentiful and visible than the GR11 trail markers.

After negotiating a final tumble of rocks at the north-east shore of the tarn, you reach *Refugi Josep Montfort* (2517m), the first of several refugios you'll come across in Catalunya run by the excellent Federació d'Entitats Excursionistes de Catalunya (FEEC). It only has 12 bunks, but if you decide to overnight here you'll probably be all alone.

Continue down into the valley of the Torrent de Baiau, roughly north-east of the refugio. After about 1¼ hours from the tarn, you reach the Torrent de Baiau. Once beyond the Estanys d'Escorbes there are plenty of potential *camp sites* in the succession of meadows to the north of the track.

Soon, you see a lone cabin in the meadows of the **Pla de Boet**, near the banks of the torrent (now called the Riu Noguera de Vall Ferrera). Once a popular summer

La Trashumancia

Winter in the plains, summer in the mountains. As so many a ruined *borda* (upland cabin) eloquently tells, the annual *trashumancia* (migration) of shepherds or cowherds and their animals is a dying – but far from dead – way of life.

It's estimated that around 150 families in Andorra still depend upon the twice yearly *anant de cabanera* – the migration to the mountains of some 100,000 sheep. They follow centuries-old *camins ramaders*, tracks to the Pyrenees, nowadays sliced through by new roads, dams, housing estates and holiday developments.

In Aragón, too, there still exists a network of routes, known as *cabiñeras*. Twice a year in spring and autumn the flocks are driven some 200km between the Ebro basin down in the plains and the high Pyrenean meadows.

A strange coincidence: the dates of departure, customarily 24 June and 29 September, are almost to the day the opening and closing dates of mountain refugios for walkers. Merely obeying the weather, or some deeper instinct?

---

grazing area for livestock, it now makes an idyllic *camp site* (300 ptas per person and 300 ptas per tent, payable at the Refugi de Vall Ferrara). Otherwise, continue to meet a broad 4WD track and, after 10 minutes, a wooden bridge leading to the *Refugi de Vall Ferrera* (☎ *973 62 43 78 for reservations*). Run by the FEEC, with capacity for 30, it's 1400 ptas for a bunk and 1800 ptas for lunch or dinner.

Side Trip: Pic de la Coma Pedrosa

2 to 2½ hours, 2.5km

This is a demanding return-trip ridge walk with spectacular views to Andorra's highest point, the Pic de la Coma Pedrosa. From the south-east shore of the brooding Estany Negre, head north-east, following the yellow markers and occasional small cairns.

Side Trip: Refugi de Vall Ferrera to Áreu

2¼ to 2½ hours, 10km

While it's possible to travel to Áreu from Vall Ferrera by 4WD (for more details, see Getting to/from the Walk in the introduction to the Vall Ferrera & Vall de Cardós walk in the Catalan Pyrenees section), the gentle 10km meander down the valley to Áreu following the GR11 is a pleasure in itself.

From the refugio, return to the 4WD track and turn west for 1½ hours of walking through a beautiful forest of fir and birch trees (sections of the walking surface may be waterlogged). Leave the 4WD track some 20 minutes after the meadows of the Pla de la Selva – another possible *camp site* – and follow a grassy trail which soon becomes a walled-in track leading all the way to Áreu.

THE CATALAN PYRENEES

The Catalan Pyrenees are bounded by France to the north and the Aragonese Pyrenees to the west, sloping away to the Mediterranean in the east. They are not quite as high as the Aragonese Pyrenees, but are greener, damper and notched by deep valleys which are some of the most underpopulated and least spoilt of the whole range. Small farming communities living in relative isolation – one that was often total during the severe winter months – developed their own localised dialects and customs.

One such area was the Vall d'Aran, which still retains its own language, known as Aranese. It's not isolated any more, however, as it now enjoys year-round tourism – the ski resort of Baqueira-Beret is the largest in the Spanish Pyrenees. With its small villages, fine Romanesque churches and enough space for everyone, it's a beautiful and convenient location for a week or more of easy to medium-standard walking.

To the east, more than 50 lakes and tarns reflect the jagged peaks of the Parc Nacional d'Aigüestortes i Estany de Sant Maurici. The national park also offers enough challenge and variety for a week or more's hiking along its numerous trails.

GETTING THERE & AWAY
Bus
For the practical purposes of this chapter, there are two major bus routes accessing the Catalan Pyrenees, and two main cities – Barcelona and Lleida – which are transport hubs. At the Pyrenees end, it's possible to join and leave every walk in this section from at least one of the towns or villages covered here. For details of transport to the trailheads in the valleys, see Getting to/from the Walk in the introduction to each.

An Alsina Graells bus leaves Lleida (4.30 pm) every day except Sunday, stopping in Pobla de Segur (6.30 pm), Llavorsí (6.40 pm), passing within 8km of Espot and terminating in Esterri d'Aneu (7.30 pm). (Note that Alsina Graells buses leave Pobla de Segur from Calle Font, a 10 minute walk from the train station.) The return bus to Lleida leaves Esterri d'Aneu at 5.30 am, passing by Llavorsí at about 6.20 am and Pobla de Segur (where it interlinks with a connection for Barcelona) at 6.30 am.

In addition, two buses link Barcelona with Pobla de Segur. The first leaves daily at 7.30 am, passing by Pobla de Segur (11.45 am), Llavorsí (11.55 am) and Esterri d'Aneu (12.50 pm). Between June and October, it continues to Vielha (2.30 pm) in the Vall d'Aran. The second leaves Barcelona daily, except Sunday, at 2.30 pm and terminates in Pobla de Segur at 6.30 pm (linking with the bus from Lleida – see the preceding paragraph – which can take you further up the Vall d'Aneu).

The return bus for Barcelona leaves Esterri d'Aneu at the awful hour of 5.30 am, passing by Pobla de Segur an hour later. The summer service from Vielha sets off at 11.44 am (no sooner, no later!), calling by Esterri d'Aneu at 1.40 and Pobla de Segur at 2.55 pm.

The second bus route connects Barcelona with Vielha via the Túnel de Vielha and Lleida. Services leave Barcelona at 6.30 am and 2.30 pm, calling by Lleida at 9 am and 5 pm, and continuing on to Vielha. For the return journey from Vielha, buses depart at 5.30 am and 1.30 pm, stopping in Lleida at 8.30 am and 4.30 pm.

To confirm bus times, call Alsina Graells in Pobla de Segur (☎ 973 68 03 36), Lleida (☎ 973 26 85 00) or Barcelona (☎ 93 265 68 66).

Train
A key train access point for the Catalan Pyrenees is Pobla de Segur, from where trains depart for Lleida at 6.15 am, 12.25 and 6 pm and leave Lleida for Pobla de Segur at 8.30 am and 1.15 plus 8.45 pm.

Taxi
In Pobla de Segur, there are usually one or two taxis waiting at the station to meet incoming trains. Otherwise, ask at the cafe just across the road, or call ☎ 973 66 09 97.

INFORMATION
Weather Information
For weather information in Catalunya, call ☎ 906 33 00 03 (premium rates apply) or ☎ 93 212 57 66.

Vall Ferrera & Vall de Cardós (Days 3 to 6 of the Pyrenean Traverse)

Duration 4 days
Distance 49.25km
Standard Medium–Hard
Start Refugi de Vall Ferrera
Finish Espot
Public Transport 3rd day only
Summary Over two cols from Vall Ferrera to Vall de Cardós via a pair of high tributary valleys – the Sotllo and Sellente. Continues to the Vall d'Aneu and Espot, gateway to the Parc Nacional d'Aigüestortes i Estany de Sant Maurici.

Vall Ferrera and Vall de Cardós are two relatively isolated and unspoilt river valleys sandwiched between the more popular tourist areas of Andorra and the Parc Nacional d'Aigüestortes i Estany de Sant Maurici. Flowing from north to south, they form part of the least populated region of Catalunya and are difficult to reach by public transport. They merit the effort, however; you'll probably be the only foreigner or even the only non-Catalan around.

Graded medium-hard, the route is only really difficult at the beginning of the walking season when a few stages may be uncairned and overgrown.

This section includes a couple of superlative side trips: the popular ascent to the Pica d'Estats (3143m), the highest point in Catalunya, and a walk to Catalunya's deepest lake, the Llac de Certascan.

PLANNING
Maps

Editorial Alpina maps *Pica d'Estats* at 1:40,000 and *San Maurici* at 1:25,000 cover most of the area yet omit a significant stretch of the route between Estaon and La Guingeta in the Vall d'Aneu. Rando Éditions maps *Haute-Ariége Andorre* No 7 and *Couserans* No 6 give complete coverage at 1:50,000.

What to Bring

You'll need food for two days. After leaving Tavascan, the nearest grocery store is at La Guingeta in the Vall d'Aneu.

PLACES TO STAY & EAT
Refugi de Vall Ferrera

The *refugio* (☎ 973 62 43 78), the starting point of this stage of the Pyrenean Traverse, is run by the FEEC. It can sleep 30 and costs 1400 ptas for a bunk and 1800 ptas for lunch or dinner.

Áreu

A double room at the *Hostal Vall Ferrera* (☎ 973 62 43 43), where you can also eat, costs 5000 ptas. *Camping Pica d'Estats* (☎ 973 62 43 47) is a camping ground with exceptionally friendly staff. Jordi, the owner, is a fount of information about walking in this area. It has great *platos combinados* (a largeish serve of meat/seafood/omelette with trimmings) for around 1000

ptas. The village has a small *shop* which, with a certain hubris, styles itself a *supermercat* (Catalan for supermarket).

Espot

For information on food and accommodation in Espot at the end of this walk, see Places to Stay & Eat in the introduction to the Espot to Refugi de Colomers walk later in this section.

GETTING TO/FROM THE WALK

For information on getting to and from Llavorsí, see Getting There & Away in the introduction to the Catalan Pyrenees section. Between Llavorsí and the mountain villages of Áreu and Tavascan you're reliant upon village taxis.

Refugi de Vall Ferrera

To get to the Refugi de Vall Ferrera, ask at Camping Pica d'Estats in Áreu for a taxi or call Josep Maria Llor (☎ 973 62 43 53) or Josep Maria Lladós (☎ 973 62 44 11) based in Arins, 5km to the south. If you're leaving the valley, a phone call from the Refugi de Vall Ferrera to one of these numbers will procure a 4WD taxi.

Descending to Áreu, in season and at weekends, you stand a good chance of hitching a lift from the parking area below the Refugi de Vall Ferrera – the upper limit for vehicles and the spot where many daytrippers leave their cars.

Tavascan

A taxi from Tavascan to the nearest vehicle access point to Planell de Boavi (see Day 4), 6km north-east of Tavascan, costs 600 ptas per person.

From the parking area downstream from the Planell de Boavi, there's a fair likelihood of hitching a lift to Tavascan and beyond. For the journey from Tavascan to Llavorsí, contact the small tourist office (☎ 973 62 30 79) in Tavascan for a taxi (3000 ptas).

Espot

For information on how to get to/from Espot at the end of this walk, see Getting to/from the Walk in the Espot to Refugi de Colomers walk later in this section.

THE WALK (see maps pages 187-9)
Day 3: Refugi de Vall Ferrera to Refugi de Baborte
4½ to 5 hours, 6.5km

As far as the Estany de Sotllo (pronounced so-yo), on the much trodden main route to the Pica d'Estats, you won't be short of company. Further west, you're unlikely to see anyone for the rest of the day.

About 15 minutes from the Refugi de Vall Ferrera, turn left at a fork where a sign points east to the Estany de Areste and west to the Pica d'Estats. After an agreeable and deceptively level stretch, the track drops to meet the Barranc de Sotllo after 45 to 55 minutes from the starting point. Cross over a wooden bridge onto the true right bank of the torrent.

Before reaching the Estany de Sotllo, the path climbs over three lateral moraines straddling the valley. Tackle the first two on the west side and the last one more towards the middle. The route, in places more stream than path, is well cairned – grooved, even – by the thousands of walkers who have passed on their way to bag the Pica d'Estats.

As you cross the third ridge, two to 2¼ hours from the refugio, the **Estany de Sotllo** lies ahead of you, probably with a tent or two adding colour to its north shore. This is a popular base camp for a morning attack on the Pica d'Estats (see the side trip at the end of this day's walk description).

At the northern end of the tarn, leave the main track to head west-north-west for 40 to 50 minutes, following the lake's feeder stream. It makes a great trail marker, drawn like a length of string between the Estany de Sotllo and your intermediate goal, an unnamed pool.

From the pool, head steeply upward, aiming for the **Coll de Baborte** (2618m) to the south-west, just south of the Pic de Barbote. At the pass, reached after 45 minutes to an hour of scarcely discernible trail, a metal sign directs you towards the Refugi de Baborte (a further 45 minutes

away). As you descend into the valley, look for cairns rather than traces of the path which loses itself among the boulders.

Keeping a couple of small tarns well to your right, aim for a small gap south-west and dead ahead. After passing a pair of more substantial tarns, also on your right, the **Refugi de Baborte** (2438m) becomes visible. Resembling nothing more than a metal haulage container or giant meat locker from the exterior, the refugio can accommodate eight and is surprisingly cosy inside, with well insulated, wood-panelled walls. Campers will find plenty of *camp sites* on the springy grass near the lake.

Side Trip: Estany de Sotllo to Pica d'Estats
4½ to 5 hours, 8.5km

Catalunya's highest mountain (3143m) has a special fascination for Catalan walkers. You can either do it as a nine to 10 hour return trip from the Refugi de Vall Ferrera or camp overnight at the Estany de Sotllo and set off the next morning for a 2½ hour ascent. It's not worth leaving too early as the crust of snow and ice higher up needs time to soften. The edges of Estany d'Estats, though further up the valley, are too steep and rocky to camp on in comfort.

From the Estany de Sottlo, follow the path as far as the clearly visible pass at Port de Sotllo (2894m). From here you've two options. The shorter one requires 30 minutes of steep clambering up the ridge. The other, easier, option – despite the snow which stays on the northern slopes until much later in the season – descends to the little Estanyet de Barz in France. From here, strike right (east) until you're between, though well below, the peaks of Estats and Montcalm (3077m). Make the final push up the gentler north slope via the Coll de Riufred (2978m).

Day 4: Refugi de Baborte to Tavascan
5 to 5½ hours, 15km

From the refugio, head west and up towards a bank of distinctly red rock and scree. If you're lucky you might hit one of the vague trails – there are at least three of them – which zigzag their way through the boulder field and up to the **Coll de Sellente** (2485m). If not, it doesn't matter too much since no path is better than another. After working your way across the boulders, you should reach the pass in a little more than 30 minutes.

Once over the col, keep heading rigorously north-west. The navigation is easy, but if in doubt look for the stones topping a giant erratic (a solitary rock different from the rocks surrounding it). There's a good chance of seeing chamois here.

Shortly after the Coll de Bessero, a hump straddling the valley, the route turns right (north) and descends to the Planell de Sant Pau (2240m) with a striped pole planted at its heart and the ruins of the long-closed Sellente refugio. Continue over the brow of another minor col and drop down into the lush valley of the **Ribera de Sellente**. The path crosses several rivulets to end up on the true right bank of the stream.

Less than 2km downstream, cross back to the true left bank. The path stays level as the stream falls away below. Where the two join again, about 30 minutes later, cross once more to the true right bank over giant stepping stones of metamorphic rock.

Some 15 minutes later turn right at a T-junction and follow the path, against all your instincts, as it turns back on itself and heads north-east, away from the col. The path very soon swings north-west to cross a swift torrent by a pair of rickety logs and becomes a fine, well maintained track. This drops gently down in switchbacks through fir and pine trees to a log bridge over the Riu de Broate and into the fertile meadows of the **Planell de Boavi**. There are several gorgeous *camp sites* here.

It's a 30 minute walk from the meadow to the barrier which marks the limit for vehicles and a further 6km to the village of Tavascan (1167m). Some 15 minutes beyond the barrier is the dam and small hydroelectric plant of Montalto, driven by the Noguera de Lladorre as well as water from the Vall Ferrera transported via a subterranean pipe.

De-Trashing the Planell de Boavi

By midsummer the meadows of the Planell de Boavi would be strewn with the rubbish of day visitors and campers taking advantage of this free, accessible space. The place was also a health hazard, without toilets or other amenities.

The solution was simple; the area was declared a protected zone for hunting and fishing, and a barrier was slung across the vehicular access track, a 30 minute walk downstream.

Those 30 minutes are crucial. There's still open access for those who make the effort, and the Planell de Boavi these days is almost as pure as the more lightly trodden meadows above.

In **Tavascan**, the cheapest option is *Pensió Casa Feliu* (☎ 973 62 31 63) where prices range from 1500 ptas to 4400 ptas, followed by *Hotel Llacs de Cardós* (☎ 973 62 31 778, fax 973 62 31 26) which has singles/doubles for 4200/6000 ptas (outside the peak August holiday season). The village camping ground, *Camping Bordes de Graus* (☎ 973 62 32 06), is an inconvenient 5km from the village. There's a small grocery store in town.

Alternative Camp Sites

There are quite a few great camp sites at the top of the Ribera de Sellente valley and around the Planell de Boavi.

Side Trip: Embalse de Montalto to Llac de Certascan
5½ to 6 hours, 16km

The Llac de Certascan (2240m), 102m deep and covering an area of 58 hectares, is Catalunya's deepest and biggest lake.

Beside the Embalse de Montalto, some 15 minutes below the Planell de Boavi, take the track which climbs westward. Follow it for 5.5km until you reach a sign which reads

'Certascan 2km', pointing along the Pista de Certascan. Ignore it. Instead, take the alternative 4WD route which almost doubles back on itself, heading south-west in a series of switchback curves which can be short-cutted. (If you have transport you can do a shorter walk, leaving your vehicle here and returning along the Pista de Certascan.)

A little more than 30 minutes later you reach the small, dark and undistinguished Estanyet de Closell. Where the 4WD track becomes overgrown, about 15 minutes later, turn sharp left (west) up a steep but brief path. This climbs to the altogether more impressive **Estany de Naorte**, a blue jewel of a lake rich in trout with a pine-shaded south bank which makes an ideal rest stop. A footpath curling around the lake's west and northern perimeter leads to the **Llac de Certascan** after a further hour.

The contrast between the Estany de Naorte and this ascetic giant is extreme. Certascan, surrounded by rocky mountains, above the tree line and stippled with lingering patches of winter snow, is impressive in its sheer magnitude.

Beside the lake is the *Refugi de Certascan* (☎ 973 62 32 30, certascan@teleline.es). Staffed from mid-June to mid-September, it has capacity for 40. A bunk costs 1400 ptas, lunch or dinner is 1800 ptas and drinks and snacks are served throughout the day.

The winding, at times overgrown trail from the refugio back to the Planell de Boavi has been marked by the warden, Alejandro Gamarra, who has spent more than 15 years here as a summertime warden and winter ski instructor. In places the route is impossible to distinguish on the ground, but his frequent red trail markers are dead reliable.

Begin by following the north bank of the small tarn below the lake to descend to the Pista de Certascan which you see below you, describing a giant U around the valley. After about 30 minutes the path hits a small track 100m east of a large waterfall and heads briefly left to meet the Pista (where those who've covered the early part of the walk by vehicle turn right to rejoin their transport, 2km down the track).

At the junction, don't continue straight ahead as the Editorial Alpina map suggests; no trail exists. Instead, turn left and follow the track for about 1km until you see a sign directing you right and down. Here, the red trail markers resume. The craggy descent gradually gives way to meadow, then a forest of conifer and oak trees. About 1¼ hours beyond the refugio you pass the small Cabana de Lluri; soon after, turn right (west) to follow the fringe of a wood before plunging into it.

Take care descending a couple of steep, rocky patches. Total walking time from the lake is two to 2½ hours.

Day 5: Tavascan to Estaon
4 to 4½ hours, 11km

This relatively short and easy stage, involving roughly 700m of ascent, is a respite before the longer and more demanding walk to Espot the next day.

Cross Tavascan's fine, steeply arched stone bridge and turn almost immediately right by the village water trough. Pass under an arch to join the ancient and occasionally overgrown path connecting Tavascan and Lleret. It's still paved in places with large, rectangular slabs of rock.

About 20 minutes into the day, the trail reaches the partly ruined, partly inhabited village of Aineto. (In the valleys on both sides of the Collada de Jou, notice the frequent, abandoned bordas in varying stages of collapse.) Bear right at a sign reading 'Lleret' and some five minutes later turn sharp left up a path which climbs the hillside next to a rocky stream bed and enters a wood of hazel, ash and oak trees. The route then turns south to maintain a fairly constant level, high on the flanks of the Vall de Cardós. It passes just above the village of Lleret (1380m) after about 1½ hours.

You're now on a wide, grassy cart track which passes through a fire-damaged area. It swings north-west to climb more steeply towards the Collada de Jou (1830m). Just before the col is a drinking trough for animals. The pass, which you reach after 2¾ to three hours of walking, has impressive views in all directions and makes a great lunch stop.

The path down to the valley of the **Ribera d'Estaon** isn't easy to distinguish amid the thick broom. No matter; just head for the ruined Borda de Vidal less than 1km away in a north-westerly direction. Once you reach the small river, turn left and continue downstream along an ancient track hacked from the hillside and cobbled in places to give access to the summer dwellings upstream. On your right are the Bordas de Nibros, yet another uninhabited cluster of farm buildings. Beside a rocky outcrop, about 30 minutes after joining the valley bottom, there's an abrupt change from tangled path to a wide, though long abandoned, cart track. About 1¼ hours after reaching the Ribera d'Estaon you come to a sealed road heading west and away from the river. Continue along it to Estaon, barely 10 minutes away.

In the tiny hamlet of Estaon, *la señora* at Casa Calatxo has the key to the *old school house*, where travellers are welcome to spend the night. For greater comfort, it's a 6km walk southwards to the fleshpots of Ribera de Cardós, which has a couple of *hotels* and *places to eat*. If you're *camping wild*, either choose one of the grassy spots beside the Ribera d'Estaon, or continue beyond the village for at least another hour and pitch your tent in one of the meadows beside the disused Borda Palau.

Day 6: Estaon to Espot

6½ to 7½ hours, 17.25km

Leave Estaon by the slate steps next to the *fuente* (spring). Ensure your water bottles are full since there's no other reliable source of water until the other side of Dorve on the other side of the Coll de Calvo.

Take a vague switchback path which climbs northwards up a rocky crag. The path soon improves and veers west to climb high above the Ribera d'Estaon. About 20 minutes out it turns left into a small copse and passes the Borda Palau. As you emerge from the trees, aim for a long defunct telegraph pole (clearly visible) on which is attached a hand-painted sign, 'Dorve'. The

trail at this point becomes indistinct as you push your way thorugh thigh-high broom and dog rose bushes.

One to 1¼ hours out, the path veers north-west beside the just discernible ruins of an old borda. Thirty minutes later it enters a sparse pine wood which continues until the **Coll de Calvo** (also called the Coll de Montcaubo; 2207m), 2¼ to 2½ hours from Estaon. From here are the first views of the higher peaks within the Parc Nacional d'Aigüestortes i Estany de Sant Maurici. In the middle ground is rolling forest descending to the Vall d'Aneu and the Riu Noguera Palleresa.

The slope on the western side of the pass is less steep, the track is easier to distinguish and you can maintain a steady pace. As you emerge from the wood, a little less than an hour from the col, you can see the abandoned hamlet of Dorve and the slender, emerald Embalse de la Torrassa dam.

The GR11 at this point is badly maintained; the path, where it can be discerned, is overgrown and tangled with broom, briars and nettles. Aim for the valley's western flank where a clear track of much greater antiquity than the upstart GR11 will lead you down to **Dorve**, a forlorn, crumbling cluster of buildings. Nearby is a flowing fuente which offers the first reliable water since Estaon. From here, a clear track leads you in about 45 minutes to the lake and La Guingeta (945m).

If you want to postpone the ascent to Espot (still 2¼ to 2½ hours away) until the next day, the friendly *Hostal Cases (☎ 973 62 60 83)* in La Guingeta has singles/doubles for 1700/3300 ptas (2250/4500 ptas with bathroom). It serves meals and runs *Camping Vall d'Aneu* on the other side of the highway. You can also eat at *Hotel Poldo*.

Leave La Guingeta along the lane beside Hotel Poldo and after 200m turn right to take an old cart track. This soon narrows to become a cobbled, stepped path which leads to Jou (1305m) after 45 minutes to an hour of steady uphill climbing. From here it's 5km – an hour's walk – along a sealed,

Top: Walkers in Parc Nacional d'Aigüestortes i Estany de Sant Maurici, one of only two national parks in the Pyrenees. According to local legend, the park owes its existence to Franco's penchant for fly-fishing.
Bottom: Fine meadows and spectacular views are only a few hours away for walkers basing themselves in Canillo, in Andorra.

Landscapes of the Pyrenees: La Bassa, one of many small glacial tarns in the isolated Vall d'Aran, Catalunya (top left); village house in Vall d'Aran (top right); Refugi de Certascan, with capacity for 40, near Tavascan, Catalunya (middle left); crossing a stream near Bielsa, Aragón (middle right); looking down on Benasque, Aragón, at the end of a challenging section of the Pyrenean Traverse (bottom).

virtually traffic-free minor road to the highway linking Espot and the Vall d'Aneu. At the junction you can head straight up the main road to Espot (1320m) or, for an altogether more pleasant alternative, cross the Riu Escrita by the array of flags beside *Camping La Mola* to take a wooded track above the river's true right bank.

Espot to Refugi de Colomers (Day 7 of the Pyrenean Traverse)

Duration 6½ to 7 hours
Distance 18.5km
Standard Easy-Medium
Start Espot
Finish Refugi de Colomers
Public Transport No
Summary A five star day past the Estany de Ratera, one of the park's major jewels, up to the Port de Ratera de Colomers, then a magnificent descent into the lake-stippled perimeter of the Circ de Colomers.

Day 7 of the Pyrenean Traverse passes through the Parc Nacional d'Aigüestortes i Estany de Sant Maurici, with some of the most spectacular country in the Catalan Pyrenees. For more information on a collection of walks around the national park, see the Parc Nacional d'Aigüestortes i Estany de Sant Maurici section later in this chapter.

PLANNING
Maps
Use Editorial Alpina's *San Maurici* and *Vall de Boi* maps, both at 1:25,000. For further suggestions, see Maps under Planning in the Parc Nacional d'Aigüestortes i Estany de Sant Maurici section later in this chapter.

PLACES TO STAY & EAT
Be aware that camping is prohibited within the national park's boundaries; you'll need to keep your tent stowed away until safely beyond the Port de Ratera.

Espot
The cosy, family-run *Casa Felip* (☎ 973 62 40 93) has singles/doubles with shared bathroom for 3000/5000 ptas including breakfast. *Casa Palmira* (☎ 973 62 40 72) charges 2300 ptas per person for a room with shower. *Hotel Roya* (☎ 973 62 40 40, fax 973 62 41 44) has rooms with bathroom for 4200/6100 ptas, while rooms at *Hotel Saurat* (☎ 973 62 41 62, fax 973 62 40 37) are 7800 ptas. You may find that the two hotels refuse to take you in unless you are prepared to eat in their restaurant.

There's no shortage of camping grounds. Ascending from the Vall d'Aneu, *Camping la Mola* (☎ 973 62 40 24) is the first you pass, followed by the friendly *Sol i Neu* (☎ 973 62 40 01). On the park (north-west) side of town are the smaller *Camping Solau* (☎ 973 2 40 68) and, 1km further on, *Voraparc* (☎ 973 62 41 08). All cost between 525 ptas and 575 ptas for a tent and the same fee is levied per person.

The set menu at *Restaurante Ivan* for 1300 ptas is magnificent value. The restaurant at Casa Palmira, with its *menú del día* (daily special, usually a three course meal) for 1400 ptas, and *Juquim* are both worth a visit. In the village, you'll find three supermarkets and an ATM (Automatic Teller Machine; an automatic cash dispenser).

Refugi de Colomers
For information on food and accommodation at the Refugi de Colomers, see Places to Stay & Eat in the introduction to the Vall d'Aran walk later in this section.

GETTING TO/FROM THE WALK
For information on the main transport routes in and out of the Vall d'Aneu at the end of this walk, see Getting There & Away in the introduction to the Catalan Pyrenees section.

Espot
There are two buses in and out of the Vall d'Aneu, 8km from Espot, one serving Lleida and the other Barcelona (for more details of bus services, see Getting There &

THE PYRENEES

Away in the introduction to the Catalan Pyrenees section). The bus between Lleida and Esterri d'Aneu passes the Espot bus stop 10 minutes before or after leaving Esterri d'Aneu. The daily service for Barcelona originating in Vall d'Aran (June to October) heads through at about 1.45 pm.

If notified in advance, a 4WD from the Associació de Taxis d'Espot (☎ 973 62 41 05) on the main street will deliver you to or collect you from the bus stop on the main Vall d'Aneu road for 2000 ptas per vehicle.

Refugi de Colomers

For information on getting to and from the Refugi de Colomers at the end of this walk, see Getting to/from the Walk in the introduction to the Vall d'Aran walk later in this section.

THE WALK (see map on page 187)

Exactly 2km along the road from Espot, turn right at a sign for the lake and the Refugi Ernest Mallafré. Cross and follow the true left bank of the Riu Escrita through a mixture of broad-leaf woodland, pine trees and meadow.

About halfway to the Estany de Sant Maurici the path begins to fill up with day-trippers from the car park at **Prat de Pierró**, the limit for private vehicles. From here to the lake the track is a conduit for some 95% of visitors who walk in.

Roughly 45 minutes beyond Prat de Pierró you can take water on board at the gushing Font de l'Ermita beside a small chapel, or a little later from the Font de Sant Maurici at the lake's north-east shore.

From the spring at the dam's north-east shore follow the lakeside track. Turn right (north) at a sign, 'Cascada' (where 'cascada' in Spanish means waterfall), to refresh yourself in the Cascada de Ratera's rainbow spray after about 30 minutes. Take the left fork at a T-junction beyond the waterfall onto a 4WD track with GR11 trail markers. The views south to the Pic dels Feixans de Monestero and the Gran and Petit Encantats – so frequently photographed that they're almost symbols of the park – are unsurpassed.

At a fork soon after the splendid tarn, **Estany de Ratera** (2150m), an hour from the Estany de Sant Maurici, don't follow the virtually impassable stream-side route indicated on the Editorial Alpina map. Instead, take the right fork towards Refugi d'Amitges. After scarcely 100m strike left (north-west), aiming for a red-striped GR11 pole. Keep looking out for the poles which from here until shortly before the Port de Ratera d'Espot are the principal trail markers. Some 15 minutes after passing the Estany d'Obagues de Ratera (also known as Estany de la Munyidera) to your left, the path reaches the beginning of two boulder fields. Stick close to the stream to avoid the worst of the first boulders. The path threads its way through the second field, reducing the amount of scrambling involved.

The grade stiffens briefly as you approach the Estanyet del Port de Ratera at the top of the valley. Having curled around a bulge on the north-eastern side of the lake, you reach the **Port de Ratera d'Espot** (2534m), a mere 50m above the tarn, 2¼ to 2½ hours from the Estany de Sant Maurici.

Stroll west along the flat, grassy saddle to begin the stepped descent into the spectacular Circ de Colomers. From here on, there's an infinity of tempting *camp sites* beside the lakes which stipple the valley. The trail skirts to the south-west of each of these lakes, linked together like beads on a necklace by a stream.

After just a glimpse of Estanh Cloto and the low ranges behind the Vall d'Aran, a wooden sign directs you left (west) over a small hill and down to the Estanh Major de Colomers. Cross the dam to reach the Refugi de Colomers, some two hours after leaving the Port de Ratera d'Espot, at the end of one of the most spectacular days of walking that the Pyrenees can offer.

Side Trip: Refugi de Colomers to Salardú

2¾ to 3 hours, 12km

The village of Salardú (1268m), with groceries, accommodation and transport to the wider world, is 12km down a sealed, little trafficked road which begins scarcely 1km below the Refugi de Colomers. The road follows the beautiful valley of the Riu d'Aiguamotx.

Around 2¾km along the road, you come to the hot springs, Banys de Tredòs. The *Hotel Baños de Tredòs*, with doubles for 16,000 ptas, may not be your automatic overnight choice, but after a few days of minimal hygiene a half-hour hydromassage for 1500 ptas (2500 ptas for a couple) is a delight. From the hotel you stand a reasonable chance of hitching a lift on to Salardú, since the nearby meadows are a popular picnic ground.

For details of accommodation and food in Salardú (1268m), the 'capital' of the Naut Aran region, as well as the neighbouring village of Tredòs, see Places to Stay & Eat in the introduction to the Vall d'Aran walk which follows.

Vall d'Aran (Days 8 to 10 of the Pyrenean Traverse)

Duration 3 days
Distance 23.5km
Standard Medium
Start Refugi de Colomers
Finish Hospital de Vielha
Public Transport Finish only
Summary Walking from mountain lake to tarn, with stimulating side trips to Montardo d'Aran and the Estany de Mar. A choice of detours to the holiday villages of Salardú and Arties in the Vall d'Aran.

Naut Aran (Upper Aran), taking in the villages of Salardú, Tredòs and Arties, is the most stimulating area of the Vall d'Aran for walking. The villages have a good local bus service and are within easy access of a number of good walks. They also have a range of comfortable accommodation and good restaurants if you want to take a break before continuing westwards on the Pyrenean Traverse.

There are two alternative routes which you might consider taking, though these are not described in any detail here. The first, which arrives at the Refugio Ventosa i Calvell via the Port de Caldes, is a more popular alternative to Day 8 and is of a similar length and difficulty (3¾ to 4½ hours, 6.5km).

The second option bypasses the Refugio Ventosa i Calvell altogether and can save a day of walking time. It diverges from the first alternative at the Port de Caldes, cutting via the south side of Estany del Port de Caldes to the Port de Güellicrestada (also known as the Port d'Onlha Crestada) and joins the Day 9 route as it comes up from the Refugi Ventosa i Calvell. The whole walk takes 4¼ to 4¾ hours.

HISTORY

The lush Vall d'Aran is at the source of the Riu Garona which flows north into France to become the Garonne river, reaching the Atlantic Ocean at Bordeaux. The valley lies at the centre of Aran, a tiny region occupying only 620 sq km. Like Andorra, it was long an isolated realm and has an idiosyncratic history, relatively independent from the events which shaped the rest of Spain.

Until 1948 and the completion of the Túnel de Vielha linking Aran umbilically with Spain, the valley of the Riu Garona was the only year-round corridor to the outside world. Hence the unique language, Aranese, still spoken by many of the 6200 inhabitants; its nearest cousin is Gascon, a dialect of the old Romance language of southern France called Occitan.

Politically, the valley's rulers have leaned towards Spain, and especially Catalunya, of which Aran has been a part since the 14th century. Cultural influences, however, tend to be from the north. Nowadays many people are unconcernedly trilingual, speaking Aranese, Spanish and Catalan – often French as well.

Also like Andorra, traditional agricultural practices are now being overridden by tourism. One real disadvantage for walkers is that during the short summer season every village is a clamour of excavating, pile-driving, drilling and hammering.

NATURAL HISTORY

Aran is unusual in that its main valley runs east-west, contrary to the more usual north-south axes. Situated where the two major Pyrenean mountain chains briefly overlap, the valley falls to some extent under the influence of the distant Atlantic Ocean, enjoying a climate that's cooler and damper than any other area of the Catalan or Aragonese Pyrenees. The average daily temperature at the height of summer is a mild 17°C and the summer rains when they fall are brief, if intense.

PLANNING

Maps

The Editorial Alpina *Vall de Boí* map at 1:25,000 takes you as far as the Refugi de la Restanca, from where you'll need *Val d'Aran* at 1:40,000. The French Rando Éditions *Couserans* No 6 at 1:50,000 ends 4km west of La Restanca. Alternatively, the ICC maps *Parc Nacional d'Aigüestortes i Estany de Sant Maurici* at 1:25,000 and *Val d'Aran* at 1:50,000 cover the same region.

What to Bring

If continuing on from the previous section of the Pyrenean Traverse, you'll probably need to exit to Salardú or Arties to stock up on food since there are no shops until Benasque at the end of Day 12 on the La Ribagorça & into Aragón walk in the Aragonese Pyrenees section.

PLACES TO STAY & EAT

The walk begins at the Refugi de Colomers. If you're coming up from the Vall d'Aran, however, or if you're taking a break from the traverse, you may wish to spend the night in one of the villages of the Naut Aran: Salardú, Tredòs or Arties.

Refugi de Colomers

The *Refugi de Colomers* (☎ 973 25 30 08) has space for 40, does meals and has an area for self-caterers. The downside is that there's just one tap on the north wall and a squat toilet perched over the dam (no swimming!).

There's just enough space to pitch a tent on the lake's west bank, beyond an abandoned *refugio*. The refugio is free and will keep you dry, but that's all to be said in its favour; it's in a lamentable state.

Salardú

Bed and breakfast at the youth hostel, *Auberja Era Garona* (☎ 973 64 52 71, fax 973 64 41 36), with capacity for 190, is 2375 ptas. You need an International Youth Hostel Association (IYHA) card and it's advisable to reserve ahead. A dormitory bed is 1700 ptas at the CEC's *Xalet-Refugi Juli Soler Sanraló* (☎ 973 64 50 16) and 1925 ptas at *Refugi Rosta* (☎ 973 64 53 08, fax 973 64 58 14), where, for a 1000 ptas supplement, you can have a double room. Doubles at *Pensió Montanha* (☎ 973 64 41 08) start at 3200 ptas. The village has an ATM, grocery shop and supermarket, as well as a reasonable choice of restaurants.

Tredòs

Its three hotels are all hideously expensive. There are, however, a couple of *casas rurales* (rural houses or farmsteads with rooms to let): *Casa Eriva* (☎ 973 64 50 59) and *Casa Micalot* (☎ 973 64 53 26).

Arties

In Arties, *Pensió Montarto* (☎ 973 64 08 03) has singles/doubles for 3000/5000 ptas. *Erla Yerla d'Arties* (☎ 973 64 16 02) is the only camping ground in Naut Aran. At *Pollo Loco* you can get a half-chicken and chips for 900 ptas and at both *La Sal Gorda* and *Montagut* the menú del día costs 1700 ptas. For something special, try the *Parador* or the excellent *Biniaran*, where a meal for two with wine costs around 5500 ptas. There's a small tourist office (☎ 973 64 16 61), a supermarket and a well stocked delicatessen. When we visited, an ATM was due to be installed.

Hospital de Vielha

For information on food and accommodation at the Hospital de Vielha at the end of this walk, see Places to Stay & Eat in the introduction to the La Ribagorça & into Aragón walk in the Aragonese Pyrenees section.

GETTING TO/FROM THE WALK
Refugi de Colomers

For information on bus services to and from Vielha, see Getting There & Away in the introduction to the Catalan Pyrenees section.

From late June to mid-September, 10 buses a day (six on Sunday) connect Vielha with the villages of Naut Aran. Off the main valley road you're dependent on taxis. From Salardú take a taxi along the sealed road as far as the path leading to the Refugi de Colomers (described in the side trip following the Espot to Refugi de Colomers walk description), 1km away. For information on taxis, inquire at the Salardú tourist office or call the taxi service directly (☎ 973 64 01 95 or ☎ 908 03 97 38).

Alternatively, you can rejoin the Pyrenean Traverse at the beginning of Day 10 by passing through Arties, 2.2km west of Salardú along the main highway. Inquire at the small tourist office about the 4WD taxi which will take you as far as the Pont de Rius, roughly one hour from the Refugio de la Restanca.

Vielha

For information on transport between Barcelona and Vielha at the end of the walk, see Getting There & Away in the introduction to the Catalan Pyrenees. Buses in both directions pass through the Túnel de Vielha and stop on request at its southern exit, just below the Hospital de Vielha.

THE WALK (see map on page 186)
Day 8: Refugi de Colomers to Refugi Ventosa i Calvell via Port de Colomers

3¾ to 4¼ hours, 8km

Set out westward from the refugio following the GR11's red-and-white trail markers upstream along La Gargantera brook. After about seven minutes an aluminium pole marks a major junction where the GR11 trail divides into two branches. Disregard them both and instead bear left (south-west) to follow the red-and-yellow trail markers of a Sendero de Pequeño Recorrido (abbreviated to PR), one of a series of locally administered day walks – in this case devised and maintained by Josep Baques i Sole, warden at the Refugi de Colomers.

Cross the outlet of Estany Mort, (literally meaning 'dead pool'), seething with frogs despite its name. Where the red-and-yellow trail markers diverge, follow the red towards a multicoloured pole and continue southwards up the true right bank of a stream flowing from lake to lake. The path improves and cairns increase in number as you pass to the east of the Estany de Cabirdonats about an hour later. The number of tarns, some no bigger than puddles, multiply as you push on further into the grey moraine area at the base of the Circ de Colomers.

The trail becomes less evident as you skirt the first of a group of tarns scattered across the cirque and known collectively as the Estanyets del Port. The red markers trail away eastward, the cairns give out – or rather the base of the bowl is covered in natural cairns – and the path becomes increasingly difficult to discern as you continue heading straight.

At the unnamed lake shaped like a pulled tooth, bear south-west towards the **Port de Colomers** (2591m), distinctive against the skyline, which retains a white bib of snow until well into July. Keep heading resolutely up and south-west to reach the col 2¼ to 2½ hours into the day.

Once over the col, and after a little less than 15 minutes of steepish descent, the path crosses to and then veers away from the true left bank of a small stream. Descending by a well cairned trail, bypass the marshy flats of Tallada Llarga to reach the first of the **Estanyets de Colieto**.

The next stage of descent, hopping from lake to tarn down to the Refugi Ventosa i Calvell, is a highlight of the day's walk. Just before the brief ascent to the refugio, about 1½ to 1¾ hours from the pass, is a stretch of unavoidable boulder scrambling along the north shore of the tiny La Bassa tarn.

At 2222m, the **_Refugi Ventosa i Calvell_** (☎ 973 29 70 90) has sleeping space for 80, pay showers and serves meals. It is in refugio terms a four star option. This said, it can be crowded. The one-time water company refugio, perched 200m west, is now quite uninhabitable – nothing more than an ugly scar on the hillside.

Camping Wild in Vall d'Aran

The traverse re-enters the Parc Nacional d'Aigüestortes i Estany de Sant Maurici at the Port de Colomers – part of the area that was incorporated in the 1996 expansion of the park's boundaries. Camping within park limits is prohibited.

Side Trip: Refugi Ventosa i Calvell to Boí
3½ to 4 hours, 14km

You can interrupt or end the Pyrenean Traverse quite easily by following this entry and exit route popular among weekend walkers. A good path descends in 1½ hours from Refugi Ventosa i Calvell to the roadhead at the southern end of the Embassament de Cavallers dam (1725m). Follow the road for a further 4.5km to Caldes de Boí, a spa with luxury hotels. Boí village (1282m) is a further 5.5km south.

For accommodation and food in Boí, see Places to Stay & Eat in the Parc Nacional d'Aigüestortes i Estany de Sant Maurici section later in this chapter.

Day 9: Refugi Ventosa i Calvell to Refugi de la Restanca
2½ to 3¼ hours, 6km

This is a brief stage, allowing time for one of two strongly recommended side trips: the ascent of Montardo d'Aran or a visit to the magnificent Estany de Mar.

First make your way north past the lakes Xic, Travessani – where the path leaves the shore to climb above a large slab of granite on its south side – Clot, les Mangades and les Monges. The route, accurately marked on the Editorial Alpina map, is cairned.

Some 35 to 45 minutes into the day, after passing Estany Clot, look out for a junction

where the more lightly trodden trail to Refugi de la Restanca continues due north, splitting from the main trail which bears away north-east to the Port de Caldes. Follow the former to the refugio to the north.

As you approach the lip of Estany de les Mangades, cross the stream which drains from the lake (ignoring a red-striped pole) and head north-west towards **the Port de Güellicrestada** (2475) which must have one of the gentlest approaches to a pass in all the Catalan mountains.

At the pass, 1½ to 1¾ hours from the starting point, again pick up the red-and-white markers of the GR11. There's a sharp, 30 minute drop down a stony trail to the Estany deth Cap deth Port, passing a massive boulder field along the way. Once around the lake, follow the path beside the sluice. This drops very steeply to the **Estany de la Restanca** (2010m). The smart new *Refugi de la Restanca* (☎ 908 03 65 59) is at the near end of the dam, its older, raddled sister falling to pieces on the far side. Allow 1¼ to 1½ hours from pass to lake.

The wardens, Albert and Esther Betrán, who have been looking after walkers for more than 20 years, are very pleasant. With 80 places, the refugio does meals, snacks and drinks and accepts Visa.

The rocky area around the dam isn't conducive to camping, but it's possible to find a couple of handkerchiefs' worth of flat, stone-free ground for a *camp site*.

If you continue a further 45 minutes along the Day 10 route (described later in this walk) there's a delightful meadow ideal for camping where the track from the refugio meets the Camino deth Pont de Rius.

Alternative Camp Sites
In the Vall d'Aran the only commercial *camping ground* is in Arties (see the side trip from Refugi de la Restanca to Arties on the following page).

Side Trip: Port de Güellicrestada to Montardo d'Aran
2 to 2½ hours, 6.5km

The superb views from the summit of Montardo d'Aran (2830m) repay in full the effort expended to undertake this popular detour. About 300m before reaching the Port de Güellicrestada, break off to the right and head cross-country over the small plain to join a clear path which rises north-east quite gently before zigzagging more severely northwards. (Should you fail to find it, continue beyond the pass where you'll pick up the trail to the summit from the other side.)

After mounting a rocky couloir, the path reaches a relatively flat area leading to the base of a false summit (2781m). From here, cross a pronounced saddle and continue to the true **summit** (2830m), crowned by the yellow and red flag of Catalunya. Panoramas are superb. Allow two to 2½ hours for the return trip from the Port de Güellicrestada.

Side Trip: Refugi de la Restanca to Estany de Mar

1¾ to 2 hours, 6km

An ascent to the Estany de Mar takes a couple of hours. If you can spare an entire day, consider undertaking a popular loop walk around the lakes of Tort de Rius and Rius (at around 2350m) before returning to the refugio. Check conditions with the warden at the Refugi de la Restanca as snow can remain quite late into the season around the Collada de l'Estany de Mar.

From the refugio head south following signs marked 'Llac de Mar' past a group of old power company buildings and along the east shore of Estany de la Restanca. A good path, with one tight spot of boulder-clambering, scales the first bluff to a flat, grassy area, then zigzags up a second cliff and emerges after no more than an hour to a view over the Estany de Mar (2230m).

The forbidding Besiberri Nord peak to the south (3015m) provides a suitable backdrop to the expanse of water that merits the name 'Mar' (sea). Allow 90 minutes for the return trip. Having come this far, it's worth continuing a little further along the south-east bank of the lake on a vague, narrow trail marked by sporadic cairns.

To complete the full day circuit of the three lakes, continue along this trail as far as the Collada de l'Estany de Mar (2428m), then

descend to approach both the lakes of the Estany de Tort de Rius and the Estany de Rius from the south-east. Return to the Restanca refugio from the latter by following in reverse the first section of the Day 10 route described later in this walk. The complete loop will take a good six walking hours: an hour to the Estany de Mar, two to the Collada de l'Estany de Mar, another to skirt the two lakes, and another two hours to return to the refugio along the Barranc de Rius.

Side Trip: Refugi de la Restanca to Arties

2 to 2¼ hours, 9km

This is the second access route between the Pyrenean Traverse and the Naut Aran valley. The other route is the trail from the Refugi de Colomers to Salardú (see the side trip from Refugi de Colomers to Salardú at the end of the Espot to Refugi de Colomers walk earlier in this section). If you've been staying in refugios or camping wild for several days, you may welcome a break for rest and reprovisioning. Bear in mind that the next opportunity for stocking up is in Benasque, three days away.

From the Restanca lake, it's about 45 minutes of pleasant descent through pine trees to the pretty Riu de Valarties valley. The path meets a river at a place known as Pont de Rius (around 1700m) where, despite the name, there no longer seems to be a bridge. A further 35 to 45 minutes brings you to an informal parking area for walkers. At this point, you can either get a lift along the sealed road which runs from here to Arties (1144m) or continue on foot (allow 1½ hours at a brisk pace). For information on food and accommodation in Arties, see Places to Stay & Eat in the introduction to this walk.

Day 10: Refugi de la Restanca or Pont de Rius to Hospital de Vielha

4 to 4½ hours, 9.5km

This is a day for striding out. From the Refugi de la Restanca, the route ascends 400m to the Port de Rius. It involves a 600m climb if you begin at Pont de Rius in the Riu de Valarties valley. But the path is clear and the climb is on the whole fairly gradual.

If you've left the mountains to visit Arties and Naut Aran, rejoin the Pyrenean Traverse at Pont de Rius. Here, where the woodland trail which climbs to the Refugi de la Restanca takes off left, go straight ahead in defiance of a GR 'X' sign (no entry). Cross the river to pick up a well cairned, though in places overgrown, path running above the true left bank. You're walking the Camino deth Pont de Rius (Camino del Pont de Rius) which, until the construction of the Túnel de Vielha, was a well travelled access route to the upper Aran valley.

After about an hour and 250m of vertical ascent, you rejoin the GR11 about 2km west of the Refugi de la Restanca. Just below the junction of the two trails is a glorious meadow, ideal for a *camp site*.

El Túnel de Vielha

It took 22 years to complete the strategic road tunnel linking the Vall d'Aran with the rest of Spain. Until it opened, winter snows blocked all access to the pass from September to June, and the only way in or out was to head northwards into France.

The Vall d'Aran had been politically affiliated with Spain since the 14th century. The decision to begin construction of the tunnel in 1926 was an attempt to reinforce the valley's economic and cultural links with Spain and diminish the French influence. Plagued by accidents and financial difficulties, the boring proceeded in fits and starts. With the outbreak of the Spanish Civil War, work stopped completely. It resumed in 1941, with Republican prisoners used as forced labour. If you look around and above the tunnel entrance, you can still see traces of the bunkers used to protect the project from raids by Republican guerillas still at large.

It was finally opened in 1948 and at 5.3km it's the longest road tunnel in the Pyrenees.

If beginning the day from the Refugi de la Restanca, you have two choices. The more scenic alternative is to take in the Estany de Mar and the equally large Estany de Tort de Rius (see the side trip from Refugi de la Restanca to Estany de Mar at the end of Day 9 on this walk) and rejoin the main route at the eastern end of the Estany de Rius. This will add about two hours to what isn't a very arduous walking day.

The easier but less exciting alternative is to stick to the GR11 which crosses the dam to pass the old refugio and curl away northwestwards. Once over a hillock, the path drops steeply, parallel to the electricity pylons leading from the dam into the main valley, and joins the Camino deth Pont de Rius.

On the way up the Riu de Valarties valley from the refugio and Pont de Rius ignore all cobbled paths engineered by the power company, enticing you to go up and left; each leads to a dead end at various waterworks. One to 1¼ hours after the junction of the GR11 and the path from the Riu de Valarties valley, pass a gutted hydroelectric company shelter and a rubbish-strewn fuente beneath a small tower. Scarcely 10 minutes later, draw level with the outlet of the Estany de Rius.

From the Estany de Rius, it's well worth making a brief detour 10 minutes south-east to visit the much more appealing Estany Tort de Rius. There's many a tarn and pool ahead but these are the last substantial lakes you'll see for the next several days of the traverse.

It takes about 40 minutes to circumnavigate all the lake's arms and crannies and reach the Port de Rius (2315m). From this pass you can clearly see the road linking Pont de Suert and Vielha and beside it the large building which houses the University of Barcelona's high mountain research institute (Institut de Investigació de Alta Muntanya). For the next 45 minutes or so the trail drops sharply in switchbacks. As you descend into the Vall de Conangles, pines yield to beech and birch trees. The final 20 minutes are an easy stroll down a wide cart track, from which you take a clear path left to descend to the *Hospital de*

El Hospital

You don't have to be sick to spend the night in a *hospital*. Built at the base of important passes, their history goes back to medieval times, recalling the original meaning of the word: a place where hospitality is offered, a haven for rest and refuge. Often established and maintained by charitable foundations such as the Knights Templar, the Knights of St John of Jerusalem and the Orden (Order) de los Hospitalarios, they offered modest, safe lodging to foot travellers at a time when walking was more hazardous than it is today.

Some still serve as refugios for walkers. Two of them are overnight stops on the Pyrenean Traverse. The Hospital de Vielha was founded in 1192 at the base of an old *camino* which crosses over the Coll de Toro into the Vall d'Aran. The Hospital de Benasque sits beside a camino leading to the Portillón de Benasque, once a popular smugglers' route into France.

Vielha, also known as the *Refugi Sant Nicolau*, poised just above the southern entrance to the Túnel de Vielha. Modified over the centuries, its stone architecture is more distinctive than that of many alpine huts. In view of the difficult days to follow, you won't regret cosseting yourself for a night.

Parc Nacional d'Aigüestortes i Estany de Sant Maurici

This national park is one of only two in the Pyrenees (the other being the Parque Nacional de Ordesa y Monte Perdido, described later in this chapter) and of 10 in the whole of Spain. Despite its relatively small area (20km from east to west and a mere nine from north to south), it encompasses more than 50 lakes and tarns and includes some of the Pyrenees' most stunning scenery. The national park lies at the core of a wider wilderness area whose outer limit is known as the *zona periférica* and includes some magnificent high country to the north and south.

We describe three walks in the national park, all of which set out from the Estany de Sant Maurici, 8km west of Espot. These walks, however, far from exhaust the park's potential.

HISTORY

According to a well attested story (see the boxed text on the following page), it was by order of Generalissimo Franco himself that, in 1955, the area was declared a national park. The park was expanded in 1996 to incorporate an additional 3890 hectares, so that its total area including the buffer zone is now 40,850 hectares.

INFORMATION
Information Sources

If you intend to make Espot or even Boí the base for a walking holiday, call by the national park information office in Espot (☎ 973 62 40 36) or Boí (☎ 973 69 61 89) for more walk suggestions. Each is open from 9 am to 1.30 pm and from 3.30 to 6.45 pm daily.

The office in Espot runs an audiovisual introduction to the park at midday (Catalan), 5 pm (Spanish) and 6 pm (Catalan). Even if you don't speak a word of either, it's worth going along to enjoy the images, which will give you a general orientation and feel for the park.

PLANNING
Maps

Mapa de la Travessa dels Refugis del Parc Nacional d'Aigüestortes i Estany de Sant Maurici at 1:50,000 is more compact than its name. Excellent value at 500 ptas, it gives the lowdown on each of the park's 11 refugios. With principle trails marked, it serves as a more than satisfactory walking guide. However, since contour lines are at intervals

THE PYRENEES

The General's Will

In the early 1950s there was a flurry in the valleys when it was announced that no less a dignitary than General Franco himself would be paying a visit to inaugurate a couple of hydroelectric projects. For the first time in its long history, the track between the Estany de Sant Maurici and Aigüestortes was rolled and graded, while liberal quantities of whitewash were splashed around.

The cortège swept by. The General – a keen fly fisherman when cares of state allowed – was so impressed by the spectacle from the smart new road that he ordered the creation of the Parc Nacional d'Aigüestortes i Estany de Sant Maurici, which was duly inaugurated in 1955.

Once the dust from the cavalcade had settled, the road scarcely saw another vehicle. Eaten away by ice, sleet and rain, used again but briefly for equestrian outings, it was formally closed to all motorised traffic in 1995. Nowadays, there are still lingering traces of the General's route, but in a decade or two all evidence will be lost and nature will have reclaimed her own.

of 100m, we recommend that you use it in conjunction with another, more detailed map. If not available in the bookshops, you'll find it at either of the park information offices or at refugios.

Parc Nacional d'Aigüestortes i Estany de Sant Maurici, published by the ICC at 1:25,000, is the most reliable large-scale map. Editorial Alpina also produces a park map, *Parc Nacional d'Aigüestortes*, at 1:25,000. If following the Pyrenean Traverse, you'll need Editorial Alpina's *San Maurici* and *Vall de Boí*, both at 1:25,000, and can dispense with the general park map. The French Rando Éditions map *Couserans* No 6 at 1:50,000 gives complete and reliable coverage.

PLACES TO STAY & EAT

Espot

For food and accommodation in Espot, see Places to Stay & Eat in the introduction to the Espot to Refugi de Colomers walk in the Catalan Pyrenees section earlier in this chapter.

Estany de Sant Maurici

If you would rather avoid the trip to and from Espot, it's possible to stay at the very friendly *Refugi de Ernest Mallafré* (☎ 973 25 01 88) just above Estany de Sant Maurici. It has room for 24 but – amazingly for such a central and long established refugio – has no showers or washbasins, not even a 'giant's footstep' toilet. Consequently, the bushes within easy radius of the refugio are among the best fertilised in all the Pyrenees.

Boí

Boí has several *cases de pagès* (a Catalan name for casas rurales), or houses with rooms to let, including *Casa Guasch* (☎ 973 69 60 42), which charges 2000 ptas per person, and *Casa Cosan* (☎ 973 69 60 18), which asks 1700 ptas. Doubles at both *Pensió Pey* (☎ 973 69 60 36), which does *bocadillos* (long sandwiches) and has set menus for 1600 ptas, and *Hostal Fondevila* (☎ 973 69 60 11), cost 7000 ptas.

Capdella

If you journey to or leave the park via Capdella, your only choice of accommodation is *Casa Joan* (☎ 973 66 31 84). In central Capdella (near the electricity generating station), 1.8km below the village, is *Hostal Leo* (☎ 973 66 31 57), about which readers have reported very positively.

Refugios

There are no fewer than 11 refugios within the national park. You can pick up a good map (500 ptas) which gives details of each (see Maps in Planning earlier in this section). Most tend to be full by 3 pm in July and August and we strongly recommend that you ring in advance to reserve. The overnight fee varies from 1100 ptas to 1400 ptas and meals are around 1800 ptas. Most keep a wing open for walkers year-round but are only staffed between mid-June and mid-September.

Camping
Officially, camping within the boundaries of the park is not allowed.

GETTING TO/FROM THE WALKS
For information on the main bus services to and from Lleida, Pobla de Segur and the Vall d'Aneu, see Getting There & Away in the introduction to the Catalan Pyrenees section.

Espot
For information on transport to and from Espot, see Getting to/from the Walk in the introduction to the Espot to Refugi de Colomers walk in the Catalan Pyrenees section.

Estany de Sant Maurici
From Espot, you can undertake an agreeable walk (two hours, 8km) to the Estany de Sant Maurici (for a description, see the Espot to Refugi de Colomers walk in the Catalan Pyrenees section). However, the majority of walkers prefer to save their energy for the even more spectacular scenery within the park and invest 500 ptas in a 4WD taxi ride as far as the lake (last descent, 8 pm), which usually leaves when full. Those with transport can drive as far as the barrier and parking area at Prat de Pierró (1640m), an hour's pleasant walk from the lake along the route we describe.

Boí
For Boí, the bus (originating in Barcelona) which leaves Lleida at 9 am for Vielha, passes by Pont de Suert at 11 am. Here, it connects with a local bus which leaves at 11.15 am for Caldes de Boí. In the opposite direction, the bus departs from Caldes de Boí at 2 pm, connecting with the Lleida-bound return service at 2.30 pm.

Capdella
On weekdays during the school year, a bus departs from Pobla de Segur at 5.15 pm and returns from Capdella at 8 am. During the vacation, it runs only on Monday, Wednesday and Friday. Otherwise, you are dependent upon a taxi – ring Carles Moyes (☎ 973 66 30 02) in Capdella.

Estany Llong

Duration 5½ to 6 hours
Distance 17km
Standard Easy-Medium
Start/Finish Estany de Sant Maurici
Public Transport No
Summary A lake-to-lake traverse of the park along a classic route. Magnificent views continue from the intervening pass of Portarró d'Espot.

Crossing the park from east to west, this is a classic walk not only because of the spectacular scenery but also for its antiquity. In medieval times, the trail was a conduit for goods, people and animals travelling between the lands of the Count of Pallars in the east and those of the fiefdom of Erill to the west. In the first half of this century, it became a fashionable leisure route as visitors travelled on horseback between Espot and the small thermal spa of Caldes de Boí. Nowadays, it's closed to all motor traffic.

The walk begins from the Estany de Sant Maurici. Most walkers do this route as a return trip in a day. It's also possible to stay overnight at the Refugi d'Estany Llong (advance reservations essential) or continue via Aigüestortes to the small village of Boí, about 9km further along the trail.

PLANNING
Maps
For map references to this walk, see Maps under Planning in the introduction to this section.

THE WALK (see map on page 187)
From the Refugi de Ernest Mallafré follow the track around the south side of the Estany de Sant Maurici and through a wood. About

45 minutes from the start the track passes a turn-off on the right to the Mirador de l'Estany (where 'mirador' in Spanish means lookout) and then swings west, following and occasionally crossing the stream which tumbles down from the **Portarró d'Espot** pass (2425m).

It's worth pausing at the col to savour the views. To the west is the **Estany Llong** (2000m), 3.5km and about one hour's steep descent away. The route here, as throughout the walk, is easy to distinguish.

At the western end of the lake is the *Refugi d'Estany Llong* (☎ *973 69 61 89 or 929 37 46 52*), the only refugio run by the national park authority. With capacity for 36, reservations are essential. Serving meals, snacks and drinks, it also makes a pleasant rest stop before the return trip. If you still have energy, consider continuing for a further 1½ to two hours as far as the particularly fine scenery at Aigüestortes.

From Aigüestortes, you can pick up a Land Rover taxi which will take you as far as Boí, from where you can head out of the valley to Lleida by bus. (For details of accommodation in and transport to and from Boí, see Places to Stay & Eat and Getting to/from the Walks in the introduction to this section.)

Refugi de Colomina

Duration 2 days
Distance 22km
Standard Medium-Hard
Start Estany de Sant Maurici
Finish Espot
Public Transport Finish only
Summary Easy walking to Estany de Monastero. The gradient increases, culminating in a steep final clamber to the Coll de Peguera, then downhill all the way to the Refugi de Colomina. A return to the Riu Escrita valley via the Collada de Saburó.

We describe a two day walk starting from the Estany de Sant Maurici, graded medium-hard because of a very steep ascent

The War That Went On

It looks like the ruins of a fine, baroque chapel up there on the hillside above the Estany de Sant Maurici. In fact, until the 1960s it used to be a military barracks. Why, you may ask, in remote country not far from the frontier with a friendly neighbour and with no major population centre nearer than Lleida (several hours drive away) would anyone want to build barracks?

Their origins relate to the end of both the Spanish Civil War and WWII. In 1939, defeated Republicans and their families streamed across the passes into France, seeking refuge in exile. After 1945 Republicans returned and infiltrated the valleys along the frontier to mount a limited guerilla struggle, which was savagely suppressed by the victorious Nationalist army. For a brief time, the *guerrilleros* (guerillas) controlled the Vall d'Aran and large areas of what is now the national park.

The barracks were constructed to drive out the Republican bands and cow the valleys' residents lest they be tempted to give support to the distant, lost Republican cause.

to the Coll de Peguera, with an overnight stop at the Refugi de Colomina.

A return trip of about 2½ hours as far as the Estany de Monestero makes an easy, scenic option. Alternatively, you can stretch yourself a little more, add on another 1½ hours to the day's total time and continue to the cirque at the head of the Riu de Monestero valley before turning back.

PLANNING
Maps

For map references to this walk, see Maps under Planning in the introduction to this section.

THE WALK (see map on page 187)
Day 1: Estany de Sant Maurici to Refugi de Colomina
5½ to 6 hours, 10km

From the Refugi de Ernest Mallafré take the path southwards to follow the Riu de Monestero. Beyond a boulder field about an hour out you pass a tiny pool to reach the **Estany de Monestero** (2170m).

Climbing gently along the true left bank of a stream which flows into the Estany de Monestero, thread your way through another jumble of truly huge boulders (the massive square one marks an end to the scrambling), eventually crossing the stream to the true right bank.

Once you reach the cirque at the head of the valley the path climbs abruptly south-south-east. Stick to the east side of the bowl where the walking is easiest. Over the lip of a false col, reached after two to 2¼ hours, descend into a large, arid basin. Here begins the much steeper ascent to the **Coll de Peguera** (2726m) between Pic de Peguera (2982m), the highest summit in the park, and Pic de Mar (2803m) to its west.

From the col, follow a sign to the Refugi de Colomina and walk southwards to the **Estany de Saburó**. Ignore the dotted path along the lake's western bank marked on the Editorial Alpina map – it's sheer and impassable – and instead pass close to the eastern shore of the Estany Xic de Saburó.

Passing by the west shores of the Estany de Mar and Estany de Colomina (2408m) you reach the *Refugi de Colomina* (☎ 973 25 20 00) after less than an hour's walking from the Estany Xic de Saburó. The attractive wooden refugio has 40 places and serves meals and drinks. If you prefer camping, descend to Estany Tort, a short distance to the west, where there are plenty of *camp site* possibilities.

An alternative to continuing on to Espot is to exit via Capdella and Vall Fosca. Pick your day carefully, however, as transport options from Capdella are limited (for more details of accommodation in and transport to and from Capdella, see Getting to/from the Walks in the introduction to this section).

Day 2: Refugi de Colomina to Espot
5 to 5½ hours, 12km

After overnighting at the refugio you can either retrace your steps over the Coll de Peguera or vary the return journey by crossing back into the main valley via the Collada de Saburó.

The latter route is a variant of the GR11 and is well marked with the familiar red-and-white trail markers. Head north-east from the refugio to follow the west bank of both the Estany de Colomina and Estany de Mar. After ascending a steep, barren gully, pass a ruined building and descend to the dam head of the Estany de Saburó; cross over. Curl around the lake and climb to the **Collada de Saburó** (2670m) at the border of the national park.

Where the path divides, take the right fork. Leaving three small lakes to your left, drop to the Estany Negre. Once across the dam head, take a path which leads off north. From it, a short detour leads left to the *Refugi Josep Blanc* (☎ 973 25 01 08), with capacity for 40 and normally full to the gunnels. Here you can get a drink or snack.

Continue until you reach another small lake and a forest refugio (not open to the public), from where the path descends in parallel with the Riu de Peguera to emerge on the sealed road on the outskirts of Espot.

Port de Ratera d'Espot

Duration 4½ to 5 hours
Distance 14.5km
Standard Medium
Start/Finish Estany de Sant Maurici
Public Transport No
Summary Superb views as you leave the crowds behind, taking in Estany de Ratera, the lake and refugio of Estany Gran d'Amitges and the Port de Ratera de Colomers. A return via the Mirador de l'Estany.

This circuit of medium difficulty starts from the Refugi de Ernest Mallafré at the Estany de Sant Maurici and follows the early part of Day 7 of the Pyrenean Traverse (see the Espot to Refugi de Colomers walk in the Catalan Pyrenees section), diverging to take in the three Estanys d'Amitges on the outbound leg and the Mirador de l'Estany on the way back.

PLANNING

For map references to this walk, see Maps under Planning in the introduction to this section.

THE WALK (see map on page 187)

Follow the Day 7 route from the Estany de Sant Maurici as far as the instruction to 'take the right fork towards Refugi d'Amitges', a little beyond the **Estany de Ratera**. Here, if you fancy nothing more taxing than an easy 2½ hour stroll, you can turn left to pass by the Mirador de l'Estany and return by the south bank of the Estany de Sant Maurici. Otherwise, where the Day 7 route turns left after 100m, continue straight along the main track in the direction of the refugio. Now climbing more steeply, the track nudges out of a pine forest to enter a wild, rocky world with only an occasional copse of trees. Stay with the 4WD track all the way to the **Estany Gran d'Amitges**, the largest of a series of three tarns, behind which rise the spiky Agulles d'Amitges, the twin Pics de Bassiero and the Tuc de Saboredo.

No more than 212m of vertical distance separate the shores of lakes Ratera and Amitges, but the contrast between the former's pine-clad charm and the latter's harsh, denuded splendour is total.

The *refugio* (☎ 973 25 01 09) beside the Estany Gran d'Amitges (2362m), reached after about 1½ hours from the start, is another popular overnight spot. It does meals, snacks and drinks and makes a congenial rest stop. A trail leads from it between the two upper lakes and across scree (here lies the only difficulty in what would otherwise be an easy walk). Continue up to the **Port de Ratera d'Espot**, which you reach after a little less than another hour. At this point the trail rejoins Day 7 of the Pyrenean Traverse. It's worth following it for another

10 minutes or so along the saddle as far as the **Port de Ratera de Colomers**, from where there are great views of the necklace of lakes falling away to the south-west.

Back at Port de Ratera d'Espot, take the Day 7 route in reverse around the Estanyet del Port de Ratera and follow it until it rejoins the main track. You've now come full circle. One hundred metres beyond, where the paths meet turn right to the **Mirador de l'Estany** with its unrivalled vistas of the mountains reflected in Estany de Sant Maurici. Continuing, you soon reach the trans-park route which links Estany Llong with Sant Maurici. Turn left along it and return by the south bank of the Estany de Sant Maurici to your point of departure.

THE ARAGONESE PYRENEES

With the transition from Catalunya to Aragón on crossing the Coll de Mulleres, you enter the land of the giants. Of the 12 tallest peaks in peninsular Spain, 10 rear up from Aragón. Three of these mountains – the Pico de Aneto, Posets and the Pico de Monte Perdido – are within easy reach of the Pyrenean Traverse. The climb to Monte Perdido (335m) is described in the side trip at the end of Day 19B on the Parque Nacional de Ordesa y Monte Perdido walk later in this section.

If peak bagging and glacial heights leave you cold, there are also plenty of gentle valley walks to enjoy. This is tough country, however, with challenging passes between each valley and the probability of snow underfoot late into summer.

The rock around you subtly changes as you progress towards the setting sun. As you climb steeply out of the upper Noguera Ribagorçana valley, you'll be scrabbling over shale and slate. Further west, the original granite bedrock pokes through more frequently, especially around the Maladeta and Posets region. In some areas, such as the Parque Nacional de Ordesa y Monte Perdido, bedrock is overlaid or cut through by limestone, with its characteristic underground rivers, potholes and caves.

But nothing is regular or ordered. The clash of the European and Iberian tectonic plates and later upheavals on a scale difficult to grasp have left the land folded, crumpled and profoundly askew.

Both east and west of Benasque the route passes through the Parque Posets-Maladeta. Established in 1994, the 33,267 hectare park contains 13 glaciers, the Pyrenees' highest peak (Pico d'Aneto) – and about 2000 varieties of flora.

INFORMATION
Books
Fourteen signed walks for the Benasque region, ranging from 30 minutes to four or five hours, are summarised in the free leaflet *El Placer de Caminar* (The Pleasure of Walking), available from the tourist office. These same walks are described in detail in the excellent *Senderos de Pequeño Recorrido: Valle de Benasque* (1500 ptas), published by PRAMES, with accompanying maps at 1:25,000. Even if you don't read Spanish, the maps alone are sufficient to guide you.

Information Sources
The visitors centre at the Parque Nacional de Ordesa y Monte Perdido (see the Parque Nacional De Ordesa y Monte Perdido walk later in this section) has interactive displays on flora and fauna of the park and also sells books and trail maps. It is open daily from 9 am to 1 pm and 3.30 to 7 pm (shorter hours in winter).

The Parque Posets-Maladeta visitors centre, 1km from Benasque just off the road to Anciles, has display panels and a good video about the park. Summer hours are 10 am to 2 pm and 4 to 8 pm.

In Benasque, Els Ibons sells a range of walking books and maps, while Rodolfoto bookshop also has a good supply of maps.

ACCOMMODATION & SUPPLIES
Benasque is the only town within easy reach of the Aragonese Pyrenees which has a selection of sports and mountaineering

Camping Wild in Aragón

As everywhere in the Pyrenees, camping is normally forbidden in national parks and designated conservation areas such as the Parque Posets-Maladeta.

Outside these areas, regulation 79/1990 of 8 May 1990 decrees that above 1500m you can camp anywhere that's more than two hours walk from a vehicle access point. Below 1500m, you have the right to pitch your tent anywhere more than 5km from a designated camping ground and 1km from an urban centre. It's forbidden to camp within 100m of a river or road. If anyone should challenge you, just quote *decreto 79/1990 del ocho de mayo* back at them!

equipment shops. Deportes Aigualluts is well stocked, while Barrabés Ski Montaña has two megashops on the Avenida de Francia. (The Compañía de Guías de la Valle de Benasque, the local guides association, is based on the 2nd floor of one of them.) Vit's shop in the Plaza Mayor hires out crampons and ice axes.

GETTING THERE & AWAY
The major transport hubs of the Aragonese Pyrenees are Barbastro, Sabiñánigo and Jaca. Though of little intrinsic importance in themselves for walkers, they're linked by numerous bus services (and trains from Sabiñánigo and Jaca) to destinations beyond the Pyrenees. For information on getting between Barbastro and Sabiñánigo and different stages of the Aragonese section of the Pyrenean Traverse, see Getting to/from the Walk in the introduction to each walk.

Barbastro
Barbastro is 53km east of Huesca and 69km north of Lleida on the N240 road. There are four return trips a day to Barbastro from Barcelona, four a day from Lleida and up to seven from Huesca. There are also six services a day to and from Monzón, where you link in with the train system.

THE PYRENEES

Sabiñánigo & Jaca

Sabiñánigo, 54km to the north of Huesca and 12km east of Jaca on the N330 road, is another key access point to the Aragonese Pyrenees.

There are four return bus services a day to Sabiñánigo from both Huesca and Jaca. There are also three trains a day to Sabiñánigo and Jaca from Zaragoza (Saragossa), leaving at 7.15 am, 3.20 and 6.30 pm. In the opposite direction, trains leave Jaca at 7.36 am, 2 and 6 pm, calling by Sabiñánigo 20 to 30 minutes later. Change at Tardienta or Zaragoza for Barcelona (for Barcelona train times and connections, ring RENFE in Barcelona on ☎ 93 490 02 02). For current information on both buses and trains, ring the tourist office in Sabiñánigo (☎ 974 48 00 05).

La Ribagorça & into Aragón (Days 11 & 12 of the Pyrenean Traverse)

Duration 1½ or 2 days
Distance 13 or 36km
Standard Medium or Hard
Start Hospital de Vielha
Finish La Besurta or Benasque
Public Transport Yes
Summary Three alternative walks, each demanding in its own way and every one taking a different pass over the mountain barrier between Catalunya and Aragón.

La Ribagorça is a wild, sparsely populated area of the Pyrenees with a mere 12,000 inhabitants scattered over 2400 sq km. It includes the catchment areas of the rivers Isábena, Noguera Ribagorçana and Ésera. The Pyrenean Traverse follows the Ésera and its tributaries, Estós and Eriste, around the Posets massif.

For most of its length the Noguera Ribagorçana river delineates the frontier between Catalunya and Aragón. On the Aragonese (west) side of the river is an area known as La Franja (The Margin) where historically, linguistically and commercially Catalan influence is strong. In this transition zone you may still hear Catalan spoken and many of the natural features have Catalan names.

This is the only leg on the entire Pyrenean Traverse where we offer you three choices at three distinct levels of difficulty. Whichever you select, to undertake it comfortably allow from 1½ to two days to get to Benasque.

Options A (Days 11A & 12A) and B (Days 11B & 12B) stay north of the Glaciar de la Maladeta glacier and Pico de Aneto, while option C (Days 11C & 12C) mostly follows the less demanding GR11 which curls around the mountain's southern flank. Due to the variation in difficulty – both from one walk to another and within each walk – we suggest that you read all three walk descriptions before deciding which to take.

If you haven't got a tent and don't fancy sleeping under the stars, you'll need to take the GR11 option (C) which has three, very basic, shelters en route. The other possibility with option A is to sleep at the Refugio de Mulleres on the first day and continue to La Besurta at the end of the next day.

Maps

Best is the excellent PRAMES map *Ribagorza: Mapa Excursionista* at 1:40,000, even though it's stingy in naming natural features. Editorial Alpina's *Val d'Aran* at 1:40,000 leads onto the Editorial Alpina *Maladeta-Aneto* map at 1:25,000. The two give complete coverage if you're traversing either the Coll de Salenques or the Coll de Mulleres (see options A and B, respectively). If you intend to follow the GR11 alternative (option C), you'll also need the Editorial Alpina *La Ribagorça* map at 1:25,000, which covers the area from the Rius lakes (see Day 10, on the Vall d'Aran walk in the Catalan Pyrenees section), both of the above passes and the GR11 route via the Collada de Ballibierna.

What to Bring

If you cross by way of the Coll de Mulleres or Coll de Salenques (Sallencas), you'll need a tent. Also consider packing walking poles or crampons and ice axe in case snow remains on the ground (quite likely).

Warning

It's prudent to ask at the Hospital de Vielha about snow conditions around the Coll de Mulleres or Salenques. As always, it's more abundant on western slopes.

PLACES TO STAY & EAT
Vielha

Hospital de Vielha (☎/fax 973 69 70 52), also known as Refugi Sant Nicolau, is run by the *ajuntament* (local authority) of Vielha. It's as much modest hotel as refugio, offering a welcome touch of luxury. It has space for 50 (it even has six double rooms) and the price (1300 ptas per night, the same for a meal) is no more expensive than elsewhere. It also has a genuine bar which gives it the atmosphere of a Spanish roadside inn.

Twenty minutes south along the highway is a large picnic spot and unofficial *camp site*, set back from the road and the Institut de Investigació de Alta Muntanya beside a wrecked Instituto Nacional para la Conservación de la Naturaleza (ICONA) chalet. You may well find it rubbish-strewn.

Alternatively, there's a *camp site* 45 minutes beyond the Hospital de Vielha on the route to the Coll de Mulleres (see option A).

La Besurta & Benasque

For information on accommodation and food in La Besurta and Benasque at the end of this walk, see Places to Stay & Eat in the introduction to the Posets Massif walk later in this section.

GETTING TO/FROM THE WALK
Vielha

For information on transport between Barcelona and Vielha, see Getting There & Away in the introduction to the Catalan Pyrenees section. Buses in both directions pass through the Túnel de Vielha and stop on request at its southern exit, just below the Hospital de Vielha.

La Besurta & Benasque

For information on transport to and from La Besurta at the end of options A and B, and Benasque at the end of option C, see Getting to/from the Walk in the introduction to the Posets Massif walk later in this section.

THE WALK (see maps on pages 184-6)
Days 11A & 12A: Hospital de Vielha to La Besurta via the Coll de Mulleres

8½ to 10½ hours, 13km

If you're in good shape, it's possible to reach La Besurta and the shuttle bus service to the Hospital de Benasque in one long day from the Hospital de Vielha. It is better, however, to camp en route and take this tough walk at a less demanding pace.

This is the most challenging but also one of the most satisfying stages of the whole traverse. Over the course of two days the trails rises and falls a total of 2400m and includes 1300m of ascent. But the rewards match the considerable effort invested, and while it would be unwise to attempt the pass alone, this is nothing to shy away from. We rate this route as hard because of the difficulty in following the trail during the last 45 minutes to the Coll de Mulleres and because the last 10m to the col are steep enough to require a four-limbed clamber.

The route as far as the Estanyets de Mulleres is uncomplicated and well marked. From the Hospital de Vielha (1630m) pick your way over the rubble above the mouth of the road tunnel to join a clear cart track, which you leave after about 15 minutes to take a path to the left through a beech wood beside the stream's true left bank. Fifteen minutes later, pass the magnificent **Cascada de Mulleres** waterfall; soon afterwards there's a small, grassy flood plain which makes an ideal *camp site*.

THE PYRENEES

About two hours from the starting point the path clambers up the wall of a cirque. An hour later a fading arrow on a granite boulder above the first lake passed indicates the turn-off to the *Refugio de Mulleres* (2360m) – a bright orange, 12 person, unstaffed refugio, only five minutes away. The patch of grass just beside the refugio and the shores of the first two of the four tarns you encounter are all possible *camp sites* – the last until you're well over the col.

From the turn-off to the refugio it's two to 2½ hours to the Coll de Mulleres (2928m), the highest pass on the Pyrenean Traverse. The path is entirely over rock and loose scree, with some snow cover. Beyond the lakes, the track becomes more spindly and you're more reliant upon cairns and the occasional very discreet vermilion trail marker.

The **Coll de Mulleres** isn't easy to distinguish against the skyline. Just below the serrated rocks which mark the pass, however, lock into the tracks made other walkers and head west across a narrow snowfield. The last 10m are a true climb – especially hard if you're lugging a backpack.

The quite stupendous views of the Pico de Aneto and the Glaciar de la Maladeta to the west, the upper slopes of the Valleta de la Escaleta before you and the peaks on the border parting Aragón from Catalunya to your right justify every bead of sweat expended. If you still have energy you can leave your backpack on the ridge and make a 30 minute return trip detour south to bag the Pic (Tuc) de Mulleres at 3010m.

Many walkers make a short crest traverse north towards Coll Alfred, from where they make their way down to the highest tarn of the Valleta de la Escaleta. Alternatively, you can just head straight down the snow-covered **Glaciar de Mulleres** to the tarn, 35 to 45 minutes away. There's just enough flat space here for a *camp site*, but camping options increase in quantity and quality as you descend the Valleta de la Escaleta.

Skirt around the lake to its right. Once the glacier and snow give out, stride for a time over huge, smooth slabs of mottled granite. Shortly before drawing level with the

evident Collado dels Aranesos (2455m), which leads back into Catalunya, pass a small tarn on its left (west) side – not as Editorial Alpina indicates – then switch to the true right bank of the stream flowing from it. Beyond the tarn, the gradient becomes gentler and there's even a hint of path again.

After passing over a rocky bluff above the west bank of a larger tarn (again contradicting the Editorial Alpina map), you emerge into meadows just below the Collado del Toro, clearly visible to the east (for a detour to Collado de Toro, see the side trip at the end of this day's walk description). Interlaced with streams, this spot makes for paradise *camping*. In a little less than an hour of easy walking (look for caves in the hillside, rated highly by speleologists), you emerge into the wide **Plan de Aiguallut**. Here, where the alternative route via the Coll de Salenques (see option B) rejoins the trail, the stream from the Valleta de la Escaleta and the Río de los Barrancos merge to meander across the plain.

A green, metal ICONA shelter – even the huts are green around here – with space for eight perches above the downstream end of the meadow. Just below is the Cascada de Aiguallut down which the river hurtles before disappearing into the cave called the **Forau de Aiguallut** (where 'forau' in the local dialect means cave or pothole).

The Forau de Aiguallut

The Forau is a cauldron into which swirl all the waters flowing from the surrounding mountains – from the Glaciar de Mulleres to the Maladeta massif. Once underground, the run-off forms a subterranean river on a bed of limestone. It loses some 600m in height over only 4km before re-emerging at Artiga de Lin in the Vall d'Aran. From here the river joins the Riu Garona, called La Garonne once it crosses the French border, and flows out into the Atlantic Ocean near Bordeaux.

At La Besurta, about 30 minutes walk from the Plan de Aiguallut, there's a *kiosko*, a small stall serving beer and soft drinks, bocadillos (400 ptas to 500 ptas) and platos combinados (850 ptas) – a gastronomic delight after a few days on the trail.

It's possible to walk on from here to Benasque via the Hospital de Benasque, for the most part off-road. Most walkers, however, prefer to take the shuttle bus down the hill (for transport details, see Getting to/from the Walk in the introduction to this walk).

Side Trip: Refugio de la Renclusa
1 to 1½ hours, 3km
From La Besurta, the Refugio de la Renclusa is an undemanding walk up the eastern flank of the Barranco de la Renclusa. Just beyond it is another impressive forau, next to which a small chapel has been built. The *Refugio de la Renclusa* (☎ 974 55 14 90), with capacity for 110, is staffed from early June to the end of September and keeps a wing open year-round. It does meals, drinks and snacks. It's a very popular base camp for climbers and for those planning an ascent of the Pico de Aneto. As it's also near to vehicle access, where whole coachloads of walkers are decanted, advance booking is essential.

If heading to the refugio from the Plan de Aiguallut, you can avoid the descent to La Besurta (then having to regain height along the Barranco de la Renclusa). Instead, take a faint trail leading initially westwards from near the green metal ICONA shelter. The first part of the ascent to the Coll de la Renclusa (2270m) is steep. Navigation is not always easy but the trail is well cairned in the latter stages. Allow an hour or a little more from the Plan de Aiguallut.

Side Trip: Collado del Toro
30 to 40 minutes, 1km
Leave your backpack behind a boulder in the meadows below the Collado del Toro and take an easy side trail to this minor pass (2235m). Just beyond it, back in Catalunya, is the pretty Estany del Collado de Toro, shaped like a figure of eight. If you want to continue for a further 20 minutes, you can

Parque Posets-Maladeta

The park was declared a protected area in 1994. It covers 33,267 hectares and encompasses the two highest massifs in the Pyrenees and 13 of the range's major glaciers. Nearly all the park lies above 1800m, including the Pico de Aneto (3404m), the highest mountain in the Pyrenees.

It owes its shape, like so many other areas of the chain, to the Ice Ages which created the characteristic U-shaped valleys, giant cirques at their head, hanging valleys high on their flanks and scooped depressions, today filled by over 100 *ibóns*, or mountain tarns.

Two consequences of the region's upgrade to park status are that vehicle access is now restricted and wild camping is not allowed. Having said this, you may still encounter walkers who discreetly pitch their tents at dusk and pack up their camp site in the early morning.

skirt the lake along its north-west shore, following cairns but no path to a possible *camp site* overlooking the Vall d'Aran watershed.

Days 11B & 12B: Hospital de Vielha to La Besurta via the Coll de Salenques
10 to 12 hours, 18km
Navigation on this alternative route is not difficult. Rather, it merits its medium-hard grade for the sheer grind of traversing extensive fields of rocks and boulders on both sides of the Coll de Salenques. For the first 6.5km the walk follows the GR11 route.

From the Hospital de Vielha, follow the main N230 road south for 200m before taking a left turn onto a path and descending for 25 minutes through fir trees to a dilapidated ICONA shelter. About 15 minutes later, veer briefly east to negotiate the Barranco de Besiberri. Crossing to the true right bank of the Noguera Ribagorçana, pass a run-down forest rest house overlooking the Embalse de Basserca (Senet). Here, where the path briefly joins the main road, a GR11 sign points down the road to your destination, 'Vall de Salenques'. Cross a metal footbridge where the Río de Salenques enters the huge dam.

On the other side of the footbridge, turn onto a trail along the true right bank of the river. The path steadily worsens until, 45 minutes from the bridge, it widens slightly into a flattish patch of terrain at the confluence of the Barranc de Salenques and the river flowing down the Valle de Anglos. Leave the GR11 route which continues up the Valle de Anglos and cross the Barranc de Salenques to mount a steep path along its true left bank.

At this point, you may need to hunt for the sporadically cairned trail through a nasty mixture of boulders and undergrowth. The going's rough and involves some treacherous boulder hopping. Finally, more than three hours above the river ford, the trail reaches the brow of a hill and several high meadows with good *camp sites*. If you want to push on, there are a few more potential *camp sites* nearer to the Coll de Salenques.

Continue along the river, now on a manageable gradient and surface, for two hours until the valley narrows and you reach the base of a grassy slope beyond a waterfall. Count on another 90 minutes to two hours from here to the **Coll de Salenques** (2810m), depending on the amount of snow cover. Up top, there's a small shelter – nothing more than a low wall of stones.

Descend from the col over virtually permanent snowfields, then climb slightly to the **Colladeta de Barrancs** (2480m). Pick up the cairns again as you descend, well above the west shore of the Lago de los Barrancos, to the edge of a basin filled with glacial debris. It's also possible to *camp* north of the Lago de los Barrancos, though unless the light's failing or you're exhausted you'll probably prefer to push on to the five star turf of the Plan de Aiguallut. Don't rely on the Editorial Alpina map at this stage as it places much of the 45 minute drop to the Río de los Barrancos too far to the west.

Using the cairns as a guide, descend from the basin to the river. Cross it and follow the steadily improving path on the east (true right) bank for a final 45 minutes down to the **Plan de Aiguallut**. To continue from here to La Besurta, see the last part of the option A walk description.

Days 11C & 12C: Hospital de Vielha to Benasque via the Collada de Ballibierna
12 to 13 hours, 36km

The route follows for the most part the GR11 which, unlike the other two variants, passes to the south of the Maladeta massif. With its familiar red-and-white trail markers, it's the simplest and least demanding route to follow.

Leaving Hospital de Vielha, follow the Day 11B route until it crosses the river to head away north-west up the Barranc de Salenques. Instead, continue west up the Vall d'Anglos.

The overgrown path ascends steeply to the first of the three Estanys d'Anglíos lakes, contouring around it to the south. Just after the small *refugio* (with room for four) at the south-west corner of the lake, the main GR11 route bears away south-west. A better option, however, is to sneak between the second and third tarns, then up a grassy bank to follow the small Riu Güeno upstream. After about 1½ hours and an altitude gain of 300m, cross the Colladeta de Riu Güeno (2325m). Wind your way around the western shore of the **Ibón Cap de Llauset** (where 'ibón' in Aragonese means lake) and follow the true right bank of its outflow stream to rejoin the main GR11 route.

From the junction, it's a further 300m of ascent over granite boulders to the **Collada de Ballibierna** (Vallibierna or even Vallhiverna – Editorial Alpina manages all three!), with the possibility of snowfields on either side of the pass. Drop westwards to the grassy south-east shore of the upper of the two Ibons de Ballibierna. Continue up and over a steep rise, then down a series of giant natural steps to the north shore of the lower lake, reached one to 1¼ hours after leaving the col.

Follow the stream which emerges from the lake down to the meadows of **Pleta de Llosás** (2200m) – a pleasant place to rest or *camp* overnight. Thirty minutes later you reach the Puente de Coronas bridge over a tributary of the Barranco de Ballibierna coming in from the north. Near here (and about 8 hours walking from the Hospital de Vielha) is a fisherfolk's refugio with room for 14. The area around the hut has some inviting *camp sites*.

From this point, it's an easy stroll down the forested path along the true right bank of the Barranco de Ballibierna. The path heads north to the municipal *camping ground* at Plan de Senarta and then swings back to follow the east shore of the Embalse de Paso Nuevo reservoir. It finally joins the main road beside the Puente de San Jaime bridge, 3.75km north of Benasque. Turn left and continue along the sealed road down to Benasque, mercifully less than an hour away.

The Frontier Ridge

Duration 3½ hours
Distance 9km
Standard Easy-Medium
Start/Finish La Besurta
Public Transport Yes
Summary An ascent to the Portillón de Benasque by an ancient camino, an easy traverse along the base of Pico de la Mina and a descent to La Besurta via the western of the two Lagos de Villamorta.

You can make this a 'modular' day. To the basic walk of around 3½ hours it's possible to graft on two worthwhile side trips; these are detailed at the end of this walk description.

PLANNING
Maps

PRAMES *Ribagorza* map at 1:40,000 and Editorial Alpina's *Maladeta-Aneto* map at 1:25,000 both cover the area.

What to Bring

Be sure to leave with your water containers full as once you're above the Ésera valley there's no fresh water on the south-facing slopes of the ridge.

PLACES TO STAY & EAT

For food and accommodation at La Besurta and Benasque, see Places to Stay & Eat in the introduction to the Posets Massif walk later in this section.

GETTING TO/FROM THE WALK

For information on transport to and from La Besurta, see Getting to/from the Walk in the introduction to the Posets Massif walk later in this section.

THE WALK (see map on page 185)

From the bus stop some 300m below La Besurta on the road to Benasque, head northwards up the hill along a faint trail. After about 15 minutes a better defined track comes in from the left. This is the old and, in its time, much travelled historical link between the Ésera valley and that of Aran. These days, it's a *ruta hípica*, or pony trekking trail (signalled by red-tipped posts), which leads to the Port de la Picada and beyond.

Continue up the trail in a series of fairly gentle zigzags for 40 to 50 minutes until you arrive at a junction indicated by a pair of ruta hípica signs. Don't be seduced into following them and taking the path which heads north-east straight towards the Port de la Picada. Instead, continue zigzagging towards the **Portillón de Benasque** (2444m), now clearly in view and sitting snugly between the twin masses of Tuc de Salvaguarda (2738m) and Pico de la Mina (2707m). After skirting a reedy tarn, you should reach the pass about 1½ hours after setting out.

Surprisingly, there's little to see beyond the windy gap (for more spectacular views, see the two side trips at the end of this walk description). You can, however, clearly see the path threading eastwards from some ruined huts at the base of the Portillón de Benasque. Bizarrely marked '23' (it's part of a French trail which sneaks over the border), it heads in a dead straight line over bare rock and scree to the **Port de la Picada** (2470m), your next 'Port of call', where you stand a good chance of seeing eagles wheeling overhead.

If you're in the mood for a longer walk, 20 minutes down a well established trail from the Port de la Picada brings you to the Collado del Infierno, virtually on the frontier and just past the *clots* (ponds) of Infern.

Turning back towards home from Port de la Picada, bear left (down and south) almost immediately onto the timeworn trail which you briefly followed at the outset of the day, passing to the east of a small tarn. After 20 to 25 minutes you'll be back at this morning's junction at the top of the switchbacks. As you retrace your steps, look out for the lower (nearer) of the two Lagos de Villamorta. Fifteen minutes from the junction, turn left (south-east) beside a medium-sized cairn onto a secondary trail. After passing a stony section with stunted pine trees – and rhododendrons, juniper and heather underfoot – skirt the lower Villamorta pond on its south side. Beyond it the path is virtually invisible, but keep due south and within 10 minutes you should meet the stone 'stairs' on the main track linking the Plan d'Aigüallut and La Besurta, which you reach after a little less than an hour from the junction.

Side Trip: Portillón de Benasque to Tuc de Salvaguarda
1½ hours, 3km

For spectacular views in all directions, take the well made side trail from the Portillón de Benasque to the summit of Tuc de Salvaguarda (2738m) to the west. It's much less daunting than a first glance at the razor-edged ridge might suggest.

Side Trip: Portillón de Benasque to Refugio de Benasque
1¼ to 1½ hours, 2.5km

Less strenuously, it's worth continuing beyond the Portillón de Benasque to head down into France for a drink or a snack at

the small, staffed *Refugio de Benasque* (2249m) run by the Club Alpin Français. It's in a glorious setting at the north-east tip of the first of three lakes called the Boums du Port. It does, however, take substantially longer to reach than the 15 minutes claimed by a sign at the col.

Lago de Cregüeña

Duration 5 to 5½ hours
Distance 11km
Standard Medium
Start/Finish Puente de Cregüeña
Public Transport Yes
Summary As the route ascends, woodland briefly becomes plain before the steep climb resumes towards to the stark, rocky bowl in which the Lago de Cregüeña nestles.

PLANNING
Maps
Refer to PRAMES *Ribagorza* at 1:40,000 and Editorial Alpina's *Maladeta-Aneto* at 1:25,000, both of which cover the area.

PLACES TO STAY & EAT
For information on food and accommodation in Benasque or La Besurta, see Places to Stay & Eat in the introduction to the Posets Massif walk later in this section.

GETTING TO/FROM THE WALK
Take the shuttle bus that runs between Benasque and La Besurta and ask to be dropped off at the Puente de Cregüeña bridge. For more detail on transport between La Besurta and Benasque, see Getting to/from the Walk in the introduction to the Posets Massif walk later in this section.

THE WALK (see maps on pages 184-5)
The path begins, wide and cairned, near the Puente de Cregüeña, just off the main C139 highway between La Besurta and Benasque. It climbs almost continuously and with little scope for error all the way to the

Lago de Cregüeña. Walking along the Río Cregüeña, pass through shady woodland until you emerge into the La Pleta de Cregüeña plain.

The western fingertip of the lake, which ranks as the third largest (in terms of volume) in the Pyrenees, is only 3.5km from the Río Ésera as the eagle flies. All the same, the times given are realistic as the ascent to the lake is steep (1200m over 11km). The setting, a savage cul-de-sac occasionally scaled by technical climbers aiming for the south face of the Pico de la Maladeta, is ample compensation for the stiff climb. Return the way you came.

Posets Massif (Days 13 to 17 of the Pyrenean Traverse)

Duration 3 to 5 days
Distance 71 or 73.5km
Standard Easy-Medium or Medium-Hard
Start Benasque
Finish Valle de Pineta
Public Transport Start only
Summary A ring route around the Posets massif, taking in some of the Pyrenees' highest passes and lakes, a descent to the humdrum Valle de Bielsa and a majestic day up and over to the Valle de Pineta.

Though second in elevation to its eastern neighbour the Maladeta massif, the Posets group is possibly even more scenic. While less popular among walkers, it's undeservedly so as opportunities for camping and day walks are almost limitless. The region is as easy to get to as any of the better known Pyrenean magnets and staff at the refugios of Estós and Viadós couldn't be more pleasant.

If you have an urge to linger an extra day at the Lago de la Escarpinosa, Batisielles, Granjas de Viadós or in the Vall de Pineta, go ahead and indulge it. West of the Posets Massif you'll be venturing into hard-core (literally and figuratively) Aragón. Gone are the meadows and forests of the central

and eastern Pyrenees, which the porous, limestone rocks of the west usually refuse to support.

To explain the grading in the introductory box, the route around the Posets Massif as far as Vall de Batisielles (Days 13A, 14 and 15) is tough in terms of both altitude change and the duration of each walking day. You can, however, break the route up into shorter stages. Extra camp sites and refugios have been highlighted along the trail to allow for more flexibility in planning an itinerary.

Alternatively, you can save yourself a couple of days and a litre of two of sweat by following the GR11's gentle, attractive but much less dramatic walk up the Vall de Estós (see Day 13B). If you aren't camping, this might be your preferred option anyway, as Day 14 of the longer route offers only rudimentary shelter.

From the Barranco de Estós it's easy-medium all the way to the Vall de Pineta, except for a final steep ascent over scree to the Puerto de Gistaín (Day 15). The descent from below the Lago Ordiceto to Parzán in the Vall de Bielsa (Day 16) is not difficult in any way, just tediously long at the end of the day.

PLANNING
When to Walk

June to September is the optimum time if you take the high-level route around the Posets Massif. If you take the shorter way up the Vall de Estós, you can add at least a month on either side.

Maps

Far and away the best map, as far as it includes this walk, is the PRAMES *Mapa Excursionista: Valle de Benasque and Valle de Gistain* at 1:25,000 (550 ptas). It covers the area from La Besurta, north-east of Benasque, to the Cabaña Sallena (where 'cabaña' in Spanish means hut), west of the Granjas de Viadós (Day 16). The PRAMES *Maladetas* map at 1:40,000 also covers most of the area and links in with the PRAMES

Parque Nacional de Ordesa y Monte Perdido y Valle de Añisclo map at the same scale.

In the Editorial Alpina series, the *Posets* and *Bachimala* maps at 1:25,000 cover the region from the hamlet of Viadós to Parzán (Day 16), though the *Posets* map is at times wildly inaccurate.

Editorial Alpina's *Ordesa y Monte Perdido* at 1:40,000 will take you from Parzán all the way to and beyond the Parque Nacional de Ordesa y Monte Perdido.

What to Bring

If you want to self-cater, bring enough food to last until Parzán at the end of Day 16, where there's a small supermarket attached to the petrol station.

Warning

Public transport is thin in these parts. Unless you coincide with one of the three buses a week out of Bielsa (see opposite for details), an expensive taxi ride or hitchhiking are the only options in and out of the valley. Otherwise, you're obliged to press on to Torla beyond the Vall de Ordesa.

PLACES TO STAY & EAT
La Besurta

The choice must be *Albergue Llanos del Hospital*, the refugio wing of the less spartan *Hostal Llanos del Hospital* (☎ 974 55 20 12, fax 974 55 10 52, hospital@encomia.es). Both occupy the old Hospital de Benasque (see the boxed text 'El Hospital' at the end of the Vall d'Aran walk in the Catalan Pyrenees section) next to the terminus of the shuttle bus running down from La Besurta – conveniently handy if you're coming off the mountain. Bed and breakfast cost 2800 ptas at the Albergue and 4700 ptas at the Hostal.

Also with character and history, the *Balneario Baños de Benasque* (☎ 974 34 40 00, fax 974 34 42 49) hotel and spa has singles/doubles from 2775/4875 ptas. Though – perhaps because – it's a long haul up the hill, it represents excellent value for money. Even if you're not staying here it's worth a visit to the thermal bath (750 ptas or 950 ptas with seaweed thrown in).

Benasque

With its cobbled streets, 13th century church and old greystone houses, roofed in slates the shape of fish scales, Benasque's roots are deep. It's also a small, bustling holiday centre where most of the new blends sensitively and harmoniously with the more antique.

Pensión Barrabés (☎ 974 55 16 54) does singles/doubles for 1500/3000 ptas. *Pensión Solana* (☎ 974 55 10 19), next door, has a range of rooms costing up to 5500 ptas for a double with bathroom.

Of the casas rurales in town, a double chez *Ramón Bardanca* (☎ 974 55 13 60) costs a bargain 2500 ptas, while rooms with *Marcial Gabás* are 2000/3000 ptas.

There are four *camping grounds*, all on the north side of town and within a shortish walk of each other. The cheapest, *Ixeia*, near the Puente de San Jaim, is particularly trekker friendly.

There's a similarly wide choice of places to eat. The cheap, cheerful and popular *Bar Restaurante Bardanca* has a set menu for 950 ptas. *Restaurante Ampriu* offers Basque cuisine and does a menú del día for 1000 ptas. More upmarket, *Restaurante Fogaril*, attached to Hotel Ciria, with a menu including a range of local specialities for 2100 ptas, is exceptional value. *Pastellería Flor de Nieve* is a pastry shop where you can stuff yourself silly.

There are at least three ATMs and – perhaps worth noting, 12 sweaty days into the Pyrenean Traverse – a laundrette, the Lavandería Ecológica Ardilla on the Avenida de Francia.

Bielsa

If joining or leaving the Pyrenean Traverse at the end of Day 16, you may well need to overnight in Bielsa. It has several cheap, nondescript *hostales* (budget hotels). Try *Hostal Vidaller* (☎ 974 50 01 04), which has doubles with bathroom for 3500 ptas, or *Hostal Pirineos*, where doubles cost 4000 ptas. The tourist office (☎ 974 50 11 27) – uninformed and as unimpressive as just about everything else in town – should be able to give you details of casas rurales and hotels.

You can, however, eat reasonably. Try *Bar-Restaurante Pineta* in the main square, where the menú del día is 1500 ptas, or *Cafetería Los Valles*, with the equivalent for 1600 ptas. There are also three or four good supermarkets and a couple of banks with ATMs.

Valle de Pineta

For information on accommodation and food in the Valle de Pineta, at the end of this walk, see Places to Stay & Eat in the introduction to the Parque Nacional de Ordesa y Monte Perdido walk later in this section.

GETTING TO/FROM THE WALK

For information on transport between destinations beyond the Pyrenees and Barbastro, see Getting There & Away in the introduction to the Aragonese Pyrenees.

Benasque & La Besurta

For information on transport between destinations beyond the Pyrenees and Barbastro, see Getting There & Away in the introduction to the Aragonese Pyrenees section.

Altoaragonesa buses leave Barbastro for Benasque at 11 am and (except Sunday) 5.30 pm. Buses to Barbastro depart from Benasque at 6.45 am (except Sunday) and 3 pm.

From Benasque up to La Besurta, buses leave at 7.30 am and 1 pm. Cars are allowed to travel beyond Hospital de Benasque and as far as La Besurta only between 8 pm and 8 am.

In the other direction, a shuttle bus (200 ptas one way, 275 ptas return) travels the 5.5km from La Besurta to the Hospital de Benasque. In principle the service runs every 30 minutes in each direction, though the driver tends to adjust the schedule to suit his personal life. Buses departing La Besurta at 12.30, 5.30 and 7.30 pm (the last of the day) continue on to Benasque. At other times you shouldn't have too much trouble finding a lift down to town from the car park beside the lower bus terminal near the Hospital de Benasque.

Bielsa

It is possible to join or leave the Pyrenean Traverse from Bielsa at the end of Day 16. However, public transport is limited. From Barbastro, Autocares Cortes (☎ 974 31 15 52) runs a service to Aínsa, from where you can catch an onward connection three times a week to Bielsa. The service leaves Barbastro at 7.45 pm and Aínsa at 8.45 pm on Monday, Wednesday and Friday. In the other direction, it sets out from Bielsa at 6 am on these same days.

Schedules change and vary seasonally. We strongly recommend that you ring Altoaragonesa (☎ 974 31 12 93) or the local tourist office (☎ 974 30 83 50) for the latest information.

Valle de Pineta

For information on getting to and from Valle de Pineta at the end of the walk, see Getting to/from the Walk at the beginning of the Parque Nacional de Ordesa y Monte Perdido walk later in this section.

THE WALK (see map on pages 182-4)
Day 13A: Benasque to Refugio Ángel Orus
4½ hours, 10.5km

From Benasque, cross the ring road to follow a quiet, leafy lane called the Carretera de Anciles to **Anciles**. It's worth taking an early break to explore the village with its 17th and 18th century houses roofed in the local slate. On the west side of this charming hamlet, follow the initially cobbled track – a continuation of the main street – which leaves the village and continues past a couple of flowing fuentes. Pick up the yellow-and-white trail markers which lead along a shady lane through hayfields to a bridge over the Río Ésera near a power plant.

You should be in Eriste (1118m) within an hour. Go through the central square, to the left of the church and up to the top of the village. The trail which you follow into the ravine is signed 'Camino de la Montaña: Refugio Forcau' (a less common name for Refugio Ángel Orus).

Just less than another hour brings you to the old **Puente de Tramarrius** (1245m). Cross to the east (true left) bank of the river and ascend it to meet a 4WD track. The path marked on the Editorial Alpina map paralleling the river and this dirt track is strictly nostalgic. Once you've found the 4WD track, continue upstream along it.

Count on a bit more than another hour, or a total of two hours from Eriste, past an abandoned pyrite mine to reach the **Cascada de la Espiantosa** (1505m), an impressive waterfall. The area around the falls makes an excellent lunch stop before continuing the ascent. Cross the nearby Puente de la Espiantosa – a mundane concrete bridge which can't compare with the magnificent arch of the Puente de Tramarrius earlier. A sign above the car park gives an accurate duration of 1½ hours to the Ángel Orus refugio.

Wild flowers in this region are every bit as spectacular as they are further east and there's even the odd rhododendron bush in the canyon. But already the terrain is harsher, the forests sparser and more coniferous and the low-altitude vegetation has become decidedly scrubby.

Within 20 minutes the path levels out briefly. Complete the fourth hour of walking by arriving at the **Pleta de les Riberes** (1815m), with a domed cabaña and possible *camp site*. ('Pleta' in these parts means a place where the animals spend the night. Make of that what you will!)

A fork to the left (following a sign on a tree) takes you via an upland meadow to the *Refugio Ángel Orus* (☎ 974 34 40 44) at 2100m, with room for 50. You normally need to reserve ahead (essential at weekends) as it's the most popular base camp for an assault on Posets mountain. It's also the only accommodation other than stark huts for noncampers walking this side of the massif.

Day 13B: Benasque to Refugio de Estós

3½ to 4 hours, 12.5km

By taking this easy walk up the Valle de Estós to the refugio of the same name, you can bypass the Posets circuit (Day 13A to the early part of Day 15). It's a well trodden route – 4WD track for the most part – popular with day-trippers from Benasque. You can either savour a short stage and overnight at the Refugio de Estós, where you rejoin the main route, or continue to the Refugio de Viadós a further 11km (four to five hours) away.

Leave Benasque by the sealed road heading north to La Besurta. The Valle de Estós takes off north-west from the Río Ésera at the Puente de San Jaime, 4km north of town. After passing the small dam at its head, cross the Palanca de Aiguacari (where 'palanca' in Aragonese means bridge) onto the true right bank. Shortly beyond a pair of green metal gates is the *Cabaña de Santa Ana*, once a chapel, which can accommodate 12 for a spartan overnight stay. Soon the steepness abates and the valley broadens into fine meadows interspersed with hazel, ash and beech trees.

Forty five minutes or so from the Puente de San Jaime, pause to refill your water supplies – and if the season's right, munch a few wild strawberries at the Fuente Corona. At a junction 10 minutes later, take the right fork signed 'Refugio de Estós, 1½ hours'. Continue walking for a further hour until the 4WD track dwindles to a broad footpath just after passing a small, locked cabin. The track crosses the river to the true left bank by another wooden bridge.

Forty five minutes later, after a final 10 to 15 minutes of steep climb, you reach the *Refugio de Estós* with its welcome terrace and icy-cold drinks. For details of accommodation and the route onward to the Refugio de Viadós, see Day 15.

Day 14: Refugio Ángel Orus to Valle de Batisielles

6 to 7 hours, 9km

This is a long day. However, if the mood takes you there are a couple of spectacular spots en route where you can break off to camp.

Continue north-west from the refugio, passing after 15 minutes the spring which supplies it. The path, ill-defined as it crosses a mixture of grassy slope and scree, is lightly cairned. After climbing 230 vertical metres and crossing the Torrente de Llardaneta, it reaches the *Cabaña de Llardana*, which accommodates four plus baggage and has abundant water from nearby seeps. You'll also find space to pitch a tent nearby. Bear north-east over turfed-in boulders (somewhat to the west of the route indicated by Editorial Alpina) until you overlook the double Lago de las Alforjas (2400m). Descending, you should reach fording points at the outlet to the lake 1¼ to 1½ hours past the cabaña.

Alforjas is one of a dozen or more lakes tucked around the eastern and southern slopes of the just visible Posets and Bardamina crests. There are two to three good *camp sites* along the canal between the lake's two sections. From the lake, allow 1¼ hours to reach the obvious **Collado de la Piana** (2660m), which is just north of Pico de Escorvets (2902m). The often frozen tarn of La Piana below the saddle should help you locate it, assisted by a few cairns along the way. From Collado de la Piana there are magnificent views.

The descent to Lago de la Tartera de Perramó takes about 1¼ hours. From the pass, head south-east and don't be seduced into following cairns which lead further north towards tarns in front of the Agujas de Perramó mountain.

Though the route is downhill much of the way from the col onwards, it's surprisingly demanding. A tough 1¼ to 1½ hours separate the Lago de la Tartera de Perramó from the Lago de la Escarpinosa (2040m). Much of that time is spent wriggling between granite slabs and wrestling with rhododendrons. There are several *camp sites* by each of the Perramó lakes.

The **Lago de Escarpinosa**, where the grass is limited but luxuriant, is a justifiably popular spot for an overnight *camp*. From here, the path follows a stream which descends in a northerly direction to the Valle de Batisielles. In 30 to 40 minutes, at around 2000m, you emerge into a lush, though in places marshy, pine-ringed meadow which enfolds the **Ibonet Pequeño de Batisielles** (1950m), a reedy pond.

Here you can choose from various *camp sites*, the best and driest being on the 'island' between the two forks of the Río de Batisielles. The only drawback to otherwise idyllic camping is that it's also a favourite grazing area of local cows and consequently the hunting ground of some particularly predatory horse flies. For the tentless, there's a very basic, green metal *shelter*, sleeping three at a squeeze, on a knoll just to the south-west of the flats.

Side Trip: Ibón Gran de Batisielles
2½ hours, 4km

Beside a ruined, rubbish-filled hut on the north-west shore of the Ibón Pequeño de Batisielles, a cairned trail (don't confuse it with the trail leading to the Refugio de Estós) diverges westwards and up to the equally attractive Ibón Gran de Batisielles (2260m), another popular overnight destination for weekend walkers. It's a medium-grade return walk which snakes its way up through pine trees to cross a lengthy boulder field.

Day 15: Valle de Batisielles to Refugio de Viadós via Refugio de Estós
5½ to 6½ hours, 15.5km

A sign on the hut near the Ibón Pequeño de Batisielle's north-west shore reads, somewhat optimistically, 'Refugio de Estós, 1 hour 15 minutes'. From there, follow the bright red dots of the forest trail. As you'll soon deduce from the churned up stream crossings and fresh dung, you share the trail with pony trekkers. Be careful not to lose those dots; paths forged by horses, humans and cows diverge, converge and sometimes drift away into nothing, tempting you off course.

After an initial climb of no more than 10 minutes, there's little net altitude change as you stride through a mixture of pine forest and grassland for the next 1½ hours. The whole way, there are fine vistas across the Valle de Estós to the peaks of Pico de Gías, Pico d'Oô (no typing error!) and the mighty Perdiguero. The Refugio de Estós, perched well above the riverside meadows, comes into sight long before you ford the river and continue up the true left bank.

The **Refugio de Estós** (☎/fax 974 55 14 83) – the end of Day 13B – is a model of its kind. The friendly warden Juan Antonio Turmo has run it ever since 1984, when the new building rose from the ashes of a devastating fire. It's the largest refugio in the Pyrenees, with room for 185. Since it's a popular venue for overnighters from Benasque, reservations are essential. It serves drinks, snacks and meals, and has hot showers and its own generator powered by a nearby torrent. It accepts Visa and MasterCard.

Continue along the path on the north (true left) side of the river, which leads on and up to the Puerto de Gistaín. The Clarabide stream descends southwards down a sheer valley to meet the main Río de Estós watercourse at about 2050m, around an hour above the refugio. It's a pretty spot to rest and replenish water supplies – the last dependable water for quite some time.

Cross to the south side of the river. From here, it's a rather monotonous westward haul over scree and rock up a long, dry tube of a valley. It's not too arduous, however, if you stick to the red-and-white trail markers since the dusty path snakes smoothly between and around obstacles, avoiding any rock scrambling. The trail reaches the **Puerto de Gistaín** pass (2592m), also known as Puerto Chistén and Puerto de Chistau, after 2¼ to 2½ hours from the refugio.

There's really a double pass here, separated by a narrow moor. Soon after the second minor col, cross to the true left bank of the gully which drops steeply westwards. From here until the confluence of streams at **Añes Cruces** (2060m), you'll never come across a more oversigned stretch of trail. Just about every wayside stone, rock and boulder for the next hour is daubed with numerous sorts of trail markers. The last 10 minutes or so require some attention as the path crosses steep scree.

At the confluence, cross both tributaries, as well as an upstart little stream to the west (true right) bank of the river, from here on known as the Cinqueta de Añes Cruces. (Editorial Alpina draws the onward trail on

the east side of the river, which becomes impassable after only a few hundred metres.) Conspicuous on the hillside is a **cabaña**, adequate for emergency stays.

The path is straightforward. As you slowly round the mountain, walking through wide, floral meadows, there are unsurpassed views of the entire west face of Posets. Allow 1½ to 1¾ hours from the confluence to Granjas de Viadós, a hamlet of a dozen or so squat, scattered farmhouses.

The privately owned **Refugio de Viadós** (☎ 974 50 61 63) at 1700m is outstanding. At 700 ptas a night, it's also very reasonable. It has 65 bunks and a cosy bar and dining room. It's a friendly, popular family operation, serving filling meals for a bargain 1300 ptas. You can also buy basic foodstuffs for a modest mark-up. It's staffed from 1 July to 20 September, though the annexe kitchen is always kept open. Out of season, ring ☎ 974 50 60 82 for reservations.

The owner, Joaquin Cazcarra, also runs **Camping El Forcallo**, 1.2km down the hill, which is open from 1 July to 31 August. There's no shop but it has a pleasant bar, where meals cost 1300 ptas.

Side Trip: Lago de Millares
5 to 5½ hours, 10.5km

Allow a full day for the return trip from Refugio de Viadós, up and out of the woodland around the Barranco de Ribereta to the Lago de Millares (2400m), lying below the Pico de la Forqueta. The gradient is steep in places but you're on a path the entire way.

Side Trip: Señal de Viadós
3½ to 4 hours, 7km

Stunning, 360-degree vistas make the 840m ascent from Viadós to the Señal de Viadós (2600m) worthwhile. Allow a generous half day for this return trip, north-north-east of the Refugio de Viadós.

Day 16: Refugio de Viadós to Valle de Bielsa
5½ to 6½ hours, 20km

After the challenge of the Posets rim, you deserve this easy, uncomplicated day of attractive walking, primarily through meadow and pine forest. There's an ascent to 2300m, but it's never too strenuous. All in all, it's a gentle prelude to the altogether sterner stuff ahead. Steel yourself, however, for the final unexciting 8.5km descent down a 4WD track from below the Lago de Ordiceto to the Valle de Bielsa. Few 4WDs venture this way so you're unlikely to get a lift.

From the Refugio de Viadós, follow the road west past the children's summer camp of Virgen Blanca (1.75km), near the confluence of the Añes Cruces and Pez streams.

It's about 45 minutes from the refugio to La Sargueta turn-off (1540m), 1km downstream from Virgen Blanca. Beside a wooden noticeboard, take the track to the right which, after 30 minutes, ends at a cluster of farms, the Bordas de Lizierte. Here, bear right at a triple fork to mount a steep path and briefly enter the welcome shade of a pine wood. Within 20 to 30 minutes you reach the small pass and meadow of **Las Collás**, or Las Colladas (1846m).

The path dips briefly to the Barranco de la Basa as the *Cabaña Sallena*, the only structure on the hillside, comes into view. The cabaña is very unsanitary and offers emergency accommodation only. The countryside is an appealing mix of piny ravines and turf. A view to the west of the bare Punta Suelza (2973m) provides a sample of the terrain to come.

The trail passes near a tiny cabaña some 20 minutes beyond Las Collás, then curves above and beyond it. About 30 minutes later – or 2¼ to 2½ hours from the Refugio de Viadós – there's a deep, inviting pool, ideal for a dunk on a hot day. No more than 10 minutes further on is a tiny, solidly built stone *shelter* which could provide emergency accommodation.

As you angle your way up the ridge separating the two barrancos, Montarruegos and Sallena, the path undulates a bit before slipping through the **Paso d'es Caballos**, or Collada de Ordiceto (2326m), 3½ to four hours into the day. If you want to stay up high, there are some wonderful *camp sites* in the meadows before the pass.

Bielsa

Now a cheapo mecca for bargain-hungry shoppers, few are aware of Bielsa's tragic and not too distant past. In the late spring of 1938, as the faltering Republican army fell back from the plains, it retreated into the Pyrenees. Barbastro fell to the Nationalists, then Benasque, leaving the Republican forces in Bielsa isolated, their only escape through the passes into France.

Throughout April and into May, as civilians began to be evacuated, Bielsa was pounded by artillery and attacked from the air. Over 6000 people struggled over the snow-covered Puerto Biello (Porte Vieille) into France.

In June, the larger and better equipped Nationalist army moved in, picking off nearby villages one by one. On 16 June, after a particularly fierce bombardment, the last of the Republican troops retreated, leaving Bielsa in flames. The church, bridge and town hall are just about the only constructions left standing in Bielsa as reminders of a time before the Spanish Civil War.

Just beyond is the dirt access road which leads left to the Lago de Ordiceto (2390m) with its stark and grimly rocky terrain – not really worth a detour. There are, however, a few flat spots here for a *camp site* if you want to postpone the next stage along the road.

Otherwise, turn right down the dirt road, then almost immediately left onto a path which cuts off a couple of long zigzags before rejoining the 4WD track 30 minutes later. After another 30 minutes on the track, take a path which runs beside a small dam and hydroelectric station and soon rejoins the 4WD track. From here on it's a slog, albeit with pleasant views, all the way down to the main highway, the Carretera de Francia, 1.5km north of the small hamlet of Parzán.

Places to Stay & Eat If you intend to walk Day 17 (unless you're pushed for time it would be a pity to miss its spectacular views), your best bet is to take a *casa rural* in tiny Parzán, having phoned ahead to reserve. In Parzán, try Luis Zueras (☎ 974 50 11 90) or María Jesús Fumanal (☎ 974 50 11 24), both of whom rent out rooms. There's a *Spar supermarket* beside the garage – an essential call if you're bypassing Bielsa, since you won't meet another shop until Torla on the far side of the Ordesa valley on Day 19.

Day 17: Valle de Bielsa to Valle de Pineta
5½ to 6 hours, 16km
The route follows the GR11, giving spectacular views of the Valle de Pineta valley and its impressive cirque, the Circo de Pineta, as well as across to the Sierra de las Tucas. After an ascent of almost exactly 1000m to the Collada de Pietramula, it's an undemanding walk all the way down to the base of the Circo de Pineta.

Less than 500m north of Parzán, turn left off the Carretera de Francia and follow the sealed track until you reach the small hamlet of Chisagües 45 minutes later. It's a relief so early in the day to leave behind the noise and fumes of the passing traffic. Continue along the same graded track, originally constructed to serve the long-abandoned silver and lead mines above Chisagües. A steady and uneventful rise of 600m over 6km along the Río Real brings you to the Fuente de Pietramula. Not long afterwards, you need to leave the track to ford the Río Real.

Work your way southwards up the Barranco de las Coronetas to reach the **Collada de Pietramula**, or Piedramula (2150m), after a further 50 to 60 minutes. From here on, it's flat or a gentle slope downhill as far as a hut at the eastern limit of the Llanos de Estiva (where 'llano' in Spanish means plain). Pass the hut to your right.

The descent becomes steeper as you approach the Barranco de las Opacas. Turn sharp left (south-west) to meet a cart track and dilapidated hut near the **Llanos de la**

Larri (1560m), about 1¾ to two hours from the col. From here, it's about 30 minutes down through a wood of beech trees to the small chapel of Nuestra Señora de Pineta (1250m) and its adjacent fountain. At the head of the Valle de Pineta, you've a choice of accommodation.

Parque Nacional de Ordesa y Monte Perdido
(Days 18 & 19 of the Pyrenean Traverse)

Duration 2 days
Distance 24 or 25km
Standard Medium-Hard
Start Valle de Pineta
Finish Pradera de Ordesa
Public Transport Finish only
Summary A vertiginous ascent to the Collado de Añisclo. A stepped descent of the impressive upper Añisclo valley, recovering height via the Barranco de Fon Blanca before dropping down to the Valle de Ordesa canyon.

The Valle de Ordesa was designated a national park in 1918. In 1982 its boundaries were expanded significantly to incorporate Monte Perdido, the head of the Valle de Pineta and large slices of the valleys of Escuaín and Añisclo. The park, renamed the Parque Nacional de Ordesa y Monte Perdido, now occupies an area of 15,600 hectares.

The two days it takes to cross the national park from the Valle de Pineta are perhaps the most spectacular of the whole Pyrenean Traverse. And the trip shouldn't be restricted to two days if your schedule permits, since the park itself merits more than a couple of days exploration. Consider basing yourself in Torla at the end of this walk for a night or two longer. We grade this walk as medium-hard because of the taxing Day 18. Days 19A or 19B, though demanding in places, are considerably less arduous.

The three major valleys of the massif, Ordesa, Pineta and Gavarnie, were scoured into their typical U shape during the Quaternary period by giant glaciers. Underground, rainwater and frost have eroded the softer limestone. The hillsides are pockmarked with caves, potholes and underground streams, attracting cavers from all over Europe.

For details of the park's visitors centre, see Information Sources under Information in the introduction to the Aragonese Pyrenees section earlier in this chapter.

PLANNING
When to Walk
Comfortable passage over the Collado de Añisclo can only be guaranteed between June and September. The main section of the Valle de Ordesa, however, is accessible for a longer period and is a popular venue for winter walkers who are experienced in dealing with snow.

Maps
Parque Nacional de Ordesa y Monte Perdido y Valle de Añisclo at 1:40,000 by PRAMES is the most reliable and user-friendly of several maps of the park. Editorial Alpina's *Ordesa y Monte Perdido*, also at 1:40,000, covers much the same area.

Warnings
Before setting out, stock up on food at the small supermarket attached to Camping Pineta. You won't meet another shop until Torla (Day 19) or the small supermarket at Camping Valle de Bujaruelo (Day 20).

Since Ordesa is predominantly limestone, surface water quickly percolates underground. Away from the valley bottoms, you can't rely on finding a ready source, so fill up your containers at every opportunity.

PLACES TO STAY & EAT
Valle de Pineta
If you fancy a touch of four star luxury at equivalent prices, try the *Parador de Bielsa* (☎ 974 50 10 11, fax 974 50 11 88). Doubles with bathroom in the high season cost 16,500 ptas. The restaurant serves gourmet meals (3500 ptas for the excellent set menu) and the views are stunning.

More modest but not necessarily less agreeable, the smart *Refugio de Pineta* (☎ 974 50 12 03), run by the Federació Aragonesa de Montañismo (FAM), is 1.5km down the valley. Even though it keeps a 25% vacancy for walk-ins, it's essential to reserve ahead. You don't have to be staying to tuck into one of their copious meals (1200 ptas).

The *Camping Municipal* is a huge tented area, like the scene before the battle of Agincourt or Gettysburg. You'll have little trouble finding a quiet pitch for the bargain price of 205 ptas per tent plus 260 ptas per person. The ratio of campers to squatter toilets and cold-water washbasins, however, is lamentable. There's a small bar which serves bocadillos.

All in all, for comfort under canvas, you're much better off walking or hitching a further 3.5km from the refugio further along the road to *Camping Pineta* (☎ 974 50 10 89), where the water in the free showers is piping hot and the toilets are the fastest flushing in the west. It also has a small supermarket – useful for stocking up on essential provisions for the next stage if you want to avoid the journey to Bielsa and back.

Torla
For information on accommodation and food in Torla at the end of this walk, see Places to Stay & Eat in the introduction to the Panticosa & Beyond walk later in this section.

GETTING TO/FROM THE WALK
The only way in or out of Valle de Pineta, apart from walking or hitching, is to call a taxi in Aínsa. Phone Taxi Araujo (☎ 608-536 649), Jose María Rabal (☎ 689-761 414) or Cerezo Arcas (☎ 974 50 00 79). A taxi from Parador de Bielsa at the head of Valle de Pineta to Aínsa costs 5500 ptas (3500 ptas from Bielsa).

For information on getting to and from the Pradera de Ordesa and Torla, see Getting to/from the Walk in the introduction to the Panticosa & Beyond walk later in this section.

THE PYRENEES

THE WALK (see maps on pages 181-2)
Day 18: Valle de Pineta to Valle de Añisclo
5 to 6½ hours, 7.5km

Make no mistake, today's a tough, strenuous one which will have you clambering over fallen trees (the whole of the wood on the southern flank of the Valle de Pineta is ailing) and negotiating a minor landslide. Statistically speaking, the climb from the Pineta valley bottom to the Collado de Añisclo represents a vertical climb of just under 1200m in almost exactly 2km of walking (or scrambling).

Regard the sign 'Collado de Añisclo' on the sealed road some 200m east of the Refugio de Pineta as a cruel joke. If you follow its finger to the broad riverbed, you'll merely be adding your traces to the footprints of those who've floundered before you, seeking a way through the impenetrable shrubs and thickets.

Instead, take a broad path westwards from the refugio. After no more than 200m, a sign pointing across the river proclaims 'Añisclo 3 horas' (Añisclo 3 hours). This sign has its (at best) playful dimension, since with a full backpack it will take you as much as an hour longer to reach the col.

It's boots and socks off to ford the river, aiming just left of a waterfall on the far bank. The alternative is to take the GR11, which crosses to the true right bank by way of the bridge beside the Camping Municipal, then turns left to follow it. Once over the river, pick up this well blazed trail and turn left along it.

One hour after leaving the refugio, cross a wide stream. Fill your water bottles here as there's no more water until you're over the Añisclo pass. Shortly after the halfway mark, the path intersects with the enviably flat Faja de Tormosa route which contours around from the Circo de Pineta to your right. As the trees begin to thin out and become more stunted, you'll notice a disproportionate number lying dead. These trees aren't victims of disease or insects; the slope is renowned for its springtime avalanches which sweep everything but the most pliable, resilient vegetation before them.

Walking times to the Collado de Añisclo (2470m), with its fine views of the head of the Valle de Añisclo canyon, vary enormously; you may find you've taken rather more than four hours. If you're running short of energy, no more than 50 to 100m below the ridge is an unspoilt spot with water and some level turf for a *camp site*.

Within 10 minutes of walking from the pass, it's decision time, the high road or the low road: the original GR11 route via the Puntas de las Olas traverse, or the more trodden variant down the Añisclo canyon. We've chosen not to cover the former in this chapter and unless you're an experienced mountaineer we strongly recommend you avoid it too (see the boxed text 'The GR11 Backtracks'). Should you opt for it, take particular care when negotiating the tranche which requires cable support when there's snow around – which is most of the year. The traverse as far as the Collado Superior de Góriz takes between two and 2¼ hours.

The GR11 Backtracks

It's a principle of GR trails throughout Europe that they should be accessible to all. But from the Collado d'Añisclo, the original GR11 route followed and continues to follow a potentially dangerous 500m traverse around the usually wet, often snowbound rock of the Punta de las Olas.

In response to widespread criticism (not least in the 1st edition to this book, which described the passage as 'extremely dangerous' as well as 'reprehensibly routed and unreservedly not recommended'), the GR11 committee approved an alternative which, unlike most variants, is marked with the red and white bars of the official GR trail.

Uniquely, the 'variant' now features in the official handbook as the recommended route, while the original life-threatener has been relegated to an option in italics.

We equally strongly recommend the GR11 variant via the alluring Valle de Añisclo, despite losing some 750m in altitude, both because it's safer and for its own sake. A series of gentle descents – each ending in a waterfall with a pool deep enough to bathe in and a green stretch of grass, alpine flowers and a choice of *camp sites* at every giant step – make the upper valley one of the major highlights of the whole Pyrenees crossing. It's advisable to stay higher as the area around the Case de los Cazadores, further down the valley, tends to fill up with campers as sunset approaches.

The squat, dry hut of *Casa de los Cazadores* (The Hunters' House) is 1½ to 1¾ hours from the col. It can accommodate five snuggled close together. Just beyond it is a rocky overhang that provides *shelter* for a similar number.

Alternative Camp Sites

Should you have any energy left when you reach the Casa de los Cazadores, consider continuing for a further 1¼ hours or so as far as the alpine meadows above the bare rock of the Barranco de Fon Blanca (see Day 19A). This will leave you drained but it will allow you to descend to the Pradera de Ordesa comfortably the following day via the more attractive Faja de Pelay route (see Day 19B).

Day 19A: Valle de Añisclo to Pradera de Ordesa via the Lower Route

5½ to 6½ hours, 16.5km

Steel yourself to rejoin the madding crowd. After an ascent to the Collado Superior de Góriz, the route drops via the teeming Refugio de Góriz to the floor of the Valle de Ordesa. As you approach the shuttle bus terminal at Pradera de Ordesa, tourists seem almost to outnumber the trees.

The day begins with a steep scree scramble, just below the spectacular Cascada de Fon Blanca waterfall. As you continue to ascend the gaunt, narrow valley of the Barranco de Fon Blanca (also known as the Barrance Arrablo), the steepness eases

markedly. After a little under 45 minutes, cross to the true right bank of the shallow stream, filling your water bottles as you do so; Ordesa is strictly limestone and surface water is at a premium away from the valley bottom.

One to 1¼ hours after leaving the Valle de Añisclo, after a brief south-westerly traverse, the path leaves behind the uniform grey rock of the canyon and emerges into a green alpine meadow – a perfect *camp site*, shared only by marmots.

A short while later, there's a final, four-limbed climb, no more than five minutes long, up the face of a bluff with plenty of hand and footholds. Once you heave yourself over the ridge, it's pleasant upland striding all the way to the **Collado Superior de Góriz**, or Collado Arrablo (2343m). This is reached two to 2¼ hours into the day. From your right (east) the GR11 path from the Punta de las Olas traverse (see the boxed text 'The GR11 Backtracks' earlier in this walk) enters, deceptively innocuous in its final stage.

From the saddle you have good views of the summits to the north. From right to left these include the Punta de las Olas (3002m), the Sum de Ramond (also called the Pico de Añisclo; 3254m), the Morrón de Arrablo (or Torre de Góriz; 2792m) and, lording it over all, Monte Perdido (3355m).

Allow around 45 minutes to get down to the Refugio de Góriz along the path, having walked a total of 2½ to three hours from the Casa de los Cazadores.

About 15 minutes beyond the Collado Superior de Góriz are several fine *camp sites* where a large stream flows through a meadow.

Once you've reached the *Refugio de Góriz* (☎ 974 34 12 01), you may well wonder why you've bothered. Multilingual signs inform you, at the risk of stating the very obvious, 'This isn't a hotel or a bar or a restaurant', and with commendable directness, 'Those camping can't use any of the refugio's services'. Such a proscription, however, doesn't apply to their drinks, snacks or, if you're lucky enough to be able to order one, meals.

THE PYRENEES

Camping Wild in the Parque Nacional

Camping wild is not totally forbidden in the Parque Nacional de Ordesa y Monte Perdido. No one will object to responsible *vivac* (bivouac) camping. This means that you can pitch a small tent between dawn and dusk above certain altitudes, which vary from sector to sector:

Ordesa	2100m
Pineta	2500m
Añisclo and Escuaín	1800m

Within park boundaries, there are a handful of *abrigos* (shelters). These, however, are intended for emergency use only.

The staff are pleasant enough, but the refugio is under enormous pressure to accommodate the large numbers of visitors to the area, particularly during July and August. You may need to reserve both meals and sleeping space as much as a month in advance. The environs of the refugio are like an earthquake disaster zone from early afternoon onwards, with tents – which you can't erect until nightfall – and bodies everywhere.

It makes sense to overnight here if you're planning to use the refugio as a base for a day walk to the summit of Monte Perdido. Otherwise, however, head down the valley to the Pradera de Ordesa, between three and four hours away.

A little more than 30 minutes from the hut, heading due south on the blazed trail, the path divides in two. At around the 1900m contour, the more evident route bears right just above the Circo de Soaso. The GR11, on this occasion prudence itself, describes a zigzagging course down the valley's south-eastern flank. Some 20 to 25 minutes down the switchbacks the trail again divides. Take the path to the right which descends to the valley bottom and ends up downstream from the Cascada de Cola de Caballo. The path straight ahead is the beginning of the Day 19B alternative route.

Whichever way you reach the valley floor, the waterfall is a pleasant place for a break. From here onwards, you won't lack company for a moment.

After about 45 minutes the canyon begins to lose some of its characteristic glacial U shape and the forest becomes more dense.

Passing by the Gradas de Soaso, a series of natural steps down which the Río Arazas tumbles, another 30 minutes brings you to the signed turn-off for the Faja de Canarellos and Circo de Cotatuero (see the side trip from Pradera de Ordesa to Cascada de Cotatuera at the end of Day 19B). Beyond Cascadas de la Cueva and del Estrecho waterfalls – both good spots for a breather – cross to the stream's south bank via the Puente de Arripes. Soon after, the Mirador del Paso de los Bucardos provides excellent views towards the cliffs of the Salarons and Cotatuero peaks.

Continue along the south-bank path, a less crowded variant of the trail on the other side of the valley. At the junction with the Senda de los Cazadores trail, the final stage of the Day 19B alternative route, cross back over the river to reach the **Pradera de Ordesa**. The car park – these days satisfyingly devoid of all private cars – is the terminus for the Torla shuttle bus (for details of bus times, see Getting to/from the Walk in the introduction to the Panticosa & Beyond walk later in this section). Total time from the Refugio de Góriz is from less than three to four hours. If you'd prefer to continue the walk until Torla, follow the route description in the side trip below.

If you've been on dehydrated goo for the past two days, *Bar-Restaurante La Pradera de Ordesa*, with its rich variety of tapas and bocadillos, icy-cold draught beer and a menú del día at 1500 ptas, is a small gastronomic paradise.

Side Trip: Pradera de Ordesa to Torla

2 hours, 6.5km
The descent from the Pradera de Ordesa to Torla follows the ancient track which links the village and the bordas of the Valle de

Ordesa valley and makes a pleasant, easy alternative to the shuttle bus. At first running parallel to the Río Arazas, it then follows the Río Ara from the confluence of the two near the Puente de la Ereta.

A little west of the Pradera de Ordesa, leave the road and cross the Puente de las Fuentes to the true left bank of the Río Arazas to join the Camino de Turieto. The camino drops gently through a wood of fir trees and open meadow. To the right (east) short detours lead to a number of small waterfalls on the Río Arazas.

After about an hour the park boundary is signposted and the camino forks south to Torla (now visible) and north (right) to the Puente de los Navarros along the GR11 route. Take the turn-off towards Torla. Roughly 30 minutes after the camino blends into a sizeable dirt track, cross the river by the Puente de la Glera and go up the cobbled lane which leads to Torla.

Day 19B: Valle de Añisclo to Pradera de Ordesa via Faja de Pelay

7 to 8 hours, 17.5km

'Faja' in Spanish means belt or band and accurately describes this contour-hugging path, high above the Valle de Ordesa. The route follows it from just south of the Circo de Soaso as far as the Mirador de Calcilarruego, where you launch yourself on the steep descent down the Senda de los Cazadores, the Hunters' Track.

Follow the Day 19A route description as far as the point, well below the Refugio de Góriz, where that route to the valley bottom bears away right and downhill to the valley bottom. Instead, continue straight with no loss of height to join the main Faja de Pelay path coming up from the meadows of the Circo de Soaso.

As you join it, disregard the potentially unnerving sign '¡Atención! Senda Muy Peligroso: Hielo y Aludes' (Beware! Extremely Dangerous Path: Ice and Avalanches), which certainly isn't applicable in summertime.

After the hard, uphill work of the previous 1½ days, the Faja is an immensely enjoyable stroll. The path twists its way around one incised ravine after another, rarely rising above 1900m. The whole way, except where obscured by trees, the views are magnificent. Keep your eyes focused on the middle ground as well as the canyon and mountain scenery. On this less trodden trail you stand a good chance of spotting sarrio, as chamois are known in Aragonese, and if you're very lucky, the Pyrenean goat (see the boxed text on the following page).

From where you join the Faja de Pelay, allow between 2¼ and 2½ hours to reach the **Mirador de Calcilarruego** and the adjacent refugio with its windows broken and fireplace clogged by bags of reeking rubbish. Not a place in which to linger.

In the next 1¼ hours or so the path drops 600m on the tight switchbacks of the **Senda de los Cazadores**, as mountain pine and fir trees gradually give way to silent, shaded beech wood. As you emerge from the wood, turn left to reach the service area and shuttle bus terminus of the Pradera de Ordesa within 10 minutes. To continue to Torla on foot takes another two hours. For a description of the route, see the side trip at the end of Day 19A.

Side Trip: Pradera de Ordesa to Cascada de Cotatuero

3½ to 4 hours, 11.5km

Setting out from the Pradera de Ordesa, follow in reverse the Day 19A route for about 3km as far as the sign indicating a turn-off left to the Faja de Canarellos and Circo de Cotatuero. The path briefly ascends to meet the Faja de Canarellos trail as it works its way north-west and the beeches become sparser, giving way to box, pine and fir.

The trail contours at 1700m around the flank of Monte Arruebo and passes below the cliffs. Crossing the rims of numerous hanging valleys, the trail narrows on occasion to avoid rock overhangs. The whole way there are tremendous views of the Faja de Pelay on the opposite side of the Valle de Ordesa canyon.

It will take you around 1½ hours from the Bosque de las Hayas to reach the bridge and tiny shelter below the **Cascadas**

THE PYRENEES

The Pyrenean Goat

In Spanish it's *cabra montés pirenaica*, in scientific circles it's known as *Capra pyrenaica pyrenaica*, but the Aragonese simply call it *el bucardo* – all names for this justifiably shy mountain goat which has been all but hunted and harried into extinction.

It used to flourish throughout the Pyrenees and Cordillera Cantábrica and its long history is recorded in paleolithic cave paintings. Nowadays the Parque Nacional de Ordesa y Monte Perdido is its last enclave. Naturalists estimate that only about 20 still survive and are pessimistic about the goat's chances of holding on. If you're very lucky, you may spot one on the hillsides above the Faja de Pelay.

These wild and very agile goats have untethered access to the Pyrenees' most spectacular views.

INGRID RODDIS

---

de Cotatuero, tumbling from the awesome Circo de Cotatuero. From here, allow about 40 minutes to rejoin the main north-bank path along the Valle de Ordesa at a junction marked by a small shrine to the Virgen de Ordesa. It takes another 10 minutes to reach the Pradera de Ordesa.

Side Trip: Refugio de Góriz to Monte Perdido
7 hours, 7km
Monte Perdido (3355m) defers in height only to the Pico de Aneto and Posets, both now several days walk away to the east. This is a classic ascent, though you'll need to be in good shape to undertake it with confidence. At any time of the year it's wise to approach the walk equipped with an ice axe and crampons, or at least walking poles.

The main route sets out from the Refugio de Góriz – one of the few good reasons for overnighting with the hordes around the refugio. It's a well cairned path which heads north as far as the tiny tarn of Lago Helado (around 3050m), reached some three hours out. There, you turn sharply right (southeast) for the final ascent up a steep couloir (a deep mountain gully), then a rock-strewn snow ridge to the summit.

Panticosa & Beyond
(Days 20 to 23 of the Pyrenean Traverse)

Duration 4 days
Distance 45.75 or 50.75km
Standard Medium-Hard
Start Torla
Finish Sallent de Gállego
Public Transport Yes
Summary An easy walk up the Ara and Otal valleys, followed by a long haul over wild upland to Panticosa, then a spectacular lake-spangled two day finale across more rugged upland terrain.

After the crowds of Ordesa, these last four days take you back to the wild stuff, all alone and way up high. The trail from Balneario de Panticosa to Sallent de Gállego, in particular, makes a spectacular finale to the Pyrenean Traverse. The high mountain landscape is resolutely alpine and spangled with lakes in a concentration not seen since the Parc Nacional d'Aigüestortes i Estany de Sant Maurici in the Catalan Pyrenees.

PLANNING
Maps
The Editorial Alpina maps have an inconvenient spread. Whichever route you take, you need *Vignemale y Bujaruelo* at 1:30,000 and *Panticosa-Formigal* at 1:25,000. In addition, on the Day 20A route, the *Valle de Tena y Sierra de Tendeñera* map covers all but for about 4km of the route. This said, the track is fairly evident and the investment scarcely worthwhile unless you're a map junkie.

What to Bring
You'll need to stock up on supplies for the last two days in one of Panticosa's two small supermarkets, unless you're prepared to make the long haul to the Refugio de Respomuso in one day – and have ordered your bed and dinner in advance.

Warning
The climb down from the Cuello de Piedrafita is treacherous. The steep descent over damp, slippery scree or snow on its north side will have you on all fours. Exercise great caution and consider taking some sort of self-arrest device, even if it's nothing more sophisticated than a stout stick.

PLACES TO STAY & EAT
Torla
Refugio L'Atalaya (☎ *974 48 60 22*) has dormitory beds for 1000 ptas and a friendly bar-restaurant. Half-board is 2800 ptas, while full-board with evening meal, breakfast and a picnic lunch is a bargain 3500 ptas. A bed at the nearby *Refugio Lucien Briet* (☎ *974 48 62 21*) also costs 1000 ptas for a bed and provides similar facilities.

Otherwise, all hotels seem to charge about the same rates. Cheapest of these is *Hostal Alto Aragón* (☎ *974 48 61 72*), with doubles at 5200 ptas. The same people run the slightly dearer *Hotel Ballarín* (☎ *974 48 51 55*), across the street. It also has a good restaurant with a 1300 ptas set menu. The village has a couple of supermarkets, each with a conveniently placed ATM just outside.

There are four camping grounds in the area, of which *Camping Río Ara* is handiest for Torla and *Camping San Antón* nearest to the Parque Nacional de Ordesa y Monte Perdido entrance.

More upmarket, there's plenty of accommodation in the 5000 ptas to 6500 ptas range, though many places are fully booked during July and August.

Sallent de Gállego
On the north side of town there's a good *zona de acampada*, a simple camping ground, run by the municipality, where a night costs 250 ptas per person plus 250 ptas for a tent. There are several hotels, of which the cheapest is *Hostal El Centro* (☎ *974 48 80 19*).

GETTING TO/FROM THE WALK
Torla
A daily bus leaves Sabiñánigo at 11 am. Arriving at Torla about 11.45 am, it heads on to Aínsa. From there, you can either continue to Sabiñánigo, leaving at 2.30 pm, or catch the 3 pm run (July to September only) to Barbastro. During July and August there's a second daily service to Torla which departs from Sabiñánigo at 6.30 pm and returns from Torla which departs form Sabiñánigo at 6.30 pm and returns from Torla at about 8 pm. To confirm these times, phone Hudebus (☎ 974 212 32 77). For Torla taxis, ring Bella Vista (☎ 974 48 61 53) or Jorge Soler (☎ 974 48 62 43).

Pradera de Ordesa
A shuttle bus leaves for the Pradera de Ordesa from the car park on the south side of Torla at 6, 7 and 7.30 am, then every 15 minutes between 8 am and 8 pm. From 8 pm until the last run at 10 pm, buses only accept passengers for the downhill journey from the Pradera. The fare is 200 ptas, whether one way or return.

Balneario de Panticosa
For information on transport between Sabiñánigo and destinations beyond the Pyrenees, see Getting There & Away in the

introduction to the Aragonese Pyrenees section.

There's a daily service from Jaca via Sabiñánigo to Panticosa at the end of Day 21 leaving Sabiñánigo at 10.15 am and 6.15 pm (except weekends).

In July and August, a daily bus leaves Panticosa at 11.35 am for Balneario de Panticosa. In the other direction it leaves Balneario de Panticosa at 5.30 pm, calling by Panticosa (5.50 pm) and continuing on to Sabiñánigo and Jaca. Otherwise, there are three taxi services based in Sallent de Gállego (☎ 974 48 82 68, ☎ 974 48 80 03 or ☎ 974 48 83 69) which will take you to Balneario de Panticosa for about 3000 ptas. If all else fails, it's not a difficult route to hitch.

In the other direction during July and August a daily bus leaves Balneario de Panticosa at 5.30 pm, calling by Panticosa (5.50 pm) and continuing on to Sabiñánigo and Jaca.

Sallent de Gállego

There's a service from Jaca via Sabiñánigo to Panticosa, continuing to Sallent de Gállego. Buses leave Jaca at 10.15 am daily and 6.15 pm (except weekends). Return buses to Sabiñánigo and Jaca leave Sallent de Gállego (calling by Panticosa 15 minutes later) at 4 pm daily and 7 am (except weekends). To confirm current bus schedules, ring the Oscense company in Sabiñánigo (☎ 974 48 00 45) or Jaca (☎ 974 35 50 60).

THE WALK (see maps on pages 179-80)
Day 20: Torla to Bujaruelo
2 hours, 6.5km

Though not a full day's walk, we include this walk as a separate day because it allows for more flexibility in planning the final stage of the Pyrenean Traverse. You can either tag this walk onto the end of a descent from the Pradera de Ordesa (see the side trip from Pradera de Ordesa to Torla at the end of Day 19B) or else take time to visit Torla and leave for Bujaruelo in the afternoon. It's also possible to begin the day from the Puente de los Navarros and continue on to either Panticosa (see Day 21A)

or Balnearios de Panticosa (see Day 21B). This makes for a very long day's walk, however.

From Torla, take the shuttle bus as far as Puente de los Navarros (for bus times, see Getting to/from the Walk in the introduction to this walk). From the bridge just west of the barrier marking the park entrance, it's a pleasant walk northwards up the Valle de Bujaruelo, the attractiveness marred only by a series of giant electricity pylons.

Follow the 4WD track which runs parallel to the Río Ara. After 2.5km, where the track crosses the small Puente de Santa Elena (or Puente Nuevo), stay on the river's true left bank to take a charming footpath which leads through woodland all the way to Bujaruelo.

A kilometre from the Puente de Santa Elena, the Puente de los Abetos leads to the excellent, walker-friendly *Camping Valle de Bujaruelo* (☎ 974 48 63 48), open from Easter to mid-October. Camping costs 445 ptas for a small tent, plus the same amount per person. Alternatively, you can sleep in the refugio where rooms cost 2500/3600/4500 ptas for two, three and four people, respectively. It has a bar, a restaurant with a good menú del día for 1400 ptas and a small shop (a good place to stock up if you're heading west and wish to bypass Torla). The owner and his friends have blazed a number of nearby trails and he's a fount of useful information on day walks in the area.

Alternatively, you can push on for a further 3km to **Bujaruelo** itself, a splendid spot where the valley broadens out. The more spartan but equally friendly *Camping San Nicolas de Bujaruelo* (☎ 974 48 64 28) charges much the same as its neighbour down the valley. If there's no one around, just pitch your tent and someone may turn up next morning to collect the fee. Beside the camping ground is *Mesón San Nicolas de Bujaruelo* (☎ 974 48 60 60) on the site of what was once a *hospital* catering to pilgrims and travellers crossing into France by the Puerto de Bujaruelo. (Take time out to look at the ruins of the Romanesque chapel just behind it.) Open from Easter to mid-October, rooms sleeping four to six cost 1000 ptas per person. Though it's prudent to reserve ahead in July and August, the friendly manager will always squeeze you in (his personal record is 130 – in a place with a capacity of around 50 – one night when a Pyrenean storm raged and the adjacent camping ground was awash). Both the Mesón and the valley's camping grounds offer free hot showers.

Day 21A: Bujaruelo to Panticosa via Collado de Tendenera

7½ to 8 hours, 23km

After the hard graft and upland barrenness of the eastern approaches to Ordesa, today's walk is almost entirely one of well marked paths with scarcely a stone to clamber over. You'll work hard as you ascend from the Valle de Otal but the route's clear and once over the Collado de Tendenera it's downhill all the way to Panticosa.

Cross Bujaruelo's fine single-arched stone bridge to follow the Río Ara's true left bank upstream – if, that is, you can resist taking a dip in the limpid blue pools. At the intersection with a 4WD track, after 20 to 25 minutes, turn left to cross the river by the Puente Oncins.

Just over the bridge, head westwards across a meadow for no more than 200m to pick up a vague trail marked by equally faint GR11 trail markers (the 'official' GR route now goes much further north – see Day 21B). As it enters a wood and climbs south-westwards, navigation isn't easy. Once in open meadow again, you'll probably lose the authentic trail overrun by new grass and competing cattle paths. However, if you keep rigorously on a south-west bearing and aim for the Collado de Otal, you shouldn't go wrong. If you do, extricate yourself by heading for the 4WD track to the south which describes a series of hairpin bends up the hillside.

Once over the col, drop gently to the broad, grassy valley, through which the Río Otal snakes. The Collado de Tendenera is

obvious at the far, western end, flanked by its outriders, the Pico de Tendenera (2853m) to the south and Mallaruego (2692m) to the north. From here it's easy, level striding on a good-quality cart track all the way to the *Cabaña de Otal* – more cowshed than refugio but fine as an emergency shelter – reached after 1¼ to 1½ hours.

Continue due west, passing to the right of a small waterfall. Keep to the north (true left) bank of the stream which feeds it, passing a large metal rain gauge as you ascend to the head of the valley. Here, the path veers due north and begins to climb more steeply out of the bowl. About 50 minutes after the cabaña, just beyond a metal sheepfold and before a multicoloured pole, the path (somewhat alarmingly) turns back on itself and heads north-east, away from the col.

Finally, after a good 25 minutes or more, the route turns sharply leftwards beside a stream which crosses the main path. Overgrown and marked only by slowly decaying wooden pegs striped with the familiar red-and-white trail markers, it heads firmly north-west to become once more an evident path.

The terrain becomes increasingly dramatic as you gain altitude. There's not a sign of humanity apart from the red-roofed cabaña below and the path at your feet. A little under an hour from the turn, at about 2200m, the trail passes over a small spring seeping from the rock just below the saddle. The grass here makes a cosy lunch spot or *camp site*, if you've started the day south of Bujaruelo.

The **Collado de Tendenera** (2325m) appears deceptively close, but it takes another 20 minutes from the spring to reach the pass, where karst and sandstone meet. Take a last look east to where the border summit of Tallón (Taillon) at 3144m overlooks the Puerto de Bujaruelo.

About 40 minutes below the col, pass a small *refugio* capable of sleeping four. There's water nearby and *camping* is possible if you beat down the long grass. Ten minutes later the path crosses to the true left bank of the stream it's been following and then veers away around a small bluff. Enjoy the unexpectedness of a magnificent view over the Río Ripera valley to the north and a glimpse of Balaitous mountain (3151m) on the Franco-Spanish border.

After 15 minutes the path crosses the Río Ripera to meet the well maintained 4WD track which follows the length of the valley. Some 20 minutes from the junction you pass an *ICONA refugio* (a possible overnight stop). From here on, the challenges are over, the walking's simple and there remains only a considerable horizontal rather than vertical distance.

Some 10 minutes beyond the refugio the path crosses to the river's true right bank at a ford that may have you paddling when the river's in spate. A couple of minutes later it passes the *Refugio de Ripera*, a spartan concrete block with capacity for six. From here on the red-and-white trail markers which, fresh or fading, have been around for most of the day, are supplemented by blue-and-white, then orange-and-white markers as the path joins other trails coming up from Panticosa. Once the path widens to become a track and makes a sharp left turn as the Arroyo Laulot stream comes in from the east, it's an hour of fairly unexceptional walking to the merendero above Panticosa and a further 30 minutes into the village itself.

Places to Stay & Eat Panticosa has a couple of supermarkets, where you'll need to buy provisions unless you plan to make the next day a long one, walking from Balneario de Panticosa to Refugio de Respomuso (see Days 22 and 23). The most reasonable food and accommodation is at *Hotel Navarro* (☎ 974 48 72 20) in the Plaza de la Iglesia, where a double costs 5300 ptas.

Alternatively, once on the main road, hitch the 5.5km up the road to Balneario de Panticosa so that you're poised for tomorrow's departure. Balneario de Panticosa has restaurants and a bakery but no shops. There's a good FAM-run refugio, the *Casa de Piedra* (☎ 974 48 75 71), where despite

having room for over 100, it's wise to reserve ahead in high summer. At 1000 ptas per night and with dinner for 1300 ptas, it's the bargain of the Balneario. The cheapest of the hotels is the *Continental* (☎ 974 48 71 37), where a double costs 5400 ptas.

For taxi and bus options up the valley, see Getting to/from the Walk in the introduction to this walk.

Day 21B Bujaruelo to Balneario de Panticosa via Cuello de Brazato
6½ to 7 hours, 18km
The clearly marked GR11 route forms a sickle shape; straight up the Río Ara valley, then curving left to mount the Barranco de Batans (de los Batanes). It then crosses the watershed at the Cuello de Brazato and curls down to the spa resort of Balneario de Panticosa.

At the junction where the Day 20A route turns left to Puente Oncins, go right to follow the trail for a further 7.5km of gradual, effortless ascent of the Río Ara valley as far as the mouth of the Barranco de Batáns (2050m). The gorge becomes more attractive as you gain height, set against the imposing, unscaleable southwest face of Vignemale (3303m).

Allow about two hours from here to the **Cuello de Brazato** (2578m). Immediately west of the pass and 200m below is a level-bottomed cirque containing the two **Ibóns de Brazato**; you may want to *camp* here if you don't have sufficient daylight or stamina to reach the Balneario de Panticosa, still 90 minutes further on. For information on food and accommodation in Balneario de Panticosa, see Places to Stay & Eat at the end of Day 21A.

Day 22: Balneario de Panticosa to Ibón de Llena Cantal
6 to 6½ hours, 9km
The *GR11: Senda Pirenaica* handbook by PRAMES recommends a 21.5km marathon with over 2500m of altitude change and quotes an overly optimistic time of eight hours. We prefer to break the journey into

one longish and one shorter day with an overnight camp. If you're without a tent, a further one to 1¼ hours beyond the Ibón de Llena Cantal will bring you to the excellent Refugio de Respomuso. If you want to break earlier, there are some particularly fine *camp sites* beside every lake on the route to the east of the Collado de Piedrafita. There's no shortage of water on this stretch.

Leave Balneario de Panticosa beside the Casa de Piedra and once beyond the last of the spa buildings head north up a rocky, well established path, popular with day-trippers on their way to the Embalse de Bachimaña reservoirs.

Some 45 minutes above a mirador, cross a meadow (1900m), the first spot above the spa where *camping* is allowed. Once you've passed the Cascada d'o Fraile water-falls, a series of steep zigzags leads after two hours to the head of the lower Embalse de Bachimaña (2180m). On the eastern shore of the reservoir are a pair of simple *shelters* and a potential *camp site*.

There's another small but more substantial *refugio* with space for *camping* beside the north-eastern shore of the higher Embalse de Bachimaña. If you're thinking of staying here, approach the refugio via the lake's northern end; the east-bank trail depicted on the Editorial Alpina map follows a route that is plain dangerous. On the reservoir's west shore, just after passing a small island in the lake, there's a fork. Follow the GR11 as it ascends and resist the temptation to stay on the enticingly flat track which ends in nothingness at the lake's edge.

You're back among chunky granite boulders and slabs – hard nonporous rock where the water gurgles at surface level rather than percolating underground. The first Ibón Azul, 1½ to 1¾ hours beyond the lower Embalse de Bachimaña, is a scruffy spot with an unpleasant, doorless metal shelter daubed with racist slogans beside an ugly dam.

Turn your back on it and attack the steep 20 to 30 minute boulder ascent to the altogether different upper Ibón Azul tarn. In a stunning setting below the Picos del Infierno

and Piedrafita mountains and unmarred by human construction, its lakeside meadows offer the best *camp site* east of the pass.

It takes around 1¼ hours from Ibón Azul to reach the **Cuello d'o Infierno** (2721m), ascending through chaotic, fragmented rock where scarcely a blade or sprig of anything green grows. From the pass, nowhere near as hellish as its name implies, there are great views east over the Embalses de Bachimaña and Lagos de Bramatuero and over the often semi-frozen Ibón de Tebarray to the west.

Hell comes 20 minutes later as you ease yourself over the rim of the Collado de Piedrafita (2782m) to descend steeply down a snow-covered scree slope (the snow persists until late into summer). Negotiate this, curl around a shoulder, and heaven stretches before you: the bijou **Ibón de Llena Cantal**, the grassy, stepped meadows, and below them the Embalse de Respomuso.

It takes 1¼ to 1½ hours to descend to the Ibón de Llena Cantal (2450m). On the east shore next to a striped pole is an excellent *camp site* (note that the trail follows the west bank, not the route indicated on the Editorial Alpina map).

Day 23: Ibón de Llena Cantal to Sallent de Gállego via Refugio de Respomuso
4 to 4½ hours, 12.25km

Continue northwards and downhill over springy turf for 20 minutes until you reach a wide meadow and another five star *camp site*. A further 20 minutes along the path the GR11 splits to go both right and left around the **Embalse de Respomuso**. For the Refugio de Respomuso, take either of two clear paths heading to the right of the lake and head north over a small ridge to a small white storage hut, once a refugio. If you're planning on *camping*, stay below this building in the water meadows or beside the small, unnamed tarn to its north-east, since tents aren't allowed in the immediate environs of the refugio.

The *Refugio de Respomuso* (☎/fax 974 49 02 03), open year-round, with espresso machine, draught beer, hot showers and Rioja wines is a palace among mountain huts. The staff are friendliness itself and prices (1200 ptas per night, 1750 ptas for dinner) are refugio average. It's essential to reserve in July and August and advisable at other times since the place is often booked by school and college groups.

The west end of the dam 15 minutes beyond the refugio is full of industrial detritus from the construction of the dam. What's billed as a refugio is now dilapidated and rubble-strewn and the chapel is locked – neither merit a detour. From a sign, 'La Sarra', head straight down the valley of the Río de Aguas Limpias on a good-quality path. It's a popular trail and, with under three hours to go on this, the very last leg of the Pyrenean Traverse, you can have the satisfaction of acknowledging panting, overheated uphill toilers with a cheery, evenbreathed greeting.

An hour or so from the dam, the green bowl of the **Llano Cheto** spreads before you, watered by the cascades of the Río de Aguas Limpias and the Barranco de Arriel. At the narrows of Paso del Onso, around 1700m, the gorge bends sharply south. The path, now to the west of the water, tunnels through a fine wood of beech trees and past some attractive lunch spots.

Thirty to 40 minutes from Llano Cheto, the track rounds a shoulder to reveal the wide meadows of Llano Tornadizas and the

Hydrotrash

Purists deplore the tinkering with high mountain tarns caused by small-scale hydroelectric schemes. Though many water pipes linking one lake with another are buried deep underground, there are some monumentally ugly wide-bore tubes which drop water from dam level to turbines further down in the valley. Around the dams you'll often see the abandoned debris of their construction: a twisted stretch of narrowgauge railway line, the concrete pad of a demolished hut or the rusting pylons of long-abandoned cable lifts.

To compensate for the aesthetic disadvantages, there's a special spin-off for walkers. Several of the mountain refugios started life as rest houses for workers on the dams and were given over to walking clubs and societies once construction had ceased.

first distant, emerald glint of the Embalse de la Sarra. Another 30 minutes brings you to a car park, picnic area and fine multiheaded fuente at the head of the dam.

Take the reservoir's east bank, pass the growling turbines of the hydroelectric station and follow the sealed road down to Sallent de Gállego for a total walking time of a little more than four hours.

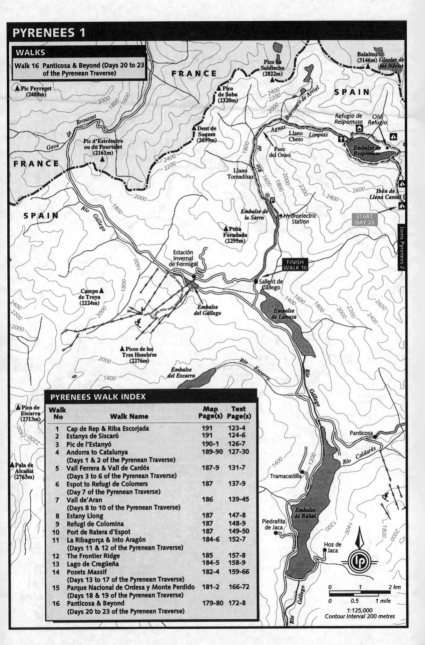

PYRENEES 1

WALKS

Walk 16 Panticosa & Beyond (Days 20 to 23
of the Pyrenean Traverse)

▲ Pic Peyreget
(2488m)

FRANCE

▲ Pico
de Soba
(2320m)

Pico de
Saldiecho
(2822m)

Balaitus
(3146m) Glacier de
los Néous

SPAIN

Barranco de Arriel

Refugio de
Respomuso

Old
Refugio

Broussel

Gave de

Pic d'Estrémère
ou du Pourtalet
(2161m)

FRANCE

▲ Dent de
Soques
(2699m)

Aguas

Llano
Cheto

Limpias

Embalse de
Respomuso

Paso
del Onso

SPAIN

Río

Llano
Tornadizas

Ibón de
Llena Cantal

Río Gállego

Embalse de
la Sarra

Hydroelectric
Station

START
DAY 23

▲ Peña
Foradada
(2295m)

Estación
Invernal
de Formigal

FINISH
WALK 16

Sallent de
Gállego

Joins Pyrenees 2

Campo
de Troya
(2224m)

Embalse
del Gállego

Embalse
de Lanuza

▲ Picos de los
Tres Hombres
(2276m)

Embalse
del Escarra

Río Escarra

Río

Río Gállego

▲ Pico de
Escarra
(2713m)

Panticosa

Río Caldarés

▲ Pala de
Alcañiz
(2763m)

Tramacastilla

Embalse
de Búbal

Piedrafita
de Jaca

Hoz de
Jaca

0   1   2 km

0   0.5   1 mile

1:125,000
Contour Interval 200 metres

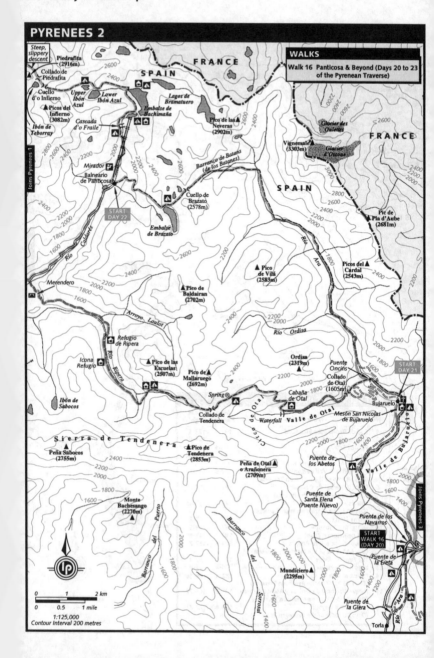

PYRENEES 2

Joins Pyrenees 1

Joins Pyrenees 3

WALKS

Walk 16 Panticosa & Beyond (Days 20 to 23
of the Pyrenean Traverse)

FRANCE

SPAIN

Steep,
slippery
descent

Piedrafita
(2916m)

Collado de
Piedrafita

Cuello
d'o Infierno

Picos del
Infierno
(3082m)

Ibón de
Teborray

Upper
Ibón Azul

Lower
Ibón Azul

Embalse
de Bachimaña

Cascada
d'o Fraile

Lagos de
Bramatuero

Pico de las
Neveras (2902m)

Glacier des
Oulettes

Vignemale
(3303m)

Glacier
d'Ossone

FRANCE

SPAIN

Mirador

Balneario
de Panticosa

Barranco de Batans
(de los Batanes)

Cuello de
Brazato
(2578m)

Pic de
Pla d'Aube
(2681m)

START
DAY 22

Río Caldarés

Embalse
de Brazato

Picos del
Cardal
(2543m)

Río Ara

Merendero

Pico de Vilá
(2583m)

Pico de
Baldairan
(2702m)

Arroyo Laulot

Río Ordisa

Refugio
de Ripera

Río Ripera

Icona
Refugio

Pico de las
Escuelas
(2507m)

Pico de
Mallaruego
(2692m)

Ordisa
(2319m)

Puente
Oncins

Collado
de Otal
(1605m)

START
DAY 21

Ibón de
Sabocos

Spring

Collado de
Tendenera

Cabaña
de Otal

Bujaruelo

Circo de Otal

Waterfall Valle de Otal

Mesón San Nicolás
de Bujaruelo

Sierra de Tendenera

Peña Sabocos
(2785m)

Pico de
Tendenera
(2853m)

Peña de Otal
o Arañonera
(2709m)

Puente de
los Abetos

Valle de Bujaruelo

Monte
Bachesango
(2270m)

Barranco del Puerto

Barranco del Sorrosal

Puente de
Santa Elena
(Puente Nuevo)

Puente de los
Navarros

START
WALK 16
(DAY 20)

Puente
de la Ereta

Mondiciero
(2295m)

Puente de
la Glera

Río Ara

Torla

0   1   2 km

0   0.5   1 mile

1:125,000
Contour Interval 200 metres

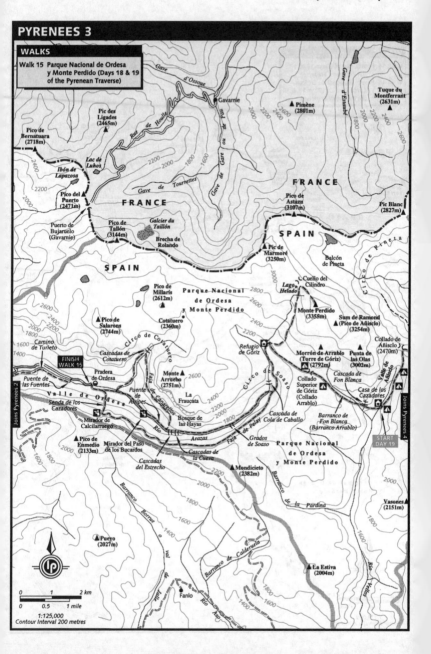

PYRENEES 3

WALKS

Walk 15 Parque Nacional de Ordesa
y Monte Perdido (Days 18 & 19
of the Pyrenean Traverse)

Tuque du
Montferrant
(2631m)

Gave d'Ossoue

Gavarnie

Pimène
(2801m)

Gave d'Estaubé

Pic des
Ligades
(2465m)

Rue de Houlla

Gave de Gare ou la Pau

Pico de
Bernatuara
(2718m)

Lac de
Luhox

Ibón de
Lapazosa

Gave de Tourrettes

FRANCE

Pic de
Astazu
(3107m)

Pic Blanc
(2827m)

Pico del
Puerto
(2471m)

FRANCE

SPAIN

Circo de Pineta

Puerto de
Bujaruelo
(Gavarnie)

Pico de
Tallón
(3144m)

Galcier du
Taillón

Brecha de
Rolando

Pic de
Marmoré
(3250m)

Balcón
de Pineta

SPAIN

Pico de
Millarís
(2612m)

Parque Nacional
de Ordesa
y Monte Perdido

Lago
Helado

Cuello del
Cilindro

Pico de
Salarons
(2744m)

Cotatuero
(2360m)

Monte Perdido
(3355m)

Sum de Ramond
(Pico de Añisclo)
(3254m)

Camino
de Turieto

Circo de Cotatuero

Cascadas de
Cotatuero

Refugio
de Góriz

Morrón de Arrablo
(Torre de Góriz)
(2792m)

Punta de
las Olas
(3002m)

Collado
de Añisclo
(2470m)

FINISH
WALK 15

Pradera
de Ordesa

Faja de Canarellos

Monte
Arruebo
(2751m)

Collado
Superior
de Góriz
(Collado
Arrablo)

Cascada de
Fon Blanca

Valle de Añisclo

Puente
de las Fuentes

Valle de Ordesa

Senda de los
Cazadores

Puente
de
Canarellos

La
Fraucata

Circo de Soaso

Casa de los
Cazadores

Mirador de
Calcilarruego

Faja de Pelay

Cascada de
Cola de Caballo

Barranco de
Fon Blanca
(Barranco Arrablo)

Pico de
Enmedio
(2133m)

Mirador del Paso
de los Bucardos

Río Arazas

Bosque
de las Hayas

Grados
de Soaso

Cascadas de
la Cueva

Parque Nacional
de Ordesa
y Monte Perdido

Cascadas
del Estrecho

Mondicieto
(2382m)

Vasones
(2151m)

Barranco Bernatuara

Barranco de la Pardina

Pueyo
(2027m)

Barranco de Calderuela

La Estiva
(2004m)

Fanlo

Río Aso

Río Aso

Joins Pyrenees 2

Joins Pyrenees 4

START
DAY 19

0   1   2 km
0   0.5   1 mile
1:125,000
Contour Interval 200 metres

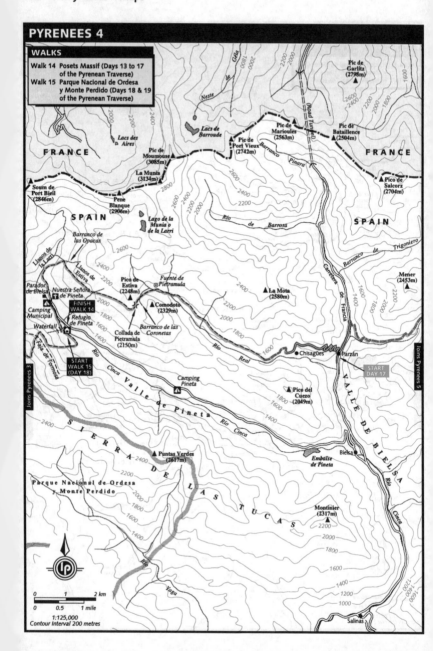

PYRENEES 4

WALKS

Walk 14 Posets Massif (Days 13 to 17
of the Pyrenean Traverse)
Walk 15 Parque Nacional de Ordesa
y Monte Perdido (Days 18 & 19
of the Pyrenean Traverse)

Gave de Neste

Lacs des
Aires

FRANCE

Lacs de
Barroude

Pic de
Moumouse
(3085m)

La Munia
(3134m)

Soum de
Port Bieil
(2846m)

Pene
Blanque
(2906m)

SPAIN

Pic de
Port Vieux
(2742m)

Pic de
Marioules
(2563m)

Barranco Pinara

(Road Tunnel)

Pic de
Garlitz
(2798m)

Pic de
Bataillence
(2504m)

FRANCE

Pico de
Salcorz
(2704m)

SPAIN

Lago de la
Munia o
de la Larri

Río de Barrosa

Barranco de
las Opacax

Llanos de
La Larri

Llanos de
Estiva

Parador
de Bielsa

Nuestra Señora
de Pineta

Camping
Municipal

Refugio
de Pineta

Waterfall

Fall de Tomosá

FINISH
WALK 14

START
WALK 15
(DAY 18)

Pico de
Estiva
(2248m)

Fuente de
Pietramula

Comodoto
(2329m)

Collada de
Pietramula
(2150m)

Barranco de las
Coronetas

La Mota
(2580m)

Barranco de Trigoniero

Mener
(2453m)

Carretera de Francia

Río Real

Valle de Pineta

Río Cinca

Camping
Pineta

Pico del
Cuezo
(2049m)

Chisagües

Parzán

START
DAY 17

VALLE DE BIELSA

SIERRA DE LAS TUCAS

Puntas Verdes
(2617m)

Parque Nacional de Ordesa
y Monte Perdido

Río Cinca

Yaga

Bielsa

Embalse
de Pineta

Montinier
(2317m)

Río Cinca

Salinas

Joins Pyrenees 3

Joins Pyrenees 5

0   1   2 km
0   0.5   1 mile
1:125,000
Contour Interval 200 metres

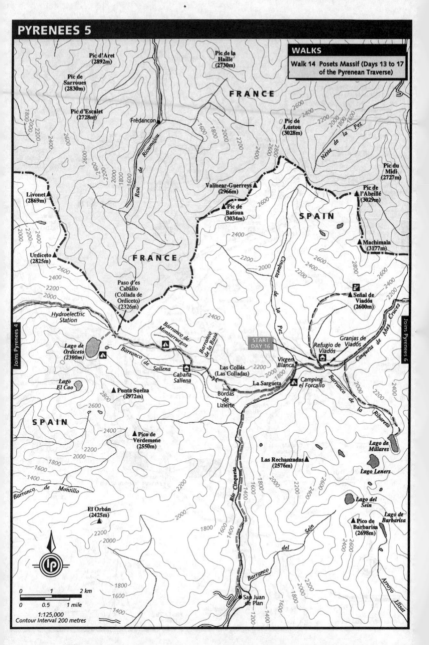

PYRENEES 5

WALKS

Walk 14 Posets Massif (Days 13 to 17 of the Pyrenean Traverse)

Pic d'Aret (2892m)

Pic de la Haille (2730m)

FRANCE

Pic de Sarroués (2830m)

Pic d'Escalet (2728m)

Frédancon

Pic de Lustou (3028m)

Neste de la Pez

Pic du Midi (2727m)

Valinear-Guerreys (2966m)

Pic de l'Abeillé (3025m)

Livonet (2869m)

Pic de Batoua (3034m)

SPAIN

Machimala (3177m)

Urdiceto (2825m)

FRANCE

Señal de Viadós (2600m)

Paso d'es Caballo (Collada de Ordiceto) (2326m)

Cinqueta de la Pez

Hydroelectric Station

Barranco de Montarruegos

Barranco de la Bada

Lago de Ordiceto (2390m)

Barranco de Sallena

START DAY 16

Granjas de Viadós

Refugio de Viadós

Joins Pyrenees 6

Lago El Cao

Cabaña Sallena

Las Collás (Las Colladas)

Virgen Blanca

Cinqueta de Añes Cruees

Punta Suelza (2972m)

Bordas de Lizierte

La Sargueta

Camping el Forcallo

Barranco de la Ribareta

SPAIN

Lago de Millares

Pico de Verdemene (2550m)

Las Rechanzadas (2576m)

Lago Leners

Río Cinqueta

Lago del Sein

El Orbán (2425m)

Sein

Lago de Barbarisa

Pico de Barbarisa (2698m)

del

Barranco

Arroyo Liliai

San Juan de Plan

Joins Pyrenees 4

0   1   2 km
0   0.5   1 mile
1:125,000
Contour Interval 200 metres

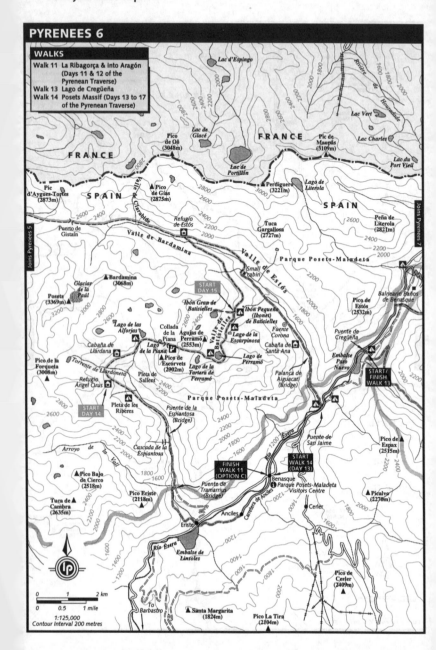

PYRENEES 6

WALKS

Walk 11 La Ribagorça & into Aragón
(Days 11 & 12 of the
Pyrenean Traverse)
Walk 13 Lago de Cregüeña
Walk 14 Posets Massif (Days 13 to 17
of the Pyrenean Traverse)

Lac d'Espingo

Rivière de Houradade

Lac Vert

Lac Charles

FRANCE

Pico de Oô
(3048m)

Pic de
Maupás
(3109m)

Lac de
Glacé

Lac du
Port Vieil

Lac de
Portillón

Pic
d'Aygues-Tortes
(2873m)

Pico
de Gías
(2875m)

SPAIN

Perdiguero
(3221m)

Lago de
Literola

SPAIN

Peña de
Literola
(2821m)

Puerto de
Gistaín

Refugio
de Estós

Tuca
Gargallosa
(2727m)

Valle de Clarabide

Valle de Bardamina

Valle de Estós

Parque Posets-Maladeta

Small
cabin

Pico de
Estós
(2532m)

Bardamina
(3068m)

Balneario Baños
de Benasque

Glaciar
de la
Paúl

Ibón Gran de
Batisielles

START
DAY 15

Ibón Pequeño
(Ibonet)
de Batisielles

Posets
(3369m)

Lago de las
Alforjas

Collada
de la
Piana

Aguja de
Perramó
(2553m)

Lago de la
Escarpinosa

Fuente
Corona

Puente de
Cregüeña

Cabaña de
Llárdana

Lago de
la Piana

Pico de
Perramó
(2902m)

Lago de la
Tartera de
Perramó

Cabaña de
Santa Ana

Lago de
Perramó

Embalse
Paso
Nuevo

Pico de la
Forqueta
(3008m)

Torrente de Llardaneta

Refugio
Ángel Orús

Pleta de
Sallent

Palanca de
Aiguacari
(Bridge)

START/
FINISH
WALK 13

START
DAY 14

Pleta de les
Ríberes

Puente de la
Espiantosa
(Bridge)

Parque Posets-Maladeta

Valle de Batisielles

Arroyo   de   la   Vall

Cascada de la
Espiantosa

Río Esera

Puente de
San Jaime

Pico de
Espás
(2515m)

Pico Bajo
de Cierco
(2518m)

FINISH
WALK 11
(OPTION C)

START
WALK 14
(DAY 13)

Tuca de la
Cambra
(2635m)

Pico Eriste
(2118m)

Puente de
Tramarrius
(Bridge)

Benasque
Parque Posets-Maladeta
Visitors Centre

Picalya
(2270m)

Ancíles

Carretera de Anciles

Cerler

Eriste

Río Esera

Embalse de
Linsóles

N

To
Barbastro

Santa Margarita
(1824m)

Pico La Tira
(2104m)

Pico de
Cerler
(2409m)

0   1   2 km
0   0.5   1 mile
1:125,000
Contour Interval 200 metres

Joins Pyrenees 5

Joins Pyrenees 7

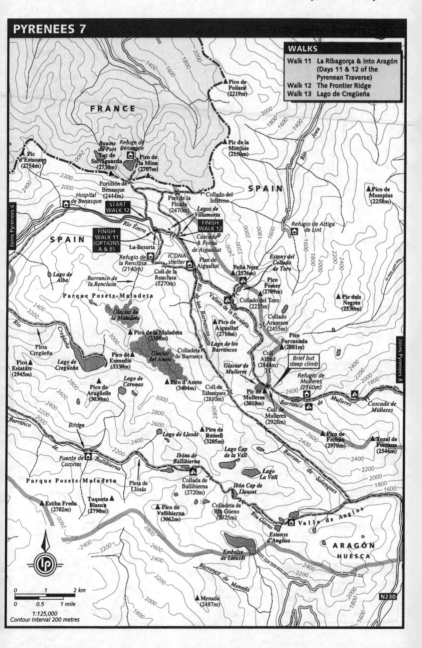

PYRENEES 7

WALKS

Walk 11 La Ribagorça & into Aragón (Days 11 & 12 of the Pyrenean Traverse)
Walk 12 The Frontier Ridge
Walk 13 Lago de Cregüeña

FRANCE

Pico de Poilané (2219m)

Pic de la Monjoie (2150m)

Pico de Mompius (2258m)

Pic d'Estaues (2754m)

Boums du Port
Tuc de Salvaguarda (2738m)
Refuge de Benasque
Pico de la Mina (2707m)

Portillon de Benasque (2444m)

Hospital de Benasque

SPAIN

Port de la Picada (2470m)

Collado del Infierno

START WALK 12

Río Ésera

Lagos de Villamorta

FINISH WALK 12

Refugio de Aitiga de Lint

La Besurta

FINISH WALK 11 (OPTIONS A & B)

ICONA shelter

Cascada & Forau de Aiguallut

Refugio de la Renclusa (2140m)

Plan de Aiguallut

Peña Nere (2576m)

Estany del Collado de Toro

SPAIN

Lago de Alba

Barranco de la Renclusa

Coll de la Renclusa (2270m)

Pico Pomer (2709m)

Collado del Toro (2235m)

Pic dels Negres (2530m)

Parque Posets-Maladeta

Glaciar de la Maladeta

Valleta de la Escaleta

Collado Aranesos (2455m)

Pico de la Maladeta (3308m)

Pico de Aiguallut (2710m)

Pico Forcanada (2881m)

Pleta Cregüeña

Pico de Enmedio (3330m)

Colladeta de Barrancs

Glaciar del Aneto

Lago de los Barrancos

Coll Alfred (2844m)

Brief but steep climb

Lago de Cregüeña

Pico Estatats (2945m)

Glaciar de Mulleres

Refugio de Mulleres (2350m)

Pico de Araguells (3030m)

Lago de Coronas

Pico d'Aneto (3404m)

Coll de Saleneus (2810m)

Pic de Mulleres (3010m)

Cascada de Mulleres

Barranco de Mulleres

Barranco

Bridge

Lago de Llosás

Pico de Russell (3205m)

Coll de Mulleres (2928m)

Pico de Fechau (2970m)

Tozal de Fontana (2546m)

Puente de Coronas

Ballibierno

Ibóns de Ballibierna

Lago Cap de la Vall

Barranc de Salenques

Parque Posets-Maladeta

Pleta de Llosás

Lago La Vall

Estiba Freda (2702m)

Tuqueta Blanca (2790m)

Collada de Ballibierna (2720m)

Ibón Cap de Llauset

Valle de Anglos

Pico de Vallibierna (3062m)

Colladeta de Ríu Güeno (2825m)

Ríu Güeno

ARAGÓN

HUESCA

Estanys d'Anglios

Embalse de Llauset

Barranco de Menada

Menada (2487m)

N230

0   1   2 km
0   0.5   1 mile

1:125,000
Contour Interval 200 metres

Joins Pyrenees 6

Joins Pyrenees 8

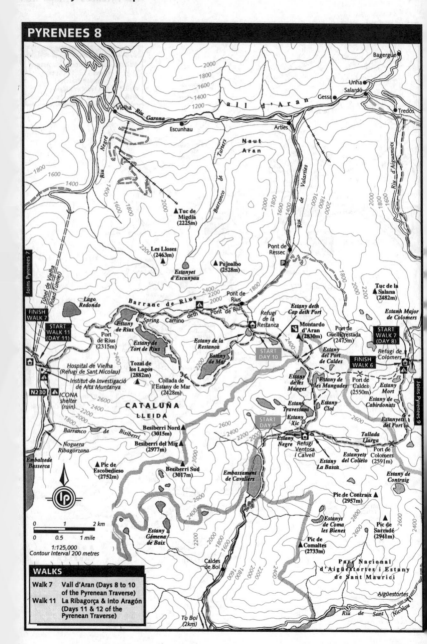

PYRENEES 8

WALKS

Walk 7   Vall d'Aran (Days 8 to 10
of the Pyrenean Traverse)
Walk 11 La Ribagorça & into Aragón
(Days 11 & 12 of the
Pyrenean Traverse)

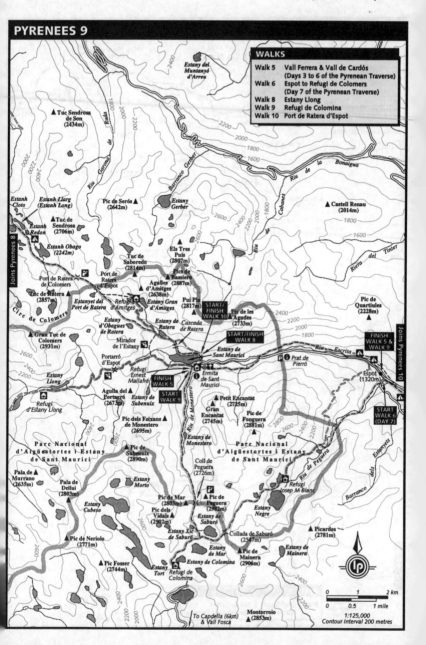

PYRENEES 9

WALKS

Walk 5	Vall Ferrera & Vall de Cardós	
	(Days 3 to 6 of the Pyrenean Traverse)	
Walk 6	Espot to Refugi de Colomers	
	(Day 7 of the Pyrenean Traverse)	
Walk 8	Estany Llong	
Walk 9	Refugi de Colomina	
Walk 10	Port de Rater d'Espot	

Estany del Muntanyó d'Arreu

Tuc Sendrosa de Son (2434m)

Riu Coronas de Ruda

Estany Gerber

Riu de la Bonaigua

Pic de Serós ▲ (2642m)

Barranco Gerber

Riu de la Bonaigua

Castell Renau ▲ (2014m)

Estanh Cloto

Estanh Llarg (Estanh Long)

Tuc de Sendrosa (2706m)

Estanh Redon

Estanh Obago (2242m)

Joins Pyrenees 8

Tuc de Saboredo (2814m)

Els Tres Puis (2807m)

Riera del Tinter

Port de Ratera de Colomers

Pic de Bassiero (2887m)

Port de Ratera d'Espot

Agulles d'Amitges (2638m)

Pui Pla (2817m)

START/FINISH WALK 10

Pic de Quartiules (2228m)

Tuc de Ratera (2857m)

Estanyet del Port de Ratera

Refugi d'Amitges

Estany Gran d'Amitges

Pic de les Agudes (2733m)

Gran Tuc de Colomers (2931m)

Circ de Colomers

Estany d'Obagues de Ratera

Estany de Ratera

Cascada de Ratera

START/FINISH WALK 8

Mirador de l'Estany

Joins Pyrenees 10

Portarró d'Espot

Estany de Sant Maurici

Riu Escrita

FINISH WALK 5 & WALK 9

Estany Llong

Refugi Ernest Mallafré

FINISH WALK 5

Ermita de Sant Maurici

Prat de Pierró

Espot (1320m)

Refugi d'Estany Llong

Agulla del Portarró (2673m)

Estany de Subenuix

START WALK 9

START WALK 10

Riu de Monestero

Petit Encantat (2725m)

START WALK 6 (DAY 7)

Pic dels Feixans de Monestero (2695m)

Gran Encantat (2745m)

Pic de Fonguera (2881m)

Pic de Subenuix (2890m)

Estany de Monestero

Parc Nacional d'Aigüestortes i Estany de Sant Maurici

Riu de Peguera

Parc Nacional d'Aigüestortes i Estany de Sant Maurici

Pala de Murrano (2635m)

Pala de Dellui (2803m)

Coll de Peguera (2726m)

Refugi Josep M Blanc

Barranco dels Estanyets

Estany Morto

Estany Cubeso

Pic de Mar (2803m)

Pic de Peguera (2982m)

Estany Negre

Pic dels Vidals (2902m)

Estany de Saburó

Picardes (2781m)

Pic de Neriolo (2771m)

Estany Xic de Saburó

Collada de Saburó (2547m)

Estany de Mainera

Pic Fosser (2744m)

Estany Tort

Estany de Mar

Pic de Mainera (2906m)

Estany de Colomina

Refugi de Colomina

To Capdella (6km) & Vall Fosca

Montorroio ▲ (2853m)

0   1   2 km
0   0.5   1 mile

1:125,000
Contour Interval 200 metres

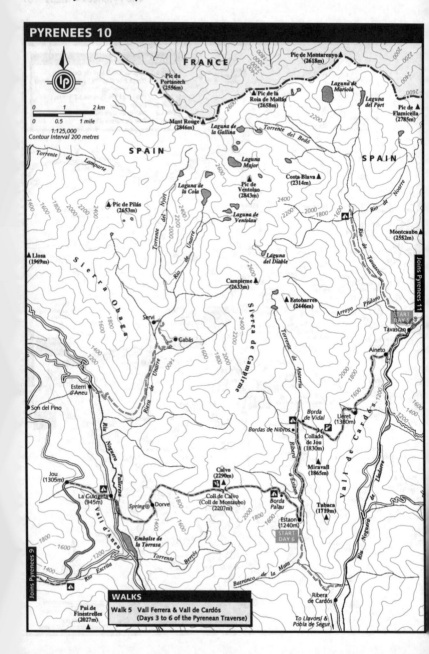

PYRENEES 10

FRANCE

Pic de Montarenyo ▲
(2618m)

Pic du
Portanech
(2556m)

▲ Pic de la Roia de Mollás
(2658m)

Laguna de
Mariola

Laguna
del Port

Pic de
Flamicella
(2785m) ▲

Mont Rouge ▲
(2846m)

Laguna de
la Gallina

Torrente del Beds

SPAIN

SPAIN

0   1   2 km
0   0.5   1 mile
1:125,000
Contour Interval 200 metres

Laguna
Major

Costa Blava ▲
(2314m)

Torrente   de   Lamparte

Pic de
Ventolao
(2843m)

Laguna de
la Cola

▲ Pic de Pilás
(2653m)

Laguna de
Ventolau

Montcaubo ▲
(2552m)

▲ Llosa
(1969m)

Laguna
del Diable

Sierra   Obaga

Campirme ▲
(2633m)

▲ Estobarres
(2446m)

Arroyo   Pauloro

START
DAY 5

Tavascan

Servi

Sierra   de   Campirme

Gabás

Aineto

Esterri
d'Aneu

Borda
de Vidal

Lleret
(1380m)

Son del Pino

Bordas de Nibrós

Collado
de Jóu
(1830m)

Miravall
(1865m)

Jou
(1305m)

Calvo
(2290m)

La Guingeta
(945m)

Spring   Dorve

Coll de Calvo
(Coll de Montaubo)
(2207m)

Borda
Palau

Tubaca
(1719m)

Estaon
(1240m)

START
DAY 6

Embalse de
la Torrasa

Torrente   Berrós

Barranco   de   la   Mata

Rio   Escrita

Ribera
de Cardós

Pui de
Finéstrelles
(2027m) ▲

To Llavorsí &
Pobla de Segur

WALKS

Walk 5   Vall Ferrera & Vall de Cardós
(Days 3 to 6 of the Pyrenean Traverse)

Joins Pyrenees 11

Joins Pyrenees 9

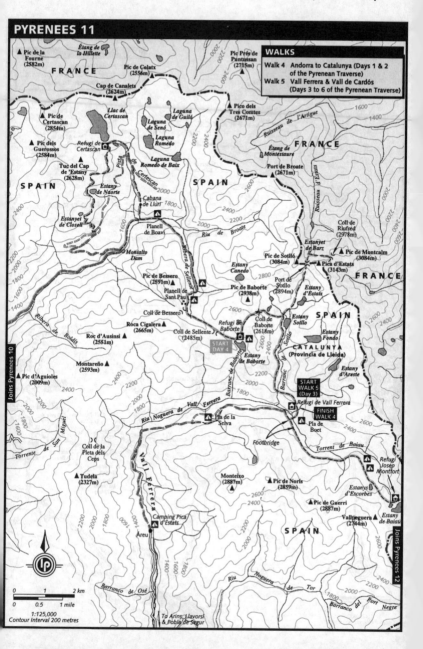

PYRENEES 11

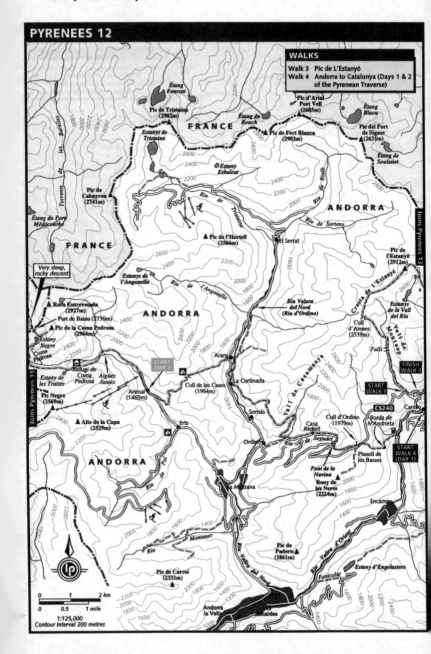

PYRENEES 12

WALKS

Walk 3   Pic de L'Estanyó
Walk 4   Andorra to Catalunya (Days 1 & 2
         of the Pyrenean Traverse)

Étang Fourcat

Pic de Tristaina (2902m)

FRANCE

Étang du Rouch

Pic d'Arial
Port Vell
(2685m)

Étang Blaou

Estany de Tristaina

Pic de Fort Blanca (2903m)

Pic del Port de Siguer (263m)

Étang de Soulanet

Estany Esbalcat

Riu de Riub

ANDORRA

Pic de Cabayrou (2741m)

Riu de Tristaina

Étang du Port Médocenthe

FRANCE

Pic de l'Hortell (2566m)

El Serrat

Riu de Sorteny

Pic de l'Estanyó (2912m)

Very steep, rocky descent

Estanys de l'Angonella

Riu de l'Angonella

Riu Valera del Nord (Riu d'Ordino)

Cresta de l'Estanyó

Estanys de la Vall del Riu

Roca Entrevessada (2927m)
Port de Baiau (2756m)
Pic de la Coma Pedrosa (2964m)

ANDORRA

Coll d'Arènes (2539m)

Vall de Montaup

Estany Negre Coma Pedrosa

Refugi de Coma Pedrosa
Aigües Juntes

Estany de les Truites

Arans

Falls

START DAY 2

Pic Negre (2569m)

Arinsal (1465m)

Coll de les Cases (1964m)

La Cortinada

FINISH WALK 3

Vall de Casamanya

START WALK 3

Alte de la Capa (2829m)

Erts

Sornás

Coll d'Ordino (1979m)

CS240

Canillo

Borda de N'Andrieta

ANDORRA

Ordino

Casa Redort

Riu de Segudet

Planell de les Basses

START WALK 4 (DAY 1)

Riu de Pal

La Massana

Font de la Navina

Bony de les Nerés (2224m)

Encamp

Montaner

Riu

Riu Valira del Nord

Pic de Padern (1861m)

Riu Valira d'Orient

Estany d'Engolasters

Pic de Carroi (2331m)

Funicular

Andorra la Vella

Escaldes

0   1   2 km
0   0.5   1 mile
1:125,000
Contour Interval 200 metres

Joins Pyrenees 11

Joins Pyrenees 13

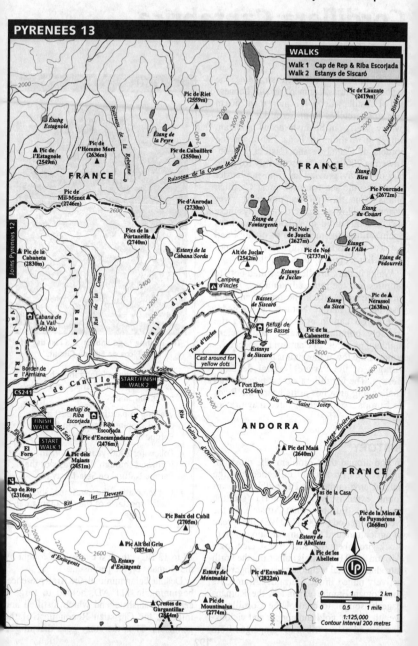

PYRENEES 13

WALKS

Walk 1   Cap de Rep & Riba Escorjada
Walk 2   Estanys de Siscaró

Étang Estagnole

▲ Pic de l'Estagnole (2549m)

Pic de l'Homme Mort (2636m)

FRANCE

Pic de Riet (2559m) ▲

Étang de la Peyre

Pic de Caballière (2550m)

Ruisseau de la Rebenne

Ruisseau de la Coume de Varilles

FRANCE

Pic de Lauzate (2419m) ▲

Nabat Rivière

Étang Bleu

Pic Fourcade (2672m) ▲

Pic de Mil-Menut (2746m) ▲

Pic d'Anrodat (2730m) ▲

Étang de Fontargente

Pic Noir de Joucla (2627m) ▲

Étangs de l'Albe

Étang du Couart

Étang de Pédourrés

Joins Pyrenees 12

Pics de la Portaneille (2740m) ▲

Estany de la Cabana Sorda

Alt de Juclar (2542m)

Pic de Noé (2737m) ▲

Estanys de Juclav

Étang du Sisca

Pic de Nérassol (2638m) ▲

▲ Pic de la Cabaneta (2830m)

Rui de la Coma

Vall de Ransol

Camping d'Incles

Basses de Siscaró

Refugi de les Basses 🏠

Pic de la Cabanette (2818m) ▲

🏠 Cabana de la Vall del Riu

Vall del Riu

Vall d'Incles

Tossa d'Incles

Cast around for yellow dots

Estanys de Siscaró

Border de l'Armiana

CS241

Vall de Canillo

START/FINISH WALK 2

Soldeu

Port Dret (2564m)

Riu de Saint Josep

FINISH WALK 1

Refugi de Riba Escorjada 🏠

Riba Escorjada

Pic d'Encampadana (2476m) ▲

Riu Valira d'Orient

ANDORRA

START WALK 1

El Forn

Pic dels Maians (2451m) ▲

Pic del Maià (2640m) ▲

FRANCE

Arget Rivière

🚉 Cap de Rep (2316m)

Riu de les Deveses

Pas de la Casa

Pic de la Mine de Puymórens (2668m) ▲

Pic Baix del Cubil (2705m) ▲

Estany de les Abelletes

Pic de les Abelletes ▲

Pic Alt del Griu (2874m) ▲

Riu d'Ensagents

Estany d'Ensagents

Estany de Montmalús

Pic d'Envalira (2822m) ▲

Crestes de Gargantillar (2864m) ▲

Pic de Mountmalus (2774m) ▲

0   1   2 km
0   0.5   1 mile
1:125,000
Contour Interval 200 metres

Cordillera Cantábrica

The Cordillera Cantábrica straddles the regions of Asturias, Cantabria and the Leonese part of Castilla y León. It is more than 250km long and stretches from Serra dos Ancares (where 'sierra' in Spanish means mountain range) in Galicia to Peña Labra on the borders of Cantabria and Castilla y León. Towering 2000m peaks rise swiftly from the Bay of Biscay, proving an imposing barrier separating the sea from the great Castilian plains. Cut through by powerful river systems and low-lying, verdant valleys these spectacular, humid mountains are perhaps Spain's finest for their wealth of flora and fauna as well as for the variety of landscapes and walking opportunities available.

Walks in the Cordillera are suited both to families and the more adventurous. In Asturias, the walks take in the gentle Senda del Oso and the Parque Natural de Somiedo, where you can lose yourself among the sparsely populated villages and ancient highland pastures. In Cantabria, expect coverage of the lower mountains and numerous villages of the Parque Natural de Saja-Besaya. The Cordillera's most popular and challenging area lies at its heart: the Picos de Europa, composed of three magnificent limestone massifs.

HISTORY

In and around the Cordillera, the most impressive early human influence on the natural environment is Paleolithic cave art found extensively in Cantabria (see the boxed text 'Europe's First Artists'). In the Neolithic period (4000-2400 BC), the spread of agriculture and the domestication of livestock provoked the first forest clearings. Around 2000 BC, immigrants from the north introduced metal technology and copper was actively mined in the Sierra del Áramo. As the Roman Empire expanded, the Romans eagerly sought to control the Cordillera's wealth of iron, gold and copper and viciously subdued native tribes in campaigns from

HIGHLIGHTS

The inviting Lago Enol on the last day of the Picos de Europa Circuit.

- Watching the indefatigable chamois as they leap around steep and rocky mountain slopes

- Walking in pastures and past abandoned shepherd's cabins in the Parque Natural de Somiedo

- Following 2000-year-old Roman highways through the forests of the Parque Natural de Saja-Besaya

- Contemplating the awesome, sheer-walled spectacle of the Garaganta del Cares gorge

29 to 13 BC – the last campaigns fought by the Romans on the peninsula.

Despite being minimal, the Arab presence, beginning in 711 AD, helped to forge a central Spanish legend which justified and initiated the Christian Reconquest of the peninsula. Thus the story goes that in 722 from Covadonga (Cave of the Holy Mother) in the Picos de Europa, the Asturian King Pelayo won the first battle against the Muslims. This great battle led in time to the end of the Muslim presence on the peninsula. Over time, the cave and its magnificent waterfall evolved into a politico-religious symbol and an exceedingly popular site of pilgrimage.

Monasteries proliferated in the 10th and 11th centuries, leaving behind superb examples of Asturian Romanesque architecture. Tracts of land were cleared to make way for urban centres and agricultural and pasture lands for the lay population. In the 16th century corn, potatoes, beans, tomatoes and peppers arrived from the New World, allowing the precarious balance between life and death in the valleys to stabilise.

Though the centuries-old cyclical practice of bringing the flocks from the low winter pastures of Castilla to the high summer pastures continues, transhumance (the oldest continuous economic activity of the Cordillera) is in decline. This becomes apparent as you walk through the villages and pastures of the mountain shepherding communities.

Much of the indigenous forests of the lower slopes were felled to supply iron production, construction and fuel needs, opening up the land to new species of conifers and eucalyptus. Eucalyptuses arrived on the Cantabrian coast 150 years ago, coincidentally introduced by the discoverer of the Altamira caves west of Santander, Marcelino Sanz de Sautuola.

The 20th century has witnessed the most aggressive transformation of the landscape as technology has made it easier to extract coal, ore and lumber and to enter areas which are ecologically fragile. The conservation

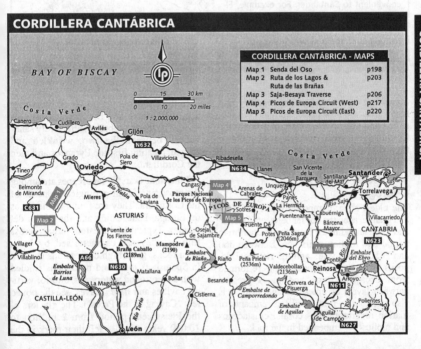

CORDILLERA CANTÁBRICA

CORDILLERA CANTÁBRICA - MAPS	
Map 1 Senda del Oso	p198
Map 2 Ruta de los Lagos &	p203
Ruta de las Brañas	
Map 3 Saja-Besaya Traverse	p206
Map 4 Picos de Europa Circuit (West)	p217
Map 5 Picos de Europa Circuit (East)	p220

Europe's First Artists

Imagine stepping back in time to Paleolithic Europe (35,000-10,000 BC). Bone-chilling cold (snow remains perpetually at 700-1000m) hits you and the land is filled with almost mythical creatures – hairy mammoth and rhinoceros – and huge herds of bison, horses and deer; a hunter's paradise. You've arrived at a pivotal moment in the history of human development. Along the Cantabrian coast, in the Pyrenees and southern France, the oldest and longest lasting art form, cave painting, is being developed.

Using magnesium or carbon to create black lines and ochre or iron oxides to create brown, red, orange and yellow earth tones, artists filled walls and ceilings with animals, human figures, isolated hands and various symbols. Using the natural relief of the rock to convey a sense of volume, the movement and realism of the naturalistic animal figures richly contrasts with the distortion of faces and abstraction of symbols in these complex works.

West of Santander is Spain's most famous cave, Altamira (open to only 20 visitors a year), discovered in 1875. Many other caves are open to visitors and are convenient to Santander. For example, El Castillo, one of four caves in Puente Viesgo 30km south of Santander, is open to the public and well worth the visit.

Frozen in time – a detail from the 14,000-year-old cave paintings at Altamira

movement also began in this century and many areas are now protected thanks to sustained and effective activism. All in all, the Cordillera is a green Spanish jewel not to be missed.

NATURAL HISTORY
Geology

The oldest zone, composed mostly of slate and granite, is on the border between Asturias and Galicia and dates from the Precambrian period 540 million years ago. Between 360 and 245 million years ago the rich coal deposits of the central Cordillera were formed from decaying ferns and moss pressed between layers of limestone and sand. It is also possible to find fossilised remnants of marine invertebrates – corals, crustaceans and molluscs – embedded in the rock.

In the Cenozoic period 40 million years ago, the African and European plates collided. The Iberian subplate, effectively sandwiched between the two, wrinkled and bulged, creating first the Pyrenees and then the Cordillera.

Limestone (karstic) landscapes are among the most significant geological features of the Cordillera. They are found in the Picos de Europa, Peña Ubiña and the Sierra del Áramo. Typical of limestone areas across Europe, they are characterised by bare, open rocks, great high depressions (known in Spanish as *jous*) and mountains riddled with underground waterways, interior vertical cavities and *simas* (caves; see the boxed text 'Caving in the Picos'). The glaciers of the Pleistocene period from 2 million to 10,000 years ago also left their mark in the

Cordillera by creating U-shaped valleys, polished walls and moraines.

Flora

Forming a natural border between the Atlantic Ocean and the more Mediterranean climate to the south, the Cordillera is exceedingly rich in flora and fauna. The dramatic variation in altitude also accounts for the great diversity of species.

Up to 500m along the valley floors and riverways, forests include common ash (*Fraxinus excelsior*), evergreen, holm oak, common oak (*Quercus robur*), beech, linden or small-leaved lime (*Tilia cordata*), chestnut, elm, alder (*Alnus glutinosa*), willow (*Salix* spp), maple and cherry trees.

Shrubs include hazel bushes (*Corylus avellana*), blackberry, sloe berry (*Prunus spinosa*), wild roses and honeysuckle. In the wetter northern valleys of Asturias, expect to see marsh orchids, globe flowers, ragged robins and marsh helleborines. In the more Mediterranean southern valleys, purple orchids and tassel hyacinths fill the meadows and the forests include strawberry trees (*Arbutus unedo*) and cork oaks (*Q. suber*).

From 500 to 1700m the plant life responds to the shorter summers and early frosts. Beech (*Fagus sylvatica*), birch (*Betula celiberica*), mountain ash (*Sorbus aria*), holly (*Ilex aquifolium*) and holm oaks dominate the forests. Shrubs include gorse, broom (*Calluna vulgaris*), genista, bell heather and tree heath (*Erica cinerea* and *E. arborea*).

In the subalpine zone from 1700 to 2300m, beech and birch trees can still be found as well as juniper bushes (*Juniperus nana*) clinging to rock walls. The alpine area (2300m and above) supports small plants including glacier fescue (*Festuca glacialis*), columbines (*Aquilegia discolour*) and toadflax (*Linaria faucicola*).

Fauna

Wildlife also varies according to ecosystem and altitude. In the forests, mammal species include brown bears, wild boars (*Sus scrofa*), mountain cats (*Felis sylvestris*), wolves (*Canis lupus*), red deers (*Cervus elaphus*) and roe deers (*Capreolus capreolus*). Smaller mammals to note are squirrels, tree martens (*Martes martes*), dormice, muskrats and forest bats.

Along the river banks, otters and muskrats dwell with kingfishers and wagtails. Birds are definitely the most diverse type of wildlife at the higher elevations. The high mountain lakes attract water rails and coots.

In the skies goshawks (*Acciptas gentiles*), golden eagles (*Aquila chrysaetos*), kestrels (*Neophron percnoptens*), common buzzards, griffon vultures (*Gyps fulvus*), peregrine falcons (*Falco peregrinus*) and woodcocks dominate. Closer to the trees, you'll find and hear green and spotted woodpeckers as well as tawny, horned and barn owls. In rocky areas, tiny birds such as hedge and alpine sparrows make their nests.

CLIMATE

Forming part of the Spanish region called 'España Verde' (Green Spain), the middle and lower elevations of the Cordillera have an Atlantic climate of temperate, wet weather. In winter and spring Atlantic cold fronts and air masses bring heavy rain and snow at high elevations. Winds tend to arrive from the north-west, showering the northern slopes and valleys. The southern slopes and valleys have a drier, warmer climate, though anywhere in the Cordillera the weather can change brusquely and rapidly. The best times for walking are outlined in When to Walk under Planning in the introduction to each walk. In general, the snow leaves the lower slopes in April and May; at the highest elevations, expect snow during June.

INFORMATION
Maps

For general orientation purposes, the Instituto Geográfico Nacional (IGN) *Asturias* at 1:200,000 and *Cantabria* maps at 1:200,000 are widely available (550 ptas each). The IGN's *Cordillera Cantábrica* at 1:200,000 map (800 ptas) is also useful.

Details of the maps for each of the walks are in Maps under Planning in the introduction to each walk.

CORDILLERA CANTÁBRICA

Books

Few books are available on the region in English. Oviedo bookshops have a couple of English books including a translation of José Ramón Patterson's *Asturias* (2400 ptas).

In Spanish, you're more likely to find books on areas within the Cordillera than specifically about the range itself. The Anaya Touring Club's *Picos de Europa y Cordillera Cantábrica* by Ramón Martín gives a general background to the area as well as suggestions on car and walking routes.

On Asturias, both VM Villar's *75 Rutas de Senderismo y Montaña en Asturias* (1800 ptas) and Juan Luis Somoano and Erik Pérez's *50 Excursiones Selectas de la Montaña Asturiana* (695 ptas) are useful for further exploration. For Cantabria, we recommend Eduardo Obregón's three volume *50 Rutas en Cantabria*.

Information Sources

Oviedo (Asturias) and Santander (Cantabria) are the most convenient major cities. Both make excellent bases for excursions in and around the Cordillera.

Oviedo The tourist office (☎ 985 21 33 85), Plaza de Alfonso II El Casto, provides information useful to walkers. The two best bookshops for maps and books are Librería Cervantes, Calle Doctor Casal 3 y 9, and Librería la Palma, next to the cathedral. Overall, the former is better but the latter has a better English-language section.

Santander The city tourist office (☎ 942 36 20 54), Jardines de Pereda, is a good source of local information. The regional tourist office (☎ 942 31 07 08), Plaza Porticada, gives accommodation and transport information as well as information on the area around Santander and the Valle de Liébana.

The best bookshop for walking information is the Librería Estudio, Avenida Calvo Sotelo 21, which also stocks English titles.

Place Names

Bable, the local Asturian dialect, can be confusing when you're trying to read signs and maps. Many local names are still used on maps, especially in the Parque Natural de Somiedo and Picos de Europa.

Weather Information

Reports in Spanish are available from park information centres listed under Information Sources in each section of this chapter.

ACCOMMODATION & SUPPLIES
Oviedo

Oviedo is a charming, slightly inland city. Decent doubles with bath cost 5900 ptas at *Hostal Los Arcos* (☎ 985 21 47 73, Magdalena 3). *Mendizábal Hostal* (☎ 985 22 01 89, Calle Mendizábal 4) charges 4500 ptas for doubles. Two very good *sidrerías* (cider bars) are *El Pigüeña*, Calle Gascona 2, and *Rimpala*, Calle Cabo Noval 10B. Both have reasonable *menús del dia* (fixed-price meals).

For last-minute walking gear requirements, both Tuñón, Calle de Campoamor 7, and Oxígeno, Calle Manuel Pedregal 4, are well equipped.

Santander

This large seaport city offers all services and can provide almost anything you may need in the way of last-minute supplies.

Pensión Angelines, Calle Atilano Rodríguez 9, has rock-bottom singles/doubles with shared bath for 2500/4000 ptas. The central and still cheap *Pensión La Corza* (☎ 942 21 29 50, Calle Hernán Cortés 25) on the 3rd floor has a variety of singles/doubles starting from 2500/4750 ptas. For good, inexpensive dining try either *Bodega Fuente Dé* or *Restaurante Versalles* on Calle Peña Herbosa (Nos 5 and 15). Set meals run from 1000 ptas to 1200 ptas.

The sports shops Límite, Calle Arrabal 20, and Eiger, Santa Lucía 21, are helpful and well stocked.

GETTING THERE & AWAY
Oviedo

To and from Madrid, ALSA (☎ 985 96 96 00) buses run every two hours from 7 am to 7 pm for 7190 ptas return. The Red Nacional de los Ferrocarriles Españoles (RENFE), or Spanish

Railway Network, has three daily trains to and from Madrid for 7000 ptas return.

By car, take the NVI from Madrid to Benavente (north-west) and then the N630 to León. Continue on the A-66 to Oviedo.

Santander

Continental Auto (☎ 915 33 04 00) runs seven daily buses to and from Madrid and Santander between 7.30 am and 8.30 pm for 5850 ptas return. Trains run to and from Madrid three times a day (6700 ptas return), arriving at Santander's main RENFE station.

If coming by car from Madrid, take the N1 to Burgos and then the N623.

Turytrans bus company (☎ 942 22 16 85) makes several daily runs between Oviedo and Santander, for 1710 ptas return.

Its name derives from the facts that it's in one of the two zones in the Cordillera where the brown bear survives and that it passes through the Monte del Oso, four enclosed hectares where two bears live in semi-liberty (see the boxed text below). A side trip to the **Casa del Oso** museum is described at the end of the walk description. Among the route's main attractions are the lush river-bank woods filled with acacia, holly, alder, maple, hazel, walnut, chestnut, holm oak, ash, willow, oak, plane, laurel and apple trees. In the dense woods, you'll hear and see a great variety of birds.

The route is described from north (Tuñón) to south (Entrago). Water is available at the beginning and along the way in Villanueva.

Senda del Oso

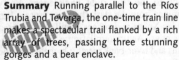

Duration 5 hours
Distance 20km
Standard Easy
Start Tuñón
Finish Entrago
Public Transport Yes
Summary Running parallel to the Ríos Trubia and Teverga, the one-time train line makes a spectacular trail flanked by a rich array of trees, passing three stunning gorges and a bear enclave.

Only 21km from Oviedo, the gentle 'Trail of the Bear' is a 20km-long cement walkway lined with river-bank trees, open fields, impressive narrow canyons, rural villages and framed by mountains up to 1300m high. In 1884 the route was a railway line carrying coal from the nearby mines of Quirós and San Martín de Teverga to the munitions factory of Trubia. To reach the mines, the 19th century engineers bored rough tunnels through the heart of several sections of rocky mountain. More than a century later, in 1995, the regional government finished the works and converted the abandoned transport route into this extraordinary trail for pedestrians.

Oso Pardo, the Brown Bear

Paca and Tola are the offspring of a brown bear disgracefully killed by a hunter in 1989 despite a 1967 prohibition to protect this endangered species. She was among 30 bears furtively hunted in the 1980s. Until two centuries ago, the brown bear (known in Spanish as *oso pardo*) inhabited nearly all of the Iberian Peninsula in large numbers, but uncontrolled hunting, habitat destruction and poisoning have caused the bears' progressive decline.

Today, counting the 10 bears in the Pyrenees, the Cordillera Cantábrica has the greatest bear population. Its habitat covers 5000 sq km divided into two zones, unfortunately isolated from one another. The eastern zone has between 20 and 25 bears; the western, 50 to 65.

Asturias, in the middle of the protected area, shelters 75% of the population and is the region most committed to the bears' recuperation. It has founded the Bear Foundation of Asturias (*Fundación Oso de Asturias*) in Casa del Oso in Proaza and established areas of protection, policing hunters. The region also compensates landowners for damage to their land caused by the bears.

CORDILLERA CANTÁBRICA

PLANNING
When to Walk
The route can be done all year though we do not recommend August when the trail overflows with walkers.

Maps & Books
IGN's maps, *Villabre* No 52-I, *Proaza* No 52-II, *Santianes* No 52-III and *La Vega* No 52-IV, cover the route at a scale of 1:25,000, but are unnecessary as it's impossible to lose your way. The Spanish booklet *Los Concejos del Trubia a través de la Senda del Oso* by Sergio Ríos and César García covers the area's history and art, the Senda del Oso and five alternative routes. It's available in Oviedo bookshops (see Information Sources in the introduction to this chapter) and in Entrago from the information kiosk (500 ptas).

What to Bring
With the hard walking surface in mind, we recommend a well padded pair of runners (training shoes).

PLACES TO STAY & EAT
Given the proximity of the walk to Oviedo and good public transport links, it's feasible to do the walk and return to Oviedo on the same day. For details of places to stay and eat in Oviedo, see Accommodation & Supplies in the introduction to this chapter.

If you'd prefer to postpone the trip back to Oviedo, the best option is San Martín de Teverga less than 1.5km south of Entrago – the route's end. The simple *Albergue San Martín* (☎ *985 76 44 54*), Calle Nueva, has bunks for 1000 ptas and the conventional *Casa Laureano* (☎ *985 76 42 13, Plaza García Miranda 23*) has singles/doubles with bath for 2000/5000 ptas. Both prepare good, home-cooked meals for 1000 ptas.

GETTING TO/FROM THE WALK
From Oviedo, ALSA runs three buses daily to Tuñón and Entrago at 8.30 am, 2 and 6.30 pm. From Entrago (passing Tuñón), buses leave for Oviedo at 7.30 and 10 am, 1 and 5.30 pm on weekdays and at varying times on the weekend. By car, head west on the N634 from Oviedo (direction Grado) to Trubia. Crossing the Río Nalón, turn left and in 8km reach Tuñón and the car park where the route begins.

THE WALK
From the car park, the route crosses to the true left bank of the Río Trubia and turns left onto the one-time train track. The 3m-wide walkway continues comfortably passing various information panels on the geomorphology of the area before crossing the river back to the true right bank again. Forty minutes from the start, the route crosses Río de las Xanas and passes a mill. The *xana*, a legendary Asturian folk figure, lived in fountains and river-bank caves. On the left as the path continues an impressive *desfiladero* (gorge), created by the Río de las Xanas,

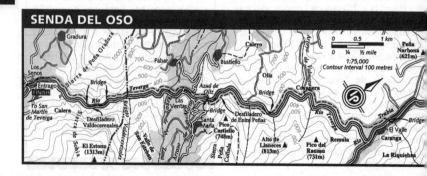

SENDA DEL OSO

appears. In 3km, the way enters the first village, **Villanueva**, which has a fountain, *hórreos* (wooden granaries) and a medieval bridge mislabelled as Roman. Crossing the bridge, continue through the village past the restored Romanesque Iglesia San Romano church on the right. Find lovely wall murals inside.

Cross by a bridge over the Río Trubia and past a recreational area (right) before reaching the **Monte del Oso**, 5.4km from the start. Enclosed by 1950m of electrified fencing, Paca and Tola live protected within. In 2km, passing the bar *La Cabaña del Oso Goloso*, which sells drinks and sandwiches, and the hydroelectric plant, the route reaches **Proaza** village. From here, the pastures diminish, the forests become fuller and there are more excavated tunnels in the surrounding rock walls. You pass the halfway point at the **Desfiladero de Peñas Juntas** gorge where the sheer walls on either side of the river nearly meet.

Cross the highway and the Río Trubia, bypassing the village of Caranga to the left. (Beware: an alternative route from here to Bárzana which has been marked on the Senda del Oso brochure is not yet complete.) In 3km, the path crosses the highway and the Río Teverga (the river it now follows) and soon reaches another stunning gorge, the **Desfiladero de Entre Peñas**. Once again, negotiate the highway and the river to the Azude de Oliz reservoir. The breathtaking **Desfiladero Valdecerezales** gorge appears

2km later. Before entering Entrago, the path crosses the Río Teverga twice more.

Side Trip: Casa del Oso Museum
30 minutes, 2km
The **Casa del Oso** museum (with bathroom, cafeteria and shop) portrays the history of the brown bear as well as the campaign for its defence. To get there, ignore the first sign for the museum in the recreational area before Proaza and pass by the Monte del Oso to see Paca and Tola. After reaching the hydroelectric plant, cross the bridge into Proaza and turn right onto the highway. Walk east 1km and find the museum on the right next to a church near a 14th century defensive tower.

Parque Natural de Somiedo

Somiedo, from the Latin *sumetum* meaning 'land of elevated mountains', lies in the south-west corner of Asturias. Established in 1988, the nature park covers some 30,000 hectares of country featuring lush oak and beech woods, high ancient pastures and low-lying settled valleys. The abrupt relief is typical of the Cordillera, with the highest peak El Cornón at 2194m and the lowest valley area Aguasmestas at 395m. Glaciers formed the highest valleys, leaving behind the greatest number of glacial lakes in Asturias. All are connected by canals for

CORDILLERA CANTÁBRICA

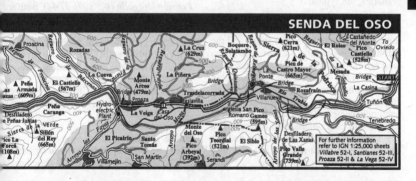

SENDA DEL OSO

hydroelectric exploitation. Looking from above, five valleys (Valle de Saliencia, Valle de Lago, Valle del Somiedo, Valle de Perlunes and Valle del Pigüeña) neatly divide the region into zones which also correspond with village organisation.

The park status of Somiedo has helped to save its valuable natural and human resources. Only decades ago, the area's population was 6000. Today 2000 people live in the 35 villages and hamlets of the valleys and some 50 families continue the traditions of transhumance, moving with their animals in an annual cycle from low winter to high summer pastures.

As part of its well conceived conservation strategy, the park has different zones of usage (indicated on the recommended map). Each of the valleys has routes marked with yellow-and-white trail markers and wooden signs that indicate route numbers.

Two marked day walks are presented in this section. Both start from Valle de Lago and take you up into the summer pastures past *brañas* (huts of the highland cowherds, known locally as *vaqueiros*), and other excellent examples of local architecture. Expect to see *teitos*, thatch-roofed stone cabins (with the thatch made from broom) and abnadoned *corros*. These circular stone buildings topped with stone are the most ancient form of summer shelter used by shepherds. Grouped in pairs, the second building was set aside for young animals. In the valleys, hórreos and *paneras*, wooden granaries, are typical.

Unusual floral species found in the nature park include the rare and fragile Somiedo centaury (*Centaurium somedanum*) and the corona del rey or king's crown (*Saxifraga longifolia*), only found in the Pyrenees and Somiedo (near Valle de Lago). In addition to being among the most ample reserves of animals in Europe with more than 40 mammal species, 100 birds and 10 types of reptiles and amphibians each, the park is a key sanctuary for the brown bear and the beautiful, local vaca roxa, or red cow, also called the Asturiana de los Valles.

INFORMATION
Books
Juan Martín's *Somiedo* is the best Spanish-language guide to the area (1995 ptas). Find it in Pola de Somiedo and Oviedo.

Information Sources
The park's information centre (☎ 985 76 37 58), open daily from 10 am to 2 pm and 4 to 8 pm, is in Pola de Somiedo in the village centre. It has maps and useful leaflets, in Spanish only, describing the park's marked routes. Free guided walks are also available.

Maps covering the nature park are available at the park's information centre, from the only bookshop in the Valle de Lago and at other locales around the village.

PLANNING
When to Walk
The climate is typical of the Cordillera's north face with high humidity and relatively temperate conditions. Snow falls above 1200m from November to April. Your best bets are July, August and September.

Maps
We recommend the *Parque Natural Somiedo* map at 1:35,000 (300 ptas). Be aware that all place names on the map are in Bable, though the signs on the trail are in Spanish.

PLACES TO STAY & EAT
Pola de Somiedo
Your best accommodation options are the *Fonda Cano* (☎ 985 76 36 61) or the *Pensión Urogallo* (☎ 985 76 37 44). Both are on the main plaza and have singles/doubles with bath for 3500/5000 ptas. A camp site was under construction at the time of writing. With 90 inhabitants, Pola de Somiedo is the area's largest village, boasting a supermarket, bank, pharmacy, fountain, ethnographic museum and public phone. Purchase any special foods or products before reaching the village.

Valle de Lago
The *Camping Lagos de Somiedo* (☎ 985 76 37 76) has a shop the size of a shoe box, a

simple bar-restaurant as well as maps and information on the park. Tariffs are 500 ptas per tent, 500 ptas per person and 450 ptas per car. The management speaks English. Two recommended hostels are *L'Auterio* (☎ 985 76 38 76) and the *Casa Cobrana* (☎ 985 76 37 48). Doubles run at 4000 ptas and 4500 ptas, respectively. The latter prepares an excellent menú for 900 ptas. Local culinary delights include *pote*, a vegetable and meat stew, beef cold cuts and steaks of the vaca roxa.

GETTING TO/FROM THE WALKS

ALSA buses go from Oviedo to Pola de Somiedo (775 ptas) at 10 am daily and at 5.30 pm every day except Sunday. Returning from Pola de Somiedo, buses leave at 5 pm daily and at 6.30 am on weekdays.

Once in Pola de Somiedo isn't a bus to Valle de Lago 8km away where the routes begin. Your best option is to catch a taxi or to hitchhike. A taxi (☎ 985 76 36 71) costs 2000 ptas each way.

By car from Oviedo, head west on the N634 to Cornellana and then south first along the AS16 and then the AS227.

Ruta de los Lagos

Duration 7 to 8 hours
Distance 26 to 28km
Standard Medium
Start/Finish Valle de Lago
Public Transport Yes
Summary Verdant pastures, unusual cowherd's cabins and bare peaks surround the gentle ascent to the isolated Lagos de Saliencia through a region containing the Cordillera's greatest concentration of glacial lakes.

The gentle route meanders through the high pastures around Valle de Lago and passes four glacial lakes. Optional returns vary the walk's length. Carry enough water for the whole day as the only options are in Valle and at a trough en route.

THE WALK

The route begins at the upper end of Valle de Lago village from a small car park. Walk south-east past the last houses of the village and turn left. The sealed road soon converts to dirt and continues along the lush valley past cultivated fields, hazel trees and broom. The first **teito** comes into sight. As the valley narrows, ignore a trail that heads to the left. At the next crossroads is a sign indicating Lago del Valle to the left and right. Turn left (you'll return from the right on the second alternative return). After briefly flattening out, the route climbs to the valley's high point near a stone wall and shepherd's hut. From here, you can see the 24 hectare **Lago del Valle** (the largest lake in Asturias) surrounded by mountains. You've now come 1½ hours from the start.

Continuing through broom, the route reaches the lake's left shore (north). Upon reaching a low stone wall it turns left (north-west), joining the PRAS10. The trail heads up the hill and back towards the Valle de Lago, offering impressive panoramic views of the valley as it climbs. On the way, it passes an animal trough (with potable water). Leaving a large peak off to the right, the trail ascends (north-west) for 30 minutes to a pass. Take a turn-off to the right (east) and traverse the flat pastures of the **Vega de Camayor** (where 'vega' in Spanish means pasture or meadow). Near the vega's limit, the trail ascends through a series of small rocks past La Cueva Camayor and then descends to cross a small valley and another field. The Lago Cerveriz appears a short distance ahead. Turn onto the dirt road that ascends past the lake and up a small hill. On reaching the summit, turn right along a stony footpath. Follow it for 10 minutes in a south-east direction until you have a beautiful view of the Lago Negro a.k.a the Lago Calabazosa. Backtrack to the dirt road and continue for another five minutes north-east, with views of the basin of the Lago de la Mina (dry in summer) and below it the Lago de la Cueva. You can still see traces of mining activity along its shores. Return by retracing your steps to the Valle de Lago.

There are two alternative routes back to the Valle de Lago. The first starts at the junction above the Lago del Valle. Instead of turning left to the lake, turn right, following the Valle de Lago sign and head directly back to the starting point.

The second route is 2km longer. After turning left at the junction, continue along the west side of the Lago del Valle. Having passed the lake's two retaining walls, turn right and follow a low wall (a feeder canal) to a shepherd's hut and teito. Bear right onto a dirt road that leads past teitos and beech woods to the crossroads (passed at the beginning of the day) east of Valle de Lago.

Ruta de las Brañas

Duration 5 to 7½ hours
Distance 13.5 to 21km
Standard Medium-Hard
Start/Finish Valle de Lago
Public Transport Yes
Summary On the remote frontier between Asturias and Castilla y León, discover ancient shepherd's cabins and highland pastures on well-marked trails.

Beginning in Valle, the route ascends to the Collado del Mojón pass (1857m), an impressive watchtower of the Sierra del Rebezo, and continues to another scenic pass from where it's possible to return to the starting point or proceed onto a vaqueiro village, Santa María del Puerto, where lodging is available. If you decide to continue to the village, the walk is rated medium-hard rather than medium because of the extra distance. Carry plenty of water.

THE WALK

An information board near the fountain in the centre of Valle de Lago contains details of the route. From the fountain, take the road which forks right and crosses the bridge over the Río del Valle, continues past a mill on the left and up towards the church. Before reaching it, bear left. The sealed road soon gives way to a dirt lane winding its way among fields.

Ignore a stony trail ascending to the left and another that descends to the right and continue climbing along the lane which briefly enters a beech forest before reaching a marvellous, natural balcony with excellent views of the valley below. The high pastures of the valley to the south are your target. Ignore two paths to the right and continue on the lane which first passes various shepherd's cabins and then rises to the **Brañas de Sousas** pastures after an hour.

A wooden sign indicates that four hours return remain to the Puerto de Somiedo on the PRAS16. From the corros in the Brañas de Sousas, the dirt lane makes a hard steep ascent south among broom, heather and wild roses. After 20 minutes, fork left at the summit of the rise and cross a scree section (a heap of weathered rock fragments). Now on a path, ignore a left-hand trail. Reward yourself with a stunning view of corros and Valle de Lago off to the right. In less than an hour, the path reaches the **Collado del Mojón** (Collau del Muñón) pass on the border between Asturias and Castilla y León.

Heading into Castilla y León, the path crosses a series of depressions and grassy mounds and in 15 minutes reaches a larger, elongated depression. Turn south and ascend to a pasture with crumbling huts. Before reaching the ruins, the path turns left (south-east) and then immediately right (south) onto an ascending trail. Soon you reach a narrow pass between the Peña Blanca and Los Comales with excellent views of a large valley ahead. Here, you have the option to turn around and retrace your footsteps or continue for another 1¼ hours to **Santa María del Puerto** (1486m).

To reach the village, descend across the valley to its western flank. Cross a wire fence and steeply descend into Asturias and Santa María. If you'd rather stay overnight and return the next day, the village has a bar, shop and fountain as well as the

RUTA DE LOS LAGOS & RUTA DE LAS BRAÑAS

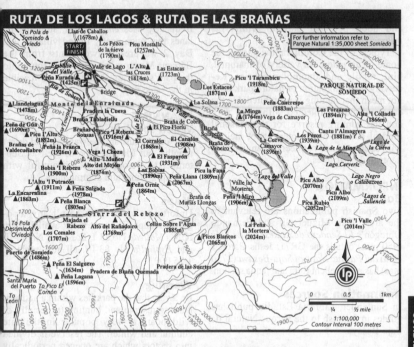

Restaurante Hotel El Coronel (☎ 985 76 37 00) with a 1000 ptas menú and doubles with bath for 5000 ptas.

Parque Natural de Saja-Besaya

From Roman roads to shepherds' wild haunts to dense beech forests, the Parque Natural de Saja-Besaya, created in 1988, offers a combination of history and infrequently visited open spaces. Nestled between two of Cantabria's great north-south rivers, the Río Saja and the Río Besaya, the park is a 24,500 hectare island in the middle of Spain's largest *reserva nacional de caza* (national hunting reserve) which occupies 30% of Cantabria.

Unlike the pinnacle-shaped Picos de Europa, the park's rounded mountains reach their highest at its southern limit: Iján (2084m) and El Cordel (2040m). The J-shaped park has two sierras (the Sierra de Bárcena Mayor and the Sierra del Cordel) and numerous permanently green valleys formed by the Ríos Besaya, Saja and their tributaries: Argoza/Lodar, Queriendo, Bayones, Cambillas and Bijoz.

The park has plenty of flora and fauna characteristic of the Cordillera in general. Hill (Atlantic shrubs and oak) and mountain (beech, holly and birch) species (500 to 1600m) dominate the area. Expect to see the shrubs spurge laurel (*Daphne laureola*) and St Daboec's heath Viola Sylvatica (*Daboecia cantábrica*), as well as various common wild flowers – wild violet (*Viola sylvatica*); primrose (*Primula vulgaris*), a cheerful, white spring bloom; foxglove (*Digitalis purpureai*); autumn crocus (*Colchium autumnale*), a joyful, pink companion in autumn; white asphodel (*Asphodelus albus*); and hoop petticoat daffodil (*Narcissus bulbocodium*).

Typical of the Cordillera, the park is the home of an extensive variety of mammal, bird, reptile and amphibian species. Receiving the designation of nature park does not mean that hunting is prohibited. On the contrary, game protected within the park and the hunting reserve for the seasonal (end of autumn and winter) shoot include wild boars, red and roe deers, chamois, wild hares and partridges.

INFORMATION
Books
Two Spanish publications are relevant to the area: Juan Miguel Gil and Fernando Obregón's *El Sendero de la Reserva de Saja* (950 ptas) details the GR71; Jesús García's *Guía del Parque Natural Saja-Besaya* (2750 ptas) has an excellent flora and fauna section.

Information Sources
In Santander, Librería Estudio publishes guides in Spanish to the Parque Natural de Saja-Besaya.

Saja-Besaya Traverse

Duration 2 to 3 days
Distance 31 to 51.5km
Standard Medium
Start Bárcena de Pie de Concha
Finish Saja
Public Transport Yes
Summary A walk from the Río Besaya to the Río Saja along Roman highways and ancient, stone-paved lanes. The trail crosses the Parque Natural de Saja-Besaya through lush forests and tiny villages.

A full traverse of the park follows part of the red-and-white trail-marked GR71 (Cantabria's first) in an eight day, 127.5km trajectory from Bárcena de Pie de Concha (where we begin) to the foot of the Picos de Europa at Potes and continuing west to Sotres. The section of the GR71 which we

describe traverses the park in three days and frequently uses *empedrados*, stone-paved lanes that once neatly linked villages. On Day 2 we present two jaunts from the Bárcena Mayor village that head south into the park's interior. Both walks are feasible in the same day.

PLANNING
When to Walk
July and August are the warmest and driest months, but May to June as well as September to October can be beautiful with their springtime and autumn hues.

Maps
Unfortunately, the park hasn't any topographic maps. The best maps available are IGN's *Molledo* No 83-I, *Los Tojos* No 82-II, and *Espinilla* No 83-IV, all at a scale of 1:25,000.

Warning
Be aware that the park lies within a national hunting reserve and hunting (especially of wild boar) is very popular in the late autumn and winter. The reserve is divided into sectors which are opened periodically and listed in local newspapers. With this said, hunting poses little if any danger to the walker and none in summer when hunting is prohibited.

PLACES TO STAY & EAT
Bárcena de Pie de Concha
The small village has a market, pharmacy, bank and public phone. To eat, try *Bar-Restaurante Casa Miguel* with an 800 ptas menú. Sleeping options are limited: *Pensión Rural Casa Ferrero* (☎ 942 84 13 03) has singles/doubles without bath for about 3000/5000 ptas.

Saja
Both the *Casa de Labranza Bijoz* (☎ 942 74 12 27) and the smaller *Casa de Labranza Seijos* (☎ 942 74 12 23), over the river, offer clean, ample rooms. The former has singles/doubles/triples with shared bath for 2500/4000/5000 ptas. Doubles with shared bath at

the latter cost 4000 ptas. Dining options are limited to the *bar-shop* over the highway and the quite good *Restaurante La Bárcena* with a generous 1000 ptas menú.

GETTING TO/FROM THE WALK

Bárcena de Pie de Concha lies 53km south of Santander and is easily accessible by bus, train and car. Twelve buses (495 ptas) with Palomera (☎ 942 88 07 63) and 11 trains (365 ptas) on the Santander-Palencia line run south daily.

By car, head south-west on the N611 towards Torrelavega and then south to Reinosa.

From Saja, public transport returns to Santander are very limited. You'll either need to hitchhike, take the Monday bus (185 ptas) with Palomera to Cabezón de Sal, where connections to Santander are numerous, or take a taxi (☎ 942 70 05 78) to Cabezón for 2900 ptas. Call Palomera to confirm times and fares.

Return by car on the northbound N625 to Cabezón de la Sal and then north-east on the N634 to Torrelavega and finally to Santander via the N611.

THE WALK

Day 1: Bárcena de Pie de Concha to Bárcena Mayor

5 to 6 hours, 19km

Water is available in the first villages along the way, but dries up after the route opens up to the ridge crest. The day entails 900m of climbing.

Begin the route by crossing the tiny village of Bárcena de Pie de Concha and following the signs for Calzada Romana and Pujayo. Before reaching the main square – which has several bars and a fountain – turn right (west) onto a sealed road that indicates Pujayo, 2.5km. En route, the road crosses the Río Besaya and then enters Pie de Concha, a one-street village. Sporadic GR71 signs appear and 500m later, the route passes a fountain and a *rollo*, a pillar where punishments were meted out for crimes committed.

In 100m, a left-hand detour leads to Cantabria's best preserved Roman *calzada*

(highway). It runs for 5km from Pie de Concha to Somaconcha further south and retains original stone paving and diagonal canals dug to prevent water erosion. You can even see old carriage wheel marks. Possibly of military origin, it was used until the 18th century to connect Castilla and Santander.

Continue along the road 2km to **Pujayo**. After its church, the route bears right towards the main plaza lined with balconied houses. Every 10 August, the village celebrates La Maya, San Lorenzo's feast day. Amid general festivities, the young men of the village cut down a beech tree, mount it in the village square, add grease to the trunk and then compete to scale it.

Cross the plaza and exit left along a street that after 100m reaches a fork. Veer right taking a slowly ascending dirt road 5km up the Barranco de Vaocerezo to a ridge with spectacular views of the valleys and foothills of the Cordillera. Grazing cattle (most likely the area's local breed, tudanca, which are grey and black with widely separated horns) and horses roaming semifreely are common in these pastures.

Once on the ridge, the dirt road ascends south-east for 1.5km to a lane on the right and a livestock corral on the left (the halfway point). Leave the road, which continues 300m to Pico de Obios (1222m), and descend west along the undulating lane for nearly one hour, crossing the **Sierra de Bárcena** to the foot of the Pico la Guarda (1085m) and a crumbling hut.

The next portion is poorly marked and it is important to follow the directions closely. Leave the lane for a left-hand (west) track and in 300m take a heather-lined trail that heads off right (north). After a gentle ascent, the trail disappears. Descend cross-country through grass, gorse bushes and heather, following a low stone wall. When the wall turns left, continue descending cross-country to a series of perpendicular horse trails (before you reach the trees below). Take one of these trails right (north), dropping towards a visible clearing (a round hill) in the forest below. Once at

CORDILLERA CANTÁBRICA

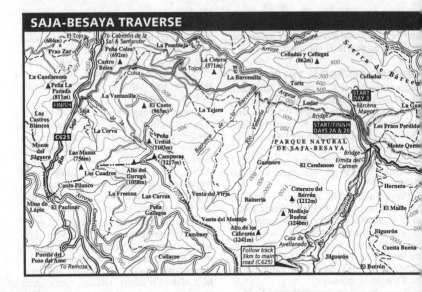

SAJA-BESAYA TRAVERSE

the clearing, descend left (west) through the low earth and stone walls of a narrow, dry (in summer) stream bed which has been made into a makeshift trail that is soon blazed.

The path zigzags through oak and beech trees and joins a once stone-paved ancient road that, for lack of use and water erosion, is littered with loose stones. Continue to **Bárcena Mayor** village, 3.5km away.

A beneficiary of an EU grant for economically depressed areas, the picturesque village received a massive face-lift and now tourism is king. The *Albergue de Bárcena Mayor* (☎ *908 18 66 57*), the cheapest option, has bunks for 1250 ptas and doubles for 4000 ptas. Alternatively, *Venta La Franca* (☎ *942 70 60 67*) provides comfortable doubles with baths for 6000 ptas and the management speaks English. For a meal along the river, try *Mesón El Puente*. *Venta La Franca* has a good menú for 1000 ptas. Find a *camping ground* 1km south of the village (with substandard bathrooms).

Day 2A: Bárcena Mayor to Venta de Mobejo

4 to 5½ hours, 14 to 20km

This unmarked forest walk runs partl[y] along an ancient Roman highway known a[s] the Camino de Reinosa. You'll need to tak[e] water with you.

After leaving Bárcena via its only ston[e] bridge, veer left onto a dirt road, passing [a] trough with potable water. The trail, bor[-] dered on either side by high walls, passes [a] horse stable, huge chestnuts, oaks and [a] series of crosses (part of a Stations of th[e] Cross). After 20 minutes, the trail reaches [a] sharp, right-hand curve. Instead of turnin[g] right, keep straight ahead along a pat[h] which soon reaches the simple **Ermita d[e] Carmen** chapel.

From the chapel, take the old, south[-] bound stone-paved trail (of Roman origi[n] that once linked Santander with Castill[a]. Keep going for 3km without detourin[g] (passing through a replanted forest) unt[il] the empedrado becomes a footpath whic[h] continues straight ahead. When you reach [a] shepherd's hut, turn right onto a path near[

SAJA-BESAYA TRAVERSE

choked with blackberry brambles and ferns that leads into a dense holly and beech forest before petering out.

Ascend west briefly through the forest cross-country, following a stone and wire wall that turns left (south) to the next cabin. From the cabin, take the footpath that undulates around the hillside to the beech forest visible on the next hill. Exit the beech forest via the empedrado to the left and follow the path towards two shepherds' huts on the next hillside. Before reaching the huts, take the right-hand trail where it divides (the left goes to the huts), and pass above the huts. In the next clearing, the **Venta de Mobejo**, a typical medieval wayside inn and stable, lies in ruins.

At this point, you can either turn around and return to Bárcena Mayor or follow the dirt and gravel road from the south side of the clearing next to the ruins. Incredibly, in 1992 this road was constructed and in the process destroyed priceless portions of the Roman calzada. It continues in a south-west direction for 3km, passing through forest and pastures. It then heads left after a cabin

to the main road (C625) near the Puerto de la Palombera (1257m). Retrace your steps back to Bárcena Mayor.

Day 2B: Bárcena Mayor to Fuente Clara

2 to 2½ hours, 6.5km

This lovely circuit walk meanders along an open hillside and then ambles back along the river.

Leave the village, heading south along a dirt road. After less than 1km, the stones in the left-hand side culvert form makeshift stairs. Ascend these stairs left and enter the pine forest, where the sight and sound of the rapids and natural pools of the Río Argoza (Lodar) below greet you. After 15 minutes, the footpath crosses a brook with a waterfall and turns left. The footpath is full of hairpin bends until halfway up the hillside before it levels out and then continues in a gentle curve south-west around the hill. Using a stile to climb over a wire fence across the footpath, drop down to cross a wooden footbridge over the **Fuente Clara** spring. Visible on the hillside are strata enveloped in ferns, heather and gorse bushes. Descend towards the Río Argoza below, crossing another wire fence on the way, and then climb to the dirt road on the other side of the river. It continues northwest for 3km through a rich mixed forest back to Bárcena Mayor.

Day 3: Bárcena Mayor to Saja
4 hours, 12km
The last day of the walk undulates through forests and several villages on more paved trails.

Leave Bárcena Mayor via its stone bridge and turn right, entering a magnificent forest. Immediately fork left, ascending a stone-paved lane which crosses a brook and enters a clearing before it disappears. Descend right along one of the visible trails, which soon rejoins the cobbled lane before it disappears again. As before, take a right-hand trail until you find the lane again. You've come 1km from Bárcena.

In five minutes, fork right at a junction onto a footpath past a large oak on the left. A barbed-wire fence to your right will be a constant reference during the next 2km. Pass a modern shepherd's cabin and descend across a stream. Continue straight ahead to the top of the next rise, ignoring a wide, perpendicular path along the way, and descend towards a hut on the other side. At the intersection with a wider trail coming in from the right, follow the trail downhill until it passes another that veers left and fords the Arroyo de Valnera.

Once across the stream, follow a wider trail uphill for five minutes to a fork. Climb steeply along the left fork. The area opens up as the track reaches a junction. Turn right. About 400m after the trail flattens, the village Los Tojos comes into sight. Fifteen minutes later, the dirt track joins a gravel and earth road that in 2km drops you in **Los Tojos** halfway through the day. Tasty, inexpensive **meals** are available in the small village (which has a public phone and fountain).

Follow a sealed road as it heads through the village and south-east for roughly 1km to Colsa village (with a fountain). Continue via a stone road that quickly ends at an enclosed monument. From here, descend left to Saja, now in sight, through a luxuriantly leafy forest. On the right is the hill called Peña Colsa.

Parque Nacional de los Picos de Europa

The Picos de Europa are the highest, most rugged and awe-inspiring of all the Cordillera. Ramón Lueje wrote of the sharpened and irregular limestone summits that it appears as though 'the earth's bones broke through its skin and emerged, cleaned of flesh'. Despite lying only 15km from the Bay of Biscay, the peaks soar dramatically to 2600m. Extending into Asturias (277 sq km), Cantabria (131 sq km) and Castilla y León (94 sq km), the Picos de Europa are 40km long (west to east) and 20km wide. The chain is separated into three massifs by rivers and deep gorges.

The Macizo Occidental (Western Massif), delimited by the rivers Sella and Cares, is the largest and arguably the most beautiful of the massifs, with the greatest variety of landscapes: forests, *majadas* (high pastures with shepherd's huts), gorges, lakes and grandiose mountains. Its highest point is the Torre de Santa de Castilla at 2596m.

The Macizo Central (Central Massif), where rock predominates over flora, lies between the rivers Cares and Duje and includes the highest peak of the Picos, the Torre de Cerredo (2648m). Its rugged and abrupt relief, dotted with rocky bowls known as *jous*, gives it a truly lunar look. The massif also harbours the Pico's signature peak El Naranjo de Bulnes, or Pico Urriellu (2519m), and Pico Tesorero (2570m), at the region's geographical centre.

Finally, the Macizo Oriental (Eastern Massif), demarcated by the rivers Duje and Deva, is the smallest, gentlest and lowest massif, though still with wild summits reaching well over 2000m.

HISTORY

On 21 July 1918 King Alfonso XIII declared, at the instigation of Pedro Pidal, Marquise of Villaviciosa, the Parque Nacional de la Montaña de Covadonga, Spain's first national park. Initially, only the Macizo Occidental fell within the 16,925 hectares of protected area. During the 1980s and 1990s, campaigns were waged by both Spanish and non-Spanish activists to bring the other two massifs under national protection. Finally, on 30 May 1995 the limits of the park were extended, creating Europe's then largest national park covering 64,660 hectares.

One of the challenges facing the park administration is to balance human and environmental needs. In 1999 Bulnes La Villa, an isolated village within the park's limits, will finally have its dream come true when a US$13 million train tunnel links it to the outside world. The train will also be used by thousands of visitors, who previously had to make the steep ascent to the village on foot. Consequences? Only time will tell.

NATURAL HISTORY

Geology

Karstification, the transformation of a limestone landscape by percolating groundwater, is the most outstanding active geological process in the Picos de Europa today. Besides causing the area's infinite cracks and caves, the process of water erosion acting upon lime also creates scree, jous and river gorges. Water filters easily through the rocks and springs forth in unlikely spots. These mountains are havens for technical rock climbers attracted to the numerous challenging peaks as well as for cavers exploring the Cordillera's innards (see the boxed text 'Caving in the Picos').

Flora

The Picos de Europa have a particularly diverse collection of flora and fauna species spread out over a wide range of different environments, from valleys to high alpine areas. Due to the lack of top soil and the large amount of land cleared for pasture, woodlands cover less than 20% of the park.

Caving in the Picos

Walking along the upper reaches of the Picos, you may be suprised to learn that under your feet the porous, limestone mountains are riddled with caves hollowed out by the effects of water erosion. Teams from (primarily) Spain, France and England have explored more than 3000 horizontal and vertical Picos cavities.

Caving began here in 1918 but did not take off until the 1960s, culminating in several major feats. In 1985, members of Oxford University's Cave Club descended 1135 spectacular metres into the Macizo Occidental's Sistema del Jito.

On Day 3 of the Picos de Europa Circuit, the trail passes El Farfao, a natural spring which surges out of a fissure in the rock wall. It's believed that this is a natural release point for water from the Sima del Trave, the deepest cave (1441m) yet to be explored in Spain and the fourth deepest in the world. The national park information office in Cangas de Onís (for details, see Information Sources on the following page) can provide further information on caving permits and speleological clubs.

Protected from extremes of climate by deep gorges, numerous river-bank species, even Mediterranean ones (strawberry, cork and holm oak), cohabit with alder, ash, willow, elm, oak and linden. There are mixed deciduous forests of oak, hazel, holly, mountain ash and yew at altitudes up to 800m. Beyond this point, find concentrations of birch and beech trees. Above the tree line heather, gorse bushes, broom, ferns, juniper bushes and grass cling on.

Finally, the abundant wild flowers deserve mention: wood anemone (*Anemone nemorosa*), purple saxifrage (*Saxifraga oppositifolia*), Cantabrian thrift (*Armeria cantabrica*), great yellow gentian (*Gentiana lutea*), pheasant's eye daffodil (*Narcissus nobilis*), iris flag (*Iris latifolia*) and green-weed, or needle furze (*Genista legionensis*).

Fauna

The most representative mammal of the Picos de Europa is without doubt the chamois, locally known as the *rebeco* (*Rupicapra pyrenaica*). Some 6500 skip along on hooves well adapted to the steep, rocky slopes. In addition, wild boars, foxes, wolves (in decline), deers, badgers, martens, hedgehogs, mountain cats and stoats scrape out a living. The skies are filled with golden eagles, griffons and Egyptian vultures, peregrine falcons, common buzzards and tawny owls. Accompanying the walker at the highest altitudes with their unmistakable caws are yellow-beaked alpine (*Pyrrhocorax graculus*) and red-beaked choughs (*P. pyrrhocorax*) as well as hedge sparrows. Closer to the ground, numerous lizards, salamanders, frogs and toads are to be found. In the rivers are trout, tench, minnow and freshwater eels.

It's easy to leave domestic animals out of a list of fauna. Cows (brown alpina and casina breeds), goats, sheep and Asturian horses (called Asturcón) are all common sights as you walk through the Picos de Europa.

INFORMATION
Books

Several books in English (original and translated) cover the Picos de Europa including *In the Picos de Europa: on Foot, on Horseback, by Bicycle, by Car, by 4WD* by V Ena Álvarez (1950 ptas). A general book laden with photos is *Picos de Europa* (1200 ptas). FJ Purroy's *The Cares Path: A Walk Along the 'Divine Gorge'* is a lovely, small volume describing this spectacular walk (650 ptas). Finally, for technical climbs, Robin Walker's *Walks and Climbs in the Picos de Europa* (US$21.95) is your best bet.

In Spanish, Miguel Adrados has two definitive works: *Picos de Europa. Ascensiones y Travesías de Dificultad Moderada* (2000 ptas) and *Picos de Europa. Ascensiones a las*

Cumbres Principales y 20 Travesías Selectas (1600 ptas).

Information Sources

In Cangas de Onís, the tourist office in Plaza Avenida Covadonga and the very helpful Parque Nacional Centro de Recepción e Interpretación (☎ 985 84 91 54), Avenida Covadonga 43, will orient you to the charming town and the Picos de Europa.

The national park information centre (987 74 05 49) is on Travesía de los Llanos in Posada de Valdeón, which is the nearest access point to Days 3 and 7 of the Picos de Europa circuit.

The Grupo de Rescate (mountain rescue group) is in Potes (☎ 942 73 00 07) at Cuartel de la Guardia Civil Calle del Obispo 7.

Maps and Books are available in Oviedo bookshops as well as in the various villages around the Picos de Europa.

Picos de Europa Circuit

Duration 9 days
Distance 104km
Standard Hard
Start/Finish Lago de la Ercina
Public Transport Yes
Summary An unforgettable route covering the Picos de Europa's most extraordinary limestone landscapes – river gorges, alpine lakes, depressions, dense beech woods, narrow canals, cliff-hanging trails and peaks with breathtaking views.

This nine day circuit offers a magnificent overview of the Macizo Occidental and Macizo Central and includes some of the classic routes of the region. You will visit several villages in the national park, explore the region's greatest gorge, Garganta del Cares, and walk through high, green pastures set against a backdrop of stunning mountain peaks.

The route is written to be done in a clockwise direction for reasons of ease and safety. There are some sections which in particular we advise you not to reverse. For instance, on Day 2 it is better to descend than ascend the 1200m Canal de Trea passage (most people only make this mistake once). Similarly, on Day 5 it's safer to climb up the fixed cable at Horcados Rojos rather than attempt to climb down it.

We've rated the route hard due to the tremendous ascents and descents and the occasionally dangerous sections of scree.

To complete the whole loop as described, the best access point is Cangas de Onís in Asturias. An ambitious, fit walker can undertake the whole walk but the circuit can also easily be divided into shorter sections and day trips. We indicate alternative entry and exit points to the Picos de Europa in Getting to/from the Walk later in this section as well as in the walk description at the beginning of each relevant day. See Other Walks at the end of this chapter for possible day excursions.

PLANNING
When to Walk
July, August and September are all good walking months, though shepherds and *refugio* (refuge or mountain hut) wardens agree that September, still clear and warm, is the ideal time as the heat lessens and crowds disappear. If you go in August and want to use the refugios, consider making reservations in advance.

Maps
Many Picos de Europa maps are riddled with errors. The best are Miguel Ángel Adrados's three maps: *El Cornión* at 1:25,000 (700 ptas), *Picos de Europa: Macizos Central y Oriental* at 1:25,000 (780 ptas) and *Picos de Europa y Costa Oriental de Asturias* at 1:80,000 (500 ptas).

What to Bring
We strongly recommend that you bring a map and compass on this walk. Especially when fog settles, it's easy to get disoriented. A tent is an important piece of equipment, particularly in August when refugios are

often full. On Day 7, a tent or full bivouac gear are imperative.

Permits & Fees
There aren't any permits or fees but a three night limit at the Lagos Enol and Ercina camping grounds is enforced. The warden passes the tents to register names and passport numbers. Designated camp sites are very near to all of the refugios. Above 1600m, it's possible to bivouac wherever you can find relatively even ground.

Warning
Mist can seriously complicate navigation and rain can increase danger, especially on steep and slippery parts of the trail. You may need to wait out such conditions for a day or two in your tent or at a refugio to ensure safety. In addition, water is scarce above 1500m and may only be available at the start and finish of each day.

PLACES TO STAY & EAT
Cangas de Onís
The *Pensión Labra* (☎ 985 84 90 47, *Avenida Castilla 1)* has doubles with shared bath for 5000 ptas. Private bath doubles at the more upmarket *Hotel Plaza* (☎ 985 84 83 08) cost 6500 ptas. *Camping Covadonga* (☎ 985 94 00 97) is 4km from Cangas in Soto de Cangas (direction Arenas de Cabrales) and charges 550 ptas per person and 475 ptas per tent. It has a supermarket and a restaurant.

Try *fabada*, a white bean-based stew made with pork, beef and sausage, and *sidra* (cider; see the boxed text 'Culinary Musts') at either the *Restaurante Los Robles*, San Pelayo 8, or *Restaurante Enol*, Avenida Covadonga 27, for excellent fare and reasonably priced menús.

Tuñón, Calle Pelayo 31, and Llosa, Avenida Castilla 36, have last-minute dry goods and sporting supplies. Find maps and books at Imagen, Avenida Covadonga 19.

Arenas de Cabrales
Casa Fermín (☎ 985 84 65 66) next to the tourist office and the nearby *Pensión*

Culinary Musts

With so many milk-producing animals running around in the high pastures of the Picos de Europa, the cheese lover will not be disappointed. The most famous cheese, Queso de Cabrales, is produced on the Picos de Europa's north side. It's part of the blue cheese family and is a semihard, pasty cheese with distinctive bluish-green veins and a pungent smell and taste. The mould (genus *Penicillium*) is crucial to the three to six month maturation process. Made with cow, goat and sheep's milk, the cheese is left in caves with 90% humidity and at a temperature of eight to 12°C.

The area is also famous for rich, steaming stews that will kill any hunger. *Pote* or *potaje*, named after the dish in which it is cooked, is a stew made with chick peas or white beans, meat, *chorizo* (red sausage), potatoes and leafy green gabbage. *Fabada* is an Asturian variant of pote and contains a mixture of pork, beef and sausage – chorizo and *morcilla* (blood sausage) – to create a tangy delight to all the senses.

To wash it down, Asturian *sidra* (cider) is a refreshing accompaniment. Dating from at least the 12th century, this lightly alcoholic cider is made from pressed apples fermented in oak barrels. Drunk during fiestas as well as simply on afternoon breaks, sidra is widely popular not only for its smooth flavour but for the social atmosphere that accompanies its drinking.

Castañeu (☎ 985 84 65 73) have doubles for 4500 ptas. The *Camping Naranjo de Bulnes* (☎ 939 07 99 43) lies 1km from Arenas (direction Panes), with a nearby restaurant, market and bar. Both the *Restaurante Cares* and the *Restaurante Hotel Picos de Europa* provide menus in English and have 1300 ptas and 1500 ptas menús, respectively. *Casa Tres Palacios* sells Queso de Cabrales for 1750 ptas/kg.

The village has supermarkets, banks, a pharmacy and a tourist office in the main street. Adradros maps are available in La Tienda Nueva (opposite the tourist office). Also find maps in two sports shops on the main street: Deportes Morán and Deportes Cendón.

Sotres

A high-altitude village in the Picos de Europa, Sotres is 16km from Arenas. Sleep and eat well in both *Pensión Perdiz* (☎ 985 94 50 11) with singles/doubles for 2500/4000 ptas and *Pensión Cipriano* (☎ 985 94 50 63), where doubles cost 4500 ptas. The Cipriano also has a *refugio*, where it costs 900 ptas to sleep. Use of the kitchen is permitted.

Potes

Potes is an ideal gateway to the southern Macizo Oriental and Macizo Central. *Pensión El Fogón De Cus* (☎ 942 73 00 60), Calle Capitán Palacios, has decent singles/doubles with shared bath for 2500/4000 ptas. The *Hostal-Residencia María Eugenia* (☎ 942 73 01 54, Calle Doctor Encinas 12) charges 4500/6000 ptas for the same. *Restaurante El Bodegón*, Calle San Roque, prepares the best reasonably priced food, though *Pensión El Fogón De Cus* has good local specialities.

Potes has all services, a sports shop (Maratón, Calle Doctor Encinas 2) and several bookshops with guidebooks (Librería Vela, Calle San Roque 2) and Adrados maps (Foto Bustamante, Plaza Capitán Palacios 10). The tourist office, Calle Independencia 30, has good descriptions of walks around Potes in the Valle de Liébana.

Fuente Dé

It has few services but sits literally at Picos de Europa's feet. *Camping El Redondo* charges 800 ptas per adult and 400 ptas each per car and tent. The other option is the high-priced *Hotel Rebeco* (☎ *942 73 66 01*) with singles/doubles for 6000/8000 ptas. The economic *Cafetería Fuente Dé,* next to the cable car, offers a wide selection of items and a 1300 ptas menú. Adrados maps are sold at Camping El Redondo and in the souvenir shop next to the cable car station.

Posada de Valdeón

Posada is closest to the city of León. The dated but comfortable *Pensión Begoña* (☎ *987 74 05 16*) offers singles/doubles with shared bath for 2200/2600 ptas and a good set menú for 1500 ptas. The *Hostal Campo* (☎ *987 74 05 02*) has doubles at 6500 ptas. The nearby *Camping Santa Marina de Valdeón* is another possibility.

The village has a *supermarket* and a pharmacy as well as the national park information centre (for location details, see Information Sources in the introduction to this section). Maps are available in summer at souvenir shops, restaurants and hostels.

Refugios

The well organised refugios serve meals and sell basic canned food. Most are close to springs. Sleeping capacities range from 3 to 96. Almost all have showers and phones. Prices tend to be higher at refugios than in the nearby villages because supplies arrive by burro or on foot. Refugio wardens are helpful and can be a useful source of walking information.

The refugios charge member and non-member rates. To receive a discount, bring your mountain club card from your country of residence. Nonmember fees are listed here. Member prices are usually half those of nonmembers' and meals are discounted.

GETTING TO/FROM THE WALK

Public transport can be a juggling act but with preparation it's feasible.

Cangas de Onís

ALSA runs nine weekday and five weekend buses from Oviedo to Cangas de Onís for 680 ptas. From 1 July to 8 September, ALSA sends five daily buses from Cangas

up to Lago de la Ercina (1, 12 am and 1, 3.30 and 5.30 pm) for 220 ptas. The first of five buses back to Oviedo is at 12.30 pm and the last at 6.30 pm. From 9 to 30 September, the weekend bus climbs the hill at 11.30 am and returns at 1 pm. Taxis to the lakes cost 3500 ptas.

By car from Oviedo, take the A8 and the N634 east to Arriondas and catch the N625 south-east to Cangas de Onís. To reach the trailhead 24km uphill, take the AS114 3km and turn right onto the AS262 in the direction of Covadonga. Continue 12km further to Lagos Enol and Ercina.

Arenas de Cabrales

From Arenas de Cabrales, join Day 3 of the walk at the northern end of the Garganta del Cares in Poncebos. To reach Poncebos from Arenas de Cabrales, hitch, walk or take a taxi (1000 ptas) 5km uphill.

Four daily ALSA buses connect Cangas de Onís to Arenas de Cabrales for 285 ptas. Coming down the Santander-Panes line with Palomera buses, descend at Panes to go west to Arenas de Cabrales and Cangas de Onís.

Sotres

To reach Sotres from Arenas, take a taxi (2500 ptas) or hitchhike. To connect to Day 4 of the walk from Sotres, walk 5km on a 4WD road to the Refugio de Terenosa via the Collado de Pandébano.

Potes

Four daily summer buses arrive from Santander. ALSA leaves at 3.30 pm and Palomera at 10.30 am and 5 pm (11 am and 3.30 pm on weekends). Return from Potes on ALSA at 11.30 am and on Palomera at 7 am, 5.45 and 9.45 pm (8 am and 6.15 pm on weekends).

Fuente Dé

Palomera buses to Fuente Dé run 22 June to 13 September at 1 and 8 pm (185 ptas) from Potes. Taxis cost 2400 ptas (☎ *942 73 04 00*). A cable car with stunning views whisks visitors 750m up in less than four minutes to the upper station, El Cable. Walk the same with much greater effort along a spectacular 1½ hour route.

From El Cable, connect to Day 5 at the Cabaña Verónica refugio in two hours. Take the wide dirt road (north) and turn left at the first crossroads. At a hairpin left turn, veer right onto a footpath through scree and pass below the Torre de los Horcados Rojos to the refugio.

Posada de Valdeón

Buses from León run daily except Sunday at 6.30 pm (6.45 am return) and on Sunday at 8.15 am (3.30 pm return). To reach Day 3 of the route at Caín 9km away or Day 7 in nearby Cordiñanes, less than 3km from Posada de Valdeón, walk, hitch or take a taxi (☎ 987 74 26 09) for 4000 ptas or 1000 ptas, respectively.

THE WALK
Day 1: Lago de la Ercina to Refugio de Vega de Ario
2½ hours, 7.5km

A classic Picos de Europa walk, the trail quickly leaves the lakes and climbs up through pastures to summits which afford stunning views of the Macizo Central. The scramble up the impressive Jultayu mountain is unforgettable. Find water at the lakes and Vega de Ario.

From the **Lago de la Ercina** (1106m) meadow near the bus stop, skirt the lake's left shore to join an eastbound footpath that gently ascends above the lake. From the cabin at the base of Pico Llucia are splendid lake views. With a maximum depth of 2m (550m long and 350m wide), the lake is a breeding ground for water birds such as coots (*Fulica atra*) and mallard ducks (*Anas plathyrynchos*). Sporadically, you'll see teals (*A. crecca*), pochards (*Aythya ferina*) and herons (*Ardea cineraria*) following their migratory patterns.

The obvious earth and stone trail begins to turn away from the lake, ascending south-east through grass, gorse, heather and blue thistles. To the south, beeches cover the high hills as the way briefly and steeply ascends. The trail levels out at the **Vega Las Bobias** meadow, distinctive for the cabins, corrals and livestock. Cross the pasture south-east to a watering trough, where the way abandons the grass and makes a serpentine ascent through stones and beeches following yellow painted trail markers and descends towards a ravine. Now halfway to Vega de Ario (3.5km, 1¼ hours), cross the Arroyo Llaguiellu to begin a hard ascent with hairpin bends for 10 minutes to the top of the rise.

Once above, continue on a moderate gradient upwards across a succession of small depressions. Limestone boulders split by water and ice dominate the landscape. Forty minutes later, the path reaches a long valley, Las Abedulas, which terminates at a rocky col, **El Jito** (1650m). Cross straight over (south-east). One of the most impressive views of the Macizo Central – its jagged peaks sawing the sky – confronts you to the east. Closer, to the south, the rounded Jultayu (1940m) appears. On the summit of El Jito, to the right of the trail, is one of three entrances to one of the deepest cave systems in the Picos (see the boxed text 'Caving in the Picos' in the introduction to the Parque Nacional de los Picos de Europa).

A bit further on, the path turns left (north-east) and in 15 minutes reaches the lengthy Vega de Ario and the **Refugio de Marqués de Villaviciosa** (☎ 989 52 45 43). It sleeps 40 (1000 ptas) and serves breakfast/lunch/dinner for 500/1500/1500 ptas. There is also a **camp site**.

Side Trip: Jultayu
2 hours, 6km

To make the two hour return trip to the top of Jultayu, cross the meadow south-east towards some huts on the opposite hillside. At the end of the meadow near one of the huts, the path veers right and winds its way through rocks with yellow trail markers. Reaching an oxidised iron sign, turn right (south) towards the mountain. At the base of the peak, 20 minutes from the start, a yellow arrow descends left (south-east). Ignore this and continue straight (south), ascending 370m to the summit following cairns along the mountain's north face. In less than an hour, you're rewarded with breathtaking views from the natural watchtower. Spread out below are the next days' goals: Caín and the end of the Valle de Valdeón to the south, the Garganta del Cares below and the Macizo Central opposite. It won't be hard to spot vultures or, with some luck, a golden eagle. Take the same trail back to the refugio.

Day 2: Refugio de Vega de Ario to Caín

3½ to 4 hours, 8.5km

Characterised by a spectacular but difficult descent of nearly 1200m along the Canal de Trea to the Garganta del Cares gorge, a deep, natural dividing line between the Occidental and Central massifs. Find water at the refugio, Fuente El Peyu (along the canal) and in Caín.

Leave Vega de Ario as though heading to Jultayu (for details of the route, see the side trip at the end of the Day 1 walk description). Upon reaching its base, follow the south-east descending arrow rather than ascend. After 5 minutes winding through large rocks along a dirt trail (marked with yellow dots), you reach the entrance to the **Canal de Trea**, a dramatic, natural balcony. Looking straight across to the Macizo Central and down towards the Río Cares, the descent begins. On the left, a rocky bluff signals the transition from yellow to red trail markers. Take great care on the slippery, loose rocks. Scree alternates with paths of dirt and stone as the passage narrows and steepens.

Pass a large cavity in the rock wall to the left used to shelter goats, known as **Cuaroble**. Soon after, the way reaches the halfway point at a beautiful spring, **Fuente El Peyu**, rising from below a boulder – one of the Río Cares' tributaries. Descend along the stream's left bank for 10 minutes and veer left into an open oak and beech wood. The canal and stream continue off to the right. Once among the trees, descend for 40 minutes following the red dots. The last portion uses natural rock stairs and beech roots to drop down to the Senda del Cares

trail (see the boxed text 'Río & Garganta del Cares'). Turn right in the direction of Caín, 2km away. En route cross the breathtaking **Puente Bolín** (where 'puente' in Spanish means bridge) which offers an unforgettable perspective on the gorge's depth and greatness. The **Puente de los Rebecos**, 10 minutes later, leads to various humid tunnels excavated in the rocks through which the walkway passes. It crosses the river twice more before entering **Caín** (460m) over the border in Castilla y León. Caín is surrounded by jagged peaks, mostly of 2000m or more. Its residents honour Gregorio Pérez (1853-1913), a shepherd from the village who made the first recorded ascent of Naranjo de Bulnes with Pedro Pidal in 1904. The village (in summer they used to vend linden blossoms) has grown

Río & Garganta del Cares

The Río Cares rises 16km south of Caín, near the Pico Gildar (2078m), and flows through the Valle de Valdeón, Posada de Valdeón, Cordiñanes and numerous lowlying winter pastures. It reaches Caín and the Garganta del Cares at its narrowest point (near the dam) and cuts through the gorge for 10km to Poncebos. Wider and calmer, it descends to Arenas de Cabrales village and continues for another 26km before joining the Río Deva in Panes.

A remarkable engineering feat, the 3mwide path running the length of the gorge was gouged out of its sheer walls in 1946 to provide access to the Canal del Cares, made by the Viesgo electric company in 1921. The canal runs from Caín at the top of the gorge to Camarmeña, from where it is funnelled in tubes to the Poncebos hydroelectric plant 230m below. Before the path was hued into the walls of the gorge, the only way along it was via a trail much higher on the slopes of the Macizo Central; a daring undertaking reserved for the shepherds of Caín.

with tourism and now has a supermarket, public phones in bars and a tourist kiosk which sells maps and books. The fountain is near the church.

To sleep, try *Posada del Montañero* (☎ 987 74 27 11) which has clean doubles (bathroom included) for 5000 ptas. In the *Casa Cuevas* (☎ 987 74 27 20), doubles without bath go for a cheap 2800 ptas, or you can camp in the fields along the river for 300 ptas. The fields' owners will come and collect the money. *Hostal la Ruta* permits free camping but you need to ask first. Both pensions also offer hearty meals for 1000 ptas and 1100 ptas, respectively.

Day 3: Caín to Bulnes La Villa
5 to 5½ hours, 13.5km

Perhaps the single most outstanding walk in the Picos de Europa, the Garganta del Cares is easily undertaken by walkers of all ages. Reaching Poncebos, the walk ascends to Bulnes La Villa. Water is available in Caín, Poncebos (in the bar) and Bulnes La Villa.

It's possible to join and leave the circuit at both Caín and Poncebos, reached later in the day. For more information on how to get to and from either of these places, see Posada de Valdeón or Arenas de Cabrales under Getting to/from the Walk in the introduction to this walk.

Leave Caín retracing yesterday's steps. The first section of the gorge is hemmed in by high, sheer walls which slowly open out towards Poncebos. After reaching the Puente Bolín, the path stays on the Río Cares' left bank. From the Castilla y León-Asturias border sign, the path remains level for 3km, passing Culiembro, a former seasonal settlement which was almost totally destroyed during the construction of the aqueduct, along the trail. A cabin and crumbling hut remain.

Continuing, two huts appear; one, converted into the *Bar Espejismo* (Mirage Bar), sells cold drinks in summer, brought in by horse and kept cold in the canal.

After another flat 1km, the wide path narrows as it climbs steeply towards Los Collados. Now halfway to Bulnes La Villa, the trail drops down 2.2km to a dirt road that leads directly to Poncebos. Eat well for 1200 ptas at the *Hospedaje-Restaurante la Garganta del Cares* (☎ 985 84 64 63). Rooms cost from 2000/4000 ptas for singles/doubles. Arenas de Cabrales is 5km downhill.

To continue to Bulnes La Villa, turn left onto the Poncebos road and after 100m, turn right and descend to the Río Cares. Once over the bridge, ascend the Arroyo Tejo, crossing to the right bank. At the base of a hill crowned by Bulnes El Castillo, ignore the bridge which leads to it and continue ahead on the gently ascending path, with scree on the left and fields on the right, to Bulnes La Villa (647m). The small village has two private refugios: *Albergue de Bulnes* (☎ 985 84 59 43) with 20 bunks and English-speaking staff and the locally run *Albergue Peña Main* (☎ 985 84 59 39) with 16 bunks. The former offers bed and breakfast for 1500 ptas and lunch and dinner for 1400 ptas each. The latter charges 1000 ptas for accommodation and 1300 ptas for lunch or dinner. The *Bar Bulnes* permits camping in a nearby field for 300 ptas and offers mattresses on the floor (but no bath or toilet) for 500 ptas. The fountain is at the end of the village on the river's true left bank.

Day 4: Bulnes La Villa to Vega de Urriellu
5 hours, 9km

A constant, 1300m climb through scenic country leads to the base of the Naranjo de Bulnes. Get water in Bulnes, La Jelguera Refugio de la Terenosa and Vega de Urriellu.

It's possible to join or leave the circuit at the Refugio de la Terenosa. The nearest village is Sotres, 5km away. (For more information on transport in or out of the valley, see Sotres under Getting to/from the Walk in the introduction to this walk.)

Leave Bulnes La Villa via the bridge and turn right, beginning the south-east ascent along the pebble path. Five minutes later, ignore a path on the right and instead continue on a lovely stone-paved lane through a forest of walnut, linden and hazelnut trees.

A cascade at the foot of Canal de Balcosín

INGRID RODDIS

INGRID RODDIS

INGRID RODDIS

Top: The towering glacial cirque at the head of the Vall de Pineta, Aragón.
Bottom Left: Cascada de Cola de Caballo in Parque Nacional de Ordesa y Monte Perdido, Aragón, is a very popular destination with day-trippers.
Bottom Right: Below Cascada de Coa de Caballo the trail descends a series of natural river terraces.

Cow and shepherd's cabin in the Vega Las Bobias, Picos de Europa (top left); Puente Romano at Villanueva, despite its name, is actually medieval (middle left); the Garganta del Cares separates the two major massifs of the Picos de Europa (top right); walkers descending to Naranjo de Bulnes, with La Jelguera ahead (bottom left); shepherds' cabins are a highlight of the Ruta de las Brañas (bottom right).

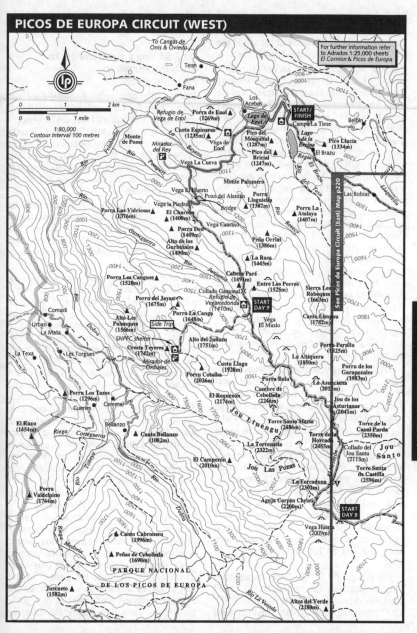

PICOS DE EUROPA CIRCUIT (WEST)

To Cangas de Onis & Oviedo

For further information refer to Adrados 1:25,000 sheets *El Cornion* & *Picos de Europa*

Teon

Fana

Los Acebos

START/FINISH

Campa La Tiese

Belbín

Refugio de Vega de Enol

Porra de Enol (1269m)

Cuetu Espineres (1235m)

Lago de Enol

Lago de la Ercina

Pico Llucia (1334m)

Monte de Pome

Mirador del Rey

Vega de Enol

Pico del Mosquital (1287m)

El Brazu

Río Pomperi

Vega La Cueva

Pico del Bricial (1247m)

Regtu

Río La Bevera

Vega El Huerto

Monte Palomero

Porra Llaguiellu (1387m)

Pozo del Alemán

Porru La Atalaya (1407m)

Las Bobias

Vega la Piedra

El Charcon (1400m)

Bridge

Porra Las Vidriosas (1376m)

Vega Canraso

Porru Deu (1409m)

Peña Orrial (1386m)

Alto de los Gurbiñales (1490m)

Río Junjumia

La Rasa (1443m)

Cabeza Paré (1491m)

Porru Les Cangues (1520m)

Entre Los Porros (1525m)

Sierra Les Robeques (1663m)

Porru del Jayau (1675m)

Collado Gamonal

Refugio de Vegaredonda (1410m)

START DAY 9

Vega El Muslo

Canto Limpiu (1782m)

Comudi

Alto Les Palanques (1566m)

Porru La Canga (1648m)

Side Trip

Urban

La Mata

SNPFC shelter

Alto del Juñazu (1751m)

Porru Perullu (1825m)

La Altiquera (1850m)

La Texa

Cresta Teyeres (1742m)

Les Torgues

Mirador de Ordiales

Cuetu Llagu (1928m)

Porru Bolu

La Asunciana (2013m)

Porru de los Garapozales (1983m)

Porru Cotalba (2026m)

Cumbre de Cebolleda (2246m)

Jou de los Asturianos (2041m)

Porru Los Tazos (1296m)

El Requexón (2174m)

Torre de la Canal Parda (2350m)

Cueries

Cerernal

Jou Lluengu

Torre Santa María (2486m)

Collado del Jou Santu (2113m)

Jou Santo

El Raxu (1454m)

Bellanzo

Canto Bellanzo (1082m)

Torre de la Horcada (2485m)

Torre Santa de Castilla (2596m)

Río Cortegueros

La Torrezuela (2322m)

Río Toneyu

Porra Valdelpino (1744m)

El Camperón (2010m)

Jou Las Pozas

La Forcadona (2302m)

Aguja Corpus Christi (2200m)

START DAY 8

Río Dobra

Canto Cabronero (1996m)

Vega Huerna (2009m)

Peñas de Cebolleda (1690m)

PARQUE NACIONAL

Jurcueto (1582m)

DE LOS PICOS DE EUROPA

Río La Verada

Altos del Verde (2180m)

0   1   2 km

0   ½   1 mile

1:80,000
Contour Interval 100 metres

See Picos de Europa Circuit (East) Map p220

CORDILLERA CANTÁBRICA

(right) marks the beginning of a steep and less scenic section of the climb to Vega de Urriellu via the Collado Camburero and the western scree slopes of the Jou Lluengo.

After 30 minutes of ascent, the first views of the imposing, cubic-looking Naranjo de Bulnes come into sight off to the right. The lane crosses the Río Tejo twice (a cabin in between sells honey) and reaches a clearing with fields and shepherd's huts. Continue east on the stone-paved lane. After 15 minutes, it turns left just before reaching a hut with a walled meadow. Twenty minutes from the meadow, the stone walkway ends. After passing a wall with a wooden door, take the dirt path which gently ascends and crosses the **La Jelguera** meadow. The second cabin on the left sells Cabrales cheese for 1300 ptas/kg and has a fountain. At the meadow's high point, **Collado Pandébano**, Sotres is visible in the distance to the east. Turn right (south-west) towards several huts, a fountain and the *Refugio de la Terenosa* (☎ 985 25 23 62). With capacity for 30, it's open all year but staffed only from May to October. If arriving from Pandébano, the shepherd in the first cabin has the keys. At this point you are halfway.

After the refugio, the trail continues south-west above a dense beech forest that descends the Monte de La Varera towards Bulnes La Villa. Further on, the forest disappears and the slope becomes more vertical.

One hour from the Refugio de la Terenosa at the base of a large scree section, the ascent steepens yet again, zigzagging between rocks and scree. Close to the Naranjo de Bulnes, the path curves briefly around its base and then heads towards the north-west face and the *Refugio Vega d'Urriellu* (1953m). From here, you'll see the first snowfields. The easiest route to the summit, still requiring ropes, is up the southern face along the Vía de los Martínez, opened in 1944.

The refugio (☎ 985 94 50 63), open from May to October, accommodates 96 (1000 ptas). Breakfast/lunch/dinner cost 350/ 1500/ 1500 ptas, respectively. It's supplied with water from a spring and nearby is a designated *camp site*.

Day 5: Vega de Urriellu to Collado Jermoso
7½ hours, 13km

This is the most arduous section of the circuit, both for its length and two difficult scrambles – one along a fixed cable. Water is available at the Refugio de la Vega d'Urriellu and at the end of the day, or buy it at Cabaña Verónica. During the whole stage, it's important to take your time and plant your feet well as erosion has caused some areas to become unstable.

You have the option of joining or leaving the circuit at the Cabaña Verónica via the El Cable cable car station above Fuente Dé, two hours away. (For more information, see Getting to/From the Walk in the introduction to this walk.)

Leave the refugio south-west along an ascending stone trail. In 30 minutes, ignore a path that heads off right and continue straight to the grandiose **Jou Sin Tierre**, an impressive lunar depression. Descend (not to the base) and cross along its left slope. Take great care with the descent into the jou and the steep ascent at the end. After a brief level section, the path reaches the **Jou de los Boches**. Cross south via its base and ascend through a scree section to the foot of **Horcados Rojos**, where yellow trail markers help to indicate the best way out. In ascending the wall, first cross through scree and then through another, more dangerous, section of sheer rock where extreme care is recommended. Halfway up is a fixed cable to help to guide you towards the exit on the right.

From the summit, the *Cabaña Verónica* (2325m), a silver-toned igloo adding to the lunar appearance of the landscape, sits on top of a rocky mound. Now in Cantabria, descend to the base of the mound and ascend south-west to the refugio, open all year. Its three sleeping spaces cost 600 ptas each. There isn't a fountain (or phone) at this height but water is sold as well as meals and expensive canned food which is brought in on foot twice a day during the summer.

Breakfast/lunch/dinner cost 600/1500/1500 ptas, respectively. The refugio was once the cannon mount for an American aircraft carrier.

Visible from the refugio are: south-east, the El Cable cable car station of Fuente Dé; north-west, the Pico Tesorero (border point of Asturias, Castilla y León, and Cantabria); and south, the Horcada Verde, our exit out of this desolate spot of earth. Leave the refugio, heading west among rocks to the circular *camp site* areas. You'll see two walls (one below the other). Cross over the higher wall (right) along its crest. After ascending the last part of the wall, follow the cairns and red trail markers that circle around to the right. When you are just opposite the refugio, take the trail descending south.

After climbing up a vertical crack, take another rocky passage (south). When it begins to widen and deepen, leave the crack, heading left. (You can continue from here down to Collado Jermoso via Tiro de Casares as seen on the Adrados map, *Macizo Central y Oriental*, but it is more difficult and less panoramic than the route we describe.) Now without cairns, ascend south to the base of the Torre del Hoyo Oscuro (2417m) and turn left towards a scree section where there is an unexpected view of the Hoyo Sin Tierra to the north-east. At the end of the scree, ascend to the **Horcada Verde** pass, either scrambling up the first vertical crack or climbing around the bluff diagonally. Again, take good care with foot and handholds. In both cases, aim for the extreme left of the pass. From the top, descend along the sporadically cairned path above the Hoyo Oscuro.

The path disappears but continue heading south (leaving off to the right a possible *camp site*) to the lowest point, which coincides with the beginning of the Canal de San Luis (east). Continue south, climbing through rocks and following cairns to the Colladina de las Nieves (2226m). At the pass, turn right (south-west) and descend on a dirt trail towards the immense Vega de Liordes. Leave it off to the left and follow a trail littered with cairns. Halfway down, the path turns right (north-west) paralleling

above the vega and soon joins a trail ascending from the vega on the left. Continue along the spectacular hillside trail. Below left, the Lago Bajero comes into sight. The path leaves the slope and begins a steep upturn to Las Colladinas. At the summit of the rise, it heads right and levels out slightly. After another brief ascent, you finally see **Collado Jermoso** and the *Refugio Diego Mella*. Follow a path up a slope to the right of the refugio. A veritable eagle's nest with incredible views of both massifs, the refugio (2046m) has space for 29 (700 ptas), a bar, fountain and *camp site*. It's open all year with all supplies arriving on human backs. Breakfast costs 700 ptas and lunch and dinner are 1400 ptas each. The wardens may speak English.

Day 6: Collado Jermoso to Cordiñanes
4 hours, 9km

Leaving behind the high mountain, the walk first steeply then gently descends (1200m) to low pastures and makes its way through one of the park's most beautiful beech forests before rejoining the Río Cares. Water is available at the beginning and end of the day.

From the refugio, head towards the fountain. Before long a sign indicates right to Cordiñanes. Follow the sign to the top of the first steep section of trail. From above, it appears more intimidating than it really is. Once at the bottom, head towards the left wall and in 10 minutes, now below, cross a stream that descends from the fountain above. Continue on the cairn-marked path to an area of irregular rocks; a rope has been fixed to help you to descend. Ten minutes later, after crossing a dry stream bed, follow the sign pointing right to Vega de la Sotín (marked with red dots).

The hillside trail crosses over a high pass and goes directly down a scree slope with protruding rocks at its base. Once at the rocks, turn right following the hillside path that leads to the irregular peak, the Torre del Collado Solano. At its base, the path makes a zigzagging descent to the halfway point, the **Vega de Asotín**. From here, turn right

PICOS DE EUROPA CIRCUIT (EAST)

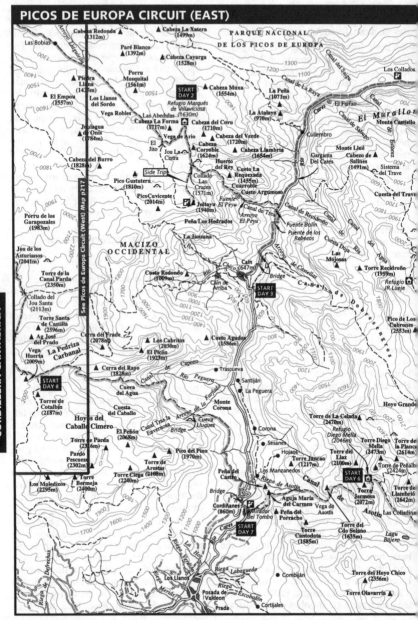

PICOS DE EUROPA CIRCUIT (EAST)

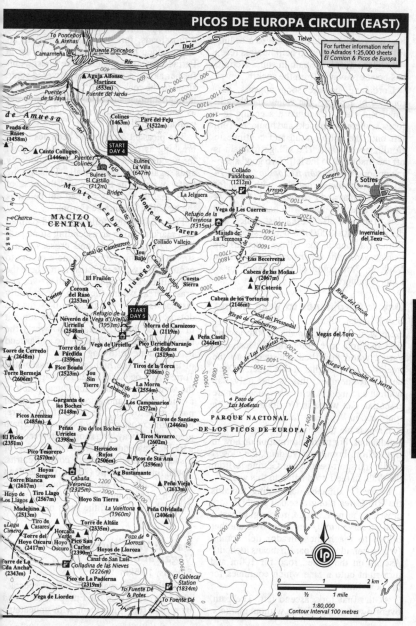

For further information refer to Adrados 1:25,000 sheets El Cornion & Picos de Europa

To Poncebos & Arenas

Camarmeña

Puente Poncebos

Tielve

Río Duje

Río Cares

de Amuesa

Aguja Alfonso Martínez (553m)

Puente del Jardu

Puente de la Jaya

Peada de Ráses (1458m)

Colines (1463m)

Paré del Feju (1522m)

Canto Collugos (1446m)

Puente Colines

START DAY 4

Bulnes La Villa (647m)

Collado Pandébano (1212m)

Sotres

Bulnes El Castillo (712m)

Bridge

La Jelguera

Monte Acebuco

Monte de La Varera

Canal de Balcosín

Refugio de la Terenosa (1315m)

Vega de Les Cuerres

Arroyo

MACIZO CENTRAL

Canal de Camburero

Jou Bajo

Collado Vallejo

Majada de La Terenosa

Invernales del Texu

Charca

Cuetos del Albo

El Fraílón

Valle del Agua

Las Becerreras

El Frailón

Jou Lluengo

Canal del Vallejo

Cuesta Sierra

Cabeza de las Moñas (2067m)

El Coterón

Corona del Raso (2253m)

Refugio de la Vega d'Urriellu (1953m)

START DAY 5

Morra del Carnizoso (2119m)

Cabeza de los Tortorios (2146m)

Canal del Fresnedal

Vegas del Toro

Neverón de Urriellu (2548m)

Torre de la Párdida (2596m)

Vega de Urriellu

Pico Urriellu/Naranjo de Bulnes (2519m)

Peña Castil (2444m)

Riega de Camburero

Torre de Cerredo (2648m)

Pico Boada (2523m)

Tiros de la Torca (2386m)

Riega de Las Moñetas

Torre Bermeja (2606m)

Jou Sin Tierre

Canal de Lebaniego

La Morra (2554m)

Riega del Oncín

Garganta de los Boches (2148m)

Los Campanarios (2572m)

Pozo de Las Moñetas

Riega del Canalón del Jierru

Picos Areniszas (2485m)

Peñas Urrieles (2398m)

Jou de los Boches

Tiros de Santiago (2446m)

PARQUE NACIONAL

El Picón (2351m)

Pico Tesorero (2570m)

Hercados Rojos (2506m)

Tiros Navarro (2602m)

DE LOS PICOS DE EUROPA

Picos de Sta Ana (2596m)

Hoyos Sengros

Cabaña Veronica (2325m)

Ag Bustamante

Torre Blanca (2617m)

Hoyo de Los Llagos

Tiro Llago (2567m)

Hoyo Sin Tierra

Peña Vieja (2613m)

Río Duje

Madejúno (2513m)

Tiro de Casares

La Vueltona (1960m)

Peña Olvidada (2406m)

Lagu Cimero

Torre de Altáiz (2335m)

Torre del Hoyo Oscuro (2417m)

Horcada Verde

Hoyo Oscuro

Pico San Carlos (2390m)

Pozo de Lloroza

Hoyos de Lloroza

Torre de La Cda Ancha (2343m)

Colladina de las Nieves (2226m)

Canal de San Luis

El Cablecar Station (1834m)

Pico de La Padierna (2319m)

Vega de Liordes

To Fuente Dé & Potes

To Fuente Dé

0   1   2 km
0   ½   1 mile

1:80,000
Contour Interval 100 metres

CORDILLERA CANTÁBRICA

(west) onto a well defined footpath that first continues above and then enters a majestic beech forest before exiting left to a beautiful hillside trail. Built to help hunters reach the high pastures, the path in some sections has been excavated from the rock.

Cordiñanes village soon appears, surrounded by pastures, the valley and the still small Río Cares. Continue descending to a forest scattered with rocks and boulders. Turn left onto the pebble road and continue to Cordiñanes (860m). The village fountain is off the first street to the left. Two good sleeping options are *Pensión El Tombo* (☎ 987 74 05 26) with singles/doubles with bath for 3500/5000 ptas and *Pensión Rojo* (☎ 987 74 05 23), where doubles with bath cost 4500 ptas. The first offers breakfast, lunch and dinner for 400/1300/1100 ptas, respectively. Without a shop in the village, supplies are available from the *supermarket* at Posada de Valdeón, 3km south of Cordiñanes, or in Caín, 6km north.

Day 7: Cordiñanes to Vega Huerta
6 to 7 hours, 10km
Hard work gets you up the 1150m ascent, first through an extraordinarily lush and varied wood and then up steeply to the treeless, rocky heights of this Macizo Occidental. Remember, this is the only day without a refugio. A tent or bivouac gear are essential. Get water in Cordiñanes, late en route and in Vega Huerta.

It's possible to join or leave the circuit in Cordiñanes. For more information on how to Get to/from Posada de Valdeón, the closest public transport centre, see Getting to/from the Walk in the introduction to this walk.

Leave Cordiñanes descending towards the Río Cares along a sealed road. Before crossing the new bridge, turn right (past a well preserved mill) and cross over another bridge to reach the Mirador del Tombo (where 'mirador' in Spanish means lookout). Ascend on the sealed road for 100m and turn right onto a lane which continues for the next 4km.

At the first fork, ascend left. The path, overgrown but still visible without markers,

continues along the slope above Monte Corona and enters a shady forest. Reaching a crossroads, fork left (north-west) to an old, wooden bridge over the Arroyo de la Farfada. The path abandons the forest. A bit further along, ascend a grass covered scree slope to the rock wall in front of you. Pass through another stretch of beech wood and as you exit, continue on the hillside footpath at the rock wall's base.

The pleasant ascent now becomes backbreaking as the footpath turns up through the woods (about 30 minutes) and suddenly ends against a sheer wall. This is the halfway point for the day and the base of the Canal de Capozo. Spread out below is the beautiful Bosque de Corona.

From this point, follow the red-painted trail markers along an ascending stone path that zigzags upwards and crosses a dry stream bed, which it begins more or less to parallel. Forty-five minutes from where the red trail markers began, the trail arrives at a grassy area, where the path occasionally disappears below the grass. Follow the red dots as the path drifts right. At the summit of the next high point, cross (west) the stone-covered base of the ravine and ascend its right slope following cairns. At the top of the ravine, the high, rocky mass of the Torre Santa de Castilla (2596m) appears to the north-west. If you want water, go left to a small pasture and a fountain. Now head north-west towards the base of the Torre, navigating cross-country as cairns and path give out. Halfway, you should intersect with a trail that ascends left (west) to the crest of a saddle marked by large, conical cairns. You'll find a *camp site* (2009m) at the **Vega Huerta** nearby. To reach the fountain, take a left-hand path and then go left again at the first fork. It's behind the ruins of a former refugio.

Day 8: Vega Huerta to Vegarredonda
5 hours, 10.5km
An initially hard walk to the most spectacular jous of the Picos de Europa is followed by a 5km (600m) descent with unbeatable

views of the northern portions of the Macizo Occidental and Asturias. Find water at the beginning and end of the day.

A clearly marked path leaves Vega Huerta north-west (another leaves south-west to Valdeón) and winds among large rocks marked with cairns, yellow slashes and blue dots. In 30 minutes, a tough scree ascent begins. Once above, at the base of the Aguja Corpus Christi (2200m), the path reaches a circular depression. Skirt around the jou to the right without descending and climb towards a group of rocks. At this point, the blue and yellow markers diverge.

If you follow the blue dots, it's possible to reach Vegarredonda via Jou las Pozas, La Torrezuela, Jou Lluengo and Porru Bolu as marked on the Adrados *El Cornión* map.

This walk follows the yellow trail markers up through the rocks and across another scree section to the north-east. The difficult ascent leads to a type of cirque without any apparent exit. Skirt around its right side and then turn left, seeing (just when you've given up hope) two yellow markers on the wall ahead at the scree's end, which lead over the **La Forcadona** pass. Even though it's necessary to scramble up one of the various cracks in the last portion, it's easier than it looks from below.

Once on top, ignore the yellow markers ascending to the Santa de Castilla, and descend north to cross a solid, year-round snowfield, **El Neverón**. Keep going north and over a small jou containing two snowfields. Climb out of the depression still heading north through rocks. There is no path but there are various cairns. From above, you can see one of the depressions to the west which make up the startling and grandiose Jou Santu. Skirt around its right side until you meet up with a path which heads left. Once on the path, we strongly recommend leaving your pack and walking back east for five minutes to contemplate, from the col, the Jou Santu in all its enormous glory.

Continue on the marked path around the right-hand side of the diminutive Jou de los Asturianos. Upon cresting its far lip, the descent begins with magnificent views of the northern and western valleys and mountains surrounding Los Picos and even the Lago de la Ercina and Vega de Enol. In the last 5km, the way descends first on stones and then earth until the black roof of the old refugio appears below. Find a fountain here and next to the new refugio below. The *Refugio de Vegarredonda* (1410m), open from May to October, has 68 bunks (1000 ptas), a bar and offers breakfast/lunch/dinner for 600/1500/1500 ptas, respectively. *Camp* around the old refugio.

Day 9: Vegarredonda to Lago de la Ercina
3 hours, 9.5km

We highly recommend beginning the day with a side trip to the Mirador de Ordiales (see the side trip to Mirador de Ordiales at the end of the day's walk description).

From behind the new refugio, walk through rocks and turn left (north) onto a path that ascends to a meadow, Collado Gamonal, and then descends past several shepherd's cabins. The path is flanked with low stone trail markers and leads first over a brook and then to a section bordered by wooden guardrails. Descend to the **Vega La Piedra** (with more cabins) named for the large, isolated boulder sitting in the field's centre. Skirt around the boulder's right side. A bit further down, near a watering trough which has the last potable water until the end of the day, a wider path begins. At the next junction, turn left among beeches. Cross the Río Pomperi to the Vega El Huerto, which has a pool called the **Pozo del Alemán** (The German's Well) dedicated by popular appeal to Robert Frassinelli (environmental champion of the Picos de Europa) on the centenary of his death in 1987.

Follow a 4WD road that leads north without turn-offs through pastures and huts for 2km to the Vega de Enol with a *refugio*, *camp site* and lake. The refugio (☎ 985 84 92 61), a large building on the left, is open all year, has 15 bunks (500 ptas) and charges 1300 ptas for lunch and dinner. It does not have showers and has portable toilets during the summer only.

To reach the Lago de la Ercina, continue along the dirt road towards the Lago Enol, veering right to reach the lake's shore (swimming area). Pick up the lovely footpath that circles around the right-hand side of the lake to the sealed road. Turn right and then left at the crossroads to reach the Lago de la Ercina. To the right of the crossroads is the bus stop.

Side Trip: Mirador de Ordiales
2½ hours, 7.5km

This is an easy return trip to a spectacular lookout and the final resting place of Pedro Pidal.

Begin the walk west of the refugio on a stone path. Climbing steadily, the trail crosses a succession of limestone hills and depressions. It's common to see chamois. After an hour or so, the path reaches a pasture with an abandoned refugio of the SNPFC (Sociedad Nacional de Pesca Fluvial y Caza). A last south-west ascent leads to the simple Mirador de Ordiales lookout with views over the peaks, forest, foothills and villages along the Río Dobra.

At the base of the lookout, Pedro Pidal's (1870-1933) remains are interred. Eight years after his death, his final wish – to be buried at this natural balcony – was fulfilled at last. Engraved in a nearby rock, he wrote (translated into English here): 'Lover of the Picos, I would love to live, die and eternally rest here in Ordiales. In the enchanted kingdom of the chamois and the eagles…' Return to Vegarredonda on the same path.

Other Walks

PARQUE NATURAL DE SOMIEDO

Five additional marked trails through the Parque Natural de Somiedo appear on the recommended map. The park's office has more information (see Information Sources in the introduction to the Parque Natural de Somiedo).

Ruta del Camín Real

Two walks leave from Puerto de San Lorenzo along the Ruta del Camín Real. Once a Roman highway linking Asturias with Astorga, the Muslims later used the road on their way to sack Oviedo. The first walk heads south-east to the Puerto de la Mesa in 21.5km; the second goes north-west for 6km to Bustariega.

Ruta de la Pornacal

Starting in Villar de Viladas (west of Pola de Somiedo), the route ascends 6km to the teito-filled pastures of La Pornacal and Los Cuartos.

Ruta de las Brañas de Arbellales

A walk to Salienca (east of Pola de Somiedo) which passes six brañas in an easy 6km.

Ruta de El Cornón

A day of climbing Somiedo's highest peak (2194m), El Cornón. From Santa María del Puerto, ascend west to the conical summit in 7km or 3½ hours. Return the same way or via the Collado los Moñones.

PARQUE NATURAL DE SAJA-BESAYA
GR71 Continuation

From Saja, the route continues to Tudanca (17km), Pejanda (16km), Cahecho (20km), Potes (8km), Bejes (16.5km) and Sotres (16km). Accommodation is available at the end of each day. For transport and lodging information in Potes and Sotres, see Places to Stay & Eat in the introduction to the Picos de Europa Circuit walk.

PARQUE NACIONAL DE LOS PICOS DE EUROPA

Using the circuit's descriptions, a number of day trips are possible. From the Lagos Ercina and Enol, there are several options. A return trip from the Lago de la Ercina to Jultayu (Day 1) is an excellent medium-hard walk feasible in six hours. A return trip from Lago Enol to the Bosque de Pome via the Mirador del Rey (see Day 9) takes three easy hours. A return trip from Lago Enol to Mirador de Ordiales (Day 9) is a walk of medium difficulty, taking 5½ hours.

Another popular option is to climb to the base of the Naranjo de Bulnes via either Sotres in eight hours return or, more strenuously, from Poncebos in nine hours (see Days 3 and 4).

Alternatively, walking the stunning Garganta del Cares gorge from Poncebos can be done in a comfortable seven hours return.

If you're still eager for more, try:

Senda Arcediano

In the 17th century the route, possibly a Roman highway, received its name when an archdeacon from Oseja de Sajambre poured money into its improvement. It connected Castilla with Asturias via the Puerto de Beza, avoiding the imposing Garganta de los Beyos gorge created by the Río Sella. We recommend starting in Soto (5km from Oseja) and continuing 15km north to Amieva. Feasible in 5 to 5½ hours, this medium route is marked part of the way with red-and-white trail markers and has stunning views of the Macizo Occidental.

From Soto, ascend to the Portillera de Beza pass and then cross the Valle de Toneyo, La Majada de Saugu, a high summer pasture, and the Collado del Cueta pass to finish in Amieva village. The Adrados map *El Cornión* at 1:25,000 and Marta Prieto's *La Senda del Arcediano* booklet cover the area.

Ascent to Treviso

Seventeen kilometres from Potes in the direction of Panes, the Río Urdón flows into the Deva. From here, a literally cliff-hanging path makes a zigzagging ascent more than 800m above the Garganta del Urdón, one of the Picos de Europa's wildest gorges, to the isolated Treviso village. Until the highway from Sotres was constructed, this thrilling path was the only link for the inhabitants of Treviso, who used it to transport cheese by burro to Potes. The footpath slowly zigzags up the nearly vertical slope, passing two natural balconies above the gorge. Vultures are common on this medium-hard 2½ hour climb. The Adrados map *Macizo Central y Oriental* at 1:25,000 is recommended.

CORDILLERA CANTÁBRICA

Galicia

Quietly nestled in Iberia's north-west, Galicia has a wealth of natural riches for the walker eager to experiment in this relatively unknown, largely rural, corner of Spain. From plunging sea cliffs and expansive dunes to deep forests and gentle mountain slopes, this startlingly beautiful area is enhanced by innumerable artistic and historical treasures: dolmens (stone tombs), Roman ruins, monasteries, medieval bridges and country mansions.

The chapter is split into two sections: the Northern Littoral and the Eastern Sierras. The coastal walks explore parts of Galicia's 1200km of coastline along the famed Costa da Morte (Death Coast), as well as into Galicia's greatest Atlantic deciduous forest, the Fraga do Eume. Walks in the Eastern Sierras offer a glimpse of Galicia's interior, exploring the range's rounded crests and enclosed, lush valleys. Despite the lure of these attractions, however, don't expect excellent walking infrastructure (good trail markers, English-language guides and an abundance of information). Unlike other parts of Spain, the development of a good network of maintained routes has been slow in coming.

HISTORY

Galicia is an archaeology buff's goldmine. Megalithic peoples left behind numerous dolmens at funerary sites. Some 3000 years later, around 2200 BC, the first petroglyphs were carved, evolving to include labyrinths, human and animal figures, and crosses. Galicia is amply sprinkled with these weighty stone monuments and carvings; their size, variety and number rival any other region along the Atlantic arch. From about the 6th century BC onwards, Indo-European peoples, including the Celts, invaded the area. This period also marked the development of *castros* – permanent, fortified, often circular settlements, coopted by the Romans upon their arrival in 137 BC. Julius Caesar sailed to present day A

Coruña province in 61 BC, where Iberia's oldest (and still functioning!) Roman lighthouse, La Torre de Hércules, stands. Roman walls still encircle Lugo.

With the decline of the Roman empire in the 5th century AD, the Germanic Suevi people took over but were swiftly dislodged by the Visigoths. During the long reign of Islam in the south, the Muslims occasionally ransacked the north but never established a governed population. Viking and Norman invaders also terrorised the coastline during the centuries around the turn of the first millennium, but left little impact. The heralded discovery in the 9th century of the tomb of the apostle James in Santiago de Compostela (see the History section in the introduction to the Camino de Santiago chapter) put Galicia forever on the map.

Thanks to the instant and unprecedented popularity of the Camino de Santiago (Way of St James) pilgrim's route, the kingdom of Galicia reached its cultural and political apex in the 12th and 13th centuries. *Galego*, the Galician language, features in key literary texts of the time.

Galicia's limelight faded in the 15th century, partly as a result of the Irmandiños (a series of bloody feudal uprisings) and also as Castilla – determined to control the various peninsular kingdoms – suppressed

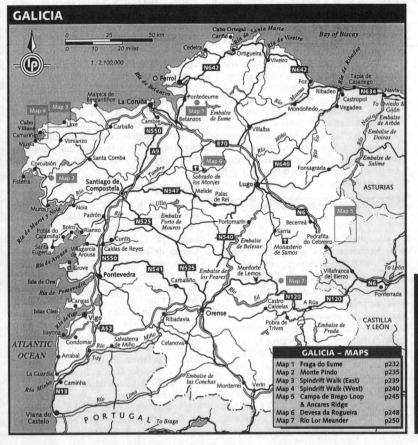

GALICIA

GALICIA – MAPS	
Map 1	Fraga do Eume	p232
Map 2	Monte Pindo	p235
Map 3	Spindrift Walk (East)	p239
Map 4	Spindrift Walk (West)	p240
Map 5	Campa de Brego Loop & Ancares Ridge	p245
Map 6	Devesa da Rogueira	p248
Map 7	Río Lor Meander	p250

GALICIA

Galician Lace-Making

Observing women (*palilleiras*) swiftly manipulate tens of bobbins (*palillos* or *bolillos*) to slowly produce intricate patterns of delicate lace is an impressive sight. Sitting at the doors of their homes or grouped together, the palilleiras practise an art – known as *encaixe de palillos* – whose origin is unclear. Some say it was imported by a Flemish soldier of Carlos I or that it was introduced via the Camino de Santiago. The most romantic version suggests that a strange, foreign woman, saved from a shipwreck by helpful locals, gave them the gift of lace in thanks.

The oblong, pillowed work board is stuffed with tightly packed hay inside a soft sack. Two wooden sticks project from the top, providing support. Around the board the women wrap the drawn pattern and position countless coloured pins at crucial intersections. Between the pins they skilfully braid linen threads, each attached to walnut palillos. A once-popular folk belief suggested that a bride who carried her rings on a lace handkerchief would be prosperous. Camariñas is the most famous centre of encaixe found throughout the Costa da Morte.

(by decapitation) the last Galician opposition. Economic and political repression from a centralised Spain reinforced the region's poverty and relative isolation.

In the mid-19th century the Galician cultural and political renaissance, known as the *Rexurdimento*, spawned a new sense of nationalism. The regime of Franco (a native of Galicia) following the Spanish Civil War discouraged expressions of regional identity, and it was not until the establishment of democracy that they began to reemerge.

Rather than industrialise, Galicia has primarily depended on the sea and its rich farm and pasture lands to sustain its population. When this has proved inadequate, many have been forced to flee to richer areas (especially during the 20th century). Money sent back from the Americas, tourism and improvements in agricultural efficiency have helped to invigorate the weak economy and, between the 1970s and 1990s, produced rapid development. Today young people head to the urban areas to seek employment and education while an ageing population tends the fields.

Galicians tend not to be avid walkers (except some younger people), explaining the nonchalant approach to route development and maintenance. The Federación Gallega de Montañismo asserts that Galicia has 500km of marked routes and 25 officially approved short-distance Sendero de Pequeno Recorrido (PR) and long-distance Sendero de Gran Recorrido (GR) trails – mostly concentrated in Pontevedra province. Unfortunately, there is no designated body maintaining them and Galician shrubbery has a remarkable knack for encroaching on sections of track. Numerous protected places are well advertised by Galicia's tourism branch but the government lacks an organised sector to regulate their protection. Hopefully, this situation will change.

NATURAL HISTORY

Split into four provinces (A Coruña, Lugo, Pontevedra and Ourense), Galicia's 29,482 sq km are bounded by sea, river and mountain. The Cantabrian Sea and Atlantic Ocean define the northern and western limits, while the great Río Miño separates Pontevedra from Portugal to the south. On the eastern limit Lugo province shares with Asturias the Río Eo, while further south in Lugo and in landlocked Ourense the last buttresses of the Cordillera Cantábrica – Serras (where 'serra' in Galician means mountain range) dos Ancares, Courel and Eixe – referred to here as the Eastern Sierras, separate Galicia from the Castilian *meseta* (high tableland of central Spain). The coastal sierras and western mountains rise to between 500 and 1100m while the interior region undulates well below this level before reaching 2000m in the Eastern

Sierras. Into the Atlantic pour some 38 rivers. Magnificent *rías*, or estuaries (more accurately defined as fjords), riddle a coast adorned with more than 50 islands.

Geology

Galicia can be separated into two geological zones. East of the 'Toad's Eye' – a 300km north-south arch of Precambrian gneiss – sandstone, quartz, slate and schists dominate, along with localised pockets of granite. West of the arch the geology is more complex, with various massifs of Precambrian metamorphosed gneiss and schists. The most common rock types throughout the western half are metamorphosed granites.

Flora

Galicia was densely covered with pine forests 8000 years ago, but after being wiped out by a blanket of glaciers, they were slowly replaced by oak forests. Humidity loving carballo, or common oak (*Quercus robur*), is the most widely distributed oak species. The Pyrenean oak (*Q. pyrenaica*) inhabits south-east Ourense, the cork oak (*Q. suber*) is found on the south-western border, while the holm oak (*Q. ilex*) occurs along the eastern slopes. Only 10% of the original oak groves remain, having been converted into agricultural land or replanted with fast-growing pines (*Pinus pinaster*, *P. sylvestris* and *P. radiata*) and eucalyptuses (*Eucalyptus globulus*), which have crowded out many indigenous species. Despite these dramatic changes, Galician forests retain species diversity, especially Atlantic forests called *fragas* (see the Fraga do Eume walk later in this chapter). Mixed Atlantic and Mediterranean forests of the south-east, called *devesas*, are found particularly in the Serra do Courel. The banks of the major rivers are lined wtih deciduous oak, alder, ash, poplar, yew, elm, birch and willow.

Between valley and mountain, Galician *monte* (low, hill country) is rich in heather, genista, broom and, the walker's nightmare, gorse (*Ulex europaeus* and *U. gallii*). During much of the year the latter two brighten the hillsides with yellow flowers. Above 300m you will find bilberry and juniper (*Juniperus nana*). Floral species are discussed more specifically in each walk section.

Fauna

The woodlands of Galicia (especially in the east) contain rare and endangered species such as pine martens (*Martes martes*), wolves and the urogallo, or capercaillie (*Tetrao urogallus*). More common species include deers, wild boar, squirrels, hares, foxes, weasels and dormice. Herds of semi-wild horses roam the coastal and interior hillsides. Looking up, various birds of prey soar: golden eagles, goshawks, sparrow hawks, peregrine falcons and kestrels. Other species include crows, great swifts, stock doves, wood pigeons and red-legged partridges. The northern coast of Galicia is a marine-bird-lover's delight (see the Costa da Morte section). Galicia's high humidity favours the presence of 20 types of amphibians. Found along the north-western coast is the golden-striped salamander (*Chioglossa lusitanica*), the fire salamander (*Salamandra salamandra*) and various newts (*Triturus* spp).

There are eight types of snakes in the region, including vipers, two of which have dangerous, though rarely fatal bites.

CLIMATE

The Atlantic gives much of Galicia a temperate, continental climate in the north and west while the south and south-eastern zones are markedly Mediterranean. Extremes in temperature are rare, though snow does fall at higher elevations on the eastern slopes in winter. Precipitation tends to be heaviest on the northern coast and in the western mountains where up to 3000mm fall annually; some 600mm fall in the south-eastern sierra. Wind and clouds from the south-west generally indicate the arrival of rain.

INFORMATION
Maps

Both Ediciones Salvora's *Mapa de Galicia* (750 ptas) and the Xunta de Galicia's *Mapa Autonómico* (850 ptas) offer comparable

1:250,000 maps suitable for general planning. These are widely available once in Galicia.

Details of the maps for individual walks are given under Planning in the introduction to each.

Books

If you can read basic Spanish then you can struggle through the only general walking guides in Galician. Paco Armada's *Rotas Para Camiñantes* cover A Coruña and Pontevedra province, while titles covering Ourense and Lugo provinces are anticipated. Be aware, though, that Armada tends to overestimate distances. Also, Enrique Vélez & María Carmen Pereiro's *As Montañas de Galicia* has a good introductory chapter to the region's geography, flora and fauna.

Information Sources

Santiago's tourist information centre is in the postmodern kiosk on the Praza de Galicia. The regional tourist information centre (☎ 981 58 40 81) at Rúa Vilar 43 has local transport and accommodation information, free brochures and maps of Galicia at 1:400,000, but little on walking routes. The apathetic Federación Gallega de Montañismo in Vigo (☎ 986 42 43 31, fax 986 42 43 38), Celso Emilio Ferreiro 9, has a booklet (in Galician) *Guía de Sendeiros de Galicia* available through their office. It very briefly describes the officially marked PRG and GR walking tracks providing basic maps and indicating points of interest.

Web sites sponsored by the regional government list, in Spanish, companies that offer guided tours (www.xunta.es/xeral/rural/castella/empresa.htm) and a guide to rural guesthouses (www.xunta.es/xeral/rural/castella/rurtoc.htm).

To buy maps and books on Galicia, both Follas Novas, Montero Ríos 37, and Abraxas, Montero Ríos 50, in Santiago de Compostela have an excellent selection.

Place Names

Road signs are in Galician. In cities you'll have no trouble finding Spanish speakers but Galician is the mother tongue of the rural population. With mutual effort you'll be able to communicate. Keep in mind that the Galician x is usually the Spanish 'j' or hard 'g', that o is 'ue', and that r may substitute 'l', for example xamón in Galician = jamón in Spanish, morte = muerte, praia = playa, and igrexa = iglesia.

Warnings

It is possible that you may encounter snakes on walks in the region. Though it's very unlikely you'll be bitten, the venom of some species is harmful. For a discussion of the treatment for snake bites, see Bites, Cuts & Stings in the Health & Safety chapter. In case of emergency in Galicia call ☎ 061.

ACCOMMODATION & SUPPLIES
Santiago de Compostela

Santiago is a good base for services and transport to and from walks. For information on accommodation and dining in Santiago, see Day 28 of the Camino de Santiago chapter. Camping grounds on Santiago's far fringes are inconvenient (the regional tourist information centre has details). Both Toribio, Hórreo 5, on the centrally located Praza de Galicia, or Piteira, just off this square at Calle Huérfanas 38, are good sports shops.

All major services are readily available within a five to 10 minute walk from the tourist information centre.

GETTING THERE & AWAY
Bus

Daily ALSA buses connect Madrid and Santiago at 8 and 10 am and 2 and 12 pm (5040 ptas). Returns run at 11 am, 2 and 9.30 pm. The bus station is in the eastern part of the city in San Caetano (☎ 981 58 77 00).

Train

A regular service runs from Madrid and Barcelona to Santiago (the station in Santiago is below the intersection of Avenida de Lugo and Calle Hórreo). See the Red Nacional de Los Ferrocarriles Españoles

(RENFE) Web site (www.renfe.es) for schedules and prices.

Car

Santiago is easy to reach via the N6 highway that connects Madrid to A Coruña.

NORTHERN LITTORAL

The northern Galician coast is broken into three sections: Rías Altas, Costa da Morte and Rías Baixas – the upper and lower rías with the Death Coast in between. All the walks in this section are in A Coruña province.

Parque Natural Fraga do Eume

Located in the Rías Altas, the Parque Natural Fraga do Eume (where 'parque natural' in Spanish means nature park) extends along the margins of the Río Eume from above where it is dammed all the way to the sea, some 30km down a gentle, granite canyon surrounded by a luxuriant forest. The river empties into the Ría de Ares and eventually flows out to the Atlantic.

Fraga is the Galician term for the Atlantic woodland that once thickly covered the littoral. Composed largely of common oak, birch, laurel, hazel, yew and holly, the fraga also includes river-bank species such as alder, maple, willow and ash. Chestnuts thrive, as do fine examples of Tertiary and Quaternary ferns (*Hymenophyllum tunbrigense, Woodwardia radicans, Culcita macrocarpa* and *Vandenboschia speciosa*). More than 100 species of mushrooms and 200 lichens dwell here, thanks to the high humidity. In addition to an abundance of otters, the forests contain wolves, martens, roe deer, mountain cats, badgers and wild boars. Above the forest floor, horned and tawny owls, falcons, merlins, short-toed eagles and goshawks predominate. In addition to a healthy salmon population, the river also has trout.

Sadly, despite being hailed as Iberia's most remarkable Atlantic forest, this magnificent woodland is seriously threatened by short-sighted economic interests which have led to logging of old-growth forests, reforestation with eucalyptus for paper production and clearing of native species for pasture land. Inefficient enforcement of environmental regulations and a lack of public outcry at the continued destruction jeopardise the park's future. In fact, many locals protested the declaration of the park, fearing an economic decline. The park has no visitors information centre.

Fraga do Eume

Duration 3½ to 4 hours
Distance 12km
Standard Easy-Medium
Start/Finish Camping Fraga do Eume
Public Transport Yes
Summary Under the lush shelter of Galicia's last great Atlantic woodland, descend to the Río Eume canyon, continuing along its river bank to reach the Mosteiro de Caaveiro.

This walk descends through the priceless fraga to one of Galicia's oldest monasteries, the 10th century Mosteiro de Caaveiro. In 987 as the Vikings were exploring the Eume, San Rosendo selected this impenetrable, mysterious forest to found one of southern Europe's most inaccessible Benedictine monasteries, intentionally hidden from civilisation and its temptations. It later passed into Augustinian hands and remained operational until the end of the 18th century. The 1836 Spanish *desamortazición*, involving the redistribution of monastic wealth and banning of monastic orders, led to its present lamentable state. Declared a national historical monument in 1975, fews sign of rehabilitation are apparent. From the monastery, an optional side trip continues to the fraga's northern fringe. There is water at the camping ground, the hydroelectric station and the monastery. Sporadic red-and-white trail markers indicate

GALICIA

the GR50 as it passes through the fraga. Note that not all the roads described in this route appear on the map. New logging tracks are opened frequently.

PLANNING
When to Walk

May to October are the best months, though in August expect the trail and camping ground to be busy. In winter, rain and fog discourage most walkers.

Maps

Though detailed maps are unnecessary, IGN *Fene* No 22-I and *Pontedeume* No 22-III maps at 1:25,000 cover the area.

PLACES TO STAY & EAT

Pontedeume is the closest sizeable town with all services. Above the medieval, two-lane stone bridge spanning the river are the worn heralds of the town, a wild boar and bear symbolising intelligence and strength.

In the old quarter, the *Casa de Huéspedes Martís* (☎ 981 43 06 37, Calle Real 23) has cheap, extremely basic singles/doubles for 1500/2500 ptas with shared bathroom. The immaculate *Hostal Allegue* (☎ 981 43 00 35, Calle Chafarís 1) has doubles with and without bath (all with TV) for 7000/4000 ptas.

Delicious, relatively inexpensive seafood is easy to find. *Yoli*, Calle Ferreiros 8, has menus in English and the excellent *cazuela mixta* (a seafood stew of monkfish and hake) costs 1200 ptas. Set menús begin at 1000 ptas. The small *Bar-Restaurante Compostela*, Calle Real 19, with a high-quality 800 ptas menú, is a sure bet.

Fifty metres from the trailhead, *Camping Fraga do Eume* (☎ 981 19 51 30) opens from June to September. The owner speaks English. Adults are charged 400 ptas and a tent and car cost 375 ptas each. Bungalows for two and four people go for 3000/5500 ptas. Simple meals and a small market can be found 2.5km away in the village of Ponte da Pedra at the *Casa Capellán*.

GETTING TO/FROM THE WALK

From Santiago five daily Castromil buses go to Pontedeume (775 ptas). Once in Pontedeume, buses go to Ponte da Pedra from Bar Martiño (175 ptas) Monday to Friday at 7.45 am and 7 pm, and at noon from Bar Pescador (near the port). A taxi (☎ 981 43 04 60) to the beginning of the walk costs 1500 ptas. From Ponte da Pedra there's a 2.5km walk to the trailhead. If you're staying at the camping ground, phone and staff will pick you up.

Return buses from Ponte da Pedra to Pontedeume leave at 8 am, 3.15 and 8.15 pm (Saturdays 9.15am, 1.45 and 8 pm) from the Casa Capellán. For a taxi back to Pontedeume ask in the bar or phone ☎ 908-98 39 09. From Pontedeume to Santiago there are four daily return buses.

By car from Santiago take the toll route A6 or the N550 towards Ferrol. Once in

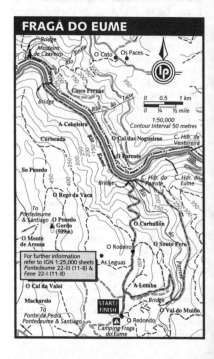

Pontedeume, take the LC144 12km towards Monfero and Taboada. Turn left in Ponte da Pedra and in 300m left again to reach the camping ground.

THE WALK

With the camping ground on your right, the trail begins as a 4WD road that descends north, curving left for 1km to a white house on the left. The road narrows and descends as it becomes a stone path walled by gorse. Steep, downhill switchbacks begin and sporadic red-and-white trail markers appear. Forty minutes from the white house the trail ends at the edge of the river. Resist the temptation to cross the wooden bridge to the tiny hydroelectric plant on the right (unless seeking water – the fountain is behind the building up a flight of stairs).

From the riverbank turn left, following the flow of water. After 15 minutes, when the trail disappears, ascend briefly left to a wide dirt road. Turn right, paralleling the river for 15 minutes and cross a cement bridge over the Eume. Veer left and uphill to the **Mosteiro de Caaveiro**. Your first vision will be its Romanesque semicircular apse and false Baroque façade. Remains of the church, wine cellars, monks' cells, kitchen and dining-hall chimneys are still visible among the ruins. There are magnificent views from the terrace.

A descending north-east (left) path from the stairs leads in three minutes to a lovely brook (crossed by a stone bridge), a fountain and the ruins of the monastery's mill.

To return, retrace your steps to the hydroelectric plant. You can either continue along the same route to the starting point or cross the wooden bridge and take the steeply ascending road straight ahead (east). The difficult incline continues for 1.3km until the road reaches a wooden gate. On the other side, take a right-hand path that quickly converts into a dirt trail. Continue for 1km to a brook and cross it. The trail soon descends over the Río de Parrote via an old wooden bridge. From the bridge ascend left to a junction of three 4WD tracks. Continue along the second from the right (north). Walking

through eucalyptus, the track hits another perpendicular dirt road. Turn left and ascend to its highpoint where it rejoins the initial 4WD road back to the camping ground.

Side Trip: Fraga's Northern Limit
1½ hours, 4km

To reach the fraga's fringe, continue on the path from the stone bridge, monastery mill and fountain, ascending for 2km to a narrow, sealed road. Here, woodlands give way to livestock pastures. Once at the road, turn around and return to the monastery.

Costa da Morte

Seeing a winter storm batter the Atlantic coast, the meaning of Costa da Morte is immediately clear. Countless ships lost on this coast are mute testimony to its treachery (see the boxed text 'The English Cemetery'). The area extends from the cliffs of Malpica, in the north-west around Cabo Fisterra, to the dazzling white dunes of Carnota. Three rías (Corme, Laxe and Corcubión) interrupt the coastline, which reaches out to the sea in a series of juts and capes; lighthouses crown seven of these. The rías are less windswept, with waveless beaches, dense woods and human settlements.

Monte Pindo

Duration 4½ to 5 hours
Distance 15 to 17km
Standard Medium-Hard
Start/Finish O Pindo
Public Transport Yes
Summary Ocean views, salty breezes, pine forests, odd granite formations, a deep river gorge and waterfalls – this loop features a stunning array of natural sculpture on one of Galicia's most celebrated coastal mountains.

Rising abruptly out of the Atlantic, Monte Pindo is Galicia's Mt Olympus. Some believe the name 'Pindo' is linked to

GALICIA

'Pyndus', the home of Apollo in Greek mythology. Local legends are extensive: Celts committed mass suicide here rather than succumb to Roman colonisation; pagan altars dotted the crown to celebrate fertility and cosmological rites; the slopes produced plants to cure complaints of the body and soul; and Celtic, Roman and even Moorish treasures are still hidden within the tantalising mount. Pindo is also known for the wondrous, erosion-produced granite formations that cover its exposed tops. The golden and rosy colour of the granite is created by the presence of iron.

The loop walk described here climbs from sea level to the mountain's high point, A Moa (627m), which offers unbeatable views of the coast from Fisterra (north) to Carnota (south). Stands of a species of oak (*Q. fruticosa*), only found again in Portugal, laurel, pines and holly accompany the climb. Wild boar live here, as do semiwild horses.

The walk continues to the magnificent Río Xallas. Its power has been harnessed since the early 20th century, culminating in its damming in 1988 which sent it below the limit of ecological viability. Diverted via tunnels and canals, the visible flow now only comes from tributaries. Nonetheless startling in its beauty, the final 100m waterfall is Europe's longest fresh water to ocean drop, forming a 20m deep pool below. Currently, the area is under consideration as a parque natural.

The walk is rated medium for the navigation required after A Moa. Sporadic painted trail markers (red and blue arrows) accompany parts of the way.

PLANNING
When to Walk
May to October are the best months, when rain and fog are at their yearly minimums.

Maps
The IGN *Brens* No 93-1 and *O Pindo* No 93-III 1:25,000 maps cover the route.

What to Bring
Long pants are advisable as gorse can be

> **Warning**
>
> Marine fog makes it easy to get lost. Additionally, the dam is opened occasionally for rain overflow in December and January and there are no warning sirens. If in doubt, take the described road return.

tough on bare legs if sections of the route are overgrown. A compass is also recommended. Get water in the village before beginning and in Fieiro, 11km into the walk.

PLACES TO STAY & EAT
Lodgings are located on the tiny O Pindo's one main road. *Pind Bar* (☎ 981 76 00 59) in the heart of the village offers clean singles/doubles, all with bathroom and TV, for 3000/4000 ptas. Doubles start at 3500 ptas at *A Revolta* (☎ 981 76 48 64), and *La Morada* (☎ 981 76 48 70), the closest to the trailhead, has tranquil rooms with bathroom for 3000/5000 ptas. Specialising in seafood, the two also serve meals for 1500/1200 ptas, respectively. The hands-down local favourite is A Revolta. O Pindo also boasts a pharmacy, ATM (Automatic Teller Machine; cash dispenser) and *supermarket*.

It is possible to pitch a tent for a night on the oceanside hillock behind O Pindo. The closest camping ground is *Camping Ancoradoiro* (☎ 981 87 88 97), between Muros and O Pindo. It's most easily reached by car and is 15km from the trailhead, nestled in a pine grove near to the sea.

GETTING TO/FROM THE WALK
To reach O Pindo from Santiago, take a Transportes Finisterre (☎ 981 56 29 24) bus to Cee for 1220 ptas (there are daily morning and afternoon connections to and from Santiago) and then a Cee bus to O Pindo (135 ptas). Times vary so phone to confirm.

By car, take the N550 towards Noia and continue along the coast, following signs to Fisterra. Past Muros, there is another 20km of stunning coastline.

GALICIA

THE WALK

From the church and fountain, head south-east into the forest, crossing a small stream bed to a narrow path. Alongside a low stone wall, wind up the hill through the lush forest, passing an abandoned house. Continue climbing for 20 minutes to the open **Olimpo Celta**. The first anthropomorphic boulders, produced by natural erosion, appear. The rocks, shaped like figures, heads and other body parts, have attracted the curiosity of passers-by for centuries. As you walk among pines the path provides sensational views of the sea.

The pines give way to low shrubs. Keep ascending for 10 minutes. **O Pedrullo**, a small peak on the right, is recognisable by the cascade of rocks at its base. Most likely the remains of the 10th century Castillo de San Xurxo, a watchtower built against Viking attacks, it was destroyed in 1467

during peasant uprisings. At the next T-junction turn left and ascend for 20 minutes. The trail enters a canyon like an inverted funnel, crowned by a large nose-shaped rock, **Outeiro Narís**. A stone wall below hems in wild horses.

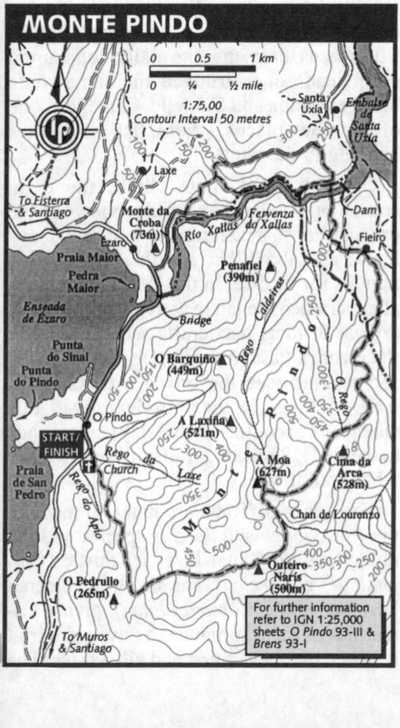

Continue for 10 minutes, winding in switchbacks through oaks and eucalyptuses. A wide tongue of grass and earth gives way to a small plain, the Chan do Lourenzo (Lorenzo's Floor). The remains of a wolfram mine exploited by the inhabitants of O Pindo desperate for pesetas during WWII, lie behind the shepherd's hut. Looking left, A Moa appears as a large mass of rounded granite lighter than the surrounding mountains. Carnota's 6km of white beach lie to the south. Continue left and, about 100m past the ruins, the most famous of the area's rock figures – the 6m **O Guerreiro** (the Warrior) – sits with his back to you.

Begin the final ascent to **A Moa** via a small pine grove and then oaks to the mountain's base. Circle round to the north-east face to reach the final summit trail. The top, punctured with erosion pools, offers excellent views. From right to left can be seen Cabo Fisterra, Illas Lobeiras (the last breeding ground of monk seals, exterminated in the 19th century), O Pindo, Quilmas and Carnota. You've walked 5.2km (1¾ to 2 hours).

Descend A Moa the same way. As you skirt back around the base, a wide dirt path set between two vertical walls (marked with graffiti) appears on the left. At first there is no clear path (horse trails maze about), though cairns mark the route. Follow the right-hand wall to its end, where a dirt way descends left through young pines to a basin studded with white trunks. Follow the horse trails along the left side – the highest peaks are on the left – and leave the basin via a small path ascending north-east. Continue north-east across the next plateau. (The A Moa summit is 15 minutes behind you.) The route descends over a fallen wall and the trail begins again. In the distance, the Embalse de Santa Uxía comes

MONTE PINDO

For further information refer to IGN 1:25,000 sheets O Pindo 93-III & Brens 93-I

GALICIA

into sight. Instead of descending towards it, the path continues straight (east). Reaching two 2m-high stones on the left, the way descends again north-east along a good trail between brambles and pines. The path briefly ascends then descends north between ferns and pines until 15 minutes later it reaches a wide trail with a wooden fence. Take this descending trail, a type of zigzagging firebreak, that opens up to a flat, walled, dirt and stone road which reaches a sealed road and the hamlet of Fieiro, where you can collect water.

Continue 1km down the road, crossing the Xallas dam. You have two options to reach Ézaro: either descend on the sealed road (1 to 1½ hours, 4.5km), or take the impressive river gorge (45 minutes, 2.5km). The latter requires some initial rock hopping but is much more spectacular.

For the road option, continue on the sealed road, ignoring the right turn to Santa Uxía, and head down the steep hill past the lookout. In 1km, fork left onto a cement road and continue down to the hydroelectric plant and Ézaro.

For a descent of the gorge, cross the dam and turn left onto a descending road that turns right and then peters out at a tunnel. Take a dirt path left of the tunnel past an abandoned house to the riverbed. The imposing wall of the dam looms large on the left. Head to the river's left bank where 10 minutes of rock hopping leads to a sluice. Cross to the wall of the canal (part of the hydroelectric system) and up onto an unforgettable walkway. The vertical drop to the left reveals the magnificent **canyon** with its numerous pools and cascades. In 10 minutes you will reach a footpath which passes under water pipes and then ascends to a pumping station. The way joins the sealed road and descends for 1.7km to Ézaro.

Once at the highway turn left over the bridge to return to O Pindo. Detour to the waterfall's base by turning left onto a service road which leads to the hydroelectric plant, 100m away (visible from the main road).

Spindrift Walk

Duration 2 days
Distance 40km
Standard Easy-Medium
Start Laxe
Finish Camariñas
Public Transport Yes
Summary With the ocean never out of sight, this two day walk provides an excellent introduction to the often desolate and always hauntingly beautiful Costa da Morte.

If the sea is one of your passions, this is your walk. From start to finish, the ocean acts as a constant right-hand companion; at times only metres away. Linking the Costa da Morte's two northern rías, the walk provides peace and isolation; only fishing villages interrupt the otherwise desolate coast.

The first short day begins in Laxe, quickly leaving the village behind, and undulates from hillside to open beach. Milkmaids carrying the daily load upon their heads once trudged the same route between Traba and Camelle. Camelle is one of the few places where fish still dries hanging in the wind.

On Day 2 the route climbs the high, coastal hills and offers striking views of the pristine coast, reaching the majestic lighthouse at Cabo Vilán and then Camariñas, famous for its lace. In the 1990s the regional government began to actively promote the revival of local handcrafts such as *encaixe* (lacework), basketry, ceramics and wooden shoemaking (see the boxed text 'Galician Lace-Making' in the introduction to this chapter). Part of the second day corresponds to the PRG38 walking trail with yellow-and-white trail markers.

The dunes of Traba are home to reeds of the *Phragmites* and *Juncus* species and the ubiquitous low-lying lavender thistle (*Omphalodes gallaecica*). The small, endangered bush camariña (*Corema album*), giving Camariñas its name, produces a tiny, white fruit believed to relieve thirst and kill worms. The

Man, El Alemán de Camelle

Approaching Camelle you'll notice on the village breakwater brightly coloured circles and other eye-catching (even psychedelic) painted designs. Along the maritime walkway a sign for 'Museo' also appears, but this does not lead to any conventional place. Following the walkway, past salty types chewing the fat over fishing nets, you'll reach the completely unexpected refugio/museum of Man (Manfred), a German who came to Camelle more than 30 years ago, set himself up on the breakwater and never left. With weathered skin, long stringy blond hair and dressed only in a loincloth (both winter and summer) he has constructed a type of outdoor museum exhibiting his paintings and pinnacle-shaped sculptures made from stones and flotsam brought by the waves: tree roots, nets, floats, shoes. He asks visitors to the museum for 100 ptas and urges them to participate by drawing his face and some aspect of the museum.

Set against a backdrop of the Atlantic, Man's sculptures have been inspired by the many objects washed up on Camelle's shores.

red-berried (summer) low bush, trevisco, hangs on doors during San Juan (end of June) to foil malignant spirits. The pinkish flower, *herba de namorar*, which literally means 'falling in love herb'(*Armeria maritima*), flourishes by the sea and helps enchant the desired mate.

Light gulls (*Larus cachinnas*) and cormorants are abundant on the coast. Numerous rare and endangered species thrive on nearby islets and inaccessible cliffs. Especially in spring (May to June), Cabo Vilán is the breeding ground for thousands of migratory birds such as the near-extinct guillemot (*Uria aalge*), the rare and exquisite fisher, the crested cormorant (*Phalacrocorax aristotelis*) and various gulls.

PLANNING
When to Walk

The walk is best made from May to October, the coast's driest months.

Maps

The IGN *Laxe* No 43-IV and *Muxía* No 67-II 1:50,000 maps are useful.

PLACES TO STAY & EAT
Laxe

The *Hostal Bahía* (☎ *981 72 83 04, Calle Generalísimo 24*), north past the church, has spotless doubles with bathroom starting at 5000 ptas. The central, 2nd floor *Hostal Beira Mar* (☎ 981 72 81 09, *Rosalía de Castro 30*) offers doubles with breakfast for 5000 ptas.

Laxe has supermarkets, a fruit shop, bakery and pharmacy. For sandwiches overlooking the ocean try *Bahía*, Calle Rosalía de Castro 18. *Restaurante Plaza* on the main square has a decent 1000 ptas menú or seafood specialities à la carte with spectacular views. Find excellent coastal Galician fare in a welcoming atmosphere at *La Sardiñeira*, Rosalía de Castro 51. The menú costs 1000 ptas.

Camariñas

From July to September *Scala* (☎ 981 73 71 09, *Calle Tras Praia 6*) offers a variety of doubles from 4000 ptas. Open all year, both *Hostal A Marina* (☎ 981 73 60 30) and *Hostal Dársena* (☎ 981 73 62 63) offer comfortable rooms; the latter's are cheaper, with 4000 ptas doubles.

The local salts head to *Dársena* on the north part of the port for tasty caldeiradas and a reasonable 900 ptas menú. Tiny *Bar Praia*, mid-bay, has good *tapas* (bar snacks) and *bocadillos* (long sandwiches). The sleek, pricier *La Marina*, south bay, serves high quality seafood and caters to foreign tourists. Without a doubt the jewel in the rough is *4 Vientos*, Calle Molino de Viento 81, serving a wide range of fish, seafood and caldeiradas as well as a 1500 ptas menú. Walk south out of town (500m) to a recessed building on the left.

GETTING TO/FROM THE WALK

To reach Laxe by bus, take the Autos Carballo service to Carballo (morning and afternoon). Transportes Finisterre (☎ 981 70 01 95) buses then go from Carballo to Laxe (morning and afternoon). Beware of infrequent Sunday runs.

By car from Santiago, take the C545 north-west to Santa Comba, Zas. At the next junction take the AC431 north and then the AC432 west to Laxe.

From Camariñas, a Transportes Finisterre bus returns to Santiago daily at 4pm. If you

parked a car in Laxe, a taxi back from Camariñas will cost around 3000 ptas. The taxi stand in Camariñas is next to Bar Praia. There is no direct bus between Laxe and Camariñas, though it is possible to return via transfers in Carballo or Ponte do Porto.

By car from Camariñas, take the N552 to Vimianzo (via Ponte do Porto). Continue to Baio on the N545 (via Santa Comba) and south-east to Santiago.

THE WALK
Day 1: Laxe to Camelle
3½ hours, 13km

Get sufficient water for the first short day in Laxe.

The Capilla Santa Cruz da Rosa chapel sits on the hill behind Laxe. To reach it, leave the main Praza Ramón Juega along the Rúa Río between a mishmash of old stone and new brick houses and ascend 600m along the road. Numerous candles burn in devotion to the 'fisherfolk's protectress'.

From the chapel, avoid the wide southbound dirt and grass lane and take the narrow grass footpath (south-west) bordered by stone walls separating fallow fields. The long stretch of gorgeous, rolling coastline, a symphony of blue, green and white, lies on the trail ahead. Gorse, blackberry briars and trevisco replace the walls as the Praia Soesto appears. Ten minutes from the chapel, enter a pine and eucalyptus grove. The poorly marked path turns right, reaching an open hillside with reforested pine and eucalyptus. Descend through the plantation to the beach and cross it parallel to the dunes. O Catasol lies ahead. Instead of ascending, the footpath impressively borders the edge of the coast; spindrift may brush your skin.

At a small stone beach the path becomes a dirt lane and at the next sandy beach, adorned with wooden boats and fishing huts, the lane becomes wider and newer. Approximately 1km further, when the road separates from the sea, take a right-hand path towards the beach and cross the great stretch (2.5km) of white sand, the **Praia de Traba**. Halfway down the beach is an optional detour up the

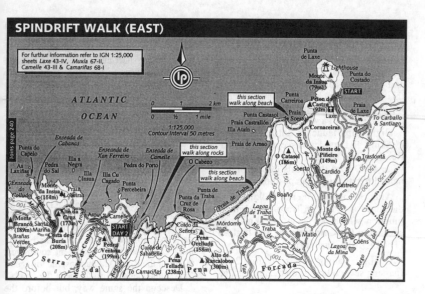

SPINDRIFT WALK (EAST)

For furthur information refer to IGN 1:25,000 sheets Laxe 43-IV, Muxía 67-II, Camelle 43-III & Camariñas 68-I

ATLANTIC OCEAN

1:125,000
Contour Interval 50 metres

this section walk along beach

this section walk along rocks

this section walk along beach

dunes to **Lagoa de Traba** freshwater lagoon where marsh birds (coots, marsh hens and grebes) thrive. A photo in the small bar at the west end of the beach shows that on this same beach in 1944 an American fighter plane was forced to land.

At the beach's end, you're halfway through the day. Continue on a right-hand dirt lane that promptly forks right onto a narrow access trail. An alternative, wider stone trail continues straight on from the fork and rejoins the narrow path in 1km. At their junction, continue for 15 minutes. With Camelle in sight, turn right onto a trail lined with gorse and blackberries, reaching a stony beach. To reach Camelle, either take the sealed road for 500m, turning right down a dirt road to the maritime walkway, or veer right onto a fishing trail which soon disappears. Pick your way along the rocky shore to three fishers' sheds, an old sardine salting factory and the maritime walkway. Both routes curve around the bay of Camelle, leading to its port and commercial centre (see the boxed text 'Man, El Alemán de Camelle').

From July to September in Camelle **Bar Rotterdam** at Calle del Muelle 20 offers delicious, inexpensive meals, specialising in *caldeiradas* (seafood stews) and *paella* (a delicious, saffron-coloured rice dish). For a light but adequate meal try *A Molinera* (☎ 981 71 04 92, Calle Principal 79). It also has the best lodging bargain on the coast – three immaculate apartments (two with ocean views), each with two bedrooms, bathroom and full kitchen cost 4000 ptas nightly. If it is full, *La Chalana*, several doors away, has good rooms and meals.

Day 2: Camelle to Camariñas
7 to 7½ hours, 27km
Water bottles can be filled in Camelle and Santa Mariña.

Leave Camelle's port via the Rúa do Porto. Climb for 200m and make a hairpin right turn onto a sealed road that leads to Arou (1.8km). At the beach ascend along the Rúa Praia and then turn right onto Rúa d'Abaixo, which leaves Arou as a sealed road. In 1.2km the way turns left onto an ascending 4WD road; 50m later the route

GALICIA

heads right onto another 4WD road. A strenuous 30 minute ascent leads to an even wider dirt road. Turn right and in another kilometre Santa Mariña fills the steep valley stretching below. The road becomes sealed and curves in hairpins right down through this lonesome enclave. Continue descending towards the port and, about 300m above it, turn left down a wide dirt path that, after a slight dip, launches into the longest (1.5km) and hardest ascent of the day. Reaching the summit, turn right onto the wide 4WD road that skirts Monte Branco, named for its sandy composition.

After 30 minutes of easy walking above the dunes and Praia do Trece, turn right at a junction which descends for 2km to the ocean and the **Cemiterio de los Ingleses** (The English Cemetery).

Continue along the road for 2.7km (passing several houses on the left) and at a junction turn right. You are now halfway. In 1km, when the road begins to ascend and curve left, continue straight along a narrow footpath that short-cuts up the steep hillside and then returns to the road. Cresting the hill, the windmills, the lighthouse of Cabo Vilán and the islets off the cape dominate the horizon. In 2km the dirt road passes between two windmills and turns right to the **lighthouse** (1km) along a sealed road (see the boxed text 'Faro do Cabo Vilán').

Backtrack from the lighthouse to just before the dirt road and turn right (south) onto a footpath. The path approaches and then parallels the shore, becoming littered with stones. Trail markers are helpful. In 30 minutes you reach a soccer field. Turn right onto a 500m-long ascending trail to **Capela da Virxe do Monte**, also dedicated to the mariner's protectress. Excellent south-west views of the Ría de Camariñas, the village of Muxía and Cabo Touriñán merit the climb.

Descend the same way, but before the soccer field turn right onto a descending sea-access road, skirt the beach and then ascend along low, stone walls. At the first junction, fork right and at the second, 15 minutes later at a modern house, fork right again. Descend along a cement road and turn left onto the

SPINDRIFT WALK (WEST)

For furthur information refer to IGN 1:25,000 sheets Camelle 43-III, Camariñas 68-I & Muxía 67-II

0   1   2 km
0   ½   1 mile

1:125,000
Contour Interval 50 metres

The English Cemetery

On 10 November 1890 the British training vessel *Serpent* sank off the coast between Cabo Vilán and the Praia do Trece. The attempts of nearby villagers to help were futile. Of the 173 hands on board all but three were lost. The few whose remains were found rest in the humble cemetery at the foot of the rocks where the ship foundered. In thanks for the heroics of the local people and the burial of the sailors, the British Admiralty gave a rifle to the priest of nearby Xaviña, a gold watch to the mayor and a barometer to the town hall. In addition, whenever a British military ship passed the area it was to sound cannon in honour of the lost sailors.

Faro do Cabo Vilán

On a rocky promontory which appears like the frozen prow of a stranded ship, the Faro do Cabo Vilán lighthouse sits 135m above the ceaselessly crashing sea. Considered to be among the most majestic of the whole Galician coast, the lighthouse is 25m high and was the first in Spain (1896) to function with electricity. Ships can see this comforting beacon from more than 60km away.

first dirt road. Fork right again at the corner walls of a house, and upon reaching another dirt road turn right again. In 200m pass the 17th century ruins of Carlos III's Castillo del Soberano. The first houses of Camariñas (the port was partially constructed from the castle's stones) appear.

EASTERN SIERRAS

The magnificent, extensive forests, the unprecedented abundance of flora and fauna and the fascinating culture of the Serras dos Ancares and Courel (or Caurel) offer a unique window into rural, historical Galicia and an exquisite retreat from better known walking areas. Both ranges are on an unusual north-east to south-west axis. The Ancares range runs for 30km and covers an area of 12,775 hectares, reaching its maximum heights at Pico Cuiña (1987m) in León and O Mostallar (1924m) in Lugo. In contrast, the more southern Courel (21,000 hecatres) is a lower but steeper range, with Pico Formigueiros (1643m) as its highest peak.

The Eastern Sierras create a natural border between Galicia and Castilla y León. A noteworthy feature of both is the abundance of rivers wedged between deep valleys, creating the possibility of panoramic ridge walks, lush forest excursions and strolls along rivers and canyons. In the Ancares, the westward flowing rivers include the Ser, Rao and Navia while the Cua, Ancares and Burbia head east. The Courel is divided and demarcated by three powerful rivers – the Lor (west), Quiroga (centre), and Sor (east). Unfortunately, these regions are difficult to reach by inexpensive public transport; their inaccessibility in part explains their pristine state, which in turn makes them well worth the effort to visit.

HISTORY

Both sierras show numerous remnants of their prehistoric and Roman, as well as medieval, past. Castros, inhabited by Celts and pre-Roman peoples, dot the countryside. The Romans, eager for ore, built numerous mining sites, routes and foundries (on rivers), and Romanised the castros. These are especially visible in Courel, a region richer in precious metals. The Carbedo castle in Courel dates from medieval times.

One of Galicia's poorest areas, the Eastern Sierras retained, until the 1980s, its traditional dwellings (for example, in the Ancares the *pallozas* – see the boxed text 'Galician Vernacular Architecture' later in this section) and lifestyle. Due to the isolation, ruggedness of life and the flight of young people to urban areas, the mountain hamlets were slow to modernise, maintaining ancient forms of building construction and water mills with few services or amenities. In fact, one village in the Ancares, Piornedo (the goal of the Ancares Ridge walk), is called the *Aldea Prerromana* (Pre-Roman Hamlet) and retains numerous pallozas. In the 1990s the area began to receive EU development grants and the government's tourism branch realised that 'the past' sells. Rather than invest the funds in the protection and conservation of the area's overwhelming natural assets (neither has achieved parque natural status), money has been funnelled into rural guesthouses and the renovation of 'sights' to appeal to the car visitor. Courel is unprotected and Ancares is a *reserva de caza* (national hunting reserve), though it is optimistically advertised by the Club de Ancares (a group which has played an active role in saving the sierra's environment) as a parque natural on area signs, stickers and its logo.

Galician Vernacular Architecture

Inhabited until the late 1980s, *pallozas* are dwellings first developed during pre-Roman times which have been well adapted to the Ancares. They had 1m-high stone walls built round an oval floor, and an elevated, conical roof of rye thatch that prevented the accumulation of snow and water. People shared the inside – which also acted as a granary – with their animals, taking advantage of their heat. Constructed with a southern exposure and on a slant to improve drainage, they had small windows but no chimneys; smoke filtered up through the hay.

Near to the dwellings are *hórreos*, free-standing granaries elevated on columns or solid blocks and used to store the harvest free from humidity. Between the column and the granary's base a projecting horizontal rock prevents hungry rodents from gaining access. The Asturian hórreos are square with wooden walls and a four-sided tile, slate or even thatch roof. The Galician ones are quite diverse but are usually rectangular and made of stone, with a two-sided tile roof often decorated with a cross.

Constructed on river banks, *molinos* were used to mill corn and wheat grains to flour using the force of water. The river's water was diverted through a canal, then channelled onto a turbine that moved a huge stone wheel which ground the grain. The mills either had one owner, who kept a percentage of the flour milled, or several who took turns milling. In the 19th century more than 8200 molinos functioned in Galicia.

Cortines, appearing strangely on the sierra's hillsides near villages, are circular or oval stone walls up to 1.5m high with horizontally projecting stones rimming their tops. They were built to prevent sweet-toothed bears from taking honey out of the beehives kept inside.

The palloza is one example of local architecture, well adapted to the Galician climate and rural lifestyle, which pre-dates Roman times.

NATURAL HISTORY

The ranges date from the Paleozoic period and were reshaped during the Quaternary. Deposits of glacial moraine in the form of huge, granite boulders laid down by glacial action have subsequently been exposed by erosion.

Flora & Fauna

While both ranges are fine floral reserves, the Courel has the greater diversity of species. A combination of orientation, steep slopes, soil content, minimal pollution and the convergence of two climate systems (Atlantic and Mediterranean) have created an extraordinary ecological phenomenon: more than 1000 floral species flourish between 400 and 1600m. Remarkably, 40% of Galicia's floral species are represented in the Courel, which constitutes only 1% of the total territory.

Devesas – humid, north facing mixed woodlands – are composed of *carballo* (common oak), maples, hazel, beech (Spain's westernmost examples), holly, birch and yew trees. Holly, a crucial part of the forest, is the only species that retains its leaves and fruit in winter, providing 50% of the herbivores' nourishment and shelter; during winter it's 5°C warmer under its canopy. The Mediterranean species, concentrated in valleys, include holm oaks – thriving in limy soils – cork oaks and strawberry trees. Around the villages, cultivated *soutos* (chestnut groves) grow in abundance – once the key carbohydrate in the local diet. At the river's edge poplars, willows and alders abound. Not overwhelmed by eucalyptuses and pines, the exquisite – even magical – forests of the Ancares are distinctly Atlantic.

Shrubbery occupies more than half of both sierras, due to human exploitation of the environment (cutting trees for timber and pastures). Broom, uces, heather, gorse, as well as bilberry (*Vaccinium myrtillus*) and juniper, fill the slopes. The Courel also has the aromatic rock rose and lavender. The most notable flower mat-grass (*Nardus* sp) flourishes in fields. Wildflowers, particularly rich in the Courel, include *Narcissus tridentatum* and flag iris (*Iris latidifolius*); lichen, fern and reed species are also well represented.

The symbol of the Ancares is the highly endangered urogallo, locally called the *pita do monte* (mountain chicken). It is known for its spectacular nuptial song. Protected from hunting since 1971, only 20 pairs are believed still to exist. Brown bears visiting from the Cordillera Cantábrica make occasional appearances, though there is no stable local population. Roe deer are especially common. In addition, there are plenty of wolves, foxes, otters, martens, badgers,

wild boars, partridges, eagle owls, goshawks and sparrow hawks.

With more than 160 vertebrates, the Serra do Courel is very similar to the Ancares, with the exception of the bear and urogallo (not found here).

Serra dos Ancares

Two one-day walks are described in this range, both beginning from the Refuxio dos Ancares near Degrada.

PLANNING
When to Walk
With its continental climate and significant altitude, winters are long, cold and wet (1500 to 2000mm of rainfall per year); snow is common from November to March. Summers tend to be short and cool and the best walking months are June to October. In autumn the deciduous forests are particularly striking.

Maps & Books
The IGN *Sierra de Ancares* map at 1:50,000 is your best option. The *Mapa Turístico-Montañero de los Ancares* 1:50,000 map by G García Pardo is inadequate.

Two books in Spanish could be helpful for providing additional information on the Ancares: JL Coedo's *31 Rutas de Senderismo por Los Ancares Lucenses*, and A González's *Guía e Rutas Dos Ancares*, which includes 30 routes and covers flora and fauna extensively. The former is not reliable with regard to times and distances.

Maps and books are widely available in the local restaurants and hostels of Piornedo, Degrada and Becerreá.

What to Bring
A compass is useful for both walks.

PLACES TO STAY & EAT
Becerreá
Nicknamed the 'Door to the Ancares', Becerreá is the closest sizeable village and the best spot for last-minute basic supplies. To

sleep in the village, try the convenient *Hostal Herbón* (☎ 982 36 00 35) across from the bus stop where singles/doubles cost 1500/3500 ptas. *Restaurante Vila* offers good local fare and a decent set meal for 950 ptas.

Degrada

The *Refuxio Dos Ancares* (☎ 982 18 11 13) is 1.5km from Degrada. It has no information centre. It has singles/doubles with bath for 2000/3000 ptas as well as 70 bunks for 600 ptas. Meals cost around 1200 ptas. In Degrada itself, the *Mesón Novo* has cheap rooms (1250/2500 ptas) and meals for 1000 ptas. The closest camping ground, *Camping Os Ancares*, is 23km from Degrada towards Doiras.

Piornedo

The village has three rural guesthouses and a hostal. Try *Mustallar* (☎ 982 15 17 17), which has doubles with and without bath for 2800/3800 ptas. Home-cooked meals cost about 1100 ptas. *Casa Casoa* (☎ 982 15 16 43) has a homey atmosphere and rooms with bath for 3000/4000 ptas. The owner will drive you back to Degrada at a cheaper price than the local taxi.

GETTING TO/FROM THE WALK

Both walks begin near Degrada at the refugio and use it as a base. To reach the small village it is necessary to pass through Becerreá. Leaving from Madrid, ALSA has five daily return buses to Becerreá for 3690 ptas. If coming from Santiago, ALSA buses run direct to Becerreá at 11 am and 9.30 pm (1770 ptas).

In Becerreá, Bus Ancares connects Degrada and Piornedo at 6 pm Monday, Wednesday and Friday from the Bar Claudio (500 ptas). A taxi from Becerreá to Degrada costs 3000 ptas and can be hired from Calle Carlos III.

By car from Santiago, take the N547 to Lugo and then the NVI to Becerreá. From Madrid, the NVI goes direct to Becerreá. To reach Degrada, head north-east (towards Navia de Suarna) for 9km and turn right, continuing via Cervantes.

After the Ancares Ridge walk you'll need to take a taxi or bus or hitch back to the refugio from Piornedo. Returns from Piornedo or Degrada to Becerreá on Bus Ancares cost 600 ptas and leave Monday, Wednesday and Friday at 7 am from Piornedo. Another option to return from Piornedo to Degrada is to hire a private car from Pedrete (☎ 982 15 13 59) for 2000 ptas. Taxis are also available (☎ 982 36 45 46). Return buses from Becerreá to Santiago leave at 5.40 am and 1.55 and 4.05 pm.

Campa de Brego Loop

Duration 4½ hours
Distance 15.5km
Standard Easy-Medium
Start/Finish Refuxio dos Ancares, Degrada
Public Transport Yes
Summary Gentle hillsides descend to tranquil valleys within the most well preserved and beautiful forest of the range. Optionally ascend the lofty lookout, Pena Rubia.

We've rated this walk, through exquisite woodland and valleys, as easy-medium for its relatively short distance, gentle ascents and the good terrain. The optional climb to Pena Rubia adds a bit more of a challenge and a bird's eye view of the sierra. (*Campa* means meadow or pasture and *golada* is saddle or pass.)

Bring water for the day or get water at two fountain troughs near the start and finish of the walk.

THE WALK

From the foot of the refugio (1350m), take the sealed road that heads south-east between broom, ferns and heather for 1.3km, where the sealed surface turns to dirt and stone. Continue for 5km, without deviations, passing a fountain trough, the Campa de Ortigosa and a holly and oak forest. The way dies out at the **Campa de Tres Obispos** (1579m) at the base of Pico Tres Obispos. Here you have a spectacular panoramic view

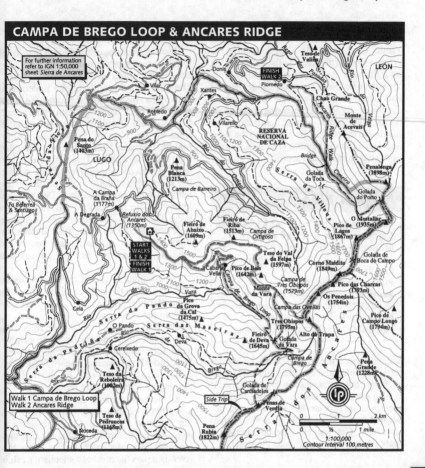

CAMPA DE BREGO LOOP & ANCARES RIDGE

For further information refer to IGN 1:50,000 sheet *Sierra de Ancares*

1:100,000
Contour Interval 100 metres

Walk 1 Campa de Brego Loop
Walk 2 Ancares Ridge

of the sierra's highest peaks. From left to right are Cuíña, O Mostallar, Lagos, Corno Maldito, As Charcas, Penedois, Tres Obispos and, on the far right, the hooked Pena Rubia.

Ignoring the path that ascends to Tres Obispos, take a right-hand (south) footpath and enter an enchanted birch and oak forest, descending to a grassy clearing called the **Golada de Vara**. Continue on the dirt road that heads left (south-east) and drops down to the hidden valley of the **Campa de Brego** with a tiny refugio.

Return along the same road to the meadow Golada de Vara and continue straight on a path that descends north-west through holly, ash and oak trees: the forest is a veritable jewel of the Ancares. The path approaches the Río Vara from its right side and then begins a gentle, zigzagging ascent for 4km, separating from the river. The trail passes the ruins of a sawmill, with potable water at a fountain trough, before it reaches the same sealed road walked in the morning. Turn left onto the road; the refugio is 1km away.

GALICIA

Side Trip: Pico Pena Rubia
3 hours, 4.5km
From the Campa de Brego, follow the Arroyo Brego (that crosses the valley) along its right bank. At the end of the valley cross the stream before it disappears under heather and take a path that ascends the hillside to the forest. Reaching a clearing dwarfed by surrounding peaks, ascend south along the hillside to the crest. Turn right onto the ridge and ascend to the summit (1822m). Retrace your steps to the main route.

Ancares Ridge

Duration 5½ to 6 hours
Distance 19km
Standard Medium-Hard
Start Refuxio dos Ancares, Degrada
Finish Piornedo
Public Transport Yes
Summary Walking with the clouds – the south-north traverse climbs five high peaks before descending to the hamlet of Piornedo with its pre-Roman-style dwellings.

This inspiring medium-hard walk includes terrific ascents and descents on some rough surfaces, but the reward is superb views. It is also possible to start in Piornedo and do the route in reverse but the direction described here takes advantage of the refugio as a base. Get water before beginning the walk (there's a fountain near the start).

THE WALK
Follow the Campa de Brego Loop walk described previously to the Campa de Tres Obispos. Take the southbound footpath that ascends the **Pico Tres Obispos** (1795m). For 20 minutes climb through heather along the peak's ridge and then its right slope to a small meadow at the base of the summit. Follow another trail exiting left and climb to the rocky summit. Excellent views of the sierra and a good part of León and Lugo provinces greet you on this legendary gathering spot of the bishops of Astorga, Lugo and León – the shared corner of their dioceses.

Descend south-east briefly and then take the ridge trail north-east, crossing the rocky and irregular peaks of **Os Penedois** (1754m). The trail sometimes disappears underneath the stones. Instead of ascending the next peak, Pico das Charcas (1793m), take a trail from its base and pass along its left-hand slope to the base of the conical **Corno Maldito** (Damned Horn). Continue along the right slope to a field. Turn left, ascending north-east to the ridge. Once above, detour left and in five minutes you'll reach a cairn marking the summit (1849m). Descend the route you have just climbed and return to the ridge. Follow the left slope of the next peak as it descends to an open field, **Golada de Boca do Campo**. A small cirque lies off to the right. You are now halfway through the walk.

For 20 minutes ascend to **Pico de Lagos** (1867m). From the summit, also cairned, **Corno Mostallar** (1935m) comes into spectacular view to the north-east. Descend towards it. To reach its summit, first take the ridge and then its left slope and finally make a right-hand turn and head directly to the top. Descend along its opposite (north) face, either cross-country or on a footpath running parallel to a wire fence.

At the base, **Golada do Porto**, continue along the wire to a small, grassy field and turn left onto a footpath. Cross the valley at its lowest point, turning right at the first two junctions you encounter. Below, cross the river then pass the ruins of a shepherd's cabin (on the right) and take a rocky path. Soon after entering the forest, the path widens and returns to the river, crossing it via an old wooden bridge. Continue straight ahead; the wide path reaches Piornedo in 3km.

Serra do Courel

The Courel is fortunate to have the active Asociación Río Lor which has marked routes and provides logistical and route information. It has two branches: on the highway in Seoane (☎ 982 43 31 17) and at the town hall in Folgoso (☎ 982 43 30 02). Following yellow-and-white trail markers, the described walks roughly follow the PR50 and PR51. In Moreda, the Centro de Interpretación opens from June to September. All information is in Galician or Spanish.

PLANNING
When to Walk
Being further south and lower than the Ancares, the temperatures are higher and annual rainfall less. Walking is best from May to October. Snows dust the mountains from December to February. The devesas are especially magnificent in spring and autumn.

Maps
The IGN *Seoane do Courel* No 157-I and *Salcedo* No 156-IV maps at 1:25,000 cover the walks. The *Mapa Turístico-Montañero del Courel* by G García Pardo is an informative 1:50,000 scale map, though it is inadequate on its own.

What to Bring
Bring a compass on both walks.

PLACES TO STAY & EAT
Seoane do Courel
This village 25km south of Piedrafita do Cebreiro has a small market, bank and pharmacy. *Camping O Caurel* (☎ 982 43 31 01) is 1.5km from Seoane towards Visuña. Tariffs are 440 ptas per adult and 400 ptas per car and per tent. Two and four person bungalows cost 5000/8000 ptas. The owners will provide information sheets with maps and details of nearby short walks. The village's budget option is the *Restaurante-Hospedaje Fontiña* (☎ 982 43 31 06), where doubles start at 2000 ptas. On the road, *Casa Ferreiro* (☎ 982 43 30 65) has singles/doubles for 2000/4000 ptas. The first pension does meals for around 1000 ptas. *Restaurante Anduriña* on the highway has a 900 ptas menú.

Folgoso do Courel
Folgoso has a market, bank and pharmacy and two recommended spots to sleep and eat. *Casa Constantino* (☎ 982 43 30 05), in the upper part of the village, has the most character. Rooms with shared bath go for 1200/2500 ptas. Home-cooked meals start at 1000 ptas. Also try *Bar-Hospedaje Novo* (☎ 982 43 30 07), where rooms with bath cost 1500/3000 ptas. Meals begin at 1300 ptas.

Vilamor
There are no shops or services here though you can find lodging and meals. Both *Casa Carlos* (☎ 982 15 56 18), with doubles for 3000 ptas, and *Casa Comerciante* have the same owner. In the second, rent the small house (room for four, kitchen and bathroom) for 6000 ptas per night. Breakfast (400 ptas), lunch and dinner (1500 ptas) can be arranged through the owner.

GETTING TO/FROM THE WALKS
The walks described in this section leave from the hamlets of Moreda and Vilamor, respectively. The closest villages are Seoane de Courel (7km from Moreda) and Folgoso do Courel (6km from Vilamor), 19km apart. Moreda has no services.

Unfortunately, public transport to the Serra do Courel is abysmal and requires bus-taxi combinations. By bus, either take an ALSA service from Santiago (11 am and 9.30 pm) or Madrid (8 and midday) to Piedrafita do Cebreiro and a taxi south to Seoane or Vilamor. Alternatively, take an Empresa Monforte (☎ 981 56 42 96) bus from Santiago to Quiroga via Monforte (daily at 3 pm) for 1435 ptas. In Quiroga, Empresa Courel buses (☎ 982 42 82 11) make runs to Folgoso and Seoane on Monday, Wednesday and Friday at 2.30pm (phone to confirm).

Taxis to and from Seoane via Bar Hydra (☎ 982 16 52 52) connect to Piedrafita (2500 ptas), Moreda (1000 ptas), Vilamor (2500 ptas) and Folgoso (2500 ptas). To link Folgoso and Vilamor (1000 ptas), contact ☎ 982 43 30 87; from Vilamor to either Seoane (2000 ptas) or Piedrafita (5000 ptas), phone ☎ 982 15 56 18.

Return ALSA buses from Piedrafita to Madrid run at 2.25 pm and 12.50 am and to

Santiago at 5.20 am and 1.35 pm. Empresa Courel buses leave Seoane (passing Folgoso) at 7.30 am on Monday, Wednesday and Friday, and Empresa Monforte buses return to Santiago from Quiroga daily at 7.20 am and weekdays at 9.15 am.

The most direct route by car is to Piedrafita via Lugo and then south on the LU651 to Seoane.

Devesa da Rogueira

Duration 5 to 5½ hours
Distance 16.5km
Level of Difficulty Medium-Hard
Start/Finish Moreda
Public Transport Yes
Summary Reaching the Serra do Courel's highest peaks and its glacial lagoon, the walk traverses this incredible forest harbouring more than 1000 species of flora.

An 870m ascent gives this walk it's medium-hard rating. Initially gentle, the walk (on the PR50) quickly ascends through the magnificent devesa before climbing out to the ridge. Just after halfway you reach a glacial lagoon. Moreda's fountain doesn't work so bring water to the trailhead.

THE WALK

The trail begins at Moreda's information centre and heads south-east into the forest, passing chestnuts before reaching a stream. After a cabin, cross the stream and keep it on the left during the long ascent. The way passes several winter grain-storage huts; soon the 2 sq km Devesa da Rogueira and the peaks to be climbed come into view. After crossing the brook ignore a left-hand footpath where the wooden PR50 signs begin. Beginning a series of ascending switchbacks, the track passes through holly, oak, birch and yew. Reaching a junction after 2km, fork right. In five minutes turn right at a T-junction and soon join another left-hand path.

Descending, the trail reaches the fascinating fountain, **Fonte do Cervo**. From the rocky wall gush two distinct springs – one red (iron rich) the other clear (calcareous) – out of parallel, round openings. They taste and smell different and both are said to have curative powers.

Begin climbing again, leaving the devesa and the last birch behind to enter an open area of low shrubs; continue to a slate road that runs along the sierra's ridge. To the left the rounded Formigueiros peak (1639m) is

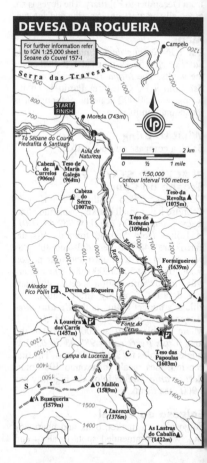

DEVESA DA ROGUEIRA

For further information refer to IGN 1:25,000 sheet Seoane do Courel 157-I

NANCY FREY

JOSE PLACER

JOSE PLACER

JOSE PLACER

Top: The Spindrift Walk, a must for ocean-lovers, begins in the village of Laxe.
Middle Left: Fishing boats moored in a cove on the beautiful Río Xallas.
Middle Right: Hillside village in the remote Serra do Courel, Galicia, an area rich with wild flowers.
Bottom: The still waters of Laguna A Lucenza in the forested hills of the Serra do Courel.

View along Bernia ridge in Valencia's La Marina mountains (top left); El Boixar village in Els Ports, Valencia (top right); Guadalest, La Marina Alta, overlooked by a fortified castle and the rugged Sierra de Aixorta (middle left); the steep descent to Torrent de Pareis, Mallorca (middle right); the invasion of 'moros' festival, Port de Sóller (bottom left); Torrent de Pareis, Mallorca's 'major' watercourse (bottom right).

visible. Turn right (south-west), ascending to **Teso das Papoulas** (1603m). Descend along the slate road to a small level area, Campa da Lucenza, and continue straight ahead, ignoring a left-hand 4WD road and ditch. Turn left onto an unmarked grassy area. The path quickly appears and descends to the base of a hill (the halfway point of the walk). Take a right-hand footpath to reach the shore of the **Laguna A Lucenza** (1376m), surrounded by broom (in summer the water level drops). Return to the Campa da Lucenza, take the 4WD road ahead (north-west) and immediately fork right, descending without turn-offs until very close (parallel) to a wider road on the left. Turn right on a lane that, after crossing a small slate quarry, enters the devesa along a south-east footpath. Soon, the path reaches a fork. Descend left on the already familiar path followed earlier in the day to the Fonte do Cervo.

Río Lor Meander

Duration 5 to 5½ hours
Distance 19km
Standard Medium
Start/Finish Vilamor
Public Transport Yes
Summary Stunning river walk along the sinuous Río Lor and its canyon, passing through thousand-year-old villages, chestnut groves and the strategically placed Castro Portela.

Marked in part as the PR51, we've added an additional side trip to continue the jaunt through the gorgeous forest, rivers and canyons to the *aldeas* (hamlets) Vilar, Froxán and Castro Portela. Water is readily available all along the route.

THE WALK

One hundred metres below Vilamor's church, on the sealed road, the slate trail descends south-east through pastures. In five minutes the trail reaches a crossing surrounded by chestnuts. Take the first footpath to the right, making a pronounced descent to the **Río Lor**, which you cross via an old wooden bridge. On the other side of the canyon, ascend for 300m along a footpath thickly hemmed in with heather and broom. The path then opens up to the chestnuts of Vilar. At the hamlet's first houses, turn right (to the left there's a fountain) and head out again. First pass through trees and pastures and then past the tiny Ermita de San Roque chapel before reaching the 2nd or 4th century **Castro de Vilar** ruins upon a rocky spur above the Lor. In spite of the overgrowth its possible to visualise the defensive walls and circular houses.

Back at the chapel, take the footpath that soon heads right (west) and descends to the Río Lor. Cross the wooden bridge (the last PR51 sign) and ascend left along a wider path to the summit, crowned with oaks. At the next fork veer left, entering **Froxán**, a hamlet of medieval appearance and descend its left side. The fountain is in the high part of the village. After the last house turn left and immediately take a right-hand footpath that dies out at a small, sealed road on the banks of the Lor.

Cross the Río Lor by way of the road and continue for 1km. Turn right onto a descending lane that appears when the road makes its first left turn, initiating the 2.5km loop of Castro Portela. At the first right-hand curve continue straight on a hillside trail above the Lor among chestnuts. Reaching a zone of pastures and huts, the trail forks. Ascend left to Castro Portela. You're now halfway through the walk. Cross through the village on its high side, passing a fountain, until reaching the sealed road. Turn left and retrace your steps back to Vilamor.

Side Trip: Lor Continuation
1½ hours, 5km

From the bridge over the Lor (near Castro Portela) continue on the sealed road towards Froxán and in 400m you will reach cork oaks and a *cortín*, or bear screen (see the boxed text 'Galician Vernacular Architecture'

GALICIA

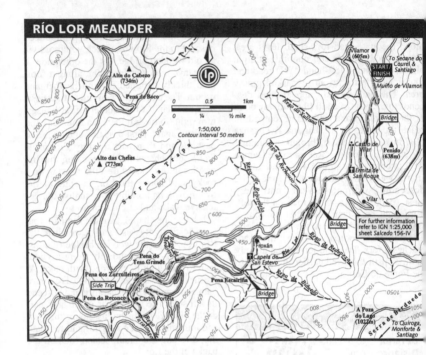

RÍO LOR MEANDER

earlier in this section). Turn left along an ancient lane that once linked the villages and descend towards the river. The path parallels the river, offering spectacular views for 2km until it reaches some cabins in a field surrounded by chestnuts. Return the same way.

Other Walks

EASTERN SIERRAS
Picos Cuíña & Penalonga

In the Ancares east of Piornedo, accessible by car and just within León's borders, is the Porto dos Ancares. From here a trail (at first poorly marked) heads south (constantly veering right) and ascends two large hills before reaching the summit of Picos Cuíña (1998m), the highest peak in the Serra dos Ancares. From its base, a right-hand trail leads to the summit of Penalonga (1898m). This hard return trip takes seven hours. Use the IGN *Sierra de Ancares* 1:50,000 mapa-guía.

Courel Ridge

Ten kilometres from Seoane, along the highway from the camping ground (toward Visuña) in the Alto do Couto, a dirt road turns off right. Over the course of 10km, the track snakes along the crest of the sierra, passing Formigueiros, Mallón, Pía Paxaro, Cobalud and ending at the Alto do Boi (10km from Folgoso). Use the *Montañeros de Los Ancares* map by G García Pardo. This 20km return trip is feasible in a day.

SANTIAGO DE COMPOSTELA AREA

If based in Santiago you may want to consider trying several easy day trips in the area that weave in and out of villages, quiet forests and the gentle, rolling hills of this largely rural zone. For additional information on the three routes listed below consult the *Rotas par Camiñantes* (see Books under Information in the introduction to this chapter) or ask in the town halls where the routes start: Cunti

(☎ 986 54 80 05), Toques (☎ 981 50 58 26) and Sobrado (☎ 981 78 90 08).

Cuntis Panoramic

Thirty kilometres south of Santiago is the Cuntis township. Here are three officially marked routes (PRGs). The most interesting is a 20km loop (PRG20) that illustrates well the rural life of southern Galicia, passing through numerous hamlets linked by ancient trails, wild rivers and rich landscapes. IGN maps *Caldass de Res* No 152-II and *Codeseda* No 153-I are useful. The easy loop leaves from Cuntis.

Route of the Megaliths

To the east of Santiago and north of Melide, in the township of Toques, there are three marked routes. The most attractive is the Sendero de los Megalitos which in 15km passes two castros (Brañas and Os Castros), a dolmen (Forno dos Mouros) and various megalithic formations (the Penas de Moura, Redonda and Cabra), all within fragas filled with mills and streams. The route leaves from A Riba in the parish of As Brañas. IGN maps *As Cruces* No 71-IV and *Melide* No 96-II cover the route.

Sobrado dos Monxes

Near the Route of the Megaliths to the north of Melide, but reached from Arzúa, is one of the best conserved (and still inhabited) monasteries of Galicia, Sobrado dos Monxes. Around the monastery is a 12km loop. Leaving from the Barrio de Alvariza the trail covers the monastery's lands, a lagoon, oak woods and various hamlets. IGN maps *Sobrado* No 71-III and *As Cruces* No 71-IV cover the walk.

Valencia

Without a 'star' mountain range, Valencia is not a place that springs to mind when thinking about walking in Spain. Images of sun, sea and sangría on the Costa Blanca belie the fact that much of Valencia's interior is extremely beautiful and rugged, and well covered by long and short-distance footpaths.

On Valencia's western boundary with Aragón and Castilla, the ends of the Iberian and Baetic mountains form a corridor of ravines and craggy summits. The Sierra de Espadán and Alto Milares near Montanejos are crossed by countless footpaths.

In Valencia's north, the medieval walled city of Morella, in the north El Maestrazgo region, is the focus of long-distance walks in Els Ports (known as 'the region of the mountain passes'), an area of seemingly endless rolling *sierras* (mountain ranges). North of Alicante, close to the rolling hills of the Sierra Mariola in Valencia's south, the arid La Marina mountains tower above the Mediterranean. A variety of routes across challenging terrain and a long walking season make this a great alternative to the sun lounges of the Costa Blanca.

HISTORY

The Iberian peoples on the Mediterranean were already trading with Greek and Phoenician merchants by 800 BC, and the Mediterranean shore ensured prosperity for Valencian communities through the Roman, Visigoth and Muslim occupations. Of those ancient peoples, the Muslims have had the most lasting influence. It was 709 AD when they captured Valencia, and in 1021 the city became the capital of a new, independent Muslim kingdom with the legendary El Cid in control during the latter part of the 10th century (see the boxed text 'El Cid' later in this section).

In 1238 the city of Valencia fell to the Christian king Jaume I of Aragón and by 1245 the Christian Reconquista (Reconquest) of the whole region was complete,

HIGHLIGHTS

The view north-east to Confrides with sierras Serrella and Aixorta beyond.

- Ridge walking on the spectacular Sierra de Bernia before climbing down to the warm waters of the Mediterranean

- Eating excellent Valenciano cuisine in the mountain restaurant of El Trestellador, Benimantell, while overlooking the Valle de Guadalest

- Walking under the huge, overhanging limestone cliffs leading to the Portell de l'Infern, Els Ports

- Looking out across waves of remote mountain ranges from the medieval, walled city of Morella

though Valencia maintained an independent parliament and legal system. The marriage of Fernando II of Aragón and Isabel I of Castilla in 1469 unified Castilla and Valencia, with other counties of the Aragones crown following suit in 1479.

VALENCIA

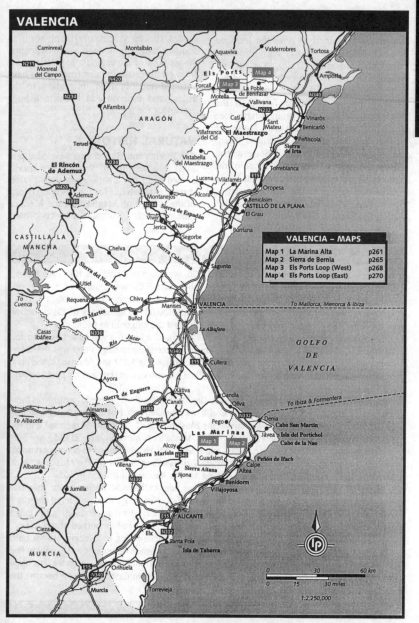

VALENCIA – MAPS

0   30   60 km
0   15   30 miles

1:2,250,000

Intensive irrigation began in pre-Roman times and continued under the Muslims, and many remained to tend the terraced *huertas* (market gardens) until the final Muslim expulsion in 1609. Agricultural production declined thereafter and did not fully recover until the 19th century. The land is among the most fertile in the Mediterranean and today oranges have once again become an important crop. Huge rice paddies are also common in central Valencia and dry-farmed crops include wheat, olives and grapes from which some of the country's best wine is produced. Valencia, a prosperous city and the third largest in Spain, was briefly the Republican capital during the Spanish Civil War.

The Comunidad Valenciana (region of Valencia) was established in 1982 and includes the provinces of (from north to south) Castellón, Valencia and Alicante. About 80% of the region's population now lives on the coastal plains (rural areas have suffered terribly from migration to the cities) and tourism has become a huge earner for the region.

NATURAL HISTORY

The Iberian and Baetic mountains that protrude into the west of Valencia are heavily eroded and form a network of deep ravines that provide habitats for species more typical of the valleys of Aragón than the Mediterranean coast. Lusitanian and cork oaks,

El Cid

Rodrigo Díaz de Vivar, popularly known as El Cid, was born in Castilla in 1043. His father, Diego Laíez, was a member of Castilla's minor nobility and El Cid was brought up in the court of Fernando I, along with the king's eldest son, the future Sancho II of Castilla. In 1065, Sancho succeeded to the Castilian throne – and put El Cid, at the tender age of 22, in control of the army. His younger brother, Alfonso VI, inherited the kingdom of León.

Sancho and Alfonso were not close, and in 1067 Sancho began a war to annex León for Castilla. El Cid played a prominent role in Sancho's successful campaigns and was therefore in an awkward position when the childless Sancho was killed in 1072 and Alfonso VI, the only possible heir, became King of Castilla. El Cid joined Alfonso's court, but lost his post as commander of the army.

In 1081, El Cid led an unauthorised raid on the Muslim kingdom of Toledo, which was then under the protection of Alfonso, and the Christian king exiled him. Not one to sit on his hands, El Cid offered his services to al-Mu'tamin, the Muslim ruler of Zaragosa (Saragossa) and for nearly a decade served him and his successor, al-Musta'in. During this time, El Cid gained an understanding of Hispanic-Arabic politics and Islamic law. He also added to his reputation as an outstanding military commander by inflicting devastating defeats on the Muslim king of Lérida in 1082 and the Christian army of King Sancho Ramírez of Aragón in 1084.

However, what he really wanted was to become ruler of the Muslim kingdom of Valencia. His chance came in 1092 when Ibn Jahháf, Valencia's chief magistrate, murdered the city's ruler, al-Qádir. El Cid besieged the city and in May 1094 Ibn Jahháf surrendered in the belief that his safety was guaranteed. He was mistaken, and El Cid had him burned at the stake.

From then until his death in 1099, El Cid ruled Valencia, acting as a magistrate for both Christians and Muslims. On hearing of his death, Muslim armies besieged the city only to flee in terror when his body, propped on a horse, was led out through the city gates. His body was finally taken to the monastery of San Pedro de Cardeña in Castilla, where it became the centre of a lively tomb cult.

cluster and black pines all occur in these highland areas, with stands of holm oak occupying the lower sierras of El Maestrazgo. The more remote mountain areas contain several rare species of animal – such as the pardel lynx and Spanish ibex – as well as wildcats, wild boar (which often conduct nightly raids on village vegetable patches and rubbish bins), red deer and red squirrels.

In early summer, Mediterranean *monte-bájo* (dry, rocky terrain) delights the senses with the smell of herbs such as lavender, thyme, sage, rue and curry plant. At this time of year, look out for lime-resistant plants such as black vanilla, mirror and frog orchids, Bertoloni's bee and, later in the year, lady's tresses.

While much of Valencia's coastal strip is devoted to the irrigated cultivation of oranges, some areas have been converted into huge rice paddies. Near one such rice-growing area is the serenely beautiful freshwater lagoon Parc Natural de La Albufera, which is the temporary home of multitudes of wintering birds. Also popular with migrating birds are the salt flats of Santa Pola, close to Alicante, where you will see flamingos.

CLIMATE

Coastal Valencia has a mild, Mediterranean climate, an average maximum temperature in winter of 13°C and an average maximum in summer of around 29°C. It gets warmer further south, where temperatures can reach 40°C. Annual precipitation is low, from 400 to 500mm per year, of which a large percentage falls between September and November. The western and northern mountains have far harsher winters and more changeable weather. Though coastal regions enjoy a mild winter, the peaks of La Marina Alta are occasionally covered with snow.

INFORMATION
Maps

Three Instituto Geográfico Nacional (IGN) *Mapa Provincial* 1:200,000 maps cover Valencia, but for planning your trip buy Michelin's *Central and Southern Spain* No

445 map at 1:400,000. Almost all of Valencia (with the exception of some areas north of Castellón de la Plana, including Els Ports) is now covered by the IGN 1:25,000 map project, as well as by new editions of the Servicio Geográfico del Ejército (SGE) 1:50,000 maps.

Books

Few books in English cover walking in the Valencia region and none covers Els Ports. Spanish readers will have a better choice including the comprehensive *Montañas Valencianas* series by Rafael Cebrían. Lonely Planet's *Spain* guidebook offers a basic outline of the most popular walking areas, as well as everything you could want to know about travelling in this country.

The Centre Excursionista de Valencia (☎ 96 391 16 43, fax 96 391 18 53), at Plaza Tavernes de Valldigna 4 in Valencia city, produces a range of tourist-oriented walking literature, including the *Topo-Guía* series which covers in detail popular sections of the long-distance footpath Sendero de Gran Recorrido (GR) 7. The general GR7 pamphlet is a good reference for walking in the Valencia region. Also useful are the parchment-coloured leaflets on rural walking areas available from most tourist information offices.

Information Sources

Librería Patagonia (☎/fax 96 391 52 47), Calle Guillem de Castro 106, is the best shop for maps and books in the city of Valencia. Also try Papelería Regolf on Calle Del Mar 2. In Alicante, try Librería International, Altmir 6, or Clan Natura on Calle Forlietti.

There are two regional tourist information offices in Valencia city, one at Paz 48 (☎ 96 394 22 22) and a smaller one in Estacíon del Norte (☎ 96 352 85 73). The main tourist office in Castellón de la Plana (☎ 964 22 10 00) is at María Agustina 5; in Alicante it is at Explanada de España 2 (☎ 96 520 00 00).

Place Names

Since the end of Franco's dictatorship, Valenciano (a dialect of Catalan), like many regional languages in Spain, has become increasingly popular. It is now common for features and place names to appear in Valenciano on local signs, but in Catalan on maps. Luckily Valenciano is not *too* different from Catalan. See also Place Names in the Facts for the Walker chapter.

ACCOMMODATION & SUPPLIES
Valencia
The Barrio del Carmen, midway between the train and bus stations and in the heart of Valencia's vibrant nightlife, has plenty of accommodation. *Hostal El Rincón* (☎ 96 391 79 98, Calle de la Carda 11) is one of Valencia's oldest hostels and has a dingy charm (singles/doubles for 1500/2800 ptas). Lock-up parking is available. *Hospedería del Pilar* (☎ 96 391 66 00, Plaza del Mercado 19) is a similar sort of place.

Valencia's metro and suburban trains make tracking down supplies relatively easy. Deportes Altarriba (☎ 96 392 21 99), Calle Paz 11, is a good central choice, while the owner of La Tienda, Calle Cordellats 6 (close to Librería Patagonia), is very helpful and holds a fair stock of equipment, maps and books.

Benidorm
Benidorm is one big tourist nightmare, but does have direct bus links with La Marina. If you really want to stay here, try *Hostal La Santa Faz* (☎ 96 585 40 63) or *Hostal Calpí* (☎ 96 585 78 48), which are both quite expensive, or *Hotel Camposol Park* (☎ 96 585 01 95) or *Hotel Easo* (☎ 96 680 70 03), which are a bit less so. Librería Francés at Ruzafa 4 stocks some GSE and IGN maps, and Benialgar Sports (an Intersport shop) at Calle Mercado 3 has some good walking equipment.

Calpe
Calpe, just along the coast, is almost as convenient and more pleasant. The English-run *Pensión Centric* (☎ 96 583 55 28) on the Plaza de Ifach is friendly, central and clean, has singles/doubles for a fixed price of 1500/3000 ptas, and is recommended. Alternatives are *Le Vieux Bruxelles* (☎ 96 583 43 57) above the port and *Hostal Crespo* (☎ 96 583 39 31) on Casa La Pinta. If you'd rather pitch a tent, *Camping Levante* (☎/fax 96 583 22 72) and *Camping Ifach* (☎ 96 583 04 77) are on the north-east side of Calpe.

For supplies, Ifac Sport (☎ 96 583 05 89) on Avenida Gabriel Miró has a limited range of walking equipment.

Alicante
If you are travelling to La Marina, you don't need to spend the night in Alicante. However, if you're stuck there for the night, try the *hostales* (budget hotels) and *pensiones* (guesthouses) in the old part of town, including *Pensión La Milagrosa* (☎ 96 521 69 18, Calle de Villavieja 8).

Close to the bus station, on Calle Foglietti, Clan Natura sells a wide range of maps and gas canisters.

Castellón de la Plana
If you're spending the night in Castellón, try the friendly and convenient *Fonda La Granadina* (☎ 964 21 21 41, Calle Navarra 99) – look for the house number; there is no sign. Singles/doubles cost 1400/2800 ptas. If it's full, try *Hostal La Esperanza* (☎ 964 22 20 31, Calle Ximénez 26), above a reasonable restaurant; the *menu del día* is good value. *Cafe Teatro* (☎ 964 24 39 52, Ramón Llull 21) is a music venue. The owner also runs the *Hostal Samana* next door.

The city hasn't the same range of walking supplies as is available elsewhere, but there are a number of sports shops which may have what you need.

GETTING THERE & AWAY
Alicante is the gateway to the Costa Blanca and there are frequent flights to and from all major centres including Palma de Mallorca, Ibiza City, Valencia, Barcelona and Madrid, as well as many destinations in Europe. Phone ☎ 96 528 50 11 for information.

In Valencia, Aeropuerto de Manises (☎ 96 360 95 00) is 15km west of the centre. Regular flights connect Valencia with Madrid, Barcelona, Palma de Mallorca and Ibiza.

Good train and bus services between Alicante, Valencia and Castellón – as well as other major Spanish cities – make getting to the major walking regions relatively easy. (See Getting to/from the Walk in the introduction to each walk for more information.)

The Valencia region is a cheap place to hire a car – very useful if you want to reach the more remote walking areas. All along the coast international companies and local firms are engaged in fierce competition for the car rental market. Auriga Rent A Car (☎ 96 583 00 91, fax 96 583 00 91, info@aurigacar.com) and Neptuno Car SL (☎ 96 583 00 91) offer small cars for less than 20,000 ptas per week, fully inclusive. Both operate at Valencia and Alicante airports. Centauro (☎ 96 585 15 90, fax 96 586 00 76) also has offices all along the Costa Blanca.

Trasmediterránea (☎ 96 367 65 12) and Flebasa (☎ 96 578 40 11) run ferries from the cities of Valencia and Denia (the closest port to Alicante), respectively, to the Islas Baleares (Balearic Islands).

La Marina

North of the high-rise blocks, sun lounges and all-night discos of Benidorm is the mountainous area known locally as La Marina. Made up of numerous east-west ridges and divided between La Marina Baja and La Marina Alta (lower and higher) the range occupies a huge headland that juts out into the Mediterranean between Alicante and Valencia.

These mountains are not giants – the highest peak is Aitana at 1558m – but the area has a variety of interesting terrain and the village hospitality is first class. Dry, rocky montebájo terrain is common, but away from the ridges and high mountain passes much of the walking is along quiet forestry tracks. High ridge walks, gorge walks and treks from mountain peak to seashore are all possible, and despite the tourist hordes a stone's throw away it's perfectly possible to pick up your pack, disappear into the mountains and not speak to another person for days on end. And this is possible for nine months of the year.

HISTORY

Before the tourist boom, when Benidorm was just a poor fishing village, Callosa d'En Sarriá was the cultural and administrative centre of La Marina region. The townspeople, who thrived thanks to the pure waters of the Río Algar, had a hand in much of the commerce occurring in and around the mountains. Archaeologists date the earliest occupation of the area to 5000 BC, with evidence of early Bronze Age, Iberian, Roman, Paleoandalusian, Islamic and Christian occupations. However, like most of Valencia, the greatest historical and cultural influence comes from the period of Muslim occupation that lasted from 714 AD to the 13th century.

Evidence of the struggle between Christian and Muslim is dotted around the mountains, mainly in the guise of hill forts. Other interesting archaeological finds include Mozarabic trails (see the boxed text 'Mozarabic Trails' on the following page) and the watchtowers built to warn of piracy and raiding parties – common in the 17th century when the whole of Valencia lacked stability and strong leadership.

Rural migration to the cities has shrunk mountain village populations, which in turn has affected the landscape. With fewer people working the land, much of the stone terracing that once covered almost every hectare of fertile land has fallen into disrepair.

NATURAL HISTORY

The rocky, arid limestone slopes of La Marina, scarred by fissures and crags, support many spiky plants, making walking in shorts unpleasant, though gorse and broom are beautiful during late spring. Plants unique to the area include the rusty foxglove (*Digitalis obscura*) found on scree, and the tiny, rush-leaved daffodil (*Narcissus requienii*). The area is home to a large number of lime-tolerant plants including yellow anthyllis, which produces carpets of colour in early spring. The summer heat limits the range of wild flowers, but sage, thyme, rue, curry plant and cotton lavender do well on this montebájo terrain. Even in the fierce heat of July,

VALENCIA

Mozarabic Trails

During the early centuries of the Islamic occupation of southern and Mediterranean Spain, a large percentage of the local population converted to Islam. Those who chose to remain Christian were not persecuted, but given full legal protection secured by the payment of tax. Local Christians mixed freely with the Muslims and slowly became indistinguishable in appearance from their Arab neighbours, causing the Christians of northern Spain to name them the *mozárabes*, the 'Arabised' or Arab-like. The mozárabes also adopted elements of the Arab culture including craft skills and building techniques (which over time filtered into the northern Christian kingdoms) and even built their churches in an Arabic style.

Ancient stepped tracks through the mountains of Valencia (and Andalucía) are also the work of the mozárabes. Typically, these trails zigzag across the steepest slopes and down into the deepest ravines, tracing routes that would be treacherous if cobbled stone paths had not been built. It's also likely that many of these trails were constructed by the Mudéjars, Muslim settlers who stayed after the Reconquista and converted to Christianity.

Many of these paths are still in good condition, standing testament to the merits of solid construction and the skills of mozárabe and Muslim craftsmen. A good example of a mozárabic trail is in the Valle de Laguart to the north of the Las Marinas mountains, where the Camino de Juvias descends to the Barranco del Infierno.

pink century (*Centaurium erythrae*) and red valerian (*Centranthus ruber*) bloom, along with rock roses and potentilla.

In the mountains, you may see rabbits, hares and foxes, but you'll be lucky if wildcats and wild boar cross your path. As in many places in Spain, widespread hunting has affected wildlife diversity and numbers, but this doesn't mean that you won't see the bold, brown-and-black hoopoe (which brings bad luck if killed), along with eagles, many species of harriers and warblers. Colourful rollers and bee-eaters can be seen in the valleys and you will often stumble across a startled partridge.

Vibora hocicuda – which is yellow with a triangular head and a wavy line down the spine – is the only poisonous viper found here. The caterpillar of the pine processionary moth (*Thaumet opea pitycampa*), which weaves its nest in pine trees, secretes a poisonous powder that causes severe skin rashes – vinegar is an effective antidote.

INFORMATION
Maps
The following SGE 1:50,000 maps cover La Marina: *Alcoy* No 29-32 (821), *Beniasa* No 30-32 (822), *Altea* (also labelled as *Benidorm*) No 30-33 (848) and *Villajoyosa* No 29-33 (847). However, the SGE 1:50,000 maps give little indication of the landscape's severity.

Books
Guidebooks worth considering are *Landscapes of the Costa Blanca* by J Oldfield and the excellent *Mountain Walks on the Costa Blanca* by Bob Stansfield. Both are intended for the day-tripper. *Costa Blanca Climbs* by Chris Craggs is a good guide to climbing in the region.

Information Sources
If you want a good insight into walking in the region, contact the Costa Blanca Mountain Walkers. This informal group of mostly British expats have been exploring La Marina for more than 10 years. Tony Jarrey (☎/fax 96 597 33 89) is the club secretary.

In Callosa, the tourist information centre (☎ 96 597 21 29) is inside the main town hall; the main tourist office in Calpe (☎ 96 583 69 20, fax 96 583 12 50) is on Avenida Ejércitos Españoles; the Benidorm tourist office (☎ 96 585 13 11, turdorm@gva.es) is at Martínez Alejos 16.

Some IGN 1:25,000 maps are available in Calpe at Papelería Vasquez on Avenida Gabriel Miró, though it's best to buy your maps in Alicante or Valencia (see Maps and Books under Information earlier in this chapter).

La Marina Alta

Duration 3 to 4 days
Distance 56km
Standard Medium
Start Confrides
Finish Callosa
Public Transport Yes
Summary This S-shaped exploration of La Marina Alta starts a short bus ride from the Costa Blanca and includes the highest peak in Alicante province, the intriguing ruins of Muslim and Christian castles, a number of ridge walks and La Marina's best restaurant.

This four day walk gives a good taste of the major limestone sierras of La Marina Alta, all a short bus ride from the Costa Blanca. The route includes the highest peak in the province of Alicante, ruins of Muslim and Christian castles, ridge traverses, tranquil high-mountain camp sites, and probably the best restaurant in La Marina.

It follows forestry tracks and marked paths across the Sierra de Aitana and Valle de Guadalest before passing over the Sierra de Serrella and descending to Castell de Castells. The final leg is a traverse around the Sierra de Aixorta to Callosa, from where there's the further option of a day's walk along the Sierra de Bernia ridge (see the Sierra de Bernia walk later in this section) and a descent to the sea. Hostal accommodation can be found in the valleys each night and campers will not have trouble finding suitable sites, which gives wider scope for exploration away from the main trail. While it is possible to do this walk in three very long days (as described here), it is better spread across four or five days as the considerable changes in altitude may take their toll.

PLANNING
When to Walk

From mid-June to mid-September, temperatures can soar to more than 35°C, even at altitude, and few people are crazy enough to go walking in July, August or September. The mild winters on the Costa Blanca mean that the walking season runs from October to June (though be prepared for 7°C, regular frosts and occasional snowfalls on the higher peaks). March to May is probably ideal as wild flowers are then in bloom. Much of the region's 490mm of rainfall is during *gota fria*, a stormy period in September and October.

Maps

The IGN map *Altea* No 848-I at 1:25,000 is useful for the traverse around the end of the Sierra de Aixorta.

Warnings

If walking during summer, when most of the rivers and streams dry up and many lesser *fuentes* (springs) are unreliable, set off at dawn and be aware of sunstroke, sunburn, heat exhaustion and cramps. Carry plenty of water (double the amount you think you'll need) and keep your salt levels up. Rehydration sachets are an excellent idea.

Also be aware that much of the rock here is friable and safe-looking holds can sometimes crumble and come away in your hand. Bring cold-weather gear for winter walking.

PLACES TO STAY & EAT
Confrides

Confrides, at the start of the walk, is not a big place, but there's a small bank, *grocery store* and several bars and restaurants. *Hostal-Pensión El Pirineo* (☎ 96 588 58 58) is reasonably priced, but often closes in midsummer. There isn't a camping ground. The bus service from Benidorm (via Callosa) is variable at best, so it's wise to book accommodation at El Pirineo for the night before you start the route.

Callosa d'En Sarriá

Callosa, the end point of this walk, is just south of the mountains and makes a good base. *Hostal Avenida* (☎ 96 588 00 53, *Carretera Alicante 9*), opposite the bus stop, has singles/doubles for 1500/3000 ptas (4000 ptas with a bath), while *Fonda Galiana* (☎ 96 588 01 55) on Calle Collon specialises in local cuisine and is similarly priced. *Mesón San José* on Carretera de Bolulla is also good for regional cuisine. For a drink, try *Bar Moros y Cristianos* on the Plaza del Convent. The nearest official *camping ground* is 3km east of town at Fuentes del Agar at the start of the Sierra de Bernia Traverse (for more details, see Places to Stay & Eat in the introduction to that walk later in this section). Callosa is also a good place to stock up on supplies.

GETTING TO/FROM THE WALK

Unless you're driving, the trailhead at the village of Confrides is best approached via Valencia or Alicante. Almost hourly UBESA (☎ 96 680 39 55) buses connect Alicante and Valencia with Calpe and Benidorm, and another hourly service connects Benidorm (departing from Avenida Europa) to Callosa (125 ptas). During the week in winter, half of these buses continue to Guadalest (100 ptas extra) and only one continues to Confrides (175 ptas extra), arriving at 7.45 pm. For an early morning start you may have to negotiate a lift from Guadalest to Confrides, a 10km trip. It may nevertheless be necessary to break Day 1 by camping at Fuente Arbols or Fuente Forata. In summer, times may change; inquire locally.

One bus every weekday runs from Benidorm to Pego (via Calpe), should you want to explore La Marina Baja and the unspoilt cherry-growing Valle de Gallinera west of the town. Be warned, though: the returning bus bypasses Benidorm, so you'll need to change at Calpe.

THE WALK
Day 1: Confrides to Fuente Partagas

7 to 7½ hours, 17km

Walk up Calle San Antonio, opposite El Pirineo, past the fuente and take the first

---

Nevera: the Original Fridges

Nevera are deep, cylindrical pits, usually constructed on the northern slopes of high mountains, used to make ice from snow. Normally about 15m deep and 10m wide, the larger ones had supporting stone beams and wooden tiled roofs. Smaller nevera had domed, dry-stone roofs

In winter, the pits were filled with snow, then insulated with straw and sealed. During the summer months, local men would come up from the villages and spend the night cutting the ice into blocks, insulating it with straw and sacking and transporting it by mule down to the valleys before sunrise.

Nevera were mainly used during the 17th and 18th centuries, but older men in the village of Confrides maintain that the practice continued into the early part of the 20th century. The nevera fell into decay with the introduction of electric refrigeration, but good examples remain below the cliffs of Aitana. The best example of an arched nevera is near the Refugio Santiago Reig del Mural, below Monte Cabre.

---

turn on your right, cutting back west. Fork right past the gate of El Pouet San Ignacio, then bear right at the next junction above the village and continue on this well made dirt road for 6km (1½ hours).

As you approach the shaded Fuente Arbols (marked as Fuente Aitana on some maps) at **Casas de Aitana** you'll have views of the radar domes and antennae on the Sierra Aitana to your right. It's perfectly acceptable to find a *camp site* among the picnic benches, but it's a popular spot.

From the fuente, zigzag up the forestry track directly south, then follow it east below the cliffs, passing a *nevera* (see the boxed text 'Nevera: the Original Fridges') after 25 minutes.

Ignore two left turns, then fork left directly under the radar domes onto a minor track which leads to the **Fuente Forata**. A *forat* (hole through the rock) is clearly visible to the south-east. This flat area, with views across Valle de Guadalest to the Sierra Serrella and north-west to the Sierra Bernia and beyond, is an ideal *camp site*. Those planning to undertake the side trip to Alto de la Peña de Sella may wish to cut the first day short and camp here. The signposted PRV21 route to Benifato offers an alternative descent (west) to Fuente Partagas and the end of this stage.

From Fuente Forata, two well worn paths lead south-east across scree slopes to a boulder-strewn gully. Halfway up the gully a yew marks the point where the route bears left to 'Fat Man's Agony', a narrow pass. Squeeze through, turn left and traverse east above a large fissure down to a marked, chest-high rock face. Here, the route leads east to Peña Alta, but it's worth climbing up the less distinct path on the right (west) towards the summit of **Aitana** (1557m). The radar installation may restrict access to the

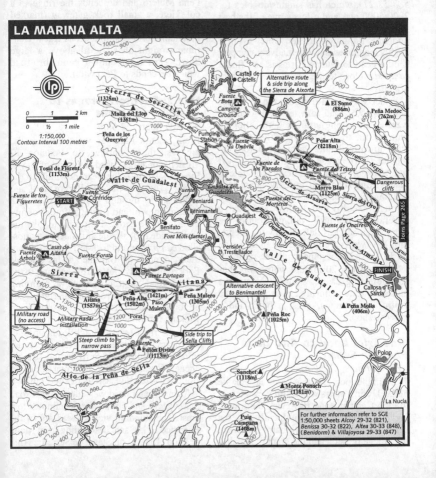

LA MARINA ALTA

summit, but the undulating peaks of the ridge are only slightly lower and give uninterrupted views of the major ranges of La Marina. Particularly impressive is Puig Campana (1408m), the second-highest peak in the province, to the south-east.

From the painted rock face, head east on the obvious path (stay close to the cliff edge where the scrub is sparse) over Peña Alta to Paso Mulero, where the route descends to a forestry road linking Benifato and Sella.

The nearest comfortable bed is in Benimantell at *Pensión El Trestellador* (☎ 96 588 52 21), which has singles/doubles for 2000/5000 ptas and offers some of the best Valencian cooking in the region. There's a poolside bungalow if the hotel is full. Highly recommended. Alternatively, campers should head to Fuente Partagas and find a *camp site* close to the beautiful, overhanging cliffs.

Either way, upon reaching the Benifato-Sella forestry road turn left and follow it west down a long straight until, after 25 minutes, the track turns right, then zigzags west down to **Fuente Partagas**. Before the second (left) zigzag, two tracks bear off right. Take the first, well made (concrete in places) dirt road that quickly bears left, heading east across a depression, down through a cultivated hollow and past a nevera to Font Moli. Walk east out of the picnic area and turn left. Below the fuente, turn left (west) along the road until a sign for El Trestellador appears on the right.

Guadalest, a 20 minute walk away, has an interesting castle, a clutch of strange museums (one featuring an ant playing the violin), restaurants, bars, a bank and a grocery shop.

Side Trip: Loop to Alto de la Peña de Sella

4½ to 5 hours, 13.5km

This simple loop across Alto de la Peña de Sella (1105m) offers wonderful views across to Puig Campana and El Realet, the row of jagged pinnacles (known locally as 'the shark's teeth') that forms a barrier between the village of Sella and the giant mountain.

At Paso Mulero, descend south-west along the dirt road to the fuente below the Alto de la Peña de Sella ridge. Fork left, turn left beside a farm building, then climb south-east to a col. Turn right (west) and begin to work your way along the rocky, scrub-covered ridge, a simple and enjoyable traverse culminating in the ascent of **Alto de la Peña de Sella**. After an hour, the ridge meets a dirt road. Turn right (east) and walk down to the fuente and then back to Paso Mulero. From here, an alternative route to Benimantell crosses the summit of Peña Mulero and descends the ridge to a col. Here, a small rock gateway (marked with a red square) offers a way off the mountain north-east to a broad track. Continue straight ahead until above a large bowl. Turn right onto a good dirt road which descends to Font Moli.

Day 2: Fuente Partagas to Castell de Castells

5 to 5½ hours, 22.5km

From Fuente Partagas walk east up the zigzags, then continue to Pensión El Trestellador as described at the end of Day 1. From El Trestellador, head downhill to the C3313. Turn left through Benimantell and right (north) through Beniardá, passing a swimming pool and fuente before crossing the Río de Beniardá. Turn right to take the road beside Embalse de Guadalest past possible *camp sites* and fork left (north) where the road meets the Barranco de las Cuevas. Fork right shortly afterwards, keeping to the sealed road as it climbs to a pumping station, where a dirt road on the right leads up to Puerto del Castillo. You've now been walking for three hours.

To the right (east) a track leads up onto the Sierra de Aixorta; to the left (west) are ruins of Castillo de la Serrella and straight ahead a forestry track leads down to Fuente Bota in Castell de Castells (a short cut).

Turn left and head west along a dirt road that zigzags and climbs for 30 minutes to a crest. The stunning views ahead are of the Barranco de la Canal descending from Mallá de Llop (1361m) on Sierra de Serrella. High on the cliffs behind you are the ruins of **Castillo de la Serrella**, one of the last strongholds of the Muslims in the La Marina region. The cistern remains intact, but be wary if you climb to the exposed lookout – the walls are 500 years old and the southern cliffs sheer. From the castle, a dirt road leads west towards Barranco de la Canal before descending north to meet a sealed road a little more than 3km west of Castell de Castells.

El Castellet camping ground (☎ 96 551 80 67) is directly south of the village, behind the swimming pool. English speakers may wish to stay overnight at the *Pensión Castells* (☎ 96 551 82 54) on Calle San Vincente 18. Doubles cost 6000 ptas, breakfast 500 ptas. The owners, Camilla and Martin Darburn, have extensive knowledge of the area and run adventure holidays. *Tasca Bigot Vell* (☎ 96 551 8216) on Avenida de Alcoy is another option. *Bar-Restaurant La Macarena*, Calle Mayor 23, has a good menu and the street outside is marked for Raspat, a Valencian version of the Basque game of handball in which strapped hands are used to strike the ball down the street.

Side Trip: Sierra de Aixorta Loop
6 hours, 14.5km
From Puerto del Castillo ascend east on a well made forestry track past Fuente La Umbría (it's difficult to find: after 700m, the track descends to a right-hand bend and the fuente is 40m below the road about 50m further east), a beautiful, overhanging cliff (a possible *camp site*) and a well kept *casita* (small farm shack). Continue east below Aixorta's magnificent cliffs, with views north of Arc del Atanços and across to Castillo de Bolulla and Castillo de Tarbena. After 45 minutes, the road starts to bend and a track on the right leads up to the shady Fuente de Teixos, a good *camp site*.

From the western end of the picnic area, follow the marked track south-west up to a col. **Peña Alta** (1218m) is a rocky scramble west-north-west from here, but the views (especially across to Sierra Bernia and the Mediterranean) are worth the effort. From

the col traverse west, not losing too much height, past a ruined farmhouse and threshing circle, then bear right along a small canal which descends to the saddle El Pas del Xic and a large threshing circle, from where a more distinct path leads north-west to the casita passed earlier and the forestry track leading down to Castell de Castells.

For an alternative route, don't turn left but turn right (east), then take the first left (north) down a forestry track that descends to agricultural land close to El Somo (886m). Once on the valley floor, turn left off the forestry road onto a lesser track and head north-west over a hillock, past a ruined farmhouse, left at a T-junction and descend to the new road which links Castell de Castells (2.5km to the west) and Tárbera.

Day 3: Castell de Castells to Callosa
6½ to 7 hours, 16.5km
Retrace the last stage of the Sierra de Aixorta Loop until you reach the main forestry road that descends from Sierra de Aixorta. Turn left onto it (this track eventually emerges at the 7km mark on the Castell de Castells road) and follow it through a number of zigzags and past a large farmhouse to a flat area of cleared land beyond which the road passes between two pines. Narrow, rocky gorges lie to the south-east and south-west. Proceed south-east across the clearing, heading towards Arc del Atanços (a natural rock arch on the eastern side) on a track that climbs diagonally up the western side of the gully and through a huge rock gateway. Once in a flatter, boggy area, cross the stream and climb west to a set of ruins marked by a solitary pine. Continue south-east to an overgrown track that passes another solitary pine before being joined by a track from the right. The severity of the surrounding terrain, dominated by cliffs and deep ravines, is not reflected on the SGE 1:50,000 map, and the views are stunning. Continue to traverse south-east, descending slightly, then traverse south to a small saddle at the beginning of a rocky spur

(a large cairn marks the spot). To the east, through the multitude of ravines and sheer drops, a forestry track picks its way south from El Somo to **Bolulla**. This is an alternative route to Callosa, and further tracks from Bolulla also offer a short cut to Fuentes del Algar.

From the saddle, descend south-west from a faint path into a deep, terraced gully. Turn left and follow the tumbling stream on a path marked with yellow-and-white trail markers south-east around the buttress of **Morro Blau** (1125m), across a spur that emanates from that peak, and down to a wide track close to some farm buildings. The marked trail cuts back west before turning south and zigzagging down the eastern side of a wooded gully to a sealed road. Turn right and walk past two reservoirs down to a T-junction. Turn left for Callosa.

Sierra de Bernia

Duration 6½ to 7½ hours
Distance 12km
Standard Hard
Start/Finish Fuentes del Algar
Public Transport Yes
Summary A hard but extremely enjoyable ridge walk requiring a degree of nerve and agility, but offering excellent views across La Marina mountains and down to the coast – Benidorm looks oddly magnificent from Bernia peak.

This exhilarating, one day traverse of the jagged western ridge of Sierra de Bernia begins at the popular Fuentes del Algar, 3km from Callosa. A few simple climbing moves and a head for heights are required, but the route is not beyond the average walker and is well marked with cairns and trail markers. Extensions to and deviations from the route are possible including a complete loop of the sierra and an exit south down to the sea (though ridge walking with a heavy pack is not recommended).

See the introduction to the La Marina Alta walk earlier in this section for more details of the history of the area, when to walk and the maps you will require.

PLANNING
Maps
The IGN *Tárbera* No 822-III 1:25,000 map covers the walk along the Sierra de Bernia.

PLACES TO STAY & EAT
The waterfalls and gorges of the Fuentes del Algar are a good place to relax after the walk. There's a well equipped *camping ground* (600 ptas per person including entrance to the Fuentes del Algar) and restaurants and bars are on the valley floor.

For information on food and accommodation in Callosa, see Places to Stay & Eat in the La Marina Alta walk.

GETTING TO/FROM THE WALK
UBESA buses leave the Avenida Europa in Benidorm for Fuentes del Algar (via Callosa) at 9.35 am, noon and 5.05 pm. The journey takes 30 minutes from Benidorm and 10 minutes from Callosa. The bus stop is 20 minutes walk from the main gorge and 30 minutes from the camping ground. Buses rarely wait for long before returning to Benidorm. The last returning service leaves at 6.20 pm. Though this gives enough time to complete the walk in one day from Benidorm if you hurry, it's far better to spend the night at Fuentes del Algar or Callosa, 40 minutes walk away, and take the time to explore Bernia properly.

THE WALK
The walk entails 976m of ascent. From the *camping ground*, walk up the hill. Ignore the first left turn but take the second, which heads north before forking right onto a dirt road overlooking the camping ground. Follow the yellow-and-white trail markers right onto a path and up a scree slope – reaching a sign for Cova del Bardalet in 20 minutes – then east past a ruined farmhouse and threshing circle and onto a wide track. Where the track descends south in a clearing, a path (slightly hidden) leads north up

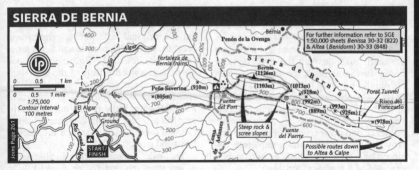

to **Fortaleza de Bernia**, which is reached after 20 minutes.

The fort was built for King Felipe II in 1562, but was subsequently occupied by Muslims escaping persecution and expulsion. Felipe III had it dismantled in 1612 to deny the fugitives the use of it, but substantial sections remain and provide emergency shelter. East of the fort is Fuente del Fuente, a not-very-private *camp site*.

From the ruins, head north-east and zigzag up to the top left corner of a scree slope where red arrows point north-west along a cliff-edge path. This rounds the western buttress of Sierra de Bernia, then ascends east straight up the rock, gaining the ridge after some simple climbing. Then it's a straightforward (30 minute) walk to **Bernia** peak (1126m) and a pleasant traverse across the 1103 and 1013m peaks – though keep to the northern side of the ridge when crossing the jagged gap between the two lower peaks.

Shortly before the 1007m peak, descents to the north and south are marked. The southern descent cuts back south-west into a wide gully that narrows to a boulder field. It is not difficult if approached from the eastern side of the gully which descends onto the very top of the boulder field. Halfway down the boulder field a marked path leads west back to Fortaleza de Bernia.

The more popular route descends to the north on a path that swings north-west, then east below the cliffs down to a broad track

leading to the hamlet of **Bernia**, where there are several *bar-restaurants*. Shortly before the hamlet, a track on the left leads back west to Fortaleza de Bernia. Retrace your steps from Fortaleza de Bernia to Fuentes del Algar.

Els Ports

While the walled town of Morella dominates the cultural and physical landscape of Els Ports, it's its network of footpaths and long-distance trails that makes walking in this mountainous region attractive. Morella is a fantastic launching point for walks in the area, which for the most part are not concerned with peak bagging but rather a matter of crossing mountain passes, walking along ancient tracks and walled lanes, traversing along cliff tops and negotiating long river valleys. This is sparsely populated country and walking in Els Ports can feel extremely remote, despite the generous local village hospitality and the 'real' Spain (to use a cliché), usually just a couple of hours away.

HISTORY

Morella is one of Spain's oldest towns, in one of the country's earliest inhabited regions. Prehistoric cave paintings at Morella la Vella mark the place where the region's first inhabitants are thought to have lived and evidence of Mediterranean man has also been found in the Río Cenía gorge close to

VALENCIA

Bellestar. Furthermore, archaeologists believe that the walking path snaking up from the Río Cenía has been used since 300 BC.

At 1000m above sea level and sitting on the main road through the mountains to Zaragoza (Saragossa), the fairy-tale town of Morella has long been the capital of Els Ports. People and produce travelling through the area usually passed through the city's gates, enabling the city to maintain its influence and power. Perched on a hill top, crowned by a castle and completely enclosed by a wall, Morella is an outstanding example of a medieval fortress.

A deep cultural history is reflected in the numerous religious and civic monuments in and around Morella – particularly impressive is the Gothic Basílica de Santa María la Mayor –which stem from the power of the church after the Reconquista. This was helped by King Jaume I, who ordered the construction of the first Cistercian foundation in Valencia, the Monasterio Santa María de Benifassá in La Tinença de Benifassá (also known as the 'Seven Settlements of Benifassá') shortly after the end of Muslim domination. The abbot was given direct control over the surrounding villages. Today the monastery is still used by Carthusian nuns, and religious monuments, sanctuaries and *ermitas* (chapels) are found across Els Ports.

The contemporary picture is again one of rural dereliction, with the pull of the cities depleting the local population. In an effort to keep mountain communities together, the EU and the Spanish government provide grants for village maintenance and housing renovation – the hope is that this will in turn boost rural tourism. However, as housing in Spain is typically passed down through families, much of the property in rural Els Ports now serves as second homes for city dwellers. Much of Fredes and El Boixar is deserted in winter.

NATURAL HISTORY

In the north-eastern corner of the province of Castellón, Els Ports is a region of rough limestone peaks, sharp ravines and wide gorges. A lot of the holm, gall and kermes oaks may have gone, but in the more remote valleys original oak forests remain and beeches, yew, holly, poplars and Scots pines can also be found. El Boixar was named after the boxwood forests of the surrounding area, which once provided wood for craftsmen making ploughing equipment and tableware. Little of this once magnificent forest is left, though the route to nearby Coratxá takes walkers through a tunnel of boxwood trees.

This wild, remote area has an abundance of unique plants and you're more likely to see a lynx, wildcat or wild boar here than anywhere else in Valencia (wild boar and Spanish ibex have been known to forage in the mountain villages). Birds to look out for include the golden eagle, the tawny vulture and numerous falcons (which nest on mountain peaks), robins, coal tits and nightingales.

PLANNING
Books

There aren't any English-language walking guides to the region, though most major Spain guides mention Morella. In Spanish, *Els Ports de Morella y Benifassá – Ports de Beceite* describes some walking routes in the region, while *Las Rutas del Cid* by Guillermo García recreates the journeys of the legendary Castillian nobleman (see the boxed text 'El Cid' in the introduction to this chapter). Also useful are the *Topo-Guía* series which detail the different sections of the GR7.

Information Sources

The tourist office in Morella (☎ 964 17 30 32) at Torre de San Miguel sells the *Els Port* map (950 ptas) referred to in the following Maps section, and can offer advice on accommodation throughout the area. It also sells a range of walking and mountain biking route guides.

Morella's Web site (www.morella.net) has some basic information. For more detailed information, contact the Centre Excursionista de Valencia (see Information Sources in the introduction to this chapter).

Els Ports Loop

Duration 4 to 5 days
Distance 91.5km
Standard Medium
Start/Finish Morella
Public Transport Yes
Summary From the medieval, walled city of Morella, this flexible walk loops through 'the region of the mountain passes' along walled paths, crossing through spectacular gorges and over narrow passes.

For much of the beginning and end of this walk the route follows the red-and-white trail markers of the GR7 long-distance path, which runs almost the whole length of Valencia. From Fredes the yellow-and-white trail markers typical of the PR routes take over and lead through Portell de l'Infern before looping through the picturesque villages of La Tinença de Benifassá to El Boixar.

Days 3 and 4 are long, but the duration of all the stages can easily be altered by allowing another day to complete the walk. A number of alternative routes avoid too much repetition on this out-and-back route, as well as wet feet on Day 2 (between November and April) where the GR7 follows the course of the Barranco de la Gatellera for a solid two hours.

Refugio Font Ferrera, beyond Fredes on the GR7, is a good launching point for walks north-east across Els Ports, and the paths around El Boixar are worth at least two days exploration.

PLANNING
When to Walk

Els Ports experiences far harsher winters and milder summers than one would expect from a region so close to the Mediterranean. The main walking season is from spring to late autumn, though both ends of the season are susceptible to the occasional snow shower. Between November and April the rivers and *barrancos* (gullies or

ravines) flow. Late April to June is probably the best time to walk, though walking through the oak woodlands in early autumn is recommended.

Maps

The greater part of the walk is covered by the Piolet *Els Port* 1:40,000 map available at the Morella tourist office. This shows footpaths, forestry tracks and PR and GR routes to good effect, though the positions of a few roads and geographical features differ from the SGE maps for the area. Changes to GR and PR routes and numbers are not shown. Also necessary is the SGE *Morella* No 30-21 (545) map. Little of this area is covered by the IGN 1:25,000 series. (See also Maps and Books under Information in the introduction to this chapter.)

PLACES TO STAY & EAT

The walk begins and ends in Morella. The cheapest place to stay (and eat) here is *Fonda Morena* (☎ 964 16 01 05, Calle San Nicolás 12). Singles/doubles cost 1400/2800 ptas and there is a menu del día of 900 ptas. Consequently, it's always full. *Hostal El Cid* (☎ 964 16 01 25), just inside Portal de Sant Mateu, is a spartan, abrupt affair, but usually has vacant rooms (1600/3200 ptas). The bar is full of retired men playing cards. *Pensión La Muralla* (☎ 964 16 02 43) is just round the corner. Built in the 16th century as the cardinal's palace, *Hotel Cardinal Rum* (☎ 964 17 30 85) on Cuesta Suñer is well worth a splurge. It charges 4500/7500 ptas.

There's a free *camp site* (with one tap) north of the castle beside the municipal swimming pool. Entrance to the swimming pool (and showers) costs 300 ptas.

The town's best restaurant is *Restaurante Casa Rouge*, Segura Barreda 8. The local specialities include *sopa morellana con buñuelos* (broth with dumplings) and *gallina trufada* (chicken with locally dug truffles). Expect to pay upwards of 2500 ptas.

Basic supplies can be bought in Morella and camping gas cartridges are available from Regalos Ma Mercedes on Calle de la

Virgen. A number of banks are along Calle Blasco de Alagón, and there is a post office at Calle San Nicolás 13.

GETTING TO/FROM THE WALK

The easiest way to get to Morella from the south is via Castellón. Trains to Castellón from Valencia (480 ptas) leave Estacíon del Norte every 30 minutes. From Castellón, buses leave for Morella (1055 ptas) from Calle Maestro Ripollés, next to Plaza de Fadrell, 20 minutes from the train station. On weekdays during summer Autos Mediterráneo (☎ 964 22 05 36) buses depart at 7.15 am, 1.25 and 3.30 pm (the 3.30 pm is the only service on Saturday).

If coming from the north, head to Vìnaros on the coast, which also has excellent rail connections – almost hourly services to Tarragona and direct services to Barcelona, Madrid (5100 ptas, 5½ hours) and Alicante – and then catch one of three Autos Mediterráneo buses to Morella (670ptas). Be warned that the Vìnaros train station (☎ 964 25 02 02) is a good 25 minute walk out of the town centre (if you

are returning to Vìnaros by bus, tell the driver and he'll stop before entering the town centre).

Monday to Friday during the summer, buses from Morella to Vìnaros and Castellón leave at 7.30, 11.30 am and 4 pm. There's an 11.30 am departure on Saturday and Sunday. There are also occasional Autos Mediterráneo buses to Alcañiz in Aragón (phone for details).

THE WALK
Day 1: Morella to Villabona
6 to 6½ hours, 22km

Go through Portal de Sant Mateu and follow the red-and-white markers of the GR7 down an alley, then left along a road to a T-junction and the N232. From 50m south of the junction, a dirt track leads east past a dog kennel to Masía San Vincente, an old mill above a fuente built in 1410. The marked route then leads east over the hill and down to a dirt track. Turn right, then left along the N232, forking left onto a dirt road before a bridge, then right across a stream beneath a grove of poplars. Continue north-east to the Río

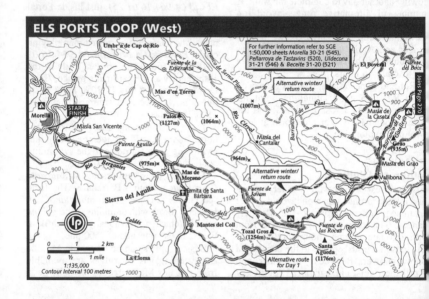

Bergantes. Cross it and walk upstream to a beautiful waterfall below a farmhouse.

Here, the route splits. The GR7 continues along the main track and offers an alternative route to Villabona (see Day 4), while green trail markers (that soon vanish) lead south-west across a field to a minor road. Cross the stream and small rock wall and head west through a meadow and into a surreal landscape dotted with *cádec* (*Juniperus oxyledrus*) that look like escapees from an ornamental garden.

Follow the Río Bergantes south through a narrow, wooded valley and meadow (north of Ermita de Santa Bárbara) and cross to the true right bank of the river. Then, before a yew copse, turn left (south-east) down a track above a walled stream, heading past a farmhouse to a ruined house and ermita before looping east to a minor road. Turn left and after a 3km walk along the road, turn left again along a dirt road leading west around the southern flank of **Tozal Gros** (1254m). Directly south of the peak, cut up through the scrub to the triangulation point and great views of the Sierra del Monte, Turmell and Morella.

Walk north from the summit, then head west along the ridge until you reach a goatherd's shelter. Double back along the GR7, which descends south-east through oak woodland to Fuente de las Rocas and a possible *camp site*. The GR7 is now well marked and leads off the main track, south down a spur and east around several gullies, through a group of houses to a road. Cross the road and pick up a well worn path that zigzags down a gully to the **Río Cérvol** and **Villabona**.

The *Hostal-Restaurante La Carbonera* (☎ 964 17 20 00) is on Plaza Sant Antoni. Singles/doubles cost 2000/4000 ptas and there is also in the plaza a lively *bar-restaurant*. Villabona has one basic shop.

Day 2: Villabona to Fredes
6½ to 7 hours, 20km
Turn right out of the hostal, past the school, then right onto a road leading north to a ford across the Barranco de la Gatellera.

Take the road up the gorge's eastern side, then follow the GR7 up an ancient path emerging west of Masía del Grao farmhouse. Walk to the dirt road and turn left, then right (north) and begin walking upstream along Barranco de la Gatellera. By continuing either left or right along the dirt road that crosses the stream, you can take one of two alternative routes (not described, but indicated on the map).

A fuente is reached after 15 minutes. For the next 1¼ hours follow the GR7 along the dry riverbed until an unmarked path on the true left (east) bank cuts up and around a set of waterfalls and a fork in the river. Continue north-east, bearing left through a bowl (30 minutes later), then up to a dirt road and a farmhouse perched on a spur. East of this point, the ground drops down to the Arroyo de Bel in a dramatic gorge. Looking south, a dirt road (the eastern alternative route mentioned previously) leads south to Villabona.

Head north-east from the farmhouse, then turn right onto a marked path. This zigzags up the pine-covered slope past another farmhouse onto a dirt road that winds north-east to a junction. A fuente is quickly reached by turning left (the western alternative route), but continue straight on, past a vague left turn and across the next junction along what is in fact the Penarroya de Tastavins Villabona. The GR7 peels off to the right and leads north-east across a clearing, past a wall and out into a large bowl. Meadows, terraced in places, and a muddy spring lie to the south (a beautiful *camp site* if clean water could be found).

Continue north-east across the bowl, then right onto a forestry track that zigzags between the summit of Aguila (1248m) and a lesser peak (1225m) before turning left and winding roughly north to a sealed road. Cross the road and head north-east onto the hill and then through waist-high scrub to **El Boixar** (Bojar). Below the village is a fuente, and there's a bar on the road above it – but don't expect it to be open in winter.

Walk past Casa-Refugio El Boixar, through the village, across the road and down (south-east) a walled lane to a junction. Turn left along a track past an orchard to the Barranco del Canal. Pick up a rough path on the true left (west) bank heading downstream and joining a wide dirt track above the true left (west) bank. After 15 minutes, bear right, skirting a meadow and a large, ruined farmhouse, and climb steeply through holm oak and pine forest to a viewpoint. This is followed by a heavily terraced saddle, complete with a couple of ruins and a fuente (a possible *camp site*). Join a dirt

road leading east to **Fredes**, which is reached after 40 minutes.

Fredes hasn't any accommodation, but suitable *camp sites* abound. At the time of writing, a *casa rural* was being built by José, a keen walker and owner of *Bar Santa María* (☎ *977 72 90 22*). Phone for up-to-date information.

If the casa rural is not yet open, you'll need to walk an extra three hours (6km) to Refugio Font Ferraro along the GR7 (see the side trip on the opposite page).

ELS PORTS LOOP (East)

Side Trip: Refugio Font Ferrera
3 hours, 12km

The route is well marked as it winds up around the gullies and cliff tops of **Roca Blanca** before descending through the Reserva Nacional de Caza to the *Refugio Font Ferrera* (☎ *977 26 71 10 or mobile 908 63 46 74*). Bunks are 1200 ptas per person; there's a kitchen and hot water. Open daily between June and October and at weekends year-round. Phone ahead to secure a bunk. For Spanish speakers, Gabriel (warden and accomplished mountaineer) is a mine of information. (A worthwhile side trip from here is described in Other Walks at the end of this chapter.)

Day 3: Fredes to El Boixar
6½ to 7 hours, 21.5km

Heading south-east from Fredes, south from Bar Santa María, two paths wind their way to Embalse de Ulldecona. The first soon peels off east into the gorge to reach the source of the Barranco del Salt, while the PRV75.16 (marked as the PR16 on the *Els Ports* map) climbs over a saddle to a ruined farmhouse and a dramatic viewpoint, before cutting east into the Reserva Nacional de Caza (unmarked on all maps) and then south-east below overhanging cliffs through the Portell de l'Infern. This traverse gives splendid views down to the Barranco del Salt. Idyllic as it would be to stay overnight in the caves (there is a fuente in one), camping here is prohibited.

Once through the Portell de l'Infern, the path zigzags south, then heads south-east parallel to the pinnacles of Punta Sola d'en Brull. Towering cliffs soon appear on the left as the track follows the Barranco de la Ronyosa to Embalse de Ulldecona. Shortly before reaching the lake, a track leads right over to the **Monasterio de Santa María de Benifassá** (the church is open between 1 and 3 pm on Thursdays).

Once beside the lake, turn right and head south (past an official *camp site*) and turn right onto a sealed road. Left, beside the dam, is *Mesón-Hotel Molí l'Abad* (☎ *977 71 34 18*), which dates back to the 15th

century and can cater for up to 160 diners. There is expensive accommodation for 18 guests. *Camping La Tinença*, also run by the hotel, is 2km east.

Walk west along the road, then left down the driveway of Vivers Forestals Forn del Vidre, a forestry nursery (Monasterio de Santa María de Benifassá is further along the road). Ford the river, then fork left through metal gates and loop right (west) around the old mill on a track that follows the Río Cenía upstream. Cross the river after 30 minutes and pick up a path that winds west beneath sandstone cliffs (and soaring raptors). Fork left (south-west) where the river divides, past Fuente Canalenta (unreliable in summer) and across the river onto an ancient path that leads up the side of the gorge to Bellestar. The village has a couple of bar-restaurants, *Mesón Bellestar* (☎ *977 72 90 92*) and *Font de Sant Pere* (☎ *977 71 33 04*). Phone ahead in winter.

West of the village, yellow-and-white markers lead to Pobla de Benifassá, which has a grocery shop, a municipal swimming pool and a couple of bar-restaurants (try *Fonda la Morena*). *Hotel Tinença de Benifassá* (☎/fax *977 72 90 44*) provides the only (expensive) accommodation.

At the western end of Calle Mayor in Poble de Benifassá, the PRV75.4 (well marked with yellow-and-white trail markers) leads north-west along a dirt road parallel to a stream. Turn right at a T-junction and ascend north-west up to a cliff-top sealed road which links El Boixar and Bellestar (reached after about an hour). El Boixar is a further 1km north-west along a flat road – a couple of marked short cuts ease the final push. *Casa-Refugio El Boixar* (☎ *977 70 31 40*) on Calle Mayor has doubles for 3700 ptas per person and dormitory space for 2900 ptas, which includes breakfast, dinner and wine.

Day 4: El Boixar to Morella
7 to 8 hours, 28km

On the return leg to Morella, a couple of variations avoid some repetition of the route.

Dirt roads on either side of the Barranco de la Gatellera lead to Villabona (as outlined in Day 1). The more complicated of these two alternatives is the route that leads west from the GR7 and follows yellow-and-white trail markers to Fuente del Boix, then takes a well used dirt road over El Boveral back to Villabona.

From the Telefónica building outside Villabona, a PR route marked with yellow-and-white trail markers (faint in places) offers an alternative way back to the Tozal Gros ridge. Heading west, the path quickly rises above the Río Cérvol to an ermita. Turn left soon afterwards and cross the river via a large boulder. Continue upstream (west) alongside a fine stone wall, crossing three streams before turning left into an overgrown gully (steps have been cut into the turf).

Cross a dirt track and continue south-west up through a gorge. After 30 minutes, cross to the true left bank to meet overhanging cliffs which in places have been turned into livestock pens. Fork right at the end of the gorge and follow the yellow-and-white markers up a walled stream, then south-west through oak woodland on a wide, walled lane. Go through a gate, past a farmhouse and into woodland and a gully. Turn right onto a dirt road and loop west around to **Fuente de Jovani**. A signpost and shrine on the ridge are reached after another 15 minute climb. Morella is visible to the west.

Red-and-white trail markers run off in three directions. Follow the set heading north-west to the northern side of a gully. After climbing a small incline and heading north-west through oak woodland, the route becomes a steady descent west to a sealed road. For the few minutes after passing through Mas de Moreno farm there are spectacular views of Morella, raised above the surrounding landscape.

Turn left (south) onto the road, pass a copse of poplar trees, then turn right onto a farm track and retrace your steps to Morella.

Other Walks

LA MARINA
Costa Blanca Way

Devised by the Costa Blanca Mountain Walkers (for contact details, see Information Sources in the introduction to La Marina), this long (over 130km) six day route zigzags south across La Marina from Villalonga (reached by bus from Gandía) to Sella (there are two buses a day from here to Villajoyosa on the coast) mostly on good forestry roads. Included is a traverse of Caballo Verde ridge, a descent on Mozarabic trails to the Barranco del Infierno (a collapsed cave system) and side trips to a number of ancient castles. Accommodation can be found in mountain villages en route though be prepared to camp. In addition to the other La Marina maps you'll need the SGE *Játiva* No 29-31 (795) map at 1:50,000.

Sierra de Serrella

The magnificent Sierra de Serrella ridge on the northern side of the Valle de Guadalest, parallel to Sierra de Aitana, has tremendous scope for exploration. Easy access is from Puerto de Confrides (4km west of Confrides) and it is possible, I was told, to traverse the whole of the Sierra de Serrella to Castillo de la Serrella. The northern slopes, lined by a row of *aguille* (jagged peaks), have other interesting possibilities; one would be an ascent of Plá de la Casa and a descent to Cuatroretondeta, where the Fonda Els Fraires (☎ 96 551 12 34) provides accommodation. All this opens up the mouth-watering possibility of a huge loop from Benimantell, along the Sierra de Aitana north to the Sierra de Serrella and then a long traverse east to the sea.

Puig Campana

Seen from the Sierra de Aitana, Puig Campana (1408m) has a classic shape and begs to be climbed. It may be a slog, but if you want to bag the second-highest peak in the region and sample unrivalled views it's a must. Most ascents begin from Finestrat, 12km north-west from Benidorm. If you're experienced enough it's possible to descend via a 300m scree run to a climbers' hut on the northern slope. This walk can be extended east to include an ascent of Monte Ponoch (1181m) and an exit to Polop, which is serviced by regular UBESA buses.

ELS PORTS

Chiva de Morella & Morella la Vella

These two simple day walks take in interesting local history while giving a taste of the surrounding countryside. The first walk heads north-east from Morella, passing the 13th century aqueduct on the way, to the picturesque village of Chiva de Morella and the Santuario de Roser before returning to the city. The second walk heads north-west to the summit of Morella la Vella and the prehistoric cave paintings close by. Both walks could be incorporated into a longer loop through Forcall on the PRV2 and are covered by the SGE map *Morella* No 30-21 (545).

Ares del Maestre Loop

A number of variations are possible along this route, which follows the GR7 south through Ares del Maestre, Benasal and Culla and then heads north-west to Villafranca del Cid on a PR trail. From the beautiful village of Villafranca del Cid, it's a matter of negotiating the forestry tracks and paths to Portell de Morella (one of the highest settlements in the entire region) and then to Morella. Allow four to five days for the

loop, though with so many attractions (Neolithic cave paintings, historical and religious monuments, and ancient oak forest) it should not be hurried. There are plenty of places to stay en route. SGE maps *Morella* No 30-21 (545), *Albocacer* No 30-22 (570), *Villafranca del Cid* No 29-22 (569) and *Forcall* 29-21 (544) are required.

Ascent of Caro

This walk leaving from Refugio Font Ferrera (see the side trip at the end of Day 2 on the Els Ports Loop walk) heads north-east to the summit of Caro (1442m) on the GR7 and returns to Fredes on a PR route (marked as PR82 on the *Els Ports* map) via Embalse de Ulldecona and the Portell de l'Infern. It's easy to adapt this route to finish at La Sénia and begin to explore the El Maestrat district southeast of Fredes. There are refugios at Les Casetes and south of Caro. Allow three days to complete this route comfortably, possibly spending the third night camped beside Embalse de Ulldecona. Poilet's *Els Port* map at 1:40,000 covers the whole walk.

Mallorca

Mallorca is one of an archipelago of four inhabited and several smaller, deserted islands called the Islas Baleares (Balearic Islands, or Illes Balears in Catalan) which spangle the western Mediterranean off Spain's eastern coast. Menorca, the north-easternmost of the chain, is distinguished mainly by its ceaseless winds and prehistoric megaliths. Ibiza and Formentera at the south-western end are warmer, sandier and trendier, sharing with Menorca only their near-flatness. Of the four major islands, only Mallorca offers exceptional walking.

Largest and longest developed of the Islas Baleares, Mallorca measures 75km from north to south and 100km from west to east. Each year the resident population of 600,000 is swollen by more than seven million visitors. But bald statistics are misleading: most visitors are packed into the beach resorts of the south and north-east, while the upland areas of the north-west remain magically unspoiled and underpopulated. Here, the imposing Serra de Tramuntana (where 'serra' in Catalan means mountain range) – with more than 40 peaks rising above 1000m – dominates, its skirts trailing down to abrupt cliffs which plunge into the sea. This is where the good walking is.

HISTORY

Archaeological evidence from cave dwellings reveals that Mallorca has been inhabited for at least 7000 years. During the Bronze Age, people began to construct stone houses in small, extended family groupings, usually including one or more *talayots* (tall cones of stone). Archaeologists still speculate about the function of these stones, found in profusion in Menorca but also evident on Mallorca. Were they distant precursors of the 17th century defensive watchtowers, called *talayas* or *atalayas*, which protrude round its coast? Were they ritualistic monuments built over a funerary chamber? Or

HIGHLIGHTS

The Torrent de Pareis snakes its way through spectacular walking country.

- Clambering down the Torrent de Pareis, Mallorca's deepest gorge

- Strolling the Camino del Archiduque and enjoying the superb seascapes

- A pause to savour the views of the Sóller valley, way below, from the Mirador d'en Quesada

- Rewarding yourself with a celebratory ice cream at the end of the day at Sa Fabrica de Gelats in Sóller

could they even have been the piles of a wooden house of which no trace remains?

Exposed, underpopulated and difficult to defend, Mallorca, like Spain's Mediterranean coast and the other Islas Baleares, was occupied by wave after wave of invaders, evidence of whose passage you can see in Palma de Mallorca's excellent museum. Phoenicians, Carthaginians,

Romans, Visigoths and Arabs have all left their mark upon the island. Despite frequent changes of master, the island lies at the heart of the western Mediterranean sea routes and has at times been a prosperous and important trading centre.

The legacy of the Muslims from North Africa amounts to much more than the fine samples of pottery displayed in Palma's museum. It was the Muslims who built the first water channels for irrigation and introduced the *noria* (water wheel) to raise water from wells and underground reservoirs. They were also the first to construct the banks of terracing evident across the island, which increased cultivable space on the flanks of the steep valleys.

The Catalans first arrived with the invading army of Jaume I, king of Catalunya and Aragón, in 1229. The battle of Palma, in which more than 50,000 combatants are estimated to have been killed, put an end to more than three centuries of Muslim occupation.

After this cataclysm, Mallorca enjoyed two centuries of prosperity and relative peace. However, by the 15th century Spain's attention was being drawn more and more to its possessions in the Americas, to the neglect of its offshore Mediterranean islands. A long economic decline began and the islands were repeatedly battered by raiding Barbary pirates and Turkish warships.

In the 19th century Mallorca regained much of its prosperity both as a trading and manufacturing centre, only to share in Spain's general decline as the century closed. Mass tourism, which began as a trickle in the 1950s and has gushed in greater volume with every subsequent year, has been the economic saviour of the islands, but at very considerable environmental cost.

Throughout recent Mallorcan history the Serra Tramuntana, which also gives its name to the north-westerly wind that howls overhead in the depths of winter, was mainly the preserve of olive farmers (living in a handful of tiny stone-built farmhouses tucked below the mountain crests) of charcoal-burners and of *nevaters*, or snow-collectors. For more information on nevaters, see the boxed text

'Nevera: the Original Fridges' in La Marina Alta walk in the Valencia chapter). While olive farming survives, the other two industries have been abandoned. However, several ancient trails linking settlements, farmsteads and high pastures still exist. Many of the highland paths were originally constructed by the nevaters and most, at whatever level, have been extensively, if erratically, trail-marked by both local and foreign enthusiasts.

There's no great tradition of walking for pleasure among the Mallorcans (natives of

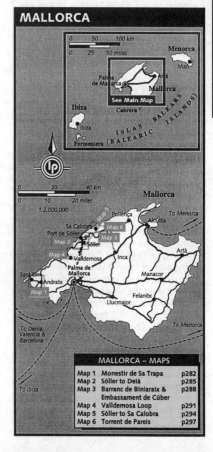

MALLORCA – MAPS		
Map 1	Monestir de Sa Trapa	p282
Map 2	Sóller to Delà	p285
Map 3	Barranc de Biniaraix &	p288
	Embassament de Cúber	
Map 4	Valldemosa Loop	p291
Map 5	Sóller to Sa Calobra	p294
Map 6	Torrent de Pareis	p297

Tourism Too Far?

In late 1998 an estimated 10% of Mallorca's population took to the streets to show their concern at the environmental and social impact of the island's sole significant industry – tourism.

The demonstration was supported by civic groups, the church, every opposition political party, and even some members of Partido Popular, the governing party. Several symptoms of the island's malaise brought people out. A newly constructed giant incinerator is already incapable of processing the 39,000 tonnes of garbage generated during peak summer months. Such a basic commodity as water now has to be shipped in from the Spanish mainland. In some rural parts – notably the prime Tramuntana walking area – what were once small farmsteads are now almost entirely first or second homes for northern Europeans, including an estimated 50,000 Germans. More generally, high property prices mean that young Mallorcans cannot afford to buy in their own birthplace. Economics apart, what touches a particularly raw nerve is that the Catalan language, so much a part of the islanders' identity, is in danger of being replaced in the capital and other coastal areas by Spanish – and by other even more remote tongues; the local government recently felt the need to pass a law banning signs and menus which are exclusively in English or German.

As Miquel Angel March, one of the organisers of the protest, eloquently phrased it, 'We want the local government to stop the island being destroyed and to protect what is still left of it from speculators and developers. That means saying no to more hotels, no to splitting up any more large farms into building plots for holiday homes, no to the motorway planned for the south of the island and no to more golf courses. If we continue to bring in ever more tourists, we'll be saying farewell to a whole way of life'.

Mallorca). Until relatively recently life was so hard for most and leisure time so limited that you walked for a purpose, to get where you needed to be, and not for the intrinsic pleasure of the journey. Two local organisations are doing their best to turn this around. Foment del Desenvolupament de Mallorca (FODESMA), a branch of the Consell Insular (the island's governing body), has produced a number of walk brochures exclusively in Catalan (see Maps later in the introduction to this chapter). The Grup Excursionista de Mallorca is an association of local walking enthusiasts (see Information Sources later in the introduction to this chapter). Despite their best efforts, however, nearly all the walkers you meet on the trails are foreign – the majority German.

FODESMA is developing a long-distance trail on the north side of the island from Andratx to Pollença. The project will link paths (such as the Camí del Castelló between Sóller and Deià and the Barranc de Biniaraix, both of which are described in this chapter) that have already been restored by teams of apprentice craftworkers. It will also create *refugios* (refuges or mountain huts) at one-day walking intervals. It will be a number of years before the final threads are joined but, once completed, the route promises to be a classic.

NATURAL HISTORY

The Islas Baleares, with similar climates, though varied geology, are much more homogeneous than Spain's other offshore territory, the Islas Canarias (Canary Islands), out in the Atlantic off the coast of Africa.

Mallorca (as well as Ibiza and Formentera) is not merely a continuation of the Andalucian mountains, also known as the Baetic Plate; it is also a consequence of tectonic movement as the African plate burrowed under the more static European one. Menorca, by contrast, has its geological roots further east in the upward thrust that produced Sardinia, off the coast of Italy.

In Mallorca's Serra de Tramuntana, limestone, uplifted from the sea floor by tectonic forces some 150 million years ago,

constitutes the core. Its north-facing crags and cliffs are much steeper than those facing south and in many places they make access to the coast impossible from the landward side. While there may be less karst than in, for example, the Picos de Europa, the serra's deep fissures, cracks and clefts have been fancifully – often forbiddingly – fashioned by wind and water. In the gullies and steep gulches, worn away by seasonal streams, you'll also find a topsoil of clay and marl.

La carrasca (evergreen oak), its leaves waxy and shiny to reduce evaporation in the heat of summer, is very different from its deciduous northern European cousin. Woods of its subspecies, the holm oak (*Quercus ilex*), give welcome shade at lower altitudes. In the past this was the tree preferred by charcoal-burners. Also thriving at the same level is the carob or locust bean (*Ceratonia siliqua*). Its seeds, which once served as food for livestock, are now mainly used as a supplement in chocolate and also as a guaranteed, flush-you-through laxative.

Nearer sea level and more restricted in its distribution, squat and more shrub than tree, the dwarf fan palm (*Chamaerops humilis*) fights for its corner, its fronds sharp and splayed just like a fan. You'll find it thriving in the north-west, on the Monestir de Sa Trapa walk, and in the north-east of the island.

The olive is tougher and can survive at higher levels. Some veterans are reputed to be more than 1000 years old. One of the joys of walking is happening upon their gnarled, twisted forms, worthy of Van Gogh's paintbrush. As you ascend, pines – a source of nourishment for squirrels and smaller mammals – begin to predominate. These trees, which appear ever more stunted and spindly as you ascend, survive up to about 1000m. The most common variety is the Aleppo pine (*Pinus halepensis*) which, despite its name, may have originated in the Islas Baleares and only later became established in Lebanon and Syria. Near the shore, in the salty soil which it favours, the tamarisk thrives. Wherever sweet water flows, elm, ash and poplar grow.

The main cultivated plants are fig trees – ponderous, pendulous and often supported by sturdy poles – and almonds, whose blossoms tint the countryside pink in springtime. There is also, of course, the ubiquitous olive. Orange and lemon trees (there's nothing more refreshing than a glass of fresh citrus juice along the route) proliferate, especially in the mild Sóller valley.

In springtime the hills blaze with the yellow of broom. Aromatic rosemary, with its characteristic blue flower, and wild rockroses stay in flower for much longer. At any level, asphodels colonise land low in nutritional value, their single, white flower with brown stipples swaying at the end of a tall stem.

Somewhere, sometime, you're bound to get your boots tangled in *Ampelodesmus mauritanica*, a grass with long, sharp-edged leaves, known locally as *callitx*.

Spring and autumn, when migratory birds use the islands as a staging post, are the best seasons for birdwatchers. Mallorca is particularly rich in birds of prey and you stand a good chance of spotting red kites, kestrels, black vultures, hawks and both Eleanor's and peregrine falcons.

Keen birdwatchers can contact fellow enthusiasts at the Grupo Ornitológico Balear (GOB), also known as the Grup Balear d'Ornitologia i Defensa de la Naturalesa, in Palma (☎ 971 72 21 77, fax 971 71 13 75).

Isolated from the main continental land mass millennia ago, Mallorca is home to a number of indigenous plants, reptiles and snails, many of which, due to their localised distribution, have no name in English.

CLIMATE

Mallorca enjoys a typical Mediterranean climate and Serra de Tramuntana, in which there is no peak higher than 1500m, is not significant enough to influence this appreciably.

The ideal months for walking are from late February to May, when the countryside is green and in blossom and the temperatures

MALLORCA

agreeable; or September and early October, after the summer crowds have gone but before the rains arrive.

Winter walking, when the average daily temperature rarely drops below 11°C, is by no means out of the question, and many aficionados actually prefer it. Routes are occasionally enlivened with a dusting of snow, and sometimes by a heavier fall. The major rains fall between late October and the end of February, when conditions can approach freezing at higher altitudes. But even December, the dampest month, has an average of only eight days of rain, a statistic that walkers from soggier climes regard with envy.

Between late June and August, when Mallorca receives its maximum number of visitors, daily average temperatures are around 25°C. Hiking the tops without even a bush for shade can be a sticky experience. But if summer, when there's no rain to speak of, is the only time you can get away, don't despair. Some walks, such as the descent of the Torrent de Pareis or the walk up the Barranc de Biniaraix, offer shade. And if you make an early enough start on others you can be cooling off in the sea by the time the sun reaches its zenith, thus contradicting the received wisdom that walking and beach lounging on Mallorca are mutually exclusive.

INFORMATION
Maps

In terms of large-scale maps, the IGN publishes a 1:200,000 map of the Islas Baleares (550 ptas) and one of Mallorca at 1:150,000 (800 ptas). If you just want to get a grip on the general lie of the land and the principal roads, you're better off picking up the free map *Las Islas Baleares* from any tourist office.

Relevant Instituto Geográfico Nacional (IGN) and Servicio Geográfico del Ejército (SGE) 1:25,000 and 1:50,000 maps are listed in the introduction to each walk. While both series are reliable for general topography, neither marks all significant paths; the 1:50,000 maps are particularly deficient. The *Mapa de Camins de Muntanya de la Valle de*

Sóller details paths in the Sóller area but is far from comprehensive.

FODESMA has produced a number of good brochures (300 ptas) in its series Itineraris a Peu Per La Serra de Tramuntana (Walking Routes in the Tramuntana Range) which, in addition to a large-scale plan of the walk and route description, highlight prominent features of interest along the route, as well as the geology, flora and fauna of the area. They're monolingual, however, and only really worth buying if you can gistread Catalan. The Consellería de Turisme's pamphlet *20 Walking Excursions in Mallorca* gives ideas for further walks but needs to be supplemented with a good map.

Discovery Walking Guides (also known as Warm Island Walking Guides), based in the UK, publishes three reliable maps, one specifically of the mountains of Mallorca, based upon IGN 1:25,000 originals together with a detailed route description in English.

Books

Walking in Mallorca by June Parker (Cicerone Press) describes more than 50 walks on the island. Great on background, it's extremely well researched and written and the text is easy to follow. Its deficiency is the spindly monochrome maps, which are difficult to read unless you're holding a better reference map in your other hand. *Mallorca* by Valerie Crespi-Green is a much slighter work. Designed as a catchall – for walkers, cyclists, picnickers and the car-bound – it has a little for everyone, but not enough for all. This said, it describes several worthwhile hikes and the colour maps at 1:40,000 are easy to follow.

If you read German, the venerable Herbert Heinrich, a long-time resident of Mallorca, has published no less than seven slim guidebooks, some of which have been translated into Spanish.

For those interested in birdwatching, whether as a hobby or just to add extra spice to a satisfying walk, *A Birdwatching Guide to Mallorca* and *A Birdwatching Guide to Menorca, Ibiza and Formentera*, both by Graham Hearl, are well worth slipping into the day-pack. Ken Stoba's *Birdwatching in Mallorca* from Cicerone Press is a worthy alternative to the former. *Wild Flowers of Majorca, Minorca and Ibiza* by Elspeth Beckett is the best guide for amateur botanists, but it's no longer easy to obtain.

For general cultural background it's worth borrowing from the library or a friend a copy of Robert Graves' sometimes sententious, scarcely integrated and increasingly time-bound *Majorca Observed*.

Information Sources

The Grup Excursionista de Mallorca (☎ 971 71 13 14), Carrer Can Cavalleria 17, has friendly members who are ready to chat. It has a good library and documentation centre. If you read or speak Spanish or Catalan you might like to drop by since the group can give you access to serious walkers. They're open from 7 to 9 pm on weekdays.

In Sóller, the tourist office (☎ 971 63 02 00) is helpful enough but not very clued up about walking. It's open from 9.30 am to 1.30 pm on weekdays. There's also a small, summer-only tourist office in Port de Sóller (☎ 971 63 30 42) on Passeig del Port. Both can provide useful leaflets on current bus and boat schedules and a list of places to stay.

La Casa del Mapa (☎ 971 46 60 61, fax 971 77 66 16) at Carrer Joan Maragall 3 in Palma is the sales centre of the IGN and has the most comprehensive selection of maps in the area. It's open from 9 am to 2 pm weekdays.

It's best to buy books before you set out. Failing this, Book Inn (☎/fax 971 71 38 98) at Calle Huertos 20 in Palma carries a few walking titles in English. If you can read Spanish, the best place is the Librería Fondevila (☎ 971 72 56 16) on Costa de la Pols, which also has a reasonable selection of maps.

In Sóller, Librería Calabruix (☎ 971 63 26 41) carries most of the recommended local guides and maps.

Place Names

Catalan is the mother tongue of most Mallorcans. However, since massive tourism is the lifeblood of the island, signs are often also, or only, in Spanish. We've used the form, whether Catalan or Spanish, which appears on signs or in brochures and timetables. Where you come across the alternative, the conversion is rarely a problem. See also Place Names & Terminology under Walking Routes in the Facts for the Walker chapter.

Warnings

Because of the porous limestone core of the island, water sources aren't always dependable and may be inconveniently located at the very beginning or end of a walk. Take plenty with you, especially in the hotter months.

Vicious thornbush or sharp callitx, the predominant grass, overgrow some paths, so consider wearing long trousers, however hot the day, to protect your legs – and make it a pair you don't mind shredding.

Lastly, access to footpaths may not be as free as in other walking regions that you are accustomed to (see the boxed text 'Mallorca's Blocked Passages' on the following page).

ACCOMMODATION & SUPPLIES

Better to bring your gear with you. If there's anything you've forgotten to pack, both Es Refugi at Vía Sindicat 21 and Intersport on Avenida Alexandre Rosselló in Palma carry a good range of walking gear and a smaller selection of walking books. The latter also has maps.

For the walks described in this chapter, Sóller is the most convenient base. Port de Sóller, at the other end of the tram line, is another alternative. You may also find yourself spending a night in the capital, Palma de Mallorca, on your way to and from the trails.

All the walks described in this chapter can be done in a day using one of these two towns as a base.

Palma de Mallorca

Hostal Apuntadores (☎ 971 71 34 91) on Carrer Apuntadors and its neighbour, *Hostal Ritzi* (☎ 971 71 46 10), are both excellent value. Singles/doubles at the former are

Mallorca's Blocked Passages

Until quite recently it was possible to do a magnificent circuit round the lip of the bowl of mountains in which Sóller nestles. But a farmer up on the tops has erected a series of locked gates to bar the way. It *is* possible to cross his territory but only as part of an organised group with a guide who pays the proprietor. It's not what walking, wild, free and harming no one, should be about.

Another favourite walk used to be the Puig Roig circuit, much of it following an old corniche path once used by smugglers. But here, too, property owners have blocked the route, allowing access on Sunday only. On another trail near the Monasteri de Lluc the landowner exacts a 500 ptas toll.

When we asked the Grup Excursionista de Mallorca, a friendly association of fellow walkers, why and how landowners can get away with restricting access, they said it was because groups of foreign walkers had abused the privilege. The tourist office in Sóller gave the same reason – while hastily adding that there were, of course, home-bred transgressors, too.

These parties are, in the main, highly responsible and organised groups of German walkers, numerous but harmless and ecologically aware. But there is little tradition of walking for walking's sake on the island. And there's no pressure group with the clout of the Ramblers Association in UK who, at the click of a barred gate, can drum up a posse of walkers to challenge closed footpaths and militate for freedom of access.

Miles Roddis

from 2200/3700 ptas; doubles with private shower are 4200 ptas. Hostal Ritzi has rooms at 2300/4200 ptas with shower, or doubles with shower/bath for 5000 ptas, and offers both laundry and kitchen facilities.

Sóller

Don't worry about the daytime crowds which more than double Sóller's population of 10,000 as the small train from Palma and the rickety tram from Puerto de Sóller decant their passengers. Come nightfall, when they've all retreated, calm returns to one of the most Mallorcan *pueblos* (villages) on the island.

Sóller has three places to stay. *Hostal Nadal* (☎/fax 971 63 11 80, Carrer Romaguera 29) has singles/doubles for 2000/3000 ptas (2400/4000 ptas with bathroom). *Casa Margarita* (☎ 971 63 42 14, Carrer Real 3) has singles for 2000 ptas and doubles from 3000 ptas, all with communal bathroom. The family-run *Hotel El Guía* (☎ 971 63 02 27), beside the train station, has rooms for 5700/8300 ptas, including breakfast. All three are popular walkers' haunts and it's advisable to book ahead except, paradoxically, between July and September, when most folk are stretched out on the beaches.

The *Celler Cas Carrete* restaurant, which occupies an old cart workshop, is a bargain with set menus for 850 ptas and 1250 ptas. One night, if not every night, refresh yourself with one of *Sa Fabrica de Gelats'* superb range of ice creams, many made with local fruit.

Port de Sóller

Port de Sóller has a wide selection of hotels but, by contrast, don't expect to find any vacancies there during the summer months. Both have good, but not very frequent, public transport connections.

GETTING THERE & AWAY

Several airlines including Air Europa and Spanair offer scheduled flights from major cities on the Spanish mainland to Palma de Mallorca, the cheapest and most frequent of which are from Barcelona and Valencia. Standard one-way fares are expensive – around 10,000 ptas. In the low season the occasional truly silly offer, such as 4000 ptas one way, comes up.

If you are travelling direct to Mallorca from Europe, charter flights are significantly cheaper than scheduled airlines. See Air in the Getting There & Away chapter for more information on direct and charter flights from outside the country.

Boat

Buquebús (☎ 902-41 42 42) is a new, sleek, high-speed ferry that rockets from Barcelona to Palma and back twice daily in just 3¼ hours. One-way tickets start at 8150 ptas (which means that it is often cheaper to book a return flight).

Otherwise, Trasmediterránea (☎ 902-45 46 45 for general information, ☎ 971 40 50 14 in Palma) is the major ferry company for the Islas Baleares. The Barcelona-Palma run has seven to nine services weekly and Valencia-Palma has six to seven services weekly. High-season fares (per person) range from 6660 ptas for a seat to 16,950 ptas for a twin cabin. Taking a small car costs 18,560 ptas.

During summer, Trasmediterránea also operates a 'Fast Ferry' service from Barcelona to Palma (8150 ptas for a seat; up to three services weekly), and Valencia to Palma (8150 ptas; four services weekly).

Flebasa (☎ 96 578 40 11 in Denia) operates a couple of daily ferries to Palma from Denia (between Valencia and Alicante) via Ibiza city, and from Vilanova i la Geltru (just south-west of Sitges on the Catalunya coast).

GETTING AROUND

Four trains a day (380 ptas) and one *tren turístico* (tourist train; 735 ptas) make the rattly 80 minute journey through a spectacular pass in the Serra de Tramuntana, connecting Sóller and Palma's station on Plaça d'Espanya.

An equally anachronistic and rumbly tram, with departures every 30 minutes until 9 pm, runs between Sóller and Port de Sóller.

Much of the island is accessible by bus and most services depart Palma from the main *estación de autobuses* (bus station; ☎ 971 71 13 93) on Plaça d'Espanya. An important exception is Bus Nord Balean (☎ 971 42 71 87), which serves towns along the north-west

coast including Deià and Sóller and has departures from Carrer del Arxiduc Lluis Salvador 1.

About 30 car rental agencies operate in Palma and you can also rent bicycles; a good mountain bike costs from 1200 ptas a day. Getting around the island by taxi is costly – prices are posted at taxi stopping points in many towns and villages.

Palma and the major resorts and beaches around the island are also connected by numerous boat and water-taxi services, required for the Sóller to Sa Calobra and Torrent de Pareis walks. See the Getting to/from the Walk sections for details of transport to and from the trailheads.

Monestir de Sa Trapa

Duration 4½ to 5 hours
Distance 12km
Standard Easy-Medium
Start Sant Elm
Finish S'Arracó
Public Transport Yes
Summary A robust ascent from the coastal resort of Sant Elm to the ex-Trappist monastery of Sa Trapa is followed by a more gentle inland return to the village of S'Arracó.

The coastal stretch of this walk, where more than 80 bird species have been recorded, is particularly rich for ornithologists; that's why a local ecological group, the Grup Balear d'Ornitologia i Defensa de la Naturalesa, purchased the dilapidated Monestir de Sa Trapa (Monastery of Sa Trapa) in 1980. With support from the Consell Insular and EU funding, it has renovated the monastery, its intricate system of irrigation, fed by a single stream, and the fine *bancales* (stone terracing).

The first part of the walk offers superb sea views to compensate for the huffing and puffing. You stand a good chance of seeing red kites, kestrels, alpine swifts and maybe even a hawk or peregrine falcon. Once you reach the *mirador* (lookout) at Cap Fabioler, it's flat or downhill all the way home, though the route is indistinct in a couple of places.

PLANNING
When to Walk
Better to avoid high summer since there's little shade until the final quarter of the walk.

Maps
The whole area is covered by the SGE *Andratx* No 37-27 (697) map at 1:50,000, though by no means all of the route is indicated.

What to Bring
Water – plenty of it – is essential since there are no springs en route. It's also well worth slipping your binoculars into your day-pack.

GETTING TO/FROM THE WALK
There are hourly buses from Palma to Andratx, which leave on the half-hour.

Buses leave Andratx for Sant Elm via S'Arracó at two-hourly intervals from 8.15 am until 6.15 pm, returning every two hours from 8.45 am until 6.45 pm. Keep in mind that this service may vary in winter. For the current bus schedule, ring Autocar Palma (☎ 971 20 45 04). Alternatively, you can take a taxi from Andratx to Sant Elm for about 2000 ptas.

THE WALK
From Sant Elm's bus terminus in Plaça Mossen Sebastiá Grau, head north-east up Avinguda de Sa Trapa, the road soon becoming a wide, dirt track. After 15 minutes, when you reach the farm of Ca'n Tomeví and a four-way junction with a signboard, go straight ahead along a narrow path and *not* right, as the sign indicates. (Both ways will, however, lead you to Sa Trapa.) The route recommended here makes for a rather

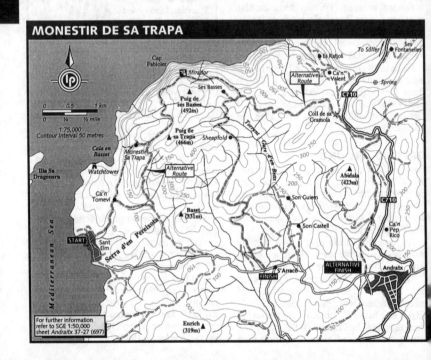

MONESTIR DE SA TRAPA

tougher ascent but it offers more shade and more spectacular views. (If you only fancy a short outing from Sant Elm, you can either ascend or descend to Sa Trapa by the alternative route.)

As the path comes out of the woods and onto a cliff, the steep stuff begins in earnest, as do the great views of the coast and the uninhabited island, Illa Sa Dragonera.

After about 1¼ hours, the track briefly levels out before leading up the side of another cliff, only to flatten out once again before the steep ascent of the last rocky crag. Just before the top, watch out for the red trail markers directing you right and up a series of large, steep boulders. Miss these and you'll find yourself facing a sheer drop to the sea.

Once over the brow the ruins of **Monestir de Sa Trapa** become visible barely 10 minutes walk away. The once-rich setting which induced a group of Trappist monks to establish their self-contained community here (see the boxed text on this page) is now bleak as a result of the devastating 1994 fire which left most of the pines no more than twisted, black fingers. Despite extensive replanting, and even though grasses and *montebajo* (scrub) are reasserting themselves, it will be a generation before the valley fully recovers. At the lower of the two miradors, beyond the monastery (1½ hours) and the old cereal mill, there's a simple plaque to one Joan Lliteras, who fell to his death when only 18.

Leave by the well defined track which mounts the eastern flank of the tight valley sweeping down to Sa Trapa. At a steep hairpin, where a sign indicates S'Arracó and Sant Elm, take instead the narrow path heading north, away from the bend. You're now at the heart of the area devastated by the 1994 fire, much of it replanted with young pines encased in chicken wire to protect them from feral goats, their principal threat.

After an undemanding ascent to 400m the route again levels out, letting you maintain a steady clip. At a giant cairn about 45 minutes from Sa Trapa, don't miss the brief diversion to the mirador at **Cap Fabioler**

Monestir de Sa Trapa

Expelled from France in 1791 in the wake of the French revolution and its anticlericalism, a small group of Trappist monks (hence the name, Sa Trapa) found their way to Tarragona on the Catalan coast, south of Barcelona. A few years later, when France invaded Spain, they were obliged to flee again and found their way to Mallorca. At the desolate south-west tip of the island, they founded a small monastery.

Never numbering more than 40, the monks returned to the mainland in 1820. But during their 10 short years of occupation they built a small monastery, chanelled the intermittent stream which flows down the San Josep valley into a network of irrigation canals, established agriculture and constructed a corn mill, threshing house and banks of terraces with dry-stone walls, all of which remain to this day.

After many years of neglect, the property and its land were acquired in 1980 by Grup Balear d'Ornitologia i Defensa de la Naturalesa, in whose trust the complex remains.

which, with its sweeping views of the sea and coast, makes an agreeable rest stop.

The views get even better only a few metres beyond the cairn, opening up to reveal the rocky coastline and Serra de Tramuntana, the south-western extremity of which you are now walking. Aim east towards the first clump of live trees since you entered the area of the fire's devastation. Among the trees is Ses Basses, 30 minutes beyond the mirador and the first intact building since Sa Trapa. Written records reveal that there has been a building on this site since 1389.

After a pair of hairpin bends less than five minutes beyond Ses Basses, you have a choice. Continuing along the wide, main track leads in about an hour to the Coll de sa Gramola at the milepost signed 'km106' on the C710 road running between Andratx and

Sóller. From here, you can walk a further 5km down an old cart track to Andratx. Alternatively, the descent to S'Arracó via Torrent Gore d'en Betts, which takes 1½ to two hours, is more varied, though you do have to cast around for the route at a couple of points. This is the option described here.

To descend to S'Arracó take a russet, sandy track to the right, which briefly doubles back before swinging south-east. After 15 minutes, where the track ends at a small quarry, take the path which veers away right over a small bluff, following an ancient wall. When you meet a side valley, follow the well cairned path up its flank. After 30 minutes you reach a ruined sheepfold, where the path all but disappears briefly under yet more burnt pines. However, if you keep the building on your right you'll soon pick it up again.

After dropping gently southwards for seven or eight minutes you enter the welcome semishade of a pine grove with a small, neglected almond orchard to your right. Just beyond here, the path runs parallel with a terrace wall, still heading southwards, to become a wide, rocky track which takes you down to S'Arracó.

Sóller to Deià

Distance 10km
Duration 3 to 4 hours
Standard Easy
Start Sóller
Finish Deià
Public Transport Yes
Summary This is an undemanding, well signed walk beside olive groves and pasture, followed by a short section of road, the coastal path to Cala de Deià and then an ascent by an ancient track to Deià.

This walk links two of the most interesting communities on Mallorca's north-western coast. It offers spectacular views of the sea – from both the mountain flank along the Camí de Castelló and from the coastal path (Camí de la Mar) which hugs the shoreline. The optional exit to Deià at the end of the Camí de Castelló saves you 3km and can make a good warm-up hike after a midday arrival in Sóller.

HISTORY

Until the highway between Sóller and Deià was thrust through in the 19th century, the Camí de Castelló was the main thoroughfare between the two pueblos. Superseded and neglected, it became the preserve of hunters, charcoal-burners and, more often, shepherds. Recently restored (note the fine dry-stone walls and repaired terraces) and rescued from oblivion, it's now a well signed and popular track for walkers.

The Camí de la Mar also has a long history. In late medieval times, for example, it was deliberately sabotaged in places to make access more difficult for Arab coastal raiders.

PLANNING
When to Walk

Despite open stretches, much of the route passes beside olive groves and through shady pine wood. It can be walked comfortably even at the height of summer, when you can also dunk yourself in one of the small coves or at the Cala de Deià.

Maps & Books

The SGE *Sóller* No 38-26 (670) map at 1:50,000 covers the whole of the route area. The IGN's 1:25,000 map of the same name (No 670-II) extends as far as Lluc Alcari. Neither, bizarrely, shows more than fragments of this well established route. FODESMA brochures, *Camí de Castelló* and *Cala de Deià*, present the route in great detail but are only really worth packing if you can gist-read Catalan.

What to Bring

Bring water, and a swimming kit if you fancy cooling off in one of the coves. This is a route which you can comfortably undertake in runners (training shoes).

GETTING TO/FROM THE WALK

Buses leave Deià daily for Sóller and Port de Sóller at 5 and 8.15 pm. If you want to do the route in reverse, they depart Port de Sóller, passing by Sóller, at 7.30 and 9.30 am plus 2.30 pm.

THE WALK

Head for the CAMPSA petrol station on the bypass road which goes to Port de Sóller. If you take Carrer de Bauça from the main Plaça Constitució in Sóller and keep heading west as straight as the turnings allow, you won't miss it.

Cross the bypass to pick up the Camí de Sa Costa Den Llorenç trail (note the stone tablet, 'Deià a Peu; Camí del Rost', which indicates the formal start of the route). About 10 minutes from the bypass and soon after a house with a couple of giant euphorbia cactuses, the sealed road narrows to a footpath which, once over a stream bed, becomes a fine stone stairway.

After 35 minutes the cobbles stop and you go through a fence, which looks temporary but has been there for ages. Descend briefly among olive trees and keep heading rigorously west-north-west, ignoring both a

potential fork and a turn to the right. The road is now a wide cart track.

Just under an hour from Sóller, you arrive at a minor crossroads, where stone tablets set in the wall indicate the way forward to Deià and back to Sóller. Nearby, you'll see the first of the red trail markers which will guide you from here onwards.

The track curls to follow the contour line of a small valley and you're once again walking with olive groves above and below – in season, a couple of giant fig trees overhanging the path offer juicy refreshment as you skirt the estate of Ca'n Carabasseta.

At a junction beside a small 17th century chapel, now sadly ruined, *don't* take the more obvious path to the right, which drops to the coastal road. Instead, go through a gate to the left of the chapel. Walk up the cobbled path which, after another gate, leads to **Son Mico** (also known as Ca'n Prohom), a large farmhouse with roots at least as deep as the 15th century. There, you can fortify yourself, at a price, with fresh orange juice, quiche and fruit tart. Queen Isabel II, who's reputed to have spent the

MALLORCA

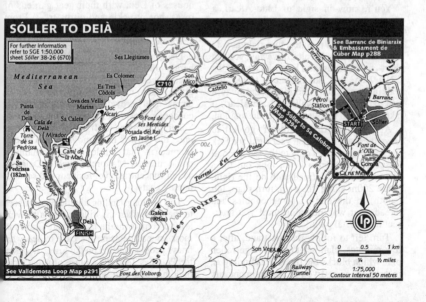

SÓLLER TO DEIÀ

night here when she visited Sóller in 1888, no doubt enjoyed more sumptuous fare.

Some 200m beyond Son Mico, leave the track and turn sharp left, just before an electricity pylon, to mount a clearly signed cobbled track beside a high wall. The walking is easy through a wood of pine and mountain oak. You're sometimes within earshot of the coastal C710 road winding below, but it doesn't intrude and you're soon rewarded with fine views over the coast to the north.

Once the cliffs of the Cala de Deià come into view (some two hours out of Sóller) there's a clearly signed potable spring, the Font de ses Mentides, in a gully no more than 50m off the route, reached by a narrow path.

Over the brow of an incline – the very last – is the **Posada del Rei en Jaume I**. Known with much greater antiquity as Son Coll, it was originally built in the 13th century shortly after the Reconquista (Reconquest), when the eponymous king Jaume I wrested Mallorca from the Muslims. It has belonged to the Coll family ever since and today's friendly descendants make this an especially pleasant juice stop.

You're now in sight of Lluc Alcari, a cluster of coastal houses whose name, derived from the Arabic, means 'the farm in the woods'. In 15 minutes, turn right at a T-junction to follow a sealed driveway; you can short-cut the bends via a lane which meets the C710. Here, you can either exit to Deià by walking west along the main road or turn east to continue the walk via Lluc Alcari. It takes about 20 minutes to either destination.

At the Lluc Alcari turn-off, go left to leave the main road, then veer right at a fork (the left option leads only to the fancy Hotel Costa d'Or). After a bend, look out for a narrow but well defined path on the right. Some 200m along this path, turn sharp left (south) at the end of some cobbles and thread your way downhill until you intersect the coastal path.

Turn left to follow the coast and, after a few minutes, clamber under a large fallen pine which blocks the track. Wayfinding is, in general, easy. Even if you momentarily

lose the track, there are plenty of red trail markers to help you relocate it. Stiles help you over boundary fences and, after 25 minutes, with the higher houses of Cala de Deià already in sight, you reach a mirador. From here, you can pick out the 17th century Torre de sa Pedrissa, a defensive tower also known as the Torre de Deià, on the headland beyond the bay. Ignore a red arrow pointing left (south) and continue straight to the small bay of **Cala de Deià** which, with its pebble beach and boathouse, may well be crowded, but what the heck – the water's clean and inviting.

There's only one way out of the tight valley; head inland along the dirt track which parallels the dry stream bed to become a narrow, sealed road. After 10 minutes cross the bed of the Torrent Major by a wooden bridge onto the true left (west) bank and ascend an excellent, recently restored cobbled path. You're now following the Camí des Ribassos, another ancient pathway linking Deià with its small sea outlet. After a brief, more rugged stretch, it joins a well defined track, where you turn left. It soon after reaches the first houses of Deià with their neat gardens of roses, honeysuckle and citrus trees. From Cala de Deià to Deià is about 40 minutes at a steady pace.

Deià, a cluster of some 75 houses with barely 300 inhabitants, retains a certain charm, even though it's now almost entirely given over to tourism. During the day it can be massively crowded as convoys of tourist coaches deposit their cargo. But, just like Sóller, it becomes itself again each evening once the crowds have moved on. The difference is that while Sóller remains a predominantly Mallorcan pueblo, Deià has a high concentration of resident and second-home expats.

This is a longstanding tradition, going back to the days when the village was a thriving artist colony, with the late Robert Graves its most famous denizen. It's easy to see what draws people. Nestled on the lower slopes of the Puig des Teix, it's a place of squat stone buildings and trim vegetable gardens, vines and orchards. And, on an island where water is a relatively scarce commodity, the place positively chuckles with irrigation channels, a wash house and springs, from which the remaining villagers draw their drinking water in preference to the town supply.

Surprisingly for a village where restaurant and gallery prices are notably higher than elsewhere, there's an affordable place to stay; *Pension Villa Verde* (☎ 971 63 90 37) on Carrer Ramon Llull, near the church, charges 2500 ptas for bed and breakfast.

Barranc de Biniaraix & Embassament de Cúber

Duration 3½ to 4 hours
Distance 13km
Standard Easy to Easy-Medium
Start Sóller
Finish Embassament de Cúber
Public Transport Yes
Summary An ascent of the tight Barranc de Biniaraix valley leads to the small upland plateau of l'Ofre. After a diversion to the Mirador d'en Quesada, the route crosses a col to join a level cart track leading to the Embassament de Cúber reservoir.

This classic walk follows part of an old pilgrim route which ran between Sóller and the Monestir de Lluc. Omitting the Mirador d'en Quesada side trip reduces total walking time by about 1½ hours.

HISTORY

Excavation of a cave in the Barranc de Biniaraix has revealed that it was home to pastoralists as early as the third millennium BC. Finds also indicate that the valley was settled continuously during the Bronze and Iron ages.

The earliest documented evidence of its use as a pilgrim route is a letter dated 1438 AD from the local bishop to his priest in So, granting an indulgence of 40 days to those who helped to maintain the track.

Until the second half of this century, it was used mainly for access to the olive groves and orange orchards in the valley's upper reaches. When these were abandoned in the late 1950s, the route, too, began to deteriorate. Nowadays, it's not only a great resource for walkers; its reconstruction and maintenance since the 1980s has led to a revival of agriculture in the valley.

NATURAL HISTORY

Few evergreen oaks, the valley's original cladding, remain. They've been superseded by olive and orange groves, carob trees and, in the upper reaches, pine trees and juniper bushes. In the more humid areas near the banks of the Torrent de Barranc is a rich variety of ferns, some of them endemic to Mallorca.

PLANNING
When to Walk

From October to May is the best period. The Barranc de Biniaraix, relatively shaded, can be walked comfortably year-round.

Maps

Both the SGE *Sóller* No 38-26 (670) 1:50,000 sheet and IGN's 1:25,000 map of the same name (No 670-II) cover the area and indicate the route.

What to Bring

Water, for once, isn't a problem on this trail. There are several springs (indicated on the map) and at a couple of points in the Barranc de Biniaraix taps have been inserted into pipes (laid on top of an older water channel) which bring fresh water from upland springs.

GETTING TO/FROM THE WALK

The twice daily bus linking Pollença and Sóller passes by Embassament de Cúber reservoir, at the end of the walk, around 5.10 pm. Miss this and it's one helluva hike home. If you opt to do the route in reverse, take the morning bus which calls by the CAMPSA petrol station on the Sóller bypass at 9.10 am and get off at the reservoir.

THE WALK

From Plaça Constitució in Sóller head north-east along Carrer de sa Lluna, which becomes Carrer de l'Alquería del Comte. Continue straight to Carrer d'Ozones. Cross over a bridge onto the true right bank of the Torrent des Barranc – the stream that you'll be following to its source. At Biniaraix, go up a flight of steps beside a telephone box and turn right up a cobbled street to emerge in Plaça de la Concepció, about 25 minutes from Sóller. Beyond it is a wash house and – mercifully upstream – a drinking-water fountain.

Take the track to the right, signposted 'Camí des Barranc' and 'A l'Ofre'. After five minutes, cross the stream and begin the long haul up well maintained cobblestone steps. During the ascent to the Cases de l'Ofre farms, there are several changes of bank and the path occasionally veers away from the stream, always to return. It should take about 1¾ hours.

After a ruined building, the going briefly gets steeper as you wind up the Seis Voletes, six steep curves which will have you panting. Throughout the valley, even in its steepest, most inhospitable sections, there are tight terraces of olive trees above neat dry-stone walls, superbly constructed and maintained.

Pass on your left the russet **Coves d'en Mena**, a huge scar on the precipitous cliff face which is clearly visible from Sóller, now in sight way below, together with the lighthouse and upper buildings of Port de Sóller.

As you pass through a green gate, ignore for once the sign saying 'l'Ofre, Propiedad Privada'. The area proclaims itself a private property at every turning, but you're grudgingly allowed through. Pay heed, however, to the bull sign onto which some walker has appended an impressively large pizzle. As you mount the upper reaches of the Torrent de l'Ofre, the track dwindles to a narrow pathway, easily followed and still progressing southward.

The splendid Mirador d'en Quesada side trip described at the end of this walk description branches off from here.

To continue to l'Embassament de Cúber, go through a green gate to bypass the farm

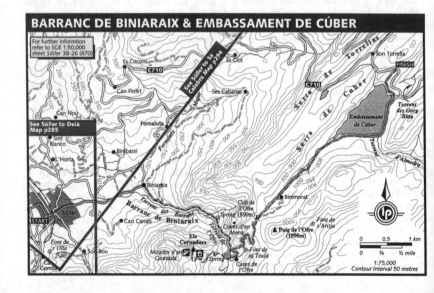

BARRANC DE BINIARAIX & EMBASSAMENT DE CÚBER

and its less-than-welcoming sign in English – bizarrely, only in English – 'Bull. Don't pass. Please don't enter. Dangerous animals' and, in Spanish, 'Propiedad Privada'. In case you're slow on the uptake, there's even a highway white-bar-on-red sign to signify 'no entry'. The good folk at Cases de l'Ofre really don't want you around.

A forest track, constructed in the 1960s, winds up through the trees, passing by the Font de sa Teula, the spring which feeds Cases de l'Ofre. From the **Coll de l'Ofre** (890m) onwards, there are fine views eastward to the Puig de l'Ofre (1090m) and, beyond the reservoir, Puig Mayor – at 1443m, the highest point on the island. Shortly after the col, you can either take a short cut on the left or continue along the wide track until both merge at a cluster of buildings, Binimorat. The route now runs parallel to one of the dam's main feeder streams. When you reach the reservoir, about 1¾ hours from Cases de l'Ofre, follow its east bank until you hit the main road which today's travellers use, with much less effort but correspondingly less satisfaction, from Sóller to the Monestir de Lluc.

Side Trip: Mirador d'en Quesada
1¼ hours, 2km

From the sign 'Mirador de'n Quesada' encountered just before bypassing the Cases de l'Ofre, head right and cross a wooden bridge just below a concrete cistern – your last opportunity to take on water until you return to this point. As you climb, you skirt and rise above the meadows of Cases de l'Ofre to meet the point where the old track, now effectively barred with wire, is reinforced by a sign, 'No pasar. Toros sueltos' (No entry. Loose bulls). It's debatable whether the bulls are there primarily to serve the cows or the farmer's interests in keeping walkers out.

From here on, there's only one point where you might go astray; at a sharp bend where the track turns west, take the turn and disregard the smaller path heading away from it. At a col about 35 minutes from the wooden bridge, take a signed path

up to the right (north-east). After passing a stone refugio, this leads you to the **mirador**.

Once you've paused for a breather and enjoyed the magnificent views of the entire Sóller basin and the coast beyond, retrace your steps to the wooden bridge.

Valldemosa Loop

Duration 5½ to 6 hours
Distance 15km
Standard Medium
Start/Finish Valldemosa
Public Transport Yes
Summary This walk takes in steepish ascent to the plateau of Es Pouet, a detour to the Mirador de ses Puntes, the splendid Camino del Archiduque, a second diversion to Es Teix and an easy descent through the Vall de Cairats.

This is a pick-and-mix day out; if you don't want to do the whole walk there are two points at which you can take a short cut. You can also omit either or both of two diversions described (in which case the difficulty of the walk is Easy-Medium); you'll still enjoy some splendid coastal views from the main section of the Camino del Archiduque.

Both landowner and villager have made their contribution to the landscape. Walkers have Archiduque Ludwig Salvator of Hapsburg, known in Spain as Luis Salvator (see the boxed text 'El Archiduque' on the following page), to thank for laying out the *camino* (way), a dramatic trail which follows the clifftops. To get there, begin by following an old charcoal burners' track to the plateau of Es Pouet, where you can still see evidence of their presence. As you drop down the Vall de Cairats, all the uphill work behind you, you pass a former *nevera*, or *casa de sa neu* (snow pit or snow house), several more charcoal-burning circles with their characteristic green moss or sward, and a *forn de calc* (lime kiln), where rock from

MALLORCA

El Archiduque

Archduke Ludwig Salvator (Luis Salvator in Spanish) of Hapsburg, Lorraine and Bourbon was much more than just another romantic, northern European aristocrat doing the Grand Tour. Captivated by the Islas Baleares, and Mallorca in particular, he bought the estate of Miramar in 1872 and made it his home for more than 40 years – notwithstanding spells at his castle outside Prague and other homes at Ramleh in Egypt and Zinis, near Trieste, plus visits to the imperial court in Vienna and long Mediterranean cruises in his prized yachts, Nixe 1 and Nixe 2.

Polymath and ecologically sensitive before the term had even been invented, he restored decaying farmhouses and dwellings, created a magnificent garden of indigenous plants and shrubs at Miramar, bought up trees that farmers were about to fell and entertained a constant procession of visitors – while still finding time to write more than 70 books and scientific treatises, of which the most famous is his Les Balears Descrites per la Paraula i el Gravat (The Balearics in Words and Images).

Es Teix used to be crushed and slow fired to make lime for whitewashing the houses.

HISTORY

In the late 19th century, Archiduque Luis Salvador built a series of paths through his estate of Miramar. In the tradition of high Romanticism, these private bridleways allowed him to ride his lands – and to impress his constant stream of visitors with spectacular coastal views and seascapes. The finest panoramas are from what is known today as the Camino del Archiduque.

PLANNING
Maps

The SGE Sóller No 38-26 (670) map at 1:50,000 covers the whole of the route area but fails to indicate even the Camino del Archiduque. At 1:25,000 you need two IGN maps: Alaró (No 670-II) and Esporlas/Valldemosa (No 670-III). There's a FODESMA brochure, available only in Catalan, on the Camino del Archiduque.

What to Bring

The broken rocks and stones used to repair and improve the camino are, paradoxically, potential ankle-twisters. While most of the walk is fine if you're wearing runners, this major stretch makes boots advisable.

GETTING TO/FROM THE WALK

Buses for Valldemosa depart Port de Sóller, passing by the Plaza America in Sóller, at 7.30 and 9.30 am. For the return journey, they call by Valldemosa at 4.45 and 8 pm.

THE WALK

From the bus stop in Valldemosa, walk towards Palma and take Carrer de la Venerable Sor Aina, the first road on your left. At the first intersection, turn right along Carrer de Joan Miró. Go straight ahead up a flight of steps beside a school, turn briefly right then left up Carrer des Ametlers, at the rear of the school, and then right onto Carrer de les Oliveres. At the end of this cul-de-sac, take the path heading north-west beside a sign which says, in English, 'Danger: Big Game'! The Spanish version is decidedly less alarming and merely warns you that you're entering a hunting zone.

Follow the path beside the sign, pass through a pair of gateposts, then over a stile, to maintain a generally north-north-west bearing along a wide, stone track, ignoring any side trails. If you've neglected to bring water you can fill up at the Font de s'Abeurada, barely 20m off the path. The ascent is, for the most part, shaded by thick oaks.

Some 45 minutes along the path go through a gap in a dry-stone wall to emerge onto a small plateau. Disregarding tracks to the right and left, continue straight ahead through spindly oak trees, passing beside a sitja (charcoal-burners' circle) to reach the well of Es Pouet (don't drink from its murky depths).

For the Mirador de ses Puntes, take the minor path which heads initially north before turning west. Alternatively, you can follow the dominant track (not described here) to the right (east) to bypass the mirador and a certain amount of easy scrambling – though you'll miss out on a spectacular view.

Climbing at first, then gently descending through pine, oak and scrub, skim the southern flank of Veiá to arrive, about 75 minutes from Valldemosa, at the **Mirador de ses Puntes**, which offers views as far as the small village of Bañalbufar to the west. Here, initially zigzagging east, the Camino del Archiduque begins.

After 15 minutes you reach the Veiá (867m), clearly identifiable by its trig marker. Ten minutes later the trail arrives at a crumbling stone shelter. As you leave the ruins the path heads briefly towards the sea before resuming its easterly progression.

After some two hours of hiking you arrive at the 'crossroads' of the Coll de s'Estret de Son Gallard with a welcome stone bench. To the right (south) is the short-cut path coming up from Es Pouet. On the left is a little used track leading to Son Gallard, Son Marroig and eventually, via the C710 road, Deià.

As you climb and begin to walk along the backbone of the archduke's promenade, the views become increasingly stunning. A 15 minute ascent leads to the most spectacular portion of the causeway, with sheer drops to one side. There are landmarks in every direction: Galatzó peak slips behind, blocking the line of sight west of Bañalbufar; the Punta de sa Foradada (the promontory with a hole punched in it) sits just above the villa besieged by tour buses at Son Marroig. Deià is a bit slow in appearing, wedged in at the bottom of sheer 700m cliffs.

After 2¾ hours of walking you skirt a copse of trees, isolated on the bleak plateau. This is about the only attractive, shaded picnic stop until you reach the Instituto Nacional para la Conservación (ICONA) grounds towards the end of the walk. To its right, a narrow path heads back to Es Pouet.

Thirty minutes later, take the turn-off left (east) at a large cairn and head for the peak of **Es Teix**, marked by two iron crosses. Es Teix means the yew tree in Catalan – a name

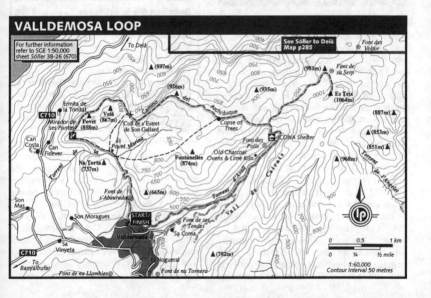

VALLDEMOSA LOOP

Valldemosa

Valldemosa, with its stone houses flanking tree-lined streets, has just as much charm as its neighbour, Deià. And, just like Deià, it is invaded daily by tourist coaches; the best time to visit is at the end of the walk, once they've all moved on.

La Cartuja, its Carthusian monastery, which has rented out rooms since the dissolution of Spain's monasteries in 1835, is an early example of holiday apartments. Here, three years after its opening, Chopin and his lover, the French writer George Sand, spent a tempestuous winter, outraging the villagers, falling out and making up. Sand's dyspeptic book, *Winter in Mallorca*, based upon her experiences, ensures that she remains unpopular with the locals to this day.

The monastery is open from 9.30 am to 1 pm and 3 to 6.30 pm (5.30 pm in winter), Monday to Saturday. The entry fee of 1000 ptas includes – nice touch, this – a piano recital and admission to the small local museum.

which is something of an anachronism nowadays since most of the yews were long ago felled by woodcutters. All the same, some remain; look out for them as you take the detour to its crest. For views toward Sóller and Ses Cornadors, be sure to climb the left-hand (easterly) summit and not the one with multiple crosses – otherwise you'll see nothing new. Some 10 minutes from the cairn is a small plain with a spring, the Font de sa Serp, where for most of the year you can replenish your water bottles.

Return to the junction with the main path at the head of the Vall de Cairats. Some 4½ hours into the day you reach the end of the archduke's path as the track widens and steepens to plunge down past a casa de sa neu.

Just below is an ICONA shelter, originally the bunkhouse for the nevaters. With benches and a hearth, it's pleasantly cool and dark on a hot day. But resist the temptation

to lunch here if you've held out this far because in 10 minutes you reach the Font des Polls (Spring of the Poplar Trees) with drinking water and shaded benches (don't confuse it with the stagnant cistern a couple of minutes below the refugio). As you continue to descend, you pass several charcoal-burning sites, another snow house and a lime kiln, all examples of now-extinct rural industries.

Five hours into the walk, you cross a large stile beside a locked gate to leave ICONA territory – and the estate of the eponymous archduke. Continue along the same track – the switchbacks of which you can short-cut – and, at a fork, bear right over a cattle grid. Once you hit a sealed road, bear right, then first left to drop to the main road. Allow about an hour from the spring to the Valldemosa bus stop, for a total of just over 5½ walking hours. This final section is rather anticlimactic but is better tackled last, rather than at the beginning of the walk.

Sóller to Sa Calobra

Duration 5½ to 6½ hours
Distance 18km
Standard Medium
Start Sóller
Finish Sa Calobra
Public Transport Yes
Summary The route climbs to the Mirador de Ses Barques, descends to the Vall de Balitx and rises to the Coll de Biniamar; it then follows the cliffside corniche to Cala Tuent and passes over the col to Sa Calobra.

A warm-up stroll through the Sóller valley is followed by a fairly hard slog up to the Mirador de ses Barques (which you can omit by taking the morning bus to this point). Woods give way to cultivation as you descend to the pleasantly fertile Vall de Balitx. Just after the Coll de Biniamar, a detour to the abandoned farm of Sa Costera (with water) makes for a pleasant lunch stop. The great views of the bay of Racó de sa Taleca continue as you walk the cliff path.

At Cala Tuent allow yourself plenty of leeway to catch the last boat back from Sa Calobra to Port de Sóller – not the least of the day's pleasures.

PLANNING
Maps

Again, the map to use is SGE's *Sóller* No 38-26 (670) at 1:50,000, supplemented by *Pollensa* No 38-25 (643); 39-25 (644) for the latter part of the corniche, Cala Tuent and Sa Costera. The IGN's *Sóller* No 670-II 1:25,000 map covers the area as far as Sa Costera and the beginning of the corniche. Eastwards from here, you need SGE's *Sa Calobra* No 643-II. None are essential and all fail to indicate segments of the walk.

PLACES TO STAY & EAT

You can overnight at the old *farmhouse* of Balitx d'Avall (sometimes also known as Balitx d' Abaix), which makes a good base for a couple of days walking. A double with half board costs 12,000 ptas.

GETTING TO/FROM THE WALK

You're constrained by the need to catch the last boat back from Sa Calobra to Port de Sóller (1100 ptas). This leaves at 4 pm outside the summer glut and 5 pm from 15 May to the end of October. From June to mid-October there's at least one boat a week to Cala Tuent and the captain may be willing to put in anyway if you're walking in a big group. For information on all sailings ring ☎ 971 63 31 09.

If you choose to begin the walk at the Mirador de Ses Barques, take the bus for Pollença, which leaves the CAMPSA petrol station on the Sóller bypass at 9.10 am, and alight at the mirador.

THE WALK

Leave the Plaça de sa Constitució in Sóller by Carrer de Sa Lluna. Take the second left onto Carrer de la Victoria 11 Maig and bear right beside a small bridge to follow the sign for Fornalutx. After about 10 minutes, turn right (north) onto Carrer de Ses Argiles,

just beyond the high wall of the football stadium.

Keep with it for 10 minutes as it meanders between fruit orchards and makes a sharp right at a T-junction. Then, just after a 90° left bend, strike right (north again; the dominant direction of the walk as far as the mirador) opposite a house called Ca's Puput. At another T-junction, a rusting sign indicating 'Camino Viejo de Balitx-Tuent-Sa Calobra' directs you left.

Climb for 10 minutes to reach the sealed C710 road. Cross and continue steadily northwards and almost straight ahead – following the red trail markers – to short-cut the twisting minor road that curls around the estate of Ca'n Costurér.

At a boundary stone an arrow directs you right, the main cart track, beside a high wall. After some 10 minutes go through a metal gate to the **Mirador de Ses Barques**. The

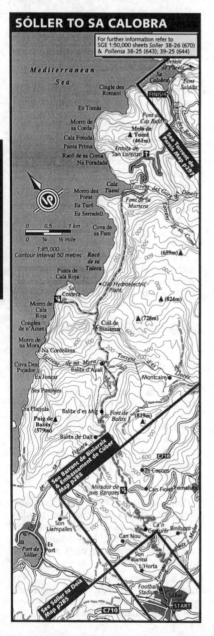

SÓLLER TO SA CALOBRA

For further information refer to
SGE 1:50,000 sheets *Sóller* 38-26 (670)
& *Pollensa* 38-25 (643); 39-25 (644)

original route has been blocked off by the owner and you have to edge yourself, quite safely, over a patch of scree along a ropeway, before picking your way through rubbish lobbed by passing motorists. This is the only disagreeable spot on the entire route.

Leave the mirador by the steps on its upper side, signed for Tuent and Sa Calobra. The path passes over a hillock to join a track, which you take to the left. Soon after it merges with a wide cart track, pass through the first of three green gates to walk beside an extensive olive plateau. Some 10 minutes later, shortly before the farm of Balitx de Dalt, fork right at a gateway to enter the richly cultivated **Vall de Balitx** valley. Savour the twisted, gnarled olive trees – some of them reputed to be 1000 years old – recalling Van Gogh's sinuous representations.

About 400m into the valley, leave the main track at a hairpin bend to go straight ahead and down some cobbled steps. A short detour leads to the Font de Balitx, a reliable source of water except towards the end of summer in particularly dry years. Rejoin the wide cart track just before the forlorn, abandoned Balitx d'es Mig. Continue to a sign 'Agroturismo, Balitx d'Avall' (also known as Balitx d'Abaix). Don't, however, follow it. Instead, turn left from the track to take the more direct pedestrian route to the farm, down several flights of stone steps. This finely engineered way descends to Balitx d'Avall to complete approximately two hours of walking from Sóller. At this substantial farm, there's accommodation (for details see Places to Stay & Eat in the introduction to this walk) and fresh orange juice from the surrounding orchards.

The track crosses the Torrent d'es Llorés stream bed to begin climbing in earnest. Blue trail markers stay with you as you toil upward until, roughly 40 minutes from the farm, you reach the Coll de Biniamar. Thick tree foliage at first obscures views in any direction, but within five minutes a red-blazed side trail, overgrown in places, meanders off left to the lonely abandoned estate at Sa Costera, a 45 minute return-trip detour.

This half-ruined farm overlooks the bay of Racó de sa Taleca, tantalisingly inaccessible some hundreds of metres below. The grounds themselves make an excellent picnic stop, with year-round water available from a spring in a cave on the terrace behind and to the right of the house.

Return to the main trail, which narrows soon after the wooded vegetation begins to dwindle and becomes an exposed but quite safe walk along the flank of the cliff. Though it appears to run parallel to the contour lines, there's a surprising amount of up and down work, though nothing too taxing, and the views are positively inspirational. About 20 minutes from the col, pass a side trail which drops to an abandoned shoreline hydro-electric plant. Continue along this fine cliff route through successive stone gates, until you reach a lone farm, 90 minutes past the Coll de Biniamar and some four hours from Sóller. Turn left (north-west) and, some minutes later, after only 20m on a newly graded track, don't miss the flight of steps leading downwards, signalled by a small cairn and a red arrow on an olive tree.

The path ends beside a *bar-restaurante*, perched on a knoll overlooking Cala Tuent. From here, it's easy to drop down to the beach of sand and pebbles for a swim, a laze or a refreshing drink.

Otherwise, take the sealed road which leads via a series of bends to Ermita de San Lorenzo (Sant Llorenç), the 13th century chapel, or hermitage, clearly visible at the breach in the saddle to the north-east. As you follow the winding road up to the pass, resist the temptation to short-cut the hairpins; the distance saved is outweighed by the energy you'll expend clambering over boulders and forging your way through the scrub. Instead, relax, resign yourself to this stretch of very lightly trafficked roadwork and enjoy the changing perspectives of Cala Tuent below you.

Once at the col, go through the gate just beyond the ermita and take an ancient paved track, now sadly overgrown, its steps and stones ill-maintained, yet still discernible. At its end, turn left at the first

house you meet, then left again when you hit the sealed road for an easy 15 minute descent to the clamour of Sa Calobra, teeming with day-trippers. Reward yourself with a drink at one of the *cafe terraces* as you wait for the boat to arrive.

Allow a generous 90 minutes to reach Sa Calobra from Cala Tuent. This gives you enough leeway to catch the late afternoon boat back to Sóller; miss it and you're in big trouble.

Torrent de Pareis

Duration 4 to 4½ hours
Distance 6km
Standard Medium-Hard
Start Escorca
Finish Sa Calobra
Public Transport Yes
Summary This is a steep descent along a switchback trail leading to the gorge of the Torrent de Pareis, Sa Calobra and the sea.

This walk is downhill all the way, and it's only a little more than 6km, but you'll expend as much energy as you negotiate the Torrent de Pareis, Mallorca's deepest canyon, as you would on a full day hike – mostly by walking but sometimes scrambling and bringing all four limbs into play.

NATURAL HISTORY

The Torrent de Pareis, believe it or not – and it is difficult to credit for much of the year, when it is reduced to a few residual pools – is the island's principal watercourse. Over the millennia rainwater has gouged a narrow gorge, in places more than 200m deep, through the soft limestone. The side valley of Sa Fosca, leading to the Torrent des Gorg Blau, is a Mallorcan mecca for cavers.

PLANNING
When to Walk

This is the one walk on Mallorca which is better done in summer. While the gorge is accessible in winter, except after heavy rain, you may have to paddle, even wade, through pools on the way down. In the hotter months, though the first part of the walk on the plateau is unshaded, the sun penetrates to the bottom of the ravine for only a few hours of each day.

Maps

Unfortunately, this short (in terms of distance) walk overlaps the borders of the SGE *Pollensa* No 38-25/39-25 (643/644) (one map) and *Inca* No 39-26 (671) 1:50,000 maps. You don't really need either.

What to Bring

Consider wearing long trousers since the sharp grasses on the first part of the walk can cut. Also think about packing a pair of runners. As well as being lighter, on the steep downhill section of the walk they may well be far less punishing on your toes.

GETTING TO/FROM THE WALK

For Escorca, take the morning bus which calls by the CAMPSA petrol station on the Sóller bypass at 9.10 am. Ask the driver to drop you off – Escorca, at the milepost signed 'km25', is only a couple of houses and is easily overrun.

To return, you need to catch the last boat back from Sa Calobra to Port de Sóller (1100 ptas). This leaves at 4 pm in winter and 5 pm from 15 May to the end of October; miss this and you're in trouble.

THE WALK

Go through a metal gate opposite Restaurante Escorca. Take lightly the litany of warnings on the adjacent sign; in particular, the advice to pack a wetsuit is overkill – presumably a defence against insurance claims by litigious walkers. Follow a level path which runs along the boundary of Ses Tanques de Baix, a series of sheepfolds.

After about 10 minutes, take a sharp left beside a large cairn and continue straight to the lip of the gorge, from where a well defined path, rocky in places, begins its zigzagging descent. After 25 minutes, you

> **Warning**
>
> After a rainstorm, or if a cloudburst is predicted, seek advice from the tourist office in Sóller since there's a risk of flash floods. Even if the gorge is practicable, the rocks can be treacherously slippery until they dry out.

reach a small, neat and round terrace with close-cropped sward. This old charcoal-burners' site is an ideal spot to pause and savour the view, where the only other evidence of humanity is the distant farm of Son Colomí on the opposite flank.

Soon after, the trail improves as you negotiate the a series of *voltes llargues* (long bends or switchbacks). A lone fig tree marks 45 minutes of unremittingly downhill hiking from the lip. Twenty metres beyond it, a seasonal spring drips from the rocks and a narrow trail, briefly much steeper and more of a clamber, begins its descent through rock and long grass to the bed of the Torrent de Lluc. Angle up onto its true left bank to find a path similar to the one you've just left. This, though heavily overgrown with sharp grasses, is less taxing than battling your way over the boulders in the riverbed.

After passing between two giant, perpendicular cliffs and feeling pretty small, return to the stream bed; 20 minutes beyond the fig tree you will reach S'Entreforc, the confluence where the smaller Torrent des Gorg Blau (Blue Ravine) joins the main valley from the south-west. Here begins the true Torrent de Pareis (where 'pareis' in the Mallorcan dialect of Catalan means pair).

On a large rock are four fading, painted arrows labelled: 'Lluch' (Lluc), pointing back upstream; 'Sa Fosca', left; 'Calobra', straight ahead; and 'Millor no anar' (which translates as 'Better not go'), pointing at the sheer, unassailable cliff wall on your right. Ho, ho!

Though the Torrent des Gorg Blau is for experienced cavers only, it's well worth briefly detouring to explore the first few hundred metres, known as Sa Fosca (The Darkness), an apt name for this narrow

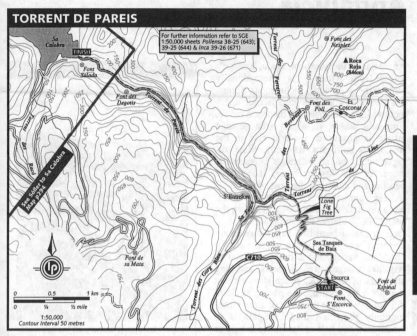

TORRENT DE PAREIS

For further information refer to SGE
1:50,000 sheets *Pollensa* 38-25 (643);
39-25 (644) & *Inca* 39-26 (671)

Sa Calobra
FINISH
Font Salada
Font des Degotis
Torrent de Pareis
See Sóller to Sa Calobra Map p294
Torrent des Niurol
Font de sa Mata
S'Entreforc
Sa Fosca
Torrent des Gorg Blau
C710
START
Escorca
Font S'Escorca
Font des Nespier
Roca Roja (846m)
Torrent des Torrents
Font des Poll
Es Cosconar
Torrent des Bovarni
Torrent de Lluc
Lone Fig Tree
Ses Tanques de Baix
Font de Espinal

0   0.5   1 km
0   ¼   ½ mile
1:50,000
Contour Interval 50 metres

MALLORCA

canyon, where the sun rarely penetrates to the base of its near-vertical walls.

Continue along the main gorge by taking a path on the true right bank, signalled by a green trail marker, in order to avoid a jumble of boulders. This threads back to the riverbed after little more than five minutes.

Now the fun really begins as you climb down the first of the three areas of giant boulders, easing yourself through a pair of narrow chimneys. Take care as the rock is slippery from the rubbing of so many boots and bums – and particularly treacherous after rain. Then comes an easy stretch where you can stride out along the stream bed before the valley narrows drastically.

When you're about 1¼ hours from the confluence, look for a path on the true left bank which will take you above and around another boulder-strewn defile. Work your way around a second huge monolith to the right of the path (courtesy of two large nails hammered into the rock), then a third giant (with the help of a strap anchored by a peg). Your reward is the Font des Degotis, a spring where water drips from the fronds on the rock wall. Here you can quench your thirst and even take a natural shower.

Two hours from the confluence you must again take evasive action, this time up the true right bank to bypass a pair of monoliths and what, in summer, may still be a couple of late-season pools. Soon after, the gorge finally opens out. A final flat stretch takes you to the small beach of Sa Calobra's eastern cove where, if you can find a spare square metre, you can relax on the shingle and cool off in the sea. A pedestrian tunnel leads to the thronged port and the boat to Port de Sóller.

Andalucía

Andalucía – the south of Spain, a stone's throw from Africa – is internationally famous for many things including its vibrant, fiesta-loving people; its great Islamic architecture; its hot climate; its flamenco music, song and dance; its sherry (the genuine article is produced nowhere else in the world); its bullfights; its pretty, white villages; and (though infamous is more the word for this last example) the packed beaches and resorts of the Costa del Sol.

Less appreciated by the outside world, but a revelation to those who get in on the secret, are Andalucía's natural attractions – large tracts of beautiful, rugged mountain country; gorgeous green river valleys; abundant, varied, and at times very visible wildlife; a huge range of plants; and long stretches of dramatic, beach-strewn coast that are a far cry from the packaged Costa del Sol. Well more than half of all environmentally protected land in Spain is in Andalucía, and half of Andalucía is hills or mountains, including mainland Spain's only 3000m-plus peaks outside the Pyrenees. The highest peak of all on the mainland, Mulhacén (3478m), is here.

Northerners might imagine Andalucía is just too hot for much walking; in fact, for about half of each year the climate is ideal. Another reason the region doesn't have the reputation it deserves among walkers is perhaps that Andalucians themselves have been slow to turn to their own backyard for recreation. Andalucía does not have the long-standing hiking and mountaineering tradition of the cooler, more industrialised northern areas such as Catalunya or the País Vasco (Basque Country). But *turismo rural* (rural tourism) has been a buzz phrase down south for quite a few years now, and the lure of their countryside and wilderness is being felt more and more by urban Andalucians.

Networks of walking trails, however, are still relatively undeveloped, and surprisingly few people take the trouble to walk away from a handful of well known trails. As

HIGHLIGHTS

Superb mountain scenery on the approach to Benaocaz in the Sierra de Grazalema.

- Traversing the black-rock wildernesses of the precipitous upper Sierra Nevada, mainland Spain's highest range

- The beautifully green valleys and endlessly varied karstic mountainscapes of the Parque Natural de Cazorla and the Sierra de Grazalema

- Unique white villages, dense green woodlands, arid hillsides, deep ravines and reminders of a fascinating history on a walk through Las Alpujarras

often as not, you'll have Andalucía's natural wonders all to yourself.

HISTORY

Andalucía was the obvious point of attack for the Muslims who arrived from Africa to oust the Visigoths in the 8th century AD. In 711 general Tariq ibn Ziyad landed at

Gibraltar with around 10,000 men, mostly Berbers (indigenous North Africans). In 711 or 712, somewhere on the Río Guadalete in western Andalucía, the Muslims decimated the Visigoth army and within a few years had taken over most of the Iberian Peninsula.

Andalucía was always the Muslim heartland on the peninsula. Córdoba (756-1031), then Sevilla (1040-1248), then Granada (1248-1492) took turns as the leading city of Muslim Spain or, as it was called, Al-Andalus (from which the modern name Andalucía is derived). At its peak in the 10th century Córdoba was easily the biggest and most dazzling and cultured city in western Europe, ruling most of Spain and Portugal. Islamic civilisation lasted longer in Andalucía than anywhere else in Europe, and the Islamic heritage is one of the region's most fascinating aspects today. This is not only a matter of great buildings such as Granada's Alhambra, Córdoba's Mezquita and Sevilla's Giralda, but also of gardens, fountains, food, music and more. Many of the villages you pass through on walks here preserve their original narrow, labyrinthine, Muslim street layout and the irrigation and terracing systems of much of the Andalucian countryside have similar roots.

The north and west of Andalucía, including Córdoba and Sevilla, fell to the Christian Reconquista (Reconquest) in the 13th century, leaving the Nasrid Emirate of Granada as the last bastion of Al-Andalus. The Nasrid Emirate, named after its 13th century founder Ibn Nasr and occupying roughly the south-eastern half of modern Andalucía, held out till 1492, when Granada fell to the Catholic Monarchs Fernando and Isabel. Despite initial promises of tolerance, the Muslims soon faced a variety of repressive measures, including forced conversion to Christianity, which sparked revolts in Andalucía in 1500 and 1568. They were finally expelled from all of Spain between 1609 and 1614.

Columbus' discovery of the Americas in 1492 brought great wealth to Sevilla, and later Cádiz, the ports through which most of the business of the new continent was conducted. But the Andalucian countryside reaped little benefit. After the Reconquista, Andalucía's new rulers had handed out great swathes of territory to their nobles, and Muslim raids from Granada, the Black Death and a series of bad 14th century harvests virtually emptied the rural north and west of people. The landowners turned much of it over to sheep, ruining formerly productive food-growing land. The vast network of *vías pecuarias* (drove roads) established in Andalucía and the rest of Spain over the following centuries – used for moving sheep between seasonal pastures – today forms the basis of some walking routes (though there's little trace of many other vías pecuarias still marked on maps).

The very backwardness and poverty of 19th century Andalucía helped stimulate travellers from elsewhere in Europe – including composers and writers such as Mozart, Rossini, Byron, Hugo, Bizet and Rimsky-Korsakov – to develop the romantic image of Andalucía as a mysterious, sensuous, materially poor but spiritually rich land of exotic adventure.

Flamenco, born out of the music and dance of the Andalucian gypsies, is one of the richest expressions of Andalucian culture.

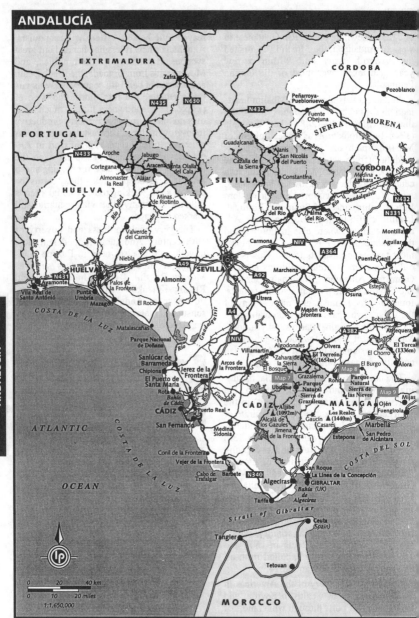

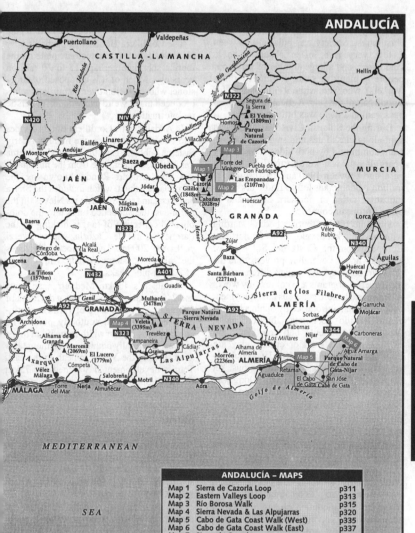

ANDALUCÍA

ANDALUCÍA

By the late 19th century rural Andalucía – especially the west – was a hotbed of anarchist unrest. Society was polarised between a few very rich, often absentee noble landowners and a large number of very poor people – many of them *jornaleros* (dayworkers), who were without employment for a good half of the year. Agriculture remained backward and there was little industry.

During the Spanish Civil War Andalucía split along class lines and savage atrocities were committed by both sides. The hungry years after the war were particularly hungry here, and between 1950 and 1970 some 1.5 million Andalucians left to find work in the industrial cities of northern Spain and in other European countries.

Since the 1960s a tourism boom – starting with mass-market developments for northern Europeans on the Costa del Sol west of Málaga – and the overall improvement in the Spanish economy have made a difference. So have a series of grants and community works schemes and a more generous unemployment benefits system introduced by Spain's left-of-centre Partido Socialista Obrera Español (PSOE) governments between 1982 and 1996. Andalucía's major cities today are bright, cosmopolitan places and its people increasingly well educated and prosperous. Yet the region remains economically a long way behind most of Spain. Unemployment (31% in 1997) is still the highest in the country.

NATURAL HISTORY

Andalucía, at 87,000 sq km, comprises 17% of Spain and, in basic terms, consists of two east-west mountain chains separated by the fertile, heavily cultivated valley of the 660km Río Guadalquivir, plus a coastal plain.

Of the two mountain chains, the Sierra Morena, rarely topping 1000m, rolls along Andalucía's northern borders, while the higher Cordillera Bética is a complicated mass of rugged *sierras* (mountain ranges) broadening out from the south-west to the east; it includes mainland Spain's highest peak, Mulhacén (3478m), in the Sierra Nevada south-east of Granada. The Guadalquivir, Andalucía's longest river, rises below the Sierra de Cazorla in north-east Andalucía and enters the Atlantic at Sanlúcar de Barrameda.

The Cordillera Bética was pushed up by pressure of the African tectonic plate on the Iberian sub-plate perhaps 15 to 20 million years ago. Much of it is composed of limestone, whose erosion over the millennia has produced many weird and wonderful karstic rock formations.

In Andalucía the Cordillera Bética divides into two main branches, the more northerly Sistema Subbético and the southerly Sistema Penibético. Both emerge from the mountainous area around Ronda known as the Serranía de Ronda, which includes the Sierra de Grazalema and Sierra de las Nieves. In the north-east the Subbético turns into the complicated collection of ranges making up the Parque Natural de Cazorla, where several peaks top 2000m. The Penibetico includes the 75km-long Sierra Nevada, with a series of 3000m-plus peaks.

Andalucía's 460km Mediterranean coast and 240km Atlantic coast meet at the Strait of Gibraltar, where the town of Tarifa is continental Europe's most southerly point. The coastal plains vary in width from 50km in the far west to virtually nothing where mountains drop sheer to the Mediterranean in the east. Tourist development has turned the 75km Costa del Sol from Málaga to Estepona into an almost-continuous developed strip.

Flora

The huge range of Andalucian flora (around 5000 species, some 150 of them unique to the region) is largely due to the fact that the last Ice Age was relatively temperate at this southerly latitude, allowing plants which were killed off further north to survive.

The mountains are responsible for a lot of the variety. When winter snows melt, zones above the tree line bloom with rock-clinging plants and pastures full of gentians, orchids, crocuses and narcissi. Many of the lower slopes are clothed in pine forests, often commercial. The rare *pinsapo* (Spanish fir), a relic of forests millions of years old, exists only in the mountains around Ronda and in northern Morocco. Many pine forests are threatened by the hairy, pine-needle-devouring caterpillars of the pine processionary moth – best steered clear of (see the Health & Safety chapter).

Along river valleys you'll often find a rich variety of deciduous trees. Poplars can be a signal of water close by. In areas such as the Sierra Morena and Sierra de Grazalema there are extensive woodland pastures known as *dehesas* with stands of cork, holm and gall oak. Dehesas were mostly created long ago when the original Mediterranean forest was burnt off or felled for pasture and replanted with these useful trees.

Where there's no woodland and no agriculture, the land is likely to be either scrub or steppe-like. Scrub occurs where forests were felled and the land then abandoned. Steppe is produced by overgrazing or occurs naturally in hot, dry areas such as Cabo de Gata. Here, plant life is sparse and scrubby, often with cacti, but bursts into colour after rain.

Fauna

A small number of wolves – probably less than 100 – survive under protection in the eastern Sierra Morena. Andalucía's ibex have weathered a deadly epidemic of scabies and now number perhaps 10,000, about half of them in the Sierra Nevada. The mouflon, a wild sheep, has been introduced to the Parque Natural de Cazorla and a couple of other areas for hunting. This park is also probably your best chance of seeing red or fallow deer and wild boar.

Andalucía is a magnet for bird-lovers, with 13 resident raptor species and several others visiting from Africa in summer. Large birds of prey in mountain regions include the golden eagle and several other eagles, the griffon vulture (with a large population in the Sierra de Grazalema) and the Egyptian vulture.

The white stork nests from spring to summer on electricity pylons, trees and towers – sometimes in the middle of towns – in western Andalucía. The much rarer black stork also nests in western Andalucía, typically on cliff ledges. Both migrate across the Strait of Gibraltar in winter and spring to breed in Spain, white storks congregating in flocks of up to 3000 to cross the strait.

Andalucía is a haven for water birds, mainly thanks to extensive wetlands along the Atlantic coast – notably the Parque Nacional de Doñana in the Guadalquivir delta, where hundreds of thousands of migratory birds, including an estimated 80% of western Europe's wild ducks, spend the winter. (Visits to the park are by 4WD tour only.)

Andalucía is the main European breeding ground of the beautiful greater flamingo, which can be seen in large numbers in several places including on the Cabo de Gata walk.

National Parks & Reserves

Andalucía has more than 80 separate areas covering some 15,000 sq km. At the end of 1998 the high Sierra Nevada joined the wetlands of Doñana to become Andalucía's second *parque national* (national park); Cabo de Gata is expected to become the third. The other most important protected category is *parque natural* (nature park). Administered by Andalucía's Agencia de Medio Ambiente (Environmental Agency), these 22 parks include much of Andalucía's most spectacular mountains and coast.

CLIMATE

Andalucía is the most southerly and, overall, warmest part of peninsular Spain. But with its range of altitudes and distances from the sea, there's variation from area to area. For one thing, temperatures differ between the coast and the interior. On the coast it's temperate in winter and hot in summer. Inland it can be cold and inclement from November to February and sizzling in July and August. Daytime temperatures in these hottest months reach 36°C in inland cities, compared to about 30°C on the coasts. In December, January and February it regularly gets down to near-freezing at night in Granada, while along the coasts it rarely falls below 8°C.

You must subtract several degrees for the extra altitude at which many of the walking areas are set. Average daily minimum temperatures in the high Sierra Nevada in winter get as low as -9°C.

ANDALUCÍA

Most places get 400 to 500mm of rain a year (a little less than London), though there are exceptions: the Sierra de Grazalema in the west – the first major elevation encountered by the prevailing south-west winds from the Atlantic – is the wettest part of Spain with more than 2000mm of rain a year, while Cabo de Gata in the east is the driest place in Europe with little more than 100mm. Most rain falls between October and March; there's little anywhere from June to September.

Expect more cloud and rain in the mountains than on the coast and plains. Most ranges get at least a dusting of snow most winters, and the upper Sierra Nevada southeast of Granada is white for eight or nine months a year.

On the whole, the best months to walk in Andalucía are April, May, June, September and October – when the weather is warm, but not too warm, and the vegetation is at its most colourful (spring flowers, autumn leaves). You *can* walk in Andalucía in July and August – but make very sure that you take adequate water and protection from the sun, and don't hesitate to rest in the shade, or even abandon the walk, if the heat dictates. The one major exception to these general rules is the Sierra Nevada.

Of course, the weather in Andalucía is no more predictable than anywhere else. Four exceptionally dry, warm winters (and drought) in the early 1990s were followed by much wetter, cooler, longer winters from 1995 to 1998. This can mean that you'll enjoy clear, sunny days in the mountains in January – or rain in June.

INFORMATION
Maps

Michelin's *Southern Spain* 1:400,000 map, updated each year, is good for overall planning. It's widely available in and outside Andalucía; in Spain, look in petrol stations and bookshops – the map costs 785 ptas.

Published large-scale maps of Andalucía should be regarded as approximations to reality – useful, but never fully to be trusted. They're basically OK on contours, courses of rivers and other natural features, but when it comes to paths and tracks, they show a lot that don't exist, and don't show many which do exist. Some maps are better than others, but none we have used are exempt from these comments.

There's a magnetic declination of between 3° and 6° west over most of Andalucía, diminishing by around six minutes a year.

Books

Lonely Planet's *Andalucía* by John Noble and Susan Forsyth fills out the picture for those who want to experience the region's cities, culture, nightlife and beaches as well as its wilder places. Among the many Spanish-language guidebook series, Libros Penthalon's El Búho Viajero walking guides and Anaya Touring Club's Ecoguías stand out. The Búho Viajero volumes are particularly useful if you're looking for more walk ideas than we have space for in this book.

Andalucía has inspired a deep fascination among foreign writers for two centuries. American Washington Irving took up residence in Granada's Alhambra palace when it was in an abandoned state in the 1820s. His *Tales of the Alhambra*, easy to find locally, weaves a series of enchanting stories around the folk with whom he shared his life there.

In the 1920s literary Englishman Gerald Brenan settled in Yegen, a remote village in Las Alpujarras, with 'a good many books and a little money', aiming to educate himself unimpeded by British traditions. *South from Granada* is his absorbing, amusing account of local life and visits from members of the Bloomsbury set.

Moorish Spain by Richard Fletcher, a fascinating short history of the country's Islamic era, concentrates to a large extent on Andalucía. Alastair Boyd's *The Sierras of the South* evokes the hill country around Ronda in the 1950s and 60s, when foreigners were a rarity. *Inside Andalusia* by David Baird is a lively recent collection of portraits of people and places.

It would be hard to better James Woodall's *In Search of the Firedance* as an introduction to that essentially Andalucian art form, flamenco. Michael Jacobs'

Andalucía runs comprehensively and entertainingly through all the important cultural and historical aspects of Andalucía, adding informed comment on the present and a good gazetteer of places and sights.

Naturalists will find both *Wild Flowers of Southern Spain* by Betty Molesworth Allen and *Where to Watch Birds in Southern Spain* by Ernest Garcia and Andrew Paterson useful, but will want a field guide with pictures to complement the latter.

Information Sources

Tourist information is provided by scores of tourist offices – usually well informed and helpful – in just about every city, town and village of any interest across Andalucía.

Most of the walks in this chapter are in parques naturales, which usually have their own *centros de interpretación* (interpretation centres) and information offices with more specific information for walkers, including routes and places to stay along the way. Useful ones are noted under individual walks.

Probably the best map and guidebook shop in Andalucía is Atlante Mapas (☎/fax 95 260 27 65), Calle Echegaray 7 in central Málaga. They have lots of Servicio Geográfco del Ejército (SGE) and Instituto Geográfico Naciona/Centro Nacional de Información Geográfica (IGN/CNIG; referred to here as IGN) maps and Spanish guidebooks to parts of Andalucía and the rest of Spain. In Granada, Cartográfica del Sur (☎ 958 20 49 01), Calle Valle Inclán 2, is the best source of maps and guidebooks. In Jaén try Librería Metrópolis, Calle del Cerón 19. In Almería try Librería Cajal (☎ 950 23 61 48), Calle Navarro Rodrigo 14.

IGN has map sales offices in Andalucía's eight provincial capitals, though with rather brief opening hours (eg Monday to Friday 10 am to 2 pm). These include:

Almería
 (☎ 950 23 45 07) Camino de la Sismológica 26
Granada
 (☎ 958 29 04 11) Avenida Divina Pastora 7
Jaén
 (☎ 953 22 18 32) Plaza de la Constitución 10, 5th floor

Málaga
 (☎ 95 231 28 08) Avenida de la Aurora 47, 7th floor
Sevilla
 (☎ 95 464 42 56) Avenida San Francisco Javier 9, Edificio Sevilla 2, 8th floor (modulo 7)

Permits

Some walks in the Sierra de Grazalema can only be done with a guide. For a brief description of these, see Other Walks at the end of the chapter.

ACCOMMODATION & SUPPLIES

Except for the Sierra de las Nieves walk, you can get supplies once you reach the walking areas. However, if you're arriving there in the evening and starting out before the shops open next morning, you'll need to take some supplies with you. Andalucian cities have plenty of shops and supermarkets, and usually at least one food market.

Youth Hostels

The 20 or so *albergues juveniles* of the Andalucian youth hostel organisation, Inturjoven, are mostly good, modern places with space for 100 to 200 people. They usually have plenty of twin rooms, often with private bathroom. Maps are provided. The hostels don't have cooking facilities but they normally serve all meals at good prices. Low/high season bed-only prices are 963/1391 ptas for under-26s and 1284/1712 ptas for others. High season is all year at Córdoba, Granada, Huelva, Málaga, Almería and Sevilla; at Jerez de la Frontera it's April to September; at Sierra Nevada it's when the ski station is open (normally early December to early May); and at the other hostels it's mid-June to mid-September, holiday weekends year-round and Semana Santa (the week leading up to Easter Sunday).

Jaén

Hostal La Española (☎ *953 23 02 54, Calle Bernardo Lopez 9*), a characterful house in the old part of town, has singles/doubles for 1600/3000 ptas, or doubles with bathroom for 4000 ptas. For its rooms,

Hotel Xauen (☎ 953 24 07 89, Plaza del Dean Mazas 3) charges 5564/7490 ptas.

Granada

The good *Camping Sierra Nevada (☎ 958 15 00 62, Avenida de Madrid 107)*, 200m from the bus station, charges around 500 ptas per adult, and the same per tent and per vehicle. It closes from November to February. The *Albergue Juvenil Granada (☎ 958 27 26 38, Calle Ramón y Cajal 2)* is 600m south-west of the train station.

Posada Doña Lupe (☎ 958 22 14 73) on Avenida del Generalife is handy for the Alhambra and has singles/doubles/triples with bathroom from 1000/1950/2950 ptas, or 700 ptas per person with your own bedding. Prices include a light breakfast. On Cuesta de Gomérez, running up to the Alhambra, *Hostal Britz (☎ 958 22 36 52)*, at No 1, has rooms from 2300/3500 ptas to 3600/5000 ptas; *Hostal Gomérez (☎ 958 22 44 37)*, at No 10, charges 1500/2500 ptas – both are good choices.

Almería

The *Albergue Juvenil Almería (☎ 950 26 97 88)*, Calle Isla de Fuerteventura, is 1.5km east of the centre; take bus No 1 ('Universidad') from Rambla del Obispo Orbera in the centre and ask for the 'albergue juvenil'.

Hostal-Residencia Americano (☎ 950 25 80 11, Avenida de la Estación 6), near the bus and train stations, is a good choice. Singles/doubles are from 2200/4200 ptas to 2800/5000 ptas. *Hostal Universal (☎ 950 23 55 57, Puerta de Purchena 3)* in the centre has simple rooms for 1500/3000 ptas.

Málaga

The *Albergue Juvenil Málaga (☎ 95 230 85 00)* is on Plaza Pío XII, 1.5km west of the centre. Bus No 18 along Avenida de Andalucía from the Alameda Principal (the central thoroughfare) goes most of the way. *Hostal Chinitas (☎ 95 221 46 83, Pasaje Chinitas 2)* off the central Plaza de la Constitución is basic but clean and friendly with rooms for 1819/3638 ptas. Also north of the Alameda Principal, *Hostal Derby (☎ 95 222 13 01, Calle San Juan de Dios 1)* has spacious rooms with bathroom from 3200/4500 ptas.

Sevilla

Many Sevilla room prices go up by anything from 20% to 200% during and around Semana Santa and April and you should book far ahead for those times.

The *Albergue Juvenil Sevilla (☎ 95 461 31 50, Calle Isaac Peral 2)* is 10 minutes south by bus No 34 from opposite the main tourist office on Avenida de la Constitución.

The attractive Barrio de Santa Cruz, east of the cathedral, has lots of *hostales* (cheap hotels). Among several on Calle Archeros, friendly *Hostal Bienvenido (☎ 95 441 36 55)*, at No 14, charges 1700/3200 ptas. *Pensión Fabiola (☎ 95 421 83 46, Calle Fabiola 16)*, with a plant-filled courtyard, has well kept rooms for 2000/4000 ptas.

There are many other places north of Plaza Nueva. *Hostal Lis II (☎ 95 456 02 28, Calle Olavide 5)* is in a beautiful house and charges 1700 ptas for small singles and 3500 ptas for doubles with toilet. *Hotel Zaida (☎ 95 421 11 38, Calle San Roque 26)* occupies an 18th century house with a lovely patio. Rooms are 3210/5350 ptas with bathroom.

Ronda

Camping El Sur (☎ 95 287 59 39), 2km out on the Algeciras road, charges 1337 ptas for two adults with a tent. Rooms are mainly in the newer part of town north of El Tajo gorge. Bright *Pensión La Purísima (☎ 95 287 10 50, Calle Sevilla 10)* has nine rooms at 2000/3000 ptas. *Hotel Virgen de los Reyes (☎ 95 287 11 40, Calle Lorenzo Borrego Gómez 13)* has solid rooms with bathroom for 3000/5000 ptas.

GETTING THERE & AWAY

The peak season for travel to Andalucía is mid-June to mid-September, with Semana Santa also busy.

Air

Málaga airport is the main international gateway in Andalucía. Almería, Sevilla, Jerez de la Frontera and Gibraltar airports also receive some international flights. Andalucía's other airport, Granada, receives internal Spanish flights only. For more information on international flights, see the Getting There & Away chapter.

Iberia flies direct from Madrid and Barcelona to all Andalucía's airports, daily in every case except Barcelona-Jerez. There are direct flights to Málaga or Sevilla from several other cities, too. Iberia's cheapest Barcelona-Málaga and Madrid-Sevilla return fares are 23,800 ptas and 14,300 ptas respectively. Air Europa undercuts Iberia by a few thousand pesetas on most of its routes, which include Barcelona to Granada, Málaga and Sevilla; Tenerife to Málaga and Sevilla; Bilbao and Madrid to Málaga; and Gran Canaria, Palma de Mallorca and Santiago de Compostela to Sevilla.

Spanair flies to Málaga direct from Madrid and from Barcelona, with Madrid-Málaga returns for 10,000 ptas.

Land

Bus For information on international routes, see the Getting There & Away chapter.

Within Spain, daily buses run, among other routes, from Madrid (Estación Sur de Autobuses) to all main and many smaller Andalucian cities and towns; from Barcelona, Valencia and other Mediterranean coast cities to Almería, Jaén, Granada, Córdoba, Sevilla and Málaga and the Costa de Sol; and to Sevilla from cities in Extremadura, Galicia and Castilla y León. Barcelona-Granada takes 14 hours for around 7600 ptas; Madrid-Málaga is 8½ hours and 2750 ptas.

Within Andalucía, buses link all the main cities. Granada-Almería, for instance, takes 2¼ hours for 1285 ptas; Granada-Sevilla is four hours for 2700 ptas. Buses reach just about every town and village, though services to small villages may run just once a day – and not at all on weekends. See individual walk sections for specifics.

Train For international routes, see the Getting There & Away chapter.

The high-speed AVE (Tren de Alta Velocidad Español) between Madrid and Sevilla is the pride of Spanish railways, covering the 471km in just 2½ hours and reaching 280km/h, with one-way fares from 8100 ptas to 16,600 ptas depending on class and time of day. Other Madrid-Sevilla trains take 3¼ to 4¼ hours for 5400 ptas to 7900 ptas in the cheapest classes.

A Talgo 200 is a normal Talgo train which uses part of the AVE track for trips between Madrid and some Andalucian destinations. On a Talgo 200, Madrid-Málaga can take as little as four hours.

Daily direct train services from Madrid include to Jaén (4½ hours, 2945 ptas), Granada (six to 8½ hours, 3100 to 3300 ptas), Almería (6½ to 9½ hours, 3800 to 3900 ptas), Málaga (four to 11½ hours, 4600 to 8000 ptas) and Ronda (8¾ hours, 4600 ptas). Fares quoted are the cheapest available.

Trains from Barcelona either funnel through Madrid or head down the Mediterranean coast to Valencia and enter Andalucía through Linares-Baeza (north-east of Jaén). There's no passenger line to Andalucía through Murcia to the east. Barcelona to Granada costs around 6300 ptas (12 to 14½ hours).

There's also a line from Cáceres and Merida in Extremadura to Sevilla. Cáceres-Sevilla costs 2165 ptas (six hours).

Within Andalucía a good network of *regionales* (regional trains) supplements the long-distance services to connect most main cities. Among regionales, a Tren Regional Diesel (TRD) is a bit quicker and dearer than an Andalucía Express (AE). Granada-Almería, for instance, takes 2¼ hours for 1710 ptas by TRD, and 2¾ hours (1550 ptas) by AE.

Car & Motorcycle A car or motorcycle is the easiest way of reaching most walks. At Málaga airport, on the Costa del Sol, in Nerja and at the Almería package resorts, you can rent a small car from a local firm for around 20,000 ptas a week all inclusive (as low as 16,000 ptas in winter). Elsewhere, and from the multinational firms, rates are often double that.

Málaga Car Hire (in the UK ☎ 0181-398 2662; from 1 June 1999, 020-8398 2662) rents cars to be picked up at Málaga airport from £90 a week all inclusive in summer (from £65 from November to January).

Parque Natural de Cazorla

The Parque Natural de las Sierras de Cazorla, Segura y Las Villas (to give it its full title) in north-east Andalucía is, at 2143 sq km, the largest environmentally protected area in Spain. It's a crinkled, pinnacled region of several complicated sierras – not extraordinarily high, but memorably beautiful – divided by high plains called *navas*, deep river valleys and lakes. Much of the park is thickly forested and wild animals abound.

The park stretches 90km from north to south and up to 35km from east to west, with most of its ranges aligned roughly north-south. The attractive old town of Cazorla, 100km east of Jaén, is the main gateway. The Río Guadalquivir rises in the south of the park between the Sierra de Cazorla and Sierra del Pozo and flows 60km north into the Embalse del Tranco de Beas reservoir, where it turns west towards the Atlantic. It's also in the south that millions of years of erosion of limestone and dolomitic rocks have created the park's most marvellous karstic mountainscapes.

It's therefore in the south that we have chosen the three day-walks described in this section. They're separate walks, not one circuit, because the park's one real disappointment is that in its southern part the only bus service and all the places to stay – including the camping grounds, which are the only places you are allowed to camp – are along the Guadalquivir valley. This means that anywhere more than half a day's walk from there or from the park's fringe towns and villages is out of reach for people without a vehicle. There *are* some good walks from Guadalquivir and the fringe settlements, and it's quite possible to devise a route of several days linking them, but the

ideal way to explore the park is to have a vehicle to reach day walks in some of its more remote areas. Many of the park's dirt roads are chained to bar motor vehicles, making them fine for walkers who have a vehicle to get them to the tracks' starts.

HISTORY

The park area has never been heavily populated. In the 18th century the sierras were turned over to the Spanish navy which had many of the native evergreen and deciduous oaks and black pine floated downriver to be made into ships at Cádiz or Cartagena. In 1960, 700 sq km in what is now the southern part of the park were declared a *coto nacional de casa* (national hunting reserve). This greatly increased the numbers of larger animals by subjecting hunting to strict controls, reintroducing species which had been hunted to extinction here such as the red deer and wild boar, and introducing new species.

By the mid-1980s the area's attractions were pulling in so many visitors – 700,000 in 1985 – that its ecology was under threat. The creation of the parque natural in 1986 was in part a response to this. The park attempts to conserve the environment while promoting compatible economic activities.

FAUNA

The big five species are the ibex, mouflon, wild boar, red deer and the smaller fallow deer (all subject to controlled hunting).

The ibex lives mainly on rocky heights. Its numbers, down to about 500 in the 1950s, grew to 10,000 in the late 1980s but were then slashed back to 500 by a scabies outbreak. Since then it has recovered to a population approaching 2000.

The other four animals prefer forests. The fallow deer and the mouflon (a large, wild sheep, reddish-brown in colour, with a very ovine bleat) were introduced here in the 1960s for hunting; but the roe deer, hunted out of existence, has not been reintroduced.

Your prospects of seeing wildlife increase as you get further from the beaten track. The chances are also higher early and late in the

Coto

You see this word scrawled all over parts of the Spanish countryside. On rocks, signs, walls, on the ground, by roadsides, in forests. With a variety of companion words – Coto Privado, Coto Nacional, Coto Deportivo de Caza, Coto Municipal San Isidro, Coto X4204, Coto Torrox – but most mysteriously on its own, over and over again: COTO, COTO, COTO, COTO.

Is this the mantra of some new mind-warping cult being subliminally infiltrated into Spain's brains? Is it a football team? A political movement? A rock group? No. Like so many things in the Spanish countryside, it's to do with hunting (*caza*). One – perhaps the original – meaning of *coto* is cairn or boundary marker, but it has come to mean an area on which hunting (shooting) rights are restricted to a certain person or group – be they private individuals (*coto privado*), a municipality (*coto municipal*), or even the nation (*coto nacional* or *reserva nacional de caza*). Cotos privados are often also signalled by small, rectangular signs divided diagonally into a black triangle and a white triangle. Publicly-owned hunting rights are normally shared out, by methods including lottery, among individuals who apply for them for a season. So that there will be animals and birds to be hunted next year, too, there are complicated regulations and rules, even on cotos privados, about what animals can be shot and where and when.

And as for when you simply see plain old 'COTO' on its own, the only thing you can be sure of is that – even if you were inclined to – you can't wander in and start blasting away at every furry or feathery thing that moves.

---

day – deer are most likely to emerge onto open grassy areas at these times.

Wild boar rarely appear till dusk – though while walking you'll very likely come across areas of upturned earth where they have rooted for food.

Some 140 bird species nest in the park.

Rocky crags are the haunt of golden and Bonelli's eagles, griffon and Egyptian vultures and peregrine falcons; in the forests you may spot buzzards, short-toed eagles, booted eagles, goshawks, sparrowhawks, and hobby or great spotted woodpeckers. One bird that's something of an emblem of the park (but which you'll be lucky to see) is the lammergeier, Europe's largest bird of prey. It disappeared from the park, its only Spanish habitat outside the Pyrenees, in 1986, but is being reintroduced.

FLORA

In dry Andalucía, the park's rich vegetation is a delight. In spring the flowers are magnificent; some areas seem a red carpet of poppies. In autumn, deciduous trees provide vivid splashes of colour.

Of the park's 2300 plant species, 24 are endemic including the beautiful *violeta de Cazorla*, or Cazorla violet, a very bright violet colour, and the *geranio* cazorlense, or Cazorla geranium. Both these like rock crevices in the drier areas.

The Parque Natural de Cazorla has Andalucía's biggest forests, with pine species predominant. The tall *pino laricio*, or black pine (*Pinus nigra*), with its horizontally-spreading branches typically clustered near the top, generally likes the higher terrain above 1300m.

The other two main pine species, introduced for timber, have largely replaced the oaks lost to shipbuilding: the *pino maritimo*, or maritime pine (*P. pinaster*; also known as *pino resinero* in Spanish), with its typically rounded top, grows at levels up to about 1500m; the *pino carrasco*, or Aleppo pine (*P. halepensis*), with a bushy top and separated, often bare branches, predominates at warmer, drier levels up to 1100m.

Some holm oak and gall oak woods remain and if you know your trees you'll find many other tree species, including wild olive, juniper, poplar, ash, willow and maple – these last four occur most commonly in river valleys. Unusually for southern Spain, some hazels, yew and even holly trees can be found growing in lower-lying, rainy areas.

Sierra de Cazorla Loop

Duration 6 to 6½ hours
Distance 18km
Standard Medium
Start/Finish Cazorla
Public Transport Yes
Summary A panoramic loop in the Sierra de Cazorla combining mountain and woodland scenery, with the option of ending in the Guadalquivir valley instead of returning to Cazorla – a good introduction to the Parque Natural de Cazorla.

This walk takes you into the hills behind Cazorla town. Especially worth a look in Cazorla itself are the Castillo de la Yedra (Castle of the Ivy), housing the Museo del Alto Guadalquivir (Museum of the Upper Guadalquivir), and Plaza de Santa María with the 400-year-old Fuente de las Cadenas and the shell of the 16th century Iglesia de Santa María, which was wrecked by Napoleonic troops.

Quercus (☎ 953 72 01 15) at Calle Juan Domingo 2, just off Plaza de la Constitución, where buses stop, provides some tourist and park information as well as selling maps and offering excursions into the park.

PLANNING
When to Walk
The walking is best from April to June and in September and October. At these times the number of other visitors (except in Semana Santa) should be well below the summer holiday peak.

Maps & Books
The Editorial Alpina *Sierra de Cazorla* 1:40,000 map, published in 1998, is the best. You should be able to find it in Cazorla town if you haven't obtained it beforehand.

What to Bring
Carry water for the whole trip – or to get you as far as the Parador El Adelantado or Fuente del Oso if you're heading down that way.

PLACES TO STAY & EAT
Cazorla has a number of options. The spick and-span *Albergue Juvenil Cazorla* (☎ 95. 72 03 29, Plaza Mauricio Martínez 6) i 200m uphill from Plaza de la Corredera.

Friendly *Hostal Betis* (☎ 953 72 05 40 Plaza de la Corredera 19) has singles. doubles from 1200/2500 ptas to 1500/2700 ptas. *La Cueva de Juan Pedro* (☎ 953 7: 12 25) on Plaza de Santa María is only mar ginally dearer. *Hotel Guadalquivir* (☎ 95: 72 02 68, Calle Nueva 6), just off Call Doctor Muñoz, is a step up in quality doubles with bathroom cost 5200 ptas.

La Forchetta (Calle de las Escuelas 2) just down from Plaza de la Constitución serves fine pizzas and pasta for 500 ptas t 800 ptas. Down on Plaza de Santa María the ancient *La Cueva de Juan Pedro* serve: up traditional Cazorla fare such as rabbit trout, *rin-rán* (a mashed concoction o bacalao, potato and dried red peppers), wil boar, venison and even mouflon – all avail able as *raciones* (meal-sized serves), done variety of ways, for 900 ptas.

In the Guadalquivir Valley, the *Compleje Turístico Puente de las Herrerías* (☎ 953 7: 70 90) at Puente de las Herrerías is the larges camping ground in the park, with room fo 1000 at 425 ptas per adult and per tent. It als has *cabañas* (cabins) and a restaurant, an opens from about mid-April to early Novem ber (plus winter holiday weekends).

The *Parador El Adelantado* (☎ 953 7: 70 75) offers all the usual parador comfort: in a pine forest setting, with rooms from 10,700/13,375 ptas to 12,840/16,050 ptas depending on season.

GETTING TO/FROM THE WALK
Alsina Graells runs two daily buses from Granada (10.30 am and 3 pm) to Cazorl: via Jaén, Baeza and Úbeda. The ride take 3½ hours from Granada and two hours (930 ptas) from Jaén.

Carcesa (☎ 953 72 11 42) runs buses daily except Sunday from Cazorla to Empalme de Valle, Arroyo Frío, Torre del Vinagre and Cot Ríos in the parque natural. At our last check buses left Cazorla in summer at 6.30 am an

2 pm, the rest of the year at 5.45 am (6.30 am on Saturday) and 2.30 pm. The bus takes about 30 minutes to Empalme del Valle, one hour to Torre del Vinagre and 1¼ hours to Coto Ríos. Buses back to Cazorla left Coto Ríos at 7.45 am (6.45 am Monday to Friday outside summer) and 4.15 pm. In Cazorla, Quercus has current timetable information.

THE WALK

Leave Cazorla's Plaza de Santa María by Camino de San Isidro, between the Fuente de las Cadenas and Restaurante La Cueva de Juan Pedro. Five minutes later, after two one-spout fountains on the left, veer left up a dirt road, then go left at another one-spout fountain. Your track climbs past idyllic-looking little farms, with the remains of Cazorla's pentagonal-towered upper castle, the Castillo de Cinco Esquinas, up to your left. Forty minutes from Plaza de Santa María, at the top of a zigzag rise, go left. The track becomes a footpath which in 10 minutes brings you to the 17th century **Monasterio de Monte Sión** in a beautiful fold of the hills. This was restored a few years ago but is now seemingly empty.

The trail rounds the monastery orchard and climbs into woods. You can begin to contemplate the sea of olive trees that covers one-third of Jaén province and produces 10% of the world's olive oil. Half an hour from the monastery you emerge on the dirt road between Riogazas and El Chorro. Go 50m to the right, then left up a faint path marked by a green arrow and small cairn. The path, immediately more distinct, climbs east and after 15 minutes meets a path coming from the left at a stone with green-and-blue paint daubs. Go right and in 40 minutes upward you reach the 1750m Puerto Gilillo (or Collado del Gilillo). Here, eastward views down towards the Guadalquivir valley and across to other ranges join the westward panoramas you have enjoyed on the way up. There's a small stone shelter just below the pass.

To cap **Gilillo** (1848m), the highest peak in this area of the park (just over 100m higher than Cazorla), head south up from the pass. The 15 minute ascent is regularly

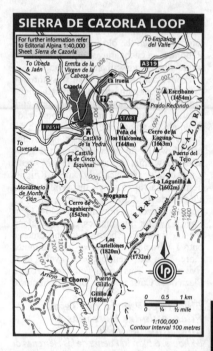

SIERRA DE CAZORLA LOOP

made by the local ungulates, judging by the number of their droppings.

Back at Puerto Gilillo, take the path north from beside the stone hut. This wends north-north-east along the **Loma de los Castellones** ridge, with alternating eastern and western panoramas. The path is mostly clear but you have to look for it going round the left side of the second hump (marked 1732m on the Editorial Alpina map). A few minutes later follow a green marker down to the left; you're soon continuing in the same direction as before. Ten minutes later ignore a right turn by three cairns, and after another 25 minutes cross a grassy basin to join a track coming from the right. A further 10 minutes along you reach the **Puerto del Tejo** (1556m) with a three-way path junction.

To head back to Cazorla, go left. The path winds round Cerro de la Laguna and then descends northward. Forty-five minutes from

Puerto del Tejo you cross a firebreak and pass under some power lines. Ten minutes later you reach the old *cortijo* (farm) **Prado Redondo**, an enchanting spot in a fold of the mountains with Escribano rising above.

From Prado Redondo head west through the trees. Your path bends a little to the right, climbing, then curves gradually left and, finally, less than 10 minutes from Prado Redondo, descends into a gully beneath the power lines you passed earlier. Follow the path down (it diverges left from the gully after a few minutes) and you'll pass above La Iruela's spectacularly sited Knights Templar castle to reach the **Ermita de la Virgen de la Cabeza**, a chapel, after 25 minutes. Cazorla is now in sight below. Continue down for five minutes, turn right along the La Iruela-El Chorro road and emerge onto La Iruela's main street in 15 minutes more. Turn left, then fork left downhill after five minutes. This brings you into Cazorla's Plaza de la Corredera in another 15 minutes.

Side Trip: Puerto del Tejo to Puente de las Herrerías & Empalme de Valle

1½ hours, 6.5km to Puente de las Herrerías or 2½ hours, 9.5km total to Empalme de Valle
This takes you down from Puerto del Tejo to the only two places to stay in the southern part of the park. If you decide to continue on to Empalme del Valle, add a further 1 hour and 3km to the walk total. Even if you don't plan to stay at either, you might enjoy a wander down towards the green Guadalquivir valley. If you're early enough you can catch a bus from Empalme del Valle down the valley or back to Cazorla.

Several worthwhile walks begin at Puente de las Herrerías; some are outlined briefly in Other Walks at the end of this chapter.

At Puerto del Tejo take the northward path, which winds 2km down to the Parador El Adelantado (1325m). From here, a paved road descends the hill. A little more than 3km down is the **Fuente del Oso** (1120m), a shady roadside fountain from which the Sendero de la Fuente del Oso footpath goes 1.4km south-east down to the **Puente de las Herrerías** (about 1000m, 1½ hours from the

Puerto del Tejo). This bridge over the upper Guadalquivir, supposedly built in one night for Queen Isabel La Católica to cross during her campaigns against Granada, stands at the south end of the Complejo Turístico Puente de las Herrerías tourist complex.

An off-road alternative between the *parador* (one of a chain of luxury state hotels) and the Puente de las Herrerías, missing out the Fuente del Oso, begins a little more than 1km down the road from the parador (800m beyond the 3km marker). On a leftward bend beneath the hill Cruz de Quique, a path heads off to the right marked by a tiny, red-paint arrow. Ten minutes along this, go left at a fork where a red arrow points right. This should have you down at the Puente de las Herrerías in another 30 minutes or so – we haven't been all the way down to confirm this, but the first few hundred metres look convincing enough.

Another path from the Fuente del Oso, the Sendero de El Empalme del Valle, strikes 1.5km north-west over the 1230m Collado del Oso to **Empalme del Valle** on the A319. Empalme del Valle is about one hour from the Puente de las Herrerías – or 1½ hours from the Puerto del Tejo if you came straight from the Fuente del Oso.

Eastern Valleys Loop

Duration 5½ to 6½ hours
Distance 21km
Standard Easy-Medium
Start/Finish 400m east of Cortijo del Tío Dionisio on the Empalme del Valle-Campos de Hernán Perea road
Public Transport No
Summary A walk combining the beautiful Valdecuevas, Valdetrillos and Guadalentín river valleys and a little mountain crossing in the less visited eastern part of the Parque Natural de Cazorla.

It's not easy to select a single route from the park's many off-the-beaten-track possibilities. We were lucky enough to see 23 deer (all fallow, we think) and six mouflon on this walk – mostly in and after the Barranco del Guadalentín (where *barranco* in Spanish means gully or ravine).

PLANNING

Recommended seasons and maps are the same as for the Sierra de Cazorla Loop walk. It's best to take enough water for the whole walk. You walk beside several streams and rivers but there's no certainty they'll be fit to drink.

PLACES TO STAY & EAT

There's a *bar* serving *comidas caseras* (home-cooked meals) at the Cortijo del Tío Dionisio, but you can't rely on it being open outside main tourist seasons.

GETTING TO/FROM THE WALK

The start/finish is just over one hour's drive from Cazorla, about 10km east of the nearest place to stay (Complejo Turístico Puente de las Herrerías) and about 15km from the nearest bus stop (Empalme del Valle).

From Empalme del Valle take the east-bound road for approximately 13.5km. You cross the Río Guadalquivir after 3.5km (ignore a turn towards Puente de las Herrerías and the Nacimiento del Guadalquivir 400m beyond), then climb through forest for 7km, the road surface changing from smooth to rough 4.5km beyond the river. The walk starts where the road turns right, about 400m past the 24km marker and the Cortijo del Tío Dionisio. At this corner a dirt road (with a chain to stop unauthorised vehicles) goes straight on.

THE WALK

Follow the dirt road from the start of the walk for 30 minutes along a pleasant wooded valley to a fork on the west side of a small bridge over the Arroyo de Valde-cuevas. Follow the straight-on track for 25 minutes up the valley until it fades into faint footpaths. Return to and cross the bridge, and wind round in 15 minutes to a bend with a view over the strange rock formations of the **Estrecho de los Perales**. Continue up the

Valdetrillos valley on this track to its end in a small clearing 35 minutes along.

Now comes the only hard bit of the walk, a steep, pathless ascent of 240m (30 minutes) to **El Pocico**, a minor pass in the forested ridge to your east. Head towards the furthest point of the curve of the ridge line and ascend the gully between two prominent rock outcrops. Occasional use of hands is needed but there's nothing difficult or dangerous about it. Rewarding views open out to the west. Veer a little to the right as you near the top, to find a slight dip in the ridge giving onto a grassy dell. Head east-north-east across the dell, picking up a thin path over its far lip, then down 80m between two lines of stones (apparently aligned naturally). Turn right (south) down a grassy valley. From the clearing visible at the foot of this, a path leads down to a longer grassy clearing; from the end of that continue down to meet a dirt road 25 minutes from the ridge top.

Walk south along the road, passing a milepost signed '31km' within a minute or so. To the east is the Sierra de la Cabrilla, the highest range in the park.

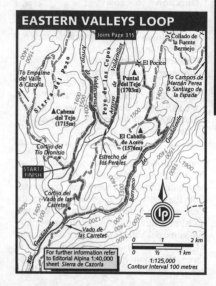

EASTERN VALLEYS LOOP

For further information refer to Editorial Alpina 1:40,000 sheet *Sierra de Cazorla*

0   1   2 km
0   ½   1 km
1:125,000
Contour Interval 100 metres

After 20 minutes turn left down a dirt track, which descends in 25 minutes to the Río Guadalentín at the bottom of its steep valley. You now have a lovely 90 minute walk south-west along the thickly wooded Barranco del Guadalentín beside the bubbling river, with high, pinnacled crags rising on both sides. Look out for deer around a ruined house by the track after 15 minutes. Forty minutes later, there's a big **natural rock arch** up to the right (you can get up to it in 15 minutes). A further 10 minutes along, where the main track crosses the river, stay on the west bank following green paint arrows. After 600m pass left of a 'Finca Particular, Prohibido el Paso' (Private Farm, No Entry) sign. At a track junction 10 minutes later, turn right following the finca's perimeter fence away from the Guadalentín and the Vado de las Carretas ford. In 35 minutes your track climbs back to the road – with a dense holm oak forest around the junction. Go left and in 15 minutes you're back at your vehicle.

Río Borosa Walk

Duration 6 to 7 hours
Distance 24km
Standard Easy-Medium
Start/Finish Centro de Interpretación Torre del Vinagre
Public Transport Yes
Summary This is the most popular walk in the Cazorla park, a day of exquisite valley and mountain scenery on the ascent of a tributary of the Guadalquivir, via a narrow gorge and two tunnels, to two beautiful mountain lakes.

The Cazorla park's best known walk follows the Río Borosa (also called Aguas Negras) upstream through scenery that progresses from the pretty to the majestic. It starts at the Centro de Interpretación Torre del Vinagre, a visitor centre on the A319, 16km north of Empalme del Valle (open daily except winter Mondays from 11 am to 2 pm, plus two or three afternoon hours depending on the season). In an adjoining building is a Museo

de Caza (Hunting Museum) with stuffed park wildlife (open the same hours), and just along the road is a botanical garden of the park's flora (open rather limited hours).

PLANNING
The large numbers of other people on the route can be a deterrent at major holiday times such as Semana Santa. Otherwise, recommended seasons and maps are the same as for the Sierra de Cazorla Loop walk.

What to Bring
The route is dotted with good track-side springs, the last of these at the Central Eléctrica. Carry a water bottle that you can fill there with enough water to take you to the top of the walk and back (about three hours). A torch (flashlight) is comforting in the darkest bits of the tunnels.

PLACES TO STAY & EAT
There's a variety of places to stay on and near the A319 within a few kilometres of Torre del Vinagre.

Hotel de Montaña La Hortizuela (☎ 953 71 31 50), 2km north from Torre del Vinagre, then 1km up a side road, is a cosy, small hotel where good singles/doubles with bathroom are 4280/5350 ptas. For 1765 ptas you can get a set dinner and breakfast thrown in. A group of wild boar comes to the hotel garden to dine on the slops thrown out after lunch.

A further 1km north on the A319, *Hostal Mirasierra* (☎ 953 71 30 44) has rooms with bathroom for 4066/5136 ptas. Within the next 4km on (or just off) the road are three riverside camping grounds, all charging around 300 ptas per car and per adult and 400 ptas per tent: *Camping Chopera Coto Ríos* (☎ 953 71 30 05), *Camping Llanos de Arance* (☎ 953 71 31 39) and *Camping Fuente de la Pascuala* (☎ 953 71 30 28). Cazorla camping grounds do not always stick to their published opening dates and from October to April it's worth ringing ahead.

Arroyo Frío, on the A319, 10km south of Torre del Vinagre, has two mid-range hotels, plus the *Complejo Turístico Los*

Enebros (☎ 953 72 71 10) which includes a hotel (rooms with bathroom for 5885/7490 ptas, including breakfast) and a small camping ground (400 ptas per adult, per tent and per car).

GETTING TO/FROM THE WALK

Using the Cazorla-Coto Ríos bus service (to Torre del Vinagre), you can do it as a day trip from Cazorla or Arroyo Frío. See the Sierra de Cazorla Loop walk for bus schedule information.

THE WALK

Opposite the Centro de Interpretación Torre del Vinagre, take a road east off the A319 signed 'Central Eléctrica'. This crosses the Guadalquivir and, 1.5km from the A319, reaches a *piscifactoría* (fish farm), with parking areas close by. Shortly past the piscifactoría the road crosses the Río Borosa and immediately on your right is the marked start of the walk.

The first section is along a dirt road which twice crosses the tumbling, trout-rich river on bridges as you move up the narrow, lushly vegetated valley. After 40 minutes, diverge to the right along a path signed 'Cerrada de Elías'. This takes you through a beautiful, 30 minute section where the valley narrows to a gorge (the **Cerrada de Elías**) and the path briefly takes to a wooden walkway to save you from swimming.

You re-emerge on the dirt road and soon pass above another gorge, the Cerrada de Fuente de Piedra. The rugged Cuerda de las Banderillas appears ahead, then the track turns south to the Central Eléctrica, a small hydroelectric transformer station 40 minutes from the Cerrada de Elías.

The path passes between the power station and river and crosses a footbridge, where a 'Nacimiento de Aguas Negras, Laguna de Valdeazores' sign directs you on upwards. The karstic mountainscape ahead begins to look increasingly like a Chinese painting as the river beside you descends in a series of high rock steps in waterfalls. Unfortunately the flow here is often diminished because some of its waters have been

diverted for the power station, and by the time you reach a curve of sheer cliffs preventing forward progress, 40 minutes from the station, the river may be completely dry. Here the path turns left and zigzags up into a **tunnel** inside the cliff. Water for the power station flows through the tunnel but a narrow path, separated from the watercourse by a fence, runs alongside. The tunnel is dimly lit for most, but not all, of its five minute length by a few openings in the rock wall.

Then there's five minutes in the open air before you enter a second tunnel, one minute long. From this you emerge just below the dam holding back the **Laguna de Aguas Negras** (or Embalse de los Órganos), a picturesque little reservoir surrounded by beautiful hills and trees. You have ascended 550m from the Río Guadalquivir to reach this point. Five minutes up the valley to the

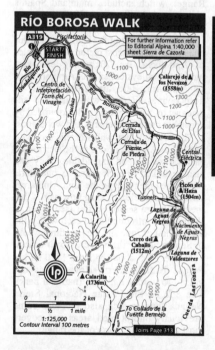

RÍO BOROSA WALK

For further information refer to Editorial Alpina 1:40,000 sheet *Sierra de Cazorla*

0   1   2 km
0   ½   1 mile
1:125,000
Contour Interval 100 metres

Joins Page 313

south-east is the **Nacimiento de Aguas Negras**, where the Río Borosa wells out from under a rock. A 15 minute walk south from the reservoir brings you to a similar-sized natural lake, the **Laguna de Valdeazores** – altogether about 3½ hours walking from Torre del Vinagre.

Return the way you came, unless you happen to have vehicle support, in which case you could continue 4km south-west to be picked up at the Collado de la Fuente Bermejo.

Sierra Nevada & Las Alpujarras

A casual visitor to the Alhambra in Granada will see, except perhaps from July to October, an imposing line of snow-topped mountains to the south-east. This is the west (high) end of the Sierra Nevada (Snowy Range), which includes mainland Spain's highest peak, Mulhacén (3478m), and many others over 3000m.

On the south side of the Sierra Nevada lies one of the oddest, most picturesque crannies of Andalucía, the 70km-long east-west jumble of valleys called Las Alpujarras, or La Alpujarra. Here, arid hillsides split by deep ravines alternate with oasis-like villages set by rapid streams and surrounded by vegetable gardens, orchards and woodlands.

The two four-day walks in this section – one in Las Alpujarras, one in the sierra – are easily divisible and extendable. They can also be linked to each other, as one starts where the other ends in the high Alpujarras village of Trevélez. A snag however is that their optimum seasons differ (see When to Walk in the introduction to each walk): the second half of June and the first three weeks of September are the best crossover times).

In late 1998 about half the 1710 sq km Parque Natural Sierra Nevada was upgraded to *parque nacional* (national park). The 862 sq km Parque Nacional Sierra Nevada thus created also includes some previously unprotected areas and covers most of the higher parts of the range.

Alpujarras Tour

Duration 4 days
Distance 57km
Standard Medium
Start Pampaneira
Finish Trevélez
Public Transport Yes
Summary A route linking many of this highly picturesque region's unique Berber-style villages. It features a variety of landscapes, from lush river valleys dotted with orchards and vegetable gardens to mountainside oak and pine forests.

The Alpujarras are not only a jumping-off point for many Sierra Nevada routes but also a fascinating area to walk in their own right. Old paths between the many intriguing, old-fashioned villages pass through constantly changing scenery. The western Alpujarras, in particular, has experienced a burst of tourism in the last decade or two, but the area remains a world apart, with a rare sense of timelessness and mystery. Reminders of the Muslim past are ubiquitous in the form of the Berber-style villages and the terracing and irrigation of the land.

The walk begins in the Barranco de Poqueira, one of the deepest of the many gashes in the south flank of the Sierra Nevada. The villages of Pampaneira, Bubión and Capileira are three of the most picturesque (albeit most touristed) in Las Alpujarras. You may want to spend a day or two exploring the Barranco de Poqueira, which reaches close up beneath the Sierra Nevada's highest peaks, before starting east eastward.

This walk takes Pampaneira, the lowest of the three villages, as its starting point simply because a useful information office, the Centro de Visitantes de Pampaneira (☎ 958 76 31 27), is located on its central Plaza de la Libertad. This normally opens from 10 am to 2 pm and 4 to 6 pm Wednesday to Saturday (other days from 10 am to 3 pm). Among other things, it can tell you about eight colour-coded walking routes of 4km to 23km marked out in the Barranco de Poqueira.

For several stretches our route follows the GR7 (see Place Names & Terminology under Walking Routes in the Facts for the Walker chapter), a long-distance footpath running from Andorra to Algeciras, as well as part of the European E4 path from Greece to Andalucía. In Andalucía the GR7 is far from complete, but the section through the Alpujarras has been marked out by posts with red and white rings and the text 'E4 GR7' and by signposts in villages. 'Wrong way' markers have a red-and-white 'X' instead of 'E4 GR7'. Here and there markers have been damaged or removed by vandals or nature.

With rarely more than two hours between villages, there is plenty of food, water and lodgings along the route. But it's best to ring ahead for rooms in the Barranco de Poqueira villages and Trevélez. Several of the bigger villages have small supermarkets and banks with ATMs (automatic teller machines; cash dispensers) – the latter including Pampaneira, Capileira, Trevélez and Cádiar.

HISTORY

In Muslim times the Alpujarras grew prosperous supplying the textile workshops of Almería, Granada and Málaga with silk thread – spun from the unravelled cocoons of caterpillars of the silk moth. Together with irrigation and agriculture, this activity probably supported a population of more than 150,000 before the fall of Granada in 1492.

Christian promises of tolerance for the conquered Muslims soon gave way to forced mass conversions and land expropriations, and in 1500 Muslims rebelled across Andalucía, with the Alpujarras in the thick of things. Afterwards, Muslims were given the choice of exile or conversion to Christianity. Most converted – to become known as *moriscos* – but the change was barely skin-deep. A 1567 decree by Felipe II forbidding use of Arabic names, dress and even the Arabic language brought a new revolt in the Alpujarras in 1568, which spread across southern Andalucía. Two years of vicious guerrilla war ensued, ending only after the rebel leader Aben Humeya was assassinated by his own cousin.

Alpujarras Villages

Travellers who have been to Morocco may notice a resemblance between villages in the Alpujarras and those in Morocco's Atlas mountains, from where the Alpujarran style was introduced in Muslim times by Berber settlers. The huddled white houses seem to clamber over each other in an effort not to slide down the hillsides. Streets too narrow for vehicles ramble between them, decked with flowery balconies.

Somewhere in most villages stands a solid 16th century *mudéjar* church – one built by Muslims living under Christian rule in medieval Spain. Most houses have two storeys, with the lower one used for storage and/or animals. The characteristic *terraos* (flat roofs), with their protruding chimney pots, consist of a layer of *launa* (a type of clay) packed onto flat stones, which are themselves laid on wooden beams. Nowadays there's often a layer of plastic between the stones and the launa for extra waterproofing.

A typical whitewashed Pitres lane in the Río Trevélez valley.

ANDALUCÍA

Almost the whole surviving Alpujarras population was then deported to other parts of Spain, and some 270 villages and hamlets were repeopled with settlers from northern Spain. Over 100 more were abandoned. Over the following centuries the silk industry fell by the wayside and swathes of the Alpujarras' woodlands were lost to mining and cereal growing.

PLANNING
When to Walk
The best times are April to mid-June and mid-September to early November. The summer months can be unpleasantly hot, and winter is often cold in the higher villages.

Maps & Books
The IGN *Sierra Nevada* 1:50,000 map shows some good paths that are missing from the appropriate IGN 1:25,000 maps (*Lanjarón* No 1042-I, *Bérchules* No 1042-II and *Ugíjar* No 1043-I). Unfortunately, at the time of writing the 1:50,000 map was getting hard to find, as it was out of print pending production of an updated version. The Centro de Visitantes de Pampaneira usually has a good selection of IGN maps, and you'll find some in the shops on the main road in Trevélez.

A fascinating read is *South From Granada* by Gerald Brenan (see Books under Information early in this chapter). One day Brenan walked home from Granada to his Alpujarras village of Yegen over the Sierra Nevada (60km, 2000m ascent) – he started out at 3 am; stopped for coffee in Güéjar Sierra; got lost in mist in the mountains; had coffee, ham and eggs in Bérchules; and was home by 10 pm.

PLACES TO STAY & EAT
Alpujarras food is hearty country fare, with lots of good meat and also local trout. The *plato alpujarreño*, found on almost every menu, consists of fried potatoes, fried eggs, sausage, ham and maybe a black pudding, usually for around 700 ptas.

Alpujarras or *costa* (coast) wine comes mainly from the Sierra de la Contraviesa and tends to be strong and fairly raw.

In Pampaneira, two good hostales face each other across Calle José Antonio at the entrance to the village from the GR421. *Hostal Alfonso* (☎ 958 76 30 02) has singles/doubles with bathroom for 2000/3000 ptas, as well as the cheapest restaurant in the village (trout 550 ptas, pork chops 650 ptas). *Hostal Ruta del Mulhacén* (☎ 958 76 30 10) charges 2900/4000 ptas. On nearby Plaza de la Libertad, *Restaurante Casa Diego* has a pleasant upstairs terrace and main dishes from 650 ptas to 1100 ptas.

In Bubión, *Hostal Las Terrazas* (☎ 958 76 30 34, Plaza del Sol 7) has pleasant little rooms with bathroom for 2515/3531 ptas. *Restaurante Teide* on the main road is good, with a three-course menu for 1100 ptas.

In Capileira, *Mesón Hostal Poqueira* (☎ 958 76 30 48, Calle Doctor Castilla 6), just off the main road, has good rooms with bathroom for 2400/4000 ptas, and a restaurant. *Hostal Paco López* (☎ 958 76 30 11, Carretera de la Sierra 5), just up the main road, has decent rooms for 2000/3000 ptas with bathroom.

Bar El Tilo on Plaza Calvario has good-value raciones. *Casa Ibero* below the church does inventive international food (mains around 700 ptas to 1100 ptas).

In Trevélez, *Camping Trevélez* (☎ 958 85 85 75), 1km from Trevélez along the GR421 towards Busquístar, seems to open and close unpredictably. You may or may not find it open.

Several places on the Plaza de Don Francisco Abellán (the main road at the foot of the village) have rooms, among them *Restaurante González* (☎ 958 85 85 33) with doubles for 2500 ptas and *Hostal Regina* (☎ 958 85 85 64) with comfier rooms with bathroom for 2800/5000 ptas. *Mesón Haraicel*, just above Plaza de Don Francisco Abellán, serves decent food in generous portions, with several main courses under 850 ptas.

Hotel La Fragua (☎ 958 85 86 26, Calle San Antonio 4) above Plaza Barrio Medio has Trevélez's most comfortable rooms at 2800/5500 ptas with bathroom, and a good restaurant, *Mesón La Fragua*.

GETTING TO/FROM THE WALK

Bus

From Granada bus station, Alsina Graells (☎ 958 18 50 10 in Granada, ☎ 958 78 50 02 in Órgiva) runs buses daily at 10.30 am, noon and 5.15 pm to Lanjarón, Órgiva, Pampaneira (two hours), Bubión, Capileira and Pitres (2¾ hours). The last two buses continue to Pórtugos, Busquístar, Trevélez (3¼ hours from Granada), Juviles, Bérchules and Alcútar (3¾ hours). Return buses to Granada start from Alcútar at 5 am and 5 pm, and from Pitres at 3.30 pm.

Another Alsina Graells service runs twice daily from Granada to Ugíjar via Lanjarón, Órgiva, Cádiar, Yegen and Valor, and vice-versa.

Daily except Sunday, Alsina Graells runs a Málaga-Lanjarón service via Órgiva and an Almería-Bérchules service via Ugíjar and Yegen.

Car & Motorcycle

The A348 (marked C333 on some signs and maps) heads east into the Alpujarras from the N323 Granada-Motril road. The GR421, which winds through the northern Alpujarras villages, leaves the A348 just west of Órgiva and rejoins it a few kilometres north of Cádiar.

It's quite common practice for walkers to leave their cars for a few days in one of the Barranco de Poqueira villages or Trevélez.

THE WALK

Day 1: Pampaneira to Pórtugos via La Taha

4½ to 5½ hours, 14km

With nine villages inviting exploration, and plenty of up-and-down (1135m ascent, 890m descent) between them, you'll fill this day more than adequately.

From Pampaneira's central square (1055m) take the uphill street beside Taberna Narciso, staying with the upward option at each division or meeting of streets. Turn right on the village edge at an information board for the blue Barranco de Poqueira walking route. Fork left 50m further on, then right after another two or three minutes, following blue

trail markers. The stone-paved path winds up among leafy orchards and poplar and chestnut trees to Bubión (1300m). About 60m down the main road from the Teide restaurant, turn up Calle Ermita, which turns into a dirt road, climbing through chestnuts and holm oaks. Ten minutes from Bubión turn right onto a path with an easily missed GR7 post; look for the 'X' (wrong way) sign on the post just past the turning.

A further 10 minutes up, the path passes a fenced enclosure, then broadens into a dirt road. Follow this as it climbs south to the ridge ahead and doubles back to the top edge of the fenced enclosure. Opposite the fence, take a path to the right, marked by a GR7 post. The path crosses the upper **Barranco de la Sangre** (Ravine of Blood; scene of a battle during the 1568-70 rebellion). Follow GR7 posts at a five-way junction among pines; at a downward right fork a few minutes further along; and down a path to the left after 10 minutes more. Three minutes down this path, ignore a broad track doubling back to the right and continue ahead down a narrower path beside a ruined building. Follow the 'Pitres 0.5' sign at the entrance to Capilerilla hamlet, go left under three arches at a fork as you descend between its houses, then turn immediately right onto a good path down to Pitres. You emerge on Pitres' plaza 1½ hours from Bubión.

Pitres (1245m) is a typical enough Alpujarras village, not quite so picturesque nor as touristed as those in the Barranco de Poqueira. *Refugio Los Albergues (☎ 958 34 31 76)*, a two minute walk (signposted) from the GR421 road on the east side of the village, is a small walkers' hostel with bunks at 1000 ptas, a double room for 3000 ptas, a kitchen and hot showers. It's open all year except 10 January to 15 February. The friendly German owner is full of local information. *Fonda Sierra Nevada (☎ 958 76 60 17)* on Pitres plaza has singles/doubles for 1700/3400 ptas. *Camping El Balcón de Pitres (☎ 958 76 61 11)* by the GR421 on the west side of the village opens from March to October and has a decent *restaurant*.

SIERRA NEVADA & LAS ALPUJARRAS

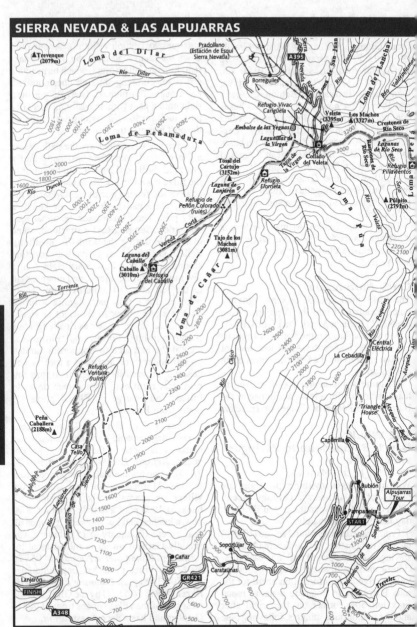

SIERRA NEVADA & LAS ALPUJARRAS

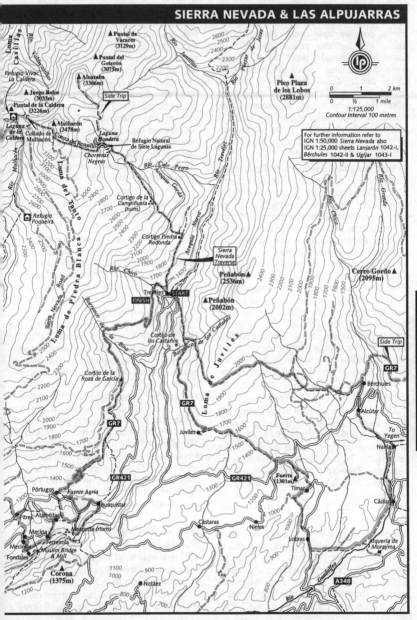

1:125,000
Contour Interval 100 metres

For further information refer to
IGN 1:50,000 *Sierra Nevada* also
IGN 1:25,000 sheets *Lanjarón* 1042-I,
Bérchules 1042-II & *Ugíjar* 1043-I

ANDALUCÍA

The five hamlets in the valley below Pitres are grouped with Pitres and Capilerilla in the *municipio* (municipality) of La Taha, a name that recalls the Muslim Emirate of Granada, when the Alpujarras were divided into 12 administrative units called *tahas*. Today these lower hamlets form a tiny world almost of their own, where the air seems thick with accumulated centuries. The tinkle of running water is ubiquitous, and ancient paths wend their way through some of the Alpujarras' lushest woods and orchards.

Take the street down beside Restaurante La Carretera on the main road below Pitres' plaza. This becomes a partly cobbled old *camino real* (state-maintained path) – not the GR7 – which will have you down in Mecina in 15 minutes. Head down the road past the church to Mecinilla, the second hamlet. At Bar Aljibe continue straight on down, by streets and then an old path. Entering Fondales, the lowest Taha village, take the first street down to the right after a single-spout fountain. Bear left to pass a four-spout fountain at the foot of the village and head on down to the Río Trevélez ravine at the bottom of this deep valley. The path reaches an old **Muslim bridge** over the gorge, with a ruined Muslim mill beside it (ask for the *puente árabe* if you need directions). You have descended 420m in 45 minutes from Pitres to reach this marvellous spot.

Take the eastward path along the river's north bank, immediately crossing a sidestream and forking left up its far bank. After 10 minutes this path meets another, more level, path. Turn right, and in five minutes you enter **Ferreirola** (1000m), perhaps the most beautiful Taha village, surrounded by lush vegetation. Your path brings you up between Ferreirola's church and a welcome fountain.

Leave Ferreirola by the uphill street beside the fountain. A 10 minute climb brings you to sleepy Atalbéitar (1140m). Turn right, go through the village and leave it on a path with a 'GR7 Pórtugos 30 min' sign. After five minutes, immediately after a bridge over a little stream, fork right where the GR7 goes

left. Two minutes after passing a ruined water mill, go left (following red paint dots) at a fork, and climb to more open land. A few metres before the GR421 road, veer right to meet a broader track. Head down to the right on this and where it bends left take a path branching right. The path passes between rocks and along the crest of a ridge to reach the so-called **Mezquita** (Mosque) after 10 minutes. This dilapidated collection of chambers around hill-top rocks has most recently been used for animal shelter, but in Muslim times this was the site of a fortification guarding the Taha villages (there are fine views over the whole valley) and of a mosque.

To complete your collection of Taha villages, head down the east side of the hill from the Mezquita and in five minutes turn left along a clear path. Fork right and down when you encounter a broader track and then almost immediately continue ahead beside a stream where the track doubles back to the right. Some 25 minutes from the Mezquita you'll be in the middle of Busquístar – larger than any village in the valley you have just left, but still a quiet place.

From Busquístar head west along the GR421 for 1.3km to the **Fuente Agria**, the best known of several mildly fizzy ferruginous (iron-bearing) springs in the district, beside a roadside chapel. Just beyond, follow the GR7 north-west off the GR421, and in a few minutes you'll arrive in Pórtugos – not the most exciting Alpujarras village but with a convenient pair of hostelries; turn right up the street to **Hostal El Mirador** (☎ 958 76 60 14) on Plaza Nueva, where basic singles/doubles with bathroom are 1750/3500 ptas; or left down to the main road for *Hotel Nuevo Malagueño* (☎ 958 76 60 98), with comfy rooms at 4815/7704 ptas, and the best *restaurant* in town.

Day 2: Pórtugos to Trevélez
3½ to 4 hours, 13km
This relatively short stage allows you time to explore the interesting village of Trevélez, or to take a side trip from there.

The GR7 from Pórtugos goes east to Busquístar, then north up the Trevélez valley by paths, but there's a short cut from Pórtugos which joins the GR7 after one hour. At the time of writing much of the short-cut route was also marked by GR7 posts, but these were 'pirate' markers placed by the Pórtugos *ayuntamiento* (town council) and may have been removed!

Leave Pórtugos by the street that goes round the back of the ayuntamiento, becoming a dirt road at the edge of the village. This passes Pórtugos cemetery about 10 minutes after and zigzags up through woods of mixed evergreen and deciduous oak. Twenty minutes (1.75km) from the cemetery, just after a left-hand bend on the 1450m contour, a path (marked at the time of writing by one of the unofficial GR7 posts) goes off to the right. Follow this through delightful dense **oak woods**, rounding several barrancos (gullies or ravines) as you go and being joined by the real GR7 after 25 minutes. After an hour you emerge on an open hillside with the Trevélez valley opening ahead.

Almost immediately you encounter two GR7 markers 10m apart. At the second take the right-hand path towards a pine wood. After 30 minutes skirting the woods and rounding another barranco or two you reach the tatty Cortijo de la Roza de García, just below the Capileira-Trevélez dirt road.

Head north on a path level with the cortijo. Soon after a GR7 marker five minutes along, the path enters oaks to round a barranco. Here, get up to the dirt road and follow it north for about 1km. Just after it rounds a barranco a GR7 post marks a path down to the right. The next bit of the GR7, down into and up out of the leafy Barranco de la Bina, is not only hard work but hard to follow and it's easier to stick with the road for a further 3.5km or so until the GR7 rejoins it, just after a left turn on the road at about 1700m. A further 700m along the road, the GR7 (marked) ducks down to the right to short-cut a long loop in the road, meeting the road (still dirt) again after five minutes. To reach the village, cross the road and spend 10 minutes winding round to Trevélez's Barrio Alto.

Entering thus at the top of Trevélez, you can enjoy its more traditional upper parts before hitting the welter of *jamón* (ham) and souvenir shops on the main road 15 minutes below.

Trevélez is the most famous Alpujarran village for three reasons: it's a frequent starting point for ascents of the high Sierra Nevada; it produces some of Spain's best *jamón serrano* (mountain-cured ham); and it's often said to be the highest village in Spain. In fact the top of Trevélez is below 1600m, so several other Spanish villages – notably Valdelinares in Aragón, which reaches above 1700m – could claim the 'highest' title.

The best thing to do with spare time and energy around Trevélez is to take a walk up the Río Trevélez valley above the village. Leave the church plaza of Trevélez's Barrio Bajo (a five minute walk up from the main road) by Calle Real and take the first street to the right, which leads to a *lavadero* (washing place). From this corner go straight on to join a track which reaches the river after about 10 minutes. This old livestock track leads right up to the 2800m Puerto de Trevélez pass over the Sierra Nevada, but the furthest you should hope to get to in one afternoon is the beginning of the Río Trevélez at the **confluence** of the Río Juntillas and Río Puerto de Jeres (1980m).

Day 3: Trevélez to Cádiar via Juviles
5½ to 6 hours, 16km

This stage takes you south and east over the Loma de Juviles and down into the much less touristed but verdant and beautiful lower Alpujarras, with a total ascent of 600m and descent of 1200m.

About 100m beyond the road bridge over the Río Trevélez, the GR7 climbs left from the road. You cross an irrigation channel after 10 minutes, following GR7 posts and the major option at each intersection. The path fades above Cortijo de los Castaños (recognisable by its nearby *castaños*, or chestnut trees), but you can see it continuing beyond the Barranco de los Castaños.

Take the steep, straight-ahead option immediately over the barranco.

Fifty minutes from the road the path reaches a rocky lookout with a cairn. Take the uppermost path from here, which soon merges with a forestry track. As you crest a rise at the end of a straight stretch, 40 minutes from the rocky lookout, look back north-north-west to Mulhacén and, to its right, the more jagged Alcazaba.

Almost immediately the pine forest ends. One minute later, turn sharp right at a crossing of tracks. Then, after just 25m, take a path to the left, opposite a GR7 post, down a scrubby hillside. GR7 posts direct you across a couple of dirt tracks above Juviles and you emerge on the GR421 road just north of the village, 2½ hours from Trevélez. **Juviles** (1250m) is a pleasant enough village barely three streets wide. In Muslim times it was renowned for its warlike people, whom one Christian chronicler described as 'the most restless in the Alpujarras, exceedingly barbarous and bestial'. The pleasant rooms at *Cafe Bar Pension Tino* (☎ 958 76 91 74) at the west end of Juviles cost 2000/3500 ptas for singles/doubles with bathroom.

A GR7 signpost to Tímar points you down Calle Escuela at the north end of Juviles. At the end of this short street, turn left at Chacinería El Granaino. Ten minutes along is a fork with a GR7 post marking the left-hand option. Go right to visit **Fuerte**, the rocky hill which was once Juviles' fortress. A clear path climbs its north-east side. As you emerge through rocks onto the top part of the hill, look down to the left: the low, rectangular structure 30m away is a Muslim-era cistern. Otherwise there's little sign that an eight-towered fort once stood here.

Return to the GR7 and continue southeast along the rugged Barranco de los Molinos to a minor pass. The path now descends south to the hamlet of Tímar. From Tímar church follow the street 700m southwest to the white-walled village cemetery, below which are abandoned mercury mine workings. The GR7 descends into a poplar-lined barranco en route to Lobras village, one hour from Fuerte.

Four hundred metres along the road south from Lobras, GR7 posts mark a left turn onto a footpath. This descends to cross two *ramblas* (seasonal watercourses) close together. Veer left along the far side of the second one and take the path heading up to the right after about 100m. This crests a ridge and starts descending towards the verdant Río Guadalfeo valley. Twenty minutes from the ridge, on a rightward bend of your track, is a GR7 post with a sign to the *Alquería de Morayma* (☎ 958 34 32 21) down to the right (off the GR7). This inn will captivate anyone who's feeling the magnetism of the Alpujarras and Sierra Nevada. An old cortijo has been lovingly renovated and expanded in meticulous alpujarreño fashion to provide a dozen comfortable rooms and apartments, each unique, costing from 5350 ptas to 8880 ptas for two. Excellent, moderately priced food is available, and there's a library and fascinating art and artefacts everywhere. To get there, follow the short path (possibly rather overgrown) indicated by the aforementioned sign, then walk a minute or so up the side of the Guadalfeo and cross it to an 'Alquería de Morayma 400m' sign: it's actually more like 600m to your goal.

For cheaper lodgings, stay on the GR7 for another 2km up the lush Guadalfeo valley to **Cádiar**, a metropolis for these parts with around 2000 people. *Café Bar Montoro* (☎ 958 75 00 68, Calle San Isidro 20), 200m from the church, has doubles with bathroom for 2033 ptas.

Side Trip: Cádiar to Bérchules via Yegen

2½ to 3 hours, 10km to Yegen or 6½ hours, 16km total to Bérchules

If the central Alpujarras appeals, you have plenty of options for extending the trip. The market town of Ugíjar and the wine-growing Sierra de Contraviesa are both within a day's walk of Cádiar, but the obvious detour is to Yegen, the village made famous by writer Gerald Brenan. From Cádiar follow the Day 4 route to Narila church, but then take the right-hand street out of the north corner of the plaza. Five minutes up, veer right where the main track turns sharp left. This path crosses the A348 and continues to Golco where you can join the GR7 to Yegen.

Brenan's house, just off Yegen's plaza, has a plaque, and there's a marked 2½ hour walking route, the Ruta de Gerald Brenan, around some spots associated with him. *El Tinao* (☎ 958 85 12 12) on the main road in Yegen has good singles/doubles with bathroom for 2000/3500 ptas, and serves food. Next day return to Golco and follow the GR7 up to Mecina Bombarón – in an attractive valley – and over a ridge to rejoin the Day 4 route at Bérchules, four hours from Yegen.

Day 4: Cádiar to Trevélez via Bérchules

5 to 5½ hours, 14km

From Cádiar church, walk north along Calle Real and, before Plaza España at the end, turn down to the left to reach a small plaza with a fountain. Here, veer right along a street which soon dwindles to a narrow track, ending at a T-junction with a footpath. Turn right then immediately left. Meeting the river, pass beneath a steep bank then head between a blackberry thicket and the water; 25m on, take a faint path round the right of an almond orchard. Continue 250m to meet a path climbing to **Narila**, the village where Aben Humeya, leader of the 1568-70 rebellion, was crowned king of the Alpujarras in an olive grove.

Leave Narila's church plaza by the left-hand street out of its north corner. After 10 minutes a GR7 sign points you across the young Río Guadalfeo. Now begins almost three hours of ascending which will take you from 1000 to 2000m. The first 30 minutes are by a steep but good path to Alcútar. Fork left at the bottom of the village, then left again at a fountain. From the church head out onto the GR421 road and up the hill into **Bérchules**, one of the bigger villages of the district and set in an attractive valley. The central *Casa Resu* (☎ 958 76 90 92, Calle Iglesia 18) has basic singles/doubles for 1000/2000 ptas.

It's easy to to go wrong finding your way out of Bérchules: when in doubt ask for the 'camino a Trevélez'. The Trevélez path starts from Bérchules' highest, westernmost point; take the first street up to the left past the Fuente de las Carmelas fountain and work your way up and leftward to a small plaza with a fenced tree in the middle. Head uphill from the plaza's far corner, go left at the top of a short section between stone walls, then left at a fountain on the very edge of the village.

Choose left at a fork five minutes further up, and right at another after two more minutes. In the next five minutes, still climbing, you cross three irrigation ditches, each bigger than the last (from the second to the third, go 10m left and pick up a path running 30m up the side of a stream bed). A clear path heads up from the third and after about seven minutes, on open moorland, crosses a dirt road. Five minutes later, go left along another dirt road, passing a cortijo on the left and bending round a barranco; 150m after the barranco, take a narrow path up to the right. When this soon meets the road again, take another track heading west up the slope.

One hour from the Fuente de las Carmelas you reach a firebreak along the edge of a pine wood. Follow this upward, crossing a good dirt road after 10 minutes; 600m further on, go left along another dirt road through the trees. One hundred metres along this, fork left along a lesser track. You soon meet another firebreak along the edge of pines; follow this up for 200m then veer left through a gate.

The dirt road you're on climbs steadily across a moor, with superb eastward views. About two hours from Bérchules, you reach the **Loma de Juviles** ridge at 2000m, with a firebreak running down it.

From here, Trevélez (which you won't see for a while yet) and Alcazaba are in line with each other to the north-north-west. There's no useful path for most of the descent – just a tangle of large and small tracks through pine woods. Keep heading a touch to the right of Alcazaba and you won't go far wrong; also make sure you keep descending. Aim to cross the Barranco de los Castaños 100m higher and 500m east of where you crossed it on Day 3; a clear path from this point leads north-westward to meet the GR7 after 900m. Turn right along the GR7 to Trevélez, which you should reach within 1½ hours from the ridge firebreak.

Sierra Nevada Traverse

Duration 4 days
Distance 50.5km
Standard Hard
Start Trevélez
Finish Lanjarón
Public Transport Yes
Summary A demanding but rewarding traverse of the heart of the high Sierra Nevada, a spectacular high-level wilderness with surprising animal and plant life; includes mainland Spain's highest and third-highest peaks.

The upper Sierra Nevada provides, in many ways, Andalucía's ultimate walking experience, not only because of its altitude and climatic conditions but also for its forbidding, wild aspect – large tracts are a rugged wilderness of black mica schist rock and stones, with plenty of sheer faces and jagged crags. To be sure, the range has its gentler aspect, and has suffered its share of attempted taming by humanity (roads, scientific installations, even a ruined chapel atop Mulhacén), but it's unlikely to fail to awe you.

The Sierra Nevada's *tresmiles* (peaks higher than 3000m) are strung along a serpentine stretch of its main ridge between Cerro Pelao (3179m), 11km north of Trevélez, and Caballo (3010m), 15km west of Trevélez. There's an infinity of routes up to the high country, including some exciting northern approaches from the Genil valley. But Trevélez, to the south, is the nearest village to the high summits. The route described heads straight up from Trevélez to the rugged heart of the tresmil zone, takes

in Mulhacén and Veleta, the two highest peaks in the range (with Alcazaba, the third highest, as an optional side trip), then traverses south-west before descending to Lanjarón. It also makes a 600m descent at the end of Day 2 to the Refugio Poqueira.

The walking times for Days 1 to 3 are not long, but you'll probably need plenty of halts because of the steepness of some of the ascents, the altitudes you reach, and the weight you're carrying for a four day trip. Energetic walkers have lots of scope for side trips, or could shorten the trip to three days – for instance by going straight from Mulhacén to Refugio Carigüela on Day 2.

Some of these alternative approaches and side trips – which would allow you to shorten or lengthen the walk described here almost at will – are briefly outlined in Other Walks at the end of this chapter.

HISTORY
During the Ice Ages Europe's most southerly glaciers formed here, the last of them surviving below the north side of Veleta until the early 20th century. Many of the Sierra Nevada's tarns (alpine lakes) lie in glacially deepened basins, or cirques. For a visual guide to some of the most recognisable glacial landforms, see the boxed text 'Signs of a Glacial Past' in the introduction to the Pyrenees chapter.

The Romans were probably the first to mine the silver and other minerals of the Minas de la Estrella (now closed) on the northern slopes. It was in Muslim times that snow began to be brought down by pack animals to Granada for refrigeration – an activity that continued well into the 20th century.

NATURAL HISTORY
The Sierra Nevada's combination of high altitude and southern latitude gives it a unique botanical variety. Among its 1700 plant species are 60-odd endemic ones – including the Sierra Nevada's own species of narcissus, clover, thistle, poppy, crocus, monkshood, saxifrage, thyme, camomile and gentian. Receding snows in the summer

uncover much of this variety; most endemic species are found above 2800m, especially on rocky crags and cliffs. Damp, grassy areas around the tarns, known as *borreguiles*, harbour many tiny flowering plants, often endemic or rare.

Preeminent among animals is the ibex, which in summer you might find anywhere above about 2800m – especially away from the paths most often trodden by humans. We counted 60 ibex in a dozen separate sightings during the walk described.

PLANNING
When to Walk

July, August and early September are best but even at these times the weather can change quickly. Try to pick a spell of settled, clear weather and keep a careful eye on any clouds that begin to settle on the sierra. Even under clear summer skies the heights of the range can be blasted by strong, cold winds and nocturnal temperatures can fall close to freezing. By late September you can expect it to get very cold at night above 2500m, perhaps with snow and storms. The first major snowfall is usually around or after mid-October. The high ground begins to thaw in May. In June there's often plenty of snow still lying, which can make the going tricky and paths hard to find, but it's a pretty month.

Winter walking over ice and snow in the high Sierra Nevada is popular among Spanish *montañeros* (mountaineers), but should definitely not be undertaken without experienced companions. Special gear needed includes ice axe, crampons, snow boots and gloves, head cover and clothing for temperatures well below freezing.

The descriptions and walk times that follow are for summer conditions.

Maps & Books

Ideally, take both the IGN *Sierra Nevada* 1:50,000 and the IGN *Pico del Veleta* No 1027-III, *Trevélez* No 1027-IV and *Lanjarón* No 1042-I 1:25,000 maps. The combination almost makes up for individual inadequacies. For approaches from the Barranco de Poqueira, you'll also need the *Bérchules* No

1042-II 1:25,000 map. See the Alpujarras Tour walk for more on maps.

Andy Walmsley's *Walking in the Sierra Nevada of Spain* is a useful little book for those who fancy getting to know the range better. In Spanish, we recommend *Excursiones por el Sur de España – I* by Juan Carlos García Gallego.

What to Bring

You'll need warm gear up here even if the skies are a cloudless blue and you've been sweltering down in the valleys. This means plenty of clothing layers – including head covering and gloves – and, for those who'll be overnighting anywhere except Refugio Poqueira, a warm sleeping bag. A small stove is advisable, to make hot drinks or food, as is a tent if you're spending any nights outside refugios.

There's plenty of water from springs, streams and tarns, but on Day 1 you should carry enough to get you to the Cañada de Siete Lagunas.

Warning

Several parts of the route, including the summits of Mulhacén and Veleta and the ridge to the summit of Alcazaba, are bordered by precipices. Consider very carefully whether to proceed if clouds or mist form.

PLACES TO STAY & EAT

See the Alpujarras Tour walk for information on Trevélez and the Barranco de Poqueira villages.

In Lanjarón, there are numerous hostales, hotels and places to eat on the main street, Avenida de Andalucía. Some of the first places you come to, about 1km from the bridge where the Camino de la Sierra emerges, are among the cheapest, including (in the order you reach them) *Hostal Dolar* (☎ 958 77 01 83), *Hotel Royal* (☎ 958 77 00 08) and *Hostal Astoria* (☎ 958 77 00 75), all with doubles between 3210 ptas and 4280 ptas.

At the Estación de Esquí Sierra Nevada, the *Albergue Juvenil Sierra Nevada* (☎ 958 48 03 05) stays open all year.

Roads & Refugios in the Sierra Nevada

The story of the road over the Sierra Nevada from Granada to Capileira and that of the range's refugios both demonstrate how official notions of 'taming' the mountains have given way since the 1980s to a philosophy of restoring the high altitudes to as wild a state as possible.

Work on the road, touted as the highest in Europe, began in the 1920s for tourist purposes. A paved section to the top of Veleta (3395m) from the Granada side was completed in 1935. In the 1960s a dirt road was built from Capileira to meet the Veleta road at about 3250m, thus creating a road right over the sierra – albeit one whose full length could open only for two or three months each summer. The Sierra Nevada ski resort began to take shape in the 1970s at Pradollano, 2100 to 2500m high, and the road on the northern slopes was used to service it. A 7km dirt spur reaching to within 800m of the top of Mulhacén was added in 1974.

Growing concern for the sierra's environment tolled the road's death knell as a public highway. In the mid-1990s, motorists started having to obtain permits to drive over the range. Today, there are barriers on both sides of the sierra to stop drivers altogether.

Related changes are taking place in the sierra's network of refugios. There are numerous refugios open to all comers – some were built by mountaineering organisations, others originally for forestry or other uses. But over the years nearly all fell into disrepair and, often, squalor – the major exception being the Refugio Félix Méndez (at around 3000m) by the Lagunas de Río Seco, a staffed refugio serving meals.

In 1997, however, the Félix Méndez was demolished in accordance with Andalucía's new Plan de Refugios de Sierra Nevada, which doesn't allow for major refugios higher than about 2500m. The new, full-service Refugio Poqueira opened in 1996 at 2500m in the upper Poqueira valley. Several other new refugios are planned, including in the upper Trevélez and Lanjarón valleys and on the Loma del Calvario. Two small stone-and-concrete *refugios vivac* (bivouac refuges), La Caldera and Carigüela – free, always open and basically just somewhere to spread out your sleeping bag – have been opened at high altitudes below Mulhacén and Veleta. Most of the older remaining refugios are dilapidated affairs, best avoided.

For current information on refugios and on how far you can drive up the Sierra Nevada road, contact the Centro de Visitantes de Pampaneira (see the Alpujarras Tour walk), or the Centro de Visitantes El Dornajo (☎ 958 34 06 25), about 10km before the ski resort on the A395 from Granada.

Opened in 1996, Refugio Poqueira is one of a new generation of refugios built to minimise the impact on the higher alpine environment.

GETTING TO/FROM THE WALK

See the Alpujarras Tour walk for information on Alpujarras transport.

On the north flank of the Sierra Nevada range, the A395 runs 33km from Granada to Estación de Esquí Sierra Nevada. Autocares Bonal (☎ 958 27 31 00) runs a bus to the ski resort daily at 8 or 9 am from Bar Ventorrillo on Paseo del Violón near Granada's Palacio de Congresos. It returns to the ski resort at about 5 pm. The one-way/return fare is 365/700 ptas.

THE WALK (See map on pages 320-1)
Day 1: Trevélez to Cañada de Siete Lagunas

4 hours, 7km

You ascend 1300m on this steep first stage. From Trevélez's Hotel La Fragua, head up the street and almost immediately turn right under an arch to a junction where you take the uphill option. Fifty metres up, turn left into a path indicated by a yellow arrow and red-and-white paint dashes. This leads you up through cultivated areas to an outlying farmlet, Cortijo Piedra Redonda, 2km from Trevélez, with one stone building on each side of the path. At a fork a few metres beyond, take the minor, left-hand option. At another fork a couple of minutes up, go left (the right-hand option has a red-paint 'X').

As you climb, keep to the right of a fence and stay with the occasional dashes of red paint. Half an hour from Cortijo Piedra Redonda the path swings northward to parallel the Acequia Gorda (where 'acequia' in Spanish means irrigation channel). It then crosses the acequia and angles up to the north-north-west. The red paint blobs disappear but small cairns help. One hour from the Acequia Gorda you pass through another fence, the red-paint trail markers reappear and you cross another irrigation channel. The path continues up to **Cortijo de la Campiñuela** (2400m), composed of two ruined stone buildings, a threshing floor (a flat area paved with stones) and a tumble-down corral, 2½ hours from Trevélez.

A clear path now climbs more gently north-west towards the Chorreras Negras, twin waterfalls tumbling over black stones. After 30 minutes you cross the Río Culo Perro and climb a path which soon heads straight for the **Chorreras Negras**. The path crosses the foot of the right-hand waterfall, 30 minutes from the river crossing, then makes a steep 25 minute climb beside the left-hand waterfall. At the top (2850m) you emerge suddenly in the Cañada de Siete Lagunas glacial basin. A shallow tarn, **Laguna Hondera**, stretches before you. The rock mass of Mulhacén looms ahead, with the jagged crags of Alcazaba to its right.

Laguna Hondera and several of the six other tarns in the basin are surrounded by grassy areas – good *camp sites*. (As alpine tarns are quite fragile environments particularly prone to pollution, your camping habits should be impeccable.) On a rise just south of Laguna Hondera is the so-called *Refugio Natural de Siete Lagunas*, a pair of shelters formed by rock walls around a boulder, with room for a few people to stretch out. There are also a number of low *rock enclosures* providing some wind shelter.

Side Trip: Alcazaba

3 to 3½ hours, 6km

If you have reached the Cañada de Siete Lagunas by lunch time and have reserves of energy, you could devote the afternoon to Alcazaba (Fortress). The name is entirely apt for this 3366m rock massif protected by awesome crags and precipices on every side but the south-east. Most of the walk is over stones and rocks (though often flat ones). Compared to Mulhacén, barely a trickle of walkers tackles this neighbouring giant.

Begin by walking up the ridge forming the north-east side of the Cañada de Siete Lagunas. As you pick your way carefully over the ridge's first lot of crags, about 1¼ hours from Laguna Hondera, Alcazaba's pyramid-shaped summit cairn appears just west of north. You can walk to the right of and below the remaining crags of the ridge before veering right (north) up the **Alcazaba summit ridge** (which has a fearsome precipice on its west side). The peak itself, two hours from Laguna Hondera, is not quite on the edge of yet another precipice, but steep walls drop away to the north and west. There are great panoramas just about every way you look.

To return, you can – after retracing your steps most of the way southward down Alcazaba's summit ridge – descend the stony valley on the north side of the ridge you ascended from the Cañada de Siete Lagunas. Make for a discernible pass in this ridge, south-east from the Alcazaba peak. Once there (30 minutes from the summit), you find that you're on a more northerly spur of the ridge than the one you ascended. Head south for some 20 minutes, losing little height, to return to your original spur, from where it's a simple 30 minute descent to Laguna Hondera.

Day 2: Cañada de Siete Lagunas to Mulhacén & Refugio Poqueira
3½ to 4 hours, 6.5km

The most sensible way up Mulhacén from the Cañada de Siete Lagunas is by the Cuesta del Resuello (Cuerda del Resuello on some maps), the rocky ridge along the south side of the cañada. A path climbs to the ridge's east end from Laguna Hondera, then follows the ridge upwards. As you climb, look down at Laguna Hondera and you'll understand the name of the Río Culo Perro (Dog's Arse River) which flows out of it.

Mulhacén's summit is 630m higher than Laguna Hondera, and the steepness and altitude make the going fairly slow. Where the path fades, dots of yellow paint show the way, keeping towards the north side of the ridge. Two hours from the cañada, you emerge 400m south of the summit on the path from the former car park at the top of the Mulhacén road (see the boxed text 'Roads & Refugios in the Sierra Nevada'). The **highest piece of rock in peninsular Spain** supports a tall, metal cross (broken and bent double when we last visited), a small shrine and a roofless stone chapel. Immediately behind the summit is a near-perpendicular 500m drop to the Hoya de Mulhacén basin.

The views take in such distant ranges as the Sierra Almijara, Sierra de las Nieves, Sierra de Cazorla and, if you're lucky, the Atlas Mountains in Morocco.

The name Mulhacén is a corruption of Moulay Abu al-Hasan (d 1485), the penultimate ruler of Muslim Granada. A legend which no one believes relates that he was buried up here.

The path down Mulhacén's steep west slope diverges from the summit-to-car-park path about 150m from the summit. About 15 minutes down, fork right to the **Collado de Mulhacén** (or Collado del Ciervo), the furthest of three obvious gaps in the rocks, where there are great views of Mulhacén's perpendicular north face, Alcazaba and the Hoya de Mulhacén. From the collado it's a straightforward few minutes down to the *Refugio Vivac La Caldera* (3100m), 40 or 50m above the Laguna de la Caldera. This simple shelter, maintained in good condition, is free, always open and has boards for 12 people to spread out sleeping bags, plus a table and benches to eat at – no more.

To reach *Refugio Poqueira* (☎ 958 34 33 49), follow the Río Mulhacén downhill for about 2.3km to the 2500m level, where a path rises slightly to the ridge on the east side of the valley, 500m away. At the ridge the refugio appears 250m ahead. It's a good, modern refugio with 87 bunk places, open all year at 1000 ptas per person, with prepared meals available (breakfast 550 ptas, dinner 1600 ptas) and some basic groceries for sale. Blankets are provided. It's rarely heavily occupied.

Day 3: Refugio Poqueira to Refugio Carigüela & Veleta
4½ hours, 12km

From Refugio Poqueira, follow the tumbling Río Mulhacén back upstream – not an unpleasant way of regaining the 600m lost descending from the Refugio Vivac La Caldera on Day 2. You can divert north-west from the river to short-cut the final 500m to the Sierra Nevada road, emerging above Laguna de la Caldera about 1½ hours from the refugio.

Turn left (south-west) along the road. Dramatic views of Veleta, Los Machos and the jagged Raspones and Crestones de Río Seco ridges unfold as you round **Loma Pela** (or Loma Pelada) 20 minutes later. By the bend in the road, *Refugio Pillavientos* is a grubby building where up to 12 people could, *in extremis*, stretch out their sleeping bags on the stone floor.

The road passes between the Crestones de Río Seco and the Lagunas de Río Seco tarns. A few minutes after you pass through a nick in the rocks where the Crestones and Raspones de Río Seco meet, a gap in the

Crestones yawns right by the road, giving dramatic views down into the Valdeinfiernos valley.

Passing under the almost sheer south-east side of Veleta, the road zigzags up to the 3200m **Collado del Veleta** (or Collado de la Carigüela del Veleta) pass, where it becomes paved and turns north to descend to the Sierra Nevada ski resort. A tremendous westward panorama opens out here, with the jagged Tajos de la Virgen ridge snaking away to the west-south-west and Granada visible 25km north-west. A few metres above the pass, 3½ hours from Refugio Poqueira, is the **Refugio Vivac Carigüela**, identical to the Refugio Vivac La Caldera encountered on Day 2.

From here it's 30 minutes to the top of Veleta (3395m), the third-highest peak in mainland Spain. A footpath up from the Collado del Veleta soon joins the paved Veleta summit road, which passes the top lifts of the Sierra Nevada ski station. The **summit** area is disfigured by a line of aerials and a small concrete building.

Day 4: Refugio Carigüela to Lanjarón

7 hours (approx), 25km

From Refugio Carigüela you could slip down the road to the ski resort in a couple of hours. But descending west to Lanjarón – a drop in altitude of 2550m – acquaints you with the impressive Río Lanjarón valley and the west end of the Sierra Nevada.

From the Collado del Veleta, a path heads west-north-west down to the **Lagunillos de la Virgen**, a group of tarns about 250m lower. This northern side of the sierra can retain substantial snow cover well into the summer, in which case the lagunillos may appear as patches of snow or even be invisible. Keep the line of tall metal poles on your left on the 25 minute descent.

From the southernmost of the lagunillos, which is visible (snow permitting) as you descend, a path climbs south-westward across the boulder-strewn slopes of Tajos de la Virgen. This is an excellent trail except for one section where it's covered by fallen

rocks (small cairns guide you across). Fifty minutes up from the Lagunillos de la Virgen you reach **Refugio Elorrieta**, on the ridge south-west of the Tajos de la Virgen crags and with great views. This multi-chambered refugio was a sorry mess on our visit, though the section inside its south-western entrance would probably be bearable.

Refugio Elorrieta stands above the Laguna de Lanjarón (or Laguna de las Tres Puertas) at the head of the Lanjarón valley, which is in a typical stony, high Sierra Nevada wilderness. Crossing into this valley from the Lagunillos de la Virgen, you cross the watershed between waters flowing to the Atlantic and waters destined for the Mediterranean.

From Refugio Elorrieta follow the clear south-westward path along the western side of the Loma de Cañar. After 10 to 15 minutes this starts to head down to the right. Fork left five minutes or so down, then right after a further five minutes. Your path leads down across the Río Lanjarón, with the Refugio Peñón Colorado (classified as ruined) a short distance downstream. Across the river the finely constructed **Vereda Corta** (Cut Path) rises along the craggy north-west flank of the valley. Twenty or 30 minutes along is the feature that earns this route its name – a steep (though not very wide) gully slicing down across the path. Negotiating this requires an all-four-limbs scramble to the path's continuation, a metre or two higher on the far side of the gully, with the aid of a length of cable fixed in place as a handhold. Another 30 or 40 minutes brings you to the **Refugio del Caballo** (official capacity: eight), even more of a last resort than Refugio Elorrieta. This refugio stands just above Laguna del Caballo and below the most westerly tresmil in mainland Spain, Caballo (3010m).

If you're not happy about the gully manoeuvre on the Vereda Corta you have two alternatives, both involving an extra descent of about 200m and ascent of 150m. One is to go left at the second fork as you descend the Loma de Cañar, and cross the Río Lanjarón at any convenient spot about 1km down. The other is to go along the Vereda Corta to the cut, and if you don't fancy it backtrack a couple of minutes, then descend the stony slope to the valley floor. In either case, then walk south-west along the valley, picking up a path which after about 15 minutes starts to climb towards Caballo. You'll reach the refugio 20 or 30 minutes later.

A clear path across the left side of Caballo leads into a steady south-westward descent. A stream 1¼ hours down, just after a pine plantation, is probably the last drinkable water before Lanjarón. Fifteen minutes later, fork left down to a concrete irrigation channel and, beyond, the *Refugio Ventura* (classified as ruined, but little worse than the Refugio del Caballo) among some grey rocks.

From Refugio Ventura continue downward on a path heading south-south-west in and out of pines. At the foot of a brief straight-downhill section after 10 to 15 minutes, the path steers to the right and becomes a dirt road. This winds downhill through pines, passing a small meteorological station 25 minutes from Refugio Ventura. From a southbound leg of the zigzag 40 minutes later, zip left down a steep firebreak with a round pool at its foot. At the bottom of the firebreak, go 800m left (northward) along a dirt road, then fork right onto a track which winds down to a group of forestry buildings, Casa Tello, the main one of which was recently in a burntout state. A big sequoia tree stands out as a landmark in the forest around Casa Tello.

From Casa Tello a path descends to a footbridge over Río Lanjarón. Cross the river, ascend the path on the east bank and take the first turn to the right. You are now on the Camino de la Sierra, an old camino real which continues 4.5km down to the bridge at the east end of Lanjarón (a descent of some 750m).

Lanjarón (population: 4000) is a spa, and its bright lights and vaguely festive air in summer and autumn certainly make a change from the black, windswept heights of the sierra.

Cabo de Gata

Andalucía's 700km coast isn't all packed throngs of pink bodies à la Costa del Sol. Far from it. The most spectacular coastal scenery of all is around the arid Cabo de Gata promontory east of Almería.

The combination of a dry, desert climate with the cliffs of the Sierra del Cabo de Gata plunging towards the azure and turquoise Mediterranean waters produces a landscape of stark, elemental grandeur. Between the cliffs and headlands are strung some of Spain's best and least crowded beaches. Cabo de Gata is not undiscovered, but it's far enough from the beaten track to feel positively deserted compared with most other Spanish beach areas. There are no towns on this coast, just a scattering of villages which – with a couple of exceptions in July and August – remain very low-key.

The Parque Natural de Cabo de Gata-Níjar has information offices in San José and at the Centro de Interpretación Las Amoladeras (☎ 950 16 04 35), north of El Cabo de Gata village, and seasonal information points at several other spots. The Las Amoladeras centre is open daily except Monday from 9.30 am to 3.30 pm (longer hours in Semana Santa and from July to September).

NATURAL HISTORY
Fauna
Cabo de Gata, especially the *salinas* (salt lagoons) south of El Cabo de Gata village, is renowned for its birds. In spring many migratory birds call at the salinas while migrating from Africa or Doñana to breeding grounds further north. A few flamingos and many others stay to breed, then others arrive in summer; by late August there can be 1000 flamingos here. Autumn brings the biggest numbers of migratory birds as they pause on their return south. In winter the salinas are relatively underpopulated as the lakes are drained after the autumn salt harvest. Black winged stilt, herons, white stork, avocet and various ducks are among the many birds you may see here. The rare Audouin's gull visits the nearby beach.

The *reserva integral* of 'coastal steppe', inland of the Retamar-El Cabo de Gata stretch of the walk, is a habitat of stone-curlew, black-bellied sandgrouse, Dupont's lark and other species favouring this country. Bonelli's eagles nest on the sierra's crags.

Flora

The dry climate and poor soil yield an unusual vegetation including the *palmito*, or dwarf fan palm (*Chamaerops humilis*), Europe's only native palm, a bush usually less than 1m high with fans of lance-shaped blades. The date palm also occurs.

Much of the peninsula is covered in scrub of thyme, lavender and rockrose. Thorny shrubs like *Ziziphus lotus*, growing in spiny hummocks, and *Periploca laevigata*, with leathery oblong leaves, are rare elsewhere in Europe. The wiry stems of false esparto grass (*Lygeum spartum*) are harvested. In the peninsula's salt-rich soils are also found some saltworts, sea blights and sea lavenders found nowhere else in Europe.

You'll come across areas of prickly pear cactus and of sisal (*Agave sisalana*), a cactus-like plant with thick spiky leaves, both of which are grown commercially here – sisal for rope-making, prickly pear for food.

Given the locations of the various places where you can stop for the night, it's impossible to divide the walk into three approximately equal days. We've opted for a short third day, giving a chance to linger at some of the more secluded beaches late in the walk or to get away from the final destination, Agua Amarga, in good time (it lacks economical accommodation). The walk can be done in two long days, especially if you start from El Cabo de Gata village (omitting the first two hours from Retamar), but that leaves little time to enjoy Cabo de Gata's inviting beaches and coves.

PLANNING
When to Walk

Given the near-permanent dry, warm weather, you can do this walk almost any time of year. July and August might be *too* warm for some people (there's hardly any shade); take it slowly and cool off at beaches along the way. Between March and June, plants bloom after the sparse winter rains. September and October have the advantage that the sea is still warm (it's warmer in October than June).

Maps

The IGN/Junta de Andalucía *Parque Natural Cabo de Gata-Níjar* 1:50,000 map is fine. The nature park information offices at Las Amoladeras and San José normally have copies but sometimes run out.

What to Bring

There's never more than 3½ hours between villages, so you only need to carry picnic food – but take plenty of water on each stage.

Walking boots are definitely worthwhile: some of the walking surfaces are rough (eg stony tracks) and some are very smooth (eg sand).

Warning

It's not advisable to do the Lobos-Cala del Bergantín or San Pedro-Cala del Plomo sections in mist or cloud – you might step over the edge of a cliff.

Cabo de Gata Coast Walk

Duration 2½ days
Distance 61km
Standard Medium
Start Retamar
Finish Agua Amarga
Public Transport Yes
Summary A coastal walk along southern Spain's most spectacular seaboard; first along the promontory's flat, beach-lined western coast; and then on the rugged southern and eastern coasts, strung with secluded beaches and coves.

This walk follows the coast from Retamar, 15km east of Almería, to Agua Amarga, combining paths, dirt roads and occasional sections of paved road.

ANDALUCÍA

PLACES TO STAY & EAT

You should call ahead for accommodation during Semana Santa and in July and August. Camping is only allowed in the four organised camping grounds, at El Cabo de Gata village, San José, Los Escullos and Las Negras.

There doesn't appear to be anywhere to stay in Retamar, so you need to spend the night before the walk in Almería (see Accommodation & Supplies in the introduction to this chapter) or in El Cabo de Gata village, then get a bus to Retamar (or start the walk from El Cabo de Gata village).

El Cabo de Gata Village

Camping Cabo de Gata (☎ 950 16 04 43), 2.5km north of the village by dirt roads, is open all year (250 sites at around 1100 ptas for two adults with a tent) and has a restaurant. *Restaurante Mediterráneo (☎ 950 37 11 37)*, towards the south end of the village seafront, has a few singles/doubles for 2500/4000 ptas. *Hostal Chiri-Bus (☎ 950 37 00 36 or ☎ 950 37 10 77, Calle La Sardina 2)*, just off the main road on the Ruescas side of the village, has nice, modern rooms with bathroom for 3500/5000 ptas. Nearby *Pizzeria Pedro*, Calle Islas de Tabarca 2, does fine pizzas and pasta at middling prices.

Agua Amarga

On Calle La Lomilla (which you pass coming down from Cerro del Cuartel), *Restaurante-Hostal René y Michèle 'El Family' (☎ 950 13 80 14)* has nine lovely doubles with bathroom for 10,000 ptas (5000 ptas from mid-September to February) including a big breakfast. An excellent four course dinner is served for 2000 ptas. *Hostal Restaurante La Palmera (☎ 950 13 82 08)* at the east end of the beach has 10 rooms with bathroom for 10,700 ptas (a bit less without a sea view).

There are several more economical hostales in Carboneras, 8km up the coast from Agua Amarga (past a big cement works).

GETTING TO/FROM THE WALK

Autocares Becerra (☎ 950 22 44 03) runs between four and six buses a day from Almería bus station to Retamar and El Cabo de Gata village. The first leaves at 9 am (10 am on Sunday) and the last at 9 pm (7 pm on Saturday, 8 pm on Sunday and holidays).

Autocares Bergarsan (☎ 950 26 42 92) runs buses from Agua Amarga to Almería from Monday and Friday only, at 6.30 am. There are buses from Carboneras to Almería from Monday to Friday at 7 am and 3 pm and on Saturday at 7 am, and from Las Negras to Almería daily except Sunday at 7.30 am. A taxi from Agua Amarga costs around 7500 ptas to Almería or 2000 ptas to Carboneras. The nearest taxis are based in San José (☎ 950 38 97 37 or ☎ 908-05 62 55) and Carboneras (☎ 950 45 41 12 or ☎ 950 45 42 25).

THE WALK
Day 1: Retamar to San José
6½ to 7 hours, 28km

Retamar is a holiday-cum-retirement settlement which, like several other villages on Cabo de Gata, only really comes alive during Spanish holiday seasons. Walk south-east from here along the beach or the dirt road just behind it and in about 15 minutes you reach an odd little cluster of buildings including the Ermita de Torre García chapel, built in 1951; the Torre García, a watchtower dating in its present form from the 18th century; and the excavated remains of a Roman *garum* factory (garum was a much-prized sauce made from fish innards).

The stretch from here to Rambla de Morales is the least inviting of the whole walk. The sandy/stony beach is so badly littered that you wonder whether it was used as a tip. The low, scrubby dunes inland are a reserva integral where you're not supposed to stray from existing tracks so as not to disturb ground-nesting birds, a regulation which makes it impractical for coast walkers to visit the interesting Centro de Interpretación Las Amoladeras, 1.75km inland. The most interesting feature is an old sisal plantation. But **Rambla de Morales** should lift your spirits: there are often greater flamingos in the lagoon at its mouth, and you'll probably get closer to the birds here than at the Salinas del Cabo de Gata.

You reach the village of El Cabo de Gata (officially San Miguel de Cabo de Gata) two hours from Retamar. Though still a fishing village, it's now more of a cluster of holiday chalets and apartments – an amiable, low-rise sort of place. There's an ATM on Calle Iglesia. The beach from here on is sandier and much cleaner. Beyond the old Guardia Civil tower immediately south of the village, you can choose between walking along the beach, the main road or a dirt road parallelling it inland. Just inland of the dirt road are the **Salinas del Cabo de Gata**, salt-extraction lagoons which have been in use since Phoenician times and are famous for their water birds (see Natural

History earlier in this section). There's a birdwatching hide in a fenced area 3km south of the village.

Ten minutes past the hide, the village of La Almadraba de Monteleva has a curious towered church at its north end. The salt from the salinas is piled up in great heaps here. *Hotel Las Salinas del Cabo de Gata* (☎ 950 37 01 03) in La Almadraba has the comfiest rooms on this side of the peninsula (the cheapest are 6420 ptas to 9630 ptas, depending on season) and a classy restaurant.

South of La Almadraba, pass through the hamlet of La Fabriquilla, after which you must resort to the road for the 45 minute section of steep coast round to the Faro del Cabo de Gata lighthouse. Five minutes before the lighthouse, *Bar José y María* does *platos combinados* (fixed-price dishes with three or four items, all served on the

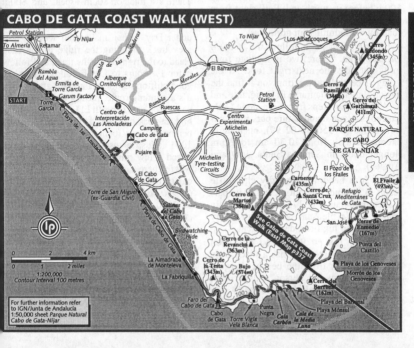

CABO DE GATA COAST WALK (WEST)

same plate), seafood raciones and the last drinks before San José.

A path beside the seasonal information kiosk at the lighthouse joins the road for the 15 minute climb up to the **Torre Vigía Vela Blanca**, an 18th century watchtower, 213m high. You can avoid the road's long last hairpin by short-cutting up a barranco. From the top, the eastward views along the next stretch of coast are magnificent. The road becomes dirt here and is barred to vehicles by a gate. It winds 25 minutes down to a similar barrier stopping traffic from the San José direction, then passes behind the enticing sandy beaches Cala Carbón, Cala de la Media Luna and Playa Mónsul, all reachable by short tracks.

When the parking area for Playa de los Genoveses appears, head cross-country to it and then onto the beach itself – a broad, 1km-long sand strip between rocky headlands, with shallow waters. Turn left along the beach and then left along a pine avenue 100m before its north end. Fork right from the avenue after about 200m to rejoin the road by a windmill 1km north-east.

Entering San José, follow the 'Centro Urbano' sign, ignore two immediate right turns but take the next right fork. At the village's central intersection you'll find the Hostal Bahía, Restaurante El Emigrante and an ATM. A few steps from here along Calle Correo is a tourist and nature park information office (☎ 950 38 02 99), open daily except Sunday from 10.30 am to 2 pm (longer hours in Semana Santa, July and August).

San José becomes a mildly chic little resort in summer, but out of season its permanent population of 175 seems decidedly sparse. It's a pleasant place, with sandy streets and no high-rise development.

Camping Tau (☎ 950 38 01 66), open from April to September, has a shady little site 400m back from the beach, charging around 450 ptas per person and per tent. The *Albergue Juvenil de San José (☎ 950 38 03 53)* on Calle Montemar, between the beach and the camping ground, is run by the local municipality, with room for 86 people

at 1000 ptas to 1300 ptas depending on the season. It opens from Semana Santa to 1 October and for winter holiday weekends.

There are seven or eight hostales and hotels. *Café Bar Fonda Costa Rica (☎ 950 38 01 03)* on Calle Correo has eight decent doubles with bathroom for 5500 ptas plus IVA in high season. Most others charge 5000/7500 ptas or more for singles/doubles.

For a bit of a hideaway, try *Refugio Mediterráneo de Gata (☎ 950 52 56 25)* on Cala Higuera, a pebbly bay about 1.25km out of town (and on the Day 2 route). Eight rustic but cosy rooms for two or three people, some with kitchen, cost from 3000 ptas to 6000 ptas. There's a summer terrace bar with food. To get there, go 200m past Camping Tau to a T-junction, then go right and follow the 'RMG' or 'Bungalow' signs.

Day 2: San José to Las Negras
7 hours, 22km

There's a total of 800m ascent and 800m descent on this stage. Follow the route to Refugio Mediterraneo de Gata described under Day 1, then make your way up to a grey track rounding the ridge to the east. Head to the right along the track and follow it for 1¾ hours to Los Escullos. There's a good clifftop section at the start, after which it's a winding route, mostly away from the coast. You pass beneath El Fraile (493m), the highest peak on Cabo de Gata, and above a bentonite quarry (bentonite is a soft clay with 1001 industrial uses). The road becomes paved a few minutes before Los Escullos, where there are two small places to stay close to the beach – *Hotel Los Escullos (☎ 950 38 97 33)*, which charges 8000 ptas or 9000 ptas a double, and *Casa Emilio (☎ 950 38 97 32)*, which has singles/doubles for 4000/6000 ptas – and the large *Camping Los Escullos (☎ 950 38 98 11)*, 900m back, open all year. Otherwise, Los Escullos consists of little more than the Batería de San Felipe (a restored 18th century fort), a ruined Guardia Civil post and the Chaman disco!

Head north along Playa del Arco. For the 1km to La Isleta del Moro village, you can continue by the water's edge except for a couple of impassable bits that you have to go over the top of. *Hostal Isleta del Moro* (☎ *950 38 97 13*) in La Isleta has rooms with bath for 3000/5000 ptas, and a restaurant. The German-run *Casa Café de la Loma* (☎ *950 52 52 11*) on a small hill just above the village has a few rooms at 3000/4500 ptas and a summer vegetarian restaurant.

From the north end of La Isleta's Playa del Peñón Blanco, a path heads inland, initially following white posts. Unless you want to visit Cala de los Toros, a small black-sand beach backed by a splash of green trees, you should continue north-east cross-country to meet the road instead of bending east with the path towards the beach. Go uphill with the road to the **Mirador de la Amatista** lookout, 1¼ hours from Los Escullos. You need to stay with the road as it heads inland towards the former gold-mining village of Rodalquilar and then bends north-east.

To head straight to **Playa del Playazo** – a good, sandy beach stretched between two headlands – turn right off the road 300m after a turning marked 'La Polacra', just past Rodalquilar. It's 2km along a level track to the beach, with the Batería de San Ramón fort (now a private home) at one end – about 1¼ hours from the Mirador de la Amatista.

It's worth the effort, however, to detour up 265m **Lobos** for magnificent views. From the 'La Polacra' turning a paved road runs right to the top (3km, 50 minutes using paths to short-cut some zigzags), with a gate barring vehicles about halfway. Lobos is topped by an 18th century watchtower converted into a lighthouse.

From Lobos you can head northward down to Cala del Bergantín (which has a stony beach), then onto Playa del Playazo by the little pass between Cerro del Romeral and Cerrico Romero. There's no real path as far as Cala del Bergantín but animal tracks help, and the going is not too rough. Just steer well away from the cliffs on your way down: they have quite an overhang in places, and in one spot the cliffline curves unexpectedly far inland. It's one hour from Lobos to Playa del Playazo this way.

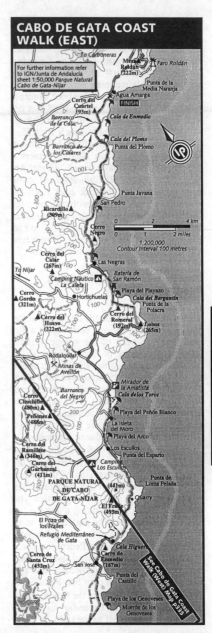

CABO DE GATA COAST WALK (EAST)

For further information refer to IGN/Junta de Andalucía sheet 1:50,000 *Parque Natural Cabo de Gata-Níjar*

To Carboneras
Mesa Roldán (222m)
Faro Roldán
Punta de la Media Naranja
Agua Amarga
FINISH
Cerro del Cuartel (93m)
Cala de Enmedio
Barranco de la Cala
Cala del Plomo
Barranco de los Cálares
Punta del Plomo
Punta Javana
Ricardillo (509m)
San Pedro
Cerro Negro
Las Negras
Cerro del Calar (267m)
To Níjar
Camping Náutico La Caleta
Batería de San Ramón
Playa del Playazo
Cerro Gordo (321m)
Hortichuelas
Cala del Bergantín
Punta de la Polacra
Cerro del Huevo (322m)
Cerro del Romeral (192m)
Lobos (265m)
Rodalquilar
Minas de Avellón
Mirador de la Amatista
Cala de los Toros
Cerro Chuchillo (480m)
Barranco del Negro
Peñones (488m)
Playa del Peñón Blanco
La Isleta del Moro
Playa del Arco
Cerro del Ramillete (346m)
Los Escullos
Punta del Esparto
Cerro del Garbanzal (411m)
Camping Los Escullos (441m)
PARQUE NATURAL DE CABO DE GATÁ-NÍJAR
Punta de Loma Pelada
Quarry
El Fraile (493m)
El Pozo de los Frailes
Refugio Mediterráneo de Gata
Cala Higuera
Cerro de Santa Cruz (432m)
Cerro de Enmedio (167m)
San José
See Cabo de Gata Coast Walk (West) Map p335
Punta del Castillo
Playa de los Genoveses
Morrón de los Genoveses

0   2   4 km
0   1   2 miles
1:200,000
Contour Interval 100 metres

At the north end of Playa del Playazo pick up the path passing the inland side of the Batería de San Ramón for an enjoyable 25 minute walk over the rocks to *Camping Nautico La Caleta* (☎ 950 52 52 37), in its own cove. This camping ground, open all year, has little shade but a nice pool. Summer prices are 530 ptas per adult and 588 ptas per tent. A road heads 1km north to Las Negras, which is set on a pebbly beach stretching towards an imposing headland of volcanic rock, Cerro Negro. Las Negras attracts a vaguely trendy holiday clientele. *Hostal Arrecife* (☎ 950 38 81 40, Calle Bahia 6) on the main street a short distance back from the beach has singles/doubles with bathroom for 4000/6000 ptas. A few houses let out *rooms* by the night – among them one (☎ 950 38 80 97) on Calle San Pedro, opposite Cerro Negro bar, with singles or doubles for 3000 ptas.

Day 3: Las Negras to Agua Amarga

3½ hours, 11km

A path climbing beside the last house at the north end of Las Negras beach joins a dirt road from the back of the village. Follow this round the back of Cerro Negro for 25 minutes. It then becomes a path high above the sea for another 25 minutes to **San Pedro**. This isolated hamlet was abandoned by its Spanish inhabitants some years ago, but its few ruined buildings (including a castle) and a couple of caves are now home to a colony of two or three dozen hippies.

There's no way out of San Pedro by land except up. A good path climbs from the round tower on the east side of the valley. You climb steeply for 25 minutes, then gently for another 15, during which you suddenly find you're walking along the top of a cliff – take care! The path is clear most of the way; where it's not, cairns guide you. Eighty minutes from San Pedro you come down to **Cala del Plomo** (sand and pebbles), with a small, scattered settlement that's in much better condition than San Pedro.

Five minutes back from the beach, a path marked by a 'Cala de Enmedio' sign and a pair of cairns turns off to the right. In a few

minutes this meets the Barranco de los Calares and follows it downstream to its meeting with the Barranco de la Cala, 20 minutes from the 'Cala de Enmedio' turning. Continue a few minutes downstream if you wish to visit the nice little **Cala de Enmedio** beach; for Agua Amarga, take an uphill path to the left at the meeting of barrancos, marked by a small cairn. This winds up and over Cerro del Cuartel and will have you removing your boots on Agua Amarga beach in 40 minutes. The village is a pleasant fishing-cum-tourist settlement stretched along a straight, sandy beach.

Side Trip: Mesa Roldán & Playa de los Muertos

3 to 3½ hours, 10km

If you're looking for extra leg-stretching, head 3km east up the Carboneras road, then 1.25km up a side road to a clifftop lighthouse, the **Faro Roldán**, which has an old watchtower for a neighbour. The views up here are marvellous. From the car park back down by the turning, you can walk down to the nudist Playa de los Muertos.

Sierra de Grazalema

The Cordillera Bética gives a final flourish west of the small hill town of Grazalema before fading away to the coastal plains of Cádiz province. The Sierra de Grazalema – actually several small sierras – is not particularly high but it contains, in a compact area dotted with white mountain villages, a great variety of beautiful landscapes, from tinkling, pastoral river valleys to deep, precipitous gorges, and from dense Mediterranean woodlands to rocky summits atop perpendicular cliffs.

This is one of the greenest parts of Andalucía. When warm, damp winds from the Atlantic meet these hills, rise, cool, condense and fall as rain (or, often in late January or February, as snow on the mountains). Grazalema town has the highest measured rainfall in Spain at an average of 2153mm a year.

The Grazalema sierras and some surrounding lowlands make up the 517 sq km

Parque Natural de la Sierra de Grazalema. Within the park, a 30 sq km *área de reserva* occupies most of the triangle between Grazalema, Benamahoma and Zahara de la Sierra, which contains much of the park's most spectacular territory. Entry to the area is only allowed with a guide, which can make planning a Grazalema visit something of a headache (see Sierra de Grazalema – Área de Reserva under Other Walks at the end of this chapter).

The two walks we describe in full are outside the reserve area and can be combined with guided walks within the reserve to give up to six days walking between the area's most attractive villages, in a sequence like this: Grazalema Loop (Grazalema to Benaocaz to Grazalema); Ascent of El Torreón (guided, with vehicle support from and back to Grazalema); Grazalema to Benamahoma via *pinsapar*, a woodland of the rare Spanish fir (guided); Benamahoma to Zahara de la Sierra; Garganta Verde (guided, with vehicle support from Zahara). Completing a circuit back to Grazalema would be a matter of a 16km road walk from Zahara (or 12km from the end of the Garganta Verde walk) – at least the road, over the 1331m Puerto de las Palomas, is spectacular.

An outline of the major guide-only routes appears in Other Walks at the end of this chapter.

HISTORY

The Romans cut into the Grazalema forests for shipbuilding, and you can still walk one of the roads they built between Benaocaz and Ubrique. In the 13th to 15th centuries, this was a Muslim/Christian frontier zone – a condition which gave rise both to the area's livestock raising tradition (animals being easier to move from conflict than crops) and to the way villages huddle into the rocky hillsides for protection. It was Zahara de la Sierra's recapture by the Granada emir Abu al-Hasan in a daring night raid in 1481 that spurred the Castilian monarchs to embark on the last phase of the Reconquista (which culminated in the fall of Granada in 1492).

In the 19th century, with land ownership concentrated in the hands of a few, the area was renowned for banditry, smuggling and poaching. Zahara was a noted hotbed of anarchism. In the mid-20th century swathes of forest were levelled for fuel and a big slice of the population departed in search of a more prosperous life elsewhere (you'll see many abandoned cortijos on your walks). Villages such as Benaocaz and Zahara lost more than half their inhabitants and Grazalema's current population of about 2300 compares with 9000 in the 18th century.

NATURAL HISTORY
Fauna

Though there are red and roe deer and more than 500 ibex in the park, your chances of spotting them are not very high unless you climb El Torreón, in which case you may see ibex. You will, however, see a lot of domesticated animals grazing in semiliberty – among them plenty of Iberian pigs, the black or dark brown breed that is turned into Spain's best ham, especially when (as it has ample opportunity to do here) it has eaten lots of acorns.

Grazalema cattle always seem to have long, sharp horns pointing in your direction. Most turn out, on second glance, to be cows, but some are bulls. If you can't keep a fence or wall between you and the bull, it makes sense to walk near some cover (thick undergrowth, trees, rocks) that you could resort to if necessary.

The star of the bird population is the griffon vulture. Around 100 pairs live in the Garganta Verde and Garganta Seca gorges south of Zahara de La Sierra. Bonelli's eagle and the peregrine falcon are two of the more common raptors.

Flora

Much of the area is covered in beautiful, dense Mediterranean woodland of holm, gall and cork oak, olive, *acebuche* (wild olive) and *algarrobo* (carob). In autumn yellow broom adds splashes of a different colour. The north flank of the Sierra del Pinar between Grazalema and Benamahoma supports a famous 3 sq km pinsapar, the best preserved woodland of the rare Spanish fir (*Abies pinsapo boiss*). This handsome, dark-green tree survives in significant numbers only in the Sierra de Grazalema, Sierra de las Nieves and Sierra Bermeja, all in south-west Andalucía, and in northern Morocco. It likes north-facing slopes up to 1800m, and can grow 30m high and live for 500 years. It's one of 10 species around the Mediterranean which are relics of the extensive fir forests of the Tertiary period (which ended about 2.5 million years ago).

Sierra de Grazalema

Duration 6½ to 7½ hours
Distance 20km
Standard Medium
Start/Finish Grazalema
Public Transport Yes
Summary A longish day walk through beautiful country of surprisingly remote valleys and passes, green woodlands and impressive limestone scenery; the Salto del Cabrero geological fault is a dramatic highlight.

There are several routes across the higher country between Grazalema and Benaocaz village, 8km south-west as the crow flies. This walk follows one outward and another returning to Grazalema, with a total ascent of 1050m. Alternative options include staying overnight in Benaocaz or getting an afternoon bus back from there.

PLANNING
When to Walk
May, June, September and October are best. The rainiest time is generally from November to mid-April, though you can be lucky and get clear, sunny weather at any time. July and August can get unpleasantly hot.

Maps
The IGN/Junta de Andalucía *Parque Natural Sierra de Grazalema* 1:50,000

mapa-guía is reasonable, though it omits some good and obvious paths and tracks. You can buy it in shops and tourist offices in Grazalema, Zahara de la Sierra and El Bosque.

What to Bring
Walking boots are best. Some sections are over rocks or loose stones. Long trousers or long socks will protect you from some prickly scrub. You certainly don't always need a waterproof garment, but if there's cloud and/or a westerly wind, you'll probably appreciate one. Carry enough water for the whole of each leg of the walk.

Permits & Fees
None are needed for the walk described.

Warning
The walk crosses pastures and woods where bulls may be grazing.

PLACES TO STAY & EAT
In Grazalema, *Camping Tajo Rodillo* (☎ 956 23 42 21) at the top of the town by the A372 charges 428 ptas per adult and per tent. In winter it only opens on weekends and holidays. In the centre, *Casa de las Piedras* (☎ 956 13 20 14, *Calle Las Piedras 32*) is a good-value hostal with plenty of rooms. Single and double rooms are 1500/3000 ptas, respectively, or 3600/4800 ptas with bathroom. The *Villa Turística de Grazalema* (☎ 956 13 21 62) on El Olivar, just above the town to the north, has rooms and apartments with all mod cons from 4708/7650 ptas, as well as a pool.

Among several places to eat and drink on Calle Agua off the central Plaza de España, *Bar La Posadilla* has very economical – and not bad – platos combinados ranging from 300 ptas to 500 ptas. *Restaurante Cádiz El Chico* (*Plaza de España 8*) is a good choice for a more expensive meal, with good meat (600 ptas to 1500 ptas), egg dishes and fish.

The *Zona de Acampada Cintillo y Aguas Nuevas* is a free camping area 2km south of

Benaocaz on the road to Villaluenga del Rosario.

Entering Benaocaz on the walk described, take the first street to the left to reach the *Refugio de Montaña El Parral* (☎ 956 12 55 65 or ☎ 908-32 25 73), which has clean, six-bunk dormitories for 963 ptas per person (bring your own sleeping bag), and a *comedor* (dining room) and bar.

Ignore the El Parral turning and in another minute you reach *Hostal San Antón* (☎ 956 46 07 64) on Plaza de San Antón, where doubles with bathroom are 3745 ptas.

A good place to eat in the centre is *La Palmera*, with a nice terrace.

GETTING TO/FROM THE WALK

The Los Amarillos company's Málaga-Ubrique buses call at Ronda, Grazalema and Benaocaz. At the time of writing buses leave Málaga from Monday to Friday at 10.30 am and 4 pm; Saturday, Sunday and holidays at 10.30 am and 3 pm. Buses leave Ronda from Monday to Friday at 12.30 and 6.15 pm; Saturday, Sunday and holidays at 1 and 5.30 pm, and Grazalema 30 minutes later.

For the return journey, buses leave Ubrique from Monday to Friday at 7.30 am and 3.30 pm; Saturday, Sunday and holidays at 8.30 am and 3.30 pm, stopping in Benaocaz after about five minutes and Grazalema after 30 minutes.

Los Amarillos also runs up to six buses a day to El Bosque and Ubrique from Jerez de la Frontera and Arcos de la Frontera, and two or three from Cádiz and Sevilla (Prado de San Sebastián bus station). From El Bosque, except on Sunday, there's a 3.15 pm Los Amarillos bus to Grazalema. The Grazalema-El Bosque bus goes from Monday to Friday at 5.30 am and Friday at 7 pm.

To confirm bus schedules, ring Los Amarillos in Cádiz (☎ 956 28 58 52) or Ronda (☎ 95 218 70 61), or the bus stations in Jerez (☎ 956 34 52 07), Málaga (☎ 95 235 00 61), Sevilla (☎ 95 441 71 11) or Ubrique (☎ 956 46 80 11).

THE WALK

Start by walking 1km west up the A372 from the top of Grazalema. At a right-hand bend just before the turning for Zahara de la Sierra, a path continues straight on and upwards, crossing the road once before meeting it again at the Puerto del Boyar (1103m), 45 minutes from the middle of Grazalema. Go 60m left down the road, then through a gate on the right with a sign 'Paso a Pie Salto del Cabrero'.

A dirt track leads 25 minutes south-west down to a white cortijo – you can glimpse the top of the Salto del Cabrero, an odd rock peak rising 3 or 4km ahead. Go down through a gate to the left of the cortijo and follow a path which starts descending through a **gall oak wood**.

Forty minutes from the cortijo, the path passes a small cottage among rocks on your right, then climbs towards the lowest point of a ridge just west of south. Just before the top of the rise, fork right to ascend between rocks (one bearing a small, green arrow and the letters 'AMA') to a gate. After the gate, the path briefly hugs a wall before veering right through country studded with limestone rocks. You descend to a flat, grassy area and curve westward through a gap between rock ridges.

Around 25 minutes from the cottage among the rocks, you're on the edge of the **Salto del Cabrero** (Goatherd's Leap) – a sloping fissure perhaps 500m long and 100m across, where the earth simply seems to have slipped 80 or 100m downwards. The path continues towards the bottom end of this canyon for those who are tempted to explore further.

Return to the flat, grassy area and veer right to leave it by its south corner. Cross a small rise and head south towards Benaocaz, which soon becomes visible. You'll reach it in roughly an hour (3¼ hours from Grazalema).

The route back to Grazalema starts eastnorth-east from Benaocaz, up the valley below the north side of the Sierra del Caillo. Make initially for Benaocaz's highest houses, north-east of the church.

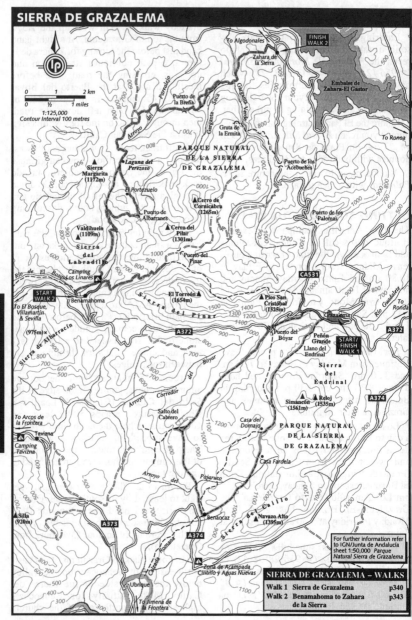

SIERRA DE GRAZALEMA

ANDALUCÍA

For further information refer to IGN/Junta de Andalucía sheet 1:50,000 *Parque Natural Sierra de Grazalema*

SIERRA DE GRAZALEMA – WALKS	
Walk 1 Sierra de Grazalema	p340
Walk 2 Benamahoma to Zahara de la Sierra	p343

From the last house, with 'BM' on its gate, a stone-walled path heads for seven minutes up to a stone water trough. Fork left here and you soon pass through a metal gate onto a clear track rising between holm oaks and limestone rock piles. Go through another metal gate, level off in open grassland, descend to two gates in quick succession, cross the small Arroyo del Parruco, then rise again to a small cortijo, Casa Fardela, an hour from Benaocaz.

The easiest way past Casa Fardela seems to be across the yard at its far end (open gates permitted this when we came through). Now head north, crossing a fence on the way, up towards a wood of holm oaks with a jumbled limestone hillock to its right and a lower ridge/wall of limestone appearing to its left.

Climbing through the holm oaks, you'll see that the limestone ridge/wall continues behind them. Head for its grassy lowest point, behind the jumbled limestone hillock. From the top of the rise, descend at about 25° to a gully running down to a few poplar trees. From the poplars, the Casa del Dornajo, a ruined cortijo, is visible two minutes west-north-west (35 minutes from Casa Fardela).

After a breather under the Dornajo trees, start out north-east and in a couple of minutes you'll pick up a path bending northward across the lower slopes of Simancón (1561m), the mountain at the head of this lovely valley strewn with holm oaks. In 30 minutes you crest a rise and the Grazalema-Benamahoma road comes into view. The path descends to a gate about 12 minutes away.

From the gate continue north-north-east (upwards now) to pick up the path again just over a little rise, where it's marked by a couple of cairns. Head down to the valley bottom where, just after a water trough by the corner of a small pine plantation, you take a lesser path up to the left. This passes beneath the rock-climbers' crag **Peñón Grande** to emerge beside Camping Tajo Rodillo at the top of Grazalema, two hours from the Casa del Dornajo.

Benamahoma to Zahara de la Sierra

Duration 5 hours
Distance 14.5km (16km via the Puerto de Albarranes)
Standard Easy-Medium
Start Benamahoma
Finish Zahara de la Sierra
Public Transport Yes
Summary The route crosses often beautiful country from Benamahoma (end-point of the guided pinsapar walk) to Zahara de la Sierra, one of the park's most attractive villages and the jumping-off point for the guided Garganta Verde walk.

This walk takes you across some surprisingly remote country of thick woodlands and high pastures just outside the área de reserva.

PLANNING
All the comments under Planning for the Grazalema Loop walk also apply to this one, except that this side of the hills is a lot less rainy.

Take enough water for the whole walk. The water running into a cattle trough a minute to the right (south) from the Puerto de Albarranes *looks* OK, but you never know what might live in it.

PLACES TO STAY & EAT
In Benamahoma, *Camping Los Linares* (☎ 956 71 62 75) about 600m up Camino del Nacimiento has cabins at 4500 ptas for two or 7000 ptas for four, and camping facilities at 481 ptas per adult and per tent. In winter it normally opens on weekends and holidays only.

There's more accommodation in El Bosque, 4km west (a path runs there alongside the Río de El Bosque from the same starting point as our Benamahoma-Zahara route). This includes the *Albergue Campamento El Bosque* youth hostel (☎ 956 71 62 12) on Molino de Enmedio, pleasantly sited by the end of the path from Benamahoma, and *Hostal Enrique Calvillo* (☎ 956 71 61 05,

Avenida Diputación 5), near the park information office, with singles/doubles with bathroom for 2000/4500 ptas.

In the centre of Zahara de la Sierra, the unsigned, friendly **Pensión González** (☎ *956 17 32 17, Calle San Juan 9)* has a few rooms with shared bathroom at 2000/3000 ptas. **Hostal Marqués de Zahara** (☎ *956 12 30 61, Calle San Juan 3)* has 10 comfy rooms at 3750/5650 ptas. *Bar Nuevo* on the same street does homely, cheap food.

GETTING TO/FROM THE WALK

Benamahoma is on the El Bosque-Grazalema bus route (see the Grazalema Loop walk).

The Comes line (☎ 95 287 19 92) runs two buses from Ronda to Zahara and vice-versa, via Algodonales, daily except Saturday, Sunday and holidays. Buses leave Ronda at 7 am and 1 pm, Zahara at 8.15 am and 2 pm. Change buses at Algodonales for Sevilla.

THE WALK

Turn north by the Venta El Bujío bar (opposite the Coop del Mueble building) at the bottom (west) end of Benamahoma. The side road crosses the Río de El Bosque and immediately divides. Take the left option, then turn right after 70m. Ignore a right fork opposite a pillared gate after three or four minutes, but almost immediately turn 90° to the right when the track passes through a fence. Go through a gate, ignore a left turn soon afterwards, and the dirt road you are now on will lead all the way to Zahara de la Sierra. However, a few worthwhile variations from the basic route are detailed in what follows.

The track soon starts climbing fairly steeply, with a few zigzags. Around 35 minutes from the last gate mentioned, with the track now more level, you pass through another gate as you head up the west side of the Breña del Agua valley. In a further 30 minutes there's a fenced enclosure on the left. Just 100m beyond this, a path branches left (north) shortly before the main track makes a sharpish right bend. Here you have a choice.

If you stay with the main track (passing a cortijo after 10 minutes or so, going left at a

junction of tracks at the Puerto de Albarranes 15 minutes later, and passing the cortijo El Portezuelo at 950m after another 10 minutes), you'll enjoy views of the Cerro del Pilar, Sierra del Pinar and Cerro de Cornicabra.

If you take the path, you save a few minutes and pass through some lovely woodlands. The path is not very clear at the start, but soon becomes so as it climbs 15 minutes to a little pass (925m). Descending, it bends a little to the right before emerging in a grassy upland valley with 1172m Sierra Margarita rising from its west side. Head for the gate in the fence across the middle of the valley, where you rejoin the main track descending from El Portezuelo.

Just through the gate is the so-called **Laguna del Perezoso**, a shallow, stone-walled depression which collects rain water but is often dry. The track continues ahead for five minutes, then begins a winding, 50 minute descent to the Arroyo del Parralejo (often dry). From the arroyo there's a 20 minute ascent through perhaps the loveliest woods of the whole walk (mainly holm oaks and olives) to the Puerto de la Breña (600m).

Then it's downhill for 50 minutes to the Arroyo de Bocaleones issuing from the Garganta Verde (Green Gorge). As you descend, to your right are some of the cliffs of the *garganta* (gorge), home to a large vulture colony. An alternative on this section, following the old Colada de la Breña livestock route and avoiding some of the main track's curves, is to take the drive down towards a cortijo on the right, six or seven minutes after Puerto de la Breña. Turn left off the drive before reaching the cortijo and follow a broad swathe north-east downhill for 10 minutes. Then pass just to the right of another cortijo, veering half-left and downhill immediately past it. Pick up a clear trail running along for 20 minutes above the Garganta Seca stream, to rejoin the main track a few minutes before the Arroyo de Bocaleones.

From the Arroyo de Bocaleones you have an up-and-down of 30 to 40 minutes (with an overall ascent of 200m) through olive groves to Zahara, passing the single remaining tower of its 12th century castle.

Top: Ibex on the slopes of Alcazaba, high above the Cañada de Siete Lagunas, Sierra Nevada, Andalucía.
Middle Left: Salt workers' church in the village of La Almadraba de Monteleva, on the Cabo de Gata.
Middle Right: Refugio Vivac Carigüela, a shelter close to Spain's third-highest peak, Veleta (3395m).
Bottom: Bubión is typical of the Berber-style villages of the Alpujarras, in Muslim-flavoured Andalucía.

JOHN NOBLE

JOHN NOBLE

JOHN NOBLE

Top Left: The Barranco del Guadalentín, Parque Natural de Cazorla, is a good place for spotting wildlife.
Top Right: The Río Borosa walk in the Parque Natural de Cazorla traverses a cliff high above the river, passing through tunnels dark enough to make a torch desirable.
Bottom: The village of Los Escullos, nestled below El Fraile, the highest peak on the Cabo de Gata.

Parque Natural Sierra de la Nieves

This 180 sq km nature park, south-east of the interesting, old hill town of Ronda, encompasses the highest mountains in the western half of Andalucía. With a vehicle, the walk can be done as a day trip from Ronda or the Costa del Sol.

NATURAL HISTORY
The park includes around 10 sq km of pinsapares (see Natural History in the Sierra de Grazalema section). Lower altitudes have extensive evergreen oak woodlands. The gall oak is quite widespread on the uplands above the pinsapares. Ibex are here, and you can scan the skies and crags for Bonelli's, short-toed, golden and booted eagles.

Torrecilla & Peñón de los Enamorados

Duration 6 to 7 hours
Distance 16km
Standard Medium-Hard
Start/Finish Área Recreativa Los Quejigales
Public Transport No
Summary A walk to the highest peak in this attractive range accessible from the Costa del Sol, with great long-distance views, taking in a beautiful ancient woodland of Spanish firs, and returning via another peak with contrasting inland views.

This walk takes you to the top of the park's highest mountain, Torrecilla, and another landmark peak, the Peñón de los Enamorados, via some of its most spectacular landscapes and panoramas.

PLANNING
When to Walk
It *can* be done any time of year, but the heat of July and August demands extra energy. Avoid cloud, mist, heavy rain or snow and

high winds: the upper parts of the route are exposed. Rain, when it falls (most often in October, December and March), is often heavy. The *nieve* (snow) after which the mountains are named usually falls between January and March. In winter, be prepared for temperatures close to freezing.

Maps & Books
The IGN/Junta de Andalucía *Parque Natural Sierra de las Nieves* map, published in 1996, covers the area at 1:50,000 but isn't always easy to find. The IGN's *Ronda* No 1051-III and *Yunquera* No 1051-IV 1:25,000 maps cover the walk, though they omit some trails and place some names inaccurately; the *Igualeja* No 1065-I map covers access to Los Quejigales from the A376.

La Sierra de las Nieves – Rutas y Leyendas by Rafael Flores Dominguez and Andrés Rodríguez González is a fine Spanish guide, with 32 walks described.

What to Bring
Carry enough water to get you as far as Cerro del Pilar.

PLACES TO STAY & EAT
Camping is allowed at the walk's start and end point, the *Área Recreativa Los Quejigales* (shown as Cortijo de los Quejigales by IGN), from about late October to late May. Los Quejigales has tap water. To camp here you need a permit from Andalucía's environmental agency, Agencia de Medio Ambiente (AMA). The AMA's Ronda office (☎ 95 287 77 78) in the Palacio de Mondragón, Plaza Mondragon, told us it will fax the permission if you supply your name and passport number by telephone. There are plans to move the camping area to Conejeras, near the start of the track from the A376 to Los Quejigales.

At the 135km milepost on the A376, just over 1km north of the Los Quejigales turn-off, *Pensión Restaurante Navasillo* (☎ 95 211 42 35) has a few singles/doubles with bathroom for 2000/4500 ptas and typical hill-country food, such as raciones of rabbit or wild boar for 800 ptas. One kilometre

ANDALUCÍA

further up the A376, at the 134km point, *Hostal-Restaurante Rincón Taurino* (☎ 95 218 10 21) has rooms for 2500/4100 ptas. The petrol station next door has an ATM and a shop with a few basic groceries.

At Yunquera, on the east side of the park, *Camping Pinsapo Azul* (☎ 95 248 27 54) charges around 400 ptas per person, per tent and per car, and *Hostal Asencio* (☎ 95 248 27 16, Calle Mesones 1), with a restaurant, charges 3850 ptas to 4710 ptas for doubles. The village's tourist office (☎ 95 248 25 01), Calle del Pozo 17, can tell you about further accommodation.

GETTING TO/FROM THE WALK

The route starts and ends at the Área Recreativa Los Quejigales, 10km by driveable track from the A376 San Pedro de Alcántara-Ronda road. The turning off the A376 is 12km from Ronda, just south of the 136km milepost. It's marked by various signs announcing the Parque Natural Sierra de las Nieves. Initially the track is fairly level, passing mainly through woodlands. After 2km it bends 90° to the right, crosses an arroyo and then forks – take the upper, left-hand track which immediately bends left again. A further 2.5km along, the track turns left (north) at the entrance to Cortijo La Nava, then zigzags over the south-west end of the Sierra de las Nieves proper before descending a little in the final 2km to Los Quejigales. Follow the major track at all junctions.

Portillo (☎ 95 287 22 62 in Ronda) runs up to six buses a day each way between Málaga and Ronda via Torremolinos, Fuengirola, Marbella and San Pedro de Alcántara. They stop at the Cruce La Ventilla stop at the petrol station at the 134km point on the A376, 2km north of the Los Quejigales turning.

Buses between Málaga and Ronda through Yunquera are run by the Sierra de las Nieves line, also called Ferrón Coin (☎ 95 287 15 93 in Ronda, ☎ 95 235 54 90 in Málaga). There are up to three daily each way.

THE WALK

The route up Torrecilla starts with a steepish 470m ascent to the Puerto de los Pilones by the Cañada de los Cuernos gully, then there's a fairly level section followed by the final, steep 230m ascent to the summit.

Start along the track running north from Los Quejigales (at the time of writing it was closed to vehicles by a chain). Two hundred metres beyond the end of the camp site/picnic area, a sign indicates the 'Sendero de los Quejigales' to Pico Torrecilla. Turn right (east) here onto a path which immediately crosses an arroyo bed and is marked by stones either side as it climbs gently through pines. It steepens a little as it enters a band of initially scattered Spanish firs (darker green than the pines below) and starts to zigzag. This pinsapar thickens as you cross the hillside and ascend the **Cañada de los Cuernos**. The route is obvious except that three or four minutes after the point where it crosses from the south side of the arroyo to the north, the path you need forks back to the right as a wider path continues northward and away from the cañada.

Soon the pinsapar thins out and one hour from Los Quejigales you emerge onto an open, shrubby hillside. Five minutes up this, your path meets a broad track. Ronda's white sprawl is visible to the west-north-west. Head left along the track, towards a radio mast. Halfway to the mast (five minutes) you are on the **Puerto de los Pilones** pass, with views as far as Gibraltar if you're lucky. Torrecilla rises 3km southeast. At the Puerto de los Pilones veer half-right (north-east) along a footpath opposite a sort of lay-by where the track briefly broadens out.

Your new path descends gradually northeastward between scattered gall oaks. On the left after 15 minutes is a round, stone-walled pit, a modern reconstruction of an old *pozo de nieve* (snow-storage pit). As late as the 1930s snow from the Sierra de las Nieves was transported as far as Málaga and the Guadalquivir valley for refrigeration purposes. About 200m beyond the pozo de nieve, the path forks beneath a gall oak; take the slightly broader right-hand option, which crosses the north flank of a small hill, with occasional small cairns. You then have a slightly downhill, south-eastward stretch before the path – still with occasional mini-cairns – veers south-west round the end of Cerro del Pilar, 45 minutes from the pozo de nieve.

The path descends the south-western side of Cerro del Pilar. There are a number of caves in the rock above you, a couple harbouring saints' images, and at least two good freshwater springs. The most reliable spring – you can trust it to flow all year – is at the foot of the south side of the Cerro del Pilar, beneath the carved image of the Virgen de la Victoria.

Fork right 150m past the Virgen de la Victoria spring for the steep path to the summit – a climb of about 30 minutes. The views from the summit of **Torrecilla** (1918m) are ample reward – on a good day as far as the Sierra Nevada and Morocco. Yunquera is clearly visible to the north-east, and part of Tolox in a dip to the east.

To start back, retrace your steps for about one hour as far as the fork in the path beneath the gall oak. Here, instead of continuing

towards the pozo de nieve, turn right (north). The clear path (Camino de la Sierra de las Nieves) descends gently into the head of a valley, then rises gradually up its left side. The Peñón de los Enamorados (1777m), a distinctive rock outcrop, comes into view 25 minutes from the gall oak fork. It's a further 15 minutes to the top of the peñón (find your own way up from the path across the hillside just below it). There are good views over the northern parts of the parque natural.

If you wish to continue from the Peñón de los Enamorados to the village of Yunquera on the eastern edge of the parque natural, head on north-eastward along the Camino de la Sierra de las Nieves. It's about 4km, much of it through pinsapar, to the Puerto del Saucillo (about 1200m), which can be reached by vehicle from Yunquera, and a further 6km down to the A366 on the northern edge of Yunquera. Camping Pinsapo Azul is about 600m before the A366.

To return from the Peñón de los Enamorados to Los Quejigales, retrace your steps to the gall oak fork and from there to the Puerto de los Pilones and down the Cañada

TORRECILLA & PEÑÓN DE LOS ENAMORADOS

de los Cuernos. A simple variant is to continue down the major track at the Puerto de los Pilones instead of going down the Cañada de los Cuernos. After 4km you meet the Los Quejigales access road, about 700m south-west of Los Quejigales.

Sierra Blanca

Much of the scenic appeal of the beach resorts of the Costa del Sol, west of Málaga, comes from the rugged hills and mountains close behind the coast. The Sierra Blanca provides the biggest and glitziest resort, Marbella, with the most impressive backdrop of any town on this coast. These mountains can look bare and brown from sea level, but turn out to be surprisingly green. There are even a couple of small pinsapares (woods of rare Spanish firs – see Natural History in the Sierra de Grazalema section).

Sierra Blanca Loop

Duration 5 to 6 hours
Distance 13.5km
Standard Medium
Start/Finish Refugio de Juanar
Public Transport No
Summary An up-and-down circuit in the unspoiled, surprisingly green and wild mountains behind Marbella; this walk offers great panoramas over the Costa del Sol and inland, and takes you through dramatic high mountain scenery and into rare Spanish fir woods.

This circuit starts and finishes at the Refugio de Juanar hotel in the heart of the sierra, with a total ascent of 900m, but alternative endings taking you down to Marbella or Ojén are also described.

PLANNING
When to Walk

Any time of year, though from November to March you may experience cloud, rain or cold. July and August can be pretty hot.

Maps

The IGN's *Marbella* No 1065-IV and *Istán* No 1065-II 1:25,000 maps cover the walk.

What to Bring

Remember that the sun can burn in the mountains just as on the beach. In winter or if it's overcast, come prepared for temperatures several degrees cooler than on the coast. There's water at El Pozuelo, about an hour from the start; at least bring a water bottle large enough to get you from there to the end of the walk. Long trousers or long socks will protect your legs from prickly scrub.

PLACES TO STAY & EAT

In Marbella, the modern *Albergue Juvenil Marbella* (☎ 95 277 14 91, Calle Trapiche 2) is between the old centre and the bus station. In the old town, *Hostal del Pilar* (☎ 95 282 99 36, Calle Mesoncillo 4) is popular among backpackers at 1500 ptas to 2000 ptas a person, while *Hostal El Castillo* (☎ 95 277 17 39, Plaza San Bernabé 2) and *Hostal Enriqueta* (☎ 95 282 75 52, Calle Los Caballeros 18) have doubles with bathroom for 5000 ptas.

El Gallo bar, Calle Lobatos 44, does egg and chips for 300 ptas and Marbella's cheapest *gambas pil pil* (prawns baked with garlic, chilli and olive oil) at 500 ptas (closed Tuesday). On Calle Huerta Chica, the *Puerta del Príncipe* does good grilled meat and fish from 850 ptas; *La Pesquera* next door concentrates on seafood for similar prices.

In Ojén there are rooms at *Pension El Solar* (☎ 95 288 11 49, Calle Córdoba 2).

The *Refugio de Juanar* (☎ 95 288 10 00) has comfortable singles/doubles for 8670/ 11,000 ptas. The menú del día in its restaurant will set you back 3210 ptas.

GETTING TO/FROM THE WALK

The Refugio de Juanar is 5.4km up a paved side road west from the Marbella-Coín A355. The turning is 2km north of the village of Ojén and 11km from Marbella. The simple way to reach the Refugio de Juanar from Marbella is by car or taxi (about 2500 ptas). Another option is a bus to Ojén, then a taxi (1600 ptas), but if Ojén's one taxi, normally found on the main plaza, is busy, you might have a wait. Walking up from Marbella or Ojén to the Refugio de Juanar is also possible (by reversing the descent routes described in the walk description), but would mean an extra ascent of more than 800 and 500m, respectively.

Buses from Marbella bus station to Ojén currently run at 7, 8 and 9.45 am and about hourly from 1.30 to 9.15 pm. There are none on Sunday. The last buses back leave Ojén at 6.45, 7.45 and 8.45 pm.

THE WALK

Start by walking 900m back from the Refugio de Juanar along its access road. Follow a path which descends beside a stone marker inscribed 'Sendero de José Lima', bends to the right across an arroyo, then steadily ascends the far (west) side of the valley, heading northward. At a little pass 30 minutes up, the path bends left (west) towards the rocky crags of Los Cuchillos. In 15 or 20 minutes you should reach El Pozuelo spring (actually a tap) and bend left

again to climb for 10 minutes to the Puerto del Pozuelo (1094m).

Those who fear for their stamina later in the day could ignore the next stage, a quick zip up the clear, northward path at the Puerto del Pozuelo. This climbs 15 minutes to the col between Picacho de los Castillejos (1238m) and the 1212m summit to its west. It's worthwhile in order to see a pinsapar, just over the col, and fine northward views from the **1212m hill**.

Back at the Puerto del Pozuelo, take the west-south-west path. Torrecilla in the Sierra de las Nieves appears away to the north-west shortly before you enter a small **pinsapar**. The path descends gently, and leftward bends about 15 and 20 minutes after the pinsapar leave you heading almost east, towards a notch in a small ridge. Continue 1½ minutes down from the notch, then hop up the rocks on the right to meet a broader track a little higher up. Head to the right along this; it soon dwindles to a narrow path descending to a basin below some jagged crags. Head for the path climbing the far (south) side of the basin, 300m away, and turn left (east) along the trail this soon meets, one hour from the Puerto del Pozuelo. This trail crosses a small pass and descends steeply into the valley where the Arroyo de Juanar rises. Ten minutes into the pines on the valley floor, turn right at an obvious fork. This path climbs the south side of the valley to arrive in 25 minutes on the panoramic saddle below the hill topped by the Cruz de Juanar.

To the south-west stretches a line of peaks ending in the rugged La Concha. Progress along this line is surprisingly difficult and the attempt is not recommended, but you can go as far as **Salto del Lobo** (35 minutes) to see why. Occasional small cairns help you onto a path climbing west towards the col between Salto del Lobo (Wolf's Leap) and the next hump to its north. The path crosses the col and turns left across the steep slope below Salto del Lobo's north-west cliffs. We don't recommend following it. Salto del Lobo's summit ridge and south-east side end

in a very steep scramble which, again, we don't recommend.

Return along the saddle and make the steep, 15 minute climb to the **Cruz de Juanar**, a metal cross on a hill top. This is the day's scenic high point with great views over Marbella, along the Costa del Sol from Mijas to Puerto Banús, and inland to Torrecilla. A path down to the north-east will have you in 20 minutes at a picnic area among pines. (A path starting here, the Camino de Puerto Rico, heads south down the valley to Marbella. It's about an hour to the cemetery beside the A355 on the north edge of town.)

At the far (east) end of the picnic area you emerge onto a broad track. Turn left, bearing north-east through the Olivar de Juanar olive grove. It's 25 minutes to the Refugio de Juanar. Halfway along, a path to the right will take you down to Ojén, a pleasant, steepish descent, through woods most of the way; after 20 minutes signposts at a fork give you the option of routes via the 'Ermita' (a chapel) or the 'Área de Acampada El Cerezal', a recreation area at the top of Ojén. It's an hour from the fork to central Ojén by the El Cerezal route, which passes under the A355 by a tunnel carrying a small stream.

Other Walks

As well as the walking areas covered in detail in this chapter (for which a few additional options are outlined below), many other parts of Andalucía have strong claims to a walker's time. Among them are the Sierra Bermeja behind the western Costa del Sol (especially the Sierra Crestellina near Casares and the Los Reales area inland of Estepona) and the Sierra Norte of Sevilla province, an attractive section of the rolling Sierra Morena. But the two areas that we most regret lacking more space for are La Axarquía and the Sierra de Aracena, and we have briefly described the walking opportunities in these areas below.

PARQUE NATURAL DE CAZORLA
Puente de las Herrerías Area

The Nacimiento del Guadalquivir, where a riverbank plaque marks the official source of the Río Guadalquivir, is just over 11km south from Puente de las Herrerías by dirt road. (Puente de las Herrerías can be reached by the described side trip off the Sierra de Cazorla Loop walk.) The trip is up a beautiful valley; off-road alternatives, to the east, are marked on the Editorial Alpina map (see Maps & Books under Planning in the Sierra de Cazorla Loop walk).

The Sierra del Pozo's panoramic highest peak, Cabañas (2028m), is 8km south-south-east of the Nacimiento, and too far for most of us to complete in a day from Puente de las Herrerías. The summit is a two hour round-trip walk from the road at Puerto Llano. More feasible one-day destinations from Puente de las Herrerías are the hill La Mesa and the Cerrada del Pintor, a gorge on the Arroyo de los Tornillos de Gualay.

A two hour walk to Vadillo Castril is described in the booklet with the Editorial Alpina map. You could follow this with the Sendero de la Cerrada del Utrero, a 2km loop which takes you under imposing cliffs to the tall Cascada de Linarejos waterfall, then back above the Embalse de la Cerrada del Utrero, a narrow reservoir on the Guadalquivir. The start of this sendero coincides with that of the Sendero de la Central de Utrero, a 1km downhill walk to a small power station on the A319, which you could use if you want to head on down the Guadalquivir valley on foot. Note that the maps of these two senderos posted at their start are juxtaposed (at least they were on our last two visits).

SIERRA NEVADA & LAS ALPUJARRAS
Capileira to Refugio Poqueira

Capileira, the highest village in the Barranco de Poqueira, is another popular starting point for walks up into the Sierra Nevada. Of several routes to the Refugio Poqueiro (at the end of Day 2 of the Sierra Nevada Traverse walk), the one which best combines interest and ease is the one known as 'por las acequias' ('by the irrigation channels'). From the middle of Capileira follow the Sierra Nevada road for 7.5km (the first 5km or so are paved) to a bend where a dirt road branches left by a stone cortijo with a swimming pool. (Walkers can short-cut some of the road's zigzags on the way up.)

Go 800m north-north-west along the branch dirt road to an unfinished house with one high triangular end – drivers can park nearby. From here follow the Acequia Baja irrigation channel along its generally northerly course, rising only slightly, for some 6km. Just 300 or 400m before the Río Mulhacén, turn right (north-north-east) up the hillside for the 420m

of ascent to the Refugio Poqueira, passing a lone farmstead then another irrigation channel, the Acequia Alta (often dry).

The refugio is about three hours from the triangle house, and five hours from Capileira.

Trevélez to Refugio Poqueira

You can reach the Sierra Nevada road by a steep climb up the Río Chico valley from Trevélez. A signposted 4km track branches north-west from the road to the Refugio Poqueira. It's about three hours from Trevélez to the refugio.

Refugio Poqueira to Mulhacén via Loma del Tanto

Follow the refugio's track 4km south-east back to its junction with the Sierra Nevada road, go 400m left along the road, then turn right up the Mulhacén summit track (closed to vehicles). The track zigzags 7km up the Loma del Tanto ridge to within 800m of Mulhacén's summit; a footpath covers the remaining distance. It's about three to 3½ hours up, 2½ hours down.

Via West Face

From the refugio a path heads 250m north-west, crosses a ridge and runs 500m north to the Río Mulhacén. Follow the river upstream to the Sierra Nevada road near Refugio Vivac La Caldera, then walk up the steep west face of Mulhacén. This route takes about 2½ hours up and 1½ hours down.

Estación de Esquí Sierra Nevada to Veleta

You can walk up the road from the Estación de Esquí (ski resort) to the top of Veleta, helped by paths short-cutting some zigzags in the road. From the bus stop in the lower part of the resort (about 2100m) to the top of Veleta takes up to four hours. Drivers can go as high as the Borreguiles turnoff (2650m) above the top of the resort, which could cut your walk to two hours.

Vereda de la Estrella

This approach to the Sierra Nevada from the north follows an old cart track which once served the Minas de la Estrella. It's a beautiful walk on which you can appreciate the grandeur of the north faces of Mulhacén and Alcazaba, and it can be done as a day trip from Granada. The path begins at the confluence (reachable by vehicle) of the Río Genil and Barranco de San Juan, 6km south-east of the town of Güéjar Sierra, which is about 15km east of Granada. The 575m ascent (three hours or so) leads to rock shelters at Cueva Secreta, at the foot of the Valdeinfiernos valley. From here various onward routes – many of them only for those with a good head for heights – lead up to Mulhacén, Alcazaba and other high peaks.

SIERRA DE GRAZALEMA – ÁREA DE RESERVA

For these walks you need a guide (Permits, Payments & Guides immediately below), but they are some of the most spectacular and interesting in the park. Walking boots are always advisable; you'll be advised by your guide company on water and food requirements. See the two walks in the Sierra de Grazalema section for accommodation, transport, season and map information.

Permits, Payments & Guides

If you want to walk in the área de reserva you must follow one of a few established routes with a guide from one of a few authorised guide companies. There are daily quotas of people per route – 60 for the pinsapar walk, for instance, and 30 for the Garganta Verde. It used to be possible to walk the established routes on your own with a free permit from the parque natural. But in 1997 the guide requirement was introduced on the grounds that it would give the área de reserva better protection and increase local employment. (It is possible, however, following a concerted campaign against the 'privatisation of the park' by a range of ecologists, walkers, youth groups and political parties, that the regulations will be changed again.)

The most prominent guide outfit is Aventerra, which also runs the nature park information offices in El Bosque (☎ 956 72 70 29, open daily from 9 am to 2 pm, and Saturday, Sunday and holidays from 4 to 6 pm) and Zahara de la Sierra (☎ 956 12 31 14, open daily from 9 am to 2 pm). Aventerra takes bookings for the pinsapar walk at the El Bosque office, and for the Garganta Verde at Zahara. Another guide company is Pinzapo (☎ 956 13 21 66), Calle Las Piedras 11, Grazalema, open from 10 am to 2 pm and 5.30 to 8 pm.

You pay far less to join an 'open' group than to hire a guide all to yourself/selves. At the time of writing Aventerra charges 900 ptas per person to join a group of 15 for the pinsapar on Wednesday, Saturday, Sunday and holidays, and 600 ptas to join a 15-person Garganta Verde walk on Thursday, Saturday, Sunday and holidays, but charges 10,950 and 9500 ptas respectively per group on other days. Pinzapar operates a similar 'two-level' scheme.

Sometimes you'll get a place in an open group if you just go along to the office first thing on the day itself, but it's better to book a few days ahead – and for times like Semana Santa and holiday weekends a few weeks notice might be needed. On the other hand, if there's no group going on the walk you want, you'll have to pay the full guide fee yourself.

Few of the guides speak foreign languages.

Ascent of El Torreón

El Torreón (1654m), the highest peak of the Grazalema region, tops the Sierra del Pinar, the most prominent of the area's ranges, stretching between Grazalema and Benamahoma. The usual route up El Torreón is from the south side, starting 100m east of the 40km marker on the Grazalema-Benamahoma road. From this point (about 850m high), it takes about 2½ hours of actual walking up to the summit and 1½ hours back down. As you climb, Mediterranean woodlands finally give way to a barer, karstic landscape where you might see ibex. Reaching the summit reveals that the northern side of the range is much steeper (sheer precipices, in fact) than the south side you have climbed. Below spreads the famous pinsapar. The views on a clear day are superb – as far as Sevilla, Cádiz, Gibraltar, Morocco's Rif Mountains and the Sierra Nevada.

Grazalema to Benamahoma via the Pinsapar

This walk of about 14km takes seven or eight hours with a guided group and is usually done from east to west because, after a couple of steepish ascents in the first one-third of the walk, it's downhill most of the way.

Normally you'll walk up from Grazalema to a point about 700m along the Zahara de la Sierra road from the A372 (this takes about 40 minutes, with an ascent of around 200m). Then you turn onto the footpath that will lead across the northern slopes of the Sierra del Pinar. There's an initial ascent of some 300m, then you stick close to the 1300m contour as you pass below Pico San Cristóbal, the pointed summit of which has long provided the first glimpse of home for Spanish sailors heading home across the Atlantic.

The thickest part of the pinsapar – blocking out long-distance views – comes in the middle third of the walk, between Pico San Cristóbal and the Puerto del Pinar, as you head west then north-west below the range's precipitous upper slopes. Mediterranean woodlands take over as you descend to Benamahoma (500m), nestling beneath the west end of the Sierra del Pinar.

Garganta Verde

The Garganta Verde (Green Gorge) is just what its name says – a lushly vegetated gorge, 100m and more deep, carved out of the limestone south of Zahara de la Sierra by the Arroyo Bocaleones. The guided itinerary of about four hours begins 3.5km from Zahara on the Grazalema road (groups travel there by car). Before descending into the gorge, you visit a viewpoint overlooking a colony of griffon vultures (around 100 pairs of these huge birds nest here and in the Garganta Seca 2km west). Then comes a steep descent of 300m. Once down in the bottom of the gorge you walk a few hundred metres to the Gruta de la Ermita, a large cavern hollowed out of the rock wall by millennia of water action. Then you go back up again! It's a beautiful walk.

LA AXARQUÍA

This area of mountains and deep valleys, behind the coast east of Málaga, has many good tracks and paths. The SGE *Zafarraya* No 18-43 and *Velez-Málaga* No 18-44 1:50,000 maps are currently the best available. Cómpeta, a village served by buses from Málaga, is a good base. Useful guides include *25 Walks in and around Cómpeta & Canillas de Albaida* by Albert & Dini Kraaijenzank, available in Cómpeta; *Sendas y Caminos por los Campos de la Axarquía* (Interguías Clave); and *Andar por La Axarquía* (El Búho Viajero).

El Lucero

This 1779m summit offers, in clear weather, views to both Granada and Morocco – about five hours up from Cómpeta (1150m ascent), and four hours down. Climb left along the track above the Cómpeta football pitch, pass below and west of a fire observation hut on the hill, La Mina, and turn right through a gap in

the rock 400m past the turning to the hut. This path leads in one hour to Puerto Blanquillo (1200m), from which a path climbs 200m to the Puerto de Cómpeta. One kilometre down from this pass, past a quarry, the summit path (1½ hours) diverges to the right across a stream bed, marked by a small cairn.

Other Routes

The shortest routes up Maroma (2069m), the highest peak hereabouts, are from villages such as Salares, Sedella and Canillas de Aceituno, or from the Alcázar picnic area above. In each case the return trip is a full day's walking of around eight to 10 hours, with an ascent of 1200 to 1400m. Two less demanding outings are to the Fabrica de Luz de Canillas de Albaida and the Fabrica de Luz de Cómpeta, each 6 or 7km from Cómpeta. These are tiny, ruined hydroelectric stations set in deep, luxuriant river valleys. From the latter you can walk onto the abandoned hamlet of Acebuchal and, if you wish, round the lower slopes of the El Fuerte hill to Frigiliana near Nerja.

SIERRA DE ARACENA

This sometimes lush, sometimes severe region in far north-west Andalucía, dotted with very old-fashioned stone villages, is the most attractive part of the rolling Sierra Morena. There's an extensive network of marked walking trails. Many villages are served by buses and have hostales. The SGE *Aracena* No 10-37 and *Aroche* No 9-37 1:50,000 maps cover the area. Local tourist offices, including the Centro de Turismo Rural y Reservas (☎ 959 12 83 55) in Aracena town, and ayuntamientos have useful material. In four or five days you could do a circuit of about 100km from Aracena to Aroche and back. An obvious route, nearly all off-road, is: Aracena, Linares de la Sierra, Alájar, Castaño del Robledo, Santa Ana la Real, Almonaster la Real, Cortegana, Aroche, Cortegana, Jabugo, Galaroza, Fuenteheridos, Los Marines, Aracena.

Islas Canarias

HISTORY

The original inhabitants of the Islas Canarias (Canary Islands) came, it's believed, from North Africa and were known as *Guanches*. European penetration began in the early 15th century, at first by colonisers from Normandy and subsequently by Spain. The demise of Guanche culture was swift as, like so many indigenous peoples around the world, they were wiped out by a combination of brute force, alien diseases and, for the fortunate, assimilation into the dominant culture.

Early Greek mariners, venturing beyond the Straits of Gibraltar, had named this archipelago of seven islands the Isles of the Blessed, while to the Romans they were the Fortunate Isles. Distant, fabled and mysterious, they were also in classical times confused or associated with the mythical Elysian fields, the Garden of the Hesperides and – until Columbus put paid to all that – the lost continent of Atlantis.

NATURAL HISTORY

The seven islands are merely the tips of a vast submarine volcanic range, created at much the same time as the Atlas mountains in North Africa. Both chains were formed in the Tertiary era, up to 65 million years ago, when the African tectonic plate slammed into the European one, crumpling along its weakest points, through which welled magma from beneath the earth's crust.

As a result of the islands' long isolation from the African continent, each has a large number of species, especially plants, which are endemic – peculiar to them alone.

CLIMATE

The islands enjoy mild weather year-round so that, apart from the upper reaches of Pico del Teide where snow lingers in winter, you can enjoy a walking holiday at any time.

A commonplace of tourist literature reckons that it's always spring in the Islas Canarias. So, indeed, it is for most of the

HIGHLIGHTS

INGRID RODDIS

The distinctive outline of Pico del Teide, Tenerife. Its enormous crater measures 14km across.

- The acrid whiff of sulphur in your raw lungs at the summit of Pico de Teide

- A healthy tot of mature Canaries rum back at sea level – to celebrate and to combat the last traces of sulphur

- The cooling, supersaturated mists and luxuriant vegetation on the upper slopes of the Parque Nacional de Garajonay

time. What the come-on doesn't tell you is that those northern flanks of the western islands can be swathed in a cloud bank more than 300m thick, supersaturated with the water vapour collected by *los alisios* (the tradewinds), as they blow over the Atlantic Ocean from the north-east. The higher points, simply because they're high, can be quite chilly. Pack a sweater, however sunny the day down below.

On the north side of both Tenerife and La Gomera, the best hours for great views as you walk are between 1 and 6 pm, once the early morning mist has dispersed and before the evening clouds come rolling in.

The ideal months for walking are February to April, when average temperatures hover around 20°C and, with most of the rest of Europe at work, you stand the best chance of finding accommodation. Wild flowers are at their best between April and June. Peak season for visitors coinciding with the lowest rainfall and higher temperatures, is between May and October.

INFORMATION
Maps
The German company Freytag and Berndt produces excellent maps of most of the islands but, at 1:75,000, the scale is a little too small for walking with confidence. For walking maps and where to buy them, see Maps under Information in the introduction to the Tenerife and La Gomera sections later in this chapter.

Books
Lonely Planet's *Canary Islands* gives detailed general background and has a host of suggestions for places to eat and stay and how to get around.

Discovery Walking Guides (also known as Warm Island Walking Guides) publishes thoroughly researched walking guides (three each for Tenerife and La Gomera) for every island except Fuerteventura. Information sheets and clear maps, based on IGN 1:25,000 originals, come in a plastic protective wallet.

Flora of the Canary Islands by David Bramwell is reliable and informative and has full colour photos. *Flowers of the Canary*

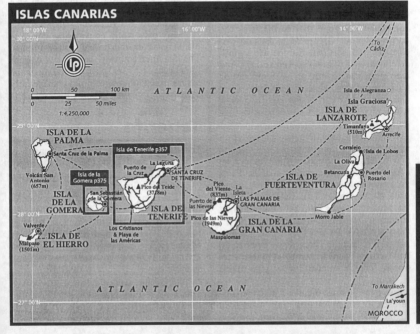

Islands by Bruno Foggi is also lavishly illustrated but is shorter on hard information. The best bird reference book specifically about the islands is *A Birdwatcher's Guide to the Canary Islands* by Tony Clarke and David Collins. If your interests are culinary, pick up *Canary Islands Cooking*, published by the Centro de la Cultura Popular.

Information Sources

Tourist offices (*oficinas de turismos*) are generally well informed and staff are cheerful and polyglot. But they tend to be somewhat insular, only carrying information on other islands that offices have bothered to send them.

For specific details of tourist offices on Tenerife and La Gomera, see Information Sources under Information in the introduction to each.

For information on guided walks on the Islas Canarias, see Organised Walks in the Getting Around chapter.

GETTING THERE & AWAY

Just about everyone flies to the Islas Canarias. Charter flights from Britain and elsewhere in northern Europe are significantly cheaper than scheduled airlines. You aren't obliged to buy an accommodation package but don't discount the idea; a bed and breakfast or half-board deal for a week will probably work out less expensive than going it alone.

Daily scheduled flights operate from major European cities to both Gran Canaria and Tenerife. From either, you can pick up a connection to the smaller islands. Fares vary enormously. For example, a standard open return fare to Tenerife from London via Madrid costs £740. Yet with the right charter at the right time of year, you can get there and back for less than £100. See also Air in the Getting There & Away chapter, and Getting There & Away in the introduction to Tenerife and La Gomera later in this chapter.

From the Spanish mainland, the price difference between charter and scheduled flights is not so significant but here, too, you can pick up some great package deals which need not inhibit your freedom to walk. There are daily scheduled flights from Madrid and Barcelona to Gran Canaria, Tenerife, Lanzarote and Fuerteventura and, less frequently, from all other major mainland cities. As with international flights, the price range can be huge. At one extreme, a one-year open return ticket with Air Europa to Tenerife costs more than 50,000 ptas from Madrid and around 65,000 ptas from Barcelona. On the other hand, a return charter fare from Madrid to Tenerife can be as low as 19,000 ptas. The seasonal variation is also substantial.

Inter-island flights are expensive. Unless you're pushed for time, it's cheaper and more interesting to island hop by boat. See the Getting There & Away sections for Tenerife and La Gomera.

A weekly Trasmediterránea freight and car ferry links Cádiz on the mainland with both Santa Cruz on Tenerife and Las Palmas on Gran Canaria. However, unless you've a passion for ships or are bringing over a car (hiring locally is significantly cheaper), it's probably only worth considering if you're planning an extended stay on the islands. The 50 hour journey, which costs from 29,000 ptas to 55,000 ptas, depending on the luxuriousness of your cabin, is considerably more expensive than hopping over by air.

Tenerife

Tenerife, the largest of the Islas Canarias, is bedded into the Atlantic Ocean like a limpet on a rock. At its apex is Pico del Teide (3718m), the highest peak in Spanish territory. Radiating from it like the grooves on the limpet shell are a number of deeply scored canyons, two of which – the Barranco del Infierno and the Barranco de Masca (where barranco in Spanish means ravine, gully or valley) – are routes featured in this chapter.

Two of the walks described here are within the Parque Nacional del Teide, the third to be designated in Spain (1954). The park was created to protect the fragile ecosystem and the wealth of endemic plant species which maintain a precarious existence on the thin, harsh volcanic soils of Teide and Las Cañadas (where cañada in Spanish means either drovers' road or gully). With an area of 13,500 hectares, it's the fifth largest in Spain. Receiving more than 3.5 million visitors a year, most of whom take a quick trip up the *Teleférico* (cable car) and move on, it's the most frequented national park in Europe.

HISTORY

Tenerife was the last island to fall to the Spanish conquest, after which it quickly attracted waves of settlers from Spain, Portugal, Italy, France and even Britain. As on other islands, sugar became the main export crop, succeeded by wine when South American sugar undercut the market. Much of this wine was produced on Tenerife – the area around Icod de los Vinos (Icod of the Wines) in the north-west of the island is an important wine growing area to this day – thus giving it an economic edge over the other islands. Thus, in 1821 Madrid declared Santa Cruz, by then Tenerife's major port, capital of the Islas Canarias.

Early in the 20th century the Islas Canarias were split into two provinces: Las Palmas, including the eastern islands, and Tenerife, incorporating the neighbouring islands of La Palma, La Gomera and El Hierro.

NATURAL HISTORY

Teide, safe from alien predators until man introduced both rabbits and mouflons, preserves a number of endemic plants. Far from being rare and threatened species, they're robust survivors, the dominant vegetation and so plentiful that you're likely literally to trip over them.

The most emblematic, almost the island's official flower, is the flamboyant *taginaste rojo*, or red tajinaste (*Echium wildpretii*), which can grow 3m high and more. When it's in flower, it's like a great red poker. After its brief, spectacular moment of glory all that remains is a thin, desiccated, spear-shaped skeleton, like a well picked-over fish. Leave these well alone; each fishbone has thousands of tiny strands as itchy as horsehair.

In the pine forests of its lower slopes, the most common undergrowth plant is escobón (*Chamaecytisus proliferus*). Out in the open, *hierba pajonera* (bird grass; *Descourainia bourgaeana*) is a tough survivor, bright yellow when in bloom and a strawlike tuft for the rest of the year. Of the shrubs, the prickly acacia like *codeso del pico*, also called *codeso de la cumbre* (*Adenocarpus viscosus* and *A. foliolosus*), also yellow flowered, can tug at the clothing. But the commonest species, surviving even where nothing else will grow, is *retama del Teide* or *retama blanca* (*Spartocytisus supranubius*), a bush of the broom family which is a riot of white and pink during its brief flowering.

Common flowers of the euphorbia family include the *cardón* (*Euphorbia canariensis*), a large, phallic growth on drier hillsides, and the altogether more delicate *tabaiba* (*E. lambii* and *E. balsamifera*) with its star-shaped leaves.

ISLA DE TENERIFE

ISLA DE TENERIFE – MAPS

Map 1	Barranco del Infierno	p361
Map 2	Barranco de Masca	p363
Map 3	Anaga Peninsula	p365
Map 4	La Caldera to El Portillo	p368
Map 5	Las Cañadas; La Rambleta & Pico del Teide	p370

ISLAS CANARIAS

Volcanoes

Volcanoes spurt in two principal ways. In the *central* variety, magma – molten material from the earth's core – wells up through a single chimney or vent to meet the air at a temperature of 700 to 1200°C. This forms the characteristic cone shape, like that of La Gomera. In *fissured* volcanoes, magma is forced through a pipe, or underground crack, within the mountain and erupts from its flank, like the Pico Viejo crater on Teide's western side. Often, a mountain may show evidence of both forms. Equally common, as in the case of Teide, today's shape may be the consequence of several eruptions over hundreds of thousands of years, each new deposit overlaying previous layers. A complex form like this is known as a *strato-volcano*.

The way a volcano erupts is largely determined by the gas content of its magma. If the material seething beneath the surface has a high gas content, the effect is like shaking a bottle of fizzy drink – once the cap is off, the contents spurt out with force. In such volcanoes, pyroclasts – cinders, ash and lightweight fragments of pumice – are hurled high into the air and scatter over a wide area. On the other hand, if the mix is more viscous, like treacle, the magma wells up, overflows a vent, then slows as it slithers down the mountain as lava flow, cooling until its progress is stopped. You'll see several such congealed rivers, composed of clinker, or volcanic slag, all spiky and irregular, around the slopes of Teide. Look also for *obsidian*, fragments or layers of smooth, shiny material like black glass and scoria, high in iron and magnesium and reddish brown in colour, since it is – quite literally – rusting.

A field of lava eggs left behind by the last lava flow on Pico del Teide, Spain's highest peak.

INFORMATION

Maps

Among the best of a shelf full of competing small and medium-scale maps of the island, suitable for general orientation, is one produced by Firestone (640 ptas) at 1:150,000.

The situation regarding walking maps isn't good. SGE or IGN maps at 1:50,000 or 1:25,000 often fail to indicate even major tracks – and some are more than 50% sea. You'll find relevant ones listed at the beginning of each walk.

There is a topographically accurate map of the Parque Nacional del Teide at 1:30,000. However it doesn't mark several major trails either and, first published in 1979, is becoming increasingly difficult to find. A successor is promised.

Distribution of maps is as dire as the range available. Librería Papyrus (☎/fax 922 37 40 62) in Puerto de la Cruz's Piramides Martianez shopping complex and the gift shop attached to Teide's El Portillo information centre are two of the very few retail outlets. Otherwise, you have to call at the map shop (☎ 922 27 66 00) of the Capitanía – the army headquarters at the junction of Avenida 25 de Julio and Calle Pérez de Rocas in Santa Cruz. It's open from 9 am to 2 pm, Monday to Friday.

Books

Landscapes of Southern Tenerife and Gomera and *Landscapes of Tenerife*, both by Noel Rochford and published by Sunflower Books, describe a number of generally gentle walks. There is also an excellent series of 23 pamphlets in English, available at tourist offices. Each has an explicit map and background notes and describes a walk of between one and four hours.

Apart from these, there isn't anything of substance in English about walking. For strolls with the emphasis on observation rather than treks for the joy of trekking, *Natural History Excursions in Tenerife* by Philip and Myrtle Ashcroft is a great source of information about Tenerife's natural history and environment. But, published in 1989, it is no longer easy to find.

In Santa Cruz, Librería Goytec (☎ 922 24 53 14), Calle Pérez Galdós 15, has a great selection of books about the islands. If you read Spanish, it's a bookworm's paradise, and if you rummage, you'll find an English walking title or two.

In Puerto de la Cruz, the small Librería Stratford on Calle Iriarte has a few titles in Spanish, English and other languages, as does Librería Papyrus (see the Maps section).

Information Sources

The large tourist office on Plaza de España in Santa Cruz (☎ 922 23 95 92, fax 922 23 98 12, nievesg@cabtfe.es) has information on the whole island and is open from 8 am to 5 pm, Monday to Friday, and from 9 am to noon on Saturday. The one in Puerto de la Cruz (☎ 922 38 60 00, fax 922 38 47 69) on Plaza de Europa is open from 9 am to 7 pm, Monday to Friday, and from 9 am to noon on Saturday. Tourist offices are also in Playa de las Américas (☎ 922 79 76 68, fax 922 38 47 69) and Los Cristianos (☎ 922 75 71 37, fax 922 75 24 92).

There are two Parque Nacional del Teide information centres. The main one at El Portillo is open daily from 9.15 am to 4 pm and has an excellent display on volcanoes, plus the park's animal and plant life. There's also an equally informative 14 minute video, 'The Sleeping Volcano', with multilingual commentary available in Spanish, English, French, German and Italian. The souvenir shop has a small stock of books and maps. Outside, take time to browse around the Jardín Botánico, where typical examples of the park's vegetation thrive.

The smaller Centro de Visitantes de Cañada Blanca, beside the Parador de Cañadas del Teide (at the end of the Las Cañadas walk), specialises in the history of the park and has the same opening hours.

ACCOMMODATION & SUPPLIES

The best base for the walks we describe is Puerto de la Cruz on the north coast, and details of some potential places to stay and eat here are listed below. Playa de Las Américas or Los Cristianos in the southwest (one runs into the other) would be a suitable second choice. The latter are no better than smaller neighbouring resorts and the unremitting rowdy hedonism may get you down. But they're the best location for public transport on this side of the island if you're without a car.

For the Anaga Peninsula, Santa Cruz, the island's capital, is the nearest base – though if you get your timing right, it's easy enough to bus into Santa Cruz from the resort in which you're staying and catch an onward connection.

Puerto de la Cruz

In Puerto de la Cruz, impeccably spruce doubles with bathroom (there aren't any singles) at *Pensión Rosamary* (☎ 922 38 32 53, Calle San Filipe 14) cost 3700 ptas. *Pensión Loly* (☎ 922 38 36 93, Calle de la Sala 4) has doubles with bathroom for 2600 ptas, while the nearby *Pensión la Platanera* (☎ 922 38 41 57, Calle Blanco 29) has singles/doubles for 3500/4600 ptas. All are often fully booked and can be reluctant to take a telephone reservation. If you draw blanks, the tourist office has further suggestions.

For typical Canarias food, try *Cafeteria Arcón* on Calle Blanco, one block south of the main square, the Plaza del Charco. Also just off the plaza, *Restaurante Carmencita* on Calle San Felipe has a good *menú del día* (fixed-price, usually three-course meal) for 1200 ptas. *El Limón* on Calle de Escivel serves great, reasonably priced vegetarian

ISLAS CANARIAS

food and juices. For something more special, try **La Herrería**, which serves good food in pleasant surroundings.

Tip Top Lavandería in Calle Teobaldo Power is one of several laundrettes in town. Open from Monday to Friday, it will wash a load for 900 ptas (returned the same day).

GETTING THERE & AWAY

Tenerife has two airports. Tenerife Norte (Los Rodeos) handles interisland flights and a few scheduled international flights. The remainder of the scheduled flights and virtually all charters are channelled to the more modern Tenerife Sur (Reina Sofia). The majority of international flights serving the islands directly are charters. From Tenerife Sur, bus No 340 runs to Puerto de la Cruz four times daily, while No 487 departs hourly until 9.20 pm for Los Cristianos and Playa de las Américas.

GETTING AROUND

Buses in the Islas Canarias are called, engagingly, *guaguas* (pronounced wa-wa). The public bus company which runs a spider's web of services all over the island is called, equally engagingly, TITSA. For the range of its network and for timekeeping, TITSA is superb. Less impressive, because there's less demand, are its services to out-of-the-way places – the sort of places where good walks begin and end – which may be limited to one or two a day. Some services change depending on the season (and some are so underpatronised that you wonder how much longer they can survive). Play safe and either ring ☎ 922 21 56 99 for the latest information or collect the current island-wide timetable at any tourist office or major bus station.

For flexibility, it's well worth investing in a week's car hire, which need not cost much more than 20,000 ptas for a small vehicle.

Typical one-way taxi fares from Puerto de la Cruz are:

El Portillo Visitors Centre	4100 ptas
Teleférico	5800 ptas
Parador de Cañadas del Teide	6000 ptas
Aeropuerto Reina Sofía	10,600 ptas

Barranco del Infierno

Duration 2½ to 3 hours
Distance 5km
Standard Easy
Start/Finish Adeje
Public Transport Yes
Summary Tenerife's most popular walk. An out-and-back route up the eponymous barranco as it narrows and becomes richer in vegetation, as far as the waterfall tumbling over the bowl at its head.

Virtually all potential danger has been removed from this diligently sanitised trail with its stairs, banking, railings and posts. Despite this, and despite being short, it will have you panting in places. And despite the almost constant company of other walkers, it's a worthwhile half-day walk – whether for its own sake, to experience the drama of the canyon, or as a 'training run' for something more demanding – such as the altogether wilder and more challenging descent of the Barranco de Masca (see the next walk).

PLANNING
When to Walk

This is a year-round walk. It's worth making an early start, both to avoid the midday heat and for the smug satisfaction of heading jauntily for home while the majority are still toiling up the valley.

Maps

SGE map *Guía de Isora* No 38-41 (1098), which covers the route at 1:50,000, is barely worth buying; it's well over 50% ocean and, on such a well travelled trail along a valley bottom with sheer walls, it would take a very particular talent to get lost.

What to Bring

A couple of pools on the way up the valley are deep enough to dunk yourself in. If the idea appeals, bring your swimming gear.

GETTING TO/FROM THE WALK

This is one route which is more accessible

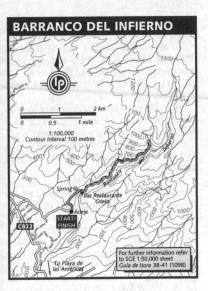

BARRANCO DEL INFIERNO

1:100,000
Contour Interval 100 metres

Spring
Bar Restaurante Otelo
Adeje
START/ FINISH
C822
To Playa de las Américas

For further information refer to SGE 1:50,000 sheet *Guía de Isora* 38-41 (1098)

Almost immediately, you enter the mouth of the gorge. At first, the path winds along the valley's northern flank to meet an irrigation channel, grooved into the rock face. Fifteen minutes later, once the path has descended and crossed the riverbed to the true left bank, the gradient briefly steepens. After five minutes, you pass under a cast-iron pipe from which fresh water gushes into a conduit.

Down at riverbed level, pick your way beside a gurgling stream along a defined track which ducks through a tunnel of ash, oleander, bramble, fern and willow. Look out, too, for the occasional fig and sweet chestnut tree.

Stay with the stream all the way to the sheer rock walls of the bowl, reached in about an hour of walking from Restaurante Otelo. This spot marks the head of the barranco and an end to progress up it. On the way are a couple of **pools**, deep and clear enough to immerse yourself and cool off.

A sign in Spanish at the base of the trickling waterfall's 100m drop reads 'One day, a group of schoolchildren cleaned up this place. Don't you be the one who fouls it.' Alas, there are always those who can't or won't read and this idyllic spot has more than its fair share of cigarette butts, tissues, eggshells and tinfoil.

from Playa de las Américas/Los Cristianos than from Puerto de la Cruz. Buses No 416 (hourly from 6.30 am) and No 473 (every 30 minutes) link the former with Adeje. From Puerto de la Cruz, you can avoid a lot of complicated interchanging by taking the 9 am bus No 343 to Playa de las Américas/Los Cristianos and picking up one of the above routes there. The last bus back to Puerto de la Cruz from Playa de las Américas is at 5.45 pm.

THE WALK

There's a difference in altitude of 300m between Adeje and the bowl at the head of the barranco. In most, but not all, places the ascent is relatively gradual and the melodramatically titled Barranco del Infierno (Hell's Valley) belies its name.

From the bus stop near the church, walk up Adeje's tree-lined main street. At its top, turn left, then sharp right. The road ends at Bar Restaurante Otelo, beside which there's limited parking space. About 50m below the restaurant is a *fuente*, flowing water channelled into a trough, where you can fill your water bottles.

Barranco de Masca

Duration 2¾ to 3 hours
Distance 4.5km
Standard Medium
Start Masca
Finish Playa de Masca (or return to Masca)
Public Transport Yes
Summary A 600m descent from the village of Masca, down the gorge of the same name to the seashore. Then back up if that's the way you want it. Otherwise, out by boat to Los Gigantes.

This route, which at least a couple of dozen walkers of average fitness undertake each day, isn't nearly so demanding as many sources would have you believe. The descent

ISLAS CANARIAS

(and corresponding ascent) are rarely steep enough to be uncomfortable and there are only a couple of points where it's helpful to bring your hands into play to negotiate the rock.

If you get your transport logistics right, it's possible to walk one way only, which we describe here. You can emulate the majority of walkers and round off the experience by taking a boat ride – a pleasure in itself – from Playa de Masca to the holiday resort of Los Gigantes. Or follow a hard-core minority who set off in the morning by boat and walk *up* the canyon (for details, see Getting to/from the Walk). The real ascetics walk both ways (count on 5½ to 6½ hours).

PLANNING
When to Walk

Any time is fine, except when heavy rain is threatening or has fallen, when it's important to seek advice from one of the tourist offices. There's a real risk of flash flooding – and stretches of the canyon's near-vertical walls wouldn't be easy to shin up in a hurry.

Maps

This walk just appears on IGN map *Guía de Isora* No 1110 at 1:50,000. It's not worth buying for this walk alone since there's only one way into the canyon and one way out. However, this map also covers the Parque Nacional del Teide.

What to Bring

Strangely, for a gorge which will probably still have at least a trickle of water splashing down its lower reaches, you should bring full flasks or sterilising tablets. Most of the pools are clogged with algae and bright green slime. Pack swimming gear for a cooling dip in the ocean from the Playa de Masca.

GETTING TO/FROM THE WALK

You can comfortably have breakfast in Puerto de la Cruz, do the walk and be home in time for dinner. Take bus No 325 from Puerto de la Cruz at 8.40 am (6.20 am weekends) to arrive in Santiago del Teide at 9.45 am (7.25 am weekends). Next, take

bus No 355 from Santiago del Teide at 10.35 am to arrive in Masca at 10.45 am.

To return, the Nashira Uno boat leaves Playa de Masca at 3.30 pm and arrives at Los Gigantes at around 4.15 pm. Bus no 325 leaves Los Gigantes for Puerto de la Cruz at 5.15 pm daily.

From Playa de las Américas, bus No 460 departs at 7.20 am (weekdays only) for Santiago del Teide, leaving you with time to kill there. To return, bus No 473 runs from Los Gigantes to Playa de las Américas every 30 minutes until 10.30 pm.

If you have your own vehicle, leave it in Santiago del Teide, take the morning bus to Masca and pick it up at the end of the day. The 3km of plunging, single lane switchbacks between Santiago and Masca are better appreciated with someone else at the wheel.

It's essential to reserve the 3.30 pm boat (1250 ptas) from Playa de Masca to Los Gigantes. Ring the Nashira Uno office on ☎ 922 86 19 18 or ☎ 670-88 99 03 the day before.

To do the walk in reverse, phone the Nashira Uno in advance to book a boat (also 1250 ptas) from Los Gigantes to the Playa de Masca, since there's no scheduled morning sailing. The last bus from Masca leaves at 4.15 pm for Santiago del Teide, from where you can connect with the 5.15 pm bus from Los Gigantes, bound for Puerto de la Cruz, or with Bus No 460, which leaves Icod at 4 pm for Playa de las Américas.

THE WALK

Unless you've lingered to enjoy the village of Masca, you reach a couple of giant, overhanging boulders after a little more than 15 minutes, having negotiated a stretch of bare rock. When you meet the stream which will be your travelling companion as far as the ocean, cross to its true left bank over a fine wooden bridge. The path stays above the valley bottom, which at this point is clogged with Indian cane and thus impenetrable. Notice, slung way up high on the hillside above the north (opposite) bank, the swathes of iron irrigation pipe and marvel at the human endeavour which made it possible. Keep an eye out, too, for the terraces of finely laid stones, untended and falling away to the chaos from which they were first selected, now that man can afford to forgo cultivating the harshest, unyielding terrain.

Some 10 minutes after the bridge, just before a lone palm tree, cross over a bed of rock to the stream's true right bank rather than taking the path straight ahead, which will lead you into an unnecessary scramble. During the course of the descent, you hop frequently from one bank to another. If in doubt, hang left; statistically, you spend more of your time on this side.

Here, the exotic Indian cane hasn't yet colonised and the dry barranco harbours indigenous and forbidding plants such as thistle, bramble, *agave*, prickly pear and other cactuses. Normally, it's not too hot – the high and increasingly sheer walls of the canyon mask the sun, except when it's at its zenith, while a cooling breeze usually huffs up from the coast.

Just less than 30 minutes from the bridge, where a steep-sided valley and tributary stream cut in from the right (north-west), there's a concrete **dam**. Here, just before the

valley begins to close in around and over you, is a pleasant place for a rest stop. Notice how the slim irrigation channel which takes off from just below the dam has been incised into the rock face. As you descend the barranco, this channel maintains a more gradual fall than the natural watercourse, and is thus ever higher above your head.

A little less than an hour later, another plunging, dry canyon comes in from the north. As in many such gorges, the water runs underground for many months of the year to nurture the roots of surface plants and reappear further down the valley. (Watch for a couple of such disappearing acts further down the Barranco de Masca). The brief luxuriance of chlorophyll rich, fleshy plants at the confluence gives way once more to tougher, spiky and more hardy specimens.

Ten minutes later, a well banked stretch of tended path briefly bypasses a potentially difficult passage along the valley bottom. Soon afterwards, up high, appears a fine rock bridge – a near-perfect circle with the sky peeking through like a bright blue eye. Then, just when it seems that you're about to walk slap bang into the sheer cliff face, the barranco turns sharply at 90° to continue its downward progress.

After another acute bend, it comes as a surprise to find neat, if crumbling, terracing up to the left. Clamber to the top briefly to join a deceptively wide path before descending – with the boom of the ocean already in your ears and its tang in your nostrils – the last short section of riverbed to the **Playa de Masca**, its black-sand beach and its mangy cats.

The Nashira Uno boat whisks away those who choose not to climb back up the valley to Masca, leaving Playa de Masca between 3.30 and 3.45 pm and arriving at Los Gigantes about 30 minutes later, depending upon the marine life to be seen en route (there's a good chance of spotting dolphins). This gives you ample time to pick up the 5.15 pm bus to Santiago del Teide and onto Puerto de la Cruz. It stops beside the Sun & Sports Centre on the south side of town, less than 15 minutes walk from the port.

BARRANCO DE MASCA

For further information refer to IGN 1:50,000 sheet *Guía de Isora* (1110)

0   1   2 km
0   0.5   1 mile
1:100,000
Contour Interval 100 metres

ISLAS CANARIAS

Anaga Peninsula

Duration 6 to 6½ hours
Distance 16km
Standard Medium
Start Taganana
Finish Punta del Hidalgo
Public Transport Yes
Summary A flexible, roller-coaster day. Three quite steep ups and downs as the route cuts across the Anaga Cordillera, 30 minutes of level striding to Chinamada, then a final, spectacular cliff-side descent to Punta del Hidalgo on the coast.

This walk leads through some of the wildest, most underpopulated parts of the Anaga Peninsula. From Taganana, it's up and over a col and down to the hamlet of Afur, followed by an ascent of a steep ridge to Taborno, a 250m altitude loss to the Barranco de Taborno, and a similar ascent to Las Carboneras, from where a stretch of road walking comes as a pleasant interlude before the dramatic descent to Punta del Hidalgo.

There are also a couple of possible side trips – a brief detour to a *mirador* (lookout) with great views of the coast (as in the body of the walk description) and a longer diversion to the Roque de Taborno – see the description following the main walk.

PLANNING
Maps

The SGE map *Punta del Hidalgo* No 79-77 at 1:25,000 covers the whole of the route.

Warning

The latter part of the walk between Chinamada and Punta del Hidalgo at first follows a footpath with a very steep, unprotected drop on one side. Though not dangerous, it can cause discomfort to sufferers of vertigo.

GETTING TO/FROM THE WALK

From the Estación de Guaguas, the main bus station in Santa Cruz, bus No 246 leaves for Taganana at 6.50 and 10.30 am, Monday to Friday, and 7.05, 9.10 and 11.40 am at weekends. Bus No 105 runs every 30 minutes until 10 pm between Punta del Hidalgo and Santa Cruz.

It's also possible to leave the walk at Las Carboneras after 4 to 4½ hours of walking. Bus No 075 runs from there to La Laguna at 4 and 7.15 pm, Monday to Friday, and 4.45 pm at weekends. From La Laguna, there are plenty of buses to Santa Cruz (for Playa de las Américas) and to Puerto de la Cruz.

THE WALK

The walk starts beside the bus stop at the entrance to Taganana, just above Restaurante Xiomara, near a small parking area and a sign describing the Parque Rural de Anaga. Cross the main road and follow the street into the village. Turn left at a T-junction, right along Calle Canónigo Juan Negrín, then left again. Just after a stone bridge, turn left up the steep, cobbled Camino Portugal to bear left when you reach a sealed road. About 15 minutes out, just before an acute bend in the road, take the track running to the right of a white house, signed No 2.

Beyond it is a fuente – the last water until the next valley. You're now following the ancient, cobbled path linking Taganana with Santa Cruz via Afur, guided here and there by rusting, yellow diamonds indicating *sendero turístico* (tourist path).

Less than 10 minutes later, turn briefly left up a stretch of ribbed concrete which has been laid over the original path. After no more than a couple of minutes, look out for an unsigned left turn, easily missed. This returns you to a cobbled path which, though it narrows significantly and is in places overgrown by ferns and brambles, remains easy to distinguish as it climbs towards the now evident col.

On entering the shade of a fine **laurisilva wood** (see the boxed text 'The Laurisilva, La Gomera's Hillside Reservoir' in the La Gomera section), the gradient slackens and, at around the one hour mark, you reach the **pass**, with great views behind and before you. Turn right along a dirt path which clings to the hillside among clumps of tree heather as it leaves the valley bottom far below. Soon, you can clearly see the irregular stump of the Roque de Taborno (706m) to the north-west and the route ahead, up the thread of path which climbs the far flank of the valley.

About 15 minutes from the col, beside the first houses of the valley, a concrete path leads down to a sealed road, where you turn right. At a bend 15 minutes later, just beyond a house with a giant oleander bush, take a flight of steps to the left to the tiny hamlet of **Afur** (320m), with a cluster of houses, a church and the very friendly *Bar José Canon* with its small, attached grocery store.

The concrete path for Taborno starts behind the church and descends between whitewashed walls to cross a stream, then passes beside a deep, dark pool at the base of a small waterfall before heading southwest up a pronounced ridge. About 15 minutes beyond Afur, the track divides to pass either side of a group of farmhouses; take your pick, since they soon rejoin.

Soon, beside a lone house, your feet will be relieved as concrete gives way to a dirt path. Barely a couple of minutes beyond,

fork right to stay with the electricity pylons which you've been following since leaving Afur. After passing another lone, white-washed farm with a troglodyte cave dwelling set into the hillside behind it, there are magnificent views back over the Afur valley, with the dark mass of Roque Negro prominent; beyond is the pass from Taganana, now more than 90 minutes walking away; to its south is Paso (934m) and, on its north side, is the Roque de Ánima (689m).

After less than 15 minutes, thread your way between a group of farm buildings to turn right along a dirt jeep track and reach **Taborno** (620m) about 30 minutes later. The route to Roque de Taborno (see the side trip at the end of this walk) leaves from the small church square, itself a pleasant place to take a rest. You can have a drink in the gloomy *Bar Abigai* – where the caged canary is the only animation – or, if it's open, in the enigmatically named *Restaurante Historias Para No Dormir* (Tales to Stop You Sleeping Restaurant).

As you leave Taborno by the only sealed road, the path which drops to the valley

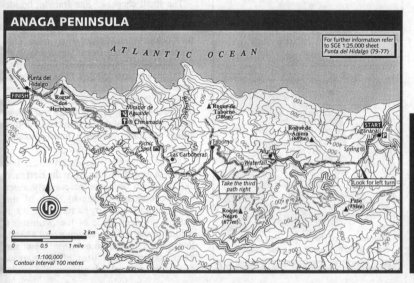

bottom isn't easy to distinguish and a mistake can mean a sweaty haul back up from some farmer's melon patch. Ignore two tempting paths which lead off and down

Tree With a Long, Shady Past

The dragon tree (*el drago* or *Dracaena draco*), an Islas Canarias curiosity, can live for hundreds of years. Indeed, one at Icod de los Vinos is reputedly 1000 years old. Slow growing, it may eventually reach up to 18m in height. As one of the few species that survived the last Ice Age, it looks different, even a touch prehistoric. In shape, it resembles a giant posy of flowers with bunches of long, narrow, silvery-green leaves. What makes the tree stranger still is the red sap or resin, known as 'dragon's blood', which was traditionally used in medicine.

The drago also played an important role in Islas Canarias life, for it was beneath the ancient branches of a dragon tree that the Guanche council of nobles gathered to administer justice.

The red sap of the dragon tree is sometimes used in making costume jewellery.

from breaks in the roadside barrier. Instead, about 150m before the first building beyond the village, take off right along and down a pronounced ridge. After a couple of minutes, you will pass a tiny shrine with a wooden cross, just beyond which you fork left to pass an electricity pylon.

Once you've found the right path, your navigational problems for the day are over. After 20 to 30 minutes and a drop in altitude of around 250m, you cross the valley bottom over an unremarkable and scarcely noticed dry stream bed, after which the path climbs steeply up to Las Carboneras (640m), reached 30 to 45 minutes later. Once you hit the sealed road, turn left to find a couple of *bars* where you can pleasurably rehydrate.

Beyond the village, the old gravel road to Chinamada has recently been sealed, but the views of the coast and the Roque de Taborno are so spectacular and the traffic so light that the pleasure of this stretch is undiminished. After 20 minutes, you pass an equally new set of picnic tables, from where the vista would be splendid – but for the bank of laurels, planted simultaneously, which completely block the view of the coast.

The small chapel of San Ramón, beside which there's a gushing tap, marks the end of the sealed road. Go straight ahead for the short detour to the Mirador de Aguaide. This brief, signed side trip from Chinamada gives fine views over the coast and will add 20 to 30 minutes to your journey. Otherwise, continue beyond the chapel, behind which a sign indicates 'Punta del Hidalgo, 1¾ horas'. The path runs between prickly pears and below some well maintained terracing, above which are the troglodyte houses of the village, set into the hillside.

As the trail maintains its level, the unprotected drop to the depths of the Barranco del Tomadero becomes increasingly sheer and the opposite (western) flank of the valley, deeply scored by barren gulches and gullies, provides some of the peninsula's wildest scenery. Then, as you round a bend, Punta del Hidalgo comes into view, the vast, plastic greenhouses of the narrow coastal agricultural belt glinting like pools.

At some of the steeper points, steps have been cut into the rock. Beside one flight, about 20 minutes from the chapel, is a deep ledge and the first of several rock overhangs, its roof blackened with the soot of generations of small camp fires. Fifteen minutes later, as you round the squat shape of the Roque Dos Hermanos, there's a magnificent seascape eastwards. The path turns inland again to continue descending steeply, crossed here and there by veins of crumbling white saltpetre, until you reach a wooden bridge. Soon after, climb above a stone building which houses a throbbing water pump to join a wide track which takes you into Punta del Hidalgo.

Side Trip: Taborno to Roque de Taborno

1 to 1¼ hours, 4km

This strongly recommended detour has great views and also allows you to approach the giant volcanic plug which you've had in your sights for the last two hours. Set off up the steps to the right of Taborno's church square. The Roque de Taborno is constantly in view and it takes a very special talent to go wrong.

La Caldera to El Portillo

Duration 5 to 5½ hours
Distance 18.5km
Standard Medium
Start La Caldera
Finish El Portillo
Public Transport Yes
Summary Strictly uphill, mainly on a cart track, for 13km through Canaries pine and, once above tree level, over thinly clad volcanic slopes. An easy, level end to the day along 5.5km of quiet road with impressive views of Pico del Teide.

You can just as easily do this walk in the opposite direction and turn a cumulative 1050m of ascent into a thousand or so downhill metres.

PLANNING
Maps

Frustratingly, this walk winds across the borders of three IGN maps: *Guía de Isora* No 1110, *Güimar* No 1111 and Santa Cruz de Tenerife y San Andrés No 1104-1105.

GETTING TO/FROM THE WALK

Bus No 345 runs every 45 minutes from Puerto de la Cruz to La Caldera between 8.45 am and 5.15 pm. The last bus from La Caldera leaves at 6.25 pm. If you plan to return to Puerto de la Cruz, you need to be at El Portillo Centro de Visitantes by 4.15 pm to catch the bus which leaves the Paradorde Cañadas del Teide at 4 pm.

THE WALK

The bowl of La Caldera is a huge picnic zone nowadays. At weekends, the smoke curls from a dozen or more fires, for all the world as though this ancient volcanic crater was about to stir again.

Take the narrow path round its western rim to meet the far side of the sealed road which circumvents the bowl. Turn left and, after no more than 25m, right at a sign announcing 'Zona de Acampada', an area where *free camping* is permitted.

From here, it's a pleasant, partly shaded walk through pine – the Canaries kind, endemic and boasting its own scientific name, *Pinus canariensis*. If you need to take water on board, ignore the gurgling pipe which transects the camping ground in favour of another pipe and water tank, some three minutes further on, where the water's more easily accessible.

After less than 30 minutes walking, turn sharp right at a sign set in stone, 'Pasada de las Bestias'. Some 10 minutes later, the spoil heap from the burrowing of an underground tunnel (see the boxed text 'Water Galleries') rears before you. This is the **Galería Chimoche**, a mine shaft from which splay a cluster of large bore pipes. You can draw water from a vent in one of them, just below the lower of two concrete blockhouses.

Around 15 minutes later, you reach a T-junction with a wide jeep track and, beside

ISLAS CANARIAS

it, Choza Chimoche – a simple, roofed structure with a wooden bench and table. Almost straight ahead, a narrow path heads steeply up and west. After barely two minutes of climbing, bear left at a fork. The path soon becomes a wide track, springy underfoot from its deep cushion of pine needles. Here and there, fading red-and-yellow metal diamonds tacked to the trees proclaim *sendero turístico* (tourist trail).

After a little more than an hour of walking, the path divides. Take your pick; the branches rejoin scarcely 100m higher. Ignore the alluring sendero turístico diamond soon after, which attempts to drag you onto a minor path heading right.

About 15 minutes later, go straight on and up beyond a metal barrier and sign, 'Pasada del Fraile'. At a T-junction and another sign, 'Cuevitas de Limón', turn left onto a more pronounced jeep track. Very soon, you get

Water Galleries

The heart of Tenerife's central mountain core is pierced by tunnels, pipes and tubes, like the aftermath of a multiple heart bypass operation. On an island where water from the skies can never be guaranteed, the inhabitants have for centuries bored beneath the crust and deep into the rock to tap rainwater, which quickly percolates down through the porous lava to hidden natural reservoirs. Look for the telltale spoil heaps and old workings.

your first glimpse of Pico del Teide, its rounded nipple dimpling the sky. Underfoot are tiny pebbles of pumice, once spewed high into the air like grapeshot during a distant gaseous, volcanic eruption. Run a handful through your fingers and feel how light and porous they are.

Around 15 minutes beyond the T-junction, curl round to the left, keeping to the main track rather than taking an equally compelling trail straight ahead. Soon the observatory complex, high on the hill tops to the south-east, comes into view as you plod over the first lava fields where, even centuries after the magma oozed and dribbled down the mountainside, nothing – not a blade of grass, not a scab of lichen – grows.

Turn sharp left at a cairn bearing two painted yellow dots and a number 5 to circle round the western flank of Montaña de Limón (Lemon Mountain), from which there are magnificent plunging views of Puerto de la Cruz and the ocean beyond. Lemon coloured it may once have been but now it's almost maroon as its high iron content literally rusts away. Once you've crossed the 2000m contour, the pines gradually become more sparse and stunted while every step dislodges several hundred pumice pellets, snapping and crackling underfoot like Rice Krispies breakfast cereal.

The path, now forging its way through retama bushes, begins to head due south

LA CALDERA TO EL PORTILLO

For further information refer to IGN 1:50,000 sheets *Guía de Isora* 1110, *Güimar* 1111 & *Santa Cruz de Tenerife y San Andres* 1104-1105

La Caldera
START
Galería Chimoche
Choza Chimoche
Spring
Barranco Barca
Montaña de Limón (2108m)
Choza J Ruiz d'Izaña
Observatory
Corral del Niño
See Las Cañadas; La Rambleta & Pico del Teide Map p370
El Portillo FINISH

0   1   2 km
0   0.5   1 mile
1:150,000
Contour Interval 100 metres

and intersects with a jeep track beside a large cairn daubed with a yellow blob. Turn left to follow the track; then, after barely 50m, swing right in order to avoid an unnecessary bend, heading for the Choza J. Ruiz d'Izaña, another picnic shelter, which you reach less than five minutes later.

Turn right and follow the jeep track for around an hour until you reach Corral del Niño (2250m), below which it's possible to camp wild if you still have sufficient water with you (the nearest source is at the visitors centre). From here you follow a good, sealed road for 5.5km of easy striding – with fine views of mountain and coast – to El Portillo. Allow time to visit the excellent visitors centre display (see Information Sources under Information in the introduction to the Tenerife section). Also, provided that you still have sufficient water with you (you can top up at the fuente beside the visitors centre), you can avoid a bus ride down to Puerto de la Cruz by camping just below *Corral del Niño*.

Side Trip: Montaña de Limón
20 minutes, 1.25km

It's an easy diversion up the south side of Montaña de Limón to the modest summit (2108m), from which there are fine views of the coast and, if the day is clear, the islands of La Palma and El Hierro.

Las Cañadas

Duration 4 to 4½ hours
Distance 15km
Standard Easy-Medium
Start Visitors Centre, El Portillo
Finish Parador de Cañadas del Teide
Public Transport Yes
Summary An easy walk below the sierra marking the park's eastern boundary, through a lunar landscape of twisted lava, minor craters and ancient volcanic plugs or chimneys.

We grade this walk medium-easy rather than easy simply because a walk of 15km at more than 2000m altitude and in high mountain sunshine takes more out of you than a similar excursion at sea level, unless you have had time to break yourself in. It can be walked in equal comfort from either direction.

Pretty, it ain't. But the stark evidence of the activity of primeval volcanoes, where nothing but the toughest grasses now grow, is deeply impressive.

PLANNING
Maps
The route appears in green and in full on the *Parque Nacional del Teide* map at 1:30,000 and also on the SGE *Guía de Isora* 1:50,000 map.

GETTING TO/FROM THE WALK
If your base is Puerto de la Cruz and you have wheels, it's better to leave your car at the Parador de Cañadas del Teide and take the morning bus back to El Portillo visitors centre, beginning your walk from there. In this way, you're not dependent on the 4 pm bus back to your vehicle and can time the walk the way you want to.

For details of the scant bus service, refer to the Getting to/from the Walk section in the introduction to the La Rambleta & Pico del Teide walk description.

THE WALK
Take the broad track which begins just across the road from the visitors centre. In a little more than five minutes, where a path leading to the much more demanding ridge walk around the bowl veers away left, stick with the main track to cross a barrier which heralds the entrance to the park.

Within 30 minutes, you're amid whorls, hanks and twists of lava, looking like melted chocolate which might have congealed only yesterday. The path, however, remains smooth and well beaten despite the chaos all around. Navigation, simplicity itself, is made even easier by the occasional corroborative plaque, 'Sendero 4' (Footpath No 4), nailed to a rock.

You're walking the inner ring of a vast bowl, of which the base – the seven plains

ISLAS CANARIAS

– and spiky, jagged walls are all that remain of a giant, primordial volcano. The most appealing of the several explanations for the mayhem is that there was, at a time our puny brains can't conceive, a volcano so big that Pico del Teide – created aeons later – is by comparison a hillock. The monster blew, the centre collapsed, imploded and became the essence of today's flat plain.

All the blobs, solid streams, hillocks and just plain jumble of lava are the result of relatively recent – at least in geological terms – volcanic disturbances, whether welling up from the valley bed or oozing down from the Teide complex. As you look east and up at the containing walls of the bowl – or, rather, at the jagged, sheered-off fragments which remain – you see what are by far the oldest rocks in the area. Though the upper parts are smashed and continue to erode and drop their debris into the plain

below, the curve of the bowl is almost complete on its southern side with one gaping exception – to the east of El Portillo visitors centre, where a whole flank of the mountain on one remote day just slid into the ocean.

Soon, in the middle ground, dwarfed by the monsters to its north, appears Montaña Mostaza (2248m), or Mustard Mountain, one side a perfect cone, the other blasted away, leaving an equally symmetrical crater. Well above it sits Montaña Blanca (White Mountain) – now more ochre, gunmetal grey and sandy – and, even higher, you can make out the Refugio Altavista and the top of the Teleférico (both landmarks if you attempt the ascent of Pico del Teide). After around 1¼ hours of walking, you meet a cluster of large cones – vents, or chimneys; all that remains of ancient volcanoes, shoving their fingers towards the sky. Until

LAS CAÑADAS; LA RAMBLETA & PICO DEL TEIDE

For further information refer to IGN 1:50,000 sheet *Guía de Isora* 1110

| Walk 1 | Las Cañadas | p369 |
| Walk 2 | La Rambleta & Pico del Teide | p371 |

the sun is directly overhead, they offer rare and welcome shade.

An hour or so beyond the cones, with the flat-topped Montaña de Guajara (2717m) already in sight to the south-west, you cross a small col to see the Cañada de la Grieta spreading below. Centuries ago, the Guanches would graze their livestock in these plains, taking advantage of the rich spring vegetation and the temporary pools which formed in the flats as the winter snowmelt tumbled down from the heights. This tradition continued until relatively recently, as you can see from the crumbling stone cabins and sheepfolds in this, the dampest, cañada where there's still a well with a firmly padlocked iron cover.

After more than three hours out, a couple of side routes branch off: on your left, the unsigned route to the summit of Montaña de Guajara and, leading away right, a track labelled 'Sendero 16' – and nothing else. Discount both and continue in a generally westerly direction. Once the track begins to wind and rise slightly, you pass a file of impressively large volcanic chimneys, their surfaces cracked and crazed like the skin of a lizard.

As you round a bend, one of the finest low-level vistas in the park unfolds: in the foreground is the Parador and – for those heading home by bus – the welcome sight of a couple of green TITSA buses. Beyond are the fingers and forearm of the Roques de García, and even more impressive remains of the central core of long-spent volcanoes. Brooding behind are the dark lava fields beneath Pico Viejo (2994m), also known as Montaña Chahorra, the last peak really to blow its top, back in 1798.

Just beyond the first bend, after a barrier marking the beginning of the sealed road, look out for a path to the right which leads within 15 minutes to the *Parador de Cañadas del Teide* (✆/fax 922 38 64 15), where you can eat or take a drink on the terrace or in the bar. If you're feeling flush, you could stay the night. Singles/doubles cost from 12,000/15,500 ptas.

La Rambleta & Pico del Teide

Duration 3¼ to 4 hours, one way
Distance 6km
Standard Medium-Hard
Start Car park for Montaña Blanca
Finish Top of Teleférico
Public Transport Yes
Summary A defined jeep track, with multiple short cuts, then a steep path to the Altavista refugio. A snaking trail through volcanic wilderness to La Rambleta. For those with permits, a further 170m of ascent to Pico del Teide's summit.

This is a classic – the big one – up Spain's highest mountain. If the atmosphere is clear, the wraparound views are soul stirring, with the islands of La Gomera, El Hierro, La Palma and Gran Canaria all peeking up from the Atlantic Ocean. If not, all you'll see below you is an aircraft window vista of cottonwool cloud and more bloody cloud.

It's quite a tough ascent, yet is within the capacity of anyone not suffering from high blood pressure or pulmonary problems. If you're fit, you'll have little problem hiking up and down in one day, though most walkers descend via the Teleférico. At the risk of stating the startlingly obvious, for an easier option, take the Teleférico up and do the route in reverse.

If these alternatives sound too daunting, you can still have a magnificent half-day out by following the route as far as the end of the jeep track and taking the easy side trip to the top of Montaña Blanca (2750m), from where there are superb views of Las Cañadas. Allow about 2½ hours altogether for this option.

PLANNING
When to Walk

Unless you're an experienced winter walker, it's inadvisable to make the attempt between November and April, when there's likely to be a considerable amount of snow underfoot on the higher reaches.

How Tenerife Missed the Evolutionary Boat

The Galápagos Islands, at the other end of the world, far off the Pacific coast of South America, are famous for having inspired Charles Darwin's theory of evolution.

Less well known is that the first port of call for his ship, the *Beagle*, was to have been Tenerife. But just as the crew were preparing to land, the island authorities told them they would have to spend a couple of weeks in quarantine. So the captain turned the bow of his boat and headed for the deep Atlantic.

Who knows? Had they landed, Tenerife's wealth of endemic plants, trees and animals, evolved over thousands of millennia in this island microcosm, might well have contributed to the development of Darwin's ideas. As he wrote regretfully in his journal: 'We have just left perhaps one of the most interesting places in the world, just at the moment when we were near enough for every object to create, without satisfying, our utmost curiosity.'

Maps

The IGN *Guía de Isora* No 1110 1:50,000 map covers the walk, as does the official park map *Parque Nacional del Teide* at 1:30,000.

What to Bring

Pack a sweater, even if it's hot and sunny down below. Also take a couple of bottles of water since there's no liquid en route until you reach the overpriced cafe at the top of the Teleférico.

Permits

If you want to walk higher than the top of the Teleférico at La Rambleta to bag Pico del Teide, you'll need a permit. It's a bureaucratic hassle, which means passing by the national park's Servicio de Uso Publico office (☎ 922 29 01 29, fax 922 24 47 78) on the 4th floor of Calle Emilio Calzadilla 5 in Santa Cruz. It observes bureaucrats' hours from 9 am to 2 pm, Monday to Friday. Take along a photocopy of the personal details pages of your passport or ID. Permits, which are free, specify both the date and the two-hour window during which you're allowed beyond the *cordon sanitaire*. Take your passport or ID with you on the walk, since you'll probably be asked to produce it.

The permit scheme restricts to 50 at any one time the number of park visitors (over 3.25 million every year) who can pass above

the barrier and into the fragile, unique ecosystem fighting to survive in such inauspicious conditions for sustaining life.

Warnings

Today above all days, remember that *actual walking time* is logged. Allow more time than you normally would for an equivalent change of altitude closer to sea level. As you get higher, not only will your pace slow but, because the air is thinner, you'll probably find yourself taking more frequent rest breaks.

PLACES TO STAY & EAT

All bookings for the *Refugio de Altavista* (☎ 922 23 98 11), a little more than an hour's walk below the top of the cable car, have to be made in person at the Oficina de Turismo (☎ 922 23 95 62) on the Plaza de España in Santa Cruz. Open between April and September – and longer if the weather remains clement – it costs 2000 ptas a night, which you can pay in at any branch of the Caja Canarias bank. You then present the receipt at the tourist office, which will log you in. All this said, you're unlikely to find the refugio full, except at weekends. It doesn't serve meals, you can't always rely on water being available and it is normally closed between 10 am and 5 pm.

If you arrive outside those times – as most walkers do – you'll find the place locked, without access to water, shelter or toilet

El Teleférico del Teide

The Teide cabin lift whisks you up from 2356 to 3555m, some 1200m of altitude change, in only eight minutes. The corresponding – and infinitely more fulfilling – foot slog from the valley will take you about 12 times as long.

If you're planning to do the Rambleta walk in reverse (downhill), get there early. The cabins, which hold around 35 passengers, start rolling at 9 am and you need to arrive before the tour buses pull in. At peak times, you can be stuck in a queue for up to two hours. The last cabin down is at 5 pm.

facilities. The cold comfort continues: a stay here is limited to one night, access to the sleeping area is restricted to between 11 pm and 6.30 am, don't move the furniture, and don't use radios or 'other appliances that emit sound'. 'There's a complaints book for any suggestions or complaints', says the sign, tautologically – but it's on the inside, so you can't get at it to suggest that the welcome could be warmer.

GETTING TO/FROM THE WALK

It is a scandal that there's only one bus a day to Parque Nacional del Teide from the south of the island and one from the north. Bus No 348 leaves Puerto de la Cruz at 9.15 am daily for the Parador de las Cañadas de Teide. Another (No 342) simultaneously sets off from Playa de las Américas, calling by Los Cristianos 15 minutes later, on its way to El Portillo. Both call by the Teleférico and will stop at intermediate points to drop off walkers. The return bus for Playa de las Américas leaves El Portillo at 3.15 pm, calling by the Teleférico at 3.40. The one bound for Puerto de la Cruz leaves the Parador de Cañadas del Teide at 4 pm.

And that, as far as public transport goes, is it. Of the park's 3.5 million annual visitors, only a tiny proportion arrive by bus;

the remainder come in courtesy of their tour company's coach, by hired car or by taxi.

The first Teleférico of the day goes up at 9 am and the last one down is at 5 pm.

THE WALK

Get off the bus or leave your car at the small parking area (signed 'Montaña Blanca' and 'Refugio de Altavista') 8km south of El Portillo visitors centre and take the jeep track leading uphill. After 15 minutes, just beyond a track leading right to a park building, ignore the well trodden path just beyond it on the left. Instead, obey the plaque 'Sendero 7' and continue on the main track.

In less than five minutes, leave this main track to take a similar unsigned path (if any place on the mountain cried out for a sign, it's here) leading north-west towards a small col. Five minutes later, eschew another tempting path which leads straight up the fawn and tawny flanks of Montaña Blanca, now clearly visible. Soon after this, treat a wider path with similar disdain, veer right, still on that north-west bearing, and pass to the left of a small hillock.

After about 45 minutes of walking – and having, satisfyingly, cut off several hairpin bends – you rejoin the jeep track beside some giant boulders, known technically as accretion balls. You've reached the **Huevos del Teide** (Eggs of Teide). For the next 20 minutes, you can either short-cut up a steepish path heading south-west or follow the more gentle curves of the track. To the west, a dark tongue of lava, product of Teide's most recent eruption, cuts through the surrounding lighter rock.

At the end of the jeep track, reached after about an hour of walking, the real uphill work begins. But before you begin to sweat, consider the brief, easy detour to the summit of Montaña Blanca (see the side trip at the end of this section).

After 30 to 40 minutes, a jumble of large boulders and a windbreak of stones provide just enough shade to escape from the sun. Soon after, you enter a sprawl of retama bushes and the trail, while still not a Sunday stroll, becomes less steep as the zigs and zags become broader. Once you have a solitary metal pole in your sights, let your spirits soar. It's not even 20m below the *Altavista refugio*, which you reach about 45 minutes after having left the boulders.

Above the refugio, pick your way between fields of pure lava, like spikes of chocolate fudge, where nothing, but *nothing*, grows. The path, however, climbs steeply again nowand is clear and easy underfoot. After 20 minutes, an easily missed, short track to the right leads to the Cueva del Hielo (Ice Cave), a sunken cavity with giant icicles. About 30 minutes later, you come to a T-junction. Turn left and in about 15 minutes you'll reach **La Rambleta** (3550m), the Teleférico's upper station and also a chain barrier which marks the beginning of the route up to Pico del Teide's crater (see the second of this walk's side trips).

Side Trip: Montaña Blanca
20 to 25 minutes, 1.25km
This easy, almost level diversion along a clear path makes a pleasant interlude between the uphill work. From the rounded summit of Montaña Blanca (2750m), there are splendid views of Las Cañadas and the sierra beyond.

Side Trip: Pico del Teide
45 minutes to 1 hour, 1.5km
It is a pity not to be able to include this as the natural and logical conclusion to an ascent of Pico del Teide's slopes. However, to preserve the summit's fragile ecosystem, there's an understandable limit of 50 people at any time. Less comprehensible is the unnecessary runaround to obtain a permit (see Permits under Information Sources in the La Rambleta & Pico del Teide walk, earlier in this section).

Almost as soon as you're above the chain barrier (have your permit plus passport or ID ready to flash when the uniformed guardians of the mountain appear from nowhere), you get the first whiff of acrid fumes in your nostrils. As you ascend, look out for patches of yellow sulphur and puffs of steam burping from the rocks, escaping from vents which are technically called *fumaroles*. After 20

Pico Viejo

Pico Viejo (Old Peak) is the last of Tenerife's volcanoes to have erupted on a grand scale. In 1798, a 700m gash split open its south-west flank. Today, you can clearly see where fragments of magma shot over 1000m into the air and fell pell-mell. Torrents of lava gushed from a secondary, lower wound to congeal on the slopes. To this day, not a blade of grass, not a stain of lichen, has recolonised their arid course.

minutes, you're rounding the lip of the summit's crater, the rocks below you stained as yellow and potash grey as old men's teeth, while the vapours rise from the cauldron like steam from a witches' brew. The two hours which your permit grants are ample time for the return trip and to savour the summit and its views.

Side Trip: Mirador del Pico Viejo
45 minutes, 1.5km
This signed trail, the most spectacular of two easy, out-and-back walks radiating from La Rambleta (the other goes to La Fortaleza overlook) leads to the Mirador del Pico Viejo (see the boxed text).

La Gomera

Without volcanic activity for millions of years, La Gomera is the most dormant of the Islas Canarias. Stretching over 354 sq km, its permanent population of less than 20,000 increases substantially around 11 am when the first ferry of the morning from Tenerife arrives. But towards dusk, when the last boat pulls out, calm returns, even to San Sebastián, the island's only major town.

Perhaps the greatest day in the island's history – though no one realised its significance at the time – was 6 September 1492. Early that morning, Christopher Columbus led his three small caravels out of San Sebastián's harbour and headed west for the

New World. He wasn't to touch land again until he reached San Salvador in what is today the Bahamas at the heart of the Caribbean.

HISTORY

Most of the walks on La Gomera follow paths which have a long history as links between pueblo and pueblo. Nowadays, many are all but abandoned. Look at the prints in the dust and sand. Sometimes, the only visible tracks are those of goats – or of the last group of trekkers to pass by.

NATURAL HISTORY

Cut off from the African mainland for millennia and despite occupying only 370 sq km, La Gomera is the home of 43 endemic plants, compared to Germany's five or Britain's 12. For more about the island's unique laurisilva, or laurel forest, see the boxed text 'The Laurisilva, La Gomera's Hillside Reservoir'.

The Parque Nacional de Garajonay was designated a national park in 1981 and its nearly 4000 hectares of semitropical rainforest were declared a UNESCO World Heritage Site five years later.

INFORMATION
Maps

Caminos de la Gomera (500 ptas) is produced by the Cabildo (local government) specifically for walkers. On the reverse, it lists principal trails and times, the island's bus timetable and other useful information. *La Gomera*, by the German company Goldstadt Wanderkarte, details 57 walking routes and is more walker friendly. Both are at 1:50,000 and use a whole minilanguage of easily understood symbols, though neither has sufficient contour information. Both are adequate to guide you through the walks we describe. Don't be tempted by the IGN's *La Gomera*. A reprint of an ancient map with an 'Edición Para el Turismo' (tourism edition) label overprinted, it is an expensive (850 ptas) and inaccurate con.

You can usually pick up Goldstadt Wanderkarte maps from the ill-tempered occupant of Kiosko Castilla, just off the main square. Foto Junonia at Avenida Colón 24 carries a few maps plus guidebooks in Spanish and German.

Books

Landscapes of Southern Tenerife and La Gomera by Noel Rochford, part of the Sunflower series, describes a number of walks. *Alternative Gomera* by Nicholas Albery is engagingly naive and anecdotal, describing just about every tree and stone on a couple of weeks' worth of trails. If you get lost, it certainly won't be the author's fault. Not easily available, you can get it from the Institute for Social Inventions in London (☎ 44 181-208 2053, fax 44 181-452 6434; from 1 June 1999 ☎ 44 020-8208 2053, fax 020-8452 6434, rhino@dial.pipex.com). *La Gomera for Walkers* by Lance Chilton is a similarly slim, less diffuse work by another committed hiker. It's available from Marengo Publications (☎ 44 1485 532 710).

Information Sources

The tourist office (☎ 922 87 02 81) at Calle Real 4 in San Sebastián is open from 9 am to 1.30 pm, Monday to Saturday, and 10 am to 1 pm on Sunday.

The Laurisilva, La Gomera's Hillside Reservoir

If you're from Florida or Georgia, at a similar latitude to the Islas Canarias, or New Zealand and the south-east coast of Australia, the *laurisilva* (roughly speaking, 'laurel forest') of La Gomera's cooler, more humid, north-facing slopes may seem familiar. But in Europe and Africa, it's about the last survivor of a vegetation which once surrounded the whole of the Mediterranean until it was wiped out by the most recent Ice Age.

The laurel, as you'd imagine, is among the dominant trees, with the local *Laurus azorica* its most common variety. The gnarled and twisted trunks of the hardy *brezo*, or heath tree (*Erica arborea*), resemble giant clumps of heather, to which it is related, as does another cousin, the *tejo* (*E. scoparia platycodon*). In season, you know when you're under a Canary wax myrtle (*Myrica faya*) by the stains of its fruit, like miniature blackberries, around its base and by its rough, cork-like bark. Another common endemic species is the Canary holly tree (*Ilex canariensis*), recognisable by the wisps of moss floating from it like grey beards. If you see a carpet of red and russet leaves at your feet, you're probably under a *viñatigo* tree (*Persea indica*), the tallest member of the laurel family.

What they all have in common is a capacity to hold the moisture which the supersaturated clouds, blown in on the tradewinds, leak onto them. They, and the mosses, lichens and ferns which grow on and around them, act like a giant sponge in a phenomenon known as 'horizontal precipitation'. This contributes more water to the island than the more usual vertical precipitation – or what we, in normal language, call rain.

The Parque Nacional de Garajonay visitors centre (☎ 922 80 09 93), though inconveniently located if you're without transport, is well worth a visit and runs a good, multilingual, 20 minute video about the park. It's open from 9.30 am to 4.30 pm daily except Monday. Ask for their free booklet, *Garajonay National Park: Self-Guider* (sic) *Paths*. Among other things, it describes the nature trail and its 16 observation points between El Contadero and Las Mimbreras on the first part of the Pajarito to Hermigua walk featured later in this section.

ACCOMMODATION & SUPPLIES

Wild camping is prohibited across the island. For details of La Gomera's only camping ground, see the Pajarito to Hermigua walk later in this chapter.

San Sebastián

Pensión Gomera (☎ 922 87 04 17), Calle del Medio, has doubles for 3000 ptas. If the fine wooden door is closed, inquire at the Centro de Ahorro supermarket opposite. On the same street, *Pensión Pajar* (☎ 922 87 02 07), noisier and more spartan, has rooms for 2500 ptas. *Pensión Colombina* (☎ 922 87 12 57, Calle Ruíz de Padrón) has singles/doubles with bathroom for 2500/4000 ptas. *Bar Restaurante Oshun* on Calle República de Chile has an intriguing gastronomic mix: pizzas, pasta and a Cuban selection. *Club Junonia*, Calle del Medio, has a pleasant garden and reasonable food.

GETTING THERE & AWAY

Linking Los Cristianos on Tenerife with La Gomera's port of San Sebastián, Líneas Fred Olsen (☎ 922 79 05 56) has four boats daily (three on Wednesday) while Trasmediterránea (☎ 902-45 46 45) has only one. Trasmediterránea also runs four hydrofoils daily (three on Sunday), which cut the journey time by half and are only slightly more expensive.

A few inter-island flights a day serve the island's new airport. The brief trip isn't worthwhile to and from Tenerife. However,

Top: Llano de Ucanca, Pico del Teide and the jagged stumps of the Roques de García.
Bottom: The Barranco de Masca cuts into the flanks of Pico del Teide, the highest peak on Tenerife.

Top: Espinal village, one of dozens of welcoming waystops along the Camino de Santiago.
Bottom Left: The Camino de Santiago winds through the Pyrenees near Roncesvalles.
Bottom Right: The village of Cebreiro, where this church stands, is famous for a 14th century miracle when the wine and host literally turned into the blood and flesh of Christ during a mass.

it may be worth considering if you're connecting there with an international flight.

GETTING AROUND

The island's bus company, El Servicio Regular de Gomera (☎ 922 87 14 18), has three bus routes, each with four services a day, leaving San Sebastián at the same time. The great inconvenience for walkers is that since they're dictated by the arrival of the first ferry from Tenerife, the first run of the day doesn't depart from San Sebastián until 11 am. Subsequent services splay out across the island at 2, 5.30 and 9.30 pm.

Hiring a car, especially if you're in a group, makes the best of a bad option. There are several agents along Calle del Medio and Calle de Ruiz de Padrón in San Sebastián. Rent a Car Piñero has an office in town and also in the ferry terminal. If you ring ☎ 922 87 01 48 in advance, they'll have a vehicle waiting for you as you step off the boat.

Typical taxi fares from La Gomera are:

Hermigua	3000 ptas
El Cedro	3000 ptas
Pajarito or El Contadero	3500 ptas
Alajeró	4000 ptas
Valle del Rey	6000 ptas

Pajarito to Hermigua

Duration 5 to 5½ hours
Distance 12km
Standard Easy-Medium
Start Pajarito
Finish Hermigua
Public Transport Yes
Summary An easy ascent to Alto de Garajonay, the island's highest point, followed by a steep descent through laurisilva to Las Mimbreras. An ascent through mixed wood to a ridge and open country before dropping to the lush Hermigua valley.

You're unlikely to be alone on what is, from El Contadero to Las Mimbreras, the most popular walk on La Gomera. If you only

want to follow the nature trail, turn around at Las Mimbreras and return to El Contadero (allow two hours).

PLANNING
Maps

The booklet *Garajonay National Park: Self-Guider Paths*, available at the Parque Nacional de Garajonay visitors centre, is the most useful map reference for this walk.

GETTING TO/FROM THE WALK

To reach the start, take the morning Valle Gran Rey bus from San Sebastián and ask to be dropped off at Pajarito. For the return to San Sebastián, buses leave Hermigua for San Sebastián at 6 and 10 pm.

THE WALK

From Pajarito, a well defined path leads to the summit of **Alto de Garajonay** (1487m), the highest point on the island. From the peak, a signed trail leads down to the road and, beyond it, to El Contadero.

Take the path downhill from the car park to El Contadero (The Counting Point) – tradition has it that shepherds would stop to count their sheep here. At first, the trail drops through *brezal* (heath tree forest) dominated by heath trees, hardy survivors common both here and in the damper laurisilva.

Soon, you're in the laurel forest proper. Some 45 minutes from El Contadero, pass a mirador overlooking a modest stream called El Cedro, one of only five brooks in the park which collect water from the laurisilva (most of the precipitation filters underground).

Veer right at a fork just beyond a sign indicating the site of an old camping ground. About 15 minutes beyond the mirador, and 2.8km from El Contadero, is Las Mimbreras (The Willows). Turn right along a jeep track, then take the first left down a path signed 'Caserío de El Cedro'.

At the **Ermita de Nuestra Señora de Lourdes** chapel refill your water containers at a flowing tap, ingeniously concealed inside a tree stump. Here, take the lower of two paths, again signed for El Cedro. At a second fork, bear right along a path which

ISLAS CANARIAS

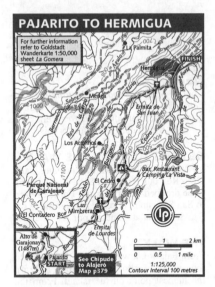

PAJARITO TO HERMIGUA

For further information
refer to Goldstadt
Wanderkarte 1:50,000
sheet La Gomera

La Palmita

FINISH

Hermigua

Ermita de
San Juan

Meriga

Los Acevinos

Bar, Restaurant
& Camping La Vista

El Cedro

Parque Nacional
de Garajonay

Las
Mimbreras

El Contadero Bco

Ermita
de Lourdes

Alto de
Garajonay
(1487m)

Pajarito
START

See Chipude
to Alajeró
Map p379

0   1   2 km

0   0.5   1 mile

1:125,000
Contour Interval 100 metres

briefly runs alongside an irrigation channel
before passing a sign, 'Límite del Parque',
to leave the national park.

At the bottom of a flight of crumbling
stone steps, turn right onto a wide track, then
left, following signs to *Bar-Restaurante La
Vista* (☎ 922 88 09 49). A pleasant, friendly
place for a drink, it has the island's only
camping ground – a site costs 300 ptas per
person. It also runs a nearby *refugio*, where
a bed costs 1500 ptas.

Continue to the end of the dirt track and
take a faint path to the right, just before the
refugio. This initially doubles back on itself
before heading up and north-east to join a
wider trail. A little beyond the highest point
– about an hour from Las Mimbreras –
ignore a tempting fork to the left marked by
two green markers. A couple of minutes
later, turn right onto a wide jeep track.

At this point you leave the forest to
enjoy open vistas of the sea and Pico del
Teide on Tenerife. About 30 minutes from
the junction, take another track right (east);
almost double back on yourself after a

sharp left-hand bend; then, within 30m,
head left down a steep path.

Five minutes later, the path joins a wider
track which briefly follows the ridge sea-
wards, giving fine views of the contrasting
valleys to the west and east; the former clad
in laurisilva and the latter, dropping towards
Hermigua, much steeper and populated by
stunted heath trees. After looping back beside
a large boulder, the track degenerates into a
footpath which dips down into the eastern
valley. Abruptly, as you round a bend, Hermigua plain spreads before you with the
pink-roofed chapel, the **Ermita de San Juan**,
on a knoll overlooking the straggling village.

After about 30 minutes of quite steep
descent, the path crosses the barranco onto its
east bank. From here on, you're following a
clear track, in part cobbled. From the small
mirador behind the ermita, where pennants
flap and fly as in some Tibetan shrine, there's
another great view of the fertile valley, its cultivation creeping right down to the seashore.

Soon afterwards, cobbles give way to
concrete steps as you pass between a
cluster of whitewashed houses to cross
over a sealed road and continue down yet
more steps. At a second sealed road, go
left and, once around an 'S' bend, take a
concrete path which leads down to the
main road and, less than 10 minutes away,
to Hermigua.

Chipude to Alajeró

Duration 5½ to 6½ hours
Distance 16.5km
Standard Medium
Start Bend, 1.25km east of Chipude
Finish Alajeró
Public Transport Yes
Summary A long descent to the hamlet
of Erquito, over the tops to El Drago, then
via a couple of steep barrancos to the level
track leading to Alajeró.

Contrasting with the walk from El Contadero
to Hermigua, which takes in the island's rich,
green central and northern slopes, this is a

day for savouring the semidesert environment of La Gomera's southern flanks – all open spaces and sweeping vistas.

PLANNING
Maps
Refer to the Goldstadt Wanderkarte *La Gomera* map at 1:50,000.

GETTING TO/FROM THE WALK
For the start, take bus No 1, Valle Gran Rey, and ask the driver to drop you at the turning for Erque and Erquito. Coming from San Sebastián, it's on a bend shortly after a sign announcing that you're leaving the national park. There *is* a road sign, 'Erque, Erquito', but it faces west and is only evident once you look back from beyond the junction. The last bus back to San Sebastián passes through Alajeró about 8.15 pm.

THE WALK
Take the dirt track which heads due south from the bend. You can avoid its long, northern loop by heading down the abandoned *bancales* (terraces) at a point about 100m before a large palm grove.

Rounding a bend, the track snakes above the largely abandoned hamlet of Erque, dominated by the flat-topped summit of La Fortaleza (1241m) across the valley. Above and below the village, bancales, tended to this day by the few villagers who remain, fill every available cleft and cranny which briefly holds water when the rains sluice off the heights.

After about 45 minutes, where the track turns sharply to the right and down to Erque, keep going straight to follow the contour of the hillside. After another 45 minutes, you reach **Erquito**, these days rather less moribund than its uphill neighbour. After zigzagging down through the village, take a stone-paved path which climbs eastwards beside the last house on the track.

Once beyond the final house up this side valley, the path begins to ascend steeply beside terraces of almond trees and tabaiba. Some 10 minutes later, a substantial fig tree,

a date palm and a large, rocky overhang cluster together. The first two give sustenance in season and all three provide welcome shade. They make a great rest stop, offering a stirring view of the seaward part of the Barranco de Erque with La Fortaleza towering above.

Soon after, the path levels out as it follows a narrow, horizontal ledge round the flank of the mountain. From here, you get spectacular views of the increasingly constricted valley below, round which water pipes snake like contour lines, and of the ocean at its mouth. A sign announces that you're leaving 'un espacio natural protegido' (an area of special conservation), then all of a sudden you're round a corner and it's all seascapes. But before walking on, take a last glance back at the deep bowl at the head of the Barranco de Erque and the mass of La Fortaleza, less regular and flat topped from this angle.

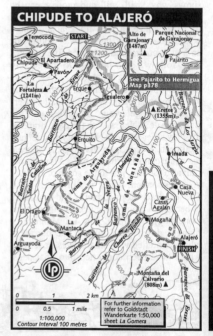

CHIPUDE TO ALAJERÓ

Before you is a ruined stone shack. Way beyond it to the south-west, the first house of El Drago peeks round the bluff, with the village of Arguayoda well to its right (west). Until quite recently, the whole hillside, an undulation of bancales mirroring the waves of the sea beyond, was intensively cultivated. But now the stones of the elaborate terraces, once the subject of so much attention and care, are tumbling back into the chaos from which they were lifted and shaped.

Ten to 15 minutes later, as you join a wider track at a hairpin bend, cast around for a path that leads down through the terracing to El Drago. The beginning is not easy to discern. If you fail to find it, just plunge down, aiming for the pueblecito's whitewashed houses and following the occasional cairn built by others who had similar ill luck. Its latter end, bounded by a stone wall and descending parallel with a water pipe, is more evident.

Follow this same path all the way through **El Drago**, an impressive little hamlet which shows what, with will and money, can be done to restore a decaying community. At its limit, you meet a jeep track at an elbow bend. Take it as it heads away south-east and, at another bend just over five minutes later, follow a sign pointing to the equally small hamlet of La Manteca.

After 150m, near a sign announcing that you're re-entering an area of special conservation, you get your first view of the Barranco de la Negra, with the dark strand of the Playa (beach) de la Negra at its outlet into the ocean. Beyond, on the horizon, appears the white chapel at the top of La Montaña del Calvario (808m), just to the south of Alajeró, your destination, which is still out of sight. The jeep track stops suddenly and arbitrarily to become a much more interesting, mature, stone-flagged path. Below La Manteca, it plunges down the flanks of the barranco, which is riddled with small caves, several of which have been converted into goat pens.

Shock-headed palms occupy the more humid clefts on each side while, where it's drier, cardón, agave, or aloe cactus, tabaiba and prickly pear compete.

Turn left when a minor path enters from the right and continue heading north-west up the valley. About 30 minutes beyond El Drago, cross Barranco de la Negra at a magnificent hunk of red rock, worked into dimples and swirls by centuries of intermittently flowing water. Fifteen minutes later, the path crosses over the smaller Barranco de Almagrero and begins to zigzag steeply up its east flank. After 15 to 20 minutes, where a block of basalt overhangs pink rock, be sure to take the upper, overgrown path rather than the more obvious one which has been beaten enticingly smooth by goats' hooves and heads away up the valley. Soon, the path becomes unpaved and less distinct as you briefly loop south-east and, it feels, away from your destination. From the **ridge**, there are fine views of the canyon, the houses of La Manteca – once again level with you on the far slope – and as far back as El Drago. Shortly after you cross the watershed, you'll need to be alert. Head due east between a huddle of abandoned houses, aiming for a lone palm, beyond which the end of a sealed road unexpectedly pops up.

After about 10 minutes, turn right at the first white building. The path follows the shoulder of the hillside north-east to pass below Magaña, a second and more substantial white house, and drops towards a tiny reservoir, an oasis of bright green at the head of **Barranco de Charco Hondo**, reached about 30 minutes after having left the sealed road.

As you reach the ridge after a steep ascent from the valley bottom, the cube of La Fortaleza appears for one last time, blocking the notch on the northern horizon. From this point, it's an easy 15 minute walk along a dirt track into Alajeró.

Camino de Santiago

The Camino de Santiago (Way of Saint James) originated as a European medieval pilgrimage. Today it is a magnificent long-distance walk spanning 738km of Spain's north from Roncesvalles on the border with France to Santiago de Compostela in Galicia. Named Europe's Premiere Cultural Itinerary in 1987 and receiving UNESCO's accolades as a World Heritage Site attest to the walk's incalculable cultural, historical and artistic value. The diversity of the regions it passes through can be seen in their cuisine, vernacular architecture, crops, climate and folk music and dance. On the route you follow scenic country roads, fields and forest tracks as well as crossing countless villages and cities born of the Camino, all overflowing with millennial treasures; it's hard to imagine a better way to enjoy Spain.

The Camino de Santiago has an exceptional infrastructure of accommodation, readily accessible services and trail marking, making the journey feasible for walkers of all ages and backgrounds. In fact, people from around the world now walk the route. For a great physical challenge, an immersion in a stunning array of landscapes, a unique perspective on rural and urban Spain, a chance to meet intriguing companions, as well as the opportunity to participate in a 1000-year-old tradition through a continuous outdoor museum, this is your walk.

It is actually incorrect to refer to the Camino de Santiago in the singular. Medieval pilgrims simply left home and picked up the closest and safest route to Santiago de Compostela. Many of these became established in and outside Spain (see Other Pilgrim Routes at the end of the chapter). In this chapter the so-called Camino Francés from the Pyrenees to Santiago de Compostela is described in 28 daily stages.

HISTORY

In the 9th century a remarkable event occurred in the poor Iberian hinterlands:

HIGHLIGHTS

DAMIEN SIMONIS

The impressive baroque façade of Catedral del Apóstol in Santiago de Compostela at the finish of the pilgrim's route.

- Reaching Santiago's historical quarter after walking 730km in one month

- The warm, animated conversation, intriguing walking companions and welcome rest in simple refugios after long days

- Sun filtering through countless stained-glass windows in León's cathedral, creating a divine kaleidoscope

- Solitude on Castilla's flat plain, with the wind combing endless fields of wheat which appear to roll off into nothing

following a shining star, a religious hermit unearthed the apostle James the Greater's tomb. (St James is from here on referred to by the Spanish Santiago.) The discovery was confirmed by the local bishop and the

Asturian king. Today it's hard to imagine the import of this news, but it made an immediate and indelible impact on European Christianity and the history of the incipient Spain.

In that age, saintly relics were highly valued, traded as commodities and even manufactured with great vigour to further ecclesiastical and monarchical interests. To see and, even better, touch a relic was a way to acquire a part of its holiness. The church cultivated the value of relics by offering the faithful who made pilgrimages to holy places an indulgence – a remittance of some or all sins committed in this life. A pilgrimage was thus partly an investment for one's future permanent retirement.

With the discovery of the apostle's tomb, Compostela (an area known to the Romans as Libredon) became the most important pilgrimage destination for Christians after Rome and Jerusalem. In addition, an 11th century papal decree increased its popularity; it received Holy Year (Año Santo or Año Jacobeo, and Xacobeo in Galician) status granting pilgrims a plenary indulgence

> ### What's in a Name?
>
> All the derivations of Santiago (Sant Iago) can be confusing. The original Latin Iacobus became Jakob in German, James in English, Jacques in French, Jaume in Catalan, Jacopo in Italian, Xacobe in Galician and even Diego (as in San Diego!) ...
>
> Another etymological conundrum is the origin of the place name Compostela. Some theorists argue that it means 'starry field' in Latin, referring to the hermit's discovery, while others suggest the more sedate Latin *compostium*, or burial ground.

– a full remission of all one's lifetime's sins. Occurring on a regular basis when Santiago's feast day (25 July) falls on a Sunday (which happens at intervals of 6, 5, 5, 6 and then 11 years): the last Año Santo of the 20th century is in 1999, followed by 2004 and 2009.

What were Santiago's remains doing in Iberia, though, when he had been martyred in

CAMINO DE SANTIAGO

CAMINO DE SANTIAGO – MAPS

Map 1	Roncesvalles to Logroño	p389
Map 2	Logroño to Hontanas	p396
Map 3	Hontanas to Terradillos de los Templarios	p400
Map 4	Terradillos de los Templarios to Molinaseca	p402
Map 5	Molinaseca to Palas do Rei	p408
Map 6	Palas do Rei to Santiago de Compostela	p411

1 : 6,000,000

Jerusalem in 44 AD? This is where medieval imagination and masterminding comes into play. The accepted story suggests that two of Santiago's disciples secreted his remains in a stone boat, sailed through the Mediterranean and moored at present-day Padrón (see the boxed text 'The Scallop Shell'). They continued inland 17km to Santiago and buried his remains, which were soon forgotten. Whether you believe this explanation or not is irrelevant: the fact that it was believed led to the mass movement of millions of pilgrims; the Camino's birth; the subsequent taming of the Iberian wilderness, unseen since the Roman colonisation; the spread of Romanesque and Gothic art styles (see the boxed text 'Romanesque & Gothic Art & Architecture' in Day 11 of this walk); and a major influx of settlers and of religious orders that established pilgrims' *hospitales* (wayside guesthouses) and monasteries.

These factors helped to ensure the safe-keeping and repopulation of the northern territories gained through the Christian Reconquista (Reconquest) of Muslim Spain. Santiago is also directly linked to the Reconquista by his appearance at several major battles as Matamoros (Moor-Slayer) who, with sword raised, descended from the clouds while mounted on a white horse. The image of Santiago as pilgrim is found throughout Europe but the association of him as the Reconquista's sponsor is limited to Spain (and South America, where the conquistadors carried his image). After its medieval heyday the pilgrimage suffered during the Reformation and had nearly died out altogether by the 19th century before its late 20th century secularised reanimation.

NATURAL HISTORY

Starting in the low western Pyrenees (1057m) of Navarra amid thick, well maintained deciduous forests (beech, hazel and linden), the Camino then drops onto rolling plains. Wild roses, stinging nettles, chickweed and blackberry brambles appear in the first days and run the length of the route. As the Río Arga river is left behind, the forests – for a time – are exchanged for the rich cultivated fields of Navarra, which produce wheat and the region's speciality, white asparagus.

Crossing over the great Río Ebro into Logroño (in La Rioja), the abrupt heights of the Cordillera Cantábrica hem in this border area between Navarra and La Rioja. Its chalky, clay (calcareous and burnt orange ferruginous) and alluvial silt soils support vineyards that produce excellent red wines; the most well known outside of Spain. The red soils also account for the large number of *alfarerías* (pottery shops and factories) found in La Rioja.

Passing through the fields of grapes, cereals and potatoes, you'll encounter common river-bank species including black poplar (*Populus nigra*), which is used for paper production, and common alder (*Alnus glutinosa*). Wild flowers which burst into

Medicinal Plants

To treat sickness among pilgrims, the great variety and richness of flora growing beside the way proved crucial for pilgrims and the staff of the *hospitales* (wayside guest-houses). The latter, who were often monks, also collected recipes from an infinite number of sources. For example, herb robert (*Geranium robertianum*) came in handy for blisters; its crumbled, fresh leaves were mixed with honey and the compound was applied over the wound three times a day.

The dull-sounding common ragwort (*Senecio jacobaea*), known in Spanish as *hierba de Santiago*, was fried in oil and then applied between the toes to sooth broken, irritated skin. Fennel (*Foeniculum vulgare*) boiled in milk was the equivalent of a modern-day power drink to counteract low energy (and also treated flatulence and indigestion when boiled in water and drunk after meals). A remedy for sore, inflamed feet – as common centuries ago as it is today – is a foot bath of cool water, vinegar and salt. Many *refugios* (refuges or mountain huts) have buckets just for this purpose.

bloom in spring and early summer include common mallow, pineapple weed, milfoil, rue and bellflower. Dotting the cereal fields with red is the ubiquitous poppy, or *amapola*. (See the boxed text 'Medicinal Plants' on the previous page.)

As the Camino rises slowly to the *meseta* (high tablelands of central Spain) of Castilla y León (Burgos lies at 860m and León at 829m), cereal crops dominate and evergreen oaks sparsely shade the plains. River species are concentrated along the north-south river systems (Ríos Carrión, Pisuerga, Cea, Bernesga and Órbigo) which cut across the Camino's route and once made the pilgrimage much more challenging. The Camino climbs again through the ore-rich Montes de León on the fringes of León; aromatic thyme, lavender, rock rose and sage grow by the way. In the El Bierzo region, nestled between two mountain systems, cherry trees, red pepper bushes and red wine grape vines thrive.

When the Camino reaches the rounded eastern sierras of Galicia, the forests begin to return: they include cultivated chestnuts (once the Galicians' main source of carbohydrate), oaks, then pines and, finally, eucalyptuses. Beyond the mountains, the land is nearly perpetually green along the undulating, gradual descent to Santiago de Compostela, the Camino's lowest point (260m). This is rich dairy and farming country, and common crops include potato, corn, cabbage and *grelos*, the leafy green vegetable that makes the famous Galician soup *caldo gallego* distinctive. Hereditary farming practices in this region produced innumerable hamlets, giving the region a distinctive feel when compared to the larger, widely scattered settlements of the meseta.

Birds are the most common visible wildlife: you'll see a rich variety of species. The most obvious is the white stork (see the boxed text 'Storks' in Day 7 of this walk), found from the Navarra-La Rioja border to the Leonese foothills. Among the numerous other birds are doves, sparrows, goshawks, kites, owls, woodpeckers and, in Galicia, black-and-white crows.

CLIMATE

The regions of Navarra, La Rioja and Galicia tend to have an Atlantic climate, whereas the high plains of Castilla y León have a Mediterranean one. The former will have wet and blustery springs, hot summers and fairly mild winters with snow in the higher elevations of Navarra and Galicia. Castilla y León has relentlessly hot summers and cold, snowy winters and is often swept by cold northern winds coming off the Cordillera Cantábrica mountain range.

INFORMATION
Maps

For information on maps and trail markers, see Maps under Planning in the introduction to the Camino Francés later in this chapter.

Books

Countless reams of paper and parchment are dedicated to the Camino. A key text is the remarkable 12th century *Codex Calixtinus*, also known as *Liber Sancti Jacobi*, a five chapter manuscript detailing the pilgrimage. The fifth chapter is considered the first guidebook to a pilgrimage in the Christian west and describes the Camino Francés and the places you pass in detail. It's available in English as *The Pilgrim's Guide to Santiago de Compostela*, translated by William Melczer. Michael Jacobs' *Northern Spain: The Road to Santiago* is a decent, compact architectural guidebook to the route.

For modern travellers' accounts, Jack Hitt's *Off the Road* is a hilarious personal account of his journey in 1993. For a spiritual perspective try Lee Hoinacki's *El Camino*. Nancy Frey's (coauthor of this chapter) *Pilgrim Stories: On and Off the Road to Santiago* analyses the Camino's present popularity, focusing on individual experiences.

The Confraternity of Saint James publishes basic, straightforward guides for walking the pilgrim roads in Spain (and France) including *Camino Francés*, *Camino Mozárabe*, *Los Caminos del Norte*, *Finisterre: Guide for Walkers* and *Camino Portugués*. To order, write or fax: 1st Floor,

1 Talbot Yard, Borough High St, London, SE1 1YP (☎ 0171-403 4500, fax 407 1468).

Information Sources

The tourist information centres (known as TICs) along the Camino (as well as the Spanish National Tourism Office) have either place or region-specific brochures. With the resurgence of interest in the Camino a number of pilgrim associations or confraternities have formed. Many have members' bulletins and may offer information to those considering the walk.

Australia
    Amigos del Camino de Santiago, c/o Bill and Lorna Hannan, 20 Shiel St, North Melbourne, Vic 3051
Canada
    The Little Company of Pilgrims, c/o Mike Henry, 6 Sandringham Drive, Don Mills, Toronto
England
    Confraternity of Saint James (see Books on the facing page)
USA
    Friends of the Road to Santiago, 2501 Kingstown Rd, Kingston, RI 02881

Camino Web sites cover topics from history to practical advice to personal experiences. Begin by connecting to www.xacobeo.es and you'll find links to others. Once in Spain, guidebooks in various languages are readily available at bookshops along the route.

Permits

Most people who walk, even if they aren't religious, carry the Credencial del Peregrino (Pilgrim's Credential). An accordion-fold document, it gives bearers access to the well organised system of *refugios* (refuges or mountain huts) along the route – see Accommodation & Supplies later in the introduction to this chapter. You can obtain the Credencial upon starting in Roncesvalles (see Day 1 of the walk description) or in major cities at a pilgrims' refugio.

The Compostela certificate, obtained from the Cathedral's Pilgrims Office in Santiago de Compostela upon finishing, is proof you have completed the journey. To receive

the Compostela, your Credencial must be stamped once daily (in refugios) during your walk, you must travel the last 100km to Santiago de Compostela on foot, and you need to affirm that the journey was made for spiritual or religious motives. Iberia Airlines and Spanair offer reduced-price one-way tickets from Santiago de Compostela's international airport to pilgrims who present the Compostela.

Place Names

In Navarra the Spanish and Basque names for settlements appear together, whereas in Galicia local signs and villages go by the Galician version. In the descriptions we provide the Spanish/Basque where appropriate; and in Galicia, only the Galician.

Warnings

Some people complain about unleashed dogs in villages acting defensively or aggressively and so carry a stick for protection. In general, they aren't a problem.

ACCOMMODATION & SUPPLIES

The Camino Francés has an extensive system of pilgrim refugios and all stages end at one. (We also list other accommodation options.) All refugios are highlighted in the text, with the number of bed spaces, the fee and whether or not it has a kitchen.

Refugios generally have sheetless bunks in communal dorms, toilets and showers (sometimes sex-segregated) and kitchens. They are run by parishes, local governments, Camino associations and private owners. Located nearly every 15km, they maintain opening hours (usually from 3 to 10 pm, closed after 8 am) and do not take reservations. Most rely on pilgrims' donations to function while others charge a nominal fee of between 300 ptas and 500 ptas. Help with maintaining and cleaning refugios is greatly appreciated. Some are staffed by a *hospitalero voluntario* (volunteer *hospital* attendant) who may spend part of a summer vacation, or may even work full-time, looking after pilgrims. To stay, present the Credencial to the hospitalero.

CAMINO DE SANTIAGO

The route regularly passes through villages and cities. In the walk description, settlements are either referred to as having *limited services*, meaning there is a bar and/or restaurant, or *all services*, signifying a bar, restaurant, pharmacy, bank, market, shops etc. With few exceptions water is readily available in bars or from village fountains. Many restaurants offer an inexpensive *menú del día* (fixed-price meal) which usually includes three courses, wine or water and bread from 900 ptas to 1200 ptas.

GETTING THERE & AWAY

All the major cities of the Camino are accessible by RENFE (Red Nacional de los Ferrocarriles Españoles) trains or buses from Madrid. The local tourist office or town hall will indicate where the closest refugio is and where the yellow trail markers begin.

To Roncesvalles

Bus Continental (☎ 91 553 04 00) at Calle de Alenza 20 in Madrid runs buses to Pamplona (3140 ptas) at 8 and 10.30 am and 3, 7 and 9.30 pm daily.

Once in Pamplona, La Montañesa buses, Avenida del Conde Oliveto, go to Roncesvalles (555 ptas) at 4 pm weekdays and Saturday at 6 pm.

Train RENFE has two daily direct trains from Madrid to Pamplona (4100 ptas), leaving at 9 am and 5 pm, from where you can catch a bus to Roncesvalles.

Car & Taxi Taxis from the Plaza del Castillo in Pamplona to Roncesvalles cost 6000 ptas. By car from Pamplona, take the N135 (towards France) to reach Roncesvalles at the milepost signed '47.6km'.

From Santiago de Compostela

Many daily train and bus services run direct to Madrid (and other major European cities) as well as to other destinations in the north of the country.

Bus ALSA buses connect Santiago de Compostela to Madrid at 11 am, 2 and 9.30 pm for 5040 ptas. SAIA buses connect Santiago de Compostela to Barcelona via Zaragoza (Saragossa) daily at 1.45 pm for 8000 ptas. The bus station (☎ 981 58 77 00) is in the eastern part of the city in San Caetano.

Train RENFE trains run from Santiago de Compostela station (below the intersection of Avendia de Lugo and Calle Hórreo) to Madrid daily at 10.25 pm. For Barcelona, take the Santiago de Compostela to La Coruña service (500 ptas) at 3.15 pm and then the 5.45 pm train from Coruña to Barcelona (6700 ptas).

Car Santiago de Compostela is easy to reach via the N6, which connects Madrid to La Coruña.

Camino Francés

Duration 28 days
Distance 733km
Standard Medium
Start Roncesvalles
Finish Santiago de Compostela
Public Transport Yes
Summary A magnificent route that traverses the north of Spain along back roads, forest tracks and agricultural fields through more than 1000 years of Spanish history, art and culture.

Feasible in a month (including rest days), this 28 day walk can be divided into fewer or more stages depending, of course, on your pace. If time is a factor, you can begin from numerous locales after Roncesvalles and continue to Santiago de Compostela. In two weeks the stretch from León (from Day 14) can be safely entertained. With one week, the spectacular Galician portion, beginning in O Cebreiro (from Day 21), offers a delightful, scenic introduction. Additionally, the initial week in Navarra, from Roncesvalles to Logroño, in the region of La Rioja, is a true highlight. If you crave solitude and desolation or have never walked in a seemingly horizonless landscape, then you might consider walking from Burgos to Hontanas (Day 11) or Castrojeriz (Day 12), especially in May or June when the high plain is still green.

PLANNING
When to Walk

Though the Camino Francés can be undertaken year-round, the best months for walking are May, June, September and October. The spring months offer long days and visual splendour: rivers are full, the hillsides burst with wild flowers and the meseta is still green. Anticipate some showers and cool mornings. By September and October the unbearable heat and crowds of July and August have diminished but shades of brown dominate the landscapes; the meseta appears a wasteland.

Feast of Santiago For those who don't mind the inevitable crowds, July is the month to be in Santiago de Compostela. The 25th is the Feast of Santiago and Galicia's 'national' day. The night before, Praza do Obradoiro comes alight with *Os Fogos do Apóstolo*, a spectacular light, music and fireworks show that dates to the 17th century and culminates in a mock burning of the Mudéjar façade to commemorate the city's razing by Muslims in 997. Fears for the safety of the cathedral's façade in the last few years have shifted the emphasis from exhilarating pyrotechnics to more sedate plays of light. The town authorities organise processions, numerous concerts, notably in Praza da Quintana, and other cultural activities.

Maps

For general orientation the Instituto Nacional de Geografía's (ING) *Mapa del Camino de Santiago* at 1:600,000 is available in the bookshops of major cities along the route for 800 ptas.

Trail marking (from bright-yellow painted arrows on trees, rocks and houses, or blue metal signs with stylised yellow shells, to ceramic shells and cement blocks) is extensive and easy to follow, making detailed maps and a compass superfluous. The

Camino Francés corresponds with the GR65 long-distance trail throughout Navarra; red-and-white slashes join the yellow trail markers.

On several days of the walk we give two alternatives (A and B). The more recommended route is always option A.

What to Bring

You need surprising little – many people, expecting hardship, find that they are carrying too much. However, pilgrims' *refugios* infrequently supply blankets; a sleeping bag is essential. Washing areas and lines are common. Stiff hiking boots are not recommended as the variety of surfaces and long stretches of relatively flat terrain require more flexible, all-round, sturdy walking shoes or boots. Supplies are readily available the whole way.

THE WALK
Day 1: Roncesvalles to Zubiri
6 to 6½ hours, 22km

This is an impressive first day, descending 440m through Navarrese forest and villages.

Roncesvalles/Orreaga (960m), one of the route's oldest pilgrim way stations, is the site of the legendary medieval epic poem, *La Chanson de Roland*. It is said that, after being killed in an ambush while protecting Charlemagne during his retreat through the Pyrenees, Roland and his soldiers were buried here. The Royal Pantheon – which contains the remains of Navarra's 13th century King Sancho (El Fuerte) – and the 14th century cloister, museum and Silo of Charlemagne (built over a pilgrims' ossuary) all attest to this history.

People beginning in Roncesvalles often arrive a day ahead and get the Credential (25 ptas) at the Oficina de Acogida (Pilgrims' Office), to the right of the *colegiata* (a type of monastery). The attendant requests statistical information and then explains the facilities of the nearby *refugio*, which has 68 places; the fee is by donation. In the restored 13th century Gothic church a 12th century pilgrims' blessing is read at the 8 pm mass. The hamlet has a souvenir store with guides, cheese shop, tourist office (☎ 948 76 03 01) and two hostels with doubles including bathroom: *Casa Sabina* (☎ 948 76 00 12) charges 6200 ptas and *La Posada* (☎ 948 76 02 25) charges 7000 ptas. Both have a 1300 ptas menú.

After 100m on the N135 (towards Pamplona), cross and enter a tree-lined pebble path continuing to the highway and Burguete/Auritz (which has all services), famous for its white and red shuttered *caseríos* (farmhouses) and as trout fishing locale in the novel by Ernest Hemingway, *The Sun Also Rises*. Near mid-village (Iglesia San Nicolás de Bari church is on the left), turn right down a paved road leaving Burguete. Cross the stream to a wide dirt lane winding left through pasture to a stream. After crossing, the path ascends through woods and then, 6.5km from Roncesvalles, descends to Espinal/Aurizberri (with all services), a picturesque hamlet founded in 1269. Mid-village, turn left after a fountain onto an ascending, narrow path. When you reach reforested firs, turn right towards a beech wood. Climb the wooden stairs to the highway (2km from Espinal) at the Alto de Mezquíriz (925m).

During the next 3km to Viscarret/Biskarreta (with a fountain), the well marked dirt path and the N135 play cat and mouse. Turn left out of Viscarret, continuing parallel to the highway. Where they join again, cross onto a white stone path that leads to Lintzoain. Note the *frontón*: a court on which *pelota vasca* – a type of handball popular in Navarra and the País Vasco – is played. Past the fountain, turn right up the street which converts to an undulating path through pine, oak, box, and beech to the **Alto de Erro** (815m). Cross the highway and continue descending on the forest and dirt path (passing the crumbling Venta del Puerto, once a pilgrim's inn and now a cow stable) to Zubiri (village of the bridge) at 526m. Enter the village by crossing the Río Arga river over the **Puente de la Rabia**, so nicknamed because livestock were circled three times around the central pillar to cure rabies. The magnesite factory, clearly visible on descent, sustains the local economy.

Places to Stay & Eat The *refugio*, with room for 20 and charging a fee by donation, is past the church and a fountain on the right. Turn right onto the highway and then left after 200m.

Pensión Goikoa (☎ 948 30 40 67) has singles/doubles with shared bathroom for 2500/3500 ptas. *Hostería de Zubiri* (☎ 948 30 43 29) charges 7000 ptas for doubles with bathroom. Both are on the highway (Nos 6 and 8). You can eat well at *Gau Txori* (next to the bridge) which has a menú for 1350 ptas.

Day 2: Zubiri to Pamplona
5½ to 6 hours, 21km

Leave Zubiri over the bridge and turn right up the lane. Soon becoming a sealed lane, the way veers left 300m and then turns right onto a dirt path above a factory. After this unpleasant area the path climbs along a winding footpath, passing two hamlets to **Larrasoaña**, where there is a fountain and a *refugio* with 34 places, a kitchen and a fee of 400 ptas.

To continue, follow the trail markers left to Akerreta. The path narrows through a pine and oak forest and slowly approaches the Río Arga, crossing at Zuriain, where there is a fountain. Exit to the highway and continue for 400m. Turn left down a paved road towards Ilurdotz. After crossing the bridge turn right onto a dirt path that leads to an abandoned mine. Turn right up the trail to Irotz, which has a fountain, and return to the N135, walking parallel to it briefly before crossing. The path ascends and skirts the hillside – passing a large, restored stone house – to the main highway. Cross via a tunnel and turn right up the road that winds down to the Río Ulzama, a tributary of the Arga. Cross the medieval bridge to Trinidad de Arre (currently a boys' seminary) and continue left. Pilgrims sometimes receive refuge here upon request. You've come 14km.

The Camino makes a beeline through the streets of Villava/Atarrabia (home town of Spanish cyclist – and several-times Tour de France winner – Miguel Indurain) and Burlada for 2km. At the Uranga municipal park (on the left), veer right onto a street flanked with trees. Pamplona's cathedral becomes visible. Where the road ends, turn right and cross the Magdalena bridge. A modern cross (*cruceiro*) dedicated to Santiago sits at the foot of the bridge. From the park the trail markers veer right, circling briefly below the city's ramparts before ascending to Pamplona's (449m) impressive, stone-gated northern entrance, the **Portal de Francia**. The way through the old quarter is well marked with blue-and-yellow trail markers.

The highlights of Pamplona, Navarra's capital, include the cathedral and its museum, the Calle Estafeta, where the running of the bulls during the Fiesta de San Fermín takes place every 7 to 14 July, and the bars and cafes around the Plaza del Castillo. The tourist office has excellent brochures and guides to the city, the Camino and Navarra.

Places to Stay & Eat The *refugio* on Calle Ansoleaga 2 has 30 places and a charge of 400 ptas.

Fonda Aragonesa (☎ 948 22 34 28, Calle San Nicolás 32) has spartan, immaculate singles/doubles for 1800/3500 ptas. Opposite, the more upmarket *Hostal Bearán* (☎ 948 22 34 28) charges 4500/5500 ptas for rooms with a bathroom. For meals, try *Montón* or *La Viña* on Calle Jarauta.

Day 3A: Pamplona to Puente la Reina via Eunate
6½ hours, 25km

Idling through wheat fields, the way climbs 320m and enters sleepy villages en route to Puente la Reina where the Camino Aragonés and Camino Francés unite.

Leave Pamplona, skirting the 16th century defensive **Ciudadela** (now a popular city park). Take the Calle Fuente de Hierro before descending past the Universidad de Navarra. When you reach a T-junction, turn right and cross the wooden bridge. In 4km you will reach Cizur Menor, which has limited services. Up the hill to the right sits the Romanesque Iglesia San Miguel – a private *refugio* with 20 places, a kitchen and a 500 ptas charge – and the ruins of a pilgrims' *hospital*.

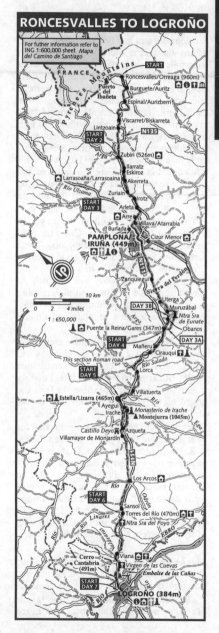

RONCESVALLES TO LOGROÑO

For futher information refer to IGN 1:600,000 sheet *Mapa del Camino de Santiago*

FRANCE

Pyrenées Mountains

START
Roncesvalles/Orreaga (960m)
Puerto del Ibañeta
Burguete/Auritz
Espinal/Aurizberri
Viscarret/Biskarreta
Lintzoain
START DAY 2
N135
Arga
Río
Zubiri (526m)
Ilarratz
Eskiroz
Larrasoaña/Larrasoaina
Akerreta
Río Ulzama
Zuriain
Irotz
START DAY 3
Arleta
Arre
Villava/Atarrabia
Burlada
PAMPLONA/IRUÑA (449m)
Cizur Menor
Zariquiegui
Sierra del Perdón
0   5   10 km
0   2   4 miles
1 : 650,000
Uterga
DAY 3B
Muruzábal
Ntra Sra de Eunate
Puente la Reina/Gares (347m)
Obanos
DAY 3A
START DAY 4
Mañeru
Cirauqui
This section Roman road
Río Salado
START DAY 5
Lorca
Estella/Lizarra (465m)
Villatuerta
Ayegui
Irache
Monasterio de Irache
Montejurra (1045m)
Castillo Deyo
Azqueta
Villamayor de Monjardín
Río
Los Arcos
START DAY 6
Ega
Oteiza
Sansol
Torres del Río (470m)
Linares
Ntra Sra del Poyo
EBRO
Cerro Cantabria (491m)
Viana
Virgen de las Cuevas
Embalse de las Cañas
START DAY 7
Río
LOGROÑO (384m)

Continue straight through the village crossroads and then veer right past a housing development and into fields of wheat. Visible 8.5km ahead, the Sierra del Perdón, with windmills spinning, makes a good reference point. The dirt lane ascends through Zariquiegui (which has a fountain) and the more pronounced ascent of the sierra begins. Near the summit the dry Fuente Reniega (Renouncement Fountain) bears witness to a 12th century pilgrim legend. The Devil tempted a dehydrated yet devout pilgrim to renounce his faith in exchange for sparkling water. He refused and in return Santiago appeared and led him to a spring. At the **summit** (780m) the Eolic wind-power company has mounted an iron sculpture depicting medieval pilgrims.

The next 10km are laid out before you in a sweeping westward view. Cross the road and descend the initially steep, loose-stone path through an oak and boxwood forest to Uterga, where there is a fountain. Exit the village to the left on a downhill dirt path. At the bottom, take a right-hand path passing cultivated fields and almond trees to Muruzábal, which has a fountain and limited services.

Follow the yellow trail markers left down a paved road for 2.5km to the highway and the octagonal, 12th century, Romanesque **Ermita Nuestra Señora de Eunate**. Possibly a Knights Templar construction (see the boxed text 'Templars' in Day 21), it was also a pilgrims' cemetery.

From the car park, follow the dirt trail for 3km parallel to the highway to reach Puente la Reina (347m). The town is an excellent example of a *sirga* (one-street village), common en route. Predictably (puente in Spanish means bridge), the name comes from its magnificent 11th century **bridge** spanning the Río Arga, constructed for pilgrims under order of, most likely, the wife of the Navarrese king, Sancho El Mayor.

Places to Stay & Eat The *refugio* at the town entrance has 60 places, a kitchen and asks for a donation. It is at the town entrance.

On Calle Mayor, along with the **Iglesia Santiago**, is the excellent restaurant *Lorca*

(at No 54) with a menú for 1500 ptas. *La Conrada*, Paseo de los Fueros 17, has comparably priced meals. The cheapest accommodation apart from the refugio is *Jakue* (☎ 948 34 01 17) on the highway, where singles/doubles with bathroom cost 6400/9500 ptas.

Day 3B: Pamplona to Puente la Reina via Obanos
5½ to 6 hours, 23km
Follow Day 3A to Muruzábal. Leave for Obanos (which has a fountain and all services) along the main road on a descending path (right) for 2km. Obanos' fame resides in the legend of fratricide between two saints, Felicia and Guillermo. The **Iglesia San Juan Bautista** houses the ghoulish relic of Guillermo (his cranium covered in silver) in the sacristy. Pass under the arch to the left of the church and descend to Puente la Reina. On the N111 a modern pilgrim statue marks the historic junction of the Camino Francés and Camino Aragonés.

Day 4: Puente la Reina to Estella
5 hours, 19km
Crossing four rivers, this lovely jaunt passes through fertile vineyards and several tranquil hill towns.

Cross the bridge and the highway to a dirt path which narrows to an ascending trail. Snake up the embankment to the summit where Mañeru's church steeple appears. Mañeru has a fountain. Leave the village via the Calle Forzosa, passing a cemetery on the left. Cemeteries in this region (and, later, in Castilla y León) are on the outskirts of town, in contrast to Galicia.

Passing between vineyards, fields of cereals and fruit trees, the dirt trail winds pleasantly for 2.7km to the compact and labyrinthine **Cirauqui** (a Basque word meaning 'nest of vipers'), where there is a fountain and limited services. The village retains some medieval walls, a hub-shaped urban plan and the **Iglesia San Román** – justifiably famous for its 13th century portal with a lobed arch. From the plaza next to the church descend left out of the village.

Cypress trees flank the impressive stretch of 2000-year-old **calzada romana** (stone-paved Roman road) that descends over a Roman bridge and ends at the highway. Cross and turn left onto a dirt then sealed road. Continue for 4km, passing under a modern aqueduct to Río Salado. The *Pilgrim's Guide* records the story of how several Frankish pilgrims, arriving at the river bank, lost their horses' skins to two Navarrese men sharpening their knives on the other side. When assured by the knife wielders that the water was potable, the Frankish horses were allowed to drink deeply – and collapsed, dead. The Franks were not in a position to argue. Cross the bridge and ascend to Lorca, where there is a fountain.

Villatuerta, which also has a fountain, lies 4km away along paths nestled among fields of cereals and plastic-covered rows of white asparagus. Exit the village along a white gravel road that turns right up to the highway. Cross and ascend along a dirt path that winds among olive trees before descending to Estella/Lizarra (465m).

The town's tourist office (on Rúa Curtidores) is housed in a building which is the finest example of civil Romanesque architecture to be found on the Camino, and offers good maps and descriptions of the city. The cloister of **Iglesia San Pedro de la Rúa** (opposite the tourist office) has excellent Romanesque capitals on top of its columns.

Places to Stay & Eat Cross the footbridge over the Río Ega and turn right past Iglesia Santo Sepulcro. The *refugio* – with 64 places, a kitchen and a 500 ptas charge – is 300m straight ahead on the Rúa Curtidores.

Both *Hostal San Andrés* (☎ 948 55 04 48, Plaza de Santiago 1) and nearby *Hostal Izarra* (☎ 948 55 00 24, Calderería 20) have doubles without bathroom for 3200 ptas and 3000 ptas, respectively. To eat, try the latter, which has a 1100 ptas menú, or *Restaurante Casanova* at Wenceslao de Oñate 8, which has a 1200 ptas menú.

Day 5: Estella to Torres del Río
7 to 7½ hours, 29km

Settlements on today's rural walk are widely spaced apart.

Leave Estella via the Rúa Curtidores and Calle San Nicolás. Cross the intersection (towards Logroño) and ascend right at the second petrol station. At the summit, either fork left to Azqueta via the 12th century Irache monastery, or veer right downhill directly to Azqueta. (We recommend and describe the former).

If you choose to head left downhill, cross the highway and continue up a lane to the ingenious **red wine and water fountain** installed by Bodegas Irache (a local winery) in 1991. Continue past the monastery along its old stone wall to a fork. At this point, you can either turn right, cross the highway and continue behind the Hotel Irache, joining the direct route to Azqueta mentioned above; or continue straight ahead, crossing a housing development and some oak woods. At the foot of Montejurra (1045m), you will reach Azqueta, with a fountain. If you reach Azqueta by the former option, the first house on the left is Pablito's, a man famous for giving pilgrims the long, hazelnut staffs which they can often be seen carrying.

Leaving the village, veer right down a dirt lane circling round a cow stable. The route gently climbs through the hills of Monjardín (894m), passing the restored 13th century Fuente de los Moros (questionably potable) below the ruins of the 10th century Castillo de Deyo. Continue to the quiet village of Villamayor (9km from Estella). A downhill left turn leads through red-soiled vineyards to an agricultural track. Los Arcos is reached after 12km through wheat, asparagus patches and an odd series of rounded hills studded with conifers.

Los Arcos, which has all services, suddenly appears. Enter the village and continue straight ahead, then turn right into the main square, dominated by the **Iglesia Santa María**, housing a magnificent organ. Leave Los Arcos under the arch from the main square, crossing over the highway and

The Scallop Shell

An important symbol since at least the 11th century, nearly all images of Santiago (the disciple James) or his followers from the 12th century onwards incorporate a scallop (shell) on the knapsack, hat or tunic. However, the origin of the symbol remains a mystery. One legend suggests that Santiago, even after his death, saved a drowning bridegroom and his horse struggling in the sea as the stone boat carrying his body arrived on the Spanish coast. When he raised them from the ocean they were covered in scallop shells.

Alternatively, the shrine's proximity to what was then considered the Finis terrum (end of the earth) made the shell a symbol of resurrection to be worn by those who returned. Or, possibly, the Santiago shrine overlayed the site of a pre-existing Venus fertility cult and the shell stuck as a common symbol representing rejuvenation and spiritual rebirth.

With the convex side out, others see in its form the back of the hand with the fingers pointing down as if engaged in an act of mercy. Whatever the truth, the symbol remains important and many pilgrims today continue to wear it.

An early engraving of pilgrims on the long road to Santiago de Compostela.

---

a bridge. The town's *refugio* – with 40 places and a 400 ptas charge – and cemetery are on the right. A macabre statement etched in the latter's archway reads: 'I was what you are. You will be what I am.'

Eight desolate kilometres remain to Torres del Río (470m). Mostly flat and straight, the wide dirt and pebble road finally reaches a gully. Veer right onto another path and then left onto the main road. In 2km you will reach Sansol. The trail markers zigzag through the streets. Descend out of town and cross the highway to a downhill footpath. The fountain at the bottom is not potable. A steep ascent through the streets of Torres leads to the **Iglesia Santo Sepulcro**, another marvellous eight-sided masterwork linked to the Templars.

Places to Stay & Eat Torres has a *bar-restaurante* and *refugio*, with a *guest house* under construction at the time of writing. As you face the church in the main square, turn left and left again to reach the refugio – it has 40 places and requests a donation – and the *bar-restaurante*, which specialises in Italian pastas.

Day 6: Torres del Río to Logroño
5 hours, 20km

Today the walk leaves behind Navarra and enters La Rioja, crossing the great Río Ebro.

Leave Torres, heading left to its highest point, and exit past the cemetery. The rural road runs parallel to the highway and then crosses it, ascending a narrow path to the **Ermita Señora del Poyo** where the Virgin of

Le Puy appeared, leaving behind her image which refused to be moved – thus compelling the locals to construct the chapel there. In medieval Catholic doctrine, saints' images and relics had their own will.

The path and road briefly coincide before the former turns right up through rock and scrub and descends through the Barranco Mataburros (Donkey-Killing Ditch). Pass the small river and the ruins of an ancient Roman settlement (both named Cornava), then cross the highway and ascend on a dirt trail. Viana's church appears, still 3km away. At the foot of this historic frontier town, the trail markers cross the highway and head up to the Plaza de los Fueros. Here there is a fountain, all services and a *refugio* – with 40 places and a kitchen; a donation is requested. The adjacent **Iglesia Santa María**, with its concave Renaissance portal and soaring Gothic interior, is especially interesting.

Logroño (384m) lies 9km from Viana, but is partially hidden behind a flan-shaped plain (Cerro de Cantabria, a pre-Roman settlement). Leave Viana, skirting the ruins of **Iglesia San Pedro**, and walk down past townhouses. Veer left with the trail markers to a path that wends through gardens, reaches the Ermita Santa María de las Cuevas, and then passes the Embalse de las Cañas. Turn right up to and cross the highway, continuing to a crossroads at the Navarra-La Rioja border. Cross onto a gravel trail (passing under two tunnels) and around Cerro de Cantabria's right side. Descend past Logroño's cemetery and enter the city over the Ebro via the **Puente de Piedra**. The façade of the **Iglesia Santiago** has an excellent image of Matamoros and the portal of the **Iglesia Bartolomé** has intriguing transition Gothic sculptures.

Places to Stay & Eat The first street to the right, Rúa Vieja, leads after 200m to the *refugio*, with 60 places, a kitchen and a 300 ptas charge.

Pensión Numantina (☎ *941 25 14 11, Calle Sagaseta 4*) and *Fonda Bilbaína* (☎ *941 25 42 26, Calle Capitán Gallarza 10*) have singles/doubles with bathroom for

3550/5500 ptas and 2500/3500 ptas, respectively. You can eat well at *Bar Moderno*, Plaza Carnicería, or *Bar Galicia*, Calle Mayor 61.

Day 7: Logroño to Nájera
7 to 7½ hours, 27km

Storks will be a familiar sight on this walk to the red cliffs of Nájera.

Follow the paving-stone scallops through the cobbled old quarter. After passing the remains of the city walls we recommend ignoring the trail markers. Instead, turn left onto Calle Once de Junio and right, briefly, onto Calle de Portales. Continue around the Plaza Alférez Provisional and onto the long Calle Marqués de Murrieta (where the official route is rejoined), reaching two petrol stations (on either side of the road). Turn left onto Calle Entrena, passing an industrial zone and the highway. Continue on a dirt road that leads to the agreeable surprise of the Embalse de la Grajera reservoir. Circling to the right, the trail ascends through vineyards to a sawmill. The large billboard bull on the hill (left) once advertised Osborne Sherry. Turn left along the highway for 250m and then cross it, descending along a path that affords views of hilltop Navarrete. Make a beeline to the village via an overpass and past the 12th century ruins of Hospital de San Juan de Acre. One of its portals serves as Navarrete's cemetery door.

Naverrete has all services and a *refugio* with 20 places and a kitchen; the charge is 300 ptas. Wrapped liked a blanket round the hill, Navarrete retains its medieval character with its cobbled, narrow streets and labyrinthine layout. Ceramic workshops, where potters use the area's red clay soil, are common. The magnificent 16th century church (on the highest plaza) offers cool relief on a hot day.

There are no fountains or villages in the next 14km to Nájera. Follow the trail markers out of Navarrete down to the N120 (towards Burgos). Three hundred metres after the cemetery turn left and weave through vineyards, and olive and fruit trees to the N120. Turn left onto the highway and follow it for

Storks

If you walk the Camino in spring or summer you'll inevitably see and hear the elegant *cigüeña* or common stork (*Ciconia ciconia*), which, after passing the winter in North Africa, flies to the Iberian Peninsula to reproduce. They almost always settle near human populations, in contrast to their shy black relatives (*C. nigra*) which hide in the woods. They construct or rein-habit huge, complex nests perched high in the most unlikely places, such as water pumps, telephone poles or chimneys. A preferred nesting site appears to be church bell-towers, sometimes crowding a single tower with three or four heavy nests.

The sociable white stork is a creature of habit, returning to the same nest for many years in a row.

nearly 3km (there are no trail markers). Finally, the route turns left and returns to vineyards and a dirt path. When you reach a fork with a large stone in the middle, veer right and begin a rocky ascent that becomes a pleasant footpath. Nájera, still 7.5km away, appears. The track descends, crosses the highway, and skirts around a telecommunications antenna and a gravel works. Cross a footbridge and continue to Nájera (485m), where a wide range of services can be found.

Places to Stay & Eat Cross the Río Najerilla and enter the old quarter, built directly into the huge, red walls rising behind the town. Parallel to both the river and the wall is the fascinating, active **Monasterio de Santa María la Real**; adjacent, on the right, is the *refugio*, with 30 places and a kitchen; the charge is 300 ptas.

Centrally located **Hostal Hispano II** (☎ *941 36 36 15, Calle La Cepa 2*) has singles/doubles with bathroom for 2900/4500 ptas and a menú for 1200 ptas. *El Mono*, Calle Mayor 45, has a good 1500 ptas menú.

Day 8: Nájera to Santo Domingo de la Calzada

4½ to 5 hours, 21km

On this stage, a stretch of uninspiring highway gives way to fields before reaching curious Santo Domingo, famous for its founder.

With the monastery on your right, ascend along the right-curving street and up a stone and dirt track bordered by pines and cliffs. Descending through a ravine, the way flattens past vineyards to a sealed road and, 5.5km from Nájera, reaches hill-top Azofra, which has a fountain, limited services and a *refugio* with 18 places and a kitchen; a donation is requested.

Leave Azofra down the main street to the highway. Turn right and after 100m turn left onto a lane passing a large *rollo* (a medieval juridical pillar used to mete out justice) converted into a cross. Climbing a small hill, the lane nears the highway and crosses a perpendicular road. You should fork left immediately and left again at the next

T-junction. The path ahead cuts a white line through wheat fields which roll away on either side. At the top, the oak-flanked trail flattens to Cirueña, where there is a fountain. As you enter the village, take the main road to the right; in 150m, where fields of hops appear on the right, the path turns left and undulates for 6km to Santo Domingo de la Calzada (639m).

The town's founder, Santo Domingo (1019-1109), was a religious hermit on the banks of the Río Oja when it lacked both bridges and roads. Rejected by the local monastery for illiteracy, he worked independently, constructing a church and pilgrims' *hospital* – now a *parador* (one of a chain of luxury hotels) – and building bridges and highways from Logroño to Burgos. A bizarre legend makes the village and the saint famous (see the boxed text 'Of Saints & Chickens').

Places to Stay & Eat To reach the town's *refugio*, turn left at the main highway and take the Calle Mayor for 1km. It has 50 places and a kitchen; a donation is requested.

For accommodation in town, ***Hostal Río*** (☎ *941 34 00 85, Calle Echegoyen 2)* has singles/doubles with shared bathroom for 2000/3200 ptas and a 900 ptas menú. ***Hostal Miguel*** (☎ *941 34 32 52, Avenida Juan Carlos I 23)* has new rooms with bathroom for 3500/5000 ptas. ***Los Arcos***, Calle Mayor 68, serves good meals for 1350 ptas.

Day 9: Santo Domingo de la Calzada to Belorado

5 hours, 22km

Entering the Burgos province within Castilla y León, the way continues through valleys surrounded by hills and high tablelands.

Head out of Santo Domingo along the N120, crossing Domingo's bridge over the Río Oja (giving La Rioja its name) and traverse 4.5km of unpleasant highway. Thankfully, the way detours left to hill-top Grañón (which has limited services), a village whose present condition belies its illustrious past. Once fully walled, it had two monasteries and a pilgrims' *hospital*. Its

---

Of Saints & Chickens

Entering Santo Domingo de la Calzada cathedral's south door, a curious pair of live white chickens (rotated weekly) are kept in an elevated niche on the western wall. This odd custom traces back to the famed miracle of Santo Domingo. A young pilgrim, travelling with his parents to Santiago, was accused of pilfering silver from a local tavern. In reality the barmaid, her amorous advances rejected, angrily slipped the silver into his knapsack and notified the authorities. To his parents' horror, the pilgrim was strung upon the gallows. Praying, they continued to Santiago and returned. Surprisingly, rather than encounter his rotting body, they found him well – yet still hanging, the saint supporting his feet. They ran to the judge who, having just sat down to roast chicken, refused to be bothered. When the pilgrims insisted, the judge exclaimed that if their son were innocent the chickens would rise from his plate and crow. And they did, giving the town its motto: 'Donde la gallina cantó después de asar' (Where the hen crowed after roasting). It is considered good luck to find a chicken feather or to hear them crowing.

---

former splendour is captured by the **Iglesia San Juan Bautista** whose restored main altar is a masterpiece of 16th century Renaissance art. The ingenious *refugio* – with 20 places and a kitchen; a donation is requested – is built into the church's southern wall; pilgrims wash laundry on top of the vault! After the church, take the first right out of village. At the first junction, head right downhill, immediately fork left and 300m later turn right. After 300m turn left onto the lane which leads towards Redecilla. A broken sign en route marks the La Rioja-Castilla y León border.

A village bisected by the highway, Redecilla has a fountain and limited services.

CAMINO DE SANTIAGO

LOGROÑO TO HONTANAS

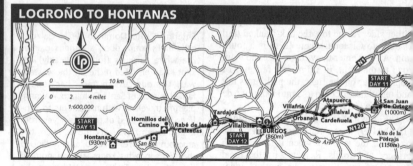

There is also a *refugio* with room for 30; a donation is requested. Cross the N120 and turn left through the village. The Iglesia Virgen de la Calle contains an exceptional 12th century baptismal font resting on eight columns. Exit to the highway and during the next 12km the route and the N120 run parallel or coincide, detouring into the villages of Castildelgado, Viloria (which has a fountain) and Villamayor del Río (also with a fountain).

Filling the Río Tirón valley, Belorado's (770m) southern cliffs and caves once housed medieval hermits, including San Caprasio – venerated in the Iglesia San Nicolás. Iglesia San Pedro is off the circular Plaza Mayor, where all services are available.

Places to Stay & Eat At the entrance to Belorado the path veers right to the *refugio*. It has 22 places and a kitchen; a donation is requested. Next door is the Iglesia Santa María. *Bar Ojarre* (☎ 947 58 03 90, *Avenida Generalísimo 10*) has singles/doubles without bathroom for 2000/3500 ptas and a menú for 900 ptas. Meals at *Etoile*, Plaza Mayor 6, cost the same.

Day 10: Belorado to San Juan de Ortega
6½ to 7½ hours, 24km
Today the Camino ventures to a secluded monastery in the heart of the Montes de Oca.

Cross the Plaza Mayor downhill and turn left onto the Calle Mayor de Santiago. Reaching the N120, cross the bridge and in

500m turn left (after a petrol station) onto a path that leads after 5km to Tosantos, where there is a fountain. The eye-catching church excavated into the hill on the right, Nuestra Señora de la Peña, contains another miraculous Romanesque image of the Virgin. In less than 2km the trail reaches deserted-looking Villambistia, which has a fountain. The first adobe houses appear in these villages and are your constant companions throughout Castilla y León. Follow the trail markers to the highway and Espinosa del Camino (with fountain).

Leave the tranquil village along a dirt road. En route an overgrown pile of rocks on the right was once a chapel flanked by a splendid horseshoe arch and the apse of **San Felices** – the vestiges of a great 10th century Mozarabic (the name given to Arabised Christians during the Islamic occupation) monastery. Continue to the highway and turn right to Villafranca Montes de Oca, where there is a fountain, limited supplies and a *refugio* with room for 18; a donation is requested. This 'Village of Franks' is named after the traders, artisans and settlers who took advantage of the reduced taxes and privileges offered by monarchs to repopulate Muslim territories after the Reconquista.

Leave Villafranca (948m) by walking right (and steeply upwards) behind the **Iglesia Santiago**, and for 12km wind through the desolate **Montes de Oca** among oaks and conifers to San Juan (1000m). The climb flattens, reaching its highest point

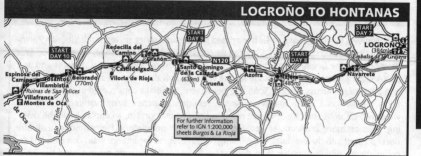

LOGROÑO TO HONTANAS

For further information refer to IGN 1:200,000 sheets *Burgos & La Rioja*

(Alto de la Pedraja; 1150m) at a cross commemorating Spanish Civil War victims. Past this point, the San Juan monastery suddenly appears.

San Juan, an 11th century disciple of Santo Domingo de la Calzada, founded the monastery on this once inhospitable stretch of the Camino. His tomb is in the Romanesque and Gothic church. (For an explanation of Romanesque and Gothic art and architecture, see the boxed text on the following page.)

Places to Stay & Eat San Juan has a *bar-restaurante* but no shop or hostel. The priest at the monastery offers *refugio* accommodation (with room for 60; a donation is requested) and a delicious bowl of *sopas de ajo*, a bread-based garlic soup. Pilgrims usually share what they have in their packs for a communal dinner.

Day 11: San Juan de Ortega to Burgos
6 hours, 25km

Today the rural Camino continues to Burgos, a town intimately linked to the epic figure, El Cid (see the boxed text 'El Cid' in the introduction to the Valencia chapter), and reeking of history.

Leave the monastery, walking along the road to a crossroads. From here, continue straight for almost 3km on a flat, dirt path enveloped in a thick forest of oak and conifers. Reaching a meadow, the way forks right and dips down to Agés (which has a fountain),

crosses it and continues for 2.5km along a paved road to Atapuerca, where there is a fountain and a *bar*. In the nearby Sierra de Atapuerca, archaeologists discovered a prehistoric burial ground with the remains of a *Homo sapiens* (dubbed 'Atapuerca Man'), believed to be Europe's oldest. Leaving the village, turn left onto a road which ascends for 2km to the **summit** (1060m), offering an exceptional lookout to Burgos.

The rough stone path descends to the valley floor. A quarry lies to the right. On reaching a fork, you can either veer right to Orbaneja on a trail that pleasantly winds through rolling fields of wheat; or fork left to Orbaneja on a partly paved road via the villages of Villalval and Cardeñuela. This last option is 1.5km longer.

From Orbaneja, where there is a fountain and a *bar*, follow the paved road for 3km to Villafría. The main N1 highway leads into Burgos (860m) along an interminable 7km stretch of first industrial park and then city streets to the old quarter.

The bustling city has all services and innumerable monuments (in the 15th century it boasted 32 pilgrims' *hospitales*). Marked with arrows, the way passes the magnificent **Gothic cathedral**, considered one of Spain's masterworks for its interior and exterior opulence. The Gothic **Iglesia San Nicolás** and the 9th century hill-top remains of the city's founding castle are definitely worth visiting. The tourist office is in the old quarter on Plaza Alfonso Martínez 7.

Romanesque & Gothic Art & Architecture

The medieval Romanesque and Gothic art and architectural styles arrived on the Iberian Peninsula via the Camino de Santiago. Christian Europe's first 'international' style, Romanesque, was developed at the beginning of the 11th century as an expression of feudal thought and as a post-millennium gesture of gratitude for the world's survival. It was spread via religious orders and pilgrimages across Europe. Solid and permanent, buildings constructed in this style used thick, regular-stone walls, massive columns, semicircular arches, barrel vaults and had few windows. Churches had three or five naves, a Latin cross floorplan, a cupola above the crossing, one or more semicircular apses and a pilgrims' ambulatory. Romanesque sculpture (incorporated into the building) and painting (which covered the interior walls completely!) accomplished a practical, rather than decorative, function; the illiterate devout 'read the Bible' through the didactic images, which sought to stimulate piety and fear of the Church. A common representation was Pantocrator (Christ) as powerful king and inflexible judge, seated on his throne and surrounded by the evangelists (Matthew, Mark, Luke and John) symbolically represented as an angel, lion, bull and eagle.

The Gothic style surfaced in the 12th century in conjunction with a general socio-economic shift of power from the country to the city. Using the pointed arch and the ribbed vault, buildings, especially cathedrals, strove for height and luminosity (representing the light of God). The basilica (rectangular) floorplan, wider at the transept, also had an ambulatory and chapels behind the altar. The high walls incorporated stained-glass and rose windows inside and flying buttresses and needle-like pinnacles on the outside. The painting and sculpture sought realism and beauty rather than presenting a message to be read. The Virgin Mary appears more frequently and Christ as judge is substituted for Christ as man who suffers on the cross. Sculptures are found on portals, chorus seats, gargoyles and altars, while painting (on wood) appears principally on altarpieces. Both reflect a greater preoccupation with light, movement, perspective and naturalism.

Places to Stay & Eat To reach the refugio, 2km from the centre, continue along the Camino, parallel to the Río Arlanzón and the Paseo de la Isla, to the Malatos bridge. Cross the highway and turn left into the El Parral park. The *refugio*, with room for 60 and which requests a donation, is in the centre. There is also a fountain here. Eat near the refugio at *Restaurante Amparo*, a bit further west.

In town, *Pensión Dallas* (☎ 947 20 54 57, *Plaza de la Vega 6*) has singles/doubles without bathroom for 2500/4400 ptas. There is spartan accommodation at *Pensión Arribas* (☎ 947 26 62 92, *Calle de los Defensores de Oviedo 6*); rooms with bathroom are 1700/2900 ptas. You can eat well and inexpensively at several places near the cathedral off the Calle Paloma.

Day 12: Burgos to Hontanas
7 to 8 hours, 29km

After the initial tramp of 10km you will reach a spectacular springtime section through a magnificent no-man's-land, where the meaning of 'meseta' becomes vividly clear. Pick up supplies in Burgos or Tardajos (much more limited) as neither Hornillos nor Hontanas have markets.

From the refugio leave the park, turning right at the Hospital del Rey to the highway. Continue for 1km and then turn right onto Calle Pérez Galdós. The street becomes dirt and winds between poplars and fields to Villalbilla, where there is a fountain. At a small train station, turn right through agricultural fields to the highway. Cross onto the main road; after 250m, the way turns left down a dirt lane to Tardajos, 7km from

Burgos, with all services and a *refugio* with room for 12; a donation is requested. Crossing the village, leave via a paved road that goes left to reach Rabé de las Calzadas after 2km.

Continue on a dirt road past a hermitage and cemetery (on the left). The way climbs a small hill, flattens out and continues for a seemingly endless 8km to Hornillos del Camino (825m). For some, this stretch (and the next to Hontanas) is mentally fatiguing as the horizon stretches to infinity. Others feel liberated, far from the sights and sounds of 'civilisation'. Hornillos has a small *refugio*, a fountain and a *bar*.

Leave Hornillos, forking right to take a dirt road for 1km. Veer left, ascending to a small meseta. The path flattens and rolls off seemingly into nothing. Crossing two minor dirt roads, continue to an unanticipated dip. Off to the left a small, solitary structure is the San Bol *refugio*, with 10 places and a fountain; a donation is requested. The way continues without turns for 6km to Hontanas (930m). The church's bell-tower pierces the sky, signalling your arrival.

Places to Stay & Eat The *refugio*, which has 20 places and a kitchen and which charges 500 ptas, is on the same street as a small, greasy *bar* offering cheap meals (700 ptas) and beds (the scrupulous should stay away). The hospitalero also arranges 1000 ptas meals.

Day 13: Hontanas to Boadilla del Camino

7 hours, 29km

Though not as dramatic as yesterday, the way continues through desolate areas with great artistic and historical value. Buy supplies for the day's end in Castrojeriz or continue for 4.5km to Frómista (see Day 14).

Leaving Hontanas, cross the highway (towards Castrojeriz) onto a parallel path. Soon, you rejoin the paved road and in 9km (from Hontanas) reach Castrojeriz. Enjoy the music of countless poplar, linden and elm leaves rustling along the way. Outside Castrojeriz, the road reaches the lamentable ruins of the impressive Gothic **Convento de San Antón**. When ergotism, or St Anthony's Fire (a gruesome disease causing reddened extremities, burning skin boils and eventually gangrene), broke out across Europe in the 10th and 11th centuries, the saint's order blessed pilgrims with their symbol, the Greek letter *tau*, as insurance against the malady. The west rose window has the tau woven into the tracery.

The road continues to monumental **Castrojeriz** (808m), a sirga wrapped round the hill's southern slope and topped with a crumbling castle. After you enter the town, pass the churches Virgen del Manzano, Santo Domingo (with a small museum) and San Juan. All services are available in town including a *refugio* with 35 places and a kitchen; a donation is requested. Descend out of town, crossing the highway to a dirt road, and over the medieval bridge.

Steeply ascend the imposing hill for 1.2km to Mostelares (900m). The dirt path slowly descends 4km through fields to a picnic area, Fuente del Piojo (Louse Fountain). Continue on the paved road for 1km and turn left onto a field road which descends past the **Ermita San Nicolás**, a tiny Romanesque church converted by an Italian Camino association into a simple *refugio* with 12 places but no electricity or running water; a donation is requested. Cross the medieval bridge with 11 arches spanning the Río Pisuerga, the natural border between Burgos and Palencia provinces.

Head right on the wide dirt road to the village of Itero de la Vega, where there is a fountain and a *refugio* with room for 12; a donation is requested.

The way leaves Itero via a paved road and continues on a wide dirt and stone road for a long 8km to Boadilla (795m). The town's visual highlights are the 16th century Iglesia Asunción and the 15th century flamboyant Gothic rollo.

Places to Stay & Eat A shady, wheeled fountain on the left offers welcome respite. The village has a *bar*, small shop and a simple *refugio* with room for 25; a donation is requested. In summer ask in the bar about lodging in the *casa rural* (rural guest house) of Jesús Marino.

Day 14: Boadilla del Camino to Carrión de los Condes

6 to 7 hours, 25km

On this day you'll see many *palomares* (dovecotes), usually cylindrical adobe structures, which are frequent along the meseta. Bird eggs and meat were once an important food source and the droppings were used as fertiliser.

Leave Boadilla via the marked dirt road. When you reach a large barn and palomar, turn left up to the 18th century canal called the **Canal de Castilla**, designed for irrigation, transport and grain milling. Continue for 4km along the canal's left shoulder to the main lock and cross it to enter Frómista, where there is a fountain, all services and a *refugio* with room for 30 and a charge of 250 ptas. Several walkways are notable for the re-cycled 4th century Roman columns supporting them. A highlight of Frómista is **Iglesia San Martín**; a pure example of Romanesque architecture, famous for its interior capitals and 315 exterior stone-sculpted figures encircling the upper eaves.

Leave along the C980 (heading towards Carrión de los Condes). Once beyond over the overpass, turn right onto the Senda de Peregrinos (Pilgrims' Path) that runs parallel to the highway. In 3.5km reach Población de Campos, with a fountain, limited services

and a *refugio* with 10 places, a kitchen and a charge of 300 ptas.

From Población to Villalcázar there are two options: either follow (roughly) the Río Ucieza's course, or return to the Senda and head straight. The former is more scenic, tranquil and 1km longer. To take this option, continue straight for 200m and veer right onto the road to Villovieco (which has a fountain), continuing past the village and over a bridge. Take the first path to the right and follow the river bank to the next bridge. Either continue straight along the river using a narrow, unmarked fisherfolk path, or turn left to the village and the Senda de Peregrinos. Following the river for 20 minutes to a sealed road and turn left. Passing the large **Ermita Virgen del Río**, continue for 1.8km to Villalcázar de Sirga. It has all services, a fountain and a *refugio* with room for 15; a donation is requested. One of the few villages with a documented Templar presence, the central remnant of their powerful past is the magnificent 13th century **Iglesia Santa María la Blanca** (see the boxed text 'Templars' in the Day 21 section). The carved southern façade, the chapel of Santiago with the seated Virgen Blanca (south transept) and the altarpiece of Santiago (north transept) are especially rich.

Continue on the Senda de Peregrinos, now the only option, for 6km to Carrión (830m). The Romanesque façade of the **Iglesia Santiago** in the main square is exquisite.

HONTANAS TO TERRADILLOS DE LOS TEMPLARIOS

Places to Stay & Eat Here are all services and two refugios: the private *Monasterio de Santa Clara*, with room for 28 and a 1000 ptas charge, and the *parish refugio*, with room for 60 and a 300 ptas charge.

El Resbalón (☎ 979 88 04 33, Calle Fernán Gómez 19) has singles/doubles without bathroom for 1500/3000 ptas. *Hostal La Corte (☎ 979 88 01 38, Calle Santa María 34)* serves meals and has rooms for 2500/6000 ptas. On the same street, *Cervecería JM* serves great food.

Day 15: Carrión de los Condes to Terradillos de los Templarios
6½ to 7 hours, 25km
With barely a curve, this is a very long, flat stretch studded with oaks, once a Roman highway; the surrounding area is littered with ruins.

The way winds down to the Río Carrión and passes the **Monasterio de San Zoilo**. Continue straight through two consecutive crossroads (towards Villotilla). Four dreary kilometres of highway lead to and pass the Abadía Benevivere, founded in 1085 and now a farm. Continue across the bridge and go straight, ignoring the road's sharp right-hand curve, onto a flat stone and dirt path – the **Vía Trajana**, the Roman highway that connected Burgundy to Astorga. In 12km you reach Calzadilla de la Cueza, where there is a fountain, limited services and a *refugio* – 25 places and a kitchen; a donation is requested – along the shadeless, stony way.

The trail markers lead to the N120. Turn right along the rolling highway and continue for 6km to Ledigos which has a fountain and a private *refugio* with room for 25 and a charge of 1000 ptas. Ignore the trail markers entering the village and instead turn left turn onto a sealed road (towards Población de Arroyo). In 200m the path turns right onto an agricultural road. A large, circular palomar sits on the left. In 300m make a sharp left onto a path that in less than 2km leads to Terradillos de los Templarios (880m). The name suggests a Templar past, but no document exists to confirm this.

Places to Stay & Eat Besides the Iglesia San Pedro, there's a small *shop*, a fountain and a private *refugio (☎ 979 88 36 62)* with room for 20 and a 1000 ptas charge. The owner prepares 1000 ptas meals (breakfast costs 300 ptas).

Day 16: Terradillos de los Templarios to Burgo Ranero
7½ to 8 hours, 29km
Called *tierra de campos*, the rolling fields of Castilla y León have been both Spain's breadbasket and an important livestock migration centre. It's common to see at least one large flock during the meseta walks.

Take the dirt path out the village's west side to the sealed road. Turn left and after 250m veer right down a lane to Moratinos (which has a fountain); 2.5km later San Nicolás del Real Camino appears. Cross the quiet village to a small poplar grove and continue west on the dirt path. Sahagún de Campos lies 7km away. At the first junction, continue straight on the dirt track; at the second, veer right. As you gently ascend to a barren plateau, Sahagún appears ahead. Descend to an unmarked T-junction and turn right to the N120. Further on, turn left and cross over the highway to the lane leading to the Ermita Virgen del Puente, which is visible amid poplars. Continue under an overpass and enter **Sahagún**.

Here there are all services including a unique municipal *refugio* (with 64 places, a kitchen and a 500 ptas charge) in the restored Trinidad church. Sahagún's monuments are excellent examples of Mudéjar architecture – medieval Christian art with a notable Islamic influence (eg brick and geometric designs). Among the celebrated examples are La Peregrina, San Tirso and San Lorenzo churches.

Leave Sahagún via the Calle Rey Don Antonio. With the Neoclassic Arco de San Benito on the right, cross the 11th century bridge over the Río Cea. Apparently, the Field of the Lances (on the right) was so dubbed for the 40,000 Christians who died fighting with Charlemagne while freeing the north from the Muslims. Continue to the N120 and then along it for 2km to a crossroads. Continue to a cross where the Senda de Peregrinos (lined with plane trees, benches and rest areas) begins again and heads due west for 32km to Mansilla de las Mulas (see Day 17).

To the right is Calzada del Coto and a rugged, poorly marked alternative route that reaches Mansilla after 35.5km. It uses the Vía Trajana, with only Calzadilla de los Hermanillos to break the monotony. Exceptionally hot in summer, during one 25km stretch the route lacks food, water or accommodation opportunities.

On the much more hospitable Senda de Peregrinos, you will reach Bercianos del Real Camino, which has a fountain, in 5.5km and Burgo Ranero (878m) 7km later. This area was once full of ponds, lagoons and – consequently – numerous frogs, giving the town its name ('*rana*' in Spanish means frog).

Places to Stay & Eat The simple village has a *refugio* with 30 places and a kitchen; a donation is requested. Both *Fonda Lozano* (☎ 987 33 00 60) and *Hostal El Peregrino* (☎ 987 33 00 69) have doubles for 3000 ptas and 3500 ptas. Meals are 1200 ptas and 1100 ptas, respectively. There is also a small *shop* in the village.

Day 17: Burgo Ranero to León
9 to 10 hours, 35.5km

This very long day through desolate countryside ends in León, a remarkable city of soaring stone.

Next to a pond at the west end of Burgo Ranero, the Senda de Peregrinos begins again. After 12.5km of solitary, uninterrupted, barren plains the way reaches sleepy Reliegos, with a fountain, limited services and a *refugio* with 30 places and a kitchen; a donation is requested. Leave Reliegos, passing the frontón to the Senda de Peregrinos, and 6km later you will enter **Mansilla de las Mulas** via the Puerta de Santiago gateway, passing a modern monument to the tired pilgrim. All services are available including a *refugio* with 26 places and kitchen; a donation is requested. The town's odd coat of arms depicts a *mano* (hand) over a *silla* (saddle). The name Mansilla, though,

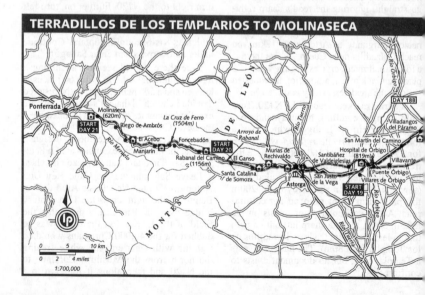

TERRADILLOS DE LOS TEMPLARIOS TO MOLINASECA

probably derives from its beginnings as a Roman *mansionella* (way station).

Leave town, crossing the bridge over the Río Esla and walk parallel to the highway on a dirt trail for 4km to Villamoros de Mansilla. Passing through, continue on the parallel highway trail, crossing a 20-arch bridge to Puente Villarente, where there is a fountain and all services. After the petrol station, the dirt trail disappears. Leave the highway and ascend to Arcabueja (with a fountain). Descend and turn left between industrial buildings to Valdelafuente (another fountain). Continue on the busy N120 for 5km to León (813m); visible from the day's high point is **Alto del Portillo** (890m). Follow the trail markers through the suburb of Puente Castro and continue over a footbridge to the Avenida del Alcalde. Veer right onto the footpaths of León; the way is marked with original bronze shells through the city.

Originally a Roman garrison town, León's most important inheritance are its fine Romanesque and Gothic monuments. The town's highlights include the **Real Basílica de San Isidoro**; the **Panteón Real**, nicknamed the

'Sistine Chapel of Spanish Romanesque' for its rare ceiling paintings; and the **Santa María de la Regla** cathedral, a Gothic masterpiece with more than 100 stained-glass windows. The tourist office is in the cathedral plaza. Leaving town, the shell-covered Monasterio and Hostal de San Marcos (a parador) abut the Río Bernesga, reminders of the Order of Santiago's 16th century presence.

Places to Stay & Eat There are two refugios: *Madres Carvajalas* on Plaza Santa María del Camino, which has room for 30, and the *Edificio Antiguos Huérfanos Ferroviarios* on Avenida del Parque, with room for 80. Each requests a donation.

Pensión Berta (☎ 987 25 70 39, *Plaza Mayor 8*) and *Hospedaje Suárez* (☎ 987 25 42 88, Calle Ancha 7) have singles/doubles without bathroom for 1800/3000 ptas and 1700/3000 ptas, respectively. You can eat well for around 1500 ptas at *La Ruta Jacobea*, El Cid 18, and *Restaurante Pozo*, Plaza San Marcelo 15.

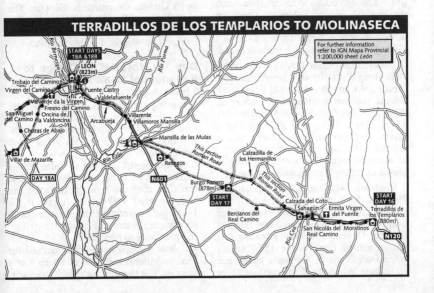

TERRADILLOS DE LOS TEMPLARIOS TO MOLINASECA

Day 18A: León to Hospital de Órbigo via Villar de Mazarife

8½ to 9½ hours, 34km

At Virgen del Camino two routes diverge, to rejoin at Hospital. Though longer, Day 18A retreats from the dangerous, dull highway and winds through Leonese villages and *páramo* – a pre-Roman term used to describe the barren, high plain.

From the Hostal de San Marcos cross the Río Bernesga to the N120, which runs between houses and high-rise buildings. When you reach a cross and small plaza, cross the train tracks via a pedestrian walkway and rejoin the N120. Veer left to avoid a dangerous curve before returning to and crossing the N120. Immediately take a paved road on the right that ascends between subterranean *bodegas*. These are excavated caves which maintain wine at optimal temperatures and humidity levels.

After the route flattens, continue for 2km on a wide dirt road to Virgen del Camino (where there is a fountain and all services) and its modern church (built in 1961). The façade contains 13 bronze statues (12 apostles – Santiago points to Compostela – and the Virgin Mary) by Subirachs. Cross the highway and descend: Day 18A (27km) turns left onto a dirt road and Day 18B (24km) continues straight on the sealed road.

Clearly marked, the Day 18A way undulates along dirt trails and minor roads past Fresno del Camino (which has a fountain), Oncina (another fountain) and Chozas de Abajo, and reaches Villar de Mazarife after 13km, where there is a fountain and a private *refugio* with 20 places and a kitchen; a donation is requested. Monseñor, an eccentric artisan who runs the refugio, makes exquisite Romanesque replicas.

Continue 14km more from Mazarife to Puente Órbigo, passing Villavante. From Puente, cross the impressive stone bridge over the dammed Río Órbigo into Hospital (819m). Dubbed the **Paso Honroso**, the bridge gained fame in the 15th century when Don Suero de Quiñones challenged all knights in honour of an unrequited love

and dispatched 300 in a jousting tournament. Hospital has all services.

Places to Stay & Eat There are two refugios: the municipal *refugio*, with 20 places and a kitchen, is to the right off the bridge; the parish *refugio*, with 30 places and a kitchen, is on the main street (on the right). Both charge 300 ptas.

Hostal Suero de Quiñones (☎ 987 38 82 38), by the bridge, charges 3500/6000 ptas for singles/doubles. Trout, the local speciality, is excellent at the *Mesón Piscifactoría* on La Vega. *Restaurante Avenida*, Fueros de León 31, has 900 ptas meals.

Day 18B: León to Hospital de Órbigo via Villadangos del Páramo

8 to 8½ hours, 31.5km

Follow Day 18A to Virgen. Roughly following the N120 west, this poorly trail-marked alternative route enters the villages of Valverde de la Virgen, San Miguel del Camino and, 14km beyond Virgen del Camino, Villadangos, which has a fountain, limited services and a *refugio* with 50 places and a kitchen; the charge is 300 ptas. The next 10km parallel the N120, passing San Martín del Camino and detouring to Puente Órbigo. Cross the bridge into Hospital.

Day 19: Hospital de Órbigo to Rabanal del Camino

9 hours, 34km

Ascending the foothills of León, the way passes through the Maragatería – a zone with distinct food, folklore and house construction. Astorga is rich in history and gastronomy.

On the edge of Hospital, two alternatives lead to Astorga: either turn right along rural roads or continue straight to reach the highway after 1.5km and follow it for 14km. Both cover the same distance but do not compare in terms of beauty, tranquillity and proximity to rural life.

Follow the first option and continue for 2km to Villares de Órbigo, which has a fountain. Cut through the village to a right-hand path that joins a paved road to Santibáñez de Valdeiglesias. Midway through the village, ascend right on a red dirt and stone lane that pleasantly wends its way through cultivated fields, bushes and oaks for nearly 8km to the **Crucero de Santo Toribio** (905m). Framed by mountains, Astorga spreads out below. Descend to and cross San Justo de la Vega, which has a fountain and limited services. After the bridge, take the first right-hand dirt road to reach Astorga in 4km.

Once a strategic Roman way station linking the ore-rich mountains with the southbound transport route (the Vía de la Plata), Astorga retains numerous Roman artefacts. Today, the town is known for its *mantecada*, a rich sweet eaten with coffee. It has all services including a *refugio* with room for 36 (charging 300 ptas). The spacious Gothic cathedral, Santa María, and Gaudí's early 20th century **Episcopal Palace** and museum are especially interesting.

Exit Astorga via Calle San Pedro and cross the NVI to the descending paved road (towards Castrillo de los Polvazares). After 4km reach Murias de Rechivaldo – with a fountain and *refugio* with room for 12; a donation is requested – a village typical of Maragateriá. Note the stone and wood construction and the buildings' distinctive door jambs. Leave Murias on a track that climbs to a junction. Fork right onto the paved road marked El Ganso and in 2km you will reach Santa Catalina de Somoza, where there is a *refugio* with room for 12; a donation is requested. On the way through the village pass the church and then continue along the Senda de Peregrinos to El Ganso. The last 6km to Rabanal (1156m) is a gentle climb and never veers from the highway.

Places to Stay & Eat At the foot of the village, fork left to the private refugio *Nuestra Señora del Pilar*, with 30 places and a kitchen; the charge is 400 ptas. Fork right to the *Refugio Gaucelmo*, constructed by the English and El Bierzo Camino associations, with 40 places and a kitchen; a donation is requested.

Also along the right fork, the first house on the left has a small market. Eat magnificently in *Mesón/Hostal el Refugio* (☎ 987 69 18 26), where singles/doubles/triples cost 4000/6000/7500 ptas and there is a 1200 ptas menú.

Day 20: Rabanal del Camino to Molinaseca

6 to 6½ hours, 24.5km

After reaching the Camino's high point (1517m), the way spectacularly descends through the first villages of El Bierzo which fills the great fertile valley below, rich in fruit groves and vineyards. Fountains en route are unreliable. Get water in Rabanal and El Acebo (17km).

Ascend the Calle Real, taking a footpath to the paved road, and continue for 5.5km to Foncebadón, a small village with a few seasonal residents. Fork left into the village. In the centre is a run-down church, now a cow stable. The 12th century hermit Gaucelmo ran a pilgrims' *hospital* here. Leave the village, veering left onto an ascending lane, lined with broom and shrubs, that soon reaches the paved road (turn left), the summit of Monte Irago (1504m) and the **Cruz de Ferro** (Iron Cross).

A highly emblematic monument of the Camino, the simple iron cross rises out of a long, wooden trunk planted in a *milladoiro* (huge mound of stones). The Romans called these cairns 'mountains of Mercury' in honour of the walker's deity. Many pilgrims add stones (like symbolic weights), continuing an age-old tradition.

The route runs parallel to the paved road for 2.4km to the largely abandoned, yet still inhabited village of Manjarín. A bell may be rung in greeting as you approach Tomás, a modern-day Knight Templar, who runs a very simple *refugio* with room for 20; he requests a donation.

Continue on the undulating highway to the crest of a hill with a military installation and fine views, before descending 11km to Molinaseca (620m). The way alternates between stretches of highway and dirt paths, passing two villages. El Acebo has a fountain, limited services and two *refugios*: the municipal, with room for 10 and which requests a donation, and the private, with room for 15 and which charges 500 ptas. Riego de Ambrós has limited services. In both villages, note the slate roofs and overhanging wooden balconies with external staircases: features typical of the area. Leaving El Acebo, an iron bicycle commemorates the death of a German pilgrim killed while cycling to Santiago de Compostela. From Riego the path zigzags downhill through groves of huge chestnut trees and aromatic rock rose.

Enter Molinaseca, a beautiful village on the banks of the Río Meruelo, by crossing the Romanesque bridge. The village has all services.

Places to Stay & Eat The municipal *refugio*, which has room for 30 and charges 300 ptas, is at the west end of town. *Hostal/Mesón El Palacio* (☎ 987 45 30 94), to the right of the bridge, has good meals and singles/doubles for 3500/4000 ptas. Doubles at *Casa San Nicolás* (☎ 929 80 40 61, Calle Iglesia 43) cost 6000 ptas. For food, also try *Mesón Real* at the end of the village.

Day 21: Molinaseca to Villafranca del Bierzo

7 to 8 hours, 30km

This relatively flat walk leads to historic Ponferrada and the gateway to Galicia.

Leave Molinaseca along the highway. After 2km of gentle ascent, Ponferrada comes into sight. Either take a left-hand dirt route on back roads, or continue along the highway directly to Ponferrada (1.5km shorter).

If you take the left option, weave for 1km between houses and grapevines to Campo. Cross to an old paved road, and continue to Escaril in 1.7km. From here, turn right onto the highway and cross Río Boeza. Once over the bridge, turn left and ascend through the streets of **Ponférrada** (Iron Bridge). You enter the town near the famed **Castillo de los Templarios**, constructed in the 12th century as one of the order's

Templars

Beginning in the 11th century as a consequence of the crusades, religio-military orders developed to combat the Muslims, recuperate and defend holy places and to protect pilgrims. Spain, thanks to the active Reconquista (Reconquest) and the Camino de Santiago, had its share of these orders. The most famous were the Knights of the Temple of Solomon (or Knights Templar) founded in Jerusalem in 1118. Despite its poor beginnings the order soon achieved great power, with numerous possessions; it became the most established bank of the period. Not surprisingly, the order attracted various enemies, among them Phillip IV of France. In 1307 he ordered the detention of the Knights Templar, torturing many and confiscating their wealth, basing his actions on ridiculous accusations including Devil worship. The order was finally suppressed in 1312.

strongholds. Circle up around the castle to reach the Plaza Virgen de la Encina. (At the time of writing there was a provisional *refugio* here with room for 80 – entry by donation – but the authorities intend to replace it with a permanent facility.)

Descend left along stairs to Ponférrada's main street. Turn left, crossing over the Río Sil, and then take the first right which ends at an avenue. Turn right and continue for 1km until the road peters out at a T-junction. Head right, passing mountains of coal, and take the first left-hand turn through Compostilla, passing in 7km Columbrianos, Fuentes Nuevas and Camponaraya, which has all services. At the end of the village leave the highway, turning left along a dirt road next to the Cooperativa de Viñas Bierzo. After the highway bridge, turn right onto another dirt road which weaves through vineyards. In 500m fork right onto a path that leads after 3km to **Cacabelos**, which has a services and a *refugio* with 60 places and a kitchen; it charges 300 ptas. Exit over the Río Cua and continue for 4km along the highway. Cross it to a marked dirt path. Fork left onto a dirt lane that leads, after a lovely 2km, to Villafranca (511m).

Here you will find the **Iglesia Santiago**. At the church's north door, **Puerta del Perdón**, 15th century pilgrims unable to continue received, by papal decree, the same privileges as if they had reached Compostela.

Places to Stay & Eat To the right of the village entrance is the municipal *refugio*, with room for 40 and charging 300 ptas. On the left, past the Iglesia Santiago, is the stone *refugio* of Jesús Jato, built by and for pilgrims; it has room for 40 and a donation is requested. Meals cost 600 ptas.

For other accommodation, try *Hostal Comercio* (☎ 987 54 00 08, Calle Puente Nuevo 2) with 2700 ptas doubles, or *Hostal Méndez* (☎ 987 54 24 08) with doubles for 4500 ptas. Both have 1200 ptas menús, as does *Mesón Don Nacho* on Calle Truqueles.

Day 22A: Villafranca del Bierzo to Cebreiro – Scenic Route

8 to 8½ hours, 29km

This is one of the most anticipated days of the Camino for its steep, 800m ascent to Cebreiro (1300m). Two alternative routes leave Villafranca and rejoin after 7km in Trabadelo. Day 22A is safer and more aesthetically pleasing.

Drop down into Villafranca and exit via the bridge over the Río Burbia. Turn right and ascend the hillside on an earth and stone road offering excellent views of Villafranca and the Valle del Valcarce. The well trail marked road climbs 3.5km through chestnuts and broom to the high point. Flattening, the way heads towards a hill topped with communication towers. Descend among chestnuts (Pradela comes into sight) and at the first fork, bear left. After 600m, fork left again and descend for 3km. You need to cross a sealed road several times until finally joining it near Trabadelo. In less than a kilometre the road meets the old

highway at the end of Trabadelo. Follow it for 2km to the NVI.

Turn right onto the NVI and in 1.5km enter Portela. Return to the NVI for 400m and turn left onto the old highway towards Ambasmestas. In the next 5km, you should enter and cross Ambasmestas, where there is a fountain; Vega de Valcarce, with a fountain and *refugio* with room for 28 and which requests a donation; and Ruitelán, with a fountain.

As you enter Herrerías (with another fountain) turn left after 100m, descending on a narrow, sealed road towards La Faba. At the end of Herrerías ascend 1km along the sealed road and then turn left onto a dirt lane that soon crosses the Río Valcarcel via a small stone bridge. The day's steepest ascent begins on a beautiful, Galician *corredoira* (wide, stone-cobbled lane). Cross La Faba, where there is a fountain, and return to the corredoira that soon disappears below a lane flanked by pastures and the high, rolling hills ahead. Ascend to Laguna de Castilla (with a fountain), the last village of León. At the edge of the village Galicia's first cement trail marker indicates that 153km remain to Santiago de Compostela. The countdown begins – every 500m there is another marker. Take the left-hand dirt trail and 1km later you will officially enter Galicia.

One kilometre away is Cebreiro. The hamlet retains several traditional dwellings (see the boxed text 'Galician Vernacular Architecture' in the Galicia chapter), one an ethnographic museum. The famous 14th century Miracle of Cebreiro occurred during a mass when the wine and host literally turned into the blood and flesh of Christ, renewing the priest's faith.

Places to Stay & Eat The village's *refugio* has 90 beds and a kitchen; a donation is requested.

Hospedería San Giraldo (☎ 982 36 71 25) and *Habitaciones Frade* (☎ 982 37 71 04) both have comfortable singles/doubles for 4000/5000 ptas. Meals at the former (1000 ptas menú) are excellent.

Day 22B: Villafranca del Bierzo to Cebreiro – Highway Route

7½ to 8 hours, 28km

Follow Day 22A over the bridge. Continue straight along the old highway (the river on your left) to the dangerous NVI. Turn right onto it and continue for 7km, entering Pereje, which has a fountain and a private *refugio* with 30 places and a kitchen; the charge is 800 ptas. Continue through Trabadelo (which has a fountain) to rejoin the Day 22A route.

Days 23A & 24A: Cebreiro to Samos & Samos to Portomarín via Aguiada

2 days, 64.5km

In Galicia, green and grey tones predominate, rain is a constant possibility and the Galician language, *gallego*, is commonly spoken. Passing countless hamlets connected by corredoiras, the recommended route winds through a spectacular region of Lugo and La Coruña provinces with numerous small parish churches, *hórreos* (granaries), stone mills and crosses marking crossroads. These usually depict Christ on one side and the Virgin on the other.

The alternative route – Days 23B & 24B, described later – diverges in Triacastela (21km from Cebreiro) and rejoins the recommended route in Aguiada. The shorter Day 23A leads to one of Spain's oldest Benedictine monasteries, while Day 23B passes seven hamlets on the stroll to Calvor.

For Day 23A (7½ to eight hours, 30.5km), leave Cebreiro on the main road (towards Triacastela), passing Liñares (founded as a linen plantation) after 3km and ascending to the Alto de San Roque. Turn right onto a path that descends 2.5km to Hospital da Condesa, which has a fountain and a *refugio* with 20 places and a kitchen; a donation is requested. Cross the hamlet and rejoin the highway. Turn right onto the road and follow it for 150m and then left onto a path that ascends to Padornelo. Climb steeply to **Alto do Poio** (1313m). Two *bar-restaurantes* mark the summit – the Camino's last high point has a large pilgrim statue. Leave along the highway, soon abandoning it for a lane that reaches Fonfría in 3.5km.

The next 9km to Triacastela are marked by brief stretches on lanes and the highway, passing Viduedo and climbing Monte Caldeirón, descending to Filloval through forests of chestnut and oak on a corredoira to Pasantes and Ramil, before finally reaching **Triacastela**, where there are all services. Immediately on the left is the *refugio* with room for 56; a donation is requested. Straight ahead is the village. No remnant of the three castles, for which the village is named, exists.

Exit Triacastela, travelling left along the highway, and remain parallel to the Río Oribio for 3km. Leave the highway and enter (on the right) San Cristobo do Real, passing its cemetery as you leave. Continue

MOLINASECA TO PALAS DO REI

on a lane flanked with chestnuts and oaks. Cross the Oribio and, on a sealed road, climb to Rente and then descend to Freituge. After the hamlet turn left, drop down to the river, and then climb to a highway tunnel. Veer left onto a dirt road that descends to Samos (510m).

This is the suggested end of Day 23A. Founded in the 6th century (the date is confirmed by a Visigothic tablet), the Samos **monastery** retains a 9th to 10th century chapel and, most notably, a wealth of Renaissance and Baroque art. The village has all services and several recommended places to stay. The monastic *refugio* has 26 beds and requests a donation. *Hostal Victoria (☎ 982 54 70 22, Calle Salvador 4)* and *Hotel A Veiga (☎ 982 54 60 52)* have doubles which cost 4000 ptas and 5000 ptas, respectively. Both serve good meals.

Day 24A (8½ to nine hours, 34km) is rejoined by the Day 24B trail in Aguiada, a hamlet 4km from Sarria. From here the two routes share the same tranquil, hamlet-laden (23 of them) trail to Portomarín.

The 8km walk to Aguiada begins on the highway (towards Sarria) and soon passes Foxos and Teiguín, which has a fountain. Follow the trail markers right to a steep, sealed road. In Pascais, turn left onto a dirt lane passing an oak grove and cultivated fields to **Aguiada**.

From Aguiada take the wide, paved road for 4km to Sarria, which has all services, passing various hamlets. Follow the trail

markers over the river to the Rúa do Peregrino; make a quick left, ascending a penitential flight of steps (Escalinata Maior) to Rúa Maior and a *refugio* at No 79 with 40 places and a kitchen; a donation is requested. Continue straight past the Santa Marina (on the right) and Salvador (on the left) churches to a fountain. Turn right onto the Avenida de la Feria, ascending to the Magdalena monastery (on the right).

Turn left down a road past the cemetery to a highway, crossing it and a medieval bridge. The path runs parallel to the train tracks, crosses them and ascends to Vilei and **Barbadelo**, 3.5km from Sarria. Its church is a fine example of rural Galician Romanesque architecture, and the hamlet has a *refugio* with 20 places and a kitchen; a donation is requested.

The Camino winds and bends along dirt, stone and sealed lanes through numerous trail-marked crossroads and hamlets. You pass through Rente, Peruscallo, Lavandeira, Brea (100km to go!), Morgade (which has a fountain), Ferreiros (where there is a *refugio* with 20 places and a kitchen; a donation is requested), Mirallos, Pena (with a fountain), Rozas, Pena dos Corvos (spectacular views and the first appearance of Galician pines), Moimentos, Mercadoiro, Parrocha and Vilachá. Finally, the route descends steeply to Portomarín.

Cross the bridge over the Río Miño. Old Portomarín, submerged below, was sacrificed in 1956 to construct a dam. Climb the

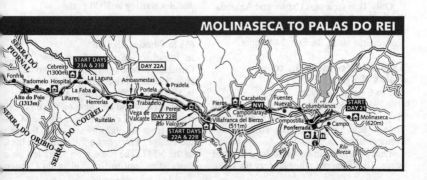

MOLINASECA TO PALAS DO REI

long stairs (topped by an image of the Virgin from the now-drowned old church) and head right up to the main plaza (350m). Parts of the village were moved stone by stone before the inundation, including the fortress-like church of San Nicolás in the main plaza. The village offers all services.

Places to Stay & Eat The *refugio* has 100 places and a kitchen; a donation is requested. For excellent meals and lodging try *Restaurante Pérez* (✆ *982 54 50 40, Plaza Aviación Española 2)*, where doubles begin at 2700 ptas. *Hostal O Mesón de Rodríguez* (✆ *982 54 50 54, Fraga Iribarne 6)* has doubles for 4300 ptas.

Days 23B & 24B: Cebreiro to Calvor via San Xil & Calvor to Portomarín via Aguiada
2 days, 62km

To begin Day 23B (8½ to nine hours, 33.5km) – the alternative route – follow Day 23A to Triacastela. Turn right at the village's west end and ascend the stream along a centuries-old path to Balsa. The way ascends to the road near a modern pilgrims' fountain and continues to San Xil, reaching the Alto do Riocabo (896m). From here, head right down a corredoira that leads to Montán, Fontearcuda and Furela. Continue on the sealed road to Calvor.

Calvor, at the end of Day 23B, has a *refugio* with 20 places and a kitchen; a donation is requested. There are no nearby services.

Only 1km separates Calvor and Aguiada. Begin Day 24B (7 to 7½ hours, 28.5km) by traversing this distance, then continue to Portomarín along the Day 24A route.

Day 25: Portomarín to Palas do Rei
5½ to 6 hours, 24.5km

The Palas do Rei township at the end of this day contains 20 Romanesque churches, though few vestiges of the village's antiquity remain.

Leave Portomarín down the long flight of steps. Turn right onto the highway for 100m

and then left onto a footpath and small bridge that crosses an arm of the reservoir. Ascend right on a dirt lane for 2km to reach the highway at a brick factory. Cross to the Senda de Peregrinos, continuing for 2km to Toixibó and 3km further to Gonzar, which has a *refugio* with 20 places and a kitchen; a donation is requested.

Past the refugio, the way turns left to Castromaior where the first eucalyptus trees appear. Continue on the sealed road to the highway, walking parallel to it before descending left in 2km to Hospital da Cruz which has a *bar* and a *refugio* with 20 places and a kitchen; a donation is requested.

Leave Hospital da Cruz and cross the highway to take a left-hand ascending sealed road that over the next 10km passes Ventas de Narón and the gentle Sierra de Ligonde (717m), then heads downhill to Lameiro, Ligonde, Airexe – which has a fountain and a *refugio* with 20 places and a kitchen; a donation is requested – Portos, Lestedo, Valos and, finally, Brea. Continue to the highway and take a parallel dirt lane to Rosario. Turn left onto a road beyond that leads downhill for 500m to Palas do Rei.

Places to Stay & Eat The small town of Palas do Rei offers all services and has a *refugio* in front of the town hall with 66 places and a kitchen; a donation is requested.

For meals, try *Casa Curro* at Avenida Orense 15, or *Guntina* (✆ *982 38 00 80, Travesía del Peregrino 8)*, which also has doubles starting at 3000 ptas.

Day 26: Palas do Rei to Ribadiso
6½ to 7 hours, 25.5km

In Ribadiso, en route from Lugo to La Coruña, there's no restaurant, hostel or shop, but all services are available en route in Melide or 1.5km further in Arzúa.

Descend to and continue on the highway past the limits of Palas. Before entering Carballal, cross the highway and climb through the village (which has a fountain) and back to the N547. The route soon veers left on a descending trail to San Xulián do Camiño (with a fountain), 3.5km from Palas. Cross a river and wind through an oak grove to Casanova, where there is a *refugio* with 20 places and a kitchen; a donation is requested. In 2.5km the way reaches the Lugo and La Coruña border. Turn left at the next crossroads along a dirt path to Leboreiro, with a fountain; its Romanesque church has a simple image of the Virgin carved in the tympanum. Leave the village over its curious bridge to a path bordered by poplars. Descend to Furelos, with a fountain. Cross the four-arched medieval bridge and continue for 1km to **Melide**, which has all services and a *refugio* with 130 places and kitchen; a donation is requested.

Cross the town via the Calle Principal to its main plaza. On fair days streetside *pulperías* (octopus boiled in copper pots and served *a la feria* on wooden plates with olive oil, red pepper and marine salt) provide a tempting excuse for a break. The free ethnographic museum packs in innumerable tidbits of Galicia 'as it was' on its two floors.

Follow the trail markers out of Melide past the cemetery and along a walled path to the highway. Cross the N547 and take the sealed road (towards San Martiño) for 100m before turning right. Over the next 5.5km you pass Carballal, Parabispo and A Peroxa. In Boente (which has limited services and a fountain), cross to the church and turn left through the village. The way undulates to Castañeda, location of the

12th century lime ovens used to construct Santiago de Compostela's cathedral. Pilgrims once carried stones from Triacastela to these ovens. On the road, the trail markers turn left to Río. The way climbs a hill, crosses the highway via an elevated bridge and then descends steeply to riverside Ribadiso (320m).

Places to Stay & Eat Cross the medieval bridge; the *refugio* has 60 places and a kitchen; a donation is requested. Originally a 15th century pilgrims' *hospital*, it is now housed in the restored complex to the right. The closest alternative accommodation is 1.5km uphill in the main street of Arzúa at *O Retiro* (☎ 981 50 05 54), with singles/doubles for 3000/5000 ptas and a 1000 ptas menú. (For directions, see Day 27.)

Day 27: Ribadiso to Arca
5½ to 6 hours, 22km

From Ribadiso, ascend to the highway, staying parallel to it briefly before crossing over and veering left onto a path that reaches the centre of Arzúa in 2.5km. Arzúa has all services and is justly famous for its *mel* (Galician for honey) and creamy *queixo de tetilla*, a breast-shaped cheese (where '*queixo*' is Galician for cheese). Leave Arzúa via the stone-paved Rúa do Carme, passing the Fuente de los Franceses, and ascend through an oak forest past the Pazo As Barrosas (a country mansion). The dirt and stone lane reaches a stream,

PALAS DO REI TO SANTIAGO DE COMPOSTELA

which runs parallel to the path, and climbs to Pregontoño. The path forks right out of the hamlet, up through a tunnel and past three houses.

In A Peroxa fork left onto the dirt road flanked by oak and fruit trees and over the next 6km wind through the sleepy hamlets of Tabernavella, Calzada, Calle (which has a fountain), Boavista and, finally, Salceda (with another fountain), where the path and highway meet. Just before Salceda, under a large chestnut tree sits a rectangular stone mortar once used to crush apples for the fermented beverage, *sidra*.

In Salceda continue on the N547, passing Alimentación Salceda (a small *shop-bar*), and turn right onto a forest track. After a 200m climb, a pair of bronzed shoes unexpectedly commemorate the spot where a 63-year-old German pilgrim took his last steps in 1993. After Xen, Ras and Brea the path joins the highway at Rabiña and runs parallel to it to two roadside *restaurants*. Turn sharp right onto a dirt track that soon passes the *refugio* (with 36 places and a kitchen; a donation is requested) of Santa Irene and continues downhill for 400m to a right-hand fork. Cross the highway to Rúa and continue downhill for 2km on a paved road to Arca. Before descending, a right turn leads to the highway and the *Hostal O Pino* (☎ 981 51 10 35) where singles/doubles with bathroom cost 4000/6000 ptas and meals cost 1000 ptas or 1300 ptas.

Places to Stay & Eat Turn left onto the highway and on the left after 100m is the *refugio*, which has 80 places and a kitchen; a donation is requested. The village has all services, and meals are available in *Bar-Restaurante Regueiro* on the highway.

Day 28: Arca to Santiago de Compostela

5 hours, 17.5km

This is the last day of the journey, culminating at the cathedral in Santiago de Compostela.

Follow the N547 to Arca's tiny main plaza and turn right at the Casa do Concello.

Follow this road past the school and turn left into the eucalyptus forest. Continue for 2km to Amenal and cross the main road, entering a natural tunnel of rich vegetation and dirt walls. This is the day's longest ascent. The dirt way winds round Santiago de Compostela's international airport to the main road and heads right down to San Paio, known for the saint born in Pontevedra, martyred in Córdoba and popular throughout Galicia. Depart to the left and climb to a dirt road and eucaplypt forest, reaching the first houses of Lavacolla. The fame of **Lavacolla** is etymological – its name aptly describes medieval pilgrims' pre-arrival ablutions (washing one's loins).

After crossing the nondescript river, the last 9km of road to Santiago de Compostela are sealed, passing Vilamaior, the large Spanish and Galician television stations and San Marcos. From here medieval pilgrims sprinted to the nearby summit of **Monte do Gozo** (Mount Joy), dubbing the first to arrive 'king'. The cathedral's three spires are now in sight (barely) for the first time. The summit's modest San Marcos chapel is overshadowed by the postmodern monument to the pilgrim and the 800 bed *refugio*, camp, amphitheatre and *bar-restaurante* below.

Four kilometres of city streets separate you from the cathedral. Descend over the highway bridge and round the left side of the roundabout. The next stage passes some interesting historical monuments. In San Lázaro, a 12th century leper's hospital borders the road; further along, the medieval centre of silver and brass artisans operated out of Rúa dos Concheiros (turn left); and finally, Rúa San Pedro leads to Porta do Camiño, one of the seven original entrances to the walled medieval city (the walls no longer exist). Granite flagstones lead up to the Praza de Cervantes and descend through the Azabacheriá – the zone of the jet (black mineral used for jewellery) artisans – then passes the cathedral's north entrance and descends a flight of stairs to the grand Praza do Obradoiro. Upon arrival, pilgrims usually mark the end with several rites: adding their hand imprint to the marble stone column at the cathedral's east end, hugging the large, baroque statue of Santiago and visiting the crypt containing his remains at the main altar. In Holy Years (see History in the introduction to this chapter) the great *botafumeiro* (incense burner) is swung every day at the Pilgrim's Mass (at noon) and is truly a sight to behold (especially from the north or south transept). Don't forget to request the Compostela in the Pilgrims' Office, Rúa do Vilar 1. The tourist office is at Rúa do Vilar 43.

Places to Stay & Eat The *Seminario Menor de Belvís* allows pilgrims to stay three nights for 400 ptas per night. *Hostal-Residencia Suso* (☎ 981 58 11 59, *Rúa do Vilar 65*) offers a hearty welcome and singles/doubles at 1800/4500 ptas. *Hospedaje La Tita* (☎ 981 58 39 8 1, *Rúa Nova 46*) has rooms without a bathroom for 2000/4500 ptas.

Options for excellent dining are almost unlimited near the cathedral along the Rúa do Franco and Rúa da Raíña. Take your pick. The cheapest and most filling meal (700 ptas) is available from a pilgrims' hotspot – *Casa Manolo* at Calle San Agustín 1. Other good places are *Restaurante San Clemente* at San Clemente 6, and *Restaurante Entre Rúas* on Calle Entrerúas (literally 'between streets').

Other Pilgrim Routes

These are some of the other popular routes followed today (though keep in mind that 95% of pilgrims walk the Camino Francés). For guides to these routes see Books under Information at the start of this chapter.

Camino Aragonés

Using the higher Somport Pass, walk 146km through Aragón, joining the Camino Francés at Puente la Reina (Day 4). The quiet, more rugged route reveals the Pyrenees as peaks rather than lumps and descends gently through fertile valleys rich in monuments. The distance, trail-marked intermittently, can be covered in five or six days – Somport/Candanchú to Jaca, 29.5/19.5km; Jaca to Puente la Reina de Jaca via San Juan de la Peña, 19.5km; Puente la Reina de Jaca to Ruesta (which entails camping), 26km; Ruesta to Sanguesa, 21km; Sanguesa to Monreal, 26.3km; and Monreal to Puente la Reina, 23.5km.

To reach Somport, take a bus to Jaca and Candanchú and hitch or walk from there. Canfranc, Jaca, Undués, Sanguesa and Monreal have refugios.

Caminos del Norte

Some pilgrims crossed the France-Spain border to Hendaya and Irún, reaching the País Vasco and taking either the coastal route via San Sebastián and Bilbao to Santander or heading inland via San Adrián's tunnel (1443m) to La Rioja and the Camino Francés. Those sailing from the north landed (eg in Santander or Gijón) and continued along the coast to Galicia or south to Fonsagrada and León via Oviedo, connecting with the Camino Francés.

Today, these routes are poorly marked, have few refugios and often coincide with the highway. For information on the País Vasco routes, contact Los Amigos del Camino de Guipúzcoa (☎ 94 34 21 396), Calle Doctor Camino 5-6, 20004 San Sebastián. In Asturias, try the Asociación Astur-Galaica (☎ 982 13 51 27), Santiago de Abres, 33379 Vegadeo.

Vía/Ruta de la Plata

From Sevilla, the Vía de la Plata (Silver Way) runs 690km north to meet the Camino Francés at Astorga via Zafra, Mérida, Cáceres, Salamanca and Zamora. Partly trail-marked with yellow arrows, the route's infrastructure gradually improves as you continue. It passes through large cities and lengthy, desolate stretches where water and people are scarce. Be prepared to carry supplies. One warning: the summer (July and August) heat in Extremadura is unbearable, often more than 40°C. The best months are April, May, mid-September and October. Michelin 1:400,000 maps *Southern Spain* No 446, *Central Spain* No 444 and *Galicia/Asturias-León* No 441 are adequate for orientation on this easy-to-follow route.

Fisterra

The 75km rural walk from Santiago de Compostela to the sea is feasible in three days.

While lodging is available in Negreira, Cée, Corcubión and Fisterra (Finisterre), about 50km separates the first two towns. Options include camping, sleeping in a cemetery (Santa Mariña) or in an old house in Olveiroa. Good

Spanish is helpful (though most villagers speak Galician). The Santiago de Compostela regional tourist office has additional information. Buses return daily from Fisterra to Santiago de Compostela.

Language

Spain has one official national language, Spanish, and three official regional languages, Basque, Catalan and Galician.

As the country's national language, Spanish (often referred to as *castellano*, or Castilian) is understood by everyone and spoken fluently by nearly all. In global terms it's the most widely spoken of the Romance languages – the group of languages derived from Latin which includes French, Italian and Portuguese.

Like Castilian, Catalan (*català*) is a Romance language; including the dialects spoken in the Islas Baleares (Balearic Islands), Andorra and much of the Valencia region (where it's usually referred to as *valenciano*), Catalan is the most widely spoken of Spain's three regional languages. It has a rich literary history and culture; you'll even find a substantial volume of writing about trekking and mountaineering, many titles unavailable in any other language. Signs in Catalunya are frequently only in Catalan – fortunately, the written forms of Catalan and Spanish are effectively very similar.

Galician (*galego*) is also a Romance language. It is very similar to Portuguese – in fact, up until the 13th century they were pretty much identical. The debate over the status of Galician as a dialect of Portuguese or a separate language still rages today.

Basque (*euskara*) has long been a conundrum for linguists. Bearing no relation to any neighbouring – or, indeed, any other – language, its origins remain obscure. It's spoken by a minority in the País Vasco (called *Euskadi* in Basque) and in Navarra.

Wherever these regional languages are spoken, people will generally be happy to converse with you in Spanish. Away from the main tourist areas and big cities, English isn't as widely spoken as many visitors seem to expect. It's therefore a good idea to try to gain some knowledge of simple conversational Spanish before you travel. It isn't difficult to pick up, particularly if you have even the most basic grounding in either French, Italian or Portuguese. Being able to communicate at any level with the people you meet will prove both useful and rewarding – even when they reply in English, they'll have appreciated the effort you made.

Take a reference book with you. Lonely Planet's pocket-sized *Spanish phrasebook* is a goldmine of information and practical phrases for coping with everyday situations; it has a two-way dictionary (not to mention special sections to cover Basque, Catalan and Galician).

If you need to ask for something in English in an out of the way place, your best bet is often to approach someone under 30 – anyone who's been through the education system since about 1985 will have studied four to five years of English.

Pronunciation

Spanish pronunciation isn't too difficult; apart from a few throat-rasping exceptions, many Spanish sounds resemble their English counterparts. There's also a very clear and consistent relationship between pronunciation and spelling; if you can read it, you can say it. Stick to the following rules and you'll have few problems making yourself understood.

Vowels

Unlike English, each of the vowels in Spanish has a uniform pronunciation, which doesn't vary. For example, the letter 'a' has one pronunciation rather than the numerous variations we find in English, such as in 'cake', 'care', 'cat', 'cart' and 'call'. Many words have a written acute accent. This accent (as in *días*) indicates a stressed syllable – it does not change the sound of the vowel. Vowels are pronounced clearly even if they are in unstressed positions or at the end of a word.

a	somewhere between the 'a' in 'cat' and the 'a' in 'cart'
e	as in 'met'
i	somewhere between the 'i' in 'marine' and the 'i' in 'flip'
o	similar to the 'o' in 'hot'
u	between the 'u' in 'put' and the 'oo' in 'loose'

Consonants

Some Spanish consonants are the same as their English counterparts. The pronunciation of others varies according to which vowel follows. The Spanish alphabet also contains the letter ñ, which isn't found in the English alphabet. Note that until recently, the clusters ch and ll were also officially separate consonants, and you're likely to encounter many situations – eg in lists and dictionaries – in which they're still treated that way.

b	soft, as the 'v' in 'van'; also (less commonly) as in 'book' when word-initial or preceded by a nasal such as m or n
c	as in 'cat' when followed by a, o, u or a consonant; before e or i as the 'th' in 'thin'
ch	as in 'choose'
d	as in 'dog' when word-initial; elsewhere as the 'th' in 'thin'
g	as in 'go' when followed by a, o, u or a consonant; before e or i, a harsh, breathy sound, like j
h	always silent, as in 'honest'
j	a harsh, guttural sound similar to the 'ch' in Scottish loch or a discreet clearing of the throat
ll	similar to the 'y' in 'yellow'
ñ	a nasal sound like the 'ni' in 'onion' or the 'ny' in 'canyon'
qu	always followed by a silent 'u' and either 'e' (as in que) or 'i' as in aquí); the combined sound of 'qu' is as the 'k' in 'kick'
r	a rolled or trilled sound; longer and stronger when initial or doubled
s	as in 'send', never as in 'fusion', 'mission' or 'miser'

v	pronounced the same as b
x	as the 'x' in 'taxi' when between two vowels; as the 's' in 'so' when it precedes a consonant
z	as the 'th' in 'thin'
y	on its own (when it means 'and') it's pronounced as 'i'; elsewhere its sound is somewhere between the 'y' in 'yonder' and the 'g' in 'beige', depending on the region – pronounce it as 'y' and you'll be understood everywhere

Greetings & Civilities

Good morning.	Buenos días.
Good afternoon.	Buenas tardes.
Hello.	Hola.
Goodbye.	Adios.
See you later.	Hasta luego.
Yes.	Sí.
No.	No.
Please.	Por favor.
Thank you.	Gracias.
That's OK/ You're welcome.	De nada.
Excuse me.	Perdón/Perdona.
I'm sorry. (forgive me)	Lo siento/Discúlpeme.
What's your name?	¿Cómo te llamas/Cómo se llama usted? (informal/polite)
My name is ...	Me llamo ...
What's the time?	¿Qué hora es?
Please wait for me here.	Espérame aquí, por favor.

Language Difficulties

Do you speak English?	¿Habla inglés?
I understand.	Entiendo.
I don't understand.	No entiendo.
Please speak more slowly.	Por favor, habla más despacio.
Could you write it down, please?	¿Puede escribirlo, por favor?
How do you say ...?	¿Cómo se dice ...?
What does ... mean?	¿Qué significa ...?

Getting Around

When does the ... leave/arrive?	¿Cuándo sale/llega el ...?
boat	barco
bus/intercity bus	autobus/autocar
train	tren
next	próximo
first	primer
last	último
timetable	horario
I'd like to hire a ...	Quisiera alquilar ...
car	un coche
motorcycle	una bicicleta
taxi	un taxi
Can you take me to ...?	¿Puedes llevarme a ...?
I'd like get off at the turn-off.	Quisiera bajar en la bifurcación.

Directions

ahead/behind	mas adelante/detrás
below/above	debajo/encima de
before/after	antes/después (de)
up/down	arriba/abajo
flat/steep	llano/empinado
ascent/descent	subida/bajada
near/far	cerca/lejos
on the other side of	al otro lado de
towards/away from	hacia/desde
north/south	norte/sur
east/west	este/oueste

Around Town

I'm looking for ...	Estoy buscando ...
a bank	un banco
a chemist/ pharmacy	una farmacia
the ... embassy	la embajada ...
the market	el mercado
the police	la policía
the post office	los correos
a telephone	un teléfono
the tourist office	la oficina de turismo
Go straight ahead.	Siga todo derecho.
Turn left.	Gire a la izquierda.
Turn right.	Gire a la derecha.

Signs

INFORMACIÓN	INFORMATION
ABIERTO	OPEN
CERRADO	CLOSED
HABITACIONES LIBRES	ROOMS AVAILABLE
COMPLETO	NO VACANCIES
COMISARÍA	POLICE STATION
SERVICIOS/ASEOS	TOILETS
HOMBRES	MEN
MUJERES	WOMEN

What time does it open/close?	¿A qué hora abren/cierran?

Accommodation

I'm looking for (a) ...	Busco ...
hotel	un hotel
guesthouse	una pensión/ casa de huéspedes
youth hostel	un albergue juvenil
How much is it ...?	¿Cuánto cuesta ...?
per night	por noche
per person	por persona
per tent	por tienda

Shopping

Where can I buy ...?	¿Dónde puedo comprar ...?
I'd like to buy ...	Quisiera comprar ...
I'm just looking.	Sólo estoy mirando.
How much is it?	¿Cuánto cuesta/ Cuánto vale?

Time, Days & Numbers

What time is it?	¿Qué hora es?
today	hoy
tomorrow	mañana
in the morning	de la mañana
in the afternoon	de la tarde
Monday	lunes
Tuesday	martes
Wednesday	miércoles
Thursday	jueves
Friday	viernes
Saturday	sábado
Sunday	domingo

0	cero	17	diecisiete
1	uno, una	18	dieciocho
2	dos	19	diecinueve
3	tres	20	veinte
4	cuatro	21	veintiuno
5	cinco	22	veintidós
6	seis	30	treinta
7	siete	31	treinta y uno
8	ocho	40	cuarenta
9	nueve	50	cincuenta
10	diez	60	sesenta
11	once	70	setenta
12	doce	80	ochenta
13	trece	90	noventa
14	catorce	100	cien/ciento
15	quince	200	doscientos
16	dieciséis	1000	mil

one million	un millón

Health

I'm ill.	Estoy enfermo/a. (m/f)
I need a doctor (who speaks English).	Necesito un doctor/ una doctora (que hable inglés).

I'm ...	Soy ...
diabetic	diabético/a
epileptic	epiléptico/a
asthmatic	asmático/a

I'm allergic to ...	Soy alérgico/a a ...
antibiotics	los antibióticos
penicillin	la penicilina

antiseptic	antiséptico
aspirin	aspirina
condoms	preservativos/condones
contraceptive	anticonceptivo

Emergencies

Help!	¡Socorro!/¡Auxilio!
Call a doctor!	¡Llame a un doctor!
Call the police!	¡Llame a la policía!
There's been an accident.	Ha habido un accidente.
Go away!	¡Váyase!
Where is the toilet?	¿Dónde está el excusado?

diarrhoea	diarrea
medicine	medicamento
nausea	náusea
tampons	tampones

WALKING
Preparations

Where can we buy supplies?	
¿Dónde podemos comprar comida?	

Can I leave some things here?
   ¿Puedo dejar algunas cosas aquí?
I'd like to talk to someone who knows this area.
   Quisiera hablar con álguien que conozca esta zona.
Where can we hire a guide?
   ¿Dónde podemos alquilar un/una guía?
We are thinking of taking this route.
   Pensamos tomar esta ruta.
Is the walk very difficult?
   ¿Es muy difícil el recorrido?
Is the track (well) marked?
   ¿Está (bien) señalizado el sendero?
Which is the shortest/easiest route?
   ¿Cuál es la ruta más corta/más fácil?
Is there much snow on the pass?
   ¿Hay mucha nieve en el collado?
We'll return in one week.
   Volverémos en una semana.

Clothing & Equipment

altimeter	altímetro
rainjacket	anorak/chubasquero
backpack	mochila
batteries	pilas
cooking pot	cazo
bootlace	cordón de bota
boots	botas
camp stove	hornillo
candle	vela
canteen/ water bottle	cantimplora
compass	brújula
crampons	crampones
gaiters	polainas
gas cartridge	cartucho de gas
ice axe	piolet
kerosene	keroseno
methylated spirits	alcohol de quemar
pocketknife	navaja

provisions (food)	*comida*
rope	*cuerda*
runners/trainers	*zapatillas*
sleeping bag	*saco de dormir*
sleeping mat	*colchoneta aislante*
sunblock	*crema solar*
sunglasses	*gafas de sol*
tent	*tienda*
torch/flashlight	*linterna*
walking poles	*palos telescópicos*

On the Walk

How many kilometres to ...?
  ¿Cuántos kilómetros hay hasta ...?
How many hours' walking?
  ¿Cuántas horas hay caminando?/
  Hace cuántas horas de marcha?
Does this track go to ...?
  ¿Va este sendero a ...?
How do you reach the summit?
  ¿Cómo se llega a la cumbre?
Where are you going to?
  ¿A dónde vas?
Can you show me on the map where we are?
  ¿Puedes señalarme en el mapa dónde
  estamos?
What is this place called?
  ¿Cómo se llama este lugar?
We're doing a walk from ... to ...
  Estamos haciendo una excursión
  desde ... a ...

bridge/footbridge	*puente/pasarela*
circuit	*circuito*
fence	*cerco/alambrado*
firebreak	*cortefuego*
refuge/mountain shelter	*refugio*
path/trail	*sendero/senda*
route	*ruta*
short cut	*atajo*
ski field	*pista de esquí*
village	*pueblo/aldea*
to carry	*llevar*
climb/to climb	*escalada/escalar*
to fish	*pescar*
to follow	*seguir*
a walk	*una excursión*
signpost	*cartel indicador*
traverse	*traversía*

Walking Signs

CAMINO PARTICULAR
  PRIVATE ROAD
CAMPING
  CAMPING GROUND
CAMPO DE TIRO
  SHOOTING RANGE
COTO PRIVADO DE CASA
  PRIVATE HUNTING AREA
CUIDADO/OJO CON EL PERRO
  BEWARE OF THE DOG
FINCA PARTICULAR
  PRIVATE FARM
PROIBIDO EL PASO
  NO ENTRY
PROPRIEDAD PRIVADA
  PRIVATE PROPERTY
TORO SUELTO
  LOOSE BULL

mountain guide	*guía de montana*
mountaineer	*montañero*
park ranger/ refugio warden	*guarda*

Map Reading

altitude difference	*desnivel*
contour lines	*curvas de nivel*
map	*mapa*
metres above sea level	*metros sobre el nivel del mar*
spot height	*cota*

Weather

What will the weather be like?
  ¿Qué tiempo hará?
Tomorrow it'll be cold.
  Mañana hará frío.
It's going to rain.
  Va a llover.
It's windy/sunny.
  Hace viento/sol.

It's raining/snowing.
Est á lloviendo/nevando.
It's clouded over.
Se ha nublado.

cloud/cloudy	*nube/nublado*
fog/mist	*neblina/niebla*
ice	*hielo*
rain (to rain)	*lluvia (llover)*
snow (to snow)	*nieve (nevar)*
wind	*viento*
clear/fine	*despejado*
high/low tide	*altamar/bajamar*
spring melt/thaw	*deshielo*
storm	*tormenta*
summer/autumn	*verano/otoño*
winter/spring	*invierno/primavera*

Camping

Where's the best place to camp?
¿Dónde está el mejor lugar para acampar?
Can we put up a tent here?
¿Podemos montar una tienda aquí?
Is it permitted to make a fire?
¿Est á permitido a hacer fuego?
I have a gas/petrol stove.
Tengo un hornillo a gas/a gasolina.
I'm going to stay here (two) days.
Voy a quedarme (dos) días aquí.

bivouac	*vivac*
to camp	*acampar*
campfire/fireplace	*hoguera*
camp site	*sitio de acampar*

Difficulties

Careful!	*¡Cuidado!*
Is it dangerous?	*¿Es peligroso?*
Can you help me?	*¿Puedes ayudarme?*
I'm thirsty/hungry.	*Tengo sed/hambre.*
I'm lost.	*Estoy perdido/a.*
Can you repair this?	*¿Puedes arreglarme ésto?*

Features

branch or tributary of lake	*afluente*
cairn	*hito*
canyon/gorge	*cañón/barranco*
cave	*cueva*
cliff	*acantilado*
coast, shoreline	*costa*
creek/small river	*arroyo*
crevasse	*grieta*
fjord/sound	*ría*
frontier/border	*frontera/límite*
glacier	*glaciar*
hill	*colina*
island	*isla*
lake	*lago*
landslide	*desprendimiento*
lookout	*mirador*
moraine	*morrena*
mountain chain	*cordillera/sierra*
mountain	*montaña*
névé/permanent snowfield	*nevero*
pass	*collado*
plain/flat terrain	*llanura/planicie*
plateau/tableland	*meseta*
range/massif	*sierra/mazico*
rapids	*catarata*
riverbank/shoreline	*orilla*
ridge/spur	*espolón/cresta*
river	*río*
slope/rise	*cuesta/pendiente*
spring	*fuente/manantial*
stream/brook	*riachuelo*
summit/peak	*cumbre/cima/pico*
thermal springs	*aguas termales*
tide	*marea*
torrent	*torrente*
valley	*valle*
volcano	*volcán*
waterfall	*cascada*
waterway junction	*confluencia*
wood/forest	*bosque*

Glossary

Unless otherwise indicated, glossary terms are in Castilian Spanish (*castellano*). Other languages are listed in brackets and are abbreviated as follows: Aran = Aranese, Arag = Aragonese, Bas = Basque, Cat = Catalan, Eng = English, Gal = Galician. Words which appear in italics within definitions have their own entries.

abrevadero – drinking trough
abrigo – shelter
acequia – irrigation channel
agua potable – drinking water
alambrada – wire fence
albergue – shelter or refuge
albergue juvenil – youth hostel
área de acampada – free camping ground, usually with no facilities
área de reserva – reserve to which access is restricted
arroyo – stream, brook or creek
ATM – (Eng) Automatic Teller Machine; cash dispenser
autopista – tollway
autovía – toll-free, dual-carriage highway
ayuntamiento – district or town council; town hall

bable – Asturian language
bahía – bay
balneario – spa or health resort
barranc – (Cat) *barranco*
barranco – gully or ravine
barrio – district or area
bocadillo – long sandwich
bodega – old-style wine bar; wine cellar
borda – mountain hut used in summer by shepherds and cowherds
bosque – forest
braña – stone hut or cabin found in the Cordillera Cantábrica

cabaña – hut
cala – cove
caldera – large, basin-shaped crater at the top of a volcano

calle – street
calzada – roadway
calzada romana – stone-paved Roman road
cambio – literally change; also currency exchange
camí – (Cat) *camino*
camino – footpath, track, path, trail or road
camino de herradura – bridle path
camino real – state-maintained *camino*
campa – (Gal) treeless land or meadow
cañada – drove road
capilla – chapel
carrer – (Cat) *calle*
carretera – public road or highway
carta – menu
casa – house or building
casa de labranza – *casa rural* in Cantabria and Asturias
casa de pagès – *casa rural* in Catalunya
casa rural – rural house or farmstead with rooms to let
cascada – waterfall or cascade
castellano – Castilian; a term often used in preference to 'español' to describe the national language
castillo – castle
castro – fortified circular village, usually pre-Roman
català – (Cat) Catalan language; a native of Catalunya
caza – hunting
cervecería – beer bar
charca – pond or pool
charco – pool or puddle
choza – simple hut or shelter with wooden bench and table in the Islas Canarias
circo – *cirque* or amphitheatre
cirque – (Eng) *corrie* or bowl at the head of a valley, typically formed by glaciation
CNIG – Centro Nacional de Información Geográfica
col – (Eng) mountain pass
coll – (Cat) *collado*
collado – pass or *col*
coma – (Cat) bowl or *cirque*
comedor – dining room

comú – local authority (Andorra)
comunidad autónoma – autonomous community
concha – shell
cordillera – mountain range
corniche – (Eng) coastal road or path
corredoira – stone-cobbled rural lane connecting hamlets in Galicia
correos – post office
corrie – (Eng) bowl or *cirque*
cortijo – farm or farmhouse, especially in Andalucía
costa – coast
coto – area where hunting rights are reserved to a specific group of people; also cairn, boundary or boundary marker
cruceiro – (Gal) stone cross marking crossroads
cuenta – bill (check)
cuesta – slope or hillside

dehesa – woodland pasture
desfiladero – gorge, defile or narrow pass between mountains
Documento Nacional de Identidad – Spanish identification card

embalse – reservoir or dam
entrada – entrance
ermita – wayside chapel or hermitage
estación de autobuses – bus station
estación de tren/ferrocarril – train station
estanh – (Aran) *estanque*
estanque – pool, small lake or tarn
estany – (Cat) *estanque*
Euskadi– (Bas) *País Vasco*

farmacia – pharmacy
faro – lighthouse
finca – building or piece of land, usually rural
font – (Cat) *fuente*
forau – (Arag) cave or pothole
fuente – spring, fountain or water source

gallego – Galician language; a native of Galicia
garganta – literally, throat; also gorge or ravine
gasolinera – petrol station

golada – (Gal) *col* or pass
guía – guide

hito – cairn; also landmark
horreo – granary in Galicia and Asturias
hospital – literally, hospital; also wayside guesthouse
hospitalero – *hospital* or *refugio* attendant on pilgrim route
hostal – inexpensive hotel
hoyo – *bable* word for *jou*
huerta – market garden or orchard

ibón – (Arag) small lake or tarn
iglesia – church
IGN – Instituto Geográfico Nacional, producing countrywide maps
IVA – Impuesto sobre el Valor Añadido, or Value-Added Tax (VAT)

jou – hollow or pothole in Asturias

karst – (Eng) characteristic landforms of a limestone region

lago – lake
laguna – pool or lagoon
lavadero – washing place, usually a public open-air sink in a village
lavandería – laundrette
librería – bookshop
lista de correos – poste restante
llano – plain
llegada – arrival
loma – low ridge

macizo – massif
madrileño/a – native of Madrid
mapa – map
marisquería – seafood restaurant
menú del día – fixed-price, usually three course meal which often includes a drink; sometimes only available at lunchtime
mercado – market
merendero – picnic spot, usually with barbecue installations
meseta – high tableland of central Spain
mesón – simple eatery with home-style cooking
mirador – lookout

mojón – boundary marker or large cairn
monasterio – monastery
montañero/a – mountaineer
montebajo – scrub or undergrowth
moraine – (Eng) rock debris swept down by glaciers and dumped as the ice melts
mudéjar – a Muslim living under Christian rule in medieval Spain; their characteristic style of architecture
municipio – municipality

nava – high plain in Andalucía
nevera – pit or building used for making ice from snow
nevero – permanent, high-level snowfield
oficina de turismo – tourist office

País Vasco – Basque Country
palloza – thatch-roofed stone dwelling in the eastern sierras of Galicia
parador – one of a chain of luxury state hotels, many of which occupy historic buildings
parque nacional – national park
parque natural – nature park
pensión – boarding house or guesthouse
peregrino – pilgrim
pico – peak or summit
piedra – stone or rock
piscina – swimming pool
pista – trail or track
pla – (Cat) *llano*
plan – (Arag) *llano*
platja – (Cat) *playa*
plato combinado – fixed-price dish with three or four items, all served on the same plate
playa – beach
port – (Cat) *puerto*
pozo de nieve – snow-storage pit
prado – meadow
praia – (Gal) *playa*
prat – (Cat) *prado*
presa – dam
pueblo – village or small town
puente – bridge
puerta – gate or door
puerto – port; also pass

ración – serving of food larger than *tapas*

rambla – seasonal watercourse; also avenue
refugi – (Cat) *refugio*
refugio – refuge or mountain hut
RENFE – Red Nacional de los Ferrocarriles Españoles, the national railway network
reserva nacional de caza – national hunting reserve, where hunting is permitted but controlled
ría – estuary in Galicia and Asturias
río – river
riu – Catalan for *río*
ruta – route
ruta hípica – pony-trekking trail

salida – exit or departure
senda – path or track
sendero – footpath
serra – (Cat) *sierra*
SGE – Servício Geográfico del Ejército, producing countrywide maps
sierra – mountain range
sima – pothole, sink hole or fissure
supermercado – supermarket

taberna – bar or tavern
tapas – bar snacks traditionally served on a saucer or lid (*tapa*)
tarn – (Eng) small mountain lake or pond
tasca – bar, particularly one specialising in *tapas*
teleférico – cable car or funicular
tienda – shop; also tent
torrente – beck, mountain stream or narrow valley
tree line – (Eng) altitude above which trees can no longer survive
true left/right bank – (Eng) side of the riverbank as you look downstream

vado – ford
vall – (Cat) *valle*
valla – fence or barrier
valle – valley
vega – pasture or meadow
via pecuaria – drove road
vivac – bivouac
volcán – volcano

zona de acampada – *área de acampada*

LONELY PLANET

ON THE ROAD

Travel Guides explore cities, regions and countries, and supply information on transport, restaurants and accommodation, covering all budgets. They come with reliable, easy-to-use maps, practical advice, cultural and historical facts and a rundown on attractions both on and off the beaten track. There are over 200 titles in this classic series, covering nearly every country in the world.

 Lonely Planet Upgrades extend the shelf life of existing travel guides by detailing any changes that may affect travel in a region since a book has been published. Upgrades can be downloaded for free from **www.lonelyplanet.com/upgrades**

For travellers with more time than money, **Shoestring** guides offer dependable, first-hand information with hundreds of detailed maps, plus insider tips for stretching money as far as possible. Covering entire continents in most cases, the six-volume shoestring guides are known around the world as 'backpackers bibles'.

For the discerning short-term visitor, **Condensed** guides highlight the best a destination has to offer in a full-colour, pocket-sized format designed for quick access. They include everything from top sights and walking tours to opinionated reviews of where to eat, stay, shop and have fun.

CitySync lets travellers use their Palm™ or Visor™ hand-held computers to guide them through a city with handy tips on transport, history, cultural life, major sights, and shopping and entertainment options. It can also quickly search and sort hundreds of reviews of hotels, restaurants and attractions, and pinpoint their location on scrollable street maps. CitySync can be downloaded from **www.citysync.com**

MAPS & ATLASES

Lonely Planet's **City Maps** feature downtown and metropolitan maps, as well as transit routes and walking tours. The maps come complete with an index of streets, a listing of sights and a plastic coat for extra durability.

Road Atlases are an essential navigation tool for serious travellers. Cross-referenced with the guidebooks, they also feature distance and climate charts and a complete site index.

LONELY PLANET

ESSENTIALS

Read This First books help new travellers to hit the road with confidence. These invaluable predeparture guides give step-by-step advice on preparing for a trip, budgeting, arranging a visa, planning an itinerary and staying safe while still getting off the beaten track.

Healthy Travel pocket guides offer a regional rundown on disease hot spots and practical advice on predeparture health measures, staying well on the road and what to do in emergencies. The guides come with a user-friendly design and helpful diagrams and tables.

Lonely Planet's **Phrasebooks** cover the essential words and phrases travellers need when they're strangers in a strange land. They come in a pocket-sized format with colour tabs for quick reference, extensive vocabulary lists, easy-to-follow pronunciation keys and two-way dictionaries.

Miffed by blurry photos of the Taj Mahal? Tired of the classic 'top of the head cut off' shot? **Travel Photography: A Guide to Taking Better Pictures** will help you turn ordinary holiday snaps into striking images and give you the know-how to capture every scene, from frenetic festivals to peaceful beach sunrises.

Lonely Planet's **Travel Journal** is a lightweight but sturdy travel diary for jotting down all those on-the-road observations and significant travel moments. It comes with a handy time-zone wheel, a world map and useful travel information.

Lonely Planet's eKno is an all-in-one communication service developed especially for travellers. It offers low-cost international calls and free email and voicemail so that you can keep in touch while on the road. Check it out on **www.ekno.lonelyplanet.com**

FOOD & RESTAURANT GUIDES

Lonely Planet's **Out to Eat** guides recommend the brightest and best places to eat and drink in top international cities. These gourmet companions are arranged by neighbourhood, packed with dependable maps, garnished with scene-setting photos and served with quirky features.

For people who live to eat, drink and travel, **World Food** guides explore the culinary culture of each country. Entertaining and adventurous, each guide is packed with detail on staples and specialities, regional cuisine and local markets, as well as sumptuous recipes, comprehensive culinary dictionaries and lavish photos good enough to eat.

LONELY PLANET

OUTDOOR GUIDES

For those who believe the best way to see the world is on foot, Lonely Planet's **Walking Guides** detail everything from family strolls to difficult treks, with 'when to go and how to do it' advice supplemented by reliable maps and essential travel information.

Cycling Guides map a destination's best bike tours, long and short, in day-by-day detail. They contain all the information a cyclist needs, including advice on bike maintenance, places to eat and stay, innovative maps with detailed cues to the rides, and elevation charts.

The **Watching Wildlife** series is perfect for travellers who want authoritative information but don't want to tote a heavy field guide. Packed with advice on where, when and how to view a region's wildlife, each title features photos of over 300 species and contains engaging comments on the local flora and fauna.

With underwater colour photos throughout, **Pisces Books** explore the world's best diving and snorkelling areas. Each book contains listings of diving services and dive resorts, detailed information on depth, visibility and difficulty of dives, and a roundup of the marine life you're likely to see through your mask.

LONELY PLANET

OFF THE ROAD

Journeys, the travel literature series written by renowned travel authors, capture the spirit of a place or illuminate a culture with a journalist's attention to detail and a novelist's flair for words. These are tales to soak up while you're actually on the road or dip into as an at-home armchair indulgence.

The range of lavishly illustrated **Pictorial** books is just the ticket for both travellers and dreamers. Off-beat tales and vivid photographs bring the adventure of travel to your doorstep long before the journey begins and long after it is over.

Lonely Planet **Videos** encourage the same independent, tough-minded approach as the guidebooks. Currently airing throughout the world, this award-winning series features innovative footage and an original soundtrack.

Yes, we know, work is tough, so do a little bit of deskside dreaming with the spiral-bound Lonely Planet **Diary** or a Lonely Planet **Wall Calendar**, filled with great photos from around the world.

TRAVELLERS NETWORK

Lonely Planet Online. Lonely Planet's award-winning Web site has insider information on hundreds of destinations, from Amsterdam to Zimbabwe, complete with interactive maps and relevant links. The site also offers the latest travel news, recent reports from travellers on the road, guidebook upgrades, a travel links site, an online book-buying option and a lively travellers bulletin board. It can be viewed at **www.lonelyplanet.com** or AOL keyword: lp.

Planet Talk is a quarterly print newsletter, full of gossip, advice, anecdotes and author articles. It provides an antidote to the being-at-home blues and lets you plan and dream for the next trip. Contact the nearest Lonely Planet office for your free copy.

Comet, the free Lonely Planet newsletter, comes via email once a month. It's loaded with travel news, advice, dispatches from authors, travel competitions and letters from readers. To subscribe, click on the Comet subscription link on the front page of the Web site.

Lonely Planet Guides by Region

Lonely Planet is known worldwide for publishing practical, reliable and no-nonsense travel information in our guides and on our Web site. The Lonely Planet list covers just about every accessible part of the world. Currently there are 16 series: Travel guides, Shoestring guides, Condensed guides, Phrasebooks, Read This First, Healthy Travel, Walking guides, Cycling guides, Watching Wildlife guides, Pisces Diving & Snorkeling guides, City Maps, Road Atlases, Out to Eat, World Food, Journeys travel literature and Pictorials.

AFRICA Africa on a shoestring • Botswana • Cairo • Cairo City Map • Cape Town • Cape Town City Map • East Africa • Egypt • Egyptian Arabic phrasebook • Ethiopia, Eritrea & Djibouti • Ethiopian Amharic phrasebook • The Gambia & Senegal • Healthy Travel Africa • Kenya • Malawi • Morocco • Moroccan Arabic phrasebook • Mozambique • Namibia • Read This First: Africa • South Africa, Lesotho & Swaziland • Southern Africa • Southern Africa Road Atlas • Swahili phrasebook • Tanzania, Zanzibar & Pemba • Trekking in East Africa • Tunisia • Watching Wildlife East Africa • Watching Wildlife Southern Africa • West Africa • World Food Morocco • Zambia • Zimbabwe, Botswana & Namibia
Travel Literature: Mali Blues: Traveling to an African Beat • The Rainbird: A Central African Journey • Songs to an African Sunset: A Zimbabwean Story

AUSTRALIA & THE PACIFIC Aboriginal Australia & the Torres Strait Islands •Auckland • Australia • Australian phrasebook • Australia Road Atlas • Cycling Australia • Cycling New Zealand • Fiji • Fijian phrasebook • Healthy Travel Australia, NZ & the Pacific • Islands of Australia's Great Barrier Reef • Melbourne • Melbourne City Map • Micronesia • New Caledonia • New South Wales • Northern Territory • Outback Australia • Out to Eat – Melbourne • Out to Eat – Sydney • Papua New Guinea • Pidgin phrasebook • Queensland • Rarotonga & the Cook Islands • Samoa • Solomon Islands • South Australia • South Pacific • South Pacific phrasebook • Sydney • Sydney City Map • Sydney Condensed • Tahiti & French Polynesia • Tasmania • Tonga • Tramping in New Zealand • Vanuatu • Victoria • Walking in Australia • Watching Wildlife Australia • Western Australia
Travel Literature: Islands in the Clouds: Travels in the Highlands of New Guinea • Kiwi Tracks: A New Zealand Journey • Sean & David's Long Drive

CENTRAL AMERICA & THE CARIBBEAN Bahamas, Turks & Caicos • Baja California • Belize, Guatemala & Yucatán • Bermuda • Central America on a shoestring • Costa Rica • Costa Rica Spanish phrasebook • Cuba • Cycling Cuba • Dominican Republic & Haiti • Eastern Caribbean • Guatemala • Havana • Healthy Travel Central & South America • Jamaica • Mexico • Mexico City • Panama • Puerto Rico • Read This First: Central & South America • Virgin Islands • World Food Caribbean • World Food Mexico • Yucatán
Travel Literature: Green Dreams: Travels in Central America

EUROPE Amsterdam • Amsterdam City Map • Amsterdam Condensed • Andalucía • Athens • Austria • Baltic States phrasebook • Barcelona • Barcelona City Map • Belgium & Luxembourg • Berlin • Berlin City Map • Britain • British phrasebook • Brussels, Bruges & Antwerp • Brussels City Map • Budapest • Budapest City Map • Canary Islands • Catalunya & the Costa Brava • Central Europe • Central Europe phrasebook • Copenhagen • Corfu & the Ionians • Corsica • Crete • Crete Condensed • Croatia • Cycling Britain • Cycling France • Cyprus • Czech & Slovak Republics • Czech phrasebook • Denmark • Dublin • Dublin City Map • Dublin Condensed • Eastern Europe • Eastern Europe phrasebook • Edinburgh • Edinburgh City Map • England • Estonia, Latvia & Lithuania • Europe on a shoestring • Europe phrasebook • Finland • Florence • Florence City Map • France • Frankfurt City Map • Frankfurt Condensed • French phrasebook • Georgia, Armenia & Azerbaijan • Germany • German phrasebook • Greece • Greek Islands • Greek phrasebook • Hungary • Iceland, Greenland & the Faroe Islands • Ireland • Italian phrasebook • Italy • Kraków • Lisbon • The Loire • London • London City Map • London Condensed • Madrid • Madrid City Map • Malta • Mediterranean Europe • Milan, Turin & Genoa • Moscow • Munich • Netherlands • Normandy • Norway • Out to Eat – London • Out to Eat – Paris • Paris • Paris City Map • Paris Condensed • Poland • Polish phrasebook • Portugal • Portuguese phrasebook • Prague • Prague City Map • Provence & the Côte d'Azur • Read This First: Europe • Rhodes & the Dodecanese • Romania & Moldova • Rome • Rome City Map • Rome Condensed • Russia, Ukraine & Belarus • Russian phrasebook • Scandinavian & Baltic Europe • Scandinavian phrasebook • Scotland • Sicily • Slovenia • South-West France • Spain • Spanish phrasebook • Stockholm • St Petersburg • St Petersburg City Map • Sweden • Switzerland • Tuscany • Ukrainian phrasebook • Venice • Vienna • Wales • Walking in Britain • Walking in France • Walking in Ireland • Walking in Italy • Walking in Scotland • Walking in Spain • Walking in Switzerland • Western Europe • World Food France • World Food Greece • World Food Ireland • World Food Italy • World Food Spain **Travel Literature:** After Yugoslavia • Love and War in the Apennines • The Olive Grove: Travels in Greece • On the Shores of the Mediterranean • Round Ireland in Low Gear • A Small Place in Italy

Lonely Planet Mail Order

Lonely Planet products are distributed worldwide. They are also available by mail order from Lonely Planet, so if you have difficulty finding a title please write to us. North and South American residents should write to 150 Linden St, Oakland, CA 94607, USA; European and African residents should write to 10a Spring Place, London NW5 3BH, UK; and residents of other countries to Locked Bag 1, Footscray, Victoria 3011, Australia.

INDIAN SUBCONTINENT & THE INDIAN OCEAN Bangladesh • Bengali phrasebook • Bhutan • Delhi • Goa • Healthy Travel Asia & India • Hindi & Urdu phrasebook • India • India & Bangladesh City Map • Indian Himalaya • Karakoram Highway • Kathmandu City Map • Kerala • Madagascar • Maldives • Mauritius, Réunion & Seychelles • Mumbai (Bombay) • Nepal • Nepali phrasebook • North India • Pakistan • Rajasthan • Read This First: Asia & India • South India • Sri Lanka • Sri Lanka phrasebook • Tibet • Tibetan phrasebook • Trekking in the Indian Himalaya • Trekking in the Karakoram & Hindukush • Trekking in the Nepal Himalaya • World Food India **Travel Literature:** The Age of Kali: Indian Travels and Encounters • Hello Goodnight: A Life of Goa • In Rajasthan • Maverick in Madagascar • A Season in Heaven: True Tales from the Road to Kathmandu • Shopping for Buddhas • A Short Walk in the Hindu Kush • Slowly Down the Ganges

MIDDLE EAST & CENTRAL ASIA Bahrain, Kuwait & Qatar • Central Asia • Central Asia phrasebook • Dubai • Farsi (Persian) phrasebook • Hebrew phrasebook • Iran • Israel & the Palestinian Territories • Istanbul • Istanbul City Map • Istanbul to Cairo • Istanbul to Kathmandu • Jerusalem • Jerusalem City Map • Jordan • Lebanon • Middle East • Oman & the United Arab Emirates • Syria • Turkey • Turkish phrasebook • World Food Turkey • Yemen **Travel Literature:** Black on Black: Iran Revisited • Breaking Ranks: Turbulent Travels in the Promised Land • The Gates of Damascus • Kingdom of the Film Stars: Journey into Jordan

NORTH AMERICA Alaska • Boston • Boston City Map • Boston Condensed • British Columbia • California & Nevada • California Condensed • Canada • Chicago • Chicago City Map • Chicago Condensed • Florida • Georgia & the Carolinas • Great Lakes • Hawaii • Hiking in Alaska • Hiking in the USA • Honolulu & Oahu City Map • Las Vegas • Los Angeles • Los Angeles City Map • Louisiana & the Deep South • Miami • Miami City Map • Montreal • New England • New Orleans • New Orleans City Map • New York City • New York City Map • New York City Condensed • New York, New Jersey & Pennsylvania • Oahu • Out to Eat – San Francisco • Pacific Northwest • Rocky Mountains • San Diego & Tijuana • San Francisco • San Francisco City Map • Seattle • Seattle City Map • Southwest • Texas • Toronto • USA • USA phrasebook • Vancouver • Vancouver City Map • Virginia & the Capital Region • Washington, DC • Washington, DC City Map • World Food New Orleans **Travel Literature**: Caught Inside: A Surfer's Year on the California Coast • Drive Thru America

NORTH-EAST ASIA Beijing • Beijing City Map • Cantonese phrasebook • China • Hiking in Japan • Hong Kong & Macau • Hong Kong City Map • Hong Kong Condensed • Japan • Japanese phrasebook • Korea • Korean phrasebook • Kyoto • Mandarin phrasebook • Mongolia • Mongolian phrasebook • Seoul • Shanghai • South-West China • Taiwan • Tokyo • Tokyo Condensed • World Food Hong Kong • World Food Japan **Travel Literature:** In Xanadu: A Quest • Lost Japan

SOUTH AMERICA Argentina, Uruguay & Paraguay • Bolivia • Brazil • Brazilian phrasebook • Buenos Aires • Buenos Aires City Map • Chile & Easter Island • Colombia • Ecuador & the Galapagos Islands • Healthy Travel Central & South America • Latin American Spanish phrasebook • Peru • Quechua phrasebook • Read This First: Central & South America • Rio de Janeiro • Rio de Janeiro City Map • Santiago de Chile • South America on a shoestring • Trekking in the Patagonian Andes • Venezuela **Travel Literature:** Full Circle: A South American Journey

SOUTH-EAST ASIA Bali & Lombok • Bangkok • Bangkok City Map • Burmese phrasebook • Cambodia • Cycling Vietnam, Laos & Cambodia • East Timor phrasebook • Hanoi • Healthy Travel Asia & India • Hill Tribes phrasebook • Ho Chi Minh City (Saigon) • Indonesia • Indonesian phrasebook • Indonesia's Eastern Islands • Java • Lao phrasebook • Laos • Malay phrasebook • Malaysia, Singapore & Brunei • Myanmar (Burma) • Philippines • Pilipino (Tagalog) phrasebook • Read This First: Asia & India • Singapore • Singapore City Map • South-East Asia on a shoestring • South-East Asia phrasebook • Thailand • Thailand's Islands & Beaches • Thailand, Vietnam, Laos & Cambodia Road Atlas • Thai phrasebook • Vietnam • Vietnamese phrasebook • World Food Indonesia • World Food Thailand • World Food Vietnam

ALSO AVAILABLE: Antarctica • The Arctic • The Blue Man: Tales of Travel, Love and Coffee • Brief Encounters: Stories of Love, Sex & Travel • Buddhist Stupas in Asia: The Shape of Perfection • Chasing Rickshaws • The Last Grain Race • Lonely Planet ... On the Edge: Adventurous Escapades from Around the World • Lonely Planet Unpacked • Lonely Planet Unpacked Again • Not the Only Planet: Science Fiction Travel Stories • Ports of Call: A Journey by Sea • Sacred India • Travel Photography: A Guide to Taking Better Pictures • Travel with Children • Tuvalu: Portrait of an Island Nation

Index

Text

Bold indicates maps.
Italics indicates boxed text.

Bold indicates maps.
Italics indicates boxed text.

Bold indicates maps.
Italics indicates boxed text.

Boxed Text

MAP LEGEND

BOUNDARIES

▬·▬·▬·▬·	International
▬··▬··▬··	Regional
▬ ▬ ▬	Disputed

HYDROGRAPHY

	Coastline
	River, Creek
	Lake
	Intermittent Lake
	Salt Lake
	Canal
⊙ ⤳	Spring, Rapids
⤙◀	Waterfalls
⚘ ⚘ ⚘ ⚘	Swamp

ROUTES & TRANSPORT

	Freeway
	Highway
	Major Road
	Minor Road
▭▭▭▭	Unsealed Road
	City Freeway
	City Highway
	City Road
	City Street, Lane
	Pedestrian Mall
⇥====:	Tunnel
⊢+++•+⊢	Train Route & Station
⊩+⊩+⊩+⊩	Cable Car or Chairlift
	Described Walk
▬ ▬ ▬	Alternative Route
▬ ▬ ▬ ▬	Walking Track
· · · · · ·	Walking Tour
▬ ▬ ▬ ▬	Ferry Route

AREA FEATURES

	Park (Regional Maps)
	Park (Walk Maps)
	Forests, Pine Plantation
	Market
	Beach
	Urban Area

MAP SYMBOLS

○	CAPITAL	National Capital	
◉	CAPITAL	Regional Capital	
●	CITY	City	
●	Town	Town	
●	Village	Village	
·		Point of Interest	

■	Place to Stay	✈	Airport	♈	National Park
⚠	Camping Area	∿	Ancient or City Wall	←	One Way Street
☕	Caravan Park	∴	Archaeological Site	🄿	Parking
⌂	Refugio	𐎛	Beach	)(	Pass
🖼	Lookout	🜨	Castle or Fort	★	Police Station
▼	Place to Eat	⌂	Cave	✉	Post Office
🍴	Pub or Bar	🏠	Church	❖	Shopping Centre
		⌇	Cliff or Escarpment	▭	Swimming Pool
		⌇500	Contour	✡	Synagogue
		○	Embassy	☎	Telephone
		✚	Hospital	⛩	Temple
		☪	Mosque	ⓘ	Tourist Information
		▲	Mountain or Hill	●	Transport
		🏛	Museum	🐘	Zoo

Note: not all symbols displayed above appear in this book

LONELY PLANET OFFICES

Australia
Locked Bag 1, Footscray, Victoria 3011
☎ 03 8379 8000 fax 03 8379 8111
email: talk2us@lonelyplanet.com.au

USA
150 Linden St, Oakland, CA 94607
☎ 510 893 8555 TOLL FREE: 800 275 8555
fax 510 893 8572
email: info@lonelyplanet.com

UK
10a Spring Place, London NW5 3BH
☎ 020 7428 4800 fax 020 7428 4828
email: go@lonelyplanet.co.uk

France
1 rue du Dahomey, 75011 Paris
☎ 01 55 25 33 00 fax 01 55 25 33 01
email: bip@lonelyplanet.fr
www.lonelyplanet.fr

World Wide Web: www.lonelyplanet.com *or* AOL keyword: lp
Lonely Planet Images: lpi@lonelyplanet.com.au